Principle #6
Internet advertising draws revenue based on the viewer's level of interactivity with the commercial message.

Principle #7
Freedom of speech for advertisers is limited by their ability to substantiate the claims that their commercials make.

Chapter 10: The Audience

Principle #1
Projecting future ratings is an early step in the development of programming.

Principle #2
As an inexact science, audience measurement is open to challenge by its stakeholders.

Principle #3
Commercial broadcasters invariably press for closer surveillance of TV viewers' behavior.

Principle #4
The characteristics of an audience usually are more important than its size.

Principle #5
Broadcasters do not give all audience members equal weight in programming decisions.

Principle #6
Industry consolidation increases pressure for high ratings.

Principle #7
No modern media—even "new" media—can escape the imperative to count and evaluate audiences.

Part Three: Electronic Media: A Broader View

Chapter 11: Theory and Research

Principle #1
The structural process of communication must be understood before the meaning of content is considered.

Principle #2
The basis of credibility is formed by audience perceptions of expertise, honesty, and sincerity.

Principle #3
The two-step flow theory says that opinion leaders interpret news for others, thereby limiting the media's direct impact.

Principle #4
Agenda setting is how news media influence the public's attention to particular issues.

Principle #5
Personal needs motivate media exposure and limit media effects.

Chapter 12: Public Broadcasting

Principle #1
The first objective of public broadcasting is to survive—but the second is public service.

Principle #2
Public broadcasters have to struggle as hard to achieve diversity as commercial broadcasters do.

Principle #3
The nonprofit status that distinguishes public broadcasting also limits its power and independence.

Principle #4
Public broadcasting's roots in education provide a natural mission that separates it from commercial media.

Principle #5
If centralized funding = centralized power, then federal funding = the threat of federal interference.

Principle #6
In a consumer economy, public broadcasting cannot escape the mandates of marketing if it is to compete for funds.

Principle #7
As an activist, volunteer-oriented fringe of public broadcasting, community radio is a true alternative to commercial media.

Chapter 13: The World

Principle #1
Electronic media can transmit across borders and thus are inherently international.

Principle #2
Electronic media internationally attract both government support and government controls.

Principle #3
Cultural imperialism and the "digital divide" are built-in issues for international electronic media.

Principle #4
Authoritarian governments always gravitate toward control of electronic media.

Principle #5
Even *laissez-faire* systems need some controls to keep electronic media working smoothly.

Principle #6
Successful global media ventures tend to be created by mergers and acquisitions.

Chapter 14: Law

Principle #1
The government licenses broadcasters to serve the public interest.

Principle #2
Public ownership of the spectrum requires government oversight over the use of its frequencies.

Principle #3
The scarcity of spectrum space limits broadcast frequencies and station licenses.

Principle #4
Competitive bidding—not the promise of performance—determines who gains access to the telecommunications channels.

Principle #5
Media consolidation leads to monopoly if left unregulated.

Principle #6
Advocacy groups influence policy and law for electronic media, including children's television.

Principle #7
There is no absolute protection for one's ownership of original and creative content.

Principle #8
Public officials and figures receive less protection for their reputations than private citizens do.

Principle #9
In granting electronic media access to the courts, jurists balance the right to a fair trial against the freedom of the press.

Principle #10
Obscenity always is illegal, but "indecent" communication is permitted when children are not in the audience.

Chapter 15: Professional Ethics

Principle #1
The golden mean recommends a middle ground between extremes.

Principle #2
Categorical imperatives such as fairness and truth guide ethical decisions.

Principle #3
Ethical decisions are based on an assessment of duty, purpose, and consequence.

Principle #4
Prescriptive ethics draw on higher principles to point us toward actions.

Principle #5
Without truth there is no trust, and without trust meaningful exchanges of information are lost.

Principle #6
Being fair means being blind to individual differences that are irrelevant to the issue.

Principle #7
A journalist who shows partisanship compromises his or her own credibility.

Principles of Electronic Media

William R. Davie
University of Louisiana at Lafayette

James R. Upshaw
University of Oregon

Boston ■ New York ■ San Francisco
Mexico City ■ Montreal ■ Toronto ■ London ■ Madrid ■ Munich ■ Paris
Hong Kong ■ Singapore ■ Tokyo ■ Cape Town ■ Sydney

Series Editor: Molly Taylor
Editorial Assistant: Michael Kish
Developmental Editor: Carol Alper
Marketing Manager: Mandee Eckersley
Production Editor: Michelle Limoges
Compositor: Omegatype Typography, Inc.
Photo Researcher: Katharine S. Cook
Composition and Prepress Buyer: Linda Cox
Manufacturing Buyer: Megan Cochran
Cover Designer: Linda Knowles

For related titles and support materials, visit our online catalog at www.ablongman.com.

Library of Congress Cataloging-in-Publication Data

Davie, William R.
    Principles of electronic media / William R. Davie, James R. Upshaw.
        p.   cm.
    Includes bibliographical references and index.
    ISBN 0-205-32738-9
    1. Broadcasting.   2. Artificial satellites in telecommunication.   3. Internet.   I. Upshaw,
Jim.   II. Title.

HE8689.4 .D38   2003
384—dc21   2002026213

Printed in the United States of America

10 9 8 7 6 5 4 3 2 1   06 05 04 03 02

CONTENTS

PART ONE: Introduction to Electronic Media

The study of broadcasting used to examine only two traditional media: radio and television. This book expands the study to include all of the newer electronic media that bring mass messages to the public: cable, satellite, and the Internet. This introductory section begins with an overview of electronic media today. Chapter 2 reviews the history of radio and television. The development of cable and satellite as mass media is explained in Chapter 3, followed by a discussion of digital delivery of media in Chapter 4. The section ends with Chapter 5, which looks at the technology by which radio and television messages are delivered today.

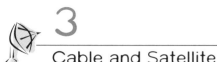

3
Cable and Satellite   54

4
Digital Domains   80

5
Radio and Television Technology   106

PART TWO: The Business of Electronic Media

This section walks students through the business of creating, promoting, and distributing electronic media messages. Chapter 6 shows how media companies are organized and how they operate. Next, Chapter 7 describes how media content is developed and distributed. The special qualities and practices of news and advertising are examined in Chapters 8 and 9. Finally, Chapter 10 explains efforts to measure and evaluate the audience that support each electronic medium.

6
The Industry   132

7

Programming and Distribution   164

8

Broadcast News   196

9

Advertising and Promotions   220

10

The Audience   248

PART THREE: Electronic Media: A Broader View

This final section highlights the ways in which electronic media have touched our society. It begins with the theories and research that help us understand how the media influence our lives. The next three chapters focus on public broadcasting, global issues, and the laws ensuring that citizens are fairly served by the media. A final chapter considers important ethical issues and concludes with a look at the principles that have guided professionals in their media careers.

11
Theory and Research   272

12
Public Broadcasting   302

15

Professional Ethics   396

PREFACE

Principles of Electronic Media enables you, the college instructor, to provide what many undergraduates need:

- To know and understand the working principles—not just the theories—on which modern professionals in electronic media make decisions and do their work
- To "hear" the voices of electronic-media professionals whose lives and careers reflect those realities across the book's wide range of content
- To gain insights into the growing array of occupations in the field
- To discover the ongoing realities of electronic media, clear and unvarnished
- To work with material that is readable—even inviting—by the standards of today's college textbooks

The title suggests our premise, which is that principles matter. We identify key principles not only to show how they work but also, sometimes, to point out when they conflict with what we might reasonably expect from the media. Some of our observations are open to debate, but we hope they at least raise important questions. Our aim is not to achieve axioms, but to provoke critical thinking about the forces that guide media worlds.

Many of the leisure hours of college students are filled with messages tailored to their tastes and social drives by the commercial media. Our book cuts through this dynamic by decoding these very media. Our goal is to lead students into deeper understanding of what these institutions are, who runs them, why, and to what effect.

Structure

Principles of Electronic Media is organized into three parts. Part One provides a foundation for understanding the origins, structures, and social roles of electronic media. It begins with an overview—dramatically illustrated by recent events—that divulges the philosophy behind the book and introduces the professional commentaries. Next is Chapter 2, our history chapter, breaking the development of broadcasting into important periods and covering its formative highlights. The third chapter charts the rise of cable and satellite television, which leads naturally into the more recent phenomenon of digital convergence. Chapter 4 addresses that, explaining the influence of the computer and its ties to the Internet. Part One closes Chapter 5, which discusses the technological principles and tools by which electronic media function.

Part Two encompasses the business of electronic media, beginning with Chapter 6, which focuses on the organization of industry. Next comes a chapter on the development and production of programming intended to attract audiences. A special category of programming—news, in which both of us are well steeped—is the sole subject of Chapter 8. Chapter 9 outlines the personnel, organization, and strategies of advertising and promotion. Chapter 10, on identifying and measuring the audience, wraps up this business-centered part of the book.

Part Three takes a broader look at electronic media. Chapter 11 shows students how the sounds and images of electronic media have influenced their lives, and explains major theories and research, both contemporary and historical. Following this, in Chapter 12, is an exploration of noncommercial media and the struggle to make public broadcasting a reality. Chapter 13 traces the increasingly global reach of broadcasting and the Internet, describing "foreign" media systems and also how the U.S. system functions internationally. Chapter 14 examines laws that sprang up in the early days of broadcasting and that now, under the eyes of federal regulators, join with newer rules to shape the media landscape. We conclude with Chapter 15, discussing professionalism and ethics—discerning right from wrong in creating and exploiting modern electronic media—to our minds a necessary emphasis at the close of this book.

Each chapter of *Principles of Electronic Media* begins with a prologue—usually anecdotal and vivid—that sets the scene for the reader and lays groundwork for the chapter. We define important terms in the margins and close each chapter's narrative with a summary of key points. Along the way, students discover:

- *Principles*—the governing ideals and realities that underlie electronic media
- *ProTalk* features built from our interviews with working professionals, illustrating media principles and practices
- *Career Focus* boxes offering practical advice to students planning careers in electronic media
- Other boxes putting forth colorful background stories or linking news developments to the chapter's topics
- *Food for Thought* questions to spark classroom discussions and suggest topics for research projects
- Photos, figures, and tables illustrating major concepts, media players, and events

Supplemental Resources

The Instructor's Manual for *Principles of Electronic Media* provides suggested syllabuses, each with a course outline, as well as ideas for research-paper assignments. The manual includes brief outlines of lectures that can be created using the Power Point presentations online. It also includes supplemental lecture topics, lists of videotapes, and other resources. Also in the manual are test bank questions, including multiple-choice, true-false, and essay questions to test critical-thinking skills.

At the *Principles of Electronic Media* companion website—which we intend as an essential companion to the book—one of us outlines each chapter, adding to it news, analysis, and further questions. Here is where instructors and students may find the freshest information related to the book's content. Along with observations that students bring in from their own media encounters, the website can keep learning current and maintain the validity and value of this book. It also includes an online practice test for each chapter for student review.

Acknowledgments

We are grateful for the helpful guidance from our support team at Allyn and Bacon. Acquisitions editor Karon Bowers nurtured us through the organizing process; development editor Carol Alper steered the book's construction; managing editor Molly Taylor advised us on our grand schemes; Kate Cook ranged far and wide to find needed photos; Maria Sas of NuGraphic Design created illustrations; production editor Michelle Limoges artfully assembled the product you're reading now, and Lynda Griffiths of TKM Productions carefully copyedited our work.

Also, we wish to thank the reviewers who provided valuable feedback throughout the writing process. They are: Terry W. Bales of Santa Ana College, Gary C. Dreibelbis of Solano College, Nancy M. Dupont of Loyola University–New Orleans, Erika Engstrom of University of Nevada–Las Vegas, Kate Fowkes of High Point University, Kathleen Fox of Southern Methodist University, Donald G. Godfrey of Arizona State University, Mark Goodman of Mississippi State University, Louisa Ha of Bowling Green State University, Susan Kehoe of George Mason University, William L. (Bill) Knowles of the University of Montana, Michael J. Laney of Lee University, Carroll Ferguson Nardone of El Paso Community College, Cathy Perron of Boston University, Stephen D. Perry of Illinois State University, Shakuntala Rao of State University of New York–Plattsburgh, James E. Reppert of Southern Arkansas University, Joseph P. Tenerelli of Indiana State University, and Thomas W. Volek of University of Kansas.

Thanks, too, to the *ProTalk* interviewees for their patience in submitting to interviews and for supplying important photos and data. Others in electronic media helped to obtain crucial materials for us, often on very short deadlines. These partners in production include Carolyn Aguayo and Debbie Davis of KTLA; Steve Behrens of *Current* magazine; Scott Berwitz of Arbitron; Bruce Bollard of KOIN-TV; Bob Bruck of the *Owensboro* (KY) *Messenger-Inquirer*; Paul Capelli and Jonathan Klein of CNBC; Sarah Colley of Turner Broadcasting; Matt Heffernan of WTVR-TV; Don Hein of KLCC-FM; Byron Holley of Dover Designs; Kelly Hudgens of General Electric; Bojana Jevtic of Radio B92; Keith Jordan of the *Fayetteville* (SC) *Observer*; Timothy J. Kurth of U.S. House of Representatives Speaker J. Dennis Hastert's office; Pamela LaBarge of WSTM-TV; Fred Lass of WRGB-TV; Jo LaVerde of Nielsen Media Research;

photographer Jack Liu of Eugene, OR; George Niesen at Kagan World Media; Bob Papper of Ball State University; Vanessa Ruiz of WGBH-TV; Chris Silvestri of Fox News Network; Graham Smith, attorney at law, Lafayette, Louisiana; Tom Somers of Gannett Television; Paul Sturlaugson of KXGN-TV; Kristen Thomas of SRI Consulting Business Intelligence; Mike Urban of the *Seattle* (WA) *Post-Intelligencer*; Noreen Welle of the Radio-Television News Directors Association, and Kim West of KETC-TV.

Also, we owe many thanks to our colleagues who—when demands of this book took us away from our faculty posts—substituted in our classes, carried extra burdens on our committees, and stepped in to advise our students. In particular, Professor Davie would like to thank—at the University of Louisiana at Lafayette—Dr. Paul Barefield, the Communication Department head, and A. David Barry, dean of the College of Liberal Arts, for granting him leave time to write this book, and the college's chief engineer, Michael Gervais, for contributing his talents to several photographs and for valuable assistance with technical issues.

At the University of Oregon, Professor Upshaw thanks the dean of the School of Journalism and Communication, Tim Gleason, for granting him leave time and remaining supportive throughout this long endeavor; Professor Alan Stavitsky for his helpful suggestions about public broadcasting; and computer experts Andre Chinn and Tom Lundberg, who kept the author safely between the white lines of the information superhighway.

Finally and fervently, we thank our families and all the friends who encouraged us—often when we really needed encouragement—and provided valuable feedback about the book as it developed.

We hope that everyone who contributed to our work will be pleased by the final outcome.

Contact Us

Now we want to invite you, the reader, to participate in improving this work. It is only through criticisms and suggestions that we can make *Principles of Electronic Media* even better in future editions. Below are our e-mail addresses and phone numbers. We hope you will use them without hesitation should you have comments. We look forward to hearing from you soon and often.

William R. Davie
Wrdavie@louisiana.edu
(337) 482-6140

James R. Upshaw
Jupshaw@ballmer.uoregon.edu
(541) 346-3745

Principles of Electronic Media

1

Overview

> We thought, because we had power, we had wisdom.

—Stephen Vincent Benet

Horror. The events of September 11, 2001, created devastation in New York, fear and anger throughout the United States, and shock everywhere as electronic media flashed images and information around the globe.

He was the new kid on the block—and what a block it was: General Electric, one of the world's largest corporations. Jeffrey Immelt was a 45-year-old GE executive when he took the helm in 2001 from Jack Welch, a legendary leader. The new boss's first few weeks in charge of the corporation featured these events:

Monday, Sept. 10: Immelt kicks off his chairmanship by conducting a "meeting" with GE's 313,000 employees worldwide via teleconference.

Tuesday, Sept. 11: Two hijacked jetliners crash into the World Trade Center.

Monday, Oct. 1: *Newsweek* publishes Immelt's crisp summary of the September 11 attacks' impact on GE: "My second day as chairman, a plane I lease, flying with engines I built, crashed into a building that I insure, and it was covered with a network that I own."[1]

It was a striking commentary on a company once known mainly for selling refrigerators and light bulbs. Four parts of the 2001 General Electric empire had an organic bond to the Manhattan attack. One of them leased jets to airlines; another manufactured jet engines;

1

a third insured commercial buildings. The fourth was called NBC. The 75-year-old network—a GE property since 1986—pulled frothy programs off the air after the "9/11" disaster and assigned journalists to describe and explain the attacks to U.S. and international audiences. TV commercials were cancelled in favor of live reports on survivor rescues, fugitive terrorists, security measures, and, soon, the threat of anthrax. NBC was pouring in immense resources with little financial return. Was there any alternative?

> NBC was pouring in immense resources with little financial return. Was there any alternative?

In his lofty perch, trying to balance corporate imperatives, Jeff Immelt may have wondered. Maybe the expensive news coverage was a public service that any network owner inevitably would have to perform and support. Maybe it would draw audiences and thus advertisers for the long run. What if the profit-oriented corporation clamped down on spending and reined in NBC at this moment of crisis—would the public suffer and then turn away?

Jeffrey Immelt. When hijacked jetliners struck the World Trade Center, Immelt was the brand new chairman of General Electric—and saw a startling convergence of company interests in the terrorist attack.

A RICH, DEEP FIELD

Questions about social effects and business dilemmas swirl daily through this age of electronic media. For the most part, these media are business driven, but they are also formally committed to public service. The two imperatives are not always a happy couple.

The United States is the most richly entertained country in the world and probably the best informed overall. Its electronic media are substantially responsible. They have sounded alarms, brought us laughter and sadness, calmed our fears, babysat children, reflected our culture, and—unevenly—helped us understand the world beyond our personal needs. The electronic media have done this despite frequent criticism, heavy competition, and fickle public support. In the bargain, they have become fabulously rich and increasingly global in scope. All of this makes electronic media a fascinating subject of study—and, for some people, an inviting world in which to pursue careers. That's why *Principles of Electronic Media* was written.

Basics

Like most complex subjects, today's electronic media cannot be fully understood simply by reading a textbook. The process requires close observation, comparison, and reflection, but most of all, *critical thinking*. This doesn't have to be especially difficult, but it must be focused and must remain at the center of the learning project.

TWO KEY WORDS

Let's start by breaking our central phrase, *electronic media*, in two and by reexamining both parts briefly. *Electronic*, as we'll use the term in this book, refers to the human manipulation of electronic energy—the flow of electrons, which can be found everywhere in the universe. We've harnessed them to create radio, television, the Internet, and more. Other electronic possibilities may lie ahead, adding to the variety of paths over which people communicate.

Media, for our purposes here, are conduits or carriers of human communication that can reach great numbers of people. Remember that *media* is the plural of *medium*. For example, the newspaper is just one medium; add in other mass communication forms, such as TV and the Internet, and you have media. We also apply the term *media* to the companies and enterprises that use and operate those paths and, usually, profit from doing so.

MESSAGES AND POWER

Electronic media basically are intermediaries; their primary functions are to record, clarify, and transmit messages among people. (You can learn more about this in Chapter 11.) However, electronic media also may *create* messages. This can complicate our task of distinguishing reality from fantasy. For example, when broadcast journalists relay news to us, we usually process those messages as real and respond accordingly. Reversing this, when TV producers or radio disc jockeys invent outrageous skits or horror tales and present them to us as such, we usually process them accurately, as fantasy. This, though, can be a shaky undertaking, because electronic media deliver both factual and fictional material and they sometimes sound and look very similar.

The most famous example of this phenomenon occurred back in 1938, when actor-producer Orson Welles electrified a national radio audience with a play about Martians landing on earth. Welles said more than once that it was a fictional yarn, but some people packed their cars and raced into remote areas to wait out an alien invasion that hadn't happened. Since then, television has presented similarly terrifying and realistic stories, and invariably some viewers miss the disclaimers and become frightened. All of this amounts to a warning: Electronic media can be terribly powerful, sometimes in unintended ways.

Observations

The breakdown of the term *electronic media* leads us to three observations:

1. There's nothing especially new about human use of electrons. People had been thinking about them long before the legend of Ben Franklin, his kite, and a bolt of lightning struck. Most modern uses of electrons to transmit pictures and sounds are derived from basic discoveries made in centuries past, as this book will explain.
2. The messages (all sorts of "content") we receive through electronic media seem to have been shaped, sometimes in subtle ways, by the nature of the

Market In broadcasting, a geographically discrete potential audience, usually identified by the name of its town, city, or metro area.

media themselves. Why, after all, do some of us prefer to read the news on paper or the Internet, whereas others prefer to hear it on radio or see it on TV? Here are three possible reasons:

- Because each form of media has a built-in limitation. *Space*-limited newspapers and magazines can provide only so many details of the news; *time*-limited broadcast media can give us only so much understanding of it.

- Because personal tastes and situations vary. Some people like to see or hear news in brief, relatively dramatic form. Others like to read it, processing its meaning at their leisure.

- Because our brains distinguish among different media. *Hearing* words and sounds on the radio, we make "pictures" in our heads to represent reality or fiction.[2] *Seeing* television lets us fuse both audio and video in our minds to construct a sense of reality or fiction. *Reading* print media is yet a third mental exercise, in which we intellectually "make meaning" that we believe decodes fact or fiction.

3. An observation central to this book: How we interact with electronic media helps to give them great influence on our lives and culture. Even if we doubt critics who claim that media and their advertisers are out to bend us to their will, we each need to ask: How many minutes or hours today did I spend with radio, TV, or the Internet?

Identities

It's hard not to have a strong identity when your hometown is Glendive, Montana. Glendive likes to call attention to its charms and its history: Lewis and Clark stopped there in 1806, so did General Custer before meeting his end at the Little Big Horn. The surroundings are rugged and picturesque; the Yellowstone River flows through town. Some 6,000 people live in Glendive, often joined by visiting anglers. However, the town is shrinking. Located at the edge of the Badlands, it's an old hub for grain growers and doesn't draw many new settlers. Perhaps appropriately, one of its chief claims to fame is the paddlefish, a spoon-billed creature that thrives in waters nearby and happens to be prehistoric.

KXGN-TV (Glendive, MT). You can't expect architectural grandeur from #210 on Nielsen's list of 210 U.S. television markets. Little KXGN-TV brings both NBC and CBS programs to viewers in rural eastern Montana.

THE "MARKET" FACTOR

Glendive is the smallest television **market** in the United States. That means it's the smallest distinct population of potential consumers of advertising—ordinary people—served by any U.S. television station, according to Nielsen Media Research. The town and a few smaller ones nearby add up to market number 210 of 210, and are unlikely to move up the list (see Table 1.1). The lone TV station, KXGN, brings in network programming and also broadcasts local news. Never mind that Jeffrey Immelt's far-off GE giant earned $12.7 billion in profits in 2000. KXGN serves the

TABLE 1.1

Sample of U.S. Television Markets (2001–2002)

RANK	DESIGNATED MARKET AREA (DMA)	TV HOUSEHOLDS
Large Market Areas		
1	New York, NY	7,301,060
2	Los Angeles, CA	5,303,490
3	Chicago, IL	3,360,770
4	Philadelphia, PA	2,801,010
5	San Francisco-Oakland-San Jose, CA	2,426,010
Middle Market Areas		
96	Johnstown-Altoona, PA	285,050
97	Evansville, IN	279,190
98	Youngstown, OH	275,410
99	Savannah, GA	273,680
100	Harlingen-Weslaco-Brownsville-McAllen, TX	273,370
Small Market Area		
206	Juneau, AK	23,990
207	Helena, MT	23,730
208	Alpena, MI	17,290
209	North Platte, NE	15,260
210	Glendive, MT	3,900
	Total	**105,444,330**

Source: Copyright © 2001 Nielsen Media Research. Reprinted by permission.

Pulling Power. A single radio set has the power to draw many people together. The resulting audience can hear not only talk, music, and information but also the advertising that supports commercial media.

people of Glendive and thus plays a part in the colorful tapestry of U.S. electronic media.

Wherever they are, in large cities or small, electronic media strive for strong identities. That's because all of them have one common objective: to catch and hold our attention. Most channels are commercial; they need to gather us into measurable audiences to "sell" to advertisers, by far the predominant source of electronic-media revenue. To achieve this, traditional broadcast networks (ABC, CBS, NBC, and others) and some cable channels and radio stations seek the widest possible audience appeal—that's why we call them *mass* media.

Brian Williams. This NBC News anchor—designated heir to long-time network star Tom Brokaw—developed his own niche on the network's cable-news outlets, MSNBC and CNBC.

That term is being redefined, however, as the media marketplace changes from one into many. In recent years, with the growth of newer networks, specialized channels, and Internet sites, the mass audience has been breaking into fragments. Each of these clusters has its own characteristics and interests, making it an identifiable target for tightly focused advertising—and a magnet to entrepreneurs who may even tailor a new channel to fit the fragmented niche.

ADAPTING TO AUDIENCES

Many cable-TV channels now carry programming only for viewers with specific concerns (health, aging, family life) or interests (sports, country music, gardening, the legal system). Some channels support what may be personal obsessions, which only the viewer's cable company knows about: golf, sex, shopping, trivia games. At this writing, the National Cable Television Association reports that channels being planned would focus on martial arts, anthropology, children's fashion—and life with puppies.

Interestingly, despite their diverse programming in recent times, electronic-media companies retain a monolithic image among many Americans. It's easier to praise or condemn stations, networks, or Internet media enterprises as just "the media"—indeed, it's easier to *remember* them that way—than as individual trees in an electronic forest. After all, many companies have changed their identities through mergers with other companies, deals that most of us can't begin to sort out. These moves toward media **consolidation** have allowed some relatively small companies to reach broader—even global—advertising markets, and have created efficiencies that increase profits for stockholders. They also have left a nucleus of mammoth corporations at the core of U.S. media control.

HOW PRINCIPLES MATTER

The title of this book is *Principles of Electronic Media*. In general, most of us probably believe that we know what a *principle* is—a rather stable rule or foundation upon which actions are or should be based. This is not a bad start on a definition. Still, we need a deeper look at the nature and function of principles before moving on.

Word and Deed

Local Reporter-Producer. Darcie Fisher of Boston's WCVB-TV prepares "Healthwatch" segments for the newscasts—an example of service to local audiences, a traditional duty of broadcasters.

Back in November 1990, the then-chairman of the Federal Communications Commission, Alfred Sikes, told an audience in Las Vegas that "one of the most fundamental American broadcasting principles . . . is **localism.**"[3]

Localism? What's that? Sikes was referring to an understanding, encoded in the Communications Act of 1934, that broadcasting's first obligation is to its local community—the people that stations are licensed to serve. To most of us, this may not appear to be an especially radical or controversial guideline for action. Critics long have complained, however, that commercial broadcasters devote less and less time to locally oriented content. One study found that less than one-half of 1 percent of total broadcast time goes to local public affairs programming, for instance.[4]

Broadcasters themselves sometimes concede privately that they have to push localism down their priority list. At the top of that list, often due to the demands of company owners and stockholders, is profit. So, is the industry's stated commitment to localism really a *principle*—or just an empty promise? Does it govern human behavior? Does it underlie the practice we see and hear on the air and in our on-line media every day? If people fail to live up to it consistently, or even now and then, can it still be considered a foundation of practice—a true principle?

One answer comes from a Random House dictionary: Its first, usually preferred, definition of *principle* is "an *accepted or professed* rule of action or conduct" (emphasis added.)[5] The word *binding* doesn't appear here. By this definition, if broadcasters generally accept localism and try to practice it or at least profess to follow it—even if they often ignore it—it can in fact be considered a principle. A doctrine, a guiding sense, and a basis for conduct: Any of these is a principle, according to the dictionary, but let's dig deeper.

Emergence

Suppose that, no matter how carefully electronic media organize their governing rules up front, they actually follow different patterns in their daily dealings. Suppose this becomes routine, systematic, and goes on for months, years, or even decades. Could that mean that *new* principles are emerging?

Our trusty dictionary suggests that a principle also may be defined as "the method of formation, operation or procedure *exhibited* in a given case" (emphasis added). The U.S. Defense Department, for example, has a policy on media access that states that "open and independent reporting shall be the principal means of coverage of U.S. military

Localism. Peter Mehegan and Mary Richardson headline the daily newsmagazine *Chronicle* on WCVB-TV, a commercial station serving Boston, Massachusetts, and surrounding communities. The show has been locally produced and broadcast for 20 years, winning awards and typically topping the ratings in its early-evening slot—and defying a long national decline in locally produced TV programs. (Photo courtesy WCVB-TV)

News Helicopters. When the terrorism of September 11, 2001, raised security concerns about the skies over the nation's cities, the government grounded these modern news tools. The ban on "chopper" flights lasted less than three months.

Consolidation The act of bringing together different entities or parts into a single or unified whole, as when media owners buy or take control of competing or complementary companies.

Localism Principle putting broadcasters' primary emphasis on serving local viewers or listeners.

operations."[6] The underlying principle is openness in a free society. Yet, in the wake of the terrorist attacks of September 11, 2001, the government temporarily grounded all aircraft, mostly helicopters, used by news organizations. Civic openness had been pushed to the rear by the military's view of a security risk.

Not just between sectors of society but even within the electronic-media community itself, bedrock principles may find themselves competing or conflicting. New circumstances may even lead to new principles. That's why this book will point out not only old and seemingly unshakable ideas but also newer patterns and precepts that arise in response to new conditions—and sometimes

ProTalk

Patrice Goya
Local TV-News Producer

"This is a very open newsroom. We can just stand up and say 'I completely disagree with you.' "

Patrice Goya was a senior in broadcasting at the University of Oregon when a disturbed teenager killed his parents and two fellow students in nearby Springfield and wounded more than 20 others. It was big national news. An NBC producer hired Goya as an assistant and sent her to find and talk with the "shooter's" older sister. Pulling up to the house where the sister was thought to be staying, the future television journalist realized that she couldn't go farther. Some *principle* inside her—involving sympathy and respect—kept her from bothering a young woman whose family had just been devastated.

Goya has not since been allowed to forget the importance of principles in electronic media. The news director who hired her at KGUN-TV in Tucson, Arizona, put out a "viewers' bill of rights"—not just for promotional reasons but out of principle, he insisted—that promised his audience ethical newsgath-

ering, privacy, and their right to hold the station accountable.

"We didn't cover a lot of crime as crime," Goya states. "There's another school of thought about that: If, in my neighborhood, I care about crime, I want to know what's behind it. How can it be prevented? Is there some reason for it being in my neighborhood? That's what we should focus on when we cover crime—not just the sensational parts."

In 2000, Tucson saw 90 murders, and violence is a tempting topic for a medium that's best at conveying emotion. However, says Goya, restraint in crime coverage allows more time for truly popular news topics, such as weather; in the desert, a few weeks of rain is a big ongoing story. Unsurprisingly, water is another well-liked news topic: Arizona struggles with the quantity and quality of its water supply. Day in and day out, TV news has plenty of issues to cover. The news producer organizes those stories into a meaningful half-hour or one-hour package.

"The hardest thing is trying to make sure everything gets done, and trusting everyone," Goya says, "knowing that if they don't come through, it's you who gets in trouble and not them. In the end it's always the producer's fault." Although there are good days and bad days producing, she adds, the September 2001 terrorist attack on the World Trade Center and Pentagon showed her that television news can be handled responsibly, no matter how grim the subject: "There were a lot of good things—like ABC choosing not to show bodies falling out of windows; I liked that . . . it surprised me."

In late 2001, at age 24, Goya was promoted to a top producing job at KGUN-TV. She was pleased to be working in a newsroom where principles mattered. "This is a very open newsroom," she says. "We can just stand up and say 'I completely disagree with you.' "

stay around. To ignore emerging principles would be like trying to describe twenty-first century American life by referring only to our eighteenth-century Constitution. Our nation and our media are still works in progress.

ELECTRONIC-MEDIA ROLES

In a process known loosely as **globalization,** U.S.-based electronic media are helping to construct a complex—and often controversial—web around the earth. To use transoceanic telephone lines or transcontinental cables, of course, is nothing new. However, for growing media giants to bring a rainbow of radio, TV, and Internet programming to dozens of countries, via satellite and with digital services to boot, is new indeed.

Electronic media never could be described very precisely in terms of *place*; their signals tend to travel too far to confine their impact to a single neighborhood or even a town.[7] Now, geography has become almost immaterial, as broadcast programming flies into previously unserved or underserved areas of the globe. *Time* is a different matter; it still both marks and limits not only messages and programs but also industry developments. Electronic media haven't been around forever and they didn't all arrive at once. Each came into being in an appropriate moment in time because people figured out how to make them and because they met pent-up personal needs.

Filling Our Needs

The main importance of our media hinges on their ability to fill demands that have existed throughout history, but that only in the past century or so have been seriously addressed. Electronic technology made that possible.

NEWS

The September 2001 attacks on the World Trade Center and the Pentagon were unprecedented; the country never had experienced large-scale terrorism. The attacks jerked the media into action and prompted Americans to use their media as never before.Fear for their own families' safety and for the security of everyday life was paramount. Panic was rare but shock and concern were almost universal.

Most Americans were working, commuting, in school, or just waking up when the carnage occurred, and they learned of it on the radio. Then came wall-to-wall TV news coverage, shoving Tuesday soap operas and then evening comedies and dramas off the air. All the while, millions of people pounded their computer keyboards, searching out details of the disaster according to their own practical and psychological needs.

These responses came as no surprise to media researchers in the electronic age. People always rush desperately to find news of a disaster in which their loved ones may have been injured or worse. What's more, the peculiar directness of electronic media—plus what seems to be a perceived intimacy—draws people to radio and TV in particular, for various deep-seated reasons. Families of air-crash victims, for example, often find healing in viewing news reports repeatedly.

Globalization Movement to deliver programming and other media services to many countries, often through international corporate partnerships or mergers.

Dan Rather. "Discovered" covering a hurricane for a Texas station in 1961, Rather built a bright network career. He reigned as top CBS anchor when audiences began shifting away from TV news.

Cultural Pertaining to the culture—the sum total of behaviors, customs, and beliefs—of a particular society or group.

Documentary Based on or relating to an actual person, era, or event and presented factually and without fictional content.

Voyeuristic Pertaining to the practice of self-gratification by viewing certain acts or situations intended to be private; traditionally applied to sexual acts, but recently broadened in media contexts to include other invasions of privacy.

Rating Size of the audience (usually in households) for a particular program.

Infotainment Blend of news (or information) and entertainment.

Even in normal times, we crave some types of news, defined broadly as fresh information about human experience and the ways in which people pass their days. **Cultural** programs that send cameras roaming the world are part of this fabric, as are thoughtful **documentary** treatments—long-form, in-depth examinations of ordinary high schools and hospitals, for example—and replays of history. Media companies have created **voyeuristic** Internet news sites: radio talk shows on which we can hear and argue with others about social issues, TV newsmagazines that trace real human stories, and "reality" shows that pit eager contestants against nature.

By now it's clear that many of today's offerings from the electronic media spill across old boundaries between news and entertainment. In fact, some have dropped boundaries and become blenders. Newsmagazines such as *Dateline NBC* use Hollywood-style visual and aural techniques to heighten their viewers' emotions over stories of true crime and personal tragedy. Don Imus, Howard Stern, and other popular radio hosts mix serious issues with colorful sexual references and personal attacks. On TV's *The McLaughlin Group* and some other programs, political analysts engage their opponents in loud, arm-waving arguments that discourage contemplation.

DIVERSION AND ENRICHMENT

Recent trends may trouble journalists, but broadcast managers see them as necessary concessions to pressure for **ratings**. However, more significant than these dry head-count numbers are the needs and urges of the people behind them: "**Infotainment**" draws millions of fans who evidently distill both the serious and the frivolous from these programs—or at least don't allow one to obscure the other.

Many people do not seem especially concerned with placing content in neat categories. Rather than focusing on news and information needs, they seek one or both of two qualities that aren't as easily boxed in: diversion and enrichment. The great majority of electronic-media content can be seen as meeting at least one of these two needs.

Diversion may be described as the process of having our attention moved from whatever's bothering us to something more pleasant. News and analysis often bother people as badly as budgets, bosses, and boyfriends or girlfriends do—and they turn it off. That helps explain why radio offers many hours a day of music as diversion while TV presents scores of comedies, game shows, and cop dramas.

Enrichment, the addition of value or significance to our lives,[8] is a more elusive notion than diversion. Commercial broadcasting is structured mainly to profit from light entertainment, not from the enrichment offered by profound music, extended and probing news treatments, arts displays, and sociopolitical

TV Argument Shows. Programs featuring noisy political arguments, such as CNN's *Crossfire,* draw criticism for putting showmanship above informing the public.

documentaries. Public broadcasting favors such fare but has been pushed toward airy content, including British comedies and *Car Talk*-style radio banter, by constantly growing pressures for bigger audiences and more donations.

However, to halt discussion here would mean taking a narrow—even elitist—view of enrichment. Whether we've received added value is determined not just by where we end up but by where we *started.* Most of what we see and hear about worlds beyond our usual routines can add significance to our lives. People with few contacts outside the home may find all broadcast programs enriching, and those of us who have "surfed" onto unfamiliar TV terrain have found that simply allowing exotic messages to roll across our brains can broaden our knowledge.

Books may be best at imparting enrichment, but it can also be found in broadcasting and is readily accessible through the Internet media, with their click-click interactivity and bottomless information pits. Their potential to connect us to troves of learning has only begun to be developed. Meanwhile, the older electronic media provide diversion and some measure of enrichment to a rushed society accustomed to *multitasking*—doing many things at once.

A SPECIAL NEED

Media scholars have found evidence that we all have a built-in **surveillance** instinct, a need to keep an eye on our surroundings. Communications scholar Pamela J. Shoemaker links this to human biological and cultural evolution and calls it being "hardwired" for news.[9] Surveillance requires us to go beyond what we usually define as news to a broader combination of information and impressions of the world we inhabit. To keep our balance in that world, so full of strangers and unexpected events, we constantly scan the people, things, and spaces around us. We are looking for reassurance, for a zone of safety, not realizing, or only half-realizing, that we're doing so.

Within this sphere of truth, rumor, and hope, electronic media hold an important place. Their directness and emotional power have helped them excel at filling our surveillance needs quickly, at presenting and sometimes even helping

Diversion The function that electronic media perform when they distract viewers from unpleasant or bothersome subjects.

Enrichment The process of adding value or significance to one's life, a function sometimes performed by electronic media.

Surveillance Observation or monitoring (of the human environment).

Entertainment Shows.
Light programs, such as *Everybody Loves Raymond,* have helped viewers escape their cares, including the national anxieties triggered by terrorism.

Streaming Digital transmission of audio or video to computer, using software decoding tool; user sees or hears transmission during download, rather than waiting for playback.

us sort out and store away the meanings of each day's events. Long-ago newspaper headlines are fascinating icons, but more often it's radio voices and television images that have burned incidents into our memory. Profiles of government officials, entrepreneurs, teachers, and fire-fighters—people against whom we can assess our own lives—all contribute to our intellectual-emotional loading.

Television often catches us at our peak levels of fear or concern and shows us vividly what has happened; that is its assumed mission. In extreme cases, this can be alarming and even damaging, as when too much local TV crime news frightens some people into hiding in their homes.[10] Most of the time, however, if our minds are otherwise in order, we take in stride the fruits of our surveillance and use them to keep living successfully.

Changing to Succeed

Broadcast audiences are getting smaller. On-line audiences are growing, but not always in predictable ways; Internet-based "new media" are struggling to assemble large and reliable groups of fans. On another front, newspapers invest in TV stations as a hedge against the future, or are joined to them by mergers. Electronic media swallow other electronic media, more out of competitive anxiety than hunger. Uncertainty reigns. Young consumers—customers of tomorrow—are adrift. Our electronic media now operate in an aggressively competitive, unstable atmosphere. The biggest enterprises use their immense buying power to get bigger (see Figure 1.1).

This kind of change matters. Today's media occupy such a large share of our popular culture—the ongoing stream of public messages, images, and social symbols in which all of us swim through our days—that each of their decisions ripples far across the cultural landscape. The way we flocked to the media in the aftermath of the 2001 terrorism onslaught helped to demonstrate this; we interact with these institutions almost automatically. What they do, for their own commercial or other purposes, has consequences for us. When one company or group takes an action that works, others are sure to imitate it, multiplying the impact on society.

Every day the business and entertainment pages of newspapers (and websites) ripple with changes brought about by the rush of technology, economic opportunities, individual ambitions, and sociocultural flux. We can track changes on several fronts, including:

- *Audiences.* With Hispanic immigrants pouring into major U.S. cities, New York's increasingly important Spanish-language radio stations compete furiously, some of them pushing limits on sexual and profane speech to grab audiences.
- *Choices.* Internet news sites go through a "shakeout," with some sites shutting down, but overall they enjoy healthy growth; they do especially well among viewers in their thirties, and have pushed video **streaming** (playback

FIGURE 1.1

One Corporation's Holdings: Tribune Company

Source: Courtesy *Columbia Journalism Review* and "Who Owns What" website, Aaron J. Moore, creator.

Broadcast and Cable

Broadcast

WPIX	New York
KTLA	Los Angeles
WGN	Chicago
WPHL	Philadelphia
WLVP	Boston
KDAF	Dallas
WGNX	Atlanta
KHTV	Houston
KTZZ	Seattle
WBZL	Miami-Ft. Lauderdale
KWGN	Denver
KTXL	Sacramento
WXIN	Indianapolis
KSWB	San Diego
WTIC	Hartford/New Haven
WTXX	Hartford
WXMI	Grand Rapids
WGNO	New Orleans
WPMT	Harrisburg
WBDC	Washington (not owned, but operated under a Lease Management Agreement)
WNOL	New Orleans

Cable

CLTV Chicago area 24-hour news and sports

TV Food Network (31%)

Central Florida News 13 (CFN 13) 24-hour local news channel—joint venture between Tribune and Time Warner Communications

Radio

WGN-AM	Chicago
KKHK-FM	Denver
KOSI-FM	Denver
KEZW-AM	Denver

Tribune Company—Publishing

Daily Newspapers
Chicago Tribune

Fort Lauderdale Sun-Sentinel

Orlando Sentinel

South Florida Newspaper Network

Daily Press (Hampton Roads, Virginia, and area)

Advocate (Stamford, CT)

Baltimore Sun

Greenwich Time (CT)

Hartford Courant

La Opinion (50% Spanish language newspaper in southern California)

Los Angeles Times

Los Angeles Times Syndicate (syndication service)

Los Angeles Times–Washington Post News Service (50%)

Morning Call (Allentown, PA)

Newsday (Long Island, NY)

Tribune Media Services (syndicated content for print and on-line)
On the Mark Media

TMS TV television programming information

TVData television programming information

Zap2it.com web site offering TV listings

Online Publications
Black Voices Afro-centric news and information

Exito South Florida Hispanic community news

Relcon listing of Chicago area apartments

US/Express weekly entertainment news

Digital City Atlanta

Digital City Boston

Digital City Chicago

Digital City Denver

Digital City Hampton Roads

Digital City Los Angeles

Digital City Orlando

Digital City South Florida

cars.com national web site for vehicle listings—venture with Times Mirror and Washington Post Co.

apartments.com national web site for apartment listings—venture with Times Mirror and Washington Post Co. (cars.com and apartments.com are part of Classified Ventures LLC)

CareerBuilder.com (with Knight Ridder)

Tribune Company—Other

Sports Franchise
Chicago Cubs

Tribune Ventures (investment in and partnerships with the following ventures; percentage indicates how much ownership Tribune Co. has with)
America Online (1.5%)

CheckFree (1.0%)—electronic payment processor

Digital City (20.1%)—local interactive content

Excite (4.3%)—World Wide Web search engine

ImageBuilder Software (23%)—software developer

Discourse Technologies (14%)—multimedia education products

Infobeat (12.6%)—customized content

iVillage (7.8%)—on-line content

Lightspan Partnership (6.6%)—new-media education products

Open Market (2.6%)—electronic commerce

Peapod (10.7%)—on-line grocery shopping service

Picture Network International (NA)—on-line content

The Learning Company (11%)—multimedia education products

SoftKey International (NA)—digital education products

StarSight TeleCast (NA)

Interealty Corp. (25%)—real estate information

Knight-Ridder/Tribune Information services (50%)—news wire

Baring Communications Equity (Asia-Pacific) Ltd. Fund (NA)

Classified Ventures LLC (33%)

of on-line video onto computer screens) into the limelight since the 2001 terrorist attacks.

- *Corporate reach.* Mogul Rupert Murdoch has been granted permission to broadcast the Phoenix Chinese Channel to 4 million people in regions of China. The channel is delivered by STAR, a wholly owned subsidiary of News Corp. Meanwhile, Murdoch's moves to control programming into Latin America have set off antitrust concerns in Mexico.

Tapping Old Currents

Not long ago (and to some extent today), bored children often played at communicating in technology-aided ways. A common pastime worked like this: Kids would fetch two empty cans from the trash, punch a hole in the bottom of each, and anchor each end with one long connecting string.

If they waxed the string and pulled it tight, the children could stand many yards apart and understand, with difficulty, the words each other spoke into his or her can. They were using long-understood principles to create a communication link from junk. Their string-and-can technology perfectly suited their content, which also was junk of a sort—grunts, howls, whistles, operational phrases such as "I can't hear you!" and maybe some risky profanity.

Simple, ridiculous, brilliant: a telephone system that cost nothing, communicated nothing of consequence, and was fun to use. There seem to be modern parallels in the adult world—media technologies that open the way for communication, wind up shaping its form, and sometimes seem to stand in for missing content.

The telegraph, for example, certainly affected the form of mass communication. It came along in the 1840s, became a tool of newspapers competing for scoops, and gave rise to terse, front-loaded news dispatches that could be transmitted quickly. They had to be sent quickly: The new system depended on thin wires crossing a rugged continent. It rapidly established a brisk journalistic writing style through which we still learn of most news events.

Now, each year, television networks produce programs by recycling basic plots, changing only faces, clothes, and details. The programs add little to our culture, but enough of us enjoy watching them—that is, at least enjoy *watching television*, as a cultural practice in front of a piece of technology—to reinforce our beliefs and memories and to guarantee profits to the networks.

Similarly, local TV stations sometimes add hours of news programming but then, instead of hiring reporters to root out more stories, hire producers to repackage stories already available. Stations put reporters on the air live from locations where news ended hours earlier or is yet to occur. Like the kids with the cans and waxed string, the reporters have nothing of consequence to say but are still compelled to speak.

Commercials, however, run as always. Broadcasters thus cleverly create new profits out of almost nothing. Our society's

Samuel F. B. Morse.
Morse's great invention, the telegraph, made it possible to communicate quickly over great distances. The telegraph led to the creation of a clipped, efficient writing style that still is found in newspapers.

fascination with the forms, rituals, and gee-whiz technologies of electronic media keeps the system going.

THE BOOK AND THE QUEST

Some people recklessly accuse today's students of having only a superficial interest in education. This is dangerous stereotyping. However, it does remind us that it's possible to examine the electronic media superficially and carry away only a loose grip of their principles—for example, that broadcasters sell audiences, not programs.

Most of us want to know more—much more. We're intrigued by the media institutions that have become so pervasive in modern life. We may have strong opinions about their motives and performance or only vague hunches that what these media do really matters. Either way, we need information and the perspectives of others. *Principles of Electronic Media* will bring much into focus by providing such material. It will do better, however, by inspiring readers to ask more questions.

This is crucial: The most important targets of inquiry are not those suggested within this book by the authors. The most important questions arise from riddles and gaps and uncharted territories exposed by each student's own discoveries and reasoning. Many questions involve not just media themselves but the communities and people affected by them. What follows are two examples—real situations from the television industry. One involves the human element inside TV news; the other holds advertising practices up to the light. Both should give rise to nagging questions about the principles involved.

Motives and a Cold Day

Will Wright was news director of WWOR-TV in Secaucus, New Jersey, when, one day in the winter of 2000–2001, a woman fell through the ice. News crews raced to the scene. The woman was rescued. She spoke only Spanish. When video of the incident arrived at the station, a writer-producer was assigned to supervise its editing. In doing so, the writer *permitted other sound to cover the rescued woman's Spanish words*. The news director saw this on the air and was displeased.

"I was bemoaning the fact that the writer didn't let the Spanish portion pass through," Wright said the next day. "That, to me, showed disrespect for that woman's culture. Are we so tight (on air time) tonight that we can't let at least 10 seconds of that language go on the air?"

So, a well-meaning manager was irked because one story on one news day omitted a touch of Spanish. That's what we learn from the anecdote—but what more do we need to learn? Here are some questions we could pose, and some answers to consider:

- *What is the station's audience?* WWOR-TV, based in New Jersey, competes for viewers in the massive New York City-area television market.
- *OK, but what are the **demographics** (the key characteristics of the audience)?* The market includes more than one million Hispanic households, about 11 percent of the total.[11]

Demographics Audience characteristics (age, gender, race, etc.) used to identify "target" audiences or consumers at which advertising is aimed.

Clutter Proliferation of advertisements that tends to overwhelm programming.

Prime time Evening hours of peak TV consumption, usually 8:00 to 11:00 P.M.

- *Did Will Wright care about that audience?* Restate the question more precisely, please.
- *Did Wright care personally about the Hispanic community?* No one could read his mind, but he was a well-known contributor to minority causes around New York and an advocate for better minority coverage by the broadcast industry. After the rescued-woman incident, he exclaimed, "Surely the entire Spanish-Latino culture in New York is worth 10 seconds!"
- *Could other factors also have been on Wright's mind?* Yes, ratings, for one; market positioning, for another. Wright was building WWOR-TV's image as a champion of minority news and issues. It was a gamble, but he believed in it, and WWOR-TV did need to distinguish itself from its competitors.
- *Still, why would a news director react so strongly to a simple editing decision?* The station and the group that owned it were to be acquired soon by Fox, which was sure to cut jobs while merging operations. Consequently, every daily decision bearing on audience perceptions and support could affect the fate of Wright and his staff. At least he hardly could be blamed for being nervous.

Will Wright left his job in the fall of 2001 after Fox bought his station and brought in its own executives. Wright went to work as the executive producer for *The Nightly News* on Black Entertainment Television (BET). He left the station, though, with credit for "attracting to the newscast the young and largely urban and minority audience," to quote an industry journalist.

When Ads Attack

Television typically suffers from what is called **clutter.** It's a condition in which ads begin to overwhelm programming. Some of these ads are "promos," created by the networks themselves to promote their upcoming shows.[12] The degree of clutter is tracked by the American Association of Advertising Agencies and the Association of National Advertisers. Their report for 1999 showed that every hour of prime-time TV programming contained nearly 17 minutes of advertising. Clutter counts had long been rising, and this new average set an unattractive all-time record. However, one year later, the 2000 report indicated a *drop* in clutter on the networks.

A decline in the number of commercial minutes we all have to endure: It seems simple and encouraging. Is that all there is to it? No; our minds fill with questions:

- *Why does clutter happen?* Clutter occurs because advertisers want to get their messages out, and because networks and stations want the advertisers' money and, to get it, are willing to squeeze programming. (This is true for publishers, too; magazines also have a clutter problem.)
- *Why does the ad industry bother to monitor clutter?* The industry well knows that some readers, viewers, and listeners do resent floods of advertising, and that clutter therefore might have a negative impact.
- *On whom?* On advertisers themselves, especially when they pay premium rates to put their ads into television's **prime time,** the evening hours when

most people watch TV. If the commercial breaks are too long or frequent, it's hard for consumers to tell the ads apart and reflect on them—so those premium dollars may go to waste.

- *Does clutter really bother TV viewers?* Yes and no. Research has established what many of us might guess: Clutter sometimes hampers our memory of commercials (bad for buyers, worse for sellers), channel switching goes up when commercials annoy us, and we especially resent ads that interrupt unusually absorbing programs. However, some TV viewers seem to consider ads a natural, tolerable, and sometimes interesting part of the viewing experience. The key is perception: Do people *feel* bothered by clutter?
- *Who regulates or controls the number of commercials?* Only the advertisers and broadcasters.

Summary

Electronic media are far more to us than suppliers of entertainment and news. They meet social and psychological needs of which we barely are aware but which are fundamental to our lives, individually and collectively. Radio, television, and the Internet both mediate and originate communication. No longer merely witnesses or storytellers, they are massive producers of culture and they are economic players; they are *active* in shaping society.

These media are connected to us through their principles—some merely professed, some usually followed; some historically grounded and some invented to suit the times. Whether and how a television station should report on violent crime are among the questions best answered through the application of principles. Media responsibility and accountability are never guaranteed.

None of us can measure the full influence of electronic media simply by consuming their products. Because media largely are businesses and adapt their behaviors to what the markets require, we can't expect to understand and keep up with them unless we examine them closely. Beyond the basic act of study—and ultimately far more important—lie daily monitoring, probing inquiry, and constant critical thinking.

FOOD FOR THOUGHT

1. Is confusion of media fact with fantasy a problem? Do streams of true and false information sometimes merge? What solutions do you see?
2. What kinds of principles should we expect in our electronic media? List a few and explain their potential importance as we consume media content.
3. Which of three content types—news, diversion, or enrichment—dominate your use of electronic media? Does this help in balancing your life? Explain.
4. Do you agree with Will Wright regarding the rescue story about the Hispanic woman? How would you address viewers' ethnic sensitivities? Explain your answer.
5. When it comes to advertising clutter, do you see any principles in conflict? For example, how can the electronic media sustain the need for increased revenue when the audience shows less tolerance for commercial interruptions?

2

History of Radio and Television

One ought to be ashamed to make use of the wonders of science embodied in a radio set, while appreciating them as little as a cow appreciates the botanic marvels in the plants she munches.

—Albert Einstein, physicist

When a new medium starts, it should be a new frontier. There should be great aspirations and high hopes.

—Lawrence K. Grossman, former television executive

The twenty-first century bears proof that many early inventors' hopes for electronic media were justified. People today increasingly work, learn, and relax among complex systems that exist only because Thomas Edison, Alexander Graham Bell, Philo T. Farnsworth, and others long ago broke ground for them. Wonders of media convergence are here or on the horizon: streams of data "bits" transmitting **satellite**-delivered radio and TV programming, wherever we happen to be; playing **digital** games through our television sets; easy ways of receiving radio and movies on our computers; accessing high-speed paths to an increasingly media-rich Internet; and much, much more. Future combinations seem unlimited.

Family around radio. Families who had sent men overseas to fight World War II felt closer to them when listening to the radio—a sign of the power and intimacy of electronic media.

Such was not always true. Our electronic media are rooted in times when tinkerers and visionaries faced limits of every kind—technological, financial, political, and cultural. Inventors and entrepreneurs surmounted these barriers through persistence, not magic or even genius alone (although some certainly were geniuses). No single inspiration or experiment held the key to all; there were many doors and many keys. The birth of our electronic media was

Our electronic media are rooted in times when tinkerers and visionaries faced limits of every kind— technological, financial, political, and cultural.

gradual, disjointed, and messy. What humans brought into being—the power to send sounds, pictures, and more across oceans and continents and then around the globe—would transform human society.

A critical event occurred May 24, 1844, in the chambers of the U.S. Supreme Court. That's where a preacher's son from Massachusetts clicked a verse of scripture on a **telegraph** key: "What hath God wrought?" The question seemed appropriate as Samuel Finley Breese Morse opened and closed his circuit breaker to transmit those words from Washington, DC, to Baltimore's Mount Clare railroad station.

Morse had hoped the government would take over and operate his invention as a national system. Instead, entrepreneurs rushed in to capitalize on this early form of "dot-com" enterprise. Western Union and American Telegraph Company launched the telecommunications industry—while fortune eluded Morse. He later told a friend that the telegraph brought him only "litigation, litigation, litigation."

Radio

The transmission of Samuel Morse's language of dots and dashes was a startling and path-breaking development. It foreshadowed radio and later forms of electronic media, but rather distantly in time. More than 30 years would pass before a speech teacher for the deaf—Alexander Graham Bell—attempted the next leap forward: a machine to amplify the human voice. First, some crucial research took place.

MAXWELL'S "ETHER"

Some of that research came from one of Bell's fellow Scots, a man named James Clerk Maxwell. He was investigating **electromagnetic waves,** which seemed promising as an invisible means of telecommunication. Maxwell wondered how an electric current could act like a magnet on a compass (as the Danish scientist Hans Christian Oersted had discovered) and how these currents could spread out in fields (as Michael Faraday observed in Great Britain).

Could it be, Maxwell wondered, that electromagnetic waves undulated in an invisible ocean of currents—"a **luminiferous ether**"? His "ether," it seems, was just a metaphor, but the idea provoked other scientists to investigate electromagnetic waves in order to discover their true identity and powers.

BELL'S TELE-TINKERING

If Alexander Graham Bell was born to be a great tinkerer, it wasn't apparent in his early years. Bell wished to follow in the footsteps of his father—an educator

---

Satellite Earth-orbiting spacecraft used to relay radio signals from one point on earth to another; permits distribution of programming or news without telephone or cable wires.

> ### Principle #1
> In the United States, government may fund electronic-media experiments, but it's up to business to apply the results.

Digital technology based on electric signals using "binary" code of 1 or 0 in combinations; indicates circuits to be switched on or off to convey a message.

Telegraph First means of electromagnetic communication; used cable wires and a coded language of dots and dashes.

Electromagnetic wave Wave produced by accelerating an electric charge, manipulating the charge by changing the intensity of nearby electric or magnetic fields.

Luminiferous ether (light-producing) James Clerk Maxwell's image of a charged ocean of air undulating with electromagnetic waves in radiating patterns; guided early thinkers.

in Scotland renowned for teaching the deaf how to use visible speech. As Bell read about electromagnetic experiments in telegraphy, he thought about the possibilities of transmitting *sounds* by telegraph. Suppose a harmonic machine could be built to vibrate in response to a voice, as the human eardrum does; could that help the deaf to hear?

In 1875, Bell, his future father-in-law, and a local businessman pooled their resources to build such a machine. Thomas A. Watson signed on to help solve mechanical problems. On March 7, 1876, Bell secured a patent for a blueprint to transmit vocal sounds telegraphically. Three days later, he recorded in his diary the moment when he first exclaimed by phone, "Mr. Watson, come here, I want you." Bell showed off his device at the Philadelphia Centennial Exposition, where it was ignored until the emperor of Brazil paused by the telephone to observe, "My word, it talks!"

Bell and his partners formed a company in 1877, introducing the name *telephone*. Seven years later, they created a subsidiary to handle long-distance communications: American Telephone & Telegraph Company. However, once the telephone drew attention as another method of making money, Bell lost interest in his invention and resumed teaching the deaf. It was others who developed the business of telegraphy and turned the telephone into the basis of a national communication system.

Alexander Graham Bell. Bell never lost interest in helping the deaf to hear, which led him to create something of immense social impact—the telephone, in 1876. Bell showed that voices could be transmitted through electrical wires.

Spark-gap detector Device that revealed electromagnetic radiation by making a spark jump a gap, emitting waves that triggered another spark-jump some distance away.

Oscillating Swinging back and forth, like energy in an alternating current.

HERTZ MAKES WAVES

Researchers continued work that eventually would tie together the strands of future electronic media. In Germany, Heinrich Rudolph Hertz decided to make the invisible visible, permitting people to *see* electromagnetic waves. Hertz used James Clerk Maxwell's formulas to create something called a **spark-gap detector.** He would use it along with **oscillating** electric circuits to turn his ideas to reality.

In a corner of his Berlin classroom in 1888, Hertz electrified a pair of metal rods. When the rods took on opposite charges, they sparked, and waves oscillated back and forth. Hertz had verified Maxwell's theorems. Electromagnetic waves existed, usually unseen, in about the form Maxwell had predicted. Interestingly, the scientist seemingly was unaware of his experiment's practical implications—and thus its historical importance. His name would endure, however, as the label for one cycle of radiated electromagnetic energy. Broadcast engineers today still call one cycle a **hertz.**

> **Principle #2**
>
> The key to telecommunications is that electromagnetic energy can be transmitted between two points.

Hertz Cycle of a radio wave; honors Heinrich Hertz for demonstrating waves' existence. (One *kiloHertz* = 1,000 waves per second; one *megaHertz* = 1,000,000 waves per second.)

MESSAGE FROM MARCONI

Meanwhile, Professor Augusto Righi of Bologna, Italy, was delving into the mysteries that Maxwell had calculated and Hertz had demonstrated. Righi was

Revisiting Alexander Graham Bell

Correspondents in Afghanistan in 2001 were reporting the fall of the Taliban regime, linked to September 2001 terrorist attacks on the United States, and the TV screen identified something called the **videophone** as the means of transmission. Its pictures were blocky and at times even frozen; words fell out of sync with the speaker's lips, as in a low-cost Kung Fu movie. However, major network news operations were using the videophone in satellite newsgathering **(SNG)** to tell the new millennium's biggest story so far.

Interestingly, in a clear connection to history, the videophone was descended directly from a device designed by Alexander Graham Bell to help the deaf hear. Bell envisioned adding pictures to his device and invented an instrument that transmitted sound by vibrations in a beam of light, the "photophone." Years later, this machine with pictures was perfected and made portable—a precursor of the videophone. In July 1999, Japan's Kyocera Corporation began marketing its VP-210 Visual Phone, the world's first mobile videophone (actually a TV camera linked to a computerized satellite-phone system). Two years later, CNN's Nic Robertson used a videophone to show a rebel strike from Kabul, the Afghan capital. Tom Aspell of NBC routinely used a videophone to cover movements of the anti-Taliban Northern Alliance, as did journalists from the British Broadcasting Corporation and Associated Press television.

How did crude pictures and hollow audio become popular so quickly in such a polished on-screen setting as TV news? First, the device permitted the networks to transmit *something* visual out of remote Afghan valleys where the U.S. war on terrorism raged. The videophone's news product was live, and it also looked (and was) digital in an age when digital was trendy. Second, a videophone could be set up or dismantled in minutes, and could operate on its own batteries or on a car's battery via the cigarette-lighter outlet. Also, the device was compact, noiseless, and easy to hide—a big advantage in hot spots where journalists sometimes were seen as targets. The videophone and its satellite-"uplink" unit could travel in four suitcases; conventional satellite newsgathering (SNG) required a truck with a large dish, with total weight measured in tons.

Best of all, in a highly cost-conscious age, a videophone cost about $15,000, whereas every ungainly satellite truck cost a network *hundreds of thousands* of dollars.

Videophone Portable camera-computer unit that can transmit news via satellite.

Satellite newsgathering (SNG) Applies to mobile satellite-relay equipment.

focused on the theoretical, and had not a visiting student begun prodding him with what today we might call "real-world" questions, he might never have earned a place in media history. The student, Guglielmo Marconi, was determined to get answers. Aware of Hertz's work, Marconi considered whether and how a *wireless* telegraph might send messages to warn ships of threatening seas, or to relay reports from distant battlefields. These large notions propelled Marconi, and his father let him use the family granary as a laboratory to begin trying out ideas.

On a summer day in 1895, Marconi sent his older brother and a tenant farmer to carry a radio receiver to the edge of the family vineyard. They were to respond with a rifle blast if they heard the receiver catch an incoming wireless signal. Marconi sent a simple message and was rewarded with the boom of a gunshot. That sharp sound from a Tuscan hillside marked the true beginning of radio, and thus of all its descendants.

Others, too, played roles in radio's creation. Mahlon Loomis won an early patent for wireless telegraphy in 1872. He had transmitted radio waves between two kites in the Blue Ridge Mountains, and founded the Loomis Aerial Telegraph

Company. Later, a Serbian inventor from Croatia, Nikola Tesla, sought a patent for his "four-tuned radio circuit." On June 21, 1943, the U.S. Supreme Court overturned Marconi's basic patent for that device, deciding Tesla had come up with it first.

That critically important inventors such as Tesla and Loomis are relatively unknown to Americans today is typical of advances in electronics and other fields: A few stars get all the headlines. Ronald Kline, a historian of technology, warns against the view that "technological change largely results from solitary, heroic acts of invention." More accurate accounts, he says, note the "simultaneity of invention, the teamwork often associated with 'lone' inventors, and the lengthy and complex process of technological development."[1]

Guglielmo Marconi. Marconi envisioned the use of radio waves for wireless telegraphy and soon spanned the ocean with messages in Morse Code, the first of them merely letters of the alphabet.

Soon after the successful wireless experiment at his family's vineyard, Marconi wrote to the Italian government, asking for funding to continue his work. A minor official in Rome dashed off a dismissive reply. So, with his Irish mother, the young inventor embarked on a journey to England to seek family help. When he showed his invention to British customs agents, the collection of wires and bolts in a telegraph box alarmed them. They dismantled the wireless transmitter and left it in a heap. Undaunted, Marconi started over again in London with the help of a cousin who introduced him to the head of British Telegraphic Services.

> **Principle #3**
> The early stage of media development is a cumulative process to which many people contribute.

The British liked his ideas, and he made good on their support—by transmitting radio waves across the Salisbury Plain in England and the Bristol Channel in 1897. Marconi formed his first company in London that year. Two years later, seeking North American sponsors for new investments, he arrived in the United States and incorporated the American Marconi Wireless Telegraph Company. Driven to transmit over greater distances, he sent the letter *S* across the Atlantic in Morse code by wireless in 1901, and began building a stronger amplifier for future transmissions.

Television

The 1800s found dreams of television drawing strength from the wireless and other inventions. Efforts to reproduce images from life had begun long before, and by the 1830s, a Frenchman named Louis-Jacque-Mandé Daguerre was perfecting photography (early photographs were dubbed *daguerrotypes*). Over the next 50 years, other advances foreshadowing *moving* images would emerge in Europe and the United States.

SCANNING

Some early innovations, such as a method of sending telegraph signals that would reproduce pictures or symbols, showed little potential. Others, though,

Lee De Forest. This American inventor pursued research on the vacuum tube—crucial to TV—by adding a third element to a glass tube, creating a "triode." It amplified and controlled electromagnetic signals.

Cathode ray Focused beam of energy from the electrode inside a vacuum tube that projects shadows (images) on the tube.

Vacuum tube Electron tube used to amplify signals; made obsolete by transistor for most uses (the cathode ray tube in TV is a vacuum tube).

Scanning Left-to-right motion of an electron beam across the face of the cathode ray tube; modulating the intensity of the beam displays TV images.

Electrode Conductor through which an electrical current enters or leaves a medium, such as a vacuum tube.

were more tantalizing. A German group discovered how the **cathode ray**—a focused beam of energy from the electrode inside a **vacuum tube**—could project shadows on the tube. As Thomas Edison's phonograph made sound recording possible, telephone creator Alexander Graham Bell and others labored to transmit not just sounds but pictures.

One of the most important contributions was the Frenchman Maurice Leblanc's 1880 revelation of **scanning.** It was a technique—still vital today—through which an image could be broken systematically into lines that were then translated into energy. Scientists and engineers were realizing that only by taking an image apart could they translate it into forms that could be transmitted to another place, where it would then be reassembled into the image. A German named Paul Nipkow soon employed scanning with encouraging results. In 1884, he patented a system of perforated disks, rotating at constant speeds, through which images could be transferred from their source to a viewing device. The mechanical approach embodied by the "Nipkow disk" lent great momentum to TV's development.

DE FOREST'S TUBE

Mechanical means of giving mobility to pictures eventually would be eclipsed by something more promising and, to the layperson, more magical: the *electronic* transmission of pictures. By the end of the nineteenth century, Lee De Forest was advancing that cause—first by way of radio. This new medium needed some way to amplify a signal as it entered the receiver inside a radio set. De Forest, an Alabama minister's son with an engineering degree, invented a tube with a new type of **electrode** that could accomplish that. He proudly dubbed his "triode" tube the **Audion.** De Forest soon faced a patent fight in court over the invention—one of the first of his many legal battles. One of them, a dispute with Columbia University's Professor Edwin Howard Armstrong over a critical circuit that increased radio signal strength, would last until 1934, when the Supreme Court awarded rights to De Forest.

1900–1930: BIRTH OF AN INDUSTRY

In 1906, De Forest patented a big improvement in the cathode ray tube. The CRT became the glowing heart of the future television set. By now, the excitement radiating from television labs was drawing brilliant minds into an international race to realize the dream. Scientists and engineers were hard at work in the United States, Europe, and Japan.

Radio

This community of scientists and engineers scarcely paused as radio stepped out of the laboratory to make public history: The first station(s) went on the air.

Thereby hangs a debate that has raged among broadcasters and scholars for nearly a century: Which station should be entitled to call itself first in the nation in terms of **broadcasting**?

WHO WAS FIRST IN THE NATION?

Station WWJ in Detroit laid its claim by documenting its initial broadcast on August 31, 1920, which announced returns from Michigan political primaries. However, in San Jose, California, an ancestor of the West Coast powerhouse KCBS had gone on the air in 1909. It broadcast Charles Herrold's farm reports to owners of **crystal sets.** These crude radio receivers were invented around 1906. Each featured an adjusting arm, two binding posts, and a string of wire called a "cat's whisker," which tickled a crystal, passing along a lot of static and occasionally radio frequencies. In Madison, Wisconsin, experimental station 9XM (later WHA) signed on at the state university's campus in 1909 as a physics department experiment, and reached a few crystal sets.

Some of the most vigorous claims to "first" status in radio surround KDKA in Pittsburgh, based on its uninterrupted service since 1920. The station's story begins when a Westinghouse engineer, Frank Conrad, built a workshop over his garage in 1916 and began transmitting. Listener letters in response to that station, then called 8XK, impressed Westinghouse Electric Corporation, which decided it could use Conrad's station to help sell its surplus of SCR-70 wireless radio sets.

Westinghouse built a 100-watt transmitter on top of its plant in east Pittsburgh, and made plans for an inaugural broadcast. A commercial license arrived from the U.S. Department of Commerce just in time for KDKA to "sign on" on November 2, 1920, and report the presidential-election returns. Vote totals were phoned to the station from the *Pittsburgh Post,* and KDKA announced that Warren G. Harding had defeated James Cox (who, ironically, would leave politics to found Cox Broadcasting Company).

It's true that other stations preceded KDKA on the air, but that 1920 event marked *the first continuous, scheduled program service by a U.S.-licensed station.* Still, others note that WBZ in Springfield, Massachusetts, another Westinghouse station, actually received its license in September of that year, nearly two months before KDKA.[2] Anyway, the news quickly spread: Radio was here. Enthusiasts lined up at electrical shops to buy receivers. They could at last begin to hear life in motion—even if they were still years away from being able to *watch* it in their living rooms.

RCA'S SARNOFF GAMBLE

As radio entered the Roaring Twenties, the Radio Corporation of America (RCA) gambled on the commercial potential for appealing to a mass audience—due, in large part, to the drive and vision of one man. Russian immigrant David Sarnoff had moved upward rapidly at American Marconi and RCA. Sarnoff imagined the idea of radio programming in his famed "music box memo," which said that the radio set would one day become a "household utility" in the same sense as the piano or phonograph.

Audion Innovation by Lee De Forest using three conducting elements (triode) in a bulb to amplify and oscillate radio waves.

Broadcasting Originally from agriculture (distribution of seed); redefined by Communications Act of 1934 as dissemination of radio communications to public.

Crystal set Early radio receiver; with a silicon crystal connected to a wire coil, antenna, and headset, hobbyists could tune in programs.

David Sarnoff. Sarnoff sparked the birth of NBC as an offspring of the Radio Corporation of America (RCA). Skilled at self-promotion, he moved from commercial manager at RCA to chairman of the corporation.

Call letters Broadcast-station identifiers; stations west of Mississippi River have call letters beginning with *K;* those east of the river begin with *W.*

Frequencies Means for counting electromagnetic waves by counting the number of times per second (frequency) they pass a particular point.

Network Group of radio or television stations (affiliates) connected by contract to a central source of programming.

Sarnoff's fierce ambition led him to become general manager of RCA in 1921. There, he proposed forming a new company, under his supervision, devoted mainly to the art and science of broadcasting. (It would become NBC, the National Broadcasting Company.) However, RCA board members required evidence that Sarnoff's vision would yield a profit on their investment. They got that evidence in the form of enthusiastic audience response to the 1922 World Series broadcast over both WJZ in Newark, New Jersey, and WGY in Schenectady, New York. In the summer of 1924, stations in 12 cities were linked to carry gavel-to-gavel coverage of political party conventions. This coalition of stations rose up because the national networks were not yet in place.

The industry was tangled up in knots over conflicting patent claims to radio technology and the lease of telephone lines to network stations. When all parties resolved their differences, two networks were formed under Sarnoff's supervision. One, "NBC Red," linked stations owned by American Telephone & Telegraph (AT&T) to RCA's station WEAF. The other network, "NBC Blue," tied a half-dozen stations to WJZ in New York. On September 9, 1926, the National Broadcasting Company celebrated the birth of its two networks by broadcasting live from New York's Waldorf-Astoria Hotel, Chicago's Drake Hotel, and the Kansas dressing room of America's favorite comic-philosopher, Will Rogers.

Radio stations were proliferating rapidly, and interference on the air was growing, so Congress in 1927 created the Federal Radio Commission (FRC), primarily to license stations in an orderly way so that their signals would not overlap. The federal government was paying closer and closer attention to the new medium, as stations eagerly colonized the public's airwaves and planted the flags of their **call letters.** Over the next few decades, the FRC and its successor, the Federal Communications Commission (FCC), created in 1934, would increase regulation of broadcasting and stand watch over the allocation of **frequencies.**

CBS AND PALEY

The story of CBS begins in 1926. That's when Arthur Judson, manager of the New York Philharmonic and of Philadelphia's symphony orchestra, joined forces with salesman-promoter George A. Coats to form the Judson Radio Program Corporation. Soon, to shore up finances, they recruited the Columbia Phonograph Company as a partner. They had 16 "affiliated" stations, and promised to change its name to the Columbia Phonograph Broadcasting System. When the **network** kept losing money, the phonograph company bailed out—leaving behind, simply, the Columbia Broadcasting System (CBS).

At about the same time, William S. Paley started thinking big. He had been infatuated with radio ever since his family's cigar company rose in sales after sponsoring a show on WCAU in Philadelphia. Hearing that the Columbia network was up for sale, Paley and his father took over a majority of its stock to see if they could turn the company around. In 1928, CBS lost more than $330,000;

but after Paley became president and moved the network's headquarters to New York, CBS balanced its books.

Paley developed affiliate-friendly ideas, giving stations the shows they needed plus money to air network advertising "spots" (commercials). He hired a professor from Princeton for research, and recruited former newspaper and wire-service journalists to build CBS News. The network pushed away advertising-agency influence, taking control of its own shows. Paley—with strong business ability and an instinct for program quality—began to build what would become known as the "Tiffany Network," after a New York jewelry company known for elegance.

Amos 'n' Andy. A pair of white performers using black dialect delighted radio audiences with humor for many years on NBC, despite the racial stereotypes they projected.

PROGRAMMING THE TWENTIES

In the decade that preceded the Great Depression, two stage performers from Illinois and Virginia kept the national mood light. Charles Correll and Freeman Gosden were white, but developed a radio serial in black dialect, *Sam and Henry*, on Chicago's WGN in 1926, and it became a hit. In 1929, NBC Red took a chance on the show—by now renamed *Amos 'n' Andy*—and put it on the network schedule. It quickly attracted a huge national audience that would follow the humorous pair for decades. Presidents Truman and Eisenhower would confess to being fans of the show. Although it had listeners of all races, and was popular among African Americans, it eventually sparked criticism for its racial stereotyping.

Elsewhere on the air, *The Eveready Hour* set the standard for musical variety in radio's early days. The National Carbon Company premiered the program on New York's WEAF in 1923. It cost up to $6,000 a week to produce—the money required to bring in telephone lines, a 16-piece orchestra, singers, and guest celebrities. Other musical variety and comedy shows would pop up on radio during the Depression, including *Rudy Vallee's Variety Hour*, *Kay Kyser's Kollege of Musical Knowledge*, *Jack Benny*, and *George Burns & Gracie Allen*.

Television

Television was moving along with deliberate speed. Systems employing the Nipkow disk were patented in the 1920s. An Englishman, John Logie Baird, fabricated the first working TV set on that mechanical principle, and earned accolades as the British "father of television." The Baird system had limited capacity to produce large, high-resolution pictures, and international brainpower increasingly was focused on achieving such quality.

Westinghouse Electric Corporation hired Vladimir Zworykin, and in 1920, he invented the iconoscope, which could scan pictures and break them into electronic signals. He conceived and created the first practical television "picture

Radio in Black and White

Some early radio shows placed African Americans in far more dramatic and substantive roles than the minstrel-show–style misadventures of *Amos 'n' Andy*:

- CBS began a network series, *John Henry, Black River Giant,* in 1933.
- An African American writer in the U.S. Office of Education produced an eight-part series for NBC, *Freedom's People,* featuring stories about prominent figures in U.S. culture, such as boxer Joe Louis and actor/singer Paul Robeson.
- New York City radio stations WMCA and WJZ broadcast African American dramas in the 1930s.
- In 1944, WMCA began airing a series of programs devoted to issues in the black community; it was titled *New World a Comin',* written by Roi Ottley and based on his book of the same name.
- In Chicago, Richard Durham developed the first African American soap opera for radio, *Here Comes Tomorrow.* Durham also produced a weekly series on WMAQ, *Destination Freedom,* spotlighting African American history makers, including baseball's Jackie Robinson, journalist Ida B. Wells, and surgeon Dr. Daniel Hale Williams.

African Americans were prominent in radio music as well. Indeed, WDIA in Memphis, Tennessee, dodged bankruptcy in 1947 by serving the city's 40 percent black population with "Negro" music. Nat D. Williams became its first popular disc jockey, B. B. King appeared as a disc jockey (Riley B. King) rather than a blues musician, and Rufus Thomas and Martha Jean "The Queen" Steinberg also were hosts.

The success of WDIA inspired imitators throughout the South. In Atlanta, WERD aired powerful personalities such as "Doctor Hep Cat" and "Chattie Hattie." They appealed not only to black audiences but also to aspiring white musicians such as Elvis Presley and Carl Perkins.

Philo Farnsworth. This former farm boy invented the image dissector tube, which brought high resolution to TV pictures, helping to ensure the medium's future.

tube." Zworykin's work transformed tiny laboratory images into large, bright pictures that could be viewed from across the room.

Another star of research was ascending: Philo T. Farnsworth. He was a Utah-born farm boy who, at age 15, realized how an image might be scanned electronically, and, at age 21, transmitted the first wholly electronic television picture. Farnsworth formed his own company, won a long patent dispute with Zworykin, and continued innovative work—but he failed to secure major financial stakes in television. His creations, notably the "image dissector" tube that improved picture resolution, greatly speeded the development of TV.

Still, television lagged well behind radio in becoming a mass medium. The audiences watching early TV programs did so

First Television Station in the Nation

The secret of broadcasting's technical advances is in the collaborative nature of science and invention. For example, a Swedish immigrant named Ernst Alexanderson went to General Electric in upstate New York and found himself working with another inventor and entrepreneur, Reginald Fessenden. On Christmas Eve, 1906, Alexanderson used his new creation, a high-frequency **alternator,** to help Fessenden transmit songs and instrumental music—the world's first radio program.

Years later, Alexanderson tried transmitting *pictures* with sounds. In 1924, "Alex's Lab" sent a wireless-telegraph picture across the Atlantic. On January 13, 1928, he inaugurated the world's first TV station, but it looked nothing like the video centers now operating across the country. Witnesses saw a large mechanical device with a tiny screen and a perforated, rotating scanning disk, a direct ancestor of television transmission today. It could send a signal 15 to 20 miles—far enough to reach an experimental TV set in Alexanderson's home in Schenectady. When that happened, it marked the first successful home television reception.

Soon came the first regular television program, making its debut on May 10, 1928, and then airing twice a day, three days a week. Alexanderson's experiment had evolved into TV station WGY. The station became famous that year for the first remote TV news report; it came from the New York state capitol in Albany as Governor Al Smith announced he would run for president on the Democratic ticket.

WGY-TV also broadcast America's first live TV drama, *The Queen's Messenger,* a blood-and-thunder play requiring more technicians than actors. Television's limitations were so great—and viewing screens so small—that only the actors' individual hands or faces could be seen at one time; three stationary cameras provided only close-up shots. Today, renamed WRGB-TV, the historic station continues to serve the capital region of New York as a CBS affiliate.

mainly at special showings in public halls. This scattered and limited the new medium's impact. It was just as well: The economy was sinking, only a handful of families could afford any of the few TV sets in existence, and technical issues had to be resolved.

Alternator Machine that converts mechanical energy into electrical energy.

AM Amplitude modulation; a way of adjusting radio waves to carry sound by changing their height and depth but not their width.

1930–1945: GROWTH, REGULATION, AND WAR

To broadcasters, the historical period from 1930 to 1945 would be pivotal—and suspenseful as well. Both radio and the fledgling television media came out of the Roaring Twenties on a technological roll that would continue.

Radio

Radio so far had been transmitted through a form called **AM** (amplitude modulation), and would remain AM-dominated for decades. In 1933, however, Edwin Howard Armstrong—a longtime competitor of Lee De Forest—unveiled an important new way of boosting the quality of radio sound.

President Franklin D. Roosevelt. The thirty-second president of the United States, FDR was a master of broadcasting who lifted the nation's spirits during the Great Depression and used radio to strengthen the country's will to fight World War II.

FM Band of 100 channels in very high frequency range, 88 to 108 megaHertz.

FROM FM TO FDR

In 1933, Armstrong obtained his first patents on radio based on **FM** transmission (frequency modulation), which minimized noise and distortion. This mode especially delighted music listeners. De Forest demonstrated his system for RCA's David Sarnoff and, by 1936, was on the air with an experimental FM station. This invention would prove critical decades later, but for now, it was obscured by bigger events.

The Great Depression had descended in 1929; with more than one-third of the work force jobless, a growing number of people tuned in their radios for relief. An estimated 12 million U.S. households invested in radio sets in 1930. President Franklin D. Roosevelt gave radio an even more powerful role in American life: He began his famous series of "fireside chats" on March 12, 1933, with a talk aimed at soothing the nation's fears as a remedy to the banking crisis. Over the next 11 years, FDR comforted and informed the nation 28 times in that way, using an intimate medium perfectly suited to his warmth and charm.

At the end of the 1930s, radios were in 51 million homes. Mystery dramas and serialized soap operas proved popular as the networks widened their hold on audiences. Hits included *Ma Perkins, Charlie Chan,* and *The Shadow.* In 1934, *Lux Radio Theater* introduced adaptations of films, with movie stars performing their roles. *The Lone Ranger* formed the cornerstone of a fourth network in 1934: The Mutual Broadcasting System started as a consortium of stations in Detroit, Chicago, Cincinnati, and Newark—all selling advertising cooperatively.

Radio gained such a grip on the nation that millions of listeners fell hard—dangerously hard—for a trick-or-treat prank. Actor Orson Welles narrated a 1938 Halloween tale of Martians landing in New Jersey, based on H. G. Welles's *War of the Worlds.* The show's reality disclaimers failed to register with Americans already primed for disaster on the eve of world war; instead, Welles's use of "news flashes" sent many frightened people scurrying for the hills.

WAR NEWS

Soon, as TV waited out a wartime license "freeze," radio began to show its highest potential. Onto the national stage stepped (of all things) reporters who had been dispatched to war posts overseas—notably, CBS's Robert Trout, William Shirer, Edward R. Murrow, Eric Sevareid, and Charles Collingwood—and who filled U.S. living rooms with battle bulletins, word portraits, and strategic analyses. (Although men ruled the age, women correspondents were rising too; Pauline Frederick would broadcast from China in 1945 and cover the United Nations from its founding in 1948.) For many families, the correspondents' reports became the next best thing to mail from their sons, brothers, and fathers on ships and in the trenches. Radio stars Bob Hope, George Burns and Gracie Allen, and Jack Benny not only comforted families at home but also visited soldiers abroad. The presence of great wooden radio boxes in millions of homes launched relationships that would continue into the explosive postwar adolescence of television.

REINING IN THE NETWORKS

A few years before World War II, the Mutual Broadcasting System had protested the tough-guy tactics CBS and NBC employed to keep stations in line, and to keep Mutual out of the big leagues. Here's how that system worked: In the average large town, CBS held an exclusive network contract with one powerful station. NBC's Red and Blue networks had two other stations locked into exclusive deals. If CBS or NBC needed to **preempt** an affiliated local station's schedule to air a network show, the network simply commandeered the slot through a "local option clause." If musicians or actors hoped for careers on network radio, NBC or CBS invited them to join an "artists' bureau"; then the network would act as both agent and employer. Taken together, all of this seemed to amount to anticompetitive behavior. It was time for the FCC to act.

On May 2, 1941, the commission's *Report on Chain Broadcasting* changed the order of the day. The ruling prevented any new licensee from affiliating with NBC Red or NBC Blue and, as a result, forced NBC to sell one of its networks. It gave local stations the right to refuse any network program, thereby nullifying the local option clause of their contracts. Furthermore, the FCC questioned the practice of the network serving as both employer and agent for radio artists. There was no FCC provision to license networks, but this report did reinforce the principle of localism—stations empowered to serve their local communities first.[3] NBC and CBS unhappily marshaled their lawyers, who went to the U.S. Supreme Court with their case—and in 1943, they lost it. The high court found nothing in the chain-broadcasting report to be unconstitutional. As a result, NBC sold its smaller NBC Blue network for $7 million to the chairman of the Life Savers Company. The network would change its name to the American Broadcasting Company and also would take Paramount studios as a partner to help it become financially viable. CBS and NBC closed their artists' bureaus and granted local affiliates the "right of first refusal" to air any network program.

KDKA station opening.
Claiming a "first" guarantees controversy—but KDKA in 1920 launched the first continuous, scheduled radio program service licensed in the United States.

Preempt Take over a show's air time to run previously unscheduled programming.

Chain broadcasting At first, simultaneous broadcasting of the same program by two or more connected stations; later used to describe group ownership.

Television

In 1935, RCA leader David Sarnoff announced plans for the first modern U.S. television station and for the manufacture of TV receivers for the masses. This was long-anticipated but still epochal news. The country was about to enter an age in which its living rooms would become audiovisual theaters, with social consequences that no one could fathom.

A SLOW START

Within the next couple of years, the British were telecasting certain events—indeed, they already had a TV chef on the air! In 1939, Sarnoff's RCA made its own splash by transmitting from an NBC camera at the opening of the World's Fair in New York. However, long after television had become technically sound, it still was not routinely available across the United States.

It didn't help that commercial and legal squabbles echoed in the boardrooms of New York and the official chambers of Washington. Among other reverses, genius Philo Farnsworth left RCA, refusing to sell the company manufacturing rights to some of his most important advances. To cool down various disputes and to fashion a national TV infrastructure, the FCC stepped in. In 1940, the agency authorized limited TV transmission over the public's "airwaves." When it became clear that competitive concerns were clouding progress, the FCC slowed the process and held hearings on technical questions.

AN FCC GREEN LIGHT

The following year brought a critical breakthrough: Members of the National Television Standards Committee, formed by manufacturers, agreed on a number of issues, including standards for home picture quality, which had been a sticking point.[4] So, despite a lingering dispute with NBC's hard-driving David Sarnoff, the FCC gave television its final go-ahead. Commercial TV across the United States was launched on July 1, 1941, when WNBT (now WNBC) in New York went on the air. CBS started telecasting that same month.

All of this activity was interrupted early in 1942, soon after the United States went to war with Japan. A government order stopped both the manufacture of television sets and the construction of TV stations. Materials needed for both processes were to be diverted to the war effort. Mass access to the delights of the still-new medium would have to wait.

1945–1960: A "GOLDEN AGE" DAWNS

World War II ended in the defeat of Germany and Japan in 1945, and broadcasters cheerfully went back on the air. A British TV announcer marked his return with "As I was saying before I was so rudely interrupted. . . ." Broadcasting, a key to American morale during the conflict, was preparing to extend its influence into a more peaceful era.

Television

In the United States, as waves of veterans returned home, industry maneuvering began to set the stage for a postwar television boom. CBS launched a series of raids to whisk away stars from the other networks. It started drawing up contracts that helped celebrities seize a tax loophole by identifying themselves as corporations. Such an incentive proved irresistible to comedians Jack Benny and Red Skelton, singer Bing Crosby, and puppet-master Edgar Bergen. CBS leader William S. Paley recruited personalities with strong name recognition who could help his TV network make a peacetime splash.

RCA chief David Sarnoff, a military reservist, had been a communications consultant to General Dwight D. Eisenhower during the war, and emerged as a brigadier general. Now "the General's" company led the big manufacturers—some of them also programmers—as they lowered prices on TV sets and began colonizing neighborhoods with the magical new electronic entertainer. (Virtually left out of the process, by the way, was Philo Farnsworth, whose major patents had expired too soon to make him rich. He would die largely unrewarded for his breakthroughs.)

The pictures on the family screen were black and white, but progress toward color TV was already moving rapidly. In 1946, CBS demonstrated a color system to the FCC. After RCA entered the fray, development of color TV accelerated, encountering the usual technical setbacks. CBS used, and promoted, a "color wheel" that spun red, green, and blue filters to create colored images. Another company, Dumont, pushed a similarly cumbersome wheel.

By now, TV was creating a new kind of excitement that both drew on and added to the good feelings that swept the United States at war's end. The return of troops to their families started a great emotional lift—and a baby boom. Goods became cheaper and more plentiful, jobs were available for the veterans, and a new kind of neighborhood, the suburb, was appearing on the edges of cities. The arrival of widespread access to movielike home entertainment, plus commercials, further inflated consumer optimism.

Television was beginning to spread through the nation's leisure hours. Baseball, the national pastime, had been televised since 1946, and the first World Series on TV triggered a rush to buy home sets. By 1948, an upstart ABC network had joined NBC, CBS, and Dumont to compete for viewers, and a cable to carry programs nationwide was installed between New York and Los Angeles. The "tube" was about to go coast to coast.

ANOTHER FREEZE

In 1948, 108 TV stations were operating. That's when the FCC once again froze the issuance of new television licenses—this time to study video and color standards, interference, frequency allocation, and educational uses. That took four years, after which the commission's *Sixth Report and Order* officially thawed the freeze, assigning more than 2,000 channels to about 1,300 communities. The new channels were not just in the existing **VHF** (very high frequency) portion of the spectrum (the whole range of wavelengths in which radio and TV can operate). Many newly allocated channels were in the **UHF** (ultra high frequency) band.

A particularly thorny topic for the FCC had been whether to hold aside part of the spectrum for noncommercial broadcasting. The forces of commercial television opposed that idea stridently. However, a new commissioner, Frieda Hennock, crusaded doggedly for the use of TV for education unaccompanied by advertising. She thus became a hero to critics of the general push for profits.

Very high frequency (VHF) Usually refers to TV channels 14 through 69.

Spectrum The array of electromagnetic "airwaves" (identified by wavelength) that broadcasters harness to transmit radio signals.

Ultra high frequency (UHF) Usually refers to TV channels 2 through 13.

Milton Berle. The broad humor of the rubber-faced Berle assembled huge audiences during national TV's infancy and turned him into "Mr. Television."

Hooper ratings Nickname for early radio-audience estimates by C. E. Hooper Company; used telephone technique to ask what respondents were hearing or had heard the night before.

Howdy Doody. The TV puppet Howdy Doody, guided by "Buffalo Bob" (Smith), starred in one of many early shows aimed at children. Howdy emerged on NBC in 1947 and his show lasted until 1960.

When the dust settled and the freeze ended, Hennock had prevailed; the FCC reserved 242 channels for noncommercial TV.

By the 1950s, radio's reign as the people's choice for comedy and drama was beginning to wane. Not only had top network radio shows and performers switched to television, but so had advertisers. From 1948 to 1958, radio's network revenues would slip by $18 million, dropping the average station's earnings to half of what it made in 1948. Music, not comedy or drama, ultimately would have to sustain radio. Americans were scurrying to position little antennas called "rabbit ears" over their small home TV screens.

A second-tier radio comedian named Milton Berle emerged on TV with the *Texaco Star Theater* in 1948. It was at about this time that broadcasters decided they had better work harder at—in theater terms—"counting the house." The **Hooper ratings** service began reporting on how many people were watching each program. This boosted Berle, whose ratings turned out to be very high; his network found it easier to sell advertising that would air during his show. The comedian also got credit for starting a national TV-buying stampede.

As programs increasingly replaced the stationary "test patterns" that TV engineers used to tune pictures, a large number of those programs were aimed at children. Such shows were simple to mount and found enthusiastic viewers who had the emotional leverage to get parents to buy advertised products. New York had been watching a kids' show since 1939. *Howdy Doody*, a cheerful puppet, began mesmerizing children in 1947. That same year, Chicago became the birthplace of *Kukla, Fran and Ollie*, a puppet-populated show that made big waves on NBC but that in 1957—like many hits to come—would fade away after losing commercial support.

NATIONAL IMPACT

When American industry stepped back from its war footing, people left farms in great numbers and settled in towns and cities where better jobs beckoned. This brought more families into contact with burgeoning electronic media. Local TV stations, still located mainly in sizable markets, did what they could to build program schedules. That took serious effort before network feeds became available.

When WTVR in Richmond, Virginia, made its debut in 1948—the first TV station in the South—it proudly advertised its schedule in the *Richmond Times-Dispatch*. "FIVE HOURS OF CONTINUOUS TELEVISION

"Five Hours of Continuous Television Programs." In 1948, WTVR in Richmond, Virginia, became the first TV station in the South and ran a splashy newspaper ad promising to fill weekday evenings with local programs.

PROGRAMS," the copy blared. All of the programs originated locally and reflected those times in that region: *Inaugural Ceremonies* (for the station) at 7:00 P.M.; *The Green Mountain Hillbillies* at 8:05; *Sing for Sweetie* at 8:20; *Spotlight* at 8:40; selections from the opera *Pagliacci* at 8:50, *Minstrel Days* at 9:00, and so on until midnight.[5] Excited Richmond viewers crowded around storefront TV monitors along Broad Street. To them, television was here, and never mind what program was on.

Part of the magnetism of TV in those early years stemmed from the fact that most of it was *live*. It had to be: Technology provided almost no way to record a program so it could be shown at a later time. Stations *did* delay and edit some shows, but they had to work from *kinescopes*—films shot off the television screen as a show was first performed. Much picture quality was lost in that process, so the "kinny" commonly took a back seat to live shows of all kinds. In 1948, the Rose Bowl game and parade were broadcast live. In 1949, viewers watched tensely on a nationwide hookup as rescuers tried for several days—in vain—to save 3-year-old Kathy Fiscus, who had fallen into an abandoned well near Los Angeles. News, wrestling, roller derby, primitive game shows, and simple music and variety programs—such was the daily fare.

Hollywood had been turning out movies in color for a decade, but television's new audiences would have to wait. The 1950s started with a technical stumble when the FCC approved CBS's mechanical pseudocolor TV system; it placed a spinning color wheel in front of black-and-white images, with disappointing results, and almost nobody bought it. RCA was working on an all-electronic system, but war in Korea drew U.S. involvement and halted most development work during the early 1950s.

Still, viewers increasingly flocked to television: There were an estimated seven million TV sets in the country by 1950. Among those who noticed this were politicians who were trying to keep up with societal trends. Broadcasters had televised national party conventions in the East in 1948 and were ready when Dwight Eisenhower launched a campaign, featuring TV appearances, that would elect him president of the United States in 1952. Conventions that year drew strong commercial support—with sponsor representatives sitting right in the control booths (as NBC producer Reuven Frank later would recall).[6]

"Someday, history will demonstrate that television was really made more by the national political conventions of 1952 than by any other single event," said Sig Mickelson, the CBS News executive who arranged the three-network coverage of the two big party conventions that year and launched an anchor-icon named Walter Cronkite.[7] Although far from complete as an entertainment medium, television already was becoming a source of vital civic information—in ways that today seem quaint in retrospect as networks trim back their political coverage.

Kathy Fiscus Vigil. In 1949, studio-size cameras brought the nation one of its first live-TV events as rescuers worked in vain to rescue a 3-year-old girl from an abandoned well near Los Angeles. (Photo courtesy KTLA-Los Angeles)

TV'S VARIETY

Television was enough of a novelty to win audiences for a wide variety of programming, including serious and even highbrow shows. CBS journalist Edward R. Murrow launched the respected *See It Now* news-documentary series in 1951. Live plays by important playwrights came to the small screen, notably in series such as *Playhouse 90.* Undemanding shows, such as *Arthur Godfrey's Talent Scouts*, drew many loyal viewers too; entertainment ruled the airwaves from the beginning. Western dramas, a growing sports menu, quiz shows (some of them, especially *Twenty-One*, secretly rigged until a national scandal broke), and family sagas also thrived and proliferated. People wisecracked, "Just the facts, ma'am," in light conversations, echoing the tough-cop series *Dragnet.*

Comedy flourished well beyond what "Uncle Milty" Berle was offering. The unique Groucho Marx and his cigar dominated the modest quiz show *You Bet Your Life.* In *The Jackie Gleason Show*, Gleason and an ensemble cast created an often darkly realistic comedy series called "The Honeymooners" that was funny as well as poignant. Other comic greats, including Sid Caesar and Carl Reiner, were hugely popular. *I Love Lucy* arrived in 1951, focusing on a Cuban American bandleader and his dizzy, manipulative wife; the show was gentle but tart, touched on familiar marital themes, and would become one of the most beloved series in TV history. It also was shot on film, making editing possible—a safety net for comic timing.

That same year, notably, TV's first all-black series premiered. *The Amos 'n' Andy Show*, a crossover from radio, featured light comic situations and stereotyped characters that raised the ire of the NAACP. Protests by black leaders failed to stop the show's production, however. African Americans were divided on the controversy, since actors of color needed the work and some assumed the show's fumbling of the English language and character buffoonery would not be mistaken for real by white audiences. It was losing viewers that eventually took *The Amos 'n' Andy Show* off the air after three seasons despite an Emmy nomination for its team of writers, who would later script such hits as *Leave It to Beaver.*[8] Another important import from radio, the soap opera, premiered on television in 1952. *The Guiding Light* would enjoy a run that (for television) was almost breathtaking, extending all the way into the twenty-first century, and even some of its rivals spanned decades.

FROM MURROW TO "DOBIE"

When RCA at last put a small-screen color set on the market in 1954, it cost one thousand precious 1954 dollars and sold very slowly nationwide. Of course, black-and-white TV was appropriate for watching white men in suits run for office, or for watching journalists, including CBS's Ed Murrow, who tended to challenge viewers' moral values. Murrow, more than any other figure in broadcast history,

I Love Lucy. The 1950s CBS-TV series, a domestic comedy featuring Lucille Ball and her bandleader-husband Desi Arnaz, created viewer loyalty that survived into the twenty-first century via reruns.

made television an essential conveyor of news and vital information to the American people. His long-form reports, such as *Harvest of Shame*, a searing close-up of migrant workers' poverty, brought startling social truths into innocently unaware living rooms.

Murrow's televised assault on Senator Joseph McCarthy's shaky grip on power and decorum took much of the steam out of early Cold War anticommunist witch-hunts. Murrow became a towering icon of broadcast journalism—yes, advocacy journalism, but a shining model for many of his professional descendants.

Elsewhere on the TV dial, the values of the Eisenhower age were being reflected and sometimes gently lampooned by growing numbers of situation comedies, known as *sitcoms*. *Ozzie and Harriet* depicted an idyllic and amusing family life for 14 seasons. *Father Knows Best* brought all problems under firm but benign paternal control. *Leave It to Beaver* featured the antics of the family's youngest son in its title and in its point of view, showcasing impish humor. *The Many Loves of Dobie Gillis* brought moony teenage angst to millions of baby boomers.

ELVIS AND QUIZ SHOWS

One of the richest years of the decade was 1956, when videotape was introduced. This technology opened television at last to top-quality editing of high-resolution pictures, permitting a high level of visual storytelling that live broadcasts couldn't attain. The first effective wireless remote-control device also surfaced in 1956. "The remote" would not become standard in U.S. homes for three decades, but producers knew better than to let their programs' pacing slacken. Among other reasons was that young audiences were warming to the new medium. Indeed, 1956 was the year of Elvis Presley: When he appeared on *The Ed Sullivan Show* on September 9, an estimated 54 million people were watching. That was evidence not only of Elvis's appeal but also of TV's massive diffusion across the country and its potential hold on all generations of viewers. Perhaps as striking was that 10 million TV-set owners did *not* tune in to see The King shake his way through rock 'n' roll songs, his hips carefully cropped out of frame.

There was a corps of businessmen behind television, and their integrity was called into question in 1958 when the great quiz-show scandal began. Some big-money shows, *The $64,000 Question* among them, had been feeding answers to contestants, largely to keep the most appealing personalities returning week after week. Critics pointed to the **Communications Act of 1934,** which required broadcasting to serve "the public interest, convenience and necessity." The quiz-show scandal set off debate as to whether television was placing its private values first, and attracted government scrutiny that would intensify for years. A fictional defense lawyer launched his

Elvis Presley. A photo of his September 9, 1956, appearance on *The Ed Sullivan Show* shows much more of "The King's" physical style than the TV camera did. Producers were nervous—but an immense audience affirmed the reach of television.

incredible courtroom career on television in 1959 in *Perry Mason*. Also that year, a talented writer named Rod Serling stepped in front of the cameras to introduce science-fiction morality tales from *The Twilight Zone*. The series would last only five seasons but paved the way for decades of TV "sci-fi" (or "s-f") ventures.

In 1950, just 9 percent of U.S. homes had television. By 1960, that figure had jumped to 87 percent—reflecting one of the biggest, fastest changes ever in American popular culture.

Radio

The radio industry, meanwhile, had scarcely been sitting on its hands. The evolution of David Sarnoff's "music box" in post-war America had a lot to do with prosperity, physical mobility, and the flight of bored teenagers from their parents' favorite tunes. In addition, however (and critically), companies that sold "records" worked steadily to develop new technologies. Their combined effect would be to free recorded music from some of its old limitations while empowering youth to get out of the house and listen to *their* favorite tunes on a new kind of radio set. Social revolt was in the air, and the fates of radio and records were intertwined.

RECORDS AND TRANSISTORS

Until the early 1950s, the standard phonograph record was made largely of shellac (a product of hardened insect secretions) and rotated on an electric turntable at 78 rpm (revolutions per minute). Then Columbia Records came up with a way of making records of *vinyl*, a plastic. What's more, the company introduced a long-playing disc that would rotate at only 33⅓ rpm. The result of all this was better sound quality, destined to be a major asset as young Americans became more and more infatuated with recorded music.

Columbia offered its new technical process to other record companies. Interestingly, RCA, Sarnoff's company, wanted no part of it. Instead, in 1949, RCA developed its own 45 rpm disc made of vinyl, seven inches in diameter with a big hole in the middle—soon to be the standard record for rock 'n' roll radio. Significantly larger than today's compact discs, the "45" was small, light, inexpensive, easy to store, and portable. Its microgroove technology put more and more music into the hands of young consumers, whetting their appetite to hear music wherever they went.

Rising to satisfy the youthful demand was a new kind of radio set. Texas Instruments in 1953 proposed something called a **transistor** radio. It was based on an amplifying device invented six years earlier by engineers who would win the Nobel Prize for it. It ran on batteries and fit nicely in the palm of the listener's hand—a personal portable radio for the Fabulous Fifties. The secret to its compact size was found in the tiny transistor buried inside it.

No major radio manufacturer was ready to take a big, expensive chance on the new idea, so a TV electronics company teamed with Texas Instruments and a design firm to build the first batch of transistor radios. They arrived in stores in time for Christmas 1954, but each cost about $61 fully equipped—equivalent to $400 today—driving away even more adventurous shoppers. Major manufacturers

Communications Act of 1934 Federal law bringing most telecommunications under oversight of one agency and board of commissioners.

Transistor Wafer-thin silicon crystal that amplified radio signals; as developed by William Shockley and his colleagues, transistors replaced tubes and led the digital revolution.

rapidly began producing competing brands, and soon the transistor revolution was on. Prices came down through mass production and parents were happy to buy "transistors" for the kids, who then could leave the house to listen to, well, whatever it was they listened to—which, by the way, was also changing rapidly.

FORMATS AND FORMULAS

By this time, radio was rethinking itself. It had held audiences spellbound for years by presenting its content—drama, comedy, sports, popular and classical music, local features, and news—in rotating "block" style: 15, 30, or 60 minutes for one genre, then on to the next. Radio had been the electronic medium that supplied all that a family could want. That was because radio had been the *only* electronic medium most people had. Now, television was sweeping the country and whisking away radio's audiences. What could be done?

One answer came from Todd Storz, an Omaha, Nebraska, radio station owner who (legend has it) made a simple discovery one day. He was in a bar near his station when he noticed patrons playing the same songs on the jukebox again and again. After the bar closed, the waitress broke out her tip change to hear the same song one more time. Storz had a stunning revelation: What seemed to be happening, when *listeners* controlled the program, was not a search for variety but the comfortable repetition of a few favorite songs. From this discovery sprang the idea of "Top 40" radio.

It's a good story, but only that, according to Richard Fatherley, who was program director at a Storz station in the 1960s. Fatherley says that the undramatic truth is this: Storz acquired a study report in 1950 from the University of Omaha in which people cited music as one of their main reasons for listening to radio. He decided to fashion programming on his Omaha station, KOWH, after a national show, *Your Hit Parade*, and a radio program at WDSU in New Orleans, *The Top 20 on 1280*.[9]

However he got the idea, Storz abandoned the variety format and focused on the 40 most popular tunes. He used local record sales, jukebox plays, and trade magazines to discover which songs people wanted to hear again and again. Storz supplemented these discs with news briefs and station "IDs"; these were identifying messages required by the FCC but also useful as promos when delivered by disc jockeys avidly hyping the station's hits. Storz added contests and treasure hunts to excite listeners. He used the same formula at six other stations and, when it worked, started selling his promotion package to other broadcasters. Soon "Top 40" ruled radio.[10]

One major contributor to this profound change in radio programming was a former U.S. Navy intelligence officer named Gordon McLendon. He moved to Dallas, Texas, in 1947, and launched KLIF radio, licensed to serve the city's Oak Cliff neighborhood. It was to be the flagship of his Liberty Broadcasting network, and it was there that McLendon added his own twists to Top 40 radio. Through a fast-moving blend of "personality" disc jockeys, news reports, and promotional contests, KLIF became one of the highest-rated stations in the country—and Liberty grew to include 458 affiliates. Imitators appeared around the country and advertising sales soared, sending local radio as a business sector into the billion-dollar stratosphere of media enterprise.[11]

1960–1980: FERMENT AND CHANGE

It was fortunate that radio in the fifties invented new ways of operating to sustain it, because the sixties increasingly drew Americans to their TV sets. Combat footage from a far-off place called Vietnam was unsettling viewers of early-evening newscasts by 1961, well before thousands of U.S. troops became embroiled there. Domestic trouble also lit up the screen: Rebellious African Americans marched through the South, braving gauntlets of screaming whites and often violent cops, and were bleeding before hordes of stunned viewers.

Television

Millions of people—along with an episode of soap opera *As the World Turns*—stopped in their tracks on November 22, 1963, when CBS anchor Walter Cronkite interrupted TV programming to announce that President Kennedy had been shot in Dallas. The next few days brought an unprecedented demonstration of broadcasting's power over Americans. Television (and radio) went everywhere and talked to everyone about the assassination, and everyone watched television in return. ABC anchor Ron Cochran later would say, "Television had actually become the window of the world so many had hoped it might be one day."[12]

AT THE "NATIONAL HEARTH"

The majestic state funeral for President Kennedy in Washington, DC, was covered live on TV. This was the first time television had etched a truly epochal event across the national consciousness. It would not be the last such occurrence, but it would be the last one conveyed entirely in black and white to a mass audience. Color television became technically feasible for network use by 1964, and color sets grew more and more affordable for much of the middle class. Some 13 months after the Kennedy assassination, all three networks broadcast in color, simultaneously, for the first time.

Viewers could now expect nearly lifelike color not only in their entertainment programs but also in the harsh hues of news reports. Coverage included the killings of President Kennedy's younger brother, Robert, and of civil rights leader Martin Luther King Jr., and the brutal handling of anti-Vietnam-war demonstrators by Chicago police outside the 1968 Democratic Party convention. These galvanizing events supported the theory that television would become a national "hearth" where, now and then, we could gather to watch, worry, and recover—together.

Television's convenience and range of programming already were pulling people away from movie theaters and back into their homes. Now the availability of color—"living color," as NBC called it—enhanced this trend. The big Hollywood studios feared television's appeal to film audiences, but also saw in it a tempting opportunity: Perhaps, by cutting deals with television, they could assure themselves bigger financial returns. Before long, Hollywood studios were cranking out most of the important series on television. The head of Twentieth Century Fox, Darryl F. Zanuck, had sneered at the new medium: "People will

The Vietnam War. Television demonstrated its public-opinion power by covering clashes over the war, including one at Kent State University in 1970. Four students died when the Ohio National Guard opened fire on protesters.

soon get tired of staring at a plywood box every night." That viewpoint had collapsed, and the film industry had no choice but to try sharing in TV's success.

TV AND SOCIETY

Throughout this period, TV technology made events visible to the public and also seemed to play a role in bringing them about. Activists made sure that television got early warnings and clear views of the many protest marches against the Vietnam war. Communication satellites launched since the mid-1960s had made live international coverage possible, and now it began to shake the world: When President Nixon went to China in 1972 to make diplomatic history, cameras went along, "going live" to beam the news globally. Television was on hand for the Olympics in Munich that year when Palestinian terrorists captured (and later executed) 11 Israeli hostages; that, too, was carried live worldwide.

The women's liberation movement launched in the sixties swept through the seventies in thousands of TV plot lines, characters, and dialogues. One must-see comedy was *The Mary Tyler Moore Show*, portraying a TV news worker whose feminism simmered near the surface; the show's success was ironic in that the seventies did not see much of an increase in the number of women employed in the *real* television industry.

On the other hand, an upsurge in black-identity movements did result in 1977 from *Roots*, an eight-night TV series of dramatized chapters in the lives of an African named Kunta Kinte and his descendants in America. At this writing, *Roots* still reigns as the third most-watched program in the history of television. Similarly, while leering jokes about homosexuality could still be heard, attempts to promote acceptance of gays began to make an impression. Billy Crystal's portrayal of the gay character, Jodie Dallas, in the 1977 comedy series *Soap* set a new standard of candor—two decades before *Ellen* came out as a lesbian on network television.

By this time, with color television routine and programmers taking risks, television was in the cultural foreground. Its resulting economic power helped prompt the FCC to force the industry to loosen its grip on the content of its shows, opening them to more perspectives. The FCC rules required networks to hand over program ideas to movie studios or other producers; *they* would then create programs and, as long as their shows lasted on networks or elsewhere, would receive license fees for them. The networks balked at this change because it would cost them a great deal of money, but the government in those days was opposing monopoly power and pushing diversity of control.

This climate suited the seventies, a decade when the interracial satire of *All in the Family* and the feminism expressed by another CBS show, *Maude*, hinted at changes that moved beyond protest marches to education and economics.

Roots. In this 1977 mini-series, author Alex Haley (played by James Earl Jones) traced his family origins to Africa. The show set an all-time viewership record, strengthened black-identity efforts, and prompted many families to seek their own roots.

Robert L. Johnson in 1979 launched Black Entertainment Television, the first network almost exclusively serving—and controlled by—African Americans; it would prosper and last. Through the electronic media, the American social fabric had become a quilt in which every vivid patch asserted its desires and demands.

MONEY AND JOURNALISM

Everyone knew that TV news could make money, but the newsmagazine *60 Minutes,* launched in 1968 and a Sunday-night staple by 1970, proved that in-depth coverage of controversial topics could win top ratings and make a *lot* of money. That was a watershed development, opening paths to success for later news programming. It made life uncomfortable for journalistic idealists who had hoped to do their work without thinking about the corporate bottom line. It also extended major network news further into the glittering realm of evening prime time, where entertainment reigned.

In the mid-seventies, about three of every four TV homes tuned in to the "Big Three" networks. Families planned their evenings around such "appointment viewing," even for the often disturbing nightly news. When the CBS documentary "The Selling of the Pentagon" exposed government efforts to win bigger military budgets through expensive public-relations campaigns, it infuriated war supporters and widened political gaps. Fortunately, the comedy show *Laugh In* and comic Flip Wilson made silly slogans such as "Sock it to me" and "Here come da judge" a safe way to laugh off stress.

Television programmers had become more inventive; they could seize a news moment and turn it into a franchise, as when ABC's coverage of the 1979–1981 Iran hostage crisis became the highly successful *Nightline* program.

**Electronic newsgathering
(ENG)** Applies to portable,
videotape-based field equipment.

A new player, Cable News Network (CNN), debuted in 1980 to the jeers of traditionalists; it would grow, slowly, into a permanent fixture. Advances in **electronic newsgathering (ENG)** fused cameras with recorders and helped send them everywhere; for example, in 1981, they captured at close range the assassination attempt on President Ronald Reagan, the shaky cameras telegraphing the frightful power of the event. Such technology, however, rarely helped voters understand government and politics; many depended heavily for their information on political *commercials*, which for some TV stations would become a lucrative stand-in for campaign news coverage.

Radio

A new era for FM dawned in April 1961with FCC approval of stereo technical standards. The government put its stamp of approval on a Zenith-General Electric stereo formula, rejecting Murray G. Crosby's competing system. The agency also ordered station owners to stop using their FM bands simply to carry what was already broadcast on AM bands. Under the nonduplication mandate, combined AM-FM stations had to air two different streams of program content for at least half of the broadcast day.

FM'S EFFECTS

These improvements rapidly increased FM's popularity as a source of unique programming with high-quality sound. In 1964, the Audience Research Bureau began "counting heads" for radio and found a surge in FM listening. As the Vietnam war and race relations sharpened political and generational divisions among Americans, so-called progressive stations, also known as "underground radio," attracted many baby boomers. By providing alternative perspectives and supporting an explosion in rock 'n' roll music, FM gradually became the setting of choice for most radio fans.

Radio as a cultural medium started to break into different parts, and one big player moved to exploit the trend. In 1967, ABC targeted different audience groups with several different programming packages for its affiliate stations: ABC Contemporary, ABC Information, ABC Entertainment, and FM formats. To make this work, ABC offered radio station managers news and public affairs material designed for each format. Soon, this strategic move by one network became an industrywide campaign to identify and gather specific groups of listeners who could be reached by well-tailored programming—and commercials.

Audience research helped to refine the new formats: new age, alternative rock, classical, urban contemporary, young country, and many more. Listeners happily adapted to the new trends in music, news, and personalities, sorting themselves into various audience groups. This made decisions simpler for programmers as well as advertisers anticipating time-buying choices. The downside was that a station had to become one of the top choices on a listener's car radio or it would be forgotten altogether. The repetition impulse that Todd Storz had noticed back in the 1950s kept many drivers, especially teenagers and young adults, punching the same few radio buttons all the time.

PUBLIC RADIO

Radio's family was about to grow. After the adoption of the Public Broadcasting Act of 1967, the FCC licensed more than 1,500 radio stations as "noncommercial educational," mostly between 88 and 92 megahertz on the FM dial. Many of these stations would receive federal money distributed through the Corporation for Public Broadcasting (a fact that annoyed commercial broadcasters who would *not* receive such subsidies). Besides local programming, the new FM stations would carry news, information, and cultural shows provided by their own source, National Public Radio (NPR). It began distributing programs to 93 member stations on April 19, 1971.

1980–PRESENT: CHALLENGES TO BROADCASTING

In the eighties, fictional cops, lawyers, doctors, and nurses filled prime-time TV, depicted in rawer, bolder terms than the only mildly racy seventies culture had allowed. Some shows featured top-notch writing and acting; series such as *Hill Street Blues*, *St. Elsewhere*, and *L.A. Law* mixed trauma and tragedy with social issues and strong characters, and developed a large fan base. It wasn't enough to offset the challenges to come, however; the struggles within commercial radio and TV would become as dramatic as anything on the air.

Television

As the networks kept proving they could do high-quality fictional shows, public-affairs treatments and long-form documentaries migrated from the broadcast networks to cable, where smaller audiences were acceptable. The 1980 retirement of the magisterial Walter Cronkite as CBS's top news anchor seemed to symbolize this shift in the media terrain.

MARKETPLACE WOES

By the eighties and early nineties, broadcast executives found themselves facing a list of troubling developments:

- Cable television was crowding "The Big Three" by carving out powerful market niches. MTV hit the air in 1981 and grabbed a large youth audience. Cable channels had a financial advantage: They not only sold commercial time but also charged subscriber fees.
- Syndication companies were selling popular dramas and sitcoms to cable as soon as they finished airing on the networks, and sometimes before then. This allowed cable to present and profit from programs that the networks themselves had once financed.
- The home VCR, which became commonplace in the eighties, was eating into broadcast revenues as viewers skipped TV offerings in favor of rented movies.

- ■ Satellite operators had begun feeding movies and sports to cable systems, which in turn fed them into home sets. What's more, direct satellite transmission to homes was getting under way.
- ■ "Fin-syn," the financial-interest-and-syndication rules Congress imposed in 1968, had become more and more burdensome. They were meant to keep networks from producing their own shows in favor of independent producers, while locking out Hollywood suppliers. To the networks, though, fin-syn was unfair—a nightmare of revenues missed.

These forces left networks ABC, CBS, and NBC weaker. Their audiences were shrinking, each company losing at least several million viewers a year and thus millions of dollars in ad revenue. This made "The Big Three" vulnerable to would-be buyers. With the *stations* they owned still making money and the FCC relaxing station-ownership limits, the networks were ripe targets. In just two years, 1985–1986, ABC merged with Capital Cities Communications, a large but relatively unknown media group; General Electric took over NBC, and Loews Corporation gained control of CBS. Disney later would purchase ABC, and CBS would become a Viacom property.

NEW RELATIONSHIPS

The networks soon found themselves among new corporate siblings. ABC shared its nest with the sports channel ESPN and the family-oriented Disney Channel, among others. In a huge radio consolidation, Westwood One acquired and combined the old NBC and Mutual Radio networks, which in turn were affiliated with more than half of the nation's commercial stations. Westwood One's chief said the megagroups gave radio more appeal to Wall Street investors—an increasingly important factor—and to Madison Avenue advertisers.

Networks desperate to ensure that their TV programming reached the right audiences got into power struggles with cable systems and affiliates that had their own scheduling ideas. In 1995, the WB and UPN networks emerged with programming aimed at youth, minorities, and other underserved viewers, further slicing up the prime-time audience. Australian press magnate Rupert Murdoch had launched Fox TV in 1986 with sexy, boundary-stretching shows; now Fox had hits (including *The Simpsons* and *The X-Files*) and was buying more stations. A seventh broadcast network, PAX, went on the air in 1998 and entered a program-sharing relationship with NBC, helping both networks.

The year 2000 found much of broadcast television reduced to running after audiences and revenue, and they often got away. Cable and direct-broadcast-satellite channels, with their uncut adult programming and sports specials, lured away viewers. The Internet siphoned leisure time that might have gone to television. Networks answered with newscasts emphasizing "news you can use" for young families and playing into populist concerns about a changing America. A genre known as *newsmagazines* mined the country for crimes and family strife that would closely mimic popular prime-time fictional dramas. Around the turn of the millennium, so-called reality programs caught fire. Notably *un*real, these shows dropped people into jungles or onto islands to test their endurance, marital fidelity, or just plain con-artistry.

Radio

Some citizens wanting more in-depth treatment of issues than commercial broadcasting supplied had begun to rely on "public" radio. National Public Radio's newsmagazines, *Morning Edition* and *All Things Considered*, had grown since their founding in the 1970s into highly regarded public-affairs programs. Another program supplier, Public Radio International (PRI) was launched in 1982, partly to get heartland programming such as Garrison Keillor's *A Prairie Home Companion* on the air nationwide. The enterprise grew to encompass more than 550 member stations. Unfortunately, people often watched or listened to noncommercial programming without sending in checks to pay for it. Also lacking advertisers, public broadcasting came under serious financial strain in the eighties and nineties.

OPINION RADIO

Commercial radio, on the other hand, had to make money on its own. Stations started searching for fresh angles back in 1978, as FM's audience eclipsed the listenership of AM. Among the relatively neglected formats was something called *news/talk* radio. It blended news segments with long, live conversations involving hot-button topics, directed by opinionated hosts, many of them politically conservative.

The news/talk format offered something few consumers had enjoyed on radio or TV—the chance to talk *back*. The genre caught fire when the vastly popular President Ronald Reagan led the country in a politically conservative direction. Americans were herded into opposing camps on gun ownership, abortion, big government, and other issues. After the 1987 repeal of the **Fairness Doctrine,** which required broadcasters to present contrasting views of a controversial issue, news/talk programming gained momentum. Some shows were syndicated nationally, snapped up by stations seeking to build loyal, engaged audiences.

The personalities emerging in talk radio knew how to stoke their listeners' peeves. Rush Limbaugh—who would become the most popular and famous "talker" of all—was a former college dropout, an ex-salesman, a sports promoter and disc jockey, and a specialist in reactionary monologues. Appearing with Limbaugh were such personalities as G. Gordon Liddy and Oliver North. Liddy had been an FBI agent and served prison time after helping to plan the Nixon-era Watergate burglary and then refusing to speak to authorities about it. North was an ex-Marine officer and a hero to some Americans for his work in secret shipments of U.S. aid to right-wing rebels in Nicaragua. None of these men suffered opposition gladly, and their "attack-and-destroy" attitudes earned them impressive ratings.

LIBERALIZED OWNERSHIP

A major feature of the 1980s was deregulation—removal of restrictions—that encouraged broadcasters to view their outlets more as financial pawns than as permanent community assets. For years, the FCC had limited every radio owner to 7 stations nationally, as a way of preserving diversity of control over an important

Fairness Doctrine FCC policy that held broadcasters responsible for covering divergent opinions on controversial issues of public importance; rescinded by FCC in 1987.

Telecommunications Act of 1996 First major piece of electronic-media legislation since 1934; liberalized radio ownership and relaxed licensing requirements.

medium. During the Reagan administration—committed to reducing government's power—the ownership limits were liberalized to 12 stations per owner. That was only the beginning: The ceiling on stations per owner was raised to 18, and finally up to 20.

These changes redrew the U.S. radio-ownership map in ways that rocked broadcasting. Centralized ownership groups sprang up and absentee control of multiple stations grew. As in other industries undergoing consolidation, bigger companies gained more political leverage as well as more financial clout in bargaining with vendors. Single-station radio ownership by local families was becoming a threatened species.

TIGHTER BELTS

Clearly, broadcasting's owners were treating their use of the airwaves more like another business than as a public service; program content would have to pull its corporate weight. Moreover, the belt-tightening begun in the seventies became more urgent. Station groups were going into debt to buy more stations; looking for revenue to repay their debts, group managers cut budgets, imposed hiring freezes, sometimes required stations to lay off workers, and put off whatever spending they could

Partly through its mergers, broadcasting had become an even bigger stakeholder in modern telecommunications advances. Its parent conglomerates invested in other media and in newer technologies—satellite, digital, wireless—wrapping all into bundles of "synergy," with the whole exceeding the sum of its parts. In the 1990s, this was aimed at surviving competition, seemingly from all directions, which just kept getting tougher.

LOOSER LIMITS

The FCC and congressional actions in the nineties opened vast opportunities for expansion of the broadcasting business. The **Telecommunications Act of 1996** eliminated the national radio-ownership "cap," a limit on the number of U.S. stations any one company could own. It also cleared the way for an owner to hold up to eight radio stations in the same market and to collect 50 percent of the advertising revenue, depending on market size. This abruptly made stations more attractive and more available to big-money ownership groups. *Radio & Records*, the leading industry trade magazine, headlined: "Let the Deals Begin!" It was understood, correctly, that the industry's new battle cry would be "Buy, sell, or get out of the way."

More than 4,000 commercial outlets changed hands in the first two years after the Telecommunications Act was signed. By 1998, nearly 70 percent of U.S. radio stations were organized in station groups or in "local marketing agreements" (also known as "leased management agreements," or LMAs); these permitted companies to run and profit from other stations without owning them outright. In half of the nation's major markets, just three companies reached 80 percent of radio listeners. Stations kept increasing in number but were held by a smaller and smaller core of powerful owners.

There are many statistics pointing to how large the major corporations in radio have grown, but one deal drives the point home. When Clear Channel Communications took over the AM-FM group of stations in September 2000, that group's control over U.S. radio channels topped 1,000. (To be exact, 1,018 stations came under one corporate umbrella headquartered in San Antonio, Texas.) In the mid-1990s, the top 25 group owners controlled a little more than 7 percent of the stations; today, they control more than 25 percent.

THE REVENUE CHASE

Radio became a $19 billion business by the end of the twentieth century, exceeding the value of either the music business or the movies. For the first time, a large group of stations could offer an advertiser more circulation than the local newspaper and a larger cumulative audience ("cume") than the leading TV station. Such a group could coordinate all of its member stations' promotional activities.

Approximately 80 percent of radio's advertising sales were based on local ad spots. Commercial clutter kept growing, and the more clearly any company dominated its market, the more it could get away with this. Westwood One's Norm Pattiz called it one of the "negative side effects of consolidation."

"When more stations in a market are owned by fewer groups," Norm Pattiz said, "those groups can, without any formal form of collusion, increase the commercial load on the radio stations—without having to worry about their competitors running limited commercial hours and attracting more audiences."[13]

Maximization of profit had become more openly the overriding objective of commercial radio stations. This often meant layoffs, since a staff could consist of little more than a sales force and one on-air person (acting as his or her own engineer) originating from distant locales. Localism diminished, with community news coverage a rarity; often, a staff announcer was left to "rip 'n' read" off the state or national wires. Syndicated program-supply services, such as Shadow Broadcast Services and Metro Networks, were set up as a substitute for local news operations.

Similar economies were applied to music programming. Satellites could relay syndicated music programs from distant studios, allowing stations to insert their own ad spots and promotional messages. Radio talent, once found mainly in local stations, now was located primarily at program centers in cities such as Chicago, Los Angeles, Atlanta, and Seattle. News and talk-formatted stations had multiplied, from an initial 200 or so to 1,350 by the mid-1990s. The resulting rebirth of radio networks and a newer wrinkle, satellite distribution, made stars of "shock jock" Howard Stern and advice giver Dr. Laura Schlessinger. In 1997, *Time Magazine* listed the gruff morning personality Don Imus among the 25 most influential people in the United States.

After the size of radio's audience peaked in 1989, it decreased by 1 percent a year through the 1990s, a gradual but steady decline. Consultant Ed Shane says only economies of scale at the lo-

Norm Pattiz. Pattiz created Westwood One, which handles radio broadcasting for CBS, CNN, Fox, Metro, NBC, and Shadow Traffic. Pattiz also oversees U.S. government radio, including the Voice of America, as a member of the Broadcasting Board of Governors.

Ed Shane, Shane Media Services. A radio industry author and consultant, Shane advises station management on sales and programming issues.

cal-station level allowed many broadcasters to make a reasonable return on investment despite a small audience share.

GLOW OF THE SATELLITE

The FCC's decision in 1997 to allow 20 channels of satellite radio spoke to a future day when Ford and General Motors cars would be equipped with digital-audio radio receivers along with AM and FM. Satellite-radio sources would then be able to compete with traditional radio in earnest. Traditional stations eagerly anticipated a federal ruling on digital standards that would allow them to improve their signals and transmit data.

There are twice as many radio sets as people in the United States, and people average 21 hours of listening per week; this makes radio competition intense. At this writing, two companies, XM and Sirius, were distributing satellite radio programming coast to coast. XM Satellite Radio launched two satellites—"Rock" and "Roll"—in September 2001, offering customers in the continental United States up to 100 digital channels for $9.99 a month on top of the $150 needed to buy a satellite radio receiver.[14] Sirius launched its service in Denver, Houston, Jackson, and Phoenix in early 2002 before expanding to the rest of the nation. Both services faced challenges in terms of their technology and customer services. Today, more than 12,600 radio stations are operating in the United States. Although only 55 percent of the commercial stations are FM, total listenership for FM is *twice* the size of AM's audience. The FCC in 2000 authorized a new class of FM in which up to 1,000 nonprofit stations using microbroadcast frequencies will operate at lower power than commercial stations do. This avenue was designed to help people whose civic groups, churches, or other interests could make good use of radio but had no access to the airwaves. The broadcast industry quickly went to court to try to block micro-radio, saying its signals would interfere with existing channels.

TOWARD A DIGITAL FUTURE

Radio, TV, and cable are moving to exploit the digital revolution, which will take forms that men named Marconi, Zworykin and Armstrong never could have conceived. Digital transmission promises to bring new programming, data services and "interactivity" to radio and TV sets as well as to home, office and portable computers. Not only broadcast companies with upgraded skills but some wholly Internet-based enterprises can be expected to join this movement. What no one yet knows is exactly which combinations of technology and content will win over enough users to make money year by year.

Radio

Most radio stations are expected to move fairly soon into digital broadcasting—and only partly to keep listeners from defecting to music sites on the Web. Digital technology should raise the fidelity of AM radio to a level approaching FM audio, and should upgrade FM to a quality nearer that of the compact disc. Possibly more important in business terms is that digital stations will be able to find new revenue. They can sell wireless data services to consumers, sending information and entertainment to their personal digital assistants and so-called smart phones.

Some radio broadcasters, however, have pushed for renovation of traditional **analog** channels rather than an all-out rush to digital operations. Responding to this, the FCC in 1999 began allowing radio stations to experiment with something called *in-band-on-channel* (IBOC) broadcasting. It's a digital technology that compresses both analog and digital signals on the same channel. More **bandwidth** is needed for IBOC than for analog radio, but an oversight body, the National Radio Systems Committee (NRSC), signaled its approval of the new approach in November 2001.

Radio stations already are meeting on-line audiences with three categories of service:

1. *Web only*, in which listeners simply click on their favorite channels according to musical group or genre
2. *Web interactive*, which gives listeners more power by customizing formats to individual tastes in music, news, and talk
3. *Web streaming* in which radio stations "simulcast" (simultaneously broadcast) programs over the air and on the Internet; on-line listeners usually receive additional material, such as song lyrics or notes on performing artists

An estimated 5,000 web-streaming radio stations were on-line, and more were registering their websites each month. The audience-measurement firm Arbitron in 1999 tallied listeners to 290 audio channels offered by nine streaming-media services. The top attraction turned out to be an adult alternative-music station in Austin, Texas, called Rebel Radio the Fan. Ranking second in listenership was another adult alternative station, KPIG-FM, in Monterey, California. In all, the Arbitron study found 850,000 web-radio listeners. Such fans sometimes encounter radio professionals who have moved to the Web. Veteran host Vin Scelsa—cut loose by WNEW-FM after more than 30 years on New York radio and now webcasting—believes his old medium has lost appeal: "So many people find commercial radio uninteresting, and unchallenging, and unenlightening."[15]

For most of 2001, a legal issue stalled commercial stations' hopes of streaming audio on the Internet. The Recording Industry of America, the American Federation of Television and Radio Artists, and other groups have filed suit over whether artists should receive fees if their commercials or records play on-line. Most broadcasters oppose paying additional fees for streaming what they've already paid for in over-the-air license fees. The dispute reminds some observers of history—specifically, a 1920s court feud over music royalties that led to the creation of the National Association of Broadcasters.

Television

Some local broadcasters have tried to learn how on-line connections might help them by launching TV station websites, a tentative toe in the water of the

Analog System that varies a signal's energy levels in a pattern of motion somewhat analogous to the original radio wave.

Bandwidth Smallest range of frequencies within a radio band that will permit transmission of a signal without distortion.

Streaming Digital transmission of audio or video to computer, using software decoding tool; user sees or hears transmission during download, rather than waiting for playback.

Video on demand (VOD)
Video ordered by viewers through an interactive digital system.

Internet. Several thousand sites now promote station personalities and offer local news and weather (mostly in text form) as the main attraction. These sites showcase ads, some of them animated, but so far, most sites have drawn only moderate attention to the advertising. A university researcher said in 2000 that "not one local station that I know of is making a profit" on-line and that the likeliest TV sites to do so were those of link-heavy, major-news-rich cable networks such as CNN and MSNBC.[16]

Cable is the primary delivery route for most television programming today, even from stations that used to be over-the-air only, and thus has something of a technical edge. Local and regional systems are being upgraded with fiber-optic cable—the key conduit for digital transmission. This gives cable companies a chance to program multiple channels and even to provide interactive services, such as video on demand (VOD), which allows viewers to "rent" movies anytime without driving to the video store. Subscriptions, as in the past, will provide a revenue stream that broadcasters can only envy.

Perhaps most important of all, broadcast television will become digital soon. Ultra-sharp TV sets with many new remote-controlled options will enliven viewers' evenings; a few network programs already are being broadcast in digital format. Given that digital compression techniques can "squeeze" a channel of video into a much smaller electronic space, broadcasters will be able to provide several programs or services simultaneously. Many stations have found it difficult to finance their FCC-mandated conversion to digital high-definition (HDTV) broadcasting, officially due to be completed by 2006. If the market grows, however, they will find ways to finish the transition. These improvements may enhance audience loyalty and bring more people to the electronic media.

Summary

Radio and television have recorded and reported much of the history of the twentieth and now the twenty-first centuries. In commercial broadcasting, reaching desirable audience demographics, rather than a mass audience, has come to be the main emphasis. Broadcasting's once-powerful unifying effect has been diffused as networks and stations entice listeners and viewers by age, gender, ethnicity, socioeconomic status, and other indicators. Large radio chains have become like ice cream shops, offering as many flavors in music as there are tastes.

History gives us an important perspective as we consider the state of commercial broadcasting today. It seems remarkable now that some founders of giant broadcast companies were intent not on chronicling history or even entertaining the masses but on peddling radio sets. Business took over most broadcasting early. Advertisements fill more minutes per broadcast hour today than ever before. Since the 1980s, the FCC has worked to loosen ownership limits to facilitate more consolidation of broadcast companies. This has coincided with increased competition and the arrival of the Internet and other uses of digital technology. These forces promise to expand the electronic media further and to continue changing their roles in American life.

FOOD FOR THOUGHT

1. Broadcasting evidently is losing the "mass" audience it began to build in the 1920s. What role do you think broadcasting will have in society in 10 years? 20 years?
2. The government struck at network power in 1941 with the Report on Chain Broadcasting. Was that move a good one? Why or why not? Is similar government action needed now? Explain.
3. FCC Commissioner Frieda Hennock fought for and won channels for public broadcasting. Could she win today? Why or why not? What factors would support or oppose her efforts?
4. Since the 1980s, competition has led to niche programming across radio and cable TV (e.g., MTV, ESPN, talk shows). Has this mattered to society? In what ways?
5. The government has been slow to set a future digital standard for radio. Should the industry be allowed to settle this for itself? Why or why not? What's at stake?

3

Cable and Satellite

Man came by to hook up my cable TV
We settled in for the night my baby and me
We switched 'round and 'round 'til half-past dawn
There was fifty-seven channels and nothin' on

—Bruce Springsteen, "57 Channels (And Nothin' On)" from
Human Touch album, 1992 Columbia Records

Satellite dish receivers.
Satellite dishes may be used to send or receive microwave signals to orbiting "birds" located above the equator approximately 23,000 miles in space, where their transponders receive audio and video signals and then bounce them back to earth.

Quick—what do cable and local television have in common that sets them apart from satellite television? If you guessed local programs, then you deserve bonus points—at least for now—although that appears to be changing rapidly.

In larger cities, small-beam **satellites** are sending local channels to "dish" customers.[1] Cable has seen its share of changes over the years, from small-town systems hooked up to community antennas to multibillion-dollar enterprises. About 10,400 cable systems weave their way across the American landscape. As systems merge, the total number has declined from a mid-1990s peak of 11,218.

What on earth gave rise to that peak in the first place? Cable was born of the government's TV "freeze" between 1948 and 1952, when there were only 108 TV stations on the air. Aspiring station owners waited patiently while the Federal Communications Commission figured out how to allocate TV channels so they wouldn't interfere with each other. Regulators also had to agree on a new system for color television and address questions concerning UHF (ultrahigh frequency) transmission.

> Cable was born of the government's TV "freeze" between 1948 and 1952.

55

Meanwhile, viewers simply could not wait to watch, and soon began looking for ways to yank TV signals from the air. Electrical engineers began installing translators—low-power transmitters—to repeat and boost signals to reach fringe pockets of rural areas blocked by mountains and hills. Translators did the job for many TV stations and still do it today, but shopkeepers with new TV sets to sell in Oregon, Arkansas, and Pennsylvania devised a different solution.

Satellites Orbiting vehicles equipped with transponders to relay microwave signals from earth stations.

Community antenna television (CATV) Term used for local cable systems until satellite and microwave distribution prompted a change to simply "cable."

EARLY DAYS OF CATV

At first, appliance store owners began to place TV antennas in high places, hoping to capture distant channels and cascade programs down to neighbors in the "white areas" where TV screens turned to snow. Who would've bet that these "mom & pop" franchises for community antenna television (**CATV**) one day would become big-money enterprises? Some people did and made a fortune; others simply lost their shirts.

First Mom and Pop System

The original "mom and pop" of cable television lived in Astoria, Oregon. Leroy "Ed" Parsons was a radio engineer; he and his wife, Grace, were impressed by a 1948 demonstration of television at a broadcasters' convention in Chicago. Grace heard that a Seattle station would be on the air soon and asked her husband to figure out a way to bring its signal to Astoria. Ed began scouting around the mouth of the Columbia River to find a point near Astoria where the TV signal could be received by an FM receiver. He not only drove around the area, he even flew his plane, searching for a point to place an antenna.

Ed finally tuned in to the Seattle station across the street from his and Grace's apartment, placing an antenna on the rooftop of the Astor Hotel. Soon, everyone in town wanted to see the Parsons's new furniture that showed a TV picture. If they were to have any peace, Ed knew he'd better drop a cable down the elevator shaft to the hotel lobby and install a television set there for neighbors and friends to watch.

Ed Parsons, CATV Engineer of Astoria.

Appliance Store Owners

The prospect of rooting for college football teams on autumn afternoons inspired a TV appliance store owner in Tuckerman, Arkansas, to build a 100-foot tower on his store's roof. Jim Y. Davidson felt sure he could capture TV signals from Memphis, only 90 miles away. He carefully strung coaxial cable down to Tuckerman's American Legion Hall for one of the first TV football parties, when Ole Miss played Tennessee. Davidson decided in 1948 to make this his new line of work; soon his firm, Davidco, began shipping ready-made cable systems to communities around the country.[2]

Meanwhile, back east, families in the hills of Pennsylvania naturally wanted to get their first peek at "seeing radio." An appliance store owner and lineman for Pennsylvania Power and Light, John Walson, hooked 700 homes to his antenna in Mahanoy City. In Lansford, Pennsylvania, another electronics appliance store owner, Robert Tarlton, was trying to figure out how to bring a signal in from Philadelphia across Summit Hill. He began rounding up appliance shopkeepers to see if they would invest in his idea. They did and, in 1950, Panther Valley CATV was born.[3]

Jerrold: CATV's Pioneer Equipment Manufacturer

Milton Jerrold Shapp, Founder of Jerrold Electronics.

The excitement surrounding this CATV system caught the eye of a Philadelphia lawyer and future governor of Pennsylvania, Milton Jerrold Shapp. Shapp watched the Panther Valley cable workers stringing lines during the Thanksgiving holiday of 1950, and decided to get involved. He named his firm Jerrold Electronics and began supplying cable wire to the Lansford system. Community antenna television was no longer an experiment now; it was well on its way to becoming a business. At first, CATV made money based on home-installation fees of between $100 and $200 rather than monthly cable bills, which then amounted to only a few dollars for system maintenance.[4]

For other CATV enterprises to get the financing they needed, Shapp invited Wall Street investors to come on board. Three venture capital firms put up money in 1952 for a system in Williamsport, Pennsylvania. Within two years, the Williamsport franchise grew to become the largest in the country. Shapp and Bob Tarlton took to the road, spreading the good news of community antenna television.

Cable's Early Wrangler

The growth of the cable industry drew on the enthusiasm and entrepreneurial spirit of big deal makers such as Bill Daniels. This ex-fighter pilot and former Golden Gloves champ was looking for work in Wyoming's oil field when, at the age of 37, he noticed something new in Denver—television. Daniels, along with other customers, came to Murphy's Restaurant every Wednesday night to watch the boxing matches. He drove in each week from Casper, hours away, where he was trying to make a go of it selling insurance in the oil industry. After reading about CATV in the newspaper, Daniels asked himself, Why not bring it to Wyoming? With an investment from AT&T and training at Jerrold Electronics, he became the first cable operator to relay TV signals 120 miles from Denver to Casper.

Daniels's salesmanship inspired others to enter the business, or at least to move forward in expanding their cable operations. In just five years, he made 147 deals for cable systems, involving $1.5 billion. Early cable giants such as TelePrompTer, Time Warner Cable, Cox Communications, Tele-Communications, Inc., and Sammons all give Daniels credit for either inspiring their original start-ups or forging deals on their companies' expansion.

In larger towns with just one TV station, community antenna systems attracted viewers with "fill-in" service. When one or more network affiliates were missing, CATV operators imported signals from a distant city, relying on **microwave** companies to bounce the signal back to the headquarters, or, as they called the building, the **headend.** The first systems carried only 2 or 3 channels, but new amplifiers and technical improvements increased the selection first to 5, and then to 12 channels.

Microwave Radio signals of at least 1,000 MHz carrying audio and video over long distances, either to satellites or to terrestrial relay towers.

Headend Technical center of a cable system where all programming is received, amplified and retransmitted.

Cable network A closed-circuit channel offering television programming via satellite to local cable systems, for delivery to the network subscribers.

Cable system A wired network for distributing television programs on a subscription basis to homes in a single community.

Broadband High-capacity networks large enough to carry channels for television, voice, data, and other digital communications.

Transponder The term is a conflation of *transmitter* and *responder.* The receiver/transmitter unit on a satellite that picks up signals on one channel and bounces them back to earth on another one.

Tiering Marketing strategy for selling levels of cable service, based on over-the-air signals at the low end and premium channels at the high end.

Public access Dedicated channels allowing residents to produce and televise programs over a community cable system.

PREMIUM CHANNELS

In the middle of the twentieth century, communication satellites were launched. Broadcast signals were bounced off the orbiting spheres and directed over long distances. Satellite technology helped solve the problem of geographic obstruction and became a key factor in cable television transmission. In 1972, the FCC allowed **cable networks** and superstations to relay their signals via satellite.

They were called **cable systems** now, and were receiving television signals from earth and space, and sending programs over a coaxial cable to viewers. Instead of receiving television by antenna, customers subscribed to a TV signal that came through a drop-line of "coax" into their homes. New technology changed that, however, as digital equipment and fiber-optic cable gave rise to higher-quality pictures and sound, greater bandwidth, and more reliable transmissions. Also, digital **broadband** technology speaks the language of computers. All of this came about because people wanted to see movies on television without commercial breaks and were willing to pay for it.

HBO's Star Is Born

A Manhattan cable operator eager to show a profit for his chief investor imagined a way to make pay cable work in the early 1970s. Marty Dolan's chief backer, Time Inc., had plowed sums of money into his Sterling Manhattan cable system, but he had only 400 customers and good faith to show for these investments. Aboard the *Queen Elizabeth II* on vacation, Dolan was struck with an idea to save his struggling enterprise—a pay channel devoted to movies and sports. It would be called the "Green Channel," he thought. After hiring a lawyer, Gerald Levin, and a marketing specialist, Tony Thompson, they decided a better name would be, at least temporarily, Home Box Office (HBO).[5]

On November 8, 1972, HBO aired its first film, *Sometimes a Great Notion,* but the premiere proved to be an inauspicious occasion. The mayor of Wilkes-Barre, Pennsylvania, where the debut was held, was forced to cancel his appearance, which really didn't matter anyway since the local newspaper thought it was unworthy of coverage. Yet the event marked the viable beginning of premium cable television, ushering in both a new format and a new revenue stream. Just three years later, in 1975, HBO was networked nationally to cable systems via satellites.

Dolan's new business reported more than $8 million in losses during its first three years of operation, so competitors were somewhat leery about joining him.

One rival, Viacom, was dedicated to becoming one of the leading programmers and producers in the industry, and it was feeding movies to cable systems and programs by videotape and microwave. Satellites opened new vistas for Viacom, and it launched a competing pay channel, Showtime, in 1978. The big winners in this arena have been satellite companies that at first auctioned off their **transponders,** the circuits that bounce signals back and forth to earth from space, for millions of dollars a year.

Satellites also created another innovation for cable television—the superstation, a local television station based in a major city that could be viewed nationwide by virtue of its signal transmission over cable systems. The same satellite carrying the HBO signal had room for more passengers, and an independent TV station owner in Atlanta, Georgia, took advantage of this by "uplinking" his UHF channel. When WTBS-TV was fed to cable systems by satellite in 1976, it became the first superstation. That, in turn, inspired more independent TV stations to seek their own satellite tickets to cable, while programmers formed new networks to join the party, offering niche channels of music, comedy, sports, news—you name it. The Atlanta broadcaster behind all this was Robert E. (Ted) Turner.

Launch of Telecom Satellite. A rocket lifts off from a base in French Guyana carrying two telecommunication satellites to send video images to viewers in India and France.

Cable Tiers

As the HBO story reveals, cable's bottom line is nurtured not by its power to retransmit local or distant channels or to offer improved reception, but by its programming options, such as premium channels and pay-per-view. One of the burdens of the cable rules of 1972, designed to mollify broadcasters, was a ban on feature films less than two years old. In addition, no movie could be delivered by cable more often than once a week. After the courts threw out such restrictions, cable began to offer customers something other than distant stations and syndicated reruns.

Pay cable enables subscribers to buy programs by paying more than the regular monthly fee. The fee structure is based on **tiering,** which gives the cable operator a list of channels to sell based on levels or tiers of service. The basic service features local TV channels, **public access,** one or more distant superstations, and advertiser-supported networks. (The average monthly fee for basic service in the United States was $33.75 in 2001, according to government sources.[6])

The cable operator then offers an expanded basic tier that often includes channels such as Nickelodeon, A&E, and the Weather Channel. Above that level

> ### Principle #2
>
> To become viable, new media create new ways of making money.

Former Time Warner Chairman and HBO Pioneer Gerald Levin.

Pay-per-view Programs sold to customers and priced according to the show requested.

Set-top box (STB) Tuning converter atop a television receiver that uses a vacant VHF broadcast channel to program cable channels.

Note: Beginning with year-end 1994, the basic and expanded basic revenues are combined as regulated basics. The graph has been revised to reflect updated information.

Source: Kagan World Media, a Media Central/Primedia Company. Reprinted by permission.

is a premium tier that offers clusters or packages of ad-free, pay-cable channels, such as HBO or Showtime. Pay or premium cable channels win "carriage" on cable systems by presenting promotion opportunities and, often, fee-splitting deals from which 60 to 70 percent of the profits go to the cable system. Pay channels are devoted entirely to either movies and sports or other special events. How, then, does Hollywood make its money on the deal? Usually, a film distributor licenses a movie for a specified number of showings over a certain period of time by the cable channel. In some cases, the distributor sells full rights to the motion picture, in much the same way as sports or concerts are sold. The **pay-per-view** channels are dedicated to movies, sports, and live performances by comedians, musicians, and magicians. In order to prevent signal piracy, each pay-cable transmission is encrypted or scrambled. Only the cable company's **set-top boxes** (STBs) can translate the signals.

As Figure 3.1 shows, in 2000, about 60 percent ($24,445,000) of cable's total revenue came from basic tier subscriptions and about 11 percent ($4,949,000) came from pay channels on higher tiers of service. More than one-third of the revenue is drawn from local and network advertising, but the network advertising revenue goes back to the programming networks.

FIGURE 3.1

Cable Revenue from Subscriber Services, 1989–2000 (in Millions)

From 1991–1998, pay revenue includes mini-pay revenue. These are channels such as Encore and Flix that are marketed at a monthly rate below that of full-priced premium channels. Total cable revenue includes local ad revenue, home shopping revenue, and other miscellaneous revenues not shown in the table. Beginning with year-end 1994, total cable revenue includes telephony.

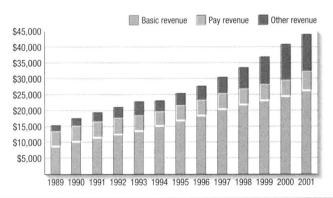

Cable Barons: Turner and Malone

Ted Turner

Station WTCG was a struggling independent station in Atlanta in 1970 when Ted Turner assumed control. He renamed it WTBS (Turner Broadcasting System) and retuned it with a lineup of sports and movies. Turner had both the foresight and finances to buy two sports franchises and place them in the national spotlight via cable. Whenever the Atlanta Hawks or Atlanta Braves ran onto the basketball court or baseball diamond, there was his superstation, shining its spotlight on the event. Turner ensured his superstation's success by taking over Southern Satellite Systems. WTBS became the bedrock for a cable empire that, in the next decade, brought forth CNN, Headline News, Turner Network Television, and a host of other enterprises.

In 1987, Turner began to turn over the keys of his business to others. First, he invited a group of investors to purchase about 35 percent of TBS so he could pay off his $1.5 billion debt to MGM/United Artists. In 1995, Time Warner CEO Gerald Levin decided to bring TBS and part of Turner's empire into his own company. In exchange, Turner would be $2 billion richer and a vice chair of the company, still in control of his Atlanta operations. Turner took the deal, only to learn five years later that he had been "reorganized" out of his job. With trademark Turner candor, he announced his regret over selling TBS and CNN to Time Warner, leaving him without a chance to fire Levin before Levin fired him. Levin resigned on his own volition just weeks after Turner's departure.

John Malone and Bob Magness

Not even the briefest overview of cable TV is complete without noting the career of John C. Malone. A Yale graduate, he made his way from the Ivy League to the board room of Jerrold Industries, a seller of cable equipment. In the early 1970s, Malone's ambitions converged with those of a former Texas rancher named Bob Magness. With his wife, Betty, Magness had built a small cable operation into Tele-Communications, Inc. (TCI), the nation's tenth largest **MSO** (multiple system operator), based in Denver.

Just as Magness was looking for a new partner, John Malone became ready to leave his job back East; the two men soon joined at the helm of TCI. They borrowed money to buy cable systems, fueling two decades of tremendous growth for the cable conglomerate. Magness died a billionaire in 1996. By the end of the 1990s, led by Malone, TCI was the largest cable system operator in the United States.

Industry dominance and his own huge fortune weren't enough to satisfy Malone. He sold TCI (to AT&T) and took the helm of one of its spinoffs, Liberty Media. Today, Liberty is expanding, mainly in Europe: Malone's acquisition maneuvers in Germany and Great Britain are part of his strategy to be a worldwide media mogul. He owns big shares of AOL Time Warner and News Corporation and holds smaller stakes in Viacom and Vivendi Universal. For anyone who ever questioned cable television's business potential, John Malone's successes has become a dramatic answer.

When cable customers decide to buy an "à la carte" option, they phone in their request, have the STB make the link or have the cable company descramble the program, then sit back to enjoy it. If viewers are able to buy the program at the time requested, it's called a *VOD (Video on Demand)* purchase. If customers have to wait a few minutes for the next showing, it is *NVOD (Near Video on Demand)*. The key to pay-per-view is its interactive technology.

Multiple system operators (MSOs) Corporations that own and operate more than one cable system.

Franchise fees Share of cable revenues dedicated to a governmental authority in exchange for an exclusive contract.

Copyright Ownership rights to literary, dramatic, musical, or artistic expressions.

Public-educational-governmental (PEG) Government term to describe dedicated-access channels on cable systems.

Pass-by rate All homes passed by a cable feeder line, as a percentage of all homes in the area.

Penetration Percentage of customers subscribing to cable, based on all the homes passed by the cable line.

Churn Dropout of pay-cable subscribers after a short period of service.

Fiber-optic cable Strands of flexible glass inside a cable transmitting pulses that carry video and audio information for cable television.

CABLE'S COSTS AND BENEFITS

Today there are more than 10,000 cable systems in the United States, serving about two out of every three households, or an estimated 175 million people. Most of these cable customers—almost 70 percent—subscribe to pay cable, which helps generate $41 billion in annual revenue. In terms of program choices, viewers watch more than 220 national cable networks, not including regional channels dedicated to news or sports coverage.

Dollars and Sense

Basic channels such as VH1 and CNN carry advertising. Others, such as American Movie Classics and HBO, rely purely on subscriber fees. Certain channels give the cable system time slots for selling spots to local businesses. Headline News, for example, offers spot breaks for commercial use by local advertisers. Compared with broadcasters, for whom ad dollars constitute 90 percent of all revenue, cable draws little support from advertising. Cable operators depend on spot sales at the local level for around 10 percent of their budgets, and subscriber fees make up most of the rest. Cable's share of television advertising dollars, however, has steadily increased, at the expense of over-the-air television.

The way it breaks down, as shown in Figure 3.2, is that advertising represents one-third of the industry's revenue, but most of that is paid to the cable networks, not the systems. In 2000, for example, they made $10,259,000 from commercial sponsors, for about 75 percent of the total picture. Local cable systems sold the rest in commercial time for retail merchants or other community interests. Sponsorship of sports programs on cable is grouped separately as a revenue source.

The money invested in cable systems requires a healthy return from subscriber fees. Cable systems need construction money for their headends, where

Source: Kagan World Media, a Media Central/Primedia Company. Reprinted by permission.

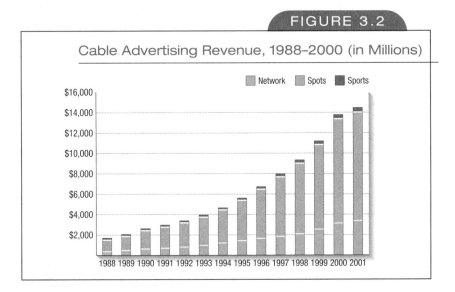

FIGURE 3.2

Cable Advertising Revenue, 1988–2000 (in Millions)

cable programs from local or network sources are received. Then there are the costs for laying cable, which can range from about $10,000 per mile in rural areas to $100,000 in a city. That figure may shoot up to $300,000 if underground cable is required.[7] There are also satellite receivers, dishes collecting the video signals, and amplifiers and converters needed to collect and send those signals. Installation of fiber-optic lines, strands of glass wire sheathed in cable-feeding coaxial drop-lines, as well as other distribution and service equipment are all part of a system's start-up costs.

Operating costs take a bite out of the cable budget, which is one reason that systems have been joining to shoulder the expenses and take advantage of their economies of scale. These consolidated groups of *multiple system operators* still factor in all of the same costs as ordinary cable systems, only on a larger scale. There are the municipal **franchise fees; copyright** licenses; satellite and microwave costs; pole attachment fees, which are charged for using utility poles and crossing public rights of way; and access channels for public, educational, and government (**PEG**) uses. In addition, there are the costs charged by cable networks to telecast their programs.

Before a cable system bids for a local contract, the system must first determine if it can make a respectable return on its investment. The cost of wiring neighborhoods is calculated according to the potential revenue, based on population density—the more people living in a neighborhood, the more potential revenue from subscriber fees. The **pass-by rate** is the number of homes passed by the cable wire that could subscribe if they wished, and **penetration** is the percentage of viewers who actually buy the cable service. The higher the penetration rate, the higher the profits, assuming sufficient numbers of customers subscribe to higher-priced premium channels, pay-per-view shows, Internet access, and other services. Another factor is the estimate of **churn,** the number of subscribers who may buy and then cancel the service.

How It All Works

To step back and view the whole distribution system, cable engineers use the metaphor of a tree with trunks and branches. These programs are packaged and fed through amplifiers into trunk and feeder cables that send the television signals to drop-lines entering the cable subscribers' homes. Replacing the tree-and-branch configuration for newer cable systems are what is described as *star patterns*, where the signal leaves the headend via **fiber-optic cable,** then goes to a hub or node where the signal is converted to analog and moves on through **coaxial cable** into the home (see Figure 3.3).

You might also think of a cable company as a distribution center, as well. Programming comes into the center by antenna from local channels, microwave relay

oaxial cable Transmission line for cable television, using a center wire of aluminum or copper surrounded by a shield to prevent signal leakage.

Fiber-Optic Cable and Telephone. Until 1996, telephone companies could not use their fiber-optic lines to deliver video programs in the same communities where they provided telephone service. The Telecommunications Act of 1996 allowed phone companies to deliver programs in the same cities where customers used their phone lines.

FIGURE 3.3

Cable System Schematics: Tree and Star

Older cable systems use a tree-and-branch style of television distribution with large trunk lines branching out to smaller feeder lines and finally drop-lines to individual homes. Newer cable systems transmit from the headend over fiber-optic cable to nodes, where digital signals are converted to analog then fed by coaxial cable to homes.

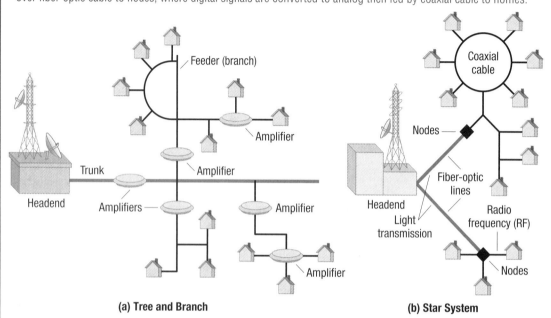

(a) Tree and Branch   **(b) Star System**

antennas bring it in from more distant stations, and by satellite from cable broadcasting networks. Programs may also be produced at the cable company's production studios but not all have such facilities.

Cable operators don't have to worry about one problem broadcasters face: interference. That's because cable TV confines its use of the spectrum to its own wires. However, cable channels are assigned frequencies, just as broadcast channels are. For example, cable channels 2 through 13 use the same frequencies as corresponding TV channels, although the UHF band and channels 23 through 64 are sent at a lower bandwidth through cable. When you turn on your cable television set, you are piping in a signal sent in one of two ways: by coaxial cable (lines that run parallel or in coaxis through a metal sheath and conducting wire) or by fiber optics.

Coaxial signals begin to fade over distances. That's why early cable systems installed amplifiers every one-third of a mile to boost the signal for each channel. These early cable systems could offer only 3 to 5 channels. As cable adopted solid-state technology, boosters were no longer required.

Fiber-optic lines are now replacing metal conductors (aluminum and copper) in cable systems. Fiber-optic cable offers greater bandwidth than older technologies and is better suited to handling digital information. Glass fibers carry laser energy generated by light-emitting diodes (LEDs), requiring fewer amplifiers. This allows more channels using less bandwidth.

Going Digital through Fiber

Digital transmission converts light into pulses suitable to the computer's binary language of ones and zeros. These pulses travel along hair-thin strands of glass through millions of miles of cable already laid in the United States. Each two-layer glass thread has both a core and a sheath. Individual fibers are braided together and polished at each end to carry light and images. They differ from coaxial cable, which uses copper and aluminum conductors, as shown in Figure 3.4.

Digital applications in fiber-optic cable are superior to analog, since converting light into pulses of equal intensity ensures greater precision than analog processes do. Also, fiber optics requires fewer repeater amplifiers to transmit video and audio signals over miles of cable. The disadvantage to this system occurs when fiber-optic cable breaks. It is difficult to splice the line, given the size and delicate nature of glass fiber.

FIGURE 3.4

Fiber-Optic and Coaxial Cable

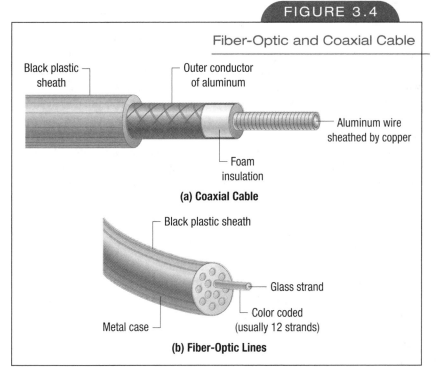

Black plastic sheath
Outer conductor of aluminum
Aluminum wire sheathed by copper
Foam insulation

(a) Coaxial Cable

Black plastic sheath
Glass strand
Color coded (usually 12 strands)
Metal case

(b) Fiber-Optic Lines

Coaxial cable contains two conducting wires: an aluminum outer conductor and a copper wire center that are in coaxis with each other. It carries far less information shorter distances than the glass strands of fiber-optic cable, which can carry up to 64,000 TV channels 300 miles without additional amplification.

MERGER MANIA AND SHAKEOUTS

How did the cable industry make its move from small, independent cable systems to media conglomerates? In some instances, the small-town cable-system owner simply could not afford to buy new equipment and facilities in order to compete with larger firms. These MSOs appeared at government meetings ready to offer an array of channels and services to win contracts that came up for renewal. Small operators had no choice but to sell their systems to businesses with greater cash flow.

Horizontal Integration

At one time, there were hundreds of cable system owners. Today, the number has shrunk to a handful of major corporations. In 1975, the 10 largest MSOs reached 40 percent of the public. In 1990, their reach had grown to 62 percent.

> **Principle #3**
> The financial lure of consolidation in the cable industry tends to eliminate single-system operators.

At last report, 80 percent of U.S. homes with cable were served by just 5 companies. AT&T Broadband & Internet Services is the largest, with about 16 million subscribers. AOL Time Warner, Comcast, Media One, and Cox Communications follow. Comcast has made a $44.5 billion offer to take over AT&T Broadband. The merger, subject to government approval, would give one cable conglomerate 22 million customers. These MSOs own more than 100 systems each.

Sometimes the growth of an MSO is subject to scrutiny by criminal investigators. Adelphia was the nation's sixth largest cable conglomerate, which was under the control of company founder John Rigas, his three sons, and his son-in-law, Peter Venetis, director of Adelphia. When Adelphia's board of directors learned that the company guaranteed billions of dollars in loans to family partnerships without bothering to indicate such on the corporate balance sheet, the house of cards began to tumble. Nasdaq removed the stock from its listing, while family members, who had financed private transactions without board approval, began making their exits. After filing for bankruptcy protection, Adelphia's directors fired its auditors and advertised for new leadership. The entire episode shows how high the stakes are when vertically integrated corporations start rolling the dice on media profits. Adelphia shares plunged more than 99 percent, and was in default on more than $7 billion in bank loans.

Vertical Integration

Huge media conglomerates are not especially interested in the day-to-day affairs of the local franchises they own. However, they are interested in the money to be made by the production interests of their companies. Greater profits are realized in programming and packaging that extends beyond just cable television to satellite and other video delivery systems. Having a hand in the affairs of production, distribution, and exhibition of media content is called *vertical integration*.[8] That term defines how media owners have grasped several links in the content chain, including the production studios, program networks, and system operators.

Multiple system operators have helped create many of the cable networks that supply programs. Because this can be a costly and risky venture, MSOs seek to become more involved in all aspects of their business. If they hedge their bets by buying cable systems to try out new channels and programs, then vertical integration protects them from the risks involved. Of the largest 25 program networks on cable, 15 are owned by MSOs.

Consider Cox Communications, for example. Cox owns and operates the Discovery Channel, the Learning Channel, and the Animal Planet Network. Naturally, these channels are more likely to be found on a Cox Cable system than on its competitors' systems. The FCC asked Congress to take a look at this practice, and the 1992 Cable Act consequently limited cable operators as to the number of channels they can carry in which their parent MSO holds a financial claim.

Network Deals

Premium channels also have had their share of mergers. The Movie Channel and Showtime merged in 1983, and A&E, the Arts and Entertainment network, is actually a merger of the Entertainment and the Arts channels. The Financial News Network (FNN) made its debut in 1981, but 10 years later filed for bankruptcy and was sold to CNBC.

Other changes have involved ownership of the means of promotion and delivery. MTV, Music Television, was sold by Time Warner to Viacom; ESPN became an ABC property; Nickelodeon moved over to Viacom from Warner. NBC started a cable channel called America's Talking Network, which became MSNBC after Microsoft Chairman Bill Gates invested in it.

In 1989, the largest pay-cable investor, Time, Inc., merged with Warner Communications to form Time Warner. In 1995, the conglomerate purchased Turner Broadcasting System. In January 2001, the FCC gave conditional approval to Time Warner's bid to join with AOL. Gerald Levin, Time Warner's chairman, took over as chief executive while AOL's Steve Case became its chairman. Within the year, Levin announced his retirement; one of the highest-ranking African Americans in corporate America, Richard Parsons, formerly with Dime Bancorp, was named Levin's successor.

FRANCHISING BATTLES

Franchising cable systems is a concern for local governments because it involves right-of-way easements and public notices. Cable companies were given protection from competition because they use city utilities and their lines cross right-of-ways. Since cable is either strung on poles or underground, elected officials must give their blessings on how and where the systems are to be built. The franchise contract is the way it is done—it is a temporary pact, usually lasting 10 or 15 years. Such deals cover everything from how many channels are offered to how much of the cable profits are paid to the franchising authority. The maximum payment, or franchise fee, has been set by law at 5 percent of gross revenues from all cable services. However, in 1996, the Telecommunications

AOL Time Warner Merger. The principal players who brought about the largest media merger in American history surround former CNN anchor Bernard Shaw. They are, from left, AOL's Steve Case, Turner Broadcasting's Ted Turner, Shaw, AOL Time Warner CEO Richard Parsons, and former CEO Gerald Levin.

Overbuild Competition between two or more cable systems with lines passing the same households.

Principle #4

Newer delivery systems undermine cable television's edge as a "natural monopoly."

Policy Act prevented cities from tacking on franchise fees to Internet and broadband services sold by cable companies.

Franchising became more than just paperwork and political maneuvering. Cities decided to raise franchise fees to shore up their budgets. Some cable companies are in competitive positions, facing potential **overbuild** situations with other cable systems vying for the service. Even though the courts have ruled in favor of cable system competition, most communities cannot financially support two systems. Local governments consequently up the ante on franchise agreements, requesting higher fees and new cable facilities if the competition warrants it. This has prompted cable operators to seek federal relief from local political pressures.

That relief came twice; first, in the form of the Cable Communications Policy Act of 1984, which allows local jurisdictions, mostly cities, to continue licensing cable franchises but limits their influence over rates and programs. The 1984 law also provides protection for franchise renewals and additional sanctions against cable piracy—hooking up to a system without paying for it.[9]

DARK CLOUDS OF CABLE

Episodes of corruption, sensational program content, and public access disputes have kept cable in the eye of the storm of public opinion. In the early days, there were more than a few charges of corruption in the franchise bidding process—one of which led to the demise of a leading MSO in cable. TelePrompTer was run by a former 20th Century Fox executive, Irving B. Kahn. Kahn's empire began to crumble after he went to jail in 1978 for trying to bribe his way into a franchise renewal contract with city leaders in Johnstown, Pennsylvania.

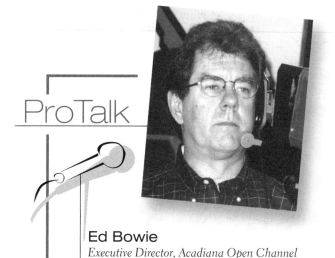

ProTalk

Ed Bowie
Executive Director, Acadiana Open Channel

"We're like the community's x-ray machine."

Ed Bowie runs the public access cable channel in the heart of Cajun country, Lafayette, Louisiana. Like the local cuisine, programming on Acadiana Open Channel (AOC) tends to be hot and spicy at times. The channel's call-in shows have been flashpoints for racial tension in the community. Bowie came on board just as the Ku Klux Klan was making a quick exit from Acadiana Open Channel; a prosecutor had brought the on-air host to trial for allowing guests to wear their hoods and masks in the studio. The Klan show was replaced by *Jabari Speaks*, a talk show that critiques the African American experience in south Louisiana.

Bowie says AOC is like the community's x-ray machine: "You don't always want to know that you have cancer but sometimes you need that x-ray machine to look inside and see that you do." Bowie, a Vietnam veteran, has to keep peace among radical factions who use the tools of his public access center. He has appeared in government chambers and before television news cameras to spread the message of tolerance that he sees embedded in the First Amendment. He believes that public access cable is vital to the community not only as an electronic soapbox but also as a means for neighbors to find out more about themselves and their community.

Acadiana Open Channel brings to cable television the civic leaders and public servants as well as the dissenters. Social service programs, produced by Goodwill and other community agencies, make up a large part of the program day at AOC, along with local government and the school board. In a media world dominated by commercial networks and homogenized content, public access is completely local and open, which is why Bowie believes it is important for cable television.

Electronic Soapbox

Public access channels are an ideal product of democracy, giving citizens the chance to produce TV shows on a first-come, first-served basis and make use of the electronic soapbox. The Supreme Court has stood by public access, declaring that cable is "an important outlet for community self expression," and a "response to the increasing concentration in public discourse." In some communities, however, America's soapbox became a pulpit for hate-mongers such as the Ku Klux Klan, which at one time threatened to shut down several public access channels with its virulent rhetoric.[10] Today, about 5,000 cable systems originate their own programming in studios, averaging 23 hours a week. In 1984, the government deregulated the cable industry, and though strongly encouraged public educational and government (PEG) channels, gave cable systems a choice in the matter.

Morality in Media

Cable's freedom from censorship allows it to take programming to new areas—some would say new depths—in terms of explicit language,

Principle #5
Cable can show more sexual or violent material because it is based on subscriber consent.

Madonna. This provocative pop singer tested the limits of censorship on cable by vivid displays of sexuality in her music videos.

sexual depictions, and gratuitous violence. Even basic channels, such as MTV—which telecasts provocative scenes of Madonna's "Justify My Love" video (1991) featuring multiple partners and erotic acts of sex—raise eyebrows from time to time. Conservative activist groups, such as Morality in Media and the Moral Majority, have sought court action to rule against obscene music videos and indecent content. Because no one is forced to subscribe to cable—much less watch it—the courts generally have given it wider First Amendment protection than the broadcasters enjoy. The state of Utah, for example, even tried to define "unfit programming" with a ban on televised nudity, but that statute was declared unconstitutional.

In 1990, an Alabama district attorney announced indictments against several satellite systems for distributing the Exxxtasy Channel to 30,000 subscribers, including almost two dozen in Montgomery County. The program supplier of the X-rated material was the Home Dish Satellite Corporation. Following the criminal indictment, Exxxtasy's main satellite distributors, GTE Spacenet and United States Satellite, opted to turn the channel off rather than risk going to jail.[11]

CABLE'S LEGISLATIVE CHRONICLE

For years, cable law has seemed like a tug of war between broadcasters and cable systems, and federal, state, and local governments, with the courts joining in the tug.[12] The Internal Revenue Service, for example, planned to levy an excise tax of 8 percent on the new industry. Cable leaders such as Shapp and Tarlton responded by forming the National Community Television Council at a hotel in Pottsville, Pennsylvania, in 1951. A district court of appeals threw out the excise tax, but the organization endured. Years later, its name was changed to the National Cable Television Association (NCTA), and to this day it continues to represent cable systems on a host of legal and political issues.

FCC Flip-Flops

The FCC originally took a hands-off position on CATV, but broadcasters persuaded the agency to rule on microwave firms' harnessing distant TV channels and importing them into local markets. In Wyoming, the Carter Mountain Transmission Company tried to relay TV shows from Denver to three cable systems. At first, the agency gave the go-ahead, but when KWRB-TV in Riverton, Wyoming, protested, the FCC turned an about-face. The agency concluded that it should evaluate the economic consequences for local broadcasters before approving any requests to import distant TV signals into their markets.[13]

Cable's Early Orders

The federal agency was now in an awkward position. It had touched a business that was supposedly beyond its reach. The FCC attempted to clear the air by issuing the First Report and Order, asserting, among other things, that the agency indeed had jurisdiction over microwave systems. CATV was "ancillary" to over-the-air television, the order said, and the FCC needed to protect the public's interest in broadcasting.[14]

Anxiety among broadcasters continued to rise as lobbyists for the NAB urged Congress to keep CATV systems from importing TV competition from distant cities. The FCC issued its second report in 1966.[15] That order effectively banned distant TV signals from large markets unless a cable system could show that such importing was in the public interest. In San Diego, one station owner, Midwest Television, complained that it was now facing competition from Los Angeles channels. The FCC responded by putting into effect its order against Southwestern Cable, but the California Supreme Court blocked the order, saying that the FCC held no jurisdiction. In *U.S.* v. *Southwestern Cable Co.* (1968),[16] the Supreme Court gave the final word by upholding FCC jurisdiction. The commission could regulate cable so long as its rules were "reasonably ancillary" to broadcast services.

Copyright Controversy

Television stations were under the impression—by virtue of licensing agreements with networks, syndicators, and producers—that the shows they aired belonged to them and that they were entitled to copyright payments. In 1976, the Copyright Act declared cable operators free to retransmit TV signals so long as they held compulsory licenses, which meant paying for programs from non-network sources. A copyright royalty panel was established to collect fees based on a share of each cable system's subscriber receipts. That money would then become royalties to the TV program's copyright holders. In 1993, Congress abolished the Copyright Royalty Tribunal and replaced it with a system based on arbitration panels appointed by the Librarian of Congress.

Must-Carry Rules

Perhaps the rule that continues to create the most controversy between broadcasters and cable companies is **must-carry.** It holds that a cable operator must carry every TV station within a certain radius of its system. Some cable owners resent the rule because it takes valuable channels away from other programming. An A/B switch was devised to allow viewers to choose between cable and antenna, but audiences wanted to have both local stations and premium channels without having to flip a switch on their television set.

At first, the 1972 report from the FCC asked cable operators to designate channels for local TV stations within a 35-mile radius. Cable was required to carry broadcast outlets that were "significantly viewed" by the local audience. In *Quincy Cable* v. *FCC* (1985),[17] a court of appeals held that must-carry rules

Must-carry Federal rule requiring cable systems to carry local broadcasters on a basic tier of channels.

Alternative delivery systems (ADS) Distribution of video and audio content other than by broadcast or cable, including satellite, telephone, and "wireless cable."

Direct broadcast satellite (DBS) Home reception of television programs distributed via satellite using small receiving dishes.

violated cable owners' First Amendment rights. A new law was drafted the following year with the support of both broadcasters and cable companies. It took into account the radius and audiences served and the channel capacity for each system. Another court held that must-carry was in violation of cable owners' First Amendment rights.

When Congress passed the Cable Television Consumer Protection and Competition Act of 1992 over President Bush's veto, a new must-carry option gave broadcasters the choice of either seeking payment from cable operators for retransmitting their signals or accepting a guarantee from each operator for a spot on its cable dial. Cable owners protested this ruling. Because local TV viewers did not pay a cent for over-the-air broadcasting, the companies argued, why should they be charged for refeeding a signal that was, after all, free? Eventually, most cable systems and broadcasters came to terms without the transfer of cash. The new law also made cable shows available to its new rivals in satellite and telephone delivery systems.

Sputnik. The space race began in earnest in 1957 when the Soviet Union launched this 184-pound aluminum sphere with nitrogen gas sealed inside. Four antennas bounced signals from the "baby moon" while it was in orbit.

ALTERNATIVES TO CABLE

There are a number of alternatives to cable for pay television programming. They include telephone companies' video services, Satellite Master Antenna Systems (SMATV), and the over-the-air system known by the curious term *wireless cable*. About 10 percent of America's television households receive their programs from sources other than cable, known collectively as **ADS** (alternative delivery systems).[18] Only about 8 percent of TV homes are linked to **DBS** (direct broadcast satellite), but that number is growing. As a result of all this competition, cable-industry leaders have urged fellow MSO owners to move ahead with digital set-top boxes in order to sell VOD (video on demand) and economical movies.

Satellite Competition

Satellite telecommunications, less than half a century old, marked the beginning of a new way to travel the television highway. The United States, however, had to have a wake-up call before it began experimenting with the new technology. The Soviet Union beat the United States into space on October 4, 1957 launching its first satellite, *Sputnik I.* The American people were shocked by the prospects of Communist superiority in space, but that jolt created a public outcry for a fast technological response.

It was 1962 before the United States entered the space race with its telecommunications satellites. AT&T's *Telstar I* was able to capture microwave signals from earth, amplify them billions of times, and bounce the waves back to receiving dishes. On July 10th, 1963, live scenes from France and England were relayed by television for several minutes before the orbiting *Telstar* satellite passed out of sight of receiving stations.

The problem this pointed up—that moving satellites "disappear"—was solved the following year, in a fashion conceived almost 20 years earlier by a young author and futurist, Arthur C. Clarke. In 1945, Clarke proposed the geostationary orbiting belt. According to the scientist, a number of satellites launched to a certain distance above the earth and "parked" there could provide uninterrupted broadcasting all over the world. The great advantage of his idea was that it required only three satellites to blanket the globe.

By 1963, Clarke's vision became a reality. The first geosynchronous, or GEO (geostationary earth orbiting), satellite was placed 22,300 miles above the planet in what is now called the *Clarke belt.* Figure 3.5 shows that at this position, higher than the LEO (lower earth orbiting) or HEO (higher earth orbiting) satellites, the GEOs stayed in phase with the earth's rotation near the equator.

There are 24 transponders on a satellite, their beams directed at different areas of the nation, as shown in Figure 3.6. The growth of cable television is directly related to this breakthrough in satellite transmission. After the "birds" were launched in the 1970s, new networks were formed to satisfy the demand for niche programming focused on areas such as comedy, law, sports, and music. Ironically, satellite transmission also introduced to subscribers one of cable's chief competitors—that powerful competitor: DBS (direct broadcast satellite) services.

In 1994, two media giants, Hughes Communication and Hubbard Communication, began DBS. Hughes called its service DirecTV, and Hubbard's competing service was named USSB (United States Satellite Broadcasting). By the end of its first year of operation, DirecTV had signed up a million subscribers. Within four years, Hughes bought out its rival and went head-to-head with EchoStar's Digital Sky Highway, or DISH.

Satellites Rising

At the end of 1999, DBS and video digital-subscriber lines had more than twice as many digital subscribers as cable, and about three million homes were converting to satellite dishes each year. While cable's stock prices were dropping, satellite companies were becoming prosperous. Cable's strategy was to compete with **bundling**—giving customers VOD, **telephony,** and high-speed Internet access all packaged together at a low price. Some cable systems even began to offer free cable if viewers would turn in their satellite dishes and decoder boxes in exchange for free digital cable service. Now, with satellites, telephone companies, and other video pipelines in the race how will local broadcast channels and cable companies stay ahead of the competition?

Telstar I. America's 171-pound sphere built by Bell Telephone Laboratories with AT&T funds was launched on July 10, 1962. The dawn of global satellite communications was reflected in its faceted solar cells. President Kennedy heralded Telstar as an "outstanding symbol of America's space achievements."

Bundling Packaging together several telecommunications services—such as television, telephone and the Internet—for a monthly fee.

Telephony Technology associated with transmitting voice, fax, or data between senders and receivers.

FIGURE 3.5

Satellite Orbit

Telecommunications satellites can be placed in geostationary (GEO) orbit 22,300 miles in space where they reach synchronous orbit with the earth. The so-called Clarke belt has no room left in its equatorial path, so telecommunications companies have contemplated higher elliptical orbits (HEOs) or lower earth orbits (LEOs) usually in polar orbits. Such paths fall out of view of the earth, and would require multiple relay satellites for data or television transmission.

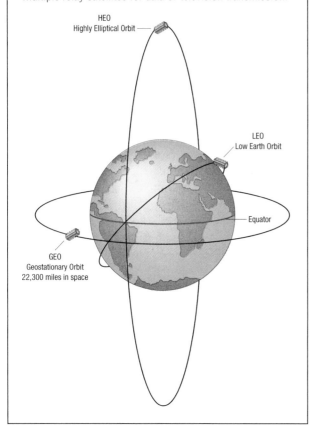

HEO
Highly Elliptical Orbit

LEO
Low Earth Orbit

Equator

GEO
Geostationary Orbit
22,300 miles in space

Open video systems (OVS)
Regulatory term describing telephone-company distribution of TV programs to home viewers.

Telephone Companies Enter the Video Business

The breakup of AT&T in 1984 gave birth to seven regional telephone systems—sometimes called the *baby bells* or *RBOCs* (Regional Bell Operating Companies). All were required to stay out of the long-distance phone and video business, something that cable companies and broadcasters lobbied to keep for themselves. Bashing cable in Congress, however, for its rates, technical problems, and indifference to customer complaints became a popular vote-getter for lawmakers in the 1980s and early 1990s. The time appeared right for telephone companies to persuade regulators to rethink their position.

The FCC in 1992 decided to modify its rules to allow the baby bells and other phone companies to slip their foot in the door of the cable enterprise.[19] At first, video dial tone services (VDTs) enabled the telephone company to serve as a carrier of programming, similar to a cable system but without any local origination of programs. Three of the baby bells—NYNEX, Pacific Telesis, and Bell Atlantic—arranged with a Hollywood agency to begin securing programs for their VDTs. With the passage of the Telecommunications Act of 1996, VDTs became **open video systems (OVS)** operators, falling under many of the same rules that apply to the cable industry. For example, OVS operaters must apply to the FCC for certification.

Phone company executives predict that the future will bring several wired and wireless forms of information and entertainment delivery. The door to such innovations swung wide open with the passage of the Telecommunications Act in 1996, which gave telephone and cable industries freedom to compete against each other. Three American telephone companies—NYNEX, Southwestern Bell, and US West—were offering cable television in Great Britain, and were more than happy to begin doing video business in their home country. Southwestern Bell stepped up first, buying two cable systems in the Washington, DC, area from Hauser Communications.

FIGURE 3.6

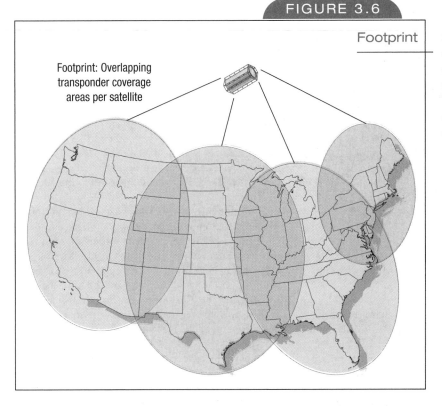

Footprint: Overlapping
transponder coverage
areas per satellite

Footprint

Satellites in geostationary
orbit use different transponders to focus at different regions of the United States.
Twenty-four transponders
on each satellite cover most
of the contiguous states.

SMATVs and MMDS

While community antenna television systems began popping up all over the country in the 1950s, another system for piping television to businesses and to residential complexes began to catch on. Master Antenna Television (MATV) was
promoted by Milton Jerrold Shapp to TV-set retailers who wanted to hook up the
in-store sets to different channels. The idea caught the attention of apartment managers and hotels, and they asked for master antenna systems to feed television signals to their housing and rental customers. After the first telecommunications
satellites were launched, Satellite Master Antenna Television (SMATV) took over
this approach and started to compete with local cable companies. Motels and
apartments began tacking television service onto tenants' bills, and realized profits from pay movies and other special events. In 1991, the FCC gave SMATV companies a boost by designating some of the microwave spectrum—73 channels—for
them to use as links between apartment complexes and hotels.[20]

A combination of microwave channels was freed up by the FCC in 1983 to
allow for another competitor in the pay-television business. The new service consisted of eight channels that had been designated to schools and universities and
were known as instructional fixed television service (IFTS); three channels used

ProTalk

Steve Creeden
Cox Cable Manager

"One way or another we're going to have the best wire to the house."

Steve Creeden manages Cox Communications for Lafayette, Louisiana. His mentor was Bob Rogers, who got into the cable business in 1954 by building TCA cable in Texas. Rogers was a pilot who flew from system to system and created his own cable business from scratch. Back then, it was a matter of teaching people basically what cable could provide for them. Mainly, the "what" was clear television reception—something rural residents couldn't get from TV stations off rabbit ears or rooftop antennas. Rogers put up towers to amplify TV signals and bring in new CATV customers.

Creeden, in the business since 1980, has managed cable systems in Texas and Louisiana. For a while, he even owned his own satellite television business. Nowadays, he finds himself competing with both satellite and telephone companies. Of satellites, he says, "Their time is now." Satellite TV companies have done an excellent job of drawing customers through promotional advertising, he says. The companies' product is relatively good and they've beat the cable industry to the digital market, but as more digital services are deployed by cable, Creeden believes, it will recoup any customers lost to the satellite companies.

The advantage for cable is having that last mile of wire into the home. It boils down to a question of bandwidth in either copper-wire or wireless transmission, compared to fiber and light, Creeden says. Cable also faces competition from telephone companies getting into the video business and offering high-speed delivery of data. Once the cable industry has all of its systems digitally upgraded, the aim is to have the best means for delivering video, high-speed data, and any other kind of digital service. This includes voice telephony, which can get to customers either through internet providers (IP) or a switched network similar to the phone company. Nearly 1.5 million Americans receive telephone service from cable systems at this point. "One way or another we're going to have the best wire to the house," he says. "And I think that's ultimately our big advantage."

Multichannel multipoint distribution service (also multipoint microwave distribution systems) (MMDS) Wireless systems for delivering TV programs and Internet service over high-frequency channels to subscribers.

by businesses for point-to-point television programs and known as operational fixed service (OFS), and eight more channels. These **multipoint multiple distribution systems** (MMDS) are similar to cable but use a microwave transmitter instead to reach rooftop antennas. At last count, there were about 90 such "wireless cable" systems in the United States, with fewer than a million subscribers.

Digital Future

Cable systems fought entry by the phone company into video delivery, but are now hoping to gain the advantage by sending more telephone and data services through the cables. Over the last decade, systems have been yanking old coaxial wires from the ground and replacing them with glass fiber to give them broadband capabilities. Most of the rebuilt cable systems are a combination of fiber and coaxial cable known as *HFC (hybrid fiber/coaxial),* but their optical-fiber backbones give them options for an array of digital services. Cable high-speed modems with fast download times have attracted businesses and consumers looking for new ways of interacting on-line through web TV and telephone.

Regardless of the delivery system, cable's bread-and-butter business is still niche networks; they have attracted a 45 percent share of the U.S. TV audience to their programming. However, a stagnant economy and other fears left optimism in short supply at the November 2001 Western Cable Show in Anaheim, California. Attendance was down by almost half, due in part to the terrorism of September 11th, but also due to industry consolidation. Ted Turner told an interviewer that one day Americans will see just two huge multiple system operators and four or five programmers. That might be dismissed as classic Turner hyperbole, but it underscored the real trend toward industry downsizing.[21]

Microwave Relay Towers.
Microwave towers are used to capture and transmit audio and video signals on earth. They may be used to repeat signals across the landscape spaced about 40 miles apart.

Summary

In its first half century, cable television became the TV-delivery choice for about 70 percent of America's households. Along the way, program producers and cable systems found themselves wrestling with customers and government regulators. Content quality and technical issues threatened their position at times, but the industry managed to keep growing. At first, it offered customers 3 or 5 channels per city, then 12 or 20, and today most systems offer 50 or more channels.

As the number of cable systems grew, so did broadcasters' fear of cable competition. In 1963, the FCC responded to lobbying by the National Association of Broadcasters, regulating cable systems using the commission's power to license microwave relays. Those relays imported distant TV signals for cable systems. In 1966, the FCC added to cable's burden by requiring systems to carry all television stations within each operator's area of coverage. The U.S. Supreme Court upheld the "must-carry rule" in 1968.

Early programming consisted of distant broadcast channels, but premium cable-only channels began with HBO's use of satellite distribution in 1975. Ted Turner's enterprises marked the beginning of cable's boom era during the 1980s. Combined groups of cable systems, known as MSOs, sprouted up as a dozen or so media conglomerates took over the cable universe. New kinds of programmers threatened cable's business, and its stocks began to sag with the rise of satellite and alternative means of video distribution.

CAREER FOCUS

Cable careers vary by their focus and by their placement in the hierarchy of the business, but they have grown substantially in number over the past 20 years, from about 40,000 in 1981 to more than 130,000 today, according to industry estimates.[22]

There are job opportunities at the local cable system level, with multiple system operators, and at cable programming networks. Generally, MSOs hire people for positions in financial and legal offices, advertising sales and marketing, corporate engineering, public affairs, and operations management.

Most MSOs are headed by a **chairman** followed by a **chief executive officer** or **president.** Below him or her are offices for the **chief operating officer** and **vice presidents** of the various departments.

The **general manager** of a local cable system supervises all aspects of the operation: policies and programming, engineering, new services, and system expansion. The **GM** is also responsible for the budget, personnel decisions, employee benefits, and planning for future growth. He or she must work effectively with managers from other offices. For example, local managers rely on an administrative staff, also called the Customer Service Department, which includes **billing clerks, accounts payable and receivable,** and **accountants.** It coordinates the technical staff's response to customer requests for new service or maintenance. Generally, a **customer service representative** handles calls about cable service and billing, and a **dispatcher** coordinates this information with the technical staff in the field.

The **chief engineer** will have working for him or her in the technical department the following personnel: **cable installers** to prepare homes for cable reception by running lines from utility poles to outlets in the home, **trunk technicians** to troubleshoot failures in the main line or feeder amplifiers, **service technicians** to respond to individual subscriber complaints, and **bench technicians** to run the cable system's repair facility.

Marketing, advertising sales and **public affairs directors** promote the image and services of the cable system in the community. The **marketing director** is charged with building the subscriber enrollment for the cable system as well as coordinating research, advertising, and promotions. This person recruits new subscribers through promotions with homes as well as hotels and apartment complexes needing hook-ups to the system. **Advertising sales** or **account executives** call on businesses, which may want to run commercial spots and reach niche audiences through cable channels. **Researchers** are often hired by cable systems to determine the demographic makeup of the local audience and determine how well the system is meeting their needs.

A **public affairs director** serves as a liaison between the cable system and the community and government leaders. This person also works with the local media to get the word out on projects and events the cable system has undertaken.

Career opportunities in television production vary from system to system. The **programming and production staff** creates local programs for some systems or works with the public access center, depending on the franchise's obligations.[23]

Primarily, cable industry jobs are found in administration and clerical offices, advertising and sales, engineering/technical services, and customer services. However, more job opportunities have been created in broadband services and web operations. These include promoting and selling the cable's broadband and on-line services as well as maintaining websites for the system.

The future holds even more wired and wireless delivery systems. Broadcast stations and cable are trying to fend off newcomers, including satellite systems, telephone companies, and Internet entrepreneurs. New delivery options for video, audio, and the Internet have made the telecommunications roadmap more intriguing and more lucrative. Yet, with billions of dollars and global enterprises at stake, it is not a game for the fainthearted or underfunded.

FOOD FOR THOUGHT

1. Early cable entrepreneurs wanted to bring distant television signals to rural customers, and recover a small profit. Today, concentration of cable systems in fewer hands has meant the virtual demise of locally owned cable companies. Do you consider that a good development? Why or why not?
2. Interactive television has been an ongoing experiment with cable companies. What types of interactive services would you like to receive?
3. Cable television recovers more of its revenue from subscribers than from advertising. Would you be willing to pay more for cable television if it were free of commercials?
4. The trend toward consolidation has meant that fewer people control both the channels we watch and how they are distributed. Do you view this as a positive or negative trend? Why?
5. The number of public access channels has declined since it became an optional requirement in 1984. Do you think that every cable system should be required to have a community access channel? Explain your reasoning.
6. Satellites are becoming more popular because of their numerous channels and digital services. What factors would determine whether you subscribe to satellite, to cable, or to video delivery by the telephone company?
7. Cable companies are now competing for telephone service using the Internet. Would you be willing to switch to a cable supplier for telephone services? Why or why not?

4

Digital Domains

We are clearly and dramatically seeing the dust rising from a multitude on the move. Species migrate both to seek more favorable environments and to escape hostile ones. Such can be observed in the Broadband Digital Migration.

—Michael K. Powell, FCC Chair, to the Progress & Freedom Foundation, December 8, 2000

Nicholas Negroponte, founder of the Media Lab at the Massachusetts Institute of Technology. Negroponte speculated on the future of the Internet and digital convergence and predicted the information age would shift the economy and society by increasing globalization and refocusing centers of power.

Every new movement must have its leader, its guru, its Martin Luther King, its Elizabeth Cady Stanton. This is usually someone who sees the world in a different light, and can prompt others to see it that way. Totally committed to their convictions, the leader persuades followers to embrace new ideas whose time has come. For the digital age, Nicholas Negroponte may be that leader. He is the professor who founded the Media Lab, the computer age's central think tank, at the Massachusetts Institute of Technology.

Negroponte spelled out his vision of the future in *Being Digital* (1995), published in more than 40 languages.[1] Read it and his reasoning becomes clear: Digital telecommunications allows data to be compressed so it becomes more efficient—no extraneous words or gestures. As Negroponte says, it works like the wink of an eye. One wink conveys mutual understanding between people without wasted information. The wink can be taken as a metaphor for compressing data, a process which, in digital technology, strips away redundant information and unnecessary detail. Negroponte used the wink example to persuade software makers to design algorithms of **compression** and stop worrying about bandwidth restrictions.

This wink also inspired the founders of a new form of interactive television (ITV) in Alameda, California.[2] For them, the term *wink*

> Every new movement must have its leader, its guru. . . . For the digital age, Nicholas Negroponte may be that leader.

was the perfect way to describe a new type of cable television that allowed viewers to do something other than become couch potatoes. They could play video games, shop over the Internet, or go on-line to find out more about the actors in shows they watched. That was all because of the interactive channels in their Wink set-top box, which allowed viewers to talk back to the television.

Today, Wink's founders are betting that U.S. viewers will become more accustomed to leaning forward and interacting with their sets—as they do with computers—than to leaning back and watching television until it lulls them to sleep. Wink was not the first experiment in ITV, but now it is in the vanguard of a new move toward television interactivity. At least that's what Negroponte's followers envision as they mine for profits from digital domains.

Compression Reduces the bandwidth needed for electromagnetic energy transmissions in video, audio, or text.

Digital convergence The trend toward merging what were separate media (radio, television, telephone, and computer) into one medium for purposes of communication and commerce.

Principle #1

Digitization allows video, audio, and text information to be compressed for more efficient transmission.

Bit Abbreviates *binary* and *digit* to represent a unit of data with two options—one or zero.

THE DIGITAL CHALLENGE

Depending on whom you ask, **digital convergence** is happening either too rapidly or too slowly. In terms of audio and video recording and editing, the conversion to point-and-click tools is moving along just fine. However, in terms of digital radio and television, there are loose ends left to be tied. Investors and owners in broadcast, telephone, and cable have embraced technology to digitally compress pictures, sounds, text, and graphics and send them over electronic highways, but using different standards.

Fiber-optic cable, for example, has been strung across North America as fast as crews can make connections. Yet compatible digital links with satellite, cable, and broadcast programming have yet to be forged. Other roadblocks involve copyright protection as well as bandwidth and spectrum limitations. However, the future in electronic media is clearly digital, so let's begin with the theory behind the practice.

Digits Defined

Simply put, digital recording and digital signal transmission are more efficient than analog. They are faster, easier, and—like a department store sale—give you more for less; in other words, more signal with less noise. When scientists and technicians began harnessing the electromagnetic spectrum, they relied on the dots and dashes of telegraphy to communicate. It's actually not that different with digital communication. The binary digit is the fundamental building block. A **bit** is simply the consolidation of two words, *binary* and *digit*. One bit is just another way of saying you have turned a switch on or off, to one or to zero. A binary computer language translates the ones and zeros into text, graphics, pictures, and sounds. Figure 4.1 shows the binary path from bits to computer code to human language. The list expands to infinity, but the point is that digital has become a universal lan-

FIGURE 4.1

Bits: The Anatomy of a Mail Message

A binary computer language, American Standard Code for Information Interchange (ASCII), translates the ones and zeros into English.

Source: Reprinted with the permission of Que Publishing, as represented by Pearson Computer Publishing, a division of Pearson Education, from *How the Internet Works, Fourth Edition, 1e,* by Preston Gralla. Copyright © 1998 by Que Publishing.

1. In the To line, type in the email address of the person to whom you're sending a message. The address must be typed in following strict rules. If you get a single letter or the syntax wrong, your message won't get to the intended recipient.

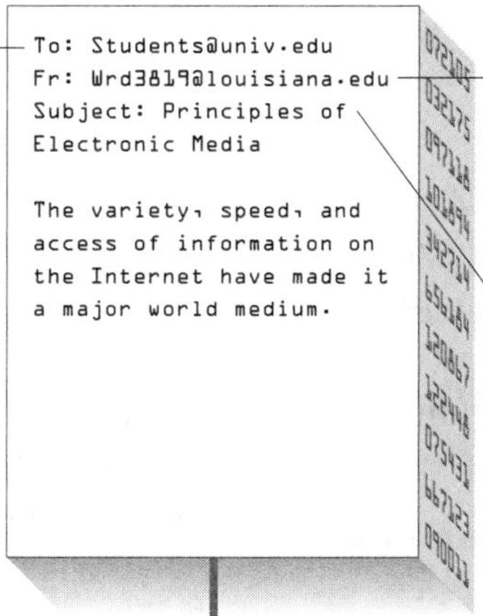

```
To: Students@univ.edu
Fr: Wrd3819@louisiana.edu
Subject: Principles of
Electronic Media

The variety, speed, and
access of information on
the Internet have made it
a major world medium.
```

2. Your email address will appear on the From line. Using this address, the recipient of your message will be able to respond to you.

3. On the Subject line, type in the subject of your message or a very brief summary.

```
01001101010111010101001100
10010000101011101011101010
01001101010111010101001100
10010000101011101011101010
01001101010111010101001100
10010000101011101011101010
01001101010111010101001100
10010000101011101011101010
01001101010111010101001100
10010000101011101011101010
01001101010111010101001100
```

4. An email message is converted to binary data, usually transmitted in the ASCII text format. ASCII is a standard that enables any computer, regardless of its operating system or hardware, to read the text. ASCII code describes the characters you see on your computer screen.

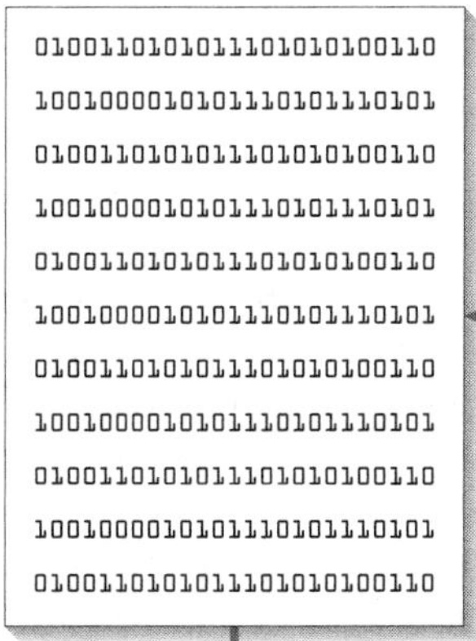

```
R Y3 J K78 H E4 V K8 L9 IO
D G N5 K E3 A4 12 FO J D2
N7 S4 F43 H M5 R Y3 J
K78 H E4 V K8 L9 IO D G
N5 K E3 A4 12 FO J D2 N7
S4 F43 H M5 R Y3 J K78 H
E4 V K8 L9 IO D G N5 K E3
A4 12 FO J D2 N7 S4 F43 H
M5 R Y3 J K78 H E4 V K8
L9 IO D G N5 K E3 A4 M5
```

5. You can also attach pictures, executable programs, sounds, videos, and other binary files to your email message. To do this, you'll have to encode the file in a way that will enable it to be sent across the Internet. The receiver will also have to be able to decode the file. A variety of encoding schemes can be used. Some email software will automatically do the encoding for you and will also do the decoding on the receiving end.

FIGURE 4.2

Bytes

Alphanumeric Character		Binary Code for Bytes
5	00110101	00110100
8	00111000	00110111
G	01100111	01000110
R	01010010	01010001
S	01010011	01010110
e	01100101	01100010
l	01101100	01101011

**Group of 8 Bits
ASCII Code**

guage of technology expressed in bits and in larger collections of bytes. A **byte** is typically eight bits of information; in Figure 4.2, the code is broken to show collections of bytes.

Beginning with the Bitstream

Speeding along the highways of digital convergence, radio and television broadcasters seize bitstreams to transport audio and video signals at volumes and speeds expressed in *bits per second*, or *bps*. Such numbers expand wider than radio frequencies, and are likewise described in *kilobits*, *megabits*, and *gigabits*. When engineers speak of *terabits*, they mean trillions of bits flowing in data streams. Figure 4.3 shows the speedometer for the Internet and spells out the bit-rate abbreviations. Now for a shorthand description of how this all came about, let's drag the cursor to the beginning.

FIGURE 4.3

Bit Rate

The flow of information on the Internet is clocked according to the flow of bits or bit rate.

20 kb	20 kbps (20,000 bits per second)	Kilobits
20 kB	20 kBs (20,000 bytes per second; 160,000 bits per second)	Kilobytes
20 Mb	20 Mbps (20,000,000 bits per second)	Megabits
20 MB	20 MBps (20,000,000 bytes per second; 160,000,000 bits per second)	Megabytes
20 Gb	20 Gbps (20,000,000,000 bits per second)	Gigabits
20 GB	20 GBps (20,000,000,000 bytes per second; 160,000,000,000 bits per second)	Gigabytes
20 Tb	20 Tbps (20,000,000,000,000 bits per second)	Terabits
20 TB	20 TBps (20,000,000,000,000 bytes per second; 160,000,000,000,000 bits per second)	Terabytes

From Tassel, Joan Van. *Digital TV over Broadband—Harvesting Bandwidth* Woburn, MA: Focal Press. 2001, 50.

Nyquist's Numbers

The theory behind the engine of the digital age belongs to a Swedish-born scientist and inventor, Harry Nyquist. He immigrated to the United States as a teenager and earned degrees in electrical engineering and physics from the North Dakota and Yale schools of engineering. Nyquist's interests covered a wide range of electrical phenomena, particularly telegraphy. After taking a job at Bell Labs, he penciled in the formulas for measuring the pulse of electromagnetic energy.[3]

BINARY IS BORN

Nyquist's idea was to rethink analogous waves of energy in terms of dots and dashes, a type of Morse code to modulate electromagnetic signals in mathematical arrays. He envisioned breaking down the waves into numbers, binary codes of ones and zeros. The key piece to the Nyquist puzzle was **sampling.** In a 1924 article, "Certain Factors Affecting Telegraph Speed," he defined sampling as the means for capturing the voltage of the original wave at fixed intervals, and coding it into pulses to represent the original signal. If the sampling rate is fast enough, the gaps between measures will not be heard or seen. Today, engineers talk about this process as **PCM (pulse code modulation)**. In other words, PCM means you're not capturing the whole wave but collecting a sample of it.

SAMPLING SOLVES THE EQUATION

Sampling is just the first step in converting an analog signal to digital. The waveform is broken into a series of narrow pulses by **quantization,** in which the amplitude is measured and converted into digits. Nyquist's theory would work so long as sampling rates were adequate and enough of the original wave was measured. The accuracy of digitization depends on the sampling rate, precision of the quantizing, and channel capacity. According to Nyquist's original theorems, channel capacity should be twice the bit rate, or 2:1. One of Nyquist's colleagues at Bell Labs, Claude Shannon, revised his calculations in 1948 when he and Warren Weaver introduced their mathematical theory of communication.

That, in a nutshell, is the beginning of digital theory. So what happened after Nyquist? Just about everything. Digital machines were invented, replaced, and reinvented—all using Nyquist's language of bits and bytes.

COMPUTER EVOLUTION

First came the computer. Just as radio and television's slow births drew on starts and stops by inquisitive thinkers and tinkerers, disputes over patents, and tedious court cases—so did the computer have its peculiar adolescence. It was more than a journey of competition and collaboration in which the lines distinguishing public and private sectors were trespassed. It involved engineers who simply gave away their source codes, the key to the machine's system of logic. And it is about ambitious entrepreneurs who converted dot-com discoveries into large profits that turned south during the shakeout of 2000–2001.

Mainframes to PCs

The early days of the invention of the computer were marked by several highlights. Computer prototypes were springing up around the United States before World War II, when branches of the military sought the precise logic of computation to solve ballistic errors in their antiaircraft guns. Bell Lab technicians in 1939 hooked up electronic relays and switches to typewriters to offer remote access. With keyboard controls, the results vaguely resembled today's personal computers. Harvard University was another center for computing design. In 1937, Harvard mathematician Howard Aiken connected his machine's electrical components to rolls of perforated paper tape. He called this the Mark 1, and with the backing of International Business Machines, Aiken's analog machine was running numbers in 1944. The British also made their contribution and have yet to receive the accolades they deserve for building the first digital computer. Colossus was invented to break the Nazi's secret codes during World War II, and it accomplished that feat using binary code.

Byte Groups bits together according to units of eight in the American Standard Code for Information Interchange (ASCII).

Sampling Digitizes analog signals through periodic measurements of continuous waves.

Pulse code modulation (PCM) The sampling process where the amplitude of an analog signal wave is converted into its numerical equivalent for digital processing.

Quantization Assigns a numerical quantity to a sample of a signal.

ENIAC—Electronic Numerical Integrator and Computer. It was built in 1946 by the University of Pennsylvania at government expense. The ENIAC was inspired by the war effort, and performed computations for the hydrogen bomb in the early 1950s.

After the war, the University of Pennsylvania set aside an auditorium to show off a tube-powered calculator that was 80 feet long. Its name seemed nearly as long: the Electronic Numerical Integrator and Computer, or ENIAC. Computer scientists John Mauchly and John Eckert of the Moore School of Electrical Engineering designed the 30-ton monstrosity with a half-million-dollar grant from the Army Ordinance Department. Like the Navy, the Army hoped for a machine that could correct the problems of artillery fire. After ENIAC, Mauchly and Eckert entered private business and designed another computer for the government. The UNIVACI (Universal Automatic Computer) in 1951 processed data collected of the U.S. population for the Census Bureau from the year before.

THE PUNCH-CARD ERA

If you're old enough to recognize the phrase "Do not fold, spindle, or mutilate," then you probably recall an era in computing that fell between the arrival of big UNIVAC machines and the age of personal computers. This era, known as the mainframe age, was marked by punch cards that tabulated numbers, and reflected IBM's dominance in computing centers. The firm held important patents on the punch-card process, but competitors eventually circumvented those patents by changing the number of rows and the shape of the holes to devise their own "electromechanical tabulators."

The Smithsonian Institution's Steven Lubar says these punch cards were binary—because their holes were either punched or not, and because their constellations figured into a larger scheme of numbers. Punch cards also symbolized an era of depersonalization in computing; the U.S. Census Bureau and other institutions started using the cards to identify people by numerical dimensions. The fear of computerized Big Brotherism was visualized in Stanley Kubrick's *2001: A Space Odyssey.* It featured the menace of a malfunctioning computer, HAL (letters preceding IBM in the alphabet).[4] The next decade would see the development of personal computers.

ADVENT OF THE PERSONAL COMPUTER

The first personal computers appeared in the United States in the 1970s. Technicians and hobbyists at Osborne, Kaypro, and Commodore companies built computers small enough to fit on a desktop. Soon, others drew on the same concept in the labs of General Electric, NCR (National Cash Register), and Xerox.

PLANTING THE APPLE SEED

The story of the personal computer hardly would be complete without the input of two California teenagers. Steve Jobs and Steve Wozniak joined a computer club, and at Jobs's insistence, they began to work on a homemade prototype. The Apple 1 was built in Jobs's garage; it was a keyboard and processing unit fitted into a briefcase. When a marketing specialist joined the team in 1977, Apple was incorporated. Jobs and Wozniak introduced a second personal computer that year; the Apple II sold more than 350,000 units.

Five years later, they combined word processing with graphic icons and business functions to create Apple's first mouse-driven computer. The Lisa desktop computer was unveiled in January 1983 and was the forerunner of the MacIntosh. It used a mouse with file menus and icons in what was described as a **GUI (graphic user interface)**. There were programs for LisaWrite, LisaDraw, LisaGraph, and so on. The name is somewhat of an enigma, since "Lisa" was either one of the designers' daughters or the abbreviation for local integrated software architecture. The Lisa computer sold for $9,995, though not very well, and was on the market for less than two years. Yet it did reflect the dawn of a new age in point-and-click computing.

The Apple Macintosh was released in 1984, with a Super Bowl commercial depicting an Olympian runner hurling a hammer at a screen where an Orwellian dictator appeared to be ordering the masses to march in lockstep. The dictator's face, shattered by the Apple runner's hammer, represented IBM.

UNIVACI Universal Automatic Computer. Scientists J. Presper Eckert and John Mauchly operate their invention for the Remington-Rand Corporation. The UNIVAC was used by the Census Bureau to tally the population, and later projected the 1952 presidential race.

Graphic user interface (GUI) Added to the computer's operating system a set of icons and visual links rather than text commands to handle data.

Big Blue versus Apple

The nation's largest computer manufacturer, IBM, famous for its big blue logo, took notice of Apple's success. In July 1980, Big Blue's executives called for a personal computer to compete in the growing market. The director of IBM's development lab in Florida recommended contracting with hardware and software suppliers from outside the company. Instead of designing its own microprocessor, IBM adapted one from the Intel model designed in Albuquerque, New Mexico.

To program the computer's operating system, IBM contacted a software company near Seattle represented by a Harvard dropout. Bill Gates of Microsoft agreed to provide the operating system—on one condition: His company would retain ownership of the license. Gates bought an OS (operating system) program written by Tim Patterson of Seattle Computer Products for his prototype, Intel 8086. Patterson had dubbed it QDOS (for quick and dirty operating system). Gates simply changed its name to MS-DOS (Microsoft-disk operating system) and reaped a fortune from his $50,000 investment.

After marketing its first personal computer (PC), IBM came up with a smaller version called the PC junior, and then dove deeper into the portable personal-computer market with its first laptop model. By 1984, IBM's desktop

Computer Developers Steve Jobs, John Scully, and Steve Wozniak. This team introduced personal computing with the Apple II in 1977. In 1984, they reconfigured it and sold the Apple IIc. Jobs holds the keyboard, while Scully and Wozniak stand behind the early monitor.

Operating system (OS) Determines how a computer's central processing unit (CPU) will read, process, and store data.

Packets Carry the information on the Internet by breaking it down into independent segments.

ARPANET Pioneered the effort to network host computers to withstand the threat of nuclear attack. It is considered the genesis of today's Internet.

models moved ahead of Apple in terms of PC sales. Apple and IBM were not alone. Soon, other electronics firms were chasing their share of the PC market—Texas Instruments, Commodore, Atari, and Radio Shack—all building machines that shared the same basic component parts.

PC COMPONENTS

The main elements of the PC are its hardware, operating system, software applications, and peripherals. The most important piece of hardware is the central processing unit, or CPU, since it's the brain of the computer. These microprocessors house one or more silicon chips to perform the CPU functions. They respond to the software applications that function through the machine's operating system.

The **operating system,** or **OS,** provides the means by which the software applications enable the computer to display graphics and text, perform calculations, and print data. Usually, an operating system is tied directly to one particular model of computer.

PC VERSUS MACINTOSH

Because of its decision to share the source code of its original operating system with software manufacturers, IBM allowed clones of its original PCs to hit the market. Apple retained all of its rights to the system technology and effectively kept clones off the market into the late 1990s. Personal computers consequently dominated the PC market because of price competition between the Dell and Gateway PCs, among others, based on the Intel CPU (chip). At this writing, IBM is now the fourth largest manufacturer of personal computers, behind Dell (first), Gateway (second) and Apple (third).

Estimates vary, but between 80 and 90 percent of all personal computers used in the United States are PC-based. Apple Macintosh, however, has kept its lead in creative applications, particularly in commercial uses for video and graphics. Apple estimates its QuickTime video system, for example, is used by 57 percent of the websites streaming video.

GLOBAL COMPUTER INDUSTRY

By the mid-1990s, more than one-third of the people in the United States had at least one personal computer, and the industry generated $100 billion in annual profits from hardware sales. Computers were globally incorporated in terms of both sales and manufacturing. IBM's printers and display monitors, for example, were manufactured and sold overseas, as were those of several of its competitors.

In brief, the computer evolved from a machine to calculate numbers to a powerful tool for storing data and moving it around the world. Its most recent incarnation as a medium of commerce and communication is due largely to the popularity of interconnected networks carrying **packets** of information by switching electrical pulses on and off.

THE INTERNET AGE

The Internet became the center of digital convergence because it merged the communication activities of the computer, telephone, radio, television, and publishing. In 1995, 8 million Americans used their computers to telecommute, and 20 million accessed the Internet each week. Internet users number more than 250 million people today, and Americans spend

1984 Macintosh Super Bowl Commercial. Based on the Orwell novel, *1984,* the commercial featured an audience of spiritless drones watching open-mouthed as a female Olympic runner (symbolizing the new Macintosh computer) hurls a sledgehammer against "Big Brother" (IBM) appearing on a gigantic television screen. The voiceover says, "On January 24, Apple Computer will introduce the Macintosh. And you will see why 1984 won't be like *1984.*"

at least one and a half hours a day on-line—twice as much time as they spend reading newspapers or magazines. How did the Internet assume such a preeminent position in the lives of people throughout the developed world?

Early Incentives

The Internet was the offspring of the Defense Advanced Research Projects Agency (DARPA), a branch of the Pentagon formed in response to a historic event occurring on October 4, 1957. That was the day the Soviet Union launched into space *Sputnik I,* the first manmade earth-orbiting satellite. This leap in space by a hostile superpower galvanized American resolve to enact a new system of defense.[5] Thus, under the watchful eye of its military leaders, DARPA was formed. The following year, the Research and Development (RAND) Corporation of California began meeting with DARPA to perfect a fail-safe system of communication in case of nuclear attack. The project was called **ARPANET,** and it was to become a system of communication links to function even if enemy missiles disabled parts of the overall infrastructure.

Military-to-College Transition

By 1966, the government was ready to establish a network of computer terminals. DARPA had initiated SAGE—the semi-automatic ground environment project exploring interactive links between computers using telephone lines and video display terminals.

> Principle #2
> **The variety, speed, and access of information on the Internet have made it a major world medium.**

In design at least, ARPANET was revolutionary because it replaced top-down hierarchies with an egalitarian model. The terminals were created equal—if any one computer went down, others would bypass it until all links were restored.

In 1969, the Advanced Research Projects Agency put its theory into practice and hooked up computers at UCLA in southern California and at Stanford in northern California. The following year, UC Santa Barbara and the University of Utah were added to the network, followed by MIT, Harvard, and

Backbone Forms the overarching route linking, by wire, smaller networks of computer terminals.

Protocols Determine how computers are going to make sense of each other's data in terms of transmission and reception.

Packet-switching Allows data to be separated into bundles and reassembled at their destination.

Uniform resource locator (URL) Finds a home page or website on the Internet.

Domain names Identifies websites with words describing their address by general application (edu = education, mil = military, org = organization, com = communication, etc.) and specific location (uoregon.edu, ablongman.com, pentagon.mil).

Carnegie-Mellon. Thus, the Internet, which began as a military secret, swiftly migrated to university campuses. Today, it covers the globe with instantly exchangeable information.

Networks on Top of Networks

The Internet has become our most familiar network, but it's actually thousands of networks cooperating with each other to direct information to a final destination. These networks link computers by copper wire, optical fiber, coaxial cable, and even microwaves. At the top level, the **backbone** networks with high-message capacity travel wide distances to link smaller networks identified by their abbreviations. Like an interstate highway, backbones cover the longest distance at the highest speeds carrying the biggest loads. Wide area networks (WANs) serve regions of the country; local area networks (LANs) interconnect computers within a building or campus area (see Figure 4.4).

PACKETS AND PROTOCOLS

Network cooperation means that networks of computers abide by the same rules, or protocols, in the language of the Internet. Protocols work because they enable computers to speak with each other through small bundles of information known as *packets* (see Figure 4.5). Packets take different routes to reach their destination, where they are reassembled by the receiving computer to make sense for the viewer. The idea of packet switching was actually the inspiration of a Welsh physicist, Donald Davies, who observed that a brain overcomes neural damage by sending messages along alternate routes. So if there is an impasse at any one juncture, the brain finds a detour to its destination. The defense system of computers was designed to cooperate in the same manner. At the National Physical Laboratory (NPL) in Great Britain, Davies applied his theory by using "packets" to transfer data.[6]

> ## Principle #3
>
> The Internet works due to the common language through which computers exchange information over a number of networks.

DETOURS IN CYBERSPACE

A science-fiction writer, William Gibson, coined the term *cyberspace* in a popular novel about crime solving called *Neuromancer*.[7] *Cyber* refers to a steersman, but to Gibson, it simply meant the journey of the mind altered by transferring thoughts to the Internet. On today's Internet, computers speak to each other in cyberspace by using a common language that obeys certain rules.

Two sets of rules, or **protocols,** make shipping information possible. Transmission control protocol (TCP) separates data into bundles of about 1,500 characters for shipping and reassembling at the destination computer. The TCP also labels the packet with a "checksum" to see if any errors contaminated its cargo during the journey. If there are flaws detected, TCP quickly discards it and asks the host computer to resend fresh bundles, which may take a waiting period at the receiving end.

Internet protocol (IP) is how information is routed along the quickest path to the receiving computer. The IP is like an address on an envelope, so that as the packets travel across the Internet, routers examine the addresses and deter-

Who Is the True Inventor of the Internet?

Sometimes politicians have to eat their own words. Vice President Al Gore was served his sound bites several times as he campaigned for the presidency in 2000. A quote extracted from a CNN interview and often played on talk shows gave the impression that Gore was taking credit for inventing the Internet. In truth, he was referring to legislation facilitating the Internet's construction. The question remains: If Al Gore didn't invent the Internet, then who did?

Several people have been credited for the groundwork that facilitated the invention of the Internet. Paul Baran of the RAND Corporation, for example, designed the plans for the package-switched network. This system required a programming code wherein computers could talk to each other. These packets of information needed computer addresses so that the routers along the way would know how to reach their destinations.

Dr. Vinton Cerf worked on the program from 1976 to 1982, and, in collaboration with Bob Kahn, developed the **packet-switching** protocols to link radio and satellite communications to the Internet. Kahn and Cerf did much to promote its development, and came up with the name: *internet*, a compression of *interconnection of networks.*

Another candidate for the Internet's founding father is a scientist who shunned publicity and was known to his friends as "Lick." Joseph Carl Robnett Licklider took over the Information Processing Techniques Office (IPTO) in 1962, and began working with the Pentagon's DARPA. While directing the IPTO, Licklider redirected government contracts away from business corporations to academic centers, who shared his vision of interactive computing. Mainframes were preferred by big business, but he thought of computers in terms of communication, not numbers, and explored concepts such as human-computer symbiosis.

Licklider prophetically nicknamed his team of specialists "the Intergalactic Network," and coauthored a paper in 1968 entitled "The Computer as a Communication Device," which was revolutionary for its day. Licklider predicted that by the year 2000, millions of people would be on-line, connected by a global network. He was wrong in the time it took to get people to go on-line. The Internet, as we know it today, actually was "born" in 1986, when the National Science Foundation took over the military lines and beefed up the Internet's capacity for handling traffic with 30 times more bandwidth. Over the next few years, Internet service providers (ISPs) such as America Online and Prodigy encouraged consumers to go on-line while technicians increased the speed of the Internet.

As with all inventions, several scientists contributed their time, talents, and creative energy to make it a reality. In addition to Licklider, Baran, Cerf, and Kahn, Leonard Kleinrock at MIT wrote the first paper and book on packet switching. Lawrence Roberts and Thomas Merrill connected the MIT computers with the California terminals. And the list goes on. If you are looking for one person, however, who holds superior claim to the title "Inventor of the Internet," J. C. R. Licklider is the name.[8]

---

mine the quickest way for them to reach their destination. On the Web, these addresses are identified by **URLs (Uniform Resource Locators).**

DOMAIN NAMES LINING UP THE ON RAMP

Every IP address is a series of four numbers separated by dots, such as 587.34.903.32. Letters replace numbers in the addressing stage. The last half of the address is called the **domain name,** and the first half is the user's identification.

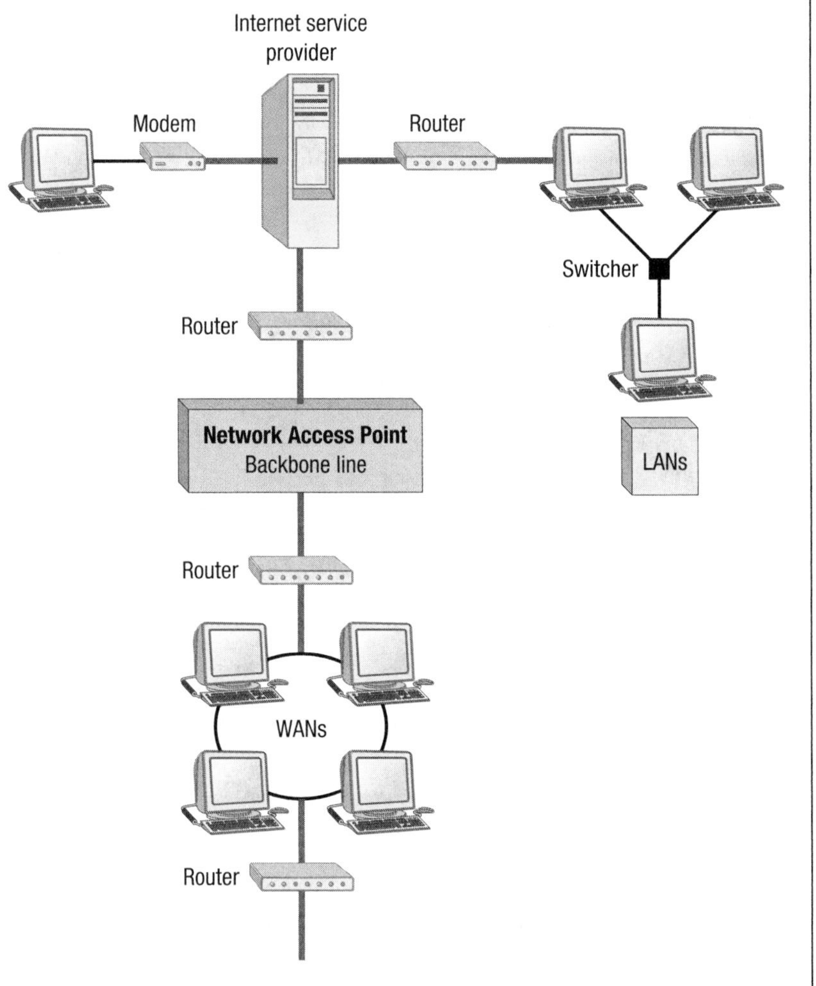

Individual computers feed information into the Internet at Internet service providers or at local area networks at schools, businesses, or other organizations. The providers and networks transmit signals through routers to wide area networks at the regional level and enter the backbone line at a network access point.

FIGURE 4.4

Local Area Networks (LANs) and Wide Area Networks (WANs)

Internet service provider

Modem   Router

Router

Network Access Point
Backbone line

Switcher

LANs

WANs

Router

Router

Router

Internet service provider (ISP) Offers Internet access to consumers by linking their home or office computer terminals to the Internet.

E-mail (electronic mail) Sends text messages digitally between two or more computers through wired or wireless networks.

Hypertext transfer protocol (HTTP) Indicates documents written in hypertext markup language (HTML) that can be linked to other sites on the Web.

To the right of the @ sign is the designation for the organization or groups of computers where the residence is located on the Internet. In the United States, it could be ".com" for commercial, ".edu" for educational, ".org" for organization, ".net" for network, ".mil" for military, and so forth. These abbreviations identify the host or server computers. Before that, comes the specific location of that application, and to the left of the @ symbol is the specific user's identification. In order to call upon these addresses, you first have to gain access to the Internet by **ISPs (internet service providers)**.

Internet service providers link together millions of people to the Internet every day. Thousands of ISPs operate in the United States: Earthlink, America

A Packet-Switched Network

The sender creates a message, which is translated into binary code by his or her computer, and assigns a destination address to receive the message. The message is transferred to the TCP (transmission control protocol) computer, which breaks the message into smaller packets of information that can travel easily through the Internet. The IP (Internet protocol) computer routes the data through a router to the receiving computer, where the information is received by the destination's computer, recombined into the original message, and translated from binary code to a readable format for the receiver.

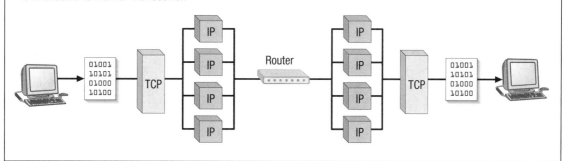

OnLine, Prodigy, and many more. The most frequent activity for an ISP is **electronic mail,** or **e-mail.** In a single year, Americans exchange trillions of e-mails, compared to mere billions of postal mail items.

Weaving the World Wide Web

The most dynamic network on the Internet is the World Wide Web (www) run by the World Wide Web Consortium (W3C). The W3C is headquartered at the Massachusetts Institute of Technology (MIT). It is an industry consortium made up of many private companies. A British software engineer, who now heads the W3C, made this his contribution to cyberspace in 1991.

Tim Berners-Lee, who is known to his friends as "TBL," developed the system for transferring documents at the CERN laboratory for particle physics in Geneva, Switzerland.[9] He named his innovation in computer programming **hypertext transfer protocol,** or **http.** It works on the idea that linking documents by clicking on key words and phrases is natural for computer users, since it follows their intuitive curiosity. Websites greet users with a homepage introducing the contents of the site while directing readers by hyperlinks to particular headings or even other web pages.

Oxford-Trained Engineer Tim Berners-Lee. He invented the World Wide Web in 1989 while trying to better organize his notes. At a Swiss think-tank, Berners-Lee designed software enabling computers to tap into each other's hard drives.

Electronic Commerce

The gold rush of the Internet's boom days during the 1990s was created by the lure of big profits through

**Amazon.com Founder
Jeff Bezos.**

**E-commerce (electronic
commerce)** Facilitates transactions of goods or services through the exchange of information or currency between computers.

electronic commerce. **E-commerce** actually predates the web, beginning with a network known as the *electronic data interchange*, or *EDI*. The creation of EDI allowed manufacturers to swap with retailers their data on prices, inventory, and shipments through computers. It grew with the expansion of the Internet into two main systems of commerce: business-to-business (B2B) and business-to-consumer (B2C). Cisco Systems, Microsoft, IBM, and Sun first began marketing B2B e-commerce solutions to their clients in the mid-1990s.

B2B COMMERCE

Cisco Systems first established an e-commerce site in 1996, but Microsoft was moving fast on its heels. Within a month, Microsoft created its "merchant system software" for making sales on the web. Then IBM elected to find its niche in e-commerce through electronic banking and financial advice. The eIntegrion Financial Network of IBM marketed "e-business strategies." Microsoft and Netscape contributed to the growth of business-to-business on the Web by offering data exchange services. There were so many firms struggling to survive in B2B e-commerce it became inevitable that many would fail, as they did during the downturn of 2000.

B2C COMMERCE

The success of e-commerce for consumers is easy to explain if you consider the pioneer work of Amazon.com. Jeffery Bezos, founder of on-line sales in books, became *Time* magazine's "Man of the Year" for 1999, based on his billion-dollar enterprise that proved the potential of e-commerce.

Bezos's original vision was to sell books on the Internet, even though he had no personal retail experience. Amazon.com grew out of his Seattle garage into a company larger than most national retail outlets. What the Princeton graduate in computer science knew how to do in 1994 was organize books on the Internet using lists of other sellers and publishing houses. His on-line store gave customers a huge selection of titles from which to choose. Bezos just added his personal touch by keeping track of trends and customer preferences, and then recommending to his buyers new titles for purchase. Amazon.com grew well beyond its book-selling roots, today offering video, music, and other retail merchandise. In so doing, it proved just how much e-commerce could sustain a lifestyle without ever leaving your home.

Downslide in the Dot-Com Economy

No one was calling it "Black December," but the last month of 2000 dug the deepest hole, closing a year of layoffs in the dot-com economy. More than 10,400 on-line employees were laid off that month, culminating in more than 41,000 job

Ebay's CEO

The silicon-valley stories of computer-class dropouts who turned fantastic ideas into huge fortunes before riding off into the Internet sunset have now faded, but there is one worth recalling. It is not a story about getting rich from B2B or B2C, but from C2C commerce. Pierre Omidyar left his major in computer science at Tufts University after interning in software programming in northern California. And yes, he did create the world's largest on-line auction house, eBay, in 1995. But then he did something different before exiting stage left—he turned it over to someone with a new perspective but who kept Omidyar's formula intact. Now, what makes this an unusual tale is that Omidyar's concept of e-commerce is a far cry from business textbooks.

Rather than acting like a profit-driven web merchant eager to grab shoppers and squeeze them for every last dime, Omidyar insisted that eBay live by the golden rule. There would be no web pitches with advertising causing "banner blindness," he said. Ebay's interactions with web customers were to be on their terms. If you had something to buy or sell at eBay, he wanted to work with you, and not the other way around. It was just that simple.

Before he moved to France in search of his family roots, Omidyar turned over the company's leadership to Margaret "Meg" Whitman. Whitman was a Princeton graduate with a Harvard MBA, who formerly held management positions at companies such as Hasbro, Disney, and Procter & Gamble. So, she was understandably shy about grabbing eBay's reins.

Whitman took over as CEO of eBay in February 1998, and eight months later the on-line auction house went public. And she has done it without compromising any of Omidyar's original vision. Success continued to follow the web company under Whitman's leadership, with market share prices rising to astronomical levels, including a secondary offering of $1.1 billion, one of the largest ever for an Internet firm. Perhaps it's not easy keeping eBay's two million-plus members happy while managing the company's brand image and employees, but Whitman made it look that way.[10]

losses in Internet-related industries for the year. Things were not a lot better in 2001. Three companies that offered high-speed Internet service by **DSL (digital subscriber lines)**—Northpoint Communications, Covad, and Rhythms—filed for bankruptcy that year, as did Excite@Home, the leading seller of broadband service over cable. Insiders knew the "gold-rush goofiness" of dot-com speculation would come to an end eventually, but no one knew for sure until the slump finally hit.

Digital subscriber line (DSL) Forms data loop, sending digital information over copper wires by bypassing the circuit-switched lines.

Bandwidth Measures the information capacity of an electromagnetic conduit.

BROADBAND FUTURE

The Internet prompted broadcasters to respect, if not embrace, the trend toward digital convergence, despite the recession in the high-tech sector. *Convergence* means that what had been viewed as independent forms of media—such as radio, television, cable, and computers—have been merging in a broadband world that relies heavily on the Internet. *Broadband* refers to the speed and **bandwidth** it takes to deliver communication and commerce on-line. Forrester Research reported in 2001 that 10.7 million American households had broadband access to the Internet by either telephone, cable modem, DSL, or satellite.[11] Faxes and

Streaming Carries audio and video information over the Internet to the computer by downloading and buffering data while playing it back.

Cache memory Acts as a buffer store of data between the CPU and computer storage.

Interactive television (ITV) Converts television from a one-way medium to one responding to viewer requests for information and entertainment.

telephony are handled on-line as well as the purchase of plane tickets and restaurant reservations.

Radio and television stations have been **streaming** their programming over the Web to encourage audiences to convert their computers into radio and television sets. Unfortunately, pictures are jerky and audio stalls while a buffer in the computer reloads the data. RealNetworks and Microsoft's Media Player report a total of more than 75 million users who have registered to click on an icon and wait the time it takes for viewers to watch Sam Donaldson on ABC.Com or listen to their favorite radio station in a distant city.

Not all computer users have embraced streaming, especially after frustrating experiences with frozen screens or awkward out-of-sync transmissions between voice and picture. Companies such as U2.burst.com experimented with new ways to take advantage of the **cache memory** on the computer and enable it to capture the video and audio content faster and play it back in real time.

Interactive Television

Interactive television holds the promise of closing the digital divide between computers and TV sets while fulfilling the vision of a user-driven medium. Advocates of this new medium hope to see a merger of the Internet and enhanced broadcasting, a blending together of downloaded music, video games, and movies. They prefer the term *t-commerce* (television commerce), rather than *e-commerce* (electronic commerce) and envision a sort of shopping mall in the TV set that entertains and informs while persuading viewers to make a purchase.

ITV Experiments

The idea of audience members interacting with radio and television programming is nothing new, of course. Early crime dramas on radio, such as *Gang Busters*, invited listeners to help police catch the bad guys by broadcasting a list of the most-wanted suspects at the end of each show. Call-in talk shows also involved audience participation beginning in the 1950s. These early interactive programs were as popular on radio then as *America's Most Wanted* and *Unsolved Mysteries* became on television much later.

Cable's potential to allow viewers to talk back to the TV sets produced an experiment in Columbus, Ohio, in 1978 called *Qube*. Warner Cable selected Columbus as a test market because its audience reflected national demographics. Cable subscribers were given 10 channels that responded to a touch-pad control. The experiment consisted of questions directed at the audience, which they could answer with their touch pad. Viewers were not particularly interested in responding to surveys, however, and preferred to just watch television instead. The Qube experiment folded in 1984.

European models of **interactive television (ITV)** used videotext and teletext to interact with the audience. Viewers could actually request information and see it displayed on the screen in text and graphic form. This forerunner of the Internet used the black bar at the bottom of the screen for transmitting messages. France's Minitel system used videotext to offer banking from home, train and airplane schedules, and even directory assistance. In Great Britain, nearly four million viewers used ITV for banking, informational services, and e-mail through a Sky Digital box.

Other ITV experiments conducted in the United States included Viewdata by GTE and Viewtron by Knight-Ridder. Both services gave customers newspaper stories, weather, and agricultural information but failed to turn profits sufficient to sustain their existence. In 1992, the FCC stepped in and assigned one megahertz of bandwidth to allow for interactive video data services. After that ruling, a number of test markets experimented with set-top boxes for ITV. What was missing was a technical standard to enable any set-top box (STB) to work with any network.

The following year there was an explosion of ITV prototypes from set-top boxes to video servers. Fourteen major players formed the Advanced Television Enhancement Forum (ATEF) to develop platform standards for the new medium.[12] After a standard evolved for creating signals to flow back and forth between interactive services, more investments in ITV followed.

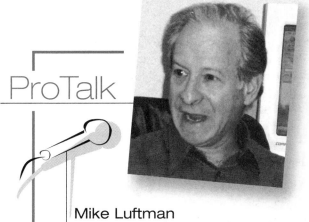

ProTalk

Mike Luftman
Vice President of Corporate Communications, Time Warner Cable

"The industry is changing dramatically from a one-product industry over a one-way pipeline . . . to a multi-service, multiple-product business."

Michael Luftman has been in corporate communications for Time Warner Cable for years. He believes that his company's merger with AOL offered a lot of promise in terms of blending the different levels of expertise of the two enterprises. "We have a lot of very complementary skill sets that that will lead us to develop a lot of interesting products."

One of those products was high-speed Internet access to Roadrunner Communication, which began in 1994 based on customer demand. Luftman reports that their research showed TV viewers wanted the full video automatically. In another words, they wanted to be able to call up a TV show or movie of their choice simply by pointing and clicking on the screen.

The cable executive says his company did not have that technology in 1994, but, through the equipment of Scientific Atlanta and Silicon Graphics, Time Warner Cable was able to upgrade its network and create the necessary Internet technology to satisfy customers. The video on demand rollout began in the markets of Boston, Honolulu, and Tampa, then spread to other Time Warner cable-franchise cities.

For professionals planning on working in the new cable industry that AOL Time Warner serves, Luftman sees a shift of attitude. "People need to know coming in that the industry is changing dramatically from a one-product industry over a one-way pipeline with limited competition into a multi-service, multiple-product business."

Even though AOL Time Warner is regarded as something of a behemoth, Luftman points out that it competes with a wide range of companies, from local phone services to direct broadcast satellite and digital service lines. "So, I think college graduates have to be comfortable operating in an environment which requires a lot more technical expertise." He says the future digital universe is more competitive and more complex.

Direct-broadcast satellites (DBS) Beams television signals in the Ku-band directly to viewers at homes, at hotels, or in businesses using dishes to receive them. Also labeled as *direct to home (DTH) satelite service* by the FCC.

The Internet, with its TCP/IP protocols, became the widely accepted open standard for ITV. Its acceptance was based on the bet that millions of Americans would want to surf the net while watching television and becoming "telewebbers." Network television continues to experiment with ITV by inviting viewers to vote during sports contests or other live events at websites associated with the network. Cable television maintains the most successful interactive ventures based on its pay-per-view business.

Digital Cable

Cable has been offering high-speed Internet access and interactive program guides through two services: TV Guide Interactive and Interactive Channel, using set-top boxes. There are also 50 digital movie channels available with *video on demand (VOD)*. Digital convergence is clearly evident in the merger of America's largest Internet service provider, America Online, and one of the nation's largest cable system operators, Time Warner. Yet, before they were allowed to merge, several loud voices were heard at the FCC.

Media watchdog groups, such as the Consumers Union and the Center for Media Education, were concerned with the competitive advantage the new AOL Time Warner giant would have over AT&T customers, since AT&T already owned one-fourth of Time Warner Entertainment. In addition, the Walt Disney Company asked the FCC to impose conditions to protect it and other interactive TV competitors. As a result, the government attached certain strings to the AOL Time Warner merger, including rules regarding interactive television.

SATELLITES IN THE DIGITAL AGE

For years, America's satellite television industry was focused on serving homes unreachable by broadcasters or cable systems. That was when several firms were competing for satellite television business in the United States. Today, consolidation is apparent in the satellite industry. Where five companies once competed for **direct-broadcast satellite (DBS)** customers, now there are only two offering digital television and data services. Both companies use small dishes to receive microwave frequencies in the Ku-band between 12 and 14 gigaHertz.[13]

DirecTV versus DISH-TV

DirecTV was launched by two of the original applicants for satellite television: Hughes Communications and United States Satellite Broadcasters (USSB). DirecTV began its DBS service in 1994 under the supervision of engineer Eddie Hartenstein and USSB's chief executive Stanley Hubbard. DirecTV's main competitor in this field then was—you guessed it—DISH-TV.

The two satellite executives, Eddy Hartenstein and Charlie Ergen, founder and chief of EchoStar's DISH-TV, were fierce competitors. They used different and incompatible technologies for talking with communication satellites, or "satcoms," in space but each believed his own to be superior. Ergen wanted to take over DirecTV, but that looked to be a monopoly to some. At this writing, the future of any DISH and DirecTV merger rests in the hands of Washington policymakers.

> **Principle #5**
>
> When a media merger creates a monopoly in restraint of trade, it is illegal.

Satellites and Digital Convergence

Satellite television has led the way in adapting to digital technology, celebrating a decade of digital video compression. In November 1992, the International Standards Organization announced its design for digital video compression, and satellite TV responded immediately. The **Motion Pictures Expert Group (MPEG)** labeled this new standard Level 1, or simply MPEG-1. The advantage of compression for satellite television was easy to understand—more content to sell to more customers. DirecTV had only 27 analog channels prior to MPEG adoption, but after digital compression, it had 216 channels available to its subscribers.

The Motion Pictures Expert Group is actually the brainchild of an international "dream team" of engineers who first met in Ottawa, Canada, in 1988. Their mission from the ISO was to design the most practical means for digitally recording and transmitting moving pictures and audio for a variety of electronic media. Toward that end, the group has met more than 50 times since 1988 and has authorized several standards important to media professionals: MPEG-1 travels at a bit rate of up to 1.5 Mbs and is used in video games, compact discs, and multimedia, but it is below broadcast standards, MPEG-2 is the standard used by satellite and high-definition television, and digital video discs (DVDs). MPEG-4 is the standard for video on demand (VOD) and mobile telecommunications, such as the wireless web.

Motion Pictures Expert Group (MPEG) Determines appropriate standard for compressing moving video images.

Personal Video Recorders

The latest example of digital convergence, the personal video recorder (PVR), is basically a set-top box that functions as a smarter VCR. Rather than use videotapes for storage, it records digitally to a hard disk with hours of storage space. Here's how it works technically: The PVR takes an incoming television signal and, on its hard drive, compresses the signal into MPEG-2 format. Doing this enables the machine to continuously record the television signal and store hours of video. It also "learns" what types of shows the viewer prefers and can record them automatically, making it unnecessary to program the device's memory. Its principal drawback is obvious: It does not play rented videos (Goodbye, Blockbuster). The other disadvantage is that once the hard drive is full, there is no place to archive the programs you would like to save. (Of course, if you don't mind buying and installing more gigabytes of memory or trashing old programs, then that's not much of a problem.)

Two major names offer PVR services: TiVo, which is manufactured by Sony and Phillips Electronics and ReplayTV, which is made by SONICblue. TiVo and ReplayTV enable the viewer to pause the recording during

Personal Digital Video Recorder. TiVo uses a hard-drive disc instead of videotape to electronically store television programs. It allows viewers to skip commercials by pausing the TV program in progress then resuming it after the commercial break.

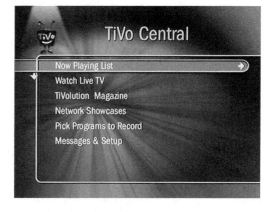

T-1 Describes size of wire linking computer networks with 1.54 megabits of bandwidth.

a live TV show, skip commercials, create instant replays, and simultaneously record and play programs. The TiVo and ReplayTV recorders both have varying speeds for fast forward and rewind, and allow viewers to move forward or backward one frame at a time. PVR prices range from around $100 to $500 per set, and TiVo also charges a monthly fee for its service.

Satellites and the Net

Both DirecTV and DISH offered customers access to the Internet. The DISH network contracted with Microsoft's WebTV networks to provide its customers the DISHPlayer 500. This is an interactive satellite TV system with a built-in hard drive that can record and play back hours of digital video. The system has some of the same features as the PVRs, including instant replay and commercial-skipping controls. DISHPlayer 500 also features video games.

The DISH Network says it was the first satellite service to offer local channels in selected cities. Meanwhile, DISH'S chief competitor, DirecTV, has teamed up with Wink and TiVo to combine its service with satellite television. DirecTV's Internet offering, known as DirecPC, uses a separate dish and receiver. AOL also has invested in DirecTV's parent company to create a joint service called UltimateTV. It, too, uses a box that serves as both a satellite receiver and a PVR/DVR.

WIRELESS NETWORKS

The vision for the future is to make the Internet as portable and mobile as a cell phone, and to remove the wires that now connect us to the Web. In order to transfer data along telephone lines, modems are used to link through the phone, the cable television line, or a special wire dedicated just for Internet access, called digital subscriber lines or DSLs. Cable and DSL lines are faster than telephone lines and have greater bandwidth for downloading audio and video.

The next generation of Internet access—third generation, or 3G—will use wireless protocols that feature even greater bandwidth. To understand the comparison, just look at the difference between a **T-1** line, which carries data at 1.54 megabits per second, and the wireless protocols, which are much faster at 7.5 megabits per second.

Third-Generation Technology

Wireless Internet was popularized by Apple Computer, which started using a high-frequency radio band that was actually faster than most wired office Internet connections over the Ethernet, which is a data network designed for short distances between offices and buildings. One popular standard is called 802.11, which was the baud rate set for wireless local area networks (LANs) by the IEEE, an engineering group standard. Colleges and universities were among the first to adopt wireless LANs to give students freedom to access the Internet in their dorms and classes without actually using a cable and socket. The future of 3G is not just in the classroom; it is where people travel, shop, or just sip a cup of coffee.

Wireless Horizons

It all began in 1971 when the Federal Communications Commission opened the way for cellular by allocating spectrum between 800 and 900 MHz. It took another decade before all cellular trials had been held and technical issues resolved. The first commercial cellular telephone services began in 1983, and according to the Cellular Telecommunications Industry Association (CTIA), usage grew to more than 68 million subscribers by 1999.

Higher frequencies were reserved for digital PCSs, and soon the newer technology was carried by phone services (e.g., Sprint) that even poked fun at analog cell phones. Television spots featured actors shouting to be heard or whose words were interrupted by static, lampooning cell phones' vulnerability to noise. By the end of the century, four wireless telcos (telephone companies) emerged as dominant players: Sprint PCS, AT&T Wireless, BellSouth/SBC Communications, and Verizon, which was a joint venture merging three companies—Bell Atlantic Mobile, AirTouch, and PrimeCo.

The focus shifted to 3G of wireless data services. It is geared toward making web browsing a wireless activity. Projections have figured a $10 billion business serving 60 million users in North America. However, the standards seeking dominance in the competition are not compatible. Cisco Systems developed a wireless network based on Internet protocol (IP). Competing firms supported

Bluetooth, the Nordic Conqueror of Digital Convergence

More than 1,000 years ago, a king by the name of Harald Blatand, known as "Bluetooth," successfully united parts of Scandinavia and ruled the peoples of Norway and Denmark until 986 A.D. In the twentieth century, Bluetooth's name was resurrected to signify a new heir to the throne of telecommunications, designed to unite computers with a new type of wireless technology.

This modern-day Bluetooth was created in 1994 by Ericsson Mobile Communications. Its goal was simply to enable laptop computers to talk to mobile telephones and other wireless devices, such as pagers and personal digital assistants (PDAs)—small handheld computers that store information such as calendars and addresses and that may use fax software or a cellular modem to send messages.

The Bluetooth consortium was formed in 1998. Nine giants in the telecommunications industry formed the Bluetooth Special Interest Group (SIG)

to demonstrate how important it is for hardware and software makers to cooperate with telecommunications providers. Intel, Nokia, Toshiba, and IBM were first to join with Ericcson, and later welcomed former rivals, Microsoft, Motorola, 3Com, and Lucent.

What it all means is that a lifestyle approaching the Jetsons family is not that far away, according to Steve McCannel writing in *Webreview*.[14] Bluetooth chips will be paired with your most basic consumer electronics so that one personal digital assistant can unlock your door, turn on your television or computer, and even start the microwave. It is all based on a wireless chip that can talk to all computerized machines in your home.

The first Bluetooth, King Harald, was killed in battle when an arrow struck him in the behind. These giant companies hope to avoid a similar fate by merging their technologies with wireless telecommunications.

ProTalk

Ashton Langlinais
President, WOW Technologies

"We need new college graduates who understand what the third generation of wireless is all about. The older guys are either retraining or seeking employment elsewhere."

WOW Technologies President Ashton Langlinais says he is not discouraged by the downturn in the dot economy because despite the companies going belly up, there are still markets—especially ones overseas—hungry for wired and wireless solutions to hook up their networks of computers. In fact, the name of his enterprise supports that claim. His business is called WOW, meaning Wired Or Wireless voice, data, and Internet solutions.

In order to become a success, though, newcomers need to stay ahead in the digital age. Langlinais says the ones who are getting left behind are professionals who still rely on old formulas for hooking up computers, telephones, and personal digital assistants. "Those solutions are passé and we need new college graduates who understand what the third generation of wireless is all about. The older guys are either retraining or seeking employment elsewhere," claims Langlinais.

What his company promises to do illustrates how wide-ranging the digital world has become. WOW promises to help companies with their web design, regional Internet service, networking between computers, and electronic commerce. It doesn't stop there. Langlinais also demonstrates how cell phones, voice-over IP (Internet protocol), and other new technologies figure in the equation.

The broadband vision of tomorrow sounds like an alphabet soup of abbreviations, and Langlinais is looking for people who decipher it all. They need to know what terms mean—such as *802.11B, Hyperland 2, 11 megs, frequency hopping, direct spectrum*, and on and on. What it all means for Langlinais is that his career, which began as an amateur ham radio operator and progressed to Internet service provider, has not slowed down at all. As far as he is concerned, the future is digital broadband, and so long as people wish to communicate around the world by voice, data, video, or fax, there is plenty of work to stay busy.

Principle #6
Greater media choice and easy access for consumers is the driving force of digital convergence.

Wireless application protocol (WAP) Transmits telephony or Internet signals using laptop computers.

wireless application protocol (**WAP**) as the new global standard. WAP is not controlled by any single firm, but it has more than 100 firms endorsing it as the best network solution for linking up desktop computers or personal digital assistants (PDAs). Still another competitor was expected to be released from five firms working under the code name "Project Rainbow." The Intel Corporation, IBM, AT&T Wireless, Cingular, and Verizon Communications appeared to prefer the 802.11 standard, also known as "WiFi." Meanwhile, Motorola said that its "Canopy" technology was superior because it could bring high-speed Internet service up to 10,000 feet from the receiving antenna or "hot spot."

Regardless of which standard becomes successful, the twenty-first century will see further convergence of cable and broadcasting with satellites, telephones, and computers. This convergence will create new ways of communicating and new jobs for telecommunicators. For broadcasters operating in the early years of the twenty-first century, the operative term is *change*. For example, network television uses videophones from the Middle East to transport images of warfare in real time through the digital convergence of video, telephones, and satellites.

Digital compression schemes are allowing migration from a wired world to a wireless one in the third generation of telecommunications. This is the age where PDAs and mobile phones can access the Internet, and where you can check on a read of your global positioning system (GPS) to find out exactly where you're driving in your car. It is more than conjecture that the wireless application protocols of the future will do for the Internet what color did for television—accelerate its adoption and integration into our daily lives.

Radio and television stations can no longer operate on rules of the game established when broadcasting was a new industry with few competitors. Technology often changes faster than government organizations can act, so major players in all electronic media will have to design some of their own solutions both in terms of technology and competition to keep up with the forces of change—digital change.

Summary

Digital theory traces its origins to a Swedish immigrant who worked in Bell Labs on the nature of telegraphy. The demand for a rapid transfer of information over long distances drove the development of digital domains. The telegraph operated as a series of dots and dashes, not unlike the ones and zeros guiding the first digital generation of telecommunications.

The wartime effort to improve ballistics and break the German code gave rise to electronic computing. Similarly, the specter of nuclear attack prompted the development of what we think of today as the Internet, based on the belief that information should be shipped across multiple pathways to escape the peril of an attack on the national telecommunications infrastructure. The Internet has developed as a means for collecting data, communicating, and conducting business. It is also the medium where traditional channels converge. Whether it is video, voice, or data, telephone, television, or computers—Americans are demanding more of digital domains to gain greater control over their information and entertainment.

Convergence means many things beyond the obvious recognition that our principal tools for electronic communication have changed from analog to digital processing, and that networks will respond more to packet switching than to circuit switching. It also means cable television and telephone networks are competing for customers by using new technologies. As one technician put it, the digital age is "pipe agnostic": Whether the binary information is transmitted by air, cable, satellites, or microwave towers, it all will be used to link radio, television, computers, telephones, and personal digital assistants to their customers. It means that distant radio stations will be streamed over telephone and cable TV networks, challenging notions of local service as well as the delineation between

C A R E E R   F O C U S

The jobs in on-line media cover areas of content, system management, and business affairs. Depending on the size and structure of the media organization, the jobs may be discretely different or may include elements of all three—maintenance of business accounts, creative design, and maintenance of the system.

Content jobs offer the most creative challenge and include graphic design, animation, and audio and video production. Others create and maintain databases for a media outlet. They are also called information providers.

System management people are more involved in the programming and software applications for websites. Those positions require technical knowledge and expertise beyond simple application skills. Then there are those who work in the business end by promoting and selling the services of the staff. Following are a few of the job descriptions in these areas:

Web managers update and maintain web sites. They set the agenda for news flow and Internet publication times in coordination with either the station news director or the newspaper editor. They develop and create content for the cable or satellite system, or the broadcast station or network, and forge links to relevant sites. Their role is to find ways to complement and enhance repurposed content on web sites. A web manager may or may not have a support staff, depending on the size of the organization.

Web/graphic designers are creative types who manipulate content by designing a website and choosing lines, images, and graphics to engage the audience. They become familiar with software applications and they translate message objectives into logos and layout designs on the computer.

In addition to knowing how to use the coding and mark-up languages, such as JavaScript, HTML, and XML, system management people, or **web authors,** decide what content will be used. They work in cooperation with **web designers.**

Web developers are familiar with software and server applications. They know how to build networks and how to place security locks into the systems. They are familiar with databases and they know how to operate PC- or MacIntosh-based computer systems, HTML/web languages (usually Java or Java Script), and a variety of software applications. This is a job for people who enjoy working at computers most of the day.

Multimedia specialists use two or more media (audio, video, graphics, text) to create content for distribution over a variety of channels, including compact discs, the Web, television, and so on. The job usually involves developing Internet-based instructional materials and websites, as well as training others in the use of instructional technology.

broadcasting and narrowcasting. It means that markets will converge with broadband access becoming the common denominator.

Digital convergence means more than a common language of binary digits; it means a convergence of consumer expectations for fast and, in many cases, free information and entertainment. It means huge corporations waging battles to see who can become the most influential and successful carriers of content and products. It means convergence of and among former competitors. In the era of digital convergence, there will be trillion-dollar empires built on combined radio, television, cable, motion picture, recorded music, magazines, newspapers, and computer access. And it is only the beginning.

FOOD FOR THOUGHT

1. Corporations are gambling on the prospect that television viewers will want to use their TV sets more and more like computers. Do you think that interactive television (ITV) is the way of the future? Why or why not?
2. One trend in Internet browsing is the growing emphasis on e-commerce. What items do you like to shop for and buy on-line, and why?
3. On-line news sites noticed an upsurge in traffic after September 11, 2001. Do you have an on-line website that you like to visit? Do you consider news stories on the web to be as credible as radio news? Television? Newspapers? Explain your answers.
4. Which would you rather have hooked up to your television set—a videocassette recorder or a personal video recorder? Why?
5. Do you listen to radio or watch television on-line? How does the experience compare to listening or viewing traditional channels of radio and television?

5

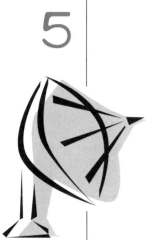

Radio and Television Technology

We live in a moment of history where change is so speeded up that we begin to see the present only when it is disappearing.

—R. D. Laing, *The Politics of Experience* (1967)

The triumphs of invention in broadcast technology owe much to a diverse collaboration of scientists and technicians. Immigrants from Sweden, Russia, Serbia, and Italy joined with Americans to overcome hurdles and make breakthroughs in radio-television technology. A recent challenge, in which the cross-fertilization of cultures played a role, involved the digital translation of video images to create a higher-definition television.

HDTV. High-definition television gives superb picture quality, but issues of cable compatibility, consumer models available, and lack of HDTV content have slowed its rollout.

A South Korean engineer led the way in compressing high-definition television into the computer language of ones and zeros. Woo Paik understood the Japanese had created an analog picture for **high-definition television (HDTV)** by more than doubling the number of scanning lines on the TV screen. He questioned why HDTV could not be transmitted digitally; not only would that be more technically efficient and economical but it also would be more challenging. Paik liked tasks others thought were too difficult for him to accomplish.

A South Korean engineer led the way in compressing high-definition television into the computer language of ones and zeros: Woo Paik.

Paik applied some of his digital know-how to compress the extra video information in order to make HDTV fit analog channels. In Joel Brinkley's account, *Defining Vision*, the moment of truth came before

107

skeptical jurors meeting at the National Association of Broadcasters Convention in Washington, DC:[1]

> Paik took the stand, a chair placed right in the center of the horseshoe. He was surrounded. The questions came fast and, though the tone was civil, it was not difficult to detect the snarl just beneath. An engineer on one side of the table posed a question and, as Paik turned to answer in his heavily accented English, someone on the opposite side of the table growled, "Huh? What was that you said?" Paik spun around and repeated his answer, only to get the same dismissive stares from the engineers on that side. So it went for half an hour.[2]

High-definition television (HDTV) Increases line resolution of standard television.

> **Principle #1**
>
> **Scientific invention is based on competition and collaboration.**

Heller successfully argued that digital signals would make television compatible with computers and might even remedy analog TV's problems, such as snow, ghosting, and other noise polluting TV pictures at home.

This chapter is aimed at providing a brief overview of technology in analog and digital television. We look at the principles guiding the waves of electronic media, including high-definition television. We also explain the government and commercial roles in shaping policy in this area, and chart the digital convergence of new media. We offer a framework based not on the actual mechanics of production but on the technical principles underlying the process.

THE BIG PICTURE: STAGES IN MEDIA PRODUCTION

Creating messages for radio and television is not just writing with words, but "writing" with sounds and pictures, as well. To do so effectively requires *media literacy*—knowing how different video clips, voices, and graphics combine to create meaningful expression. In order to do that, media professionals become familiar with the tools of their trade—microphones, recorders, cameras—what they do and how they do it. Before a radio or television program wends its way through cameras and microphones to homes and automobiles, it passes through several stages in the production process.

The first stage is *acquisition*, where raw materials in pictures and sounds are recorded for production. Radio and TV producers talk about getting good audio and video; others call it *field acquisition*. The second stage requires *editing* the raw material, when writers and producers select both visual and aural elements to convey the message clearly. This is a process of subtraction and addition. The successful writer *edits* the raw material, but also takes pains to enhance it.

The third stage requires *recording* the completed program to store it in either digital or analog formats. It may be "burned" onto a digital disc or recorded to a videotape cassette, but its quality and fidelity must be preserved for the audience. When electronic messages are amplified and conveyed to viewers and listeners, the fourth stage of *delivery* is accomplished. Finally, the audience hears and sees the messages through wired or wireless means of *reception*.

Transduction Converts sound or light energy into electrical signals.

ACQUISITION

The first stage of media production, *acquisition*, can be viewed as a search for compelling pictures and sounds to capture. In order to ensure the clarity and power of the images and sounds recorded, professionals learn the basic mechanics.

Tools for Sound Recording

Voice, music, or any variety of sound produces waves of pressure in the air. These waves bounce against a microphone's *diaphragm*, which is the circular element that acts as the "ears" of the mic. Sound pressure is transformed into electrical energy in a process known as **transduction**, which occurs inside the mic.

MICROPHONES

Three popular transducers have been created for recording sound: A moving coil of wire vibrates in *dynamic* mics; a charged plate or capacitor responds to sound waves in *condenser* mics, and a thin strip of metal ribbon converts sound to energy in *velocity* mics. Microphones react to sound in a manner similar to the human eardrum. The transducing elements—the ribbon, moving coil, and capacitor—vibrate in response to the sound waves. These vibrations trigger the flow of electrical current. The raw sound energy is then amplified and mixed with sources of music, voice, instruments, or special effects. Microphones vary both in terms of their transducing elements and in their pickup patterns—the way they hear.

PICKUP PATTERNS

Microphones absorb sounds from different directions in four principal patterns. As Figure 5.1 shows, the *cardioid*, or *unidirectional*, mic picks up sounds in a heart-shaped pattern from its front. The most focused pickup pattern is called the *supercardioid*, and it is used in shotgun and parabolic mics to pick up sounds from long distances. Natural sound is often recorded using a shotgun mic. *Bidirectional* mics pick up sounds in a figure-eight pattern on both sides, and became popular during the golden age of radio when actors in live dramas spoke into them facing each other. *Omnidirectional* mics register sound almost uniformly from any direction. They are often used as stick mics on windy days in one-on-one interviews. Omnidirectional mics are worn on the lapels of news anchors as *lavalieres* (the French term for pendant) and are often called "lavs." Lavs are usually omnidirectional and best used indoors where background noise is unlikely to cause distractions. Directional lavs, although uncommon, are useful for reduction of room ambiance.

Microphones are described by their mounts, transducers, and pickup patterns. Most common are cardioid microphones that pick up sounds in a heart-shaped pattern in front of the microphone. Supercardioid patterns are found on shotgun and parabolic mics designed to pick up sounds from greater distances. Omnidirectional pickup patterns are used on lapel mics, and bidirectional mics are least common.

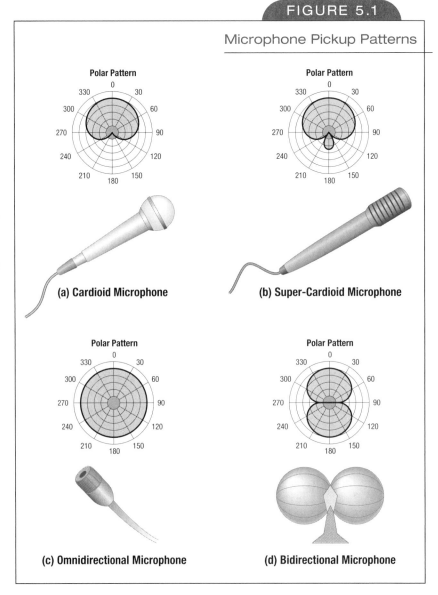

FIGURE 5.1

Microphone Pickup Patterns

(a) Cardioid Microphone

(b) Super-Cardioid Microphone

(c) Omnidirectional Microphone

(d) Bidirectional Microphone

MIC TYPES

Microphones also are described by how they are mounted. A *boom* mic extends from a crane or a fishpole; it hovers near the speaker but out of the camera's viewfinder.[3] A boom mic requires a wind screen or "blimp" to minimize wind noise. *Wireless* mics have proven popular with stage performers and musicians. They transmit from tiny antennas to receivers and amplifiers. Whether used as a stick, lavaliere, or headset, a wireless mic sends signals short distances over either a VHF or UHF frequency. These mics give television talent a chance to move freely without a cable and to meet the camera or the audience face to face.

Video Processing

The first step in processing the television picture begins when the camera lens views a scene. The rays of light captured through the lens are filtered by a mirrorlike prism called a *beam splitter*. In this block of optical glass, the light is distributed to either tubes or silicon chips called CCDs, for charge-coupled device (see Figure 5.2). In the glass tube, an electron gun shoots streams toward the *faceplate* while two deflection magnets direct the electrons across the image, converting each line of the picture into an electronic signal. The trend toward digital convergence in cameras began when these glass tubes, *vidicon* and *plumbicon*, were replaced by solid-state circuitry.

DIGITAL CONVERGENCE IN VIDEO

Television engineers developed something similar to the transistor. "Minicams" became popular for covering stories in the field in the mid-1970s. Although the first minicams used small plumbicons, they were converted to silicon chips for

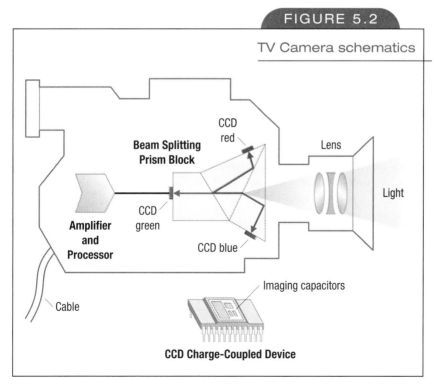

FIGURE 5.2

TV Camera schematics

CCD red

Lens

Beam Splitting Prism Block

Light

CCD green

Amplifier and Processor

CCD blue

Imaging capacitors

Cable

CCD Charge-Coupled Device

A television camera collects light through a lens that is filtered by the camera's internal optical system, which is a beam-splitting prism. The beam splitter of optical glass separates red, green, and blue elements of the scene and sends them to CCDs that react with photo-electron charges to the intensity of the primary light colors. These charges are then coupled with (transferred to) pixels to be scanned as a video image.

Charge-Coupled Device.
This is a solid-state imaging device for converting light to electronic signals. In this large format, two silver rinks encircle the black square, which is the imaging device. CCDs were first designated for electronic-news-gathering (ENG) video cameras, and later installed in studio cameras as well.

Charge-coupled devices (CCDs) Convert light into a charge pulse and code it as a number using light-sensitive chips.

Red, Green, Blue (RGB) Primary colors of light mixed to produce a video image for television and computers.

Pixels Picture elements on a television screen's scanning line illuminate phosphors in mixtures of red, green, and blue light.

Antenna Metallic rod or wires conduct sending or receiving radio signals.

portable TV cameras in the late 1980s. The minicam used a **charge-coupled device (CCD)** instead of glass tubes to convert primary colors of light into pictures.

Charge-coupled devices worked more efficiently with the camera's internal optical system, the *beam splitter*, a combination of color filters and mirrors that divides incoming rays into primary colors of light: **red, green** and **blue (RGB)**.[4] Studio TV cameras often use three chips (CCDs)—one for each color. These chips have the storage capacity of 400,000 picture elements, or **pixels.** CCDs have made TV cameras more portable and lighter so that "one-size-fits-all" shoulders.

EDITING

The next stage of media production, *editing*, occurs first in the minds of the audio technician and the camera operator. Every decision made about what images and sounds to record is a form of editing based on professional judgment. For the actual production, a second edit mixes the various pictures, sound, and text into the final program.

Audio Mix

After the sound energy is transduced—whether it is music, voice, or special effects—it is transported by cable to an audio console where it is amplified and mixed with other sound sources. Each audio console has multiple channels with *inputs, outputs,* and *monitors*. These channels, called *pots*—short for *potentiometer*—have independent volume controls and on-off switches.

The board operator, or "board op," mixes the pots that are routed to a transmitter or a recording machine. If the audio production is in a studio, there usually are between 16 and 24 channels to mix on multitrack tape recorders. For radio stations, 8 to 12 channels are mixed in the console, amplified, and sent to the station's transmitter and **antenna** tower.

ANALOG AUDIO EDITING

The audio industry has migrated from editing in analog to digital technology. For years, radio announcers, disc jockeys, and journalists sat over a splicing bar beneath reel-to-reels of audiotape, using a wax pencil and a razor blade to make diagonal slices and eliminate unwanted cuts while splicing selected sounds together. That began to change in the 1990s.

DIGITAL CONVERGENCE FOR AUDIO EDITING

Digital-audio workstations (DAWs) gave producers the chance to edit, amplify, and enhance audio programs with special effects using computers. Whether they were working with an Apple- or PC-based program, digital editing for sound simply became a matter of experimenting with an audio waveform appearing on the computer screen in horizontal tracks. The editor could cut, paste, and merge sound tracks by pointing, clicking, and dragging the sound on the screen. Gone were the days of splicing tape with a razor blade and piecing it together with adhesive strips. It was not long before computerized editing moved beyond sound to visual images.

Video Mix

After TV cameras capture the talent's image in the studio, the video signal is first routed to a switcher under the control of a director making decisions over a row of buttons called a *bus*. The director punches buttons to select a camera, a videotape, a character generator, or a network feed in various combinations. There is, for example, an option for a *chroma-key* effect, allowing a different background to be visually inserted behind the talent, such as a weather map behind a TV meteorologist.

Digital Audio Editing. Computer software programs have replaced spools of tape and splicing blocks for editing audio tape. Audio technicians use a waveform track to cut and paste blocks of audio sound for broadcast.

Fader bars on the switcher enable the director to create transitions by *fades*, *dissolves*, and *cuts*. A picture can be faded in and out of black or can dissolve to another scene. The director may choose to cut from one scene to the next or add special effects through a machine called the *digital video effects (DVE)*, which can flip a picture over, spin it around, and shrink or enlarge it in a variety of ways. If a videotape recording is made, more edits can be made to smooth the rough cuts.

ANALOG VIDEO EDITING

When mistakes flawed early television programs, technicians would cut with scissors two-inch-wide videotape and try to piece together the scenes. This technique applied special fluid to the videotape just to find where audio and video tracks were located. The cuts looked anything but clean on the air. The next phase in video editing required two engineers to synchronize the speeds of both playback and recording videotape machines to get rid of unwanted material. If both engineers were lucky enough to punch the right buttons at the right time, the result might pass the viewer's inspection.

By the time the minicam era arrived in the 1970s, a new videotape control editor was created to synchronize two videotape machines. They contained cassettes of three-quarter-inch tape in what became known as *linear editing*. The playback machine on the left and the record machine on the right responded to commands from the edit controller in the middle. Both were timed to respond to the signals of *preroll*, *roll*, and *record* sent from the edit controller. This system of linear editing also became popular for video cassettes with one-half-inch tape (VHS, S-VHS) and one-quarter-inch digital tape (Beta, DVC Pro). Now, the days of linear editing with analog or digital cassettes appear to be numbered.

DIGITAL CONVERGENCE IN VIDEO EDITING

At first it was called "desktop video," but after engineers started experimenting with the computer's capacity for digitally splicing together sounds and pictures, it became known as **nonlinear editing.** Older videotape editors followed a beginning-to-end sequence by making two passes through the videotape—one for the audio and another for the video.

Nonlinear simply meant that the editor is free to click on the screen and digitally splice the video together in random sequence. The first PC-based video editing system was the Commodore Amiga 500. In the 1990s, more advanced video editing systems hit the market, such as Avid's Media Composer, Microsoft Video for Windows, and Apple's QuickTime. Other digital editors were introduced by TV news software systems, such as Electronic News Production System (ENPS) and Cool Edit Pro. These systems moved the art of video editing to the next stage of recording.

Analog Videotape Editing. A control editor synchronizes pictures and sounds in order to electronically transfer scenes from a playback machine to a recorder with analog videotape. This linear process edits the tape from first frame to last frame of the program.

Nonlinear editing Manipulates scenes of video and audio in random fashion through computer software.

Analog Signals vary electromagnetic waves to resemble the original pattern.

Compact discs (CDs) Store information on polished metal disks by optical scanning using a laser beam.

Digital-audio tape (DAT) Scans digitally stored sound waves on a helical tape.

Digital-audio broadcasting (DAB) Uses mathematical compression to send radio signals.

RECORDING

The transition to digital continues, but for many media professionals and consumers it is still an **analog** world. Electronically converting sound and light in analog simulates the original wave patterns. Digital systems, on the other hand, apply mathematical formulas to recreate audio and video signals.

Analog Audio

Transduced waves of sound are recorded electronically on tape by magnetizing microscopic particles. The fidelity of the recording depends on the quality of the tape recorder and the speed of the recording. All things being equal, faster speeds translate into superior sound quality. Analog speed controls are gauged to inches per second, or IPS (1 ⅞, 3 ¾, 7 ½, 15, and 30). Higher speeds dispense more tape and record more information to produce a better-quality sound. The transport system moves the tape past magnetic heads to *erase, record* and *playback* audio tracks.

DIGITAL CONVERSION IN AUDIO: DAT AND CDs

The conversion to digital-audio recording began in 1983 when two recording giants, Sony Corporation of Japan and Philips Electronics of the Netherlands, started selling **compact discs (CDs)** to Japanese and European customers. The following year, CDs with the capacity to play 70 minutes of sound were marketed in the United States after Ampex opened its replication plant here. These

4.7-inch discs made of aluminum and plastic were a product of laser technology that could read binary numbers recorded in pits on one side of the CD. Compact discs soon began to replace vinyl phonograph records.

Audio labs began experimenting with another format in digital recording—one that used tape: **digital-audio tape (DAT)**. Sony introduced the new format, slightly larger than a matchbox, to end the problem of hiss and noise in analog cassettes. However, DAT met with little success on the consumer market because of its price, and it fared only slightly better among professionals in the field.

MDs AND MP3s

In 1992, a new digital audio format, the *MiniDisc (MD)*, was marketed by Sony and Philips. It looked like a CD inside a floppy diskette, only two-and-a-half inches wide. It was half the size of a CD, yet capable of storing 74 minutes of sound. Sony's MiniDisc recorders could fit into a pocket or purse, but the recorders had no speakers and required earphones and a digital volume unit (VU) meter to monitor the sound.

The most recent digital format takes advantage of the Internet. *MP3 (Motion Picture Experts Group, Audio Layer 3)* was developed in Germany as part of the Eureka project for **digital-audio broadcasting (DAB)**. It is essentially a formula for digitally compressing audio. Professor Dieter Seitzer of the University of Erlangen formulated the algorithm to compress sound waves for digital transfer and storage. MP3 encoders and players have been invading the youth market,

Nonlinear Digital Editing. Digital video editors assemble scenes using techniques combining film and video terminology in a software format. Editors cut and paste scenes and sounds moving back and forth through the production in random fashion.

DAT Recording. Digital audio tape (DAT) cassettes and recorders have proven useful for certain venues such as concerts where high-quality sound is desired in the field.

Sony MiniDisc. The MD digitally records 74 minutes of sound on software that looks like a small computer disk.

challenging older Walkmans, portable CDs, and MiniDisc players and offering greater convenience in on-line downloading and file transfers.

Analog Video

In videotape, the trend has been toward lighter, faster, and higher-fidelity recording. Ampex introduced the first two-inch videotape recorders in 1956. They used rotating heads that scanned the tape from top to bottom, recording 15 lines of video each time. Later, television engineers discovered a more efficient means of recording videotape by stripping the frames diagonally through *helical scanning*, which wrapped the tape around the recording heads at a slant. It also allowed the video to be seen while stopped or wound at high speed.

Videotape widths began to shrink from two- to one-inch formats, then to three-quarter-inch cassettes in Sony's *U-matic* model. Eventually, one-half-inch cassettes of videotape were introduced in 1976 by JVC. Consumers were enthusiastic about the Video Home System (VHS) and the Super (S-VHS) formats. These inexpensive cassettes dominated the rental market, while VHS cameras and cassettes become popular for making home videos.

DC: DIGITAL CONVERSION IN VIDEO RECORDERS

Digital videotape recording began in the late 1980s with two ¾-inch formats (D-1 and D-2). A more portable version followed when Sony introduced its Digital Betacam, which used a one-half-inch videotape, in the 1990s. Panasonic's DVC Pro added new competition by deploying even smaller, quarter-inch cassettes.

PRO-SUMER MODELS

The mini-DV camcorder was promoted as a "pro-sumer" (professional + consumer) model in 1999. This quarter-inch videotape manufactured by Canon and Panasonic began to replace S-VHS camcorders and videotapes among consumers, academic institutions, and certain professional outlets.

MiniDigital Video. The Mini-DV camcorder is becoming a popular item for academic, corporate and amateur videographers. The quarter-inch tape is easily edited with computer software programs.

VIDEO FUTURE

Will digital video recording eventually become tapeless? Engineers hope to move beyond the wear and tear of videotape and record clips easily accessible by a computer server to multiple editors in a station or production house. Avid introduced a disc-based video camera in 2000 that uses a drive that can be removed from the camera and inserted into a nonlinear editor for final production. Television stations are converting to digital storage in a central server, so that all video recordings can be dispensed to any location.

The most popular development in digital video for consumers was the **digital video (or versatile) disc (DVD)**. First released in 1995, it soon captured a major segment of the consumer market. Not only does it offer an enhanced version of motion pictures and other television programs but it also contains significantly more information. A laser beam records the signal by creating pits on *both* sides of the DVD in two layers, instead of the one-sided recording found on a CD. The introduction of computer-compatible versions, known as *DVD-RAM*, represents that format's bid to become the standard for video storage. Sensing competition, compact disc manufacturers released their own video formats for computers.

> **Principle #2**
>
> When quality, cost, and convenience meet customer expectations, then new media succeed in the marketplace.

BROADCAST DELIVERY

When a video or audio recording is finished, it must be transformed once again to be carried to the audience. Radio and TV stations transmit on channels that use electromagnetic energy to bring sounds and pictures to life. Bursts of energy emanate from a tower in pulses radiating outward in all directions. If they were visible, radio waves would resemble ripples created by tossing a stone into a pool of water.

Broadcast Waves

Sounds and images of broadcasting ripple across a busy ocean of air known as the **electromagnetic spectrum.** Radio and TV signals cruise at the speed of light— 186,000 miles per second. Scientists clocked these invisible waves according to their number of peaks per second. A single wave represents one cycle. The number of waves radiating outward in a second is the signal's **frequency.** Electromagnetic waves are measured by the frequency of cycles-per-second, called *Hertz (Hz)*. By international agreement, the term was used to honor Heinrich Hertz, the German physicist who built a spark-gap generator to display radio waves for his students.

Most humans hear sounds in a range between 15 and 15,000 cycles, but sound waves oscillate in frequencies far below the frequencies that broadcasters use. Radio and TV stations use frequencies of millions and billions of Hertz per second that grow to be such huge numbers that metric prefixes are used to make them manageable. For one thousand hertz, it's *kilo*Hertz; for a million hertz, it's *mega*Hertz, and for a billion hertz, it's *giga*Hertz. These frequencies are organized into separate bandwidths or bands.

RADIO LANES OF BANDWIDTH

There are 12 bands recognized by the International Telecommunications Union (ITU). Channels are grouped into *low, middle,* and *high* bands. There also are *very-high, ultrahigh, superhigh,* and *extremely high* bands, just as there is a *very low* band. Figure 5.3 shows how AM and short-wave radio broadcasts in the middle frequency (MF band), which covers all frequencies between 300 and 3,000 kHz. Someone living in Los Angeles, for example, listens to KABC-AM radio over 790 kHz, which is found in the middle band. FM radio broadcasts in the **very high frequency (VHF)** band. Someone listening to WRKF-FM in Baton Rouge, Louisiana, would tune in to 89.3 MHz in the VHF band.

Digital video discs (DVDs) Record with laser video and sound with more information than CDs or digital tapes.

Electromagnetic spectrum Oscillates energy from radio and television signals at the speed of light.

Frequency Wave cycles per second measured in units called Hertz (Hz).

Very high frequency (VHF) TV channels broadcasting between 30 and 300 megahertz employed for television and FM radio transmissions.

Ultrahigh Frequency (UHF) TV broadcasts on channels 14 through 69, but will scale back to 14 through 52 to give more room for wireless.

Carrier Wave The signal frequency that is imprinted with information for broadcast.

Amplitude modulation (AM) Impresses sound or picture information on a carrier wave by varying its height and depth.

> **Principle #3**
>
> The higher the frequency the shorter the wavelength.

Frequency modulation (FM) Shapes carrier waves by varying their width and occurs in the very high frequency band.

Local services AM radio channels of limited range serving single communities.

Regional stations Serve one large community and adjacent rural areas with AM radio.

Clear channel services Exclusive signal patterns assigned to one station.

TV LANES OF BANDWIDTH

Older TV stations send VHF signals that are designated as channels 2 through 13. These are arbitrary numbers, since stations actually use two different frequencies for sound and pictures. In analog television, AM signal is used to carry video, whereas TV audio is broadcast by FM carrier. In the set, they are combined to become picture and sound together.

Channels 14 through 69 travel in the **ultrahigh frequency (UHF)** band along with mobile land carriers, such as police and railroad radios.[5] In higher lanes of bandwidth are frequencies used for medical procedures, such as X-rays and ultraviolet radiation. As the frequencies increase in number, the waves become smaller and shorter in length. Higher-frequency bands carry microwaves for radar and satellite transmission. Infrared radiation, which can be used in photography, travels in even higher frequencies (see Figure 5.3).

MODULATING WAVES

Electrical impulses of sound produced in a radio studio are too weak to be transmitted without a carrier. At the transmitter, the audio waves reproducing sound are merged with **carrier waves.** This process is called *modulation*. Figure 5.4 shows how an unmodulated carrier wave oscillates symmetrically. **Amplitude modulation (AM)** shapes the wave's height and depth in order to electronically reproduce the sounds and pictures to be transmitted. In **frequency modulation (FM),** the wave's width rather than its height is varied. For that and other reasons, FM needs more bandwidth than AM radio.

AM Radio

AM radio is assigned a narrow corridor of spectrum; each channel has just 10 kHz for broadcasting. The FCC has designated 107 channels in the AM band, with just enough room on either side to protect it from adjacent channel noise. AM radio stations are tuned between 535 and 1705 kHz. Lower-frequency channels, such as 590 kHz, send out longer waves with clearer signals than higher-frequency channels, and that has figured into the government's scheme for classifying radio stations.

AM CLASSES

There are four classes of AM stations, designed to broadcast to different audiences based on **local, regional,** and **clear-channel** services. The most powerful radio stations are clear-channel broadcasting at 50,000 watts of power. They are designated *Class I*, and include the original flagships of America's broadcast networks and pioneer radio stations. They generally are found in larger cities, and include WLS in Chicago, WABC in New York, WJR in Detroit, KMOX in St. Louis, and WWL in New Orleans. There is a subtle difference between these stations and Class II stations.

Class II radio also broadcasts a clear-channel signal, but is subdivided into five categories based on frequency, power, and signal direction. Class I stations keep their signal strong both day and night, but Class II stations must pull back their power at sundown. Higher-frequency channels are defined as *Class III*, and broad-

FIGURE 5.3

Frequency Bands

Frequency bands are grouped together by the length of their waves—the shorter their waves, the higher the frequency. Microwaves, for example, are so short that the frequency of their oscillations is measured in gigaHertz. AM radio, on the other hand, generates much longer waves and their cycles can be measured in kiloHertz.

Radio Bandwidths

High Frequency (HF)
3,000 kHz–30 MHz
Shortwave radio, ham radio,
citizens band

Medium Frequency (MF)
300 kHz–3,000 kHz
AM radio, marine communications,
airplane communications,
more ham radio

Low Frequency (LF)
30 kHz–300 kHz
Air and marine communications

Very Low Frequency (VLF)
3 kHz–30 kHz
Time signals, distant military

Extremely High Frequency (EHF)
30,000 MHz–300,000 MHz
Military and future options

Super High Frequency (SHF)
3,000 MHz–30,000 MHz
Satellites, microwave relays,
air navigation, some radar

Ultrahigh Frequency (UHF)
300 MHz–3,000 MHz
UHF-TV channels, weather satellites,
police, and taxis

Very High Frequency (VHF)
30 MHz–300 MHz
FM radio, VHF television, more police
and taxis, military satellites

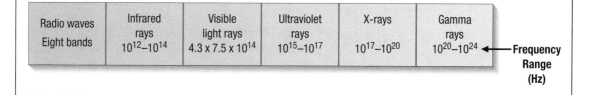

Radio waves Eight bands	Infrared rays 10^{12}–10^{14}	Visible light rays $4.3 \times 7.5 \times 10^{14}$	Ultraviolet rays 10^{15}–10^{17}	X-rays 10^{17}–10^{20}	Gamma rays 10^{20}–10^{24}

← **Frequency Range (Hz)**

cast in a range between 500 and 5,000 watts. They serve an area extending beyond the boundaries of one community, and are designated as regional stations. The smallest stations are situated at 1230 kHz and higher on the AM dial. These *Class IV* radio stations are limited to 1,000 watts during the day and 250 watts at night, and are classified as local channels. Overall, radio classifications are just one way the FCC keeps broadcasters from bumping into each other.

SIGNAL INTERFERENCE

Interference between stations is a special concern for the government when granting AM radio licenses. A station may have the same channel as another's

Principle # 4
Lower-frequency channels are desirable in AM radio because their longer waves travel farther than the waves emitted by high-frequency channels.

FIGURE 5.4

AM/FM Wave Modulation

Carrier waves are modulated to carry the information found in video and audio messages. The key difference between amplitude and frequency modulation is illustrated by the variations in height (AM) versus width (FM).

Unmodulated Carrier Waves are transmitted in a straight line until modulated by a video or audio signal.

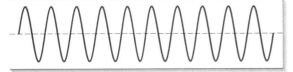

Amplitude Modulation changes the height and depth of carrier waves, but not the width.

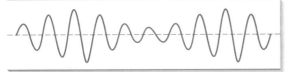

Frequency Modulation changes the width of carrier waves, but not the height or depth.

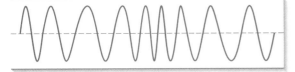

frequency, so the two must be separated by a distance and power range that prevent their interference. AM radio sends out its programs using **ground waves** radiating near the earth's surface during the day. AM radio is not bounded by the curvature of the earth or other obstructions, and so can send a signal long distances, particularly at night. AM radio transmits by **sky waves** that are produced when its signal skips off layers of the **ionosphere** and bounces back to earth. The ionosphere is an electrical layer of charged particles surrounding the earth. The ionosphere may cause interference along with other sources of "noise." Wireless transmitters from cell phones and garage doors produce what engineers call "RF clutter," or radio frequency interference.

Until 1996, the FCC licensed broadcast engineers to keep radio and TV signals centered in the middle of their channels in order to prevent interference. Even though the Telecommunications Act of 1996 took the FCC out of the licensing business, engineers still are charged with that duty. They must keep the transmitter's signal properly centered as well as investigate noises produced by atmospheric changes, ground static, or interfering signals from other stations.

Ground waves Propagate AM radio signals above earth's surface.

Sky waves Refract radio waves through the ionosphere and then return to earth.

Ionosphere Holds ions in layers of atmosphere reflecting or refracting radio waves.

Direct waves Travel in a straight line from FM radio stations or TV towers.

FM Radio

FM broadcasting uses a different technique for merging carrier waves with message output. Instead of varying the wave's height and depth, the width is modulated—hence the name *frequency modulation*. FM radio also broadcasts in a higher band than AM. FM broadcasts at millions of cycles per second with 100 channels designated between 88 and 108 MHz, which is in the VHF (very high-frequency) band. Consequently, FM not only offers higher fidelity but also escapes much of the static interference plaguing AM radio. It sends out signals using a more direct route.

FM DIRECT

Unlike AM radio, FM signals are sent out by **direct waves** rather than by the sky or ground waves. At higher frequencies, FM radio signals hold to a straighter path reaching the horizon. Since it relies on line-of-sight waves, FM must build taller towers than AM radio to avoid obstructions. Engineers for FM radio deal with the curvature of the earth when plotting coverage maps. Each FM chan-

ProTalk

Roger Helling
Radio Engineer

"It's mainly a matter of getting to know your transmitter."

The first radio station to sign on in Fort Worth, Texas, was WBAP-AM in 1922. Eighty years later, station technicians still oversee its transmitter to make sure it broadcasts at 50 kilowatts on 820 AM. Roger Helling is one of the engineers at the station whose duty is to keep the tower signals stable and respond to deviations when they occur. "It's mainly a matter of getting to know your transmitter," he says, "and the type of equipment involved."

Helling checks a 640-foot antenna that rises as high as it digs deep into the ground. Underground, it burrows and spreads out like spokes in a wheel, with 120 copper antennas—radials—propagating waves. "WBAP's signal is clear channel and nondirectional," Helling notes, "but we share the frequency of 820 kHz with stations in Florida and Canada."

Signals may wander off their channel and interfere with others. Then it becomes a question of determining which station is missing the mark. Helling recalls one time when a Kansas City broadcaster thought WBAP had veered off its course and was broadcasting too close to 810 AM, causing signal interference in Kansas City. WBAP checked the transmitter and concluded that it was the other station that had wandered into the 820 lane instead. In other words, it can be like a traffic accident when two radio signals collide.

nel is 200 kHz wide, compared to 10 kHz for AM radio, which means FM frequencies have room to spare for other services.

STEREO AND SCAs

The extra spectrum FM has to transmit allows stations to **multiplex** their signals for stereo. **Stereo** is simply multiple sound sources transmitted through two separate channels. FM has bandwidth left over to program other services through **subsidiary communication authorizations (SCAs).** These subcarriers are used to send musical atmosphere to grocery stores and retail outlets, or to provide reading services for the blind. The SCA frequencies are not found on the FM channels in your car or at home; rather, they squeeze in between those frequencies, reaching special receivers. FM broadcast stations, however, are organized into categories that differ from AM's classifications.

FM CLASSIFICATIONS

The FCC has grouped FM stations into different classifications according to their *power, antenna height,* and *coverage area. Class A* stations cover the smallest terrain, about 15 miles, and are limited to 3 kilowatts (kw) of radiated power. *Class B* stations reach twice as wide an area using 50 kilowatts (kw) of power. *Class C* stations are the most powerful, covering up to 60 miles with 100 kilowatts of power, four times as great a distance as Class A stations.

Multiplexing Transmits two or more independent signals on the same channel.

Stereo Records, transmits, and plays back audio through separate channels.

Subsidiary communication authorizations (SCAs) Carry FM subcarrier signals for atmosphere music and other specialized services.

Low-power radio Broadcasts 50- to 100-watt FM stations reaching from one to three miles.

Spectrum Management

Competing interests come into play in decisions as to what traffic will have access to the spectrum, and so domestic and international agencies have been formed to resolve disputes. Because the world's airwaves grow more congested each year, "traffic cops" are needed to keep signals from crossing lanes and bumping into each other.

ITU

The International Telecommunications Union (ITU) has the authority to oversee the world's spectrum traffic. The union dates to 1865, when stringing telegraph wires across national borders created problems requiring diplomatic solutions. With the advent of radio, the ITU became the global manager for allocation of spectrum and the arbiter of airwave disputes. Today, 150 countries comply with the ITU's decisions. The union's board allots bandwidth but leaves individual channels to nations to assign and license.

FCC

The Federal Communications Commission (FCC) handles broadcast licensing in the United States. The agency assigns to each radio and TV station its broadcast power, wattage, antenna direction, and signal pattern for its coverage area. Meeting the needs of everyone who wants to use the spectrum is not easy, since the demand exceeds the supply.

LOW-POWER SOLUTIONS

In both television and radio licensing, the government has sought to meet the needs of the "have-nots" by licensing lower-power stations. For example, community groups, such as churches and schools, have long wanted to broadcast FM radio at low-power frequencies. At the urging of FCC Chair William Kennard, the agency became amenable to this in 2000, but many commercial broadcasters did not. They claimed that **low-power radio** threatened the integrity of their signal. The issue divided engineers who testified before the FCC. Some said that interference was an unjustified concern, but Congress eventually intervened with a decision favorable to commercial broadcasters.[6]

The idea behind low-power FM was to set aside additional spectrum for stations that needed to broadcast only three or four miles from their transmitters. License applications came in from churches and schools, such as Eureka College in Illinois and the First Presbyterian Church of New Gillette, Wyoming. Some applicants had programming ideas that would not likely be found on commercial radio. An applicant in Sitka, Alaska, for example, wanted only to use his low-power station to broadcast shrill, warbling whale songs. Because of commercial protest, the FCC approved just 255 applicants from a pool of more than 1,200.

LOW-POWER TELEVISION

As in radio, there are more applications than TV channels available. The FCC began seeking ways to accommodate additional stations in the 1970s. The agency proposed its solution in 1982—**low-power television stations (LPTV).** This solution could give community broadcasters a chance to set up TV antennas to transmit at levels of power between 10 and 1,000 watts. Under ideal conditions, higher-power LPTV stations would reach viewers up to 10 miles away. The FCC was at first overwhelmed by thousands of requests for LPTV licenses. After application guidelines finally were in place, the commission granted almost 1,700 LPTV licenses. Several networks, including America One, Channel America, and Network One, began feeding LPTV stations their programs.

Low-power television (LPTV) Provides licenses to TV translators of up to 1,000 watts in VHF band.

When United Paramount Network (UPN) and Warner Brothers (WB) cobbled together their networks of affiliates, they called on some LPTV stations to carry network programs to rural areas. Critics charged this arrangement was contradictory to the spirit behind the LPTV movement—to give low-population-density areas a chance to see and produce local television. This problem persists in terms of funding such operations. Advertising models have not proven viable, and community donations are an unstable source of revenue.

> **Principle #5**
> The demand for telecommunications channels exceeds the supply controlled by the government.

Digital Radio

To most people, radio broadcasting is a simple matter of selecting their favorite AM and FM stations. The next generation of digital radio will broadcast on both old and new channels. Digital radio, or DAB (digital-audio broadcasting), has been slow in coming, due in part to the debate over whether to move it to a new location on the dial. The ITU considered that as a solution, and allotted DAB a chunk of UHF spectrum in the L-band in 1992. This move, however, did not suit the United States, since part of the L-band already was assigned to military purposes. The S-band, which is higher in the UHF range, seemed a better choice to the FCC, but broadcasters preferred still another option to using microwave channels in the UHF range. The NAB asked for an "in-band, on-channel" (IBOC) solution that would allow stations to keep their spots on the dial but make the switch to digital signals.

In 1999, three types of digital radio were proposed, but the major competitors merged to form iBiquity Digital Corporation.[7] It has taken the lead in field testing a digital radio system called iDAB, which won approval from the ITU. iBiquity also designed a system of digital compression for broadcasting radio over the Internet. In the meantime, the FCC has redesignated part of the S-band originally allotted for DAB to digital-audio radio service (DARS) satellite radio.

SATELLITE RADIO

Radio signals relayed by satellite for both car and home receivers came into being in 2001. Two companies were in competition for "sky radio": XM and Sirius. They offered channels of music, news, and talk from coast to coast in CD-quality sound. These services used microwaves, and consumers needed special receivers to tune in the channels in the S-band. Listeners also have been tuning in to stations over the World Wide Web.

STREAMING AUDIO

Streaming audio allows listeners to begin playing files while they still are being downloaded into the computer. This is possible through a process called *buffering*. With streaming audio, a file is downloaded into a buffer and then relayed to the computer's sound card. The sound card circuitry converts and synthesizes sounds for play through the computer's speaker. Streaming audio servers, such as Real Audio's Real Server, allow the file to start playing shortly after downloading begins, but if the server is overwhelmed, interruptions can occur. Web radio stations cannot compete with FM in sound quality or service, given the buffering technique used for transmission. The future promises to cure the problems of streaming audio through more efficient means of digital compression.

Analog Television Delivery

Each TV channel has 6 megaHertz of bandwidth to broadcast all of its audio and video information, which is about 600 times the width of an AM radio channel. Two-thirds of this space is used to carry video, and less than one-third of one MHz is designated for audio. Figure 5.5 illustrates how much of the 6 mega-Hertz is divided up for interference-protecting sidebands, video and color sub-carriers, and the FM audio signal.

Just as in radio, TV channels have sidebands, although not of equal size. On each channel there is a sideband beginning below the visual carrier and extending above it. In order to economize on valuable spectrum, TV engineers have devised creative solutions for compressing video and audio content onto carrier waves. One method is called *interleaving*. It alternates the video carrier's *luminance* with the subcarrier's *chrominance* signal, like compressing two messages into one telegram. These two principal features of color require inspection. Technicians judge the fidelity of the red, green, and blue hues by their richness

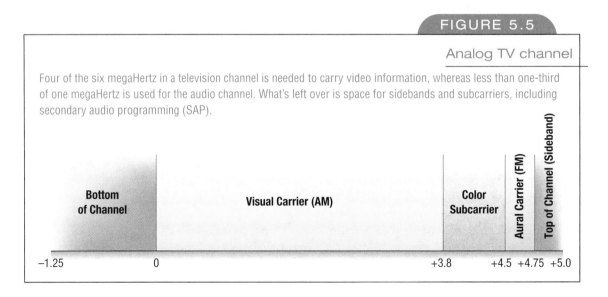

FIGURE 5.5

Analog TV channel

Four of the six megaHertz in a television channel is needed to carry video information, whereas less than one-third of one megaHertz is used for the audio channel. What's left over is space for sidebands and subcarriers, including secondary audio programming (SAP).

Bottom of Channel

Visual Carrier (AM)

Color Subcarrier

Aural Carrier (FM)

Top of Channel (Sideband)

−1.25   0   +3.8   +4.5 +4.75 +5.0

or saturation, which is called **chrominance.** They also measure the signal's brightness, or **luminance.** There are other differences in old and new television—analog and DTV.

Signal Integrity

Radio and television signals are vulnerable to deterioration, so steps must be taken to protect and stabilize them. Just as FM technicians ensure the quality of sound signals, TV engineers monitor their station's audio and video signals to check on quality and strength. Two different transmitters are used to modulate the TV picture and sound. The AM transmitter generates video while the FM transmitter carries the audio. A *diplexer* combines the sound and picture signals before they're sent to the station antenna for **propagation,** the technical term for signal distribution. Technicians look at the *amplitude* (brightness and contrast) of the picture using *waveform monitors.* They check the color phasing through a *vectorscope.*

Once the audio and video signals have merged and become a *composite signal,* they are broadcast by direct waves radiating from the TV antenna, which is positioned to avoid obstructions in the coverage area. Because UHF waves are smaller than VHF signals, they tend to attenuate easily, so the FCC affords up to five million watts of **effective radiated power (ERP).** The ERP in television is actually a measure of the station's transmitter power multiplied by the antenna gain.

A broadcast station's coverage map shows just how strong the signal is by outlining its A and B contours. The A contour represents primary coverage, and the B contour is the outer terrain. These contours are divided by the percentage of homes receiving the signal. Analog television tends to fade out over distance, and although digital signals have a longer reach the reception stops abruptly. This is called the *cliff effect*, because once a digital signal weakens to a certain point, it behaves as if it is falling off a cliff and disappearing.

Digital Television Delivery

There are other differences between how analog and digital TV signals are sent, but the most noticeable one is that two transmitters no longer are needed for **digital television (DTV).** The audio and video are compressed, meaning the redundant information has been eliminated and the signals are combined into one data stream.[8] This system of digital modulation is called **eight-level discrete amplitude vestigial sideband (8-VSB).** It fits into the 6 MHz of bandwidth, and uses a pilot signal to stabilize the data stream of audio and video. The dilemma confronting American broadcasters is not whether to broadcast digitally, but whether to do so in high definition.

Television stations were given one UHF channel to broadcast digitally in exchange for turning over their old analog channels for other uses. Some broadcasters indicated they would need the additional channel to create revenue in order to afford digital facilities. That move upset some Washington lawmakers and citizens' groups who thought broadcasters should use the extra spectrum to give viewers high-definition television (HDTV). To understand how HDTV began, we step back to early experiments in Japan.

Chrominance Contains color information in the TV signal.

Luminance Controls brightness levels in a color television signal.

Propagation Spreads radio waves from a transmitter over assigned areas.

Effective radiated power (ERP) Determines broadcast signal reach by the antenna gain measurement.

Digital television (DTV) Replaces analog signals by 2006 with video and audio compressed onto one channel in binary language compatible with computers.

Eight-level discrete amplitude vestigial sideband (8-VSB) Broadcasts digital television in the United States.

HDTV

In 1970, the technicians of NHK (Nippon Hoso Kyokai), Japan's primary public broadcasting network, began experimenting with a new format for television. Its goal was to make the resolution of the TV picture richer and more detailed. The format was called "high definition" because it increased the number of lines on the screen from 525 to 1,125. It also elongated the picture, conforming more closely with the wide screen of the cinema.

The Europeans were studying the Japanese analog system of HDTV that required more than three times as much spectrum as standard definition television channels. *Multiple sub-nyquist sample encoding (MUSE)* failed to find favor with the Europeans, who decided to perfect their own analog high-definition TV. European researchers from universities and the electronics industry came up with a system in 1986: *high-definition multiplexed analog components (HD-MAC)*. Both early Japanese and European systems used analog signals, requiring more bandwidth than digital processing.

In the United States, the FCC noticed NHK's lead in high-definition television and formed the Advisory Committee on Advanced Television Service in 1983. As noted at the beginning of this chapter, General Instrument's all-digital system met with favorable nods from American engineers. Its principal advantages were its compressible *digital* signal and its compatibility with existing television sets.

Grand Alliance

Five companies came forward with HDTV proposals, but the review panel found flaws in all of them. Consequently, a so-called Grand Alliance of U.S. firms was formed to iron out the differences and to bring together the best ideas of AT&T/Zenith, General Instrument/MIT, and Philips/Thomson/Sarnoff. In 1994, the Grand Alliance offered two systems for field testing: *quadrature amplification modulation (QAM)* and 8-VSB. Following months of testing, Zenith's 8-VSB standard was selected, but the choice met with controversy.

HDTV Controversy

The FCC chose 8-VSB despite continued protests led by the Sinclair Broadcast group of Baltimore. It was convinced that a better system existed than 8-VSB. That system was called *coded orthogonal frequency division multiplexing (COFDM)*, and it was the basis for digital HDTV in Europe. The COFDM system was favored by some because it could more easily overcome *multipath* effects. When a signal is transmitted, it strikes natural and human-made objects, causing it to scatter and take two or more paths to reach the television receiver. The COFDM system overcomes multipath problems by using different carriers to transmit the same signal. Nonetheless, more than 400 TV stations in the United States were digitally broadcasting using the 8-VSB standard by 2002.

The focus shifted from high-definition to digital television (DTV) when the government allocated new spectrum space for completion of the transition from analog to digital by 2006. In that year, old analog TV channels are to be turned over to the government for new digital uses. Meanwhile, many TV station owners were saying they would not make the deadline for the transition, and more than 600 filed for waivers. FCC Chair Powell appointed a task force to smooth the transition to DTV and called on DTV manufacturers to have sets available by 2007.

Interlace scanning Alternates odd- and even-numbered lines.

National Television System Committee (NTSC) Standard definition of 525 lines, 30 frames per second.

RECEPTION

On your TV screen, roughly 150,000 round pixels are illuminated during the scanning process. This is known as *scansion,* and it occurs so rapidly across the horizontal lines of the screen that scenes appear to meld together. The viewer's brain receives each image and retains it long enough to seamlessly link it to the next picture—a process called *persistence of vision.*

Interlace Scanning

The scanning beam skips every other line as it traverses the screen back and forth from the top down, which is **interlace scanning.** Engineers for the **National Television System Committee (NTSC)** decided in 1941 that interlacing was the best way to fit the TV picture into six megaHertz. The process divides the frame in half by sending out two fields of odd- and even-numbered lines.[9]

How fast is interlace scanning? It scans 30 frames per second (fps), and there are two fields per frame—odd and even—so there are 60 fields of video scanned

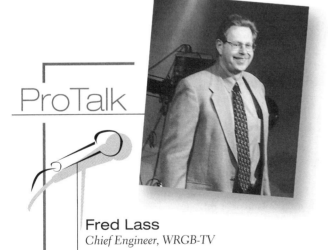

ProTalk

Fred Lass
Chief Engineer, WRGB-TV

"There's absolutely no chance whatsoever that there is going to be 85 percent penetration of digital TV by 2006."

The transition to DTV has been an awkward one for several reasons. The 8-VSB standard was incompatible with COFDM technologies in Europe and Japan,

thus creating controversy. TV station owners wondered where they would find the money to finance replacing old analog equipment with expensive, new digital facilities. Stations would need to buy everything from antenna towers to digital tapes and all of the hardware and software in between.

Chief Engineer Fred Lass of WRGB-TV in Schenectady, New York, oversees the transfer of technology for a pioneer station in broadcasting, and he sees obstacles in the road ahead. "There is no clear consensus," Lass says, pointing to the variety of digital formats available. There are decisions to be made on videotapes, sampling schemes, aspect ratios, compatibility with cable, and protecting the property rights of program owners with DTV.

Lass says even the timetable is problematic: "The FCC put the deadline of 2006 out there as a carrot so everyone would work toward it." That deadline, however, is based on the number of digital TV sets that have been bought by American consumers. "There's absolutely no chance whatsoever that there is going to be 85 percent penetration of digital TV by 2006," Lass says. "Zero chance."[10]

Sync generators Hold TV signals in order during transmission.

Vertical blanking interval (VBI) Forms a black bar when the electron gun reaches the bottom of the screen.

Progressive scanning Visual lines of output in ascending order to create one frame at a time.

Aspect ratio The width-to-height proportion of a television picture.

across the TV screen each second. Figure 5.6 illustrates the process by showing how electronic guns vary the currents to each of the dots in the pixels so that they glow at different intensities. In TV receivers, the picture information from the camera is fed to electronic guns that paint each scene one dot (or phosphor), at a time on a *kinescope*, a type of cathode ray tube (CRT). The color phosphors on the screen of the CRT illuminate the pixels in shades of red, green, blue, white, or black at the same intensity as the scene captured by the camera lens.

SECOND AUDIO PROGRAMS

Stereo and foreign language on television broadcasts come over the channel's *second audio program (SAP)* transmission. Technically, the SAP channel in television is much like radio's subsidiary communication authorizations (SCAs), noted earlier, only the sound is of a higher quality.

VERTICAL BLANKING INTERVAL: THE BLACK BAR

TV pictures are held in check by a **sync generator.** Not only does it generate horizontal and vertical pulses to keep pictures from fluttering or rolling but it also keeps the camera's output in step with the TV screen. In addition, the sync generator adds a black bar at the bottom of the frame, known as the **VBI (vertical blanking interval).** The bar appears when the scanning beam reaches the bottom of the frame. In the moment before the beam returns to the top, information is sent to the black bar, holding the picture in place along with other data, such as closed-circuit captions.[11]

Progressive Scanning

An important distinction in the scanning process separates screens for TVs and computers. Computers use **progressive scanning,** which paints the lines across one line after another in sequence to form a whole frame, unlike the half-frames or fields of even- and odd-numbered rows scanned in NTSC television. The system adopted in Europe, COFDM, uses progressive scanning. In the United States, the Advanced Television Systems Committee (ATSC) has offered specifications for several progressive scanning formats.

Aspect Ratio

The size of the screen is defined by its **aspect ratio,** which is the relationship of the horizontal to vertical dimensions. In NTSC, the ratio is four units horizontal by three units vertical (4×3). That remains consistent regardless of whether the screen is small or large, 12 or 36 inches in diameter. Television's aspect ratio one day will resemble the rectangular dimensions of a cinema screen, which is 16×9, 16 units across and 9 units down.

Digital Viewing

Chances are that your television set at home uses a kinescope picture tube, which is shaped like a narrow glass cylinder and widens to form a picture screen.

FIGURE 5.6

Scanning Systems: Interlaced and Progressive

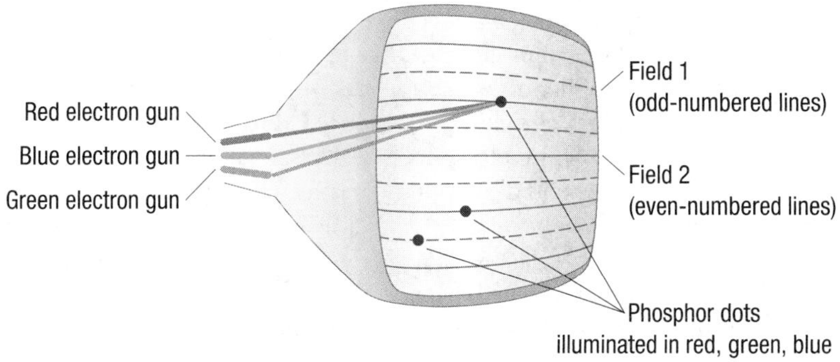

Red electron gun
Blue electron gun
Green electron gun

Field 1
(odd-numbered lines)

Field 2
(even-numbered lines)

Phosphor dots
illuminated in red, green, blue

(a) Analog Interlaced Scanning

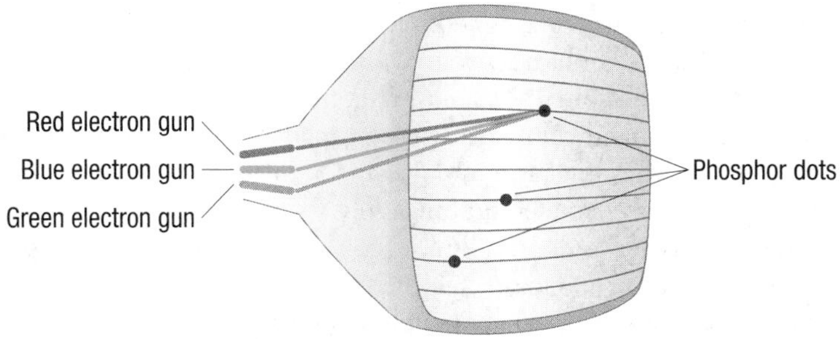

Red electron gun
Blue electron gun
Green electron gun

Phosphor dots

(b) Digital Progressive Scanning

The National Television System Committee (NTSC) uses interlaced scanning (odd- and-even numbered lines) in order to economize on the bandwidth by sending out half a picture (one field) at a time. Inside the kinescope tube, the picture process that takes place in the camera is reversed. Beams of red, blue, and green are scanned by electron guns across the screen one line at a time—first even-numbered and then odd-numbered lines. In progressive scanning, the video frame is scanned from top to bottom without skipping any lines.

(Vladimir Zworykin invented this glass screen, also known as a *cathode-ray tube [CRT]*, in 1929.) Recent research, however, has developed new technologies for producing flat screens that can be hung on a wall. The flat screens in your computer use *liquid crystal display (LCD)* technology. They are called *liquid crystal* because stored between the sheets of glass are thin films of liquid crystals with transistors etched on their surface.

Liquid crystal displays are either passive matrix, which use a continuous stream of power to the pixels, or active matrix, which are turned on and off. Active LCDs are superior in image quality, color, brightness, and stability. The LCD, however, offers limited peripheral vision to the audience. As with a computer, viewers need to be seated directly in front of the screen.

Another screen for future TV viewing is the plasma-display panel (PDP), which uses a grid of tiny pixels filled with a gas mixture. This grid illuminates red, green, and blue phosphors with ultraviolet light when charged with electricity. The PDP offers a better peripheral view and is relatively thin and light in weight, but its price is prohibitive.

Summary

The technical business of television requires taking what can be seen and heard and then converting it into signal waves to be presented through the speakers and screens of radio, television, and computers. The technical process can be broadly defined through the stages of production. In the acquisition phase, audio waves are transduced by microphones to be broadcast from digital or analog tape or discs. In television, scenes of light are transduced through a camera lens and eventually converted to picture elements on a TV screen or stored in analog or digital recordings on tapes and discs. Editing has seen the progression from reels of audiotape and videotape to digital formats using computers to manipulate scenes and sounds. Recording has seen a progression from discs of vinyl to oxide tape to metallic discs engraved with beams containing digital information.

Broadcasting delivery is basically the business of harnessing invisible waves of electromagnetic energy and encoding them with information—audio, video, graphics, and text. Radio and television are wireless communications that broadcast over the electromagnetic spectrum, which can be envisioned as lanes or channels. Broadcast stations are assigned frequencies, referring to the number of times a broadcast signal sends out cycles within one second.

The International Telecommunications Union (ITU) is the global manager of spectrum, allocating bandwidth and settling broadcasting disputes between neighboring countries. Channel assignments are left to governments to license; in the United States, the Federal Communications Commission (FCC) handles that duty. Spectrum space is constantly in demand for a variety of purposes. Commercial demand is high, and special interests seek to broadcast, as well, so the FCC has created low-power radio and television broadcasting.

Radio and television engineers constantly seek to eliminate interference, either from adjacent channels or from other sources. Television and FM radio have extra channel space to protect them from interference, as well as extra bandwidth for secondary audio programs, which allows for stereo and other services for retail outlets and the blind.

Delivery and reception of digital television (DTV) have raised a number of issues because they require retooling the broadcast industry with new facilities. TV stations are looking for new revenue to make that transition possible. The main question about DTV does not concern whether stations will choose to broadcast in high definition once the digital conversion is complete. Rather, it asks whether they should use the extra channel of bandwidth to generate revenue.

FOOD FOR THOUGHT

1. The five stages of production—acquisition, editing, recording, delivery, and reception—suggest the necessity of compatible digital technology for machines in each step of the process. Explain the role you think industry and government should play in this process.

2. In the acquisition stage, the technical emphasis is on converting sound and light waves to electronic energy. What do you think are the most important

CAREER FOCUS

An estimated 93,000 broadcast, audio, and video equipment technicians work in the United States. Television stations employ, on average, many more technicians than radio stations do. Broadcast and sound engineering technicians install, operate, maintain, and repair the equipment used to record and transmit radio, television, and cable programs. They work with TV cameras, microphones, lights, audio- and videotape recorders, transmitters, antennas, and other electronic apparatus.

In the control room of a radio or television broadcasting studio, technicians monitor the audio and video signals for strength, clarity, and stability before and during the recording and transmission of programs. In smaller stations, titles such as *operator, engineer,* or *technician* are used almost interchangeably to describe various jobs. At larger stations and networks, the jobs are more specialized.

Audio and video equipment operators are responsible for recording productions, either live television programs or studio recordings. They also edit tapes for compact discs (CDs) and cassettes, or transmit programs for radio and television broadcasting. **Transmitter operators** monitor and log television signals and operate transmitters. **Master control room operators** regulate the station's signal strength, clarity, and range of sounds and colors for TV broadcasts. They also monitor and log outgoing signals at the transmitter. **Maintenance technicians** set up, fine-tune, check, and repair electronic broadcasting equipment.

Recording engineers operate and maintain video and sound recording equipment. **Field technicians** set up and operate portable field equipment for audio and video recording outside the studio. **Chief engineers** supervise the technicians who operate and maintain broadcasting equipment. **Television and video camera operators** operate TV studio cameras or double as electronic newsgathering camera operators.

Master control engineers make sure that a television station's scheduled program elements—such as satellite and microwave feeds, prerecorded segments, and commercials—are recorded. They also are responsible for making sure these elements are inserted into the scheduled programming. **Technical directors** are in charge during the production of a program and direct the studio and control room staff.

Television station engineers generally hold college degrees in electrical engineering or associate's degrees from technical schools. Some are also members of IBEW (International Brotherhood of Electrical Workers). The FCC licenses engineers to maintain the transmitter and tower facilities. The Federal Communications Commission no longer requires the licensing of broadcast technicians; this requirement was eliminated by the Telecommunications Act of 1996. Certification by the Society of Broadcast Engineers has become the accepted standard of professional competence with experience.

things professionals need to keep in mind when recording audio and video in the field? Why?

3. In recording audio and video, the trend is away from analog tape and toward digital discs compatible with computers. Do you think there will ever be one software format that can be used for all media—television, radio, and the Web? Why or why not?

4. Issues of technology often involve issues of economics. Do you believe the government should mandate standards of technology compatible with most countries or one standard that protects our nation's manufacturers from competition? Explain your answer.

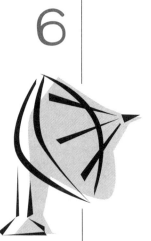

6

The Industry

Civilization and profits go hand in hand.

—Calvin Coolidge, U.S. President, 1923–1929

Broadcasters often do their finest work when other people are having a bad day. This is no news to Lucy Himstedt, vice president and general manager of WFIE-TV in Evansville, Indiana. She knows, from experience, the vital connection between broadcast workers and the ways in which they're organized to act. In January 2000, after a tornado slammed into nearby Owensboro, Kentucky, destroying or damaging hundreds of homes, Himstedt put that interaction to the test.

Broadcast Workers. In commercial radio and television, workers and managers are charged with making money by attracting viewers and advertisers. Meeting broader public-service needs is a second priority.

"We knew right away they needed help," Himstedt recalls, "and we'd been doing the Muscular Dystrophy Association **telethon** for 30 years. Now, in just two full work days, we pulled together a telethon that generated $500,000 in cash for the Red Cross."

"You love a crisis, because it proves to all the people in the station that you can work together as a team."

How did WFIE pull off such a feat so rapidly? By rallying a staff that lives in constant readiness to respond. "We got the people in news involved," says Himstedt, "as well as our (commercial-time) sales manager. The way any telethon works is that much of the money is raised *before* you go on the air. She went to local businesses beforehand and said, 'We know you'll donate; we want to put you on the air to present us with a check.'

"We gave everybody something to do. Our business office knew we would have to have guards around when we put money in the pot, and they took care of that. We ran phone banks, too. . . . You love a crisis, because it proves to all the people in the station that you can work together as a team."

FUNDAMENTALS

> **Principle #1**
>
> In commercial broadcasting, public service must support business objectives by promoting or otherwise benefiting the company.

Telethon (from "marathon") Continuous TV broadcast for hours or days, usually soliciting donations to a charity or cause.

Certainly it is important that a TV station be ready to serve its viewers with prompt, accurate news reports about any emergency. To find the energy to muster donations and other aid for disaster victims is a community-relations plus. The basic mission of the station, however, includes one more element that is paramount among the purposes of management: the underlying, never-ending mandate to make money. That's the nature of any business or industry, including the commercial electronic media.

A Dual Role

It is often hard to find a bright line dividing what broadcasters do for the public from what they do for themselves. WFIE probably gained both in goodwill and materially from the tornado experience. Owensboro's lone TV outlet had folded two years earlier, leaving an unserved audience that the Evansville station was working to woo. A fast response to the community's sudden need helped cultivate a relationship on many levels.

Here's a fact to remember: In the U.S. system, *local stations are the ONLY true broadcasters.* To win a government license to broadcast—that is, to transmit programming "over the air"—a station must have a local address and a specific geographic audience to serve. Once licensed, a broadcaster operates under an affirmative mandate from the government to serve the public interest.

Cable and satellite systems also are regulated, but far differently. That's because they can be received only by paid subscription, not through the airwaves.

Tornado, January 2000. A twister's devastating effects on Owensboro, Kentucky, were eased when WFIE-TV in nearby Evansville, Indiana, raised $500,000 for Red Cross aid to victims through a hurriedly organized "telethon."

ProTalk

Lucy Himstedt
General Manager, WFIE-TV

"The sales department and the business office are going to fight sometimes, but between those times we pull together for the good of all."

When she was hired to run WFIE-TV, Lucy Himstedt had to move quickly. First came her need to study and understand every cranny of her station to a degree of detail she had never needed as a news director.

"You only know your niche," says Himstedt, "and now, suddenly, you have to learn the big picture. What are the problems that are facing the traffic department? What are the problems Operations is dealing with? And how do we function as a *group* of departments?" She had to choose what to discard, what to change, and what to leave alone: "I had one-on-one interviews with everybody on the staff—not about work, but 'getting to know you.' That helped me learn a lot." Himstedt realized that some major tinkering was needed, but that it would take time.

Meanwhile, as the new "GM," Himstedt would have to supervise the station's overall budget and keep subordinate managers focused on the bottom line. She would need to spur ad sales, programming, and promotion staffers toward maximum performance. And there was a people-to-people dimension to the job that brought her special satisfaction. She might have a staff member help monitor community factors on which WFIE's broadcast license depended—but she wanted the buck to stop at her desk.

"Part of my job is to be on boards and to be in the community," she says, adding that she also stays personally close to the station's employees—as a broadcast manager needs to do in a business of rapid change and psychological ups and downs.

"The sales department and the business office are going to fight sometimes," Himstedt acknowledges, "but between those times we pull together for the good of all."

This means that cable customers, lacking certain federal protections, are left on their own to filter out objectionable programming and protect themselves from media misconduct. Cable and satellite providers have to heed only their consciences and professional ethics; with luck, they overlap.

The Federal Communications Commission (FCC)—the federal body charged with overseeing and regulating broadcasting—does not license networks, whether they're broadcast, cable, or satellite networks. So, stations, as a sort of chokepoint for most radio and television programming, theoretically are a fat target for government scrutiny. In reality, however, thanks in part to the Constitution's First Amendment, the FCC grants great freedom to stations to do pretty much what they want. They're expected to keep activity files open for public inspection and to show a sense of social responsibility, staying aware of local issues and informing the community about them from time to time. However, the FCC doesn't spell out how much information is enough. Nor does the government slap broadcasters' hands unless they stray into certain forbidden zones—indecency (during most of the day), obscenity anytime, rigged contests, payola, and so on—in which Congress has authorized the FCC to act.

Syndicators Agents or companies that sell programs to radio and television; most successful network programs are later sold in syndication.

Most important, perhaps, the system explicitly does *not* interfere with profit making. Unlike broadcasters in most countries, U.S. broadcasters were permitted to take a sharp turn toward private enterprise from the beginning. American radio and TV stations still operate, mostly profitably, under government policy that protects commercialism. Stations consequently decide what to broadcast based on what makes or loses money. That's why, today, a rich industry rests on their shoulders.

The Business Dynamic

Commercial broadcasting is a business, but rather than sell programs directly to audiences, stations deliver programs in exchange for people's attention. This is how stations *create* audiences, which they then sell: Businesses that want to reach crowds of potential customers pay stations for the time needed to broadcast advertising. So the broadcast industry, its individual parts and its personnel, are organized to create and profit from a seamless flow of programming and sales messages. If everything works as planned, everybody's satisfied. (As we'll see shortly, "everybody" includes an increasingly influential community of stockholders who keep money flowing into broadcast treasuries.)

WFIE, like most stations today, produces shows of its own (primarily newscasts) and reaps local ad revenues from those programs. It also buys shows from **syndicators**—companies set up to acquire programs, some newly produced and untested, some network reruns—and then sells them to stations and networks. Most of all, WFIE and most other stations need the big-name, heavily promoted entertainment that their affiliated networks provide, day by day. Network comedies and dramas draw many viewers "into the tent" of a local station, often holding their attention when local news or other non-network shows come on. Networks almost always keep control of most of the advertising time in any of their programs. However, they also release some of those commercial minutes to the affiliate stations so that they can insert local ads and make money from them. It's a barter arrangement from which both sides benefit (see Figure 6.1).

Pulling in every possible dollar of revenue has become critical to broadcasting. It's a "mature" industry, which means that virtually everyone already owns or uses its products and services, and it takes ingenuity to come up with new ways to generate cash flow. What's more, broadcasting is buffeted increasingly by competition from young rivals and by destructive infighting within its own industry. This was not always so.

Principle #2

The industry rests on a three-legged stool of economic factors: broadcaster, audience, and advertiser.

FIGURE 6.1

Network-Affiliate Ties: Relationship between a Typical Network and Its Affiliates

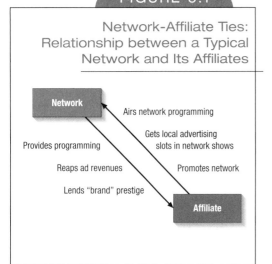

An Explosion of Choices

Broadcasting once held the deed to a "national hearth"—a metaphor for the way most Americans typically gathered to watch a single hit television show at the same hour of the same night in the mid-twentieth century. The medium was new. Channel choices were few. The hits were on at the same time every week. Everybody talked about them, so everybody watched them.

Now, not even the best television programming draws a vast and reliable horde to the same cozy metaphorical fire on a given evening. Radio programming, which galvanized families every night during and after World War II, has split up and moved into **niches** where select clusters of listeners dwell. Not many shows in either medium draw massive audiences. Most of the time, each individual watches or listens to something different from the show being enjoyed by the folks next door—even in the next *room*, since American homes average about 2 ½ TV sets apiece. What's more, neither medium dominates people's leisure moments as automatically as it once did. Too many activities are packed into the normal day, too many channel choices, too many other electronic toys—and a serious challenge from the Internet along with other new media.

As noted earlier, broadcast-style programming still begins at, or is relayed to us by, nearby broadcast stations. Many changes have come along, though, since radio and television each had its "golden age" through the mid-twentieth century:

- Since the 1970s, many people have been watching broadcast television through local and regional cable systems. These systems reach more of us geographically than over-the-air broadcasting can, and they provide clearer and more stable signals for many areas.
- The 1980s brought the start of a cable revolution in which movie companies and others created programming just for cable. This original content now competes directly with shows produced by old-line broadcast stations and networks.
- Yet another delivery technology—satellites—has captured millions of loyal fans. Companies can send us programming directly, with no stations or cables in the loop, by bouncing it off human-made objects in space to antenna dishes at our homes. Satellites also play a huge role in the delivery of programs to local cable systems, which transmit them to subscribers and place commercials in them.
- Although we still turn to either broadcast, cable, or satellite channels to swim in the pop-culture mainstream, that may be changing. Many people now use their computers to hear radio-style audio or watch **streaming** versions of TV video.
- Possibly more important, the Internet has spawned scores of news, information, and entertainment enterprises of its own. Some operate without reference to the "old" media—broadcasting, newspapers—using tools and techniques to draw young audiences, while others draw on more familiar media names.

These other pipelines haven't destroyed broadcasting, however; its access to virtually everyone and the superior value of its air time to advertisers continue to make it the nation's media powerhouse. Many sources say local stations still reap profits of 30 to 50 percent a year, so they remain among the nation's most successful businesses. Still, newer options for consumers have forced the broadcast

Niche Submarket in which radio station or TV channel can find consumers interested specifically in its unique programming (e.g., outdoor sports, foreign-language shows, etc.).

Streaming Transmission of sounds or images as continuous stream of data over Internet.

Station Group Cluster of broadcast stations owned by single company; such groups now own most U.S. radio stations.

Conglomerate Corporation made up of subsidiary companies or holdings in a number of different industries or industry sectors.

Ratings Numbers showing size of audience for particular show or time period.

Consolidation Centralization of ownership or control of a number of entities; many radio and TV stations, as well as cable channels, have been consolidated recently.

Market In broadcasting, specific population or area to which programs are targeted, as in "the Louisville market"; an industry term is *DMA*, for *designated market area*.

Synergy Process by which combining two or more units results in an outcome greater than the sum of the parts; consolidation usually is aimed at achieving synergy.

industry to review its budgets, tighten its belt, look for new revenue streams, reorganize its stations, and generally become more innovative.

LEVELS OF OPERATION

When early founders and their investors launched the first radio networks, most of the local stations around the country had local owners. Rarely were stations as homespun and intimate as a mom-and-pop general store, but their managers knew many of their audience members by name, primarily because they were neighbors.

Was such utterly local business any better for society than the widely dispersed but rather centrally controlled modern broadcast industry? Opinions about that are all over the map. So, probably, are the people who control most of the stations in *your* town. Today, companies known as **station groups** have acquired many local outlets and oversee their operations from whole time zones away. The older networks and some of the newer ones are members of much larger corporations, some of them **conglomerates**—that is, having interests in many businesses besides broadcasting. The policies and practices found at all of these levels ultimately must satisfy stockholders who pour their investment dollars into the companies.

We'll start our examination at the top level, among the largest media corporations and conglomerates. By the time we reach the local-station level, a number of important realities should be clear. One is that however WFIE-TV improves the measured size of its audience (**ratings**) in Indiana, Lucy Himstedt doesn't hold all the strings to her station's future. Far from it.

Corporations

There always has been some benevolence at the roots of the electronic media; few of their leaders, as good citizens entrusted with the public airwaves, could forget their public obligations. By the late twentieth century, however, the potential of these media as *businesses* clearly came first in the minds of the mighty. Many moved toward **consolidation** of ownership and/or control—a move to run or direct whole masses of media companies from central hubs of power.

OBJECTIVES

Media owners pursued consolidation for sound economic reasons. One was to achieve "economies of scale," the savings and earnings that only a large business could expect. It's possible that some owners also wanted to acquire *monopolies* in some media **markets** (targeted commercial areas, usually cities), hoping to control all or most of their supply of products, despite the intent of U.S. antitrust laws. There were cases, too, when acquiring a few highly successful middle-sized companies simply would improve a corporation's overall "bottom line" and make its business more lucrative and also more predictable.

That phenomenon is called **synergy**, which is when the sum of the parts is greater than the whole. For example, even a movie studio's lower-quality movies might pay off if a sister network or station group gave the movies new life on television. Or perhaps cable companies could extend the geographic reach (and advertising power) of their sibling radio and TV stations. Over recent years, FCC regulation has come closer to making most kinds of combinations permissible.

In one drive toward synergy, Time Inc., a print and broadcast concern, and Warner Communications, the cable branch of a movie/media company, merged in 1989. The major purpose was to make more money by combining movie, cable TV, and magazine units of the merged companies in creative ways. At first, it proved to be a winner. Time Warner invented programs and product lines, bought CNN and other properties from flashy media mogul Ted Turner, and went on to consummate the biggest media merger ever, joining with AOL in 2000.

The fusion of America Online, an Internet giant, with Time Warner, a titan of print, broadcast, movies, and more, produced a case study in what can happen when media conglomerates tie the knot, and fail to show a profit. This marriage brought 11 subsidiary companies under one roof (see Figure 6.2), the

> **Principle #3**
>
> U.S. commercial electronic media will oppose efforts to regulate them.

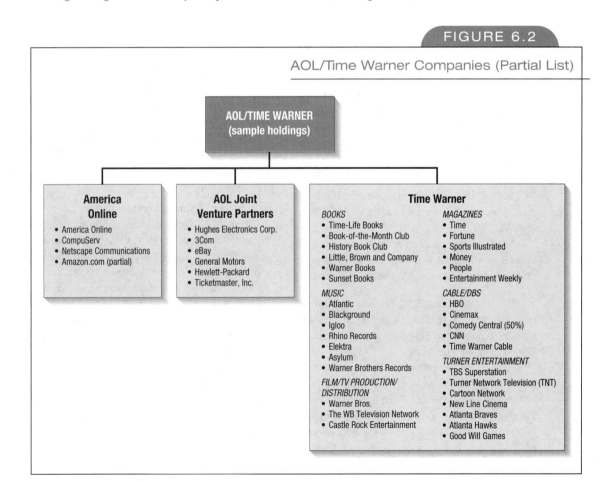

FIGURE 6.2

AOL/Time Warner Companies (Partial List)

AOL/TIME WARNER (sample holdings)

America Online
- America Online
- CompuServ
- Netscape Communications
- Amazon.com (partial)

AOL Joint Venture Partners
- Hughes Electronics Corp.
- 3Com
- eBay
- General Motors
- Hewlett-Packard
- Ticketmaster, Inc.

Time Warner

BOOKS
- Time-Life Books
- Book-of-the-Month Club
- History Book Club
- Little, Brown and Company
- Warner Books
- Sunset Books

MUSIC
- Atlantic
- Blackground
- Igloo
- Rhino Records
- Elektra
- Asylum
- Warner Brothers Records

FILM/TV PRODUCTION/ DISTRIBUTION
- Warner Bros.
- The WB Television Network
- Castle Rock Entertainment

MAGAZINES
- Time
- Fortune
- Sports Illustrated
- Money
- People
- Entertainment Weekly

CABLE/DBS
- HBO
- Cinemax
- Comedy Central (50%)
- CNN
- Time Warner Cable

TURNER ENTERTAINMENT
- TBS Superstation
- Turner Network Television (TNT)
- Cartoon Network
- New Line Cinema
- Atlanta Braves
- Atlanta Hawks
- Good Will Games

Vertical Integration Buying companies to support the buyer's business (e.g., a Hollywood studio purchasing cable systems to air the studio's films).

total value of which was estimated at $350 billion—enough money to fund the U.S defense program.

Few questioned the wisdom of the merger in business terms. AOL's experience and resources in the on-line communications business (it had 22 million subscribers) would appear to complement Time Warner's old-media strengths and its capacity to produce content of all sorts. The result, some analysts speculated, eventually could be dominance of twenty-first century media by a single supercompany.

Then blue skies turned grey. AOL Time Warner's stock prices fell 66 percent in 12 months, and the company assumed billions in debt. Some blamed over-exuberant investments in convergence technologies, such as AOLTV interactive television. Others claimed that too much power had been consolidated in New York, robbing division heads of their autonomy and ability to compete. Whatever the reason, AOL Time Warner's new CEO, Richard Parsons, faced a

Vivendi Goes Vertical

Surprising things can happen when twenty-first century electronic-media owners sit down together to make deals. Sometimes they lead to disaster.

In electronic media, **vertical integration** means owning everything in the system from creation of the product to its delivery to consumers' homes, cars, offices, or neighborhood theaters. Here's how one series of deals unfolded around the turn of the twenty-first century:

Deal: Vivendi, a French-owned global media giant, purchased Universal Studios for $30 billion in 2000.

Motive: Vivendi wanted a bigger presence in the U.S. marketplace. It already owned 43 percent of USA Networks, a cable-TV and movie company.

Deal: In December 2001, the renamed Vivendi Universal bought 10 percent of the U.S.-owned satellite broadcaster EchoStar Communications Corporation, for $1.5 billion.

Motive: Vivendi Universal, which now had plenty of production capacity, wanted more U.S. distribution for its products. Since EchoStar owned the direct-broadcast DISH Network and had just merged with DirecTV, it would have a monopoly on much noncable home service. That, in turn, would

give Vivendi Universal films and shows a great U.S. outlet.

Deal: A few days later, Vivendi Universal struck a deal with the head of USA Networks, Barry Diller, to essentially acquire his company, owning 93 percent of its stock.

Motive: More distribution. This deal would give Vivendi Universal control of USA cable, Sci-Fi, Home Shopping Network, and other channels—with access to more.

Disaster: Vivendi Universal had invested too much too fast. A big stock-market drop in mid-2002 helped to drain value from new Vivendi companies, leaving the corporation $19 billion in debt. Its chairman was forced out, and Vivendi began selling holdings he had borrowed heavily to acquire. Would the corporation recover? Executives could only say they hoped so. All of USA's and Universal's movie and television production units now would operate within a new entity, Vivendi Universal Entertainment (VUE). Diller would be its chief executive officer, as well as CEO of USA Interactive, a new unit that would operate Internet businesses, including Ticketmaster.com, Hotel Reservations Network, and more. (Diller said that unit would be "completely independent.")[1]

remarkable challenge—saving one of the world's largest media conglomerates from dying under the weight of its own obesity.

Much of commercial broadcasting now is part of a few huge corporations. One is General Electric, which was ranked by *Business Week* magazine two years running as the world's highest-valued company, worth almost $500 billion in 2001.[2] This sort of statistic tends to alarm social critics who contend that placing great media power in just a few hands is certain to reduce the diversity of voices in our popular culture. Others argue that powerful companies produce a *wider* variety of programming than smaller companies do collectively. In any case, the concentration of electronic-media control continues to this day.

Another corporate giant, Viacom, purchased the CBS network in 2000. At that time, federal regulations prohibited any company from owning stations reaching more than 35 percent of the United States—in effect, an antimonopoly rule. This meant that Viacom would have to sell off valuable CBS-owned stations. However, in 2002, a federal court ordered the FCC to reconsider the 35 percent ownership "cap." The FCC has appealed that order.

GOVERNMENT LIMITS

Within weeks of Viacom's threat, the FCC's new commissioner, Michael Powell (appointed by President George W. Bush), was calming such concerns publicly. He told Congress that he planned to scrap the 35 percent rule and other limits. Powell said repeatedly that he wanted to open broadcasting further to market forces, a signal that consolidation could continue and even accelerate. Powell was not breaking with tradition; he simply embodied what was becoming a tradition of deregulation.

The FCC, most notably since the years of Republican President Ronald Reagan, had worked to reduce or dismantle controls on group ownership of broadcast outlets. In many respects, this was in keeping with the American legacy of freedom for all. Business people with the courage, vision, and money to build media corporations would have increasing freedom to do so. Without their enterprise and risk taking, many said, the nation never would reap the full benefits of what technology and capital could produce.

By the 1980s, the FCC's rules (and loopholes) were encouraging many people—some of them with no prior interest in broadcasting—to start buying stations as investments. Looser federal controls created a sort of national license bazaar in which stations that once might have been sold one at a time, with considerable gravity, were being peddled in batches. Some that were sold were resold almost immediately at a profit.

By the late 1990s, under the 1996 Telecommunications Act, one person could buy eight stations *in a single town* and could own as many stations *nationally* as the person could afford. This attracted not only committed broadcast operators but financial speculators and absentee owners. Neither group seemed likely to contribute much to the stability of local communities or to broadcasting's public obligations.

> **Principle #4**
>
> The urge to consolidate ownership is fundamental to broadcasting, as it is to many other industries.

Most restrictions are intended to prevent monopolies and encourage diversity. However, corporations that own electronic media (for example, see Figure 6.3)

Tribune Broadcasting in 2002 owned and operated 22 major-marketing television stations, including national superstation WGN, and reached 80 percent of U.S. television households. It was the largest TV group not owned by a network. Tribune's properties also included radio stations, Tribune Entertainment, and the Chicago Cubs baseball team.

Source: http://www.tribune.com/report2000/tc2000ar02.html

FIGURE 6.3

Tribune Corporation Holdings

BROADCAST OPERATIONS

Television

WPIX (WB11) New York	KDAF (WB33) Dallas	KTWB (WB22) Seattle	WXIN (FOX59) Indianapolis	WPMT (FOX43) Harrisburg, PA
KTLA (WB5) Los Angeles	WBDC (WB50) Washington, D.C.	WZBL (WB39) Miami	WTIC (FOX61) Hartford, CT	WEWB (WB45) Albany, NY
WGN (WB9) Chicago	WATL (WB36) Atlanta	KWGN (WB2) Denver	WXMI (FOX17) Grand Rapids, MI	
WPHI (WB17) Philadelphia	KHWB (WB39) Houston	KTXL (FOX40) Sacramento, CA	WGNO (ABC26) New Orleans	
WLVI (WB56) Boston	KCPQ (FOX13) Seattle	KSWB (WB69) San Diego	WNOL (WB38) New Orleans	

Radio	**Television Programming**
WGN-AM Chicago	Tribune Entertainment Company, Los Angeles—develops and distributes first-run television programming for the Tribune station group and national syndication
KEZW-AM Denver	**Baseball**
KOSI-FM Denver	Chicago National League Ball Club Inc. (Chicago Cubs)
KKHK-FM Denver	**Investments**
	The WB Television Network (25% owned); TV Food Network (29%); The Golf Channel (9%); iBlast Networks (25%)

Carriage One medium's delivery of another medium's content, as when a cable system "carries" (delivers) a TV station's programs.

Sweeps Periods four times yearly in which measurement firms "sweep" (intensively sample ratings in) broadcast markets to measure audiences.

often argue that if they're prevented from expanding their ownership or control, then competition from rivals will engulf them and deny their services to consumers.

Some people questioned such companies' concern for service after a noisy clash-of-the-titans in the spring of 2000. Time Warner Cable, locked in a contract dispute with Disney over **carriage** of its ABC and other networks, disconnected ABC-owned stations from 96 cable systems for 40 hours. This denied programming to 3.5 million viewers in New York and other major cities. Worse, it happened during May, a **"sweeps"** month in which audience ratings determine advertising rates.

The FCC, evidently reluctant to punish Time Warner Cable severely, accepted a "voluntary" $72,000 settlement payment to the U.S. Treasury. The company also gave some free services to the affected viewers. The incident indicated graphically that media companies caught in business disputes might not always put consumers first.

SHAREHOLDER INFLUENCE

Except when someone starts and runs a small company (such as an Internet venture) using his or her own savings, media businesses need massive and continuous investment. Advertising revenue alone won't cover all corporate obligations and keep a business growing. Instead, companies sell stock to investors, use the proceeds to create and market programs, make profits (usually), pay dividends to the investors, and thus keep attracting new investors.

People have been investing money in media for centuries, often in ways that benefit society. Benjamin Franklin cofounded the *Pennsylvania Gazette* with funding from his partner's father, who is said to have chipped in on the condition that his booze-loving son keep Franklin around to provide stability.[3] Much later, in the early 1900s, Guglielmo Marconi found little support for wireless telegraphy in his native Italy. However, he was able to win over British and American backers who helped make him—in some people's eyes—"the father of radio." (If he was the father, however, it took other pioneers, such as Reginald Fessenden, to turn Marconi's breakthroughs into the mass medium of radio.)

Electronic media are based on fairly simple scientific principles but require expensive facilities and constant upgrading, mainly for competitive reasons. Most important media companies today have "gone public"; that is, issue stock on public exchanges where anyone can buy it. People willing to buy shares of stock, putting capital into a growing corporation, are crucial assets. In return, they receive voting power over corporate policy. Those with the most stock can become company directors, helping to make the biggest strategic decisions.

Throughout broadcasting, managers say that the mere knowledge that shareholders *exist* exerts tremendous influence today. Much of it is positive, through investments that lead to upgrading, but there's a long-simmering argument over the influence of investors and the profit motive on the *nature and quality* of media products. Some critics (and broadcasters) complain that shareholders, concerned about the value of their stocks, focus too much on efficiency and profits. By doing so, goes this critique, they pressure companies to lay off too many employees, slash production spending, cancel challenging programs, and otherwise compromise media quality.

The other side of this argument holds that commercial media always have been businesses first and cannot be expected to settle for inefficiency. Companies must be lean and productive to bring the public what it wants and needs. Everyone has a right to seek profits. Anyway, runs this line of defense, most shareholders simply hover in the background, hoping for financial gain as their dollars stimulate growth.

Sometimes there are apparent conflicts between private profit and public service. The Disney Company has been a target of criticism along this line. Disney's holdings

Wall Street. Trading in media stocks on the nation's financial exchanges affects the media's behavior. Shareholders want value and profits, placing demands that can lead to controversial steps to win audiences.

The Annual Meeting. A media corporation's yearly gathering of shareholders emphasizes their power to wield quiet influence over how broadcasters make decisions.

in 2000 included—by chief executive Michael Eisner's accounting—"seven theme parks (with four more in the works), 27 hotels with 36,888 rooms, two cruise ships, 728 Disney Stores, one television broadcast network, 10 television stations, 9 international Disney Channels, 42 radio stations, an Internet portal, 5 major Internet websites, interests in 9 U.S. cable networks," and more.[4]

In many respects, those widely varied leisure and media businesses help one another do business in ways that are both profitable to Disney and pleasing to society. However, among those on the corporation's megapayroll are the journalists of ABC News. They've been employees of the corporation since it acquired ABC in 1996. Some observers (including journalists) had misgivings about Mickey Mouse's entertainment empire buying a major news operation; they were concerned that corporate profit goals might influence journalistic performance. Soon, there were reports that, indeed, the network had suppressed some ABC stories that portrayed Disney negatively.

ABC denied misconduct, and the controversy died away. Today, advocates of public service over profit can find little comfort in a declaration at the corporate website: "Disney's overriding objective is to create *shareholder value* (italics added) by continuing to be the world's premier entertainment company from a creative, strategic, and financial standpoint."[5]

> **Principle #5**
>
> Consolidation increases broadcasting's dependence on approval from Wall Street investors.

Networks

NBC, CBS, and, later, ABC built much of American broadcasting. They long have made a business of producing or buying highly polished programming and broadcasting it to every corner of the country through local stations; in return, the

Katie Couric. This one-time local-TV reporter became a national sweetheart to morning TV audiences as co-host of NBC's *Today* show, signing a $15-million-a-year contract in 2002.

Monday Night Football. The savvy, often wisecracking announcers of *ABC's Monday Night Football* have been a long-term success—a rarity for a sports series in prime-time network TV.

Fin-Syn Financial Interest and Syndication Rules, which kept networks from profiting from production and sale of programs; abolished in 1995.

David Letterman. Late-night personality Letterman has brought amusement to viewers of more than one TV network.

stations granted the networks advertising time or revenue. For decades, simply gathering audiences to hear and watch satisfying shows drew enough advertising to create good business.

Now, however, the "Big Three" networks have company: Fox, the WB, UPN, and PAX all operate as networks, owning some stations and in affiliation with others. This upsurge of competition didn't happen overnight. Strong new competition and the aging of traditional audiences were eroding the traditional networks before the 1970s ended.

REGULATION'S TOLL

In those days, two FCC actions—known as the financial interest and syndication ("**fin-syn**") rules—were squeezing the networks hard. Both were intended to reduce the power of the networks to dictate programming and to profit unduly from it at the expense of its producers. The first rule prohibited networks from

PTAR The FCC's prime-time access rule, which limited network TV programming during high-viewership evening hours; abolished in 1996.

acquiring financial stakes in programs produced by others. The second rule barred networks from selling programs to local stations. This left many programs available for sale only in syndication, where others could reap profits from what the networks had created.

Another tether on the networks was the prime-time access rule (**PTAR**), which limited network programming to three hours a night during the four-hour prime-time period. Like the syndication rule, this encouraged stations to create or buy shows elsewhere. They did, and soon at least one hour every night in most cities featured inexpensive game or talk shows or other products from independent production companies.

These government limits substantially broke the big networks' choke-hold on what Americans could watch, helping to diversify TV content. The limits also badly damaged network profitability. Soon, new networks and cable TV grabbed viewers from the Big Three. Within a couple of years in the mid-1980s, ABC, CBS, and NBC were sold to or merged with richer companies. Sapped of strength, each one-time media giant had become little more than "an office building," in the assessment of media writer Ken Auletta.[6]

Auletta exaggerated: Each network still owned lucrative local stations and was affiliated with many more that would broadcast its programming. The Big Three maintained large business and production complexes in Los Angeles and New York. On the other hand, fin-syn had limited their power to make money, which would not satisfy the bottom-line–oriented corporations that bought them. So "downsizing" arrived: many rounds of cutbacks and layoffs in the interest of overall corporate efficiency.

ADAPTING TO A NEW AGE

Meanwhile, the networks were having increasing difficulty with their affiliated stations. In the 1990s, the two sectors squabbled over how revenues would be shared. However, 1995 brought the abolishment of the fin-syn rules, restoring to the networks some of their old leverage over programming. This came too late to prevent many new competitors from horning in on the marketplace.

The networks had not lost all their financial strength or their resilience, however—not even close, as is evident from today's financial statistics. NBC, for instance, despite a national advertising slowdown, reported fourth-quarter-2000 earnings of $476 million. (This contributed nicely to GE's record quarterly profit of $3.9 billion.[7]) On the other hand, the networks no longer rule alone at the summit of U.S. electronic media. Knowing this, they've moved rapidly to branch out, acquiring Internet outlets, forming alliances, and generally reinventing themselves to compete with new rivals.

ABC is interesting in the way it has blended its network geographic reach with the market efficiency of niche broadcasting. ABC News Radio, ABC Sports Radio, Radio Disney (for kids), ESPN Radio Network, the Paul Harvey "network"—testimony to a single commentator's following—all reach out to distinct audiences and thus to stations trying to reach them. This diverse national approach is not especially labor intensive in its program production; about 100 staffers at the network's New York headquarters, aided by affiliate

ProTalk

Chris Berry
Vice President, Radio, ABC News

"We have tremendous resources devoted to gathering information, and we can slice and dice it in new ways."

If Chris Berry has a problem, at least he needn't doubt that someone will listen to what he has to say. With a top network job, 3,500 radio affiliates across the United States and 100 employees near him at ABC's headquarters in New York, Berry rarely needs to plead for attention.

The scope of Berry's mission underscores the new competing interests found almost everywhere in the broadcast business. His domain covers several subnetworks, all, in his view, flourishing because they are "branded" as part of ABC News. "Our system reinforces the credibility and reliability of ABC News, but still enables us to provide differentiated stations in the same market," says Berry.

Dividing up customers at the local level is not a traditional network approach, but these are not traditional times. Networks must find revenue wherever they can and that means tapping new markets. ABC can and sometimes does target different audiences in the same town through services ranging from straight hourly newscasts to sports news to the broadcasts of Paul Harvey, who's spent half a century with ABC (see Figure 6.4).

"For instance, a country music station might not take our top-of-the-hour newscasts, but will be very interested in news that affects their audience," Berry says. ABC is developing an Internet-delivered radio service for affiliates; once a station has a password, it can "open" newscasts that arrived in digital form and put them on the air.

Berry arrived at the network after a management stint at the CBS-owned station in Chicago; radio is his only game. A normal work day finds him huddling with the New York editorial staff, phoning bureaus in Washington, Los Angeles, and Dallas, and calling stringers in overseas capitals such as London. Besides his wider news functions, he discusses specific news stories with correspondents, editors, and managers—and always makes room for the ever-growing business imperatives.

"Because we do have a very large affiliate base, and that ultimately is who we work for, I try to also keep in touch with those customers," Berry says. "I do make a lot of phone calls." His executive role also requires him to think about the future of broadcasting: "It will involve more convergence of resources. Radio has been around for 75 years and can a play a key role in that direction."

Obviously, this is not radio as it was in the days of large wooden cabinets, hushed living rooms, and the news from a World War II battlefront. Yet Chris Berry sees a future for radio at least as powerful as its past:

"We have tremendous resources devoted to gathering information, and we can slice and dice it in new ways. By combining the very personal nature of our medium with things such as the Internet and also new TV technology, we can provide our product to platforms no one's even dreamed of yet."

FIGURE 6.4
ABC Radio Networks

reporters and network correspondents, reach 3,500 stations with news around the clock. Promoting and selling its specialties as subnetworks, ABC keeps them closely tied to its long-popular national brand.

More than 600 affiliates of the Big Three charged the networks in 2001 with illegally bullying stations about programming and business decisions. The networks denied the charges and braced for what probably would become a power struggle in the courts or before the FCC. Competing for ever-smaller slices of the great media pie, networks and stations were ready to do battle—with one another if necessary. Many affiliates now acted through a newer and more powerful kind of organization: the station group.

Station Groups

We know their names from quick voice-tags that end the "station identification" messages every hour, or from graceful logos seen briefly on the TV screen: Belo, Citadel, Clear Channel, Cox, Emmis, Infinity, Jefferson-Pilot, Journal. These are companies licensed to own and operate radio or TV stations, and most of them don't seem very interested in public "brand" recognition. What little they need comes from their stations, pushing their call letters and slogans and newscasts, along with network programming and stars, to draw audiences and advertisers. A station typically sends much of its local revenue up the chain to the group that owns it.

THE TRADING GAME

It's a rich business—far richer now than before the 1980s, when changing regulatory and economic realities created more and more demand for broadcast properties (and thus, of course, higher prices for them). Television stations in particular drew attention; they long had been known as the "cash cows" of broadcasting, many of them milked for annual profits topping 30 to 40 percent and some as high as 50 percent.

Belo, a Texas-based media company, offers an example of the explosion of station trading that began as a Reagan-era FCC was starting to loosen ownership restrictions. Belo was born as a newspaper company but had launched the first network-affiliated radio station in Texas back in 1922. Even though Belo grew large in other ways, not much else in the way of broadcasting came into its fold until the 1980s. Then, in 1983, the company bought four medium/large-market TV stations in what for that period was a huge transaction. Under the FCC rules then, no one could own more than seven TV stations, so the company had to sell off two stations it already owned—but it wasn't about to stop expanding.

Belo sold some of its stock to raise capital, bought two big-city network affiliates in the early 1990s, then, in 1997, acquired the Providence Journal Company and with it eight more TV outlets. By 2002, Dallas-based Belo owned 19 TV stations and six cable news channels. Six of its stations are in top-20 markets that reach into millions of TV homes, plus its publishing enterprises, gave the company annual revenues of $1.5 *billion*.

dwarfs its competitors and results in profits no one else in radio can equal.

"It does drive the top line, the revenue line," Palmer says, "but I think the real key to our success is the fact that, now, with our overall presence, we cover the airwaves in all 50 states."

This means that an advertiser can gain maximum reach by making a single buy—that is, purchasing air time on multiple stations at once that will broadcast its message across entire regions and beyond. "So I could go to, say, Procter & Gamble in New York, and if they said, 'We want to reach the top 20 markets,' I could say, 'We can do it!' "

Clear Channel didn't exactly come out of nowhere, but close to it. In 1995, the San Antonio–based "station group" owned about 100 stations. The following year it had 173. That's when the 1996 Telecommunications Act lifted numerical limits on station ownership. By 2000, having bought companies including AMFM, Inc.—another radio mammoth, for which it paid $23.8 billion—Clear Channel had more than 1,000 stations. The company took in nearly 20 percent of the entire radio industry's revenue that year.[8] Growth continued into 2001.

"We're close to 1,200 stations," said Palmer—happily—as the first quarter of 2001 ended. By late in the year, he was happier: Clear Channel owned about 1,225 radio stations in the United States and had financial interests in 240 stations abroad.

ProTalk

Randy Palmer
Vice President, Clear Channel Communications

"And if they said, 'We want to reach the top 20 markets,' I could say, 'We can do it!' "

Randy Palmer spent years working on behalf of investors, managing mutual funds, but now his world has flipped: His job today is to *court* people with money to put into businesses. As vice president for investor relations at Clear Channel Communications, he's been at the vortex of some of the hottest financial action in broadcasting. Clear Channel is the country's largest owner of radio stations. That massive size

One industry insider decided to measure the effects of consolidation of station ownership in the mid-1990s, and came up with a startling result: Between 1994 and 1998, the number of owners of full-power commercial TV stations spiraled from 658 down to 425—a drop of more than one-third.[9] Radio stations have become especially ripe targets for consolidation of ownership. After many years when no one was permitted to own more than 40 stations, the 1996 Telecommunications Act repealed national ownership limits. Buyers were allowed to hold as many as eight stations in a local market. Within the next year, the total number of owners of U.S. radio stations dropped almost 12 percent as station groups new and old bought up all they could. For example, Citadel Communications Corporation, which owned 36 stations, in 1997 sold a million shares of its stock and bought 61 more.[10]

MOTIVES FOR GROWTH

Big groups got bigger, and even small groups strained to buy more stations, for a number of reasons, including these:

- The larger a station group becomes, the more it's able to reduce the average costs of doing business, a basic efficiency move.
- Acquiring many stations at different market levels, or in different geographic regions, allows a station to offer an advertiser a single buy that exposes her or his products or services to many audiences at once.
- When a recession hits or other events curtail advertising—the September 11th terrorist attacks had such an effect—the resulting financial stress can be spread over many stations or allocated to the most cash-rich family members.
- The more stations a group owns, the better able it is to negotiate the programming. An owner of many stations has much greater bargaining leverage against networks and syndication firms than the owner of only one or two stations has.

There can be other bonuses to bigness. Lucy Himstedt's TV station in Indiana is owned by Liberty Corporation, based in Greenville, South Carolina (see Figure 6.5). The company also owns 14 other network affiliates and also owns or controls a cable-advertising sales company, a video production house and a firm that sells broadcast equipment, as well as financial stakes in Internet-related companies. These companies can be resources for one another—for example, a

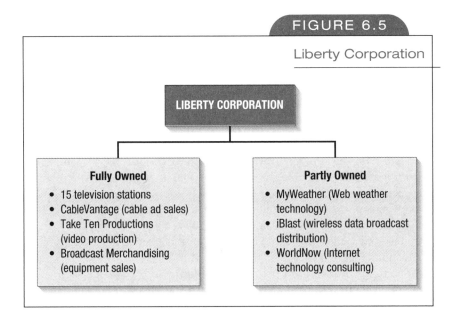

FIGURE 6.5

Liberty Corporation

LIBERTY CORPORATION

Fully Owned
- 15 television stations
- CableVantage (cable ad sales)
- Take Ten Productions (video production)
- Broadcast Merchandising (equipment sales)

Partly Owned
- MyWeather (Web weather technology)
- iBlast (wireless data broadcast distribution)
- WorldNow (Internet technology consulting)

Liberty station can buy gear from the Liberty equipment firm and the money stays in the family.

Despite their growth, some station groups have had to struggle to keep profits as high as shareholders want them. One reason is that, under FCC orders to convert gradually to high-definition TV (**HDTV**) technology, TV broadcasters have been forced to spend millions of dollars *per station*. Sinclair Broadcasting Group, owner of 62 TV stations, has had to refinance more than a billion dollars in loans to avoid defaulting on them.[11]

CONCERN FOR LOCALISM

Some critics accuse broadcasters of placing faraway owners' financial motives above the needs of local audiences. Certainly "localism" was a founding tenet of broadcasting, and some station groups maintain that they give their local managers freedom to serve their communities. However, business pressures on commercial stations appear to have eliminated most local programming except for newscasts—and have torpedoed some of those as well. Station groups also have provided the same programming to all of their members, which tends to homogenize on-air content from city to city.

The classic objection to station-group consolidation is that it reduces not only localism but *diversity*—not ethnic diversity in programming and on payrolls, but diversity of programming sources and thus of perspectives. Some critics say this results from putting too much broadcasting power in too few hands. At a Senate hearing, William Baker—an executive in *public* broadcasting—drove the point home:

> Six gigantic corporations control the vast majority of television, cable, radio, newspapers, magazines and the most popular Internet sites, and consequently, the majority of information, public discourse, and even artistic expression in the United States. We have on our hands what one might call a "merger epidemic" in the media industry. And like any other epidemic, this is an unhealthy one.[12]

Such warnings, however, have drawn rebuttals not just from industry but from the American government's top communications policymaker: FCC Chairman Michael Powell. A strong advocate of letting the marketplace dictate how the industry operates, Powell said electronic media never have been more diverse than they are now:

> Today, we've gone from three networks to seven—and nine if you count the Spanish-language networks. At the local station level we have a greater number of outlets than had ever existed before in both radio and television. Cable channel capacity, the average system in America, has 56 channels or more and passes 98 percent of the homes in the United States."[13]

What's more, Powell said, homeowner purchases of direct-broadcast-satellite (DBS) systems, with up to several hundred channels, are soaring—all of this guaranteeing diversity. At Powell's urging, the FCC moved to consider permitting more consolidation—by removing limits on newspaper-broadcasting cross-ownership and on the total percentage of homes that any company is allowed to

High-definition television (HDTV) New digital format offering exceptionally sharp pictures.

Sponsor Traditionally, advertiser who bears full cost of a program, gaining exclusive rights to commercial time, sometimes including advertiser's name in show title.

reach through all of its outlets. This would help some station groups grow larger, but others, ironically, voiced fears that *they* would be taken over—by networks.

Production Companies

This is a good point at which to consider production companies, an unsung but important sector of the electronic media that none of the other sectors can do without. Production companies that most of us rarely hear of (not the big-name networks) create most of the programming seen on television today. They literally build programming from the ground up, conceiving, shooting, editing, producing, and polishing the shows.

PIONEERING TV

Although megacorporations own some production studios today, the traditional mode, responsible for most TV programming over the past half century, is to contract with an *independent* production firm. Starting as TV first entered U.S. homes in the 1940s and 1950s, independent companies—often paid by **sponsors** (advertisers who financed entire programs)—created many important shows for the fledgling TV networks. One series, *Dragnet*, began at a company owned by its star, Jack Webb, who sold the program in 1949 to NBC Radio and later to television.[14] The classic comedy *I Love Lucy* premiered in 1951, starring Lucille Ball and her husband Desi Arnaz; again, the stars owned the production company (Desilu).

Independent producers eventually came to play an even larger role in our entertainment media, largely because of the FCC's fin-syn rules, imposed in 1971. These restraints on network control of programming created big opportunities for production companies, and soon they were mushrooming, selling completed shows to networks and to cable television. By the time the fin-syn rules were lifted in 1995, many companies were healthy and, thanks to the proliferation of cable and other nonnetwork programmers, had developed a broad customer base. Today, some production firms are so diversified that they lack only broadcast stations to get their products on the air—and, if they've become part of a huge media conglomerate, they may even have stations.

Among the success stories is Carsey-Werner-Mandabach, founded independently by two creative wizards who created 1970s–1980s ABC hit series such as *Happy Days*, *Taxi*, and *Mork & Mindy*. The company now markets the shows it produces to networks and stations globally, while investing in new ventures. Another example is the Jim Henson Company; it produces TV series and specials featuring the famous and child-friendly Muppets and also creates science-fiction programs for older audiences, selling the shows to broadcasters globally. Moreover, the Henson company has enough capacity left over to produce commercials for nonmedia clients.

This is not unusual: Having invested in expensive equipment and technical talent, a production company needs to fill in its work gaps with any income-generating projects that may be available. There is more and more demand for advanced computer skills, too, as "special effects" are needed and as HDTV looms on the horizon.

NEW OPPORTUNITY

Some companies offer not just conventional production expertise but **multimedia** design work—digitally combining audio, video, and other media—that may show up on the World Wide Web or perhaps on hybrid computer/television screens. Besides creating major TV programs, even some of the largest firms rent out their skills and facilities to nonbroadcast businesses for special projects. Disney's production arm offers moviemakers their choice of seven big stages—a synthetic business street or Western town, for example—and dozens of services.

To the aspiring electronic-media professional, it's not the huge, Hollywood-focused production companies that offer the most personal opportunity; rather, it's the medium-to-small companies scattered not only throughout Los Angeles and New York but across the continent. The smallest (look up some in your town's telephone directory) may do good business by serving short lists of customers—from area broadcast stations to nearby manufacturing plants or even used-car sales managers who want commercials taped.

In the middle range of size, companies can take on more ambitious productions. Their staffing may start with managers who prowl for business and work with creative specialists who come up with sharp program concepts and write scripts to bring them to life. There may be producers to oversee field and studio work, videographers, music specialists, graphics experts, sound designers, animation wizards, and other critical support players. Some survive as free-lancers, available to companies that can't afford to keep these specialties on their payrolls full time.

Production companies hire the most talented and ambitious (though not necessarily in that order), including new graduates. Some offer internships to students. The experience to be gained can be transferred easily to bigger production arenas or translated to other electronic-media fields.

Multimedia Computer-based presentation of integrated media; can combine text, audio, video, animation, and graphics.

THE LOCAL PICTURE

Little of what local broadcasters do every day is directly related to the organization of the industry. Using whatever resources they command, managers generally try to "fly below the radar" of large corporate concerns and keep their audiences and advertisers satisfied. Besides being practical, that's a safe strategy for advancement to the upper reaches of the business.

Like Lucy Himstedt of WFIE-TV, most local broadcasters organize their forces and facilities tightly while spending only what it takes to do so. This generally means fairly small payrolls. Even in flush times, broadcasting does not have—and never has had—a large "rank and file" by the standards of other major industries. The government found

> **Principle #6**
> Because of its technologies, broadcasting generally is more capital intensive than labor intensive.

TABLE 6.1

U.S. Broadcast Jobs, 1998–2008 (in thousands)

	1998	% OF TOTAL	EST. CHANGE, 1998–2008
Announcers	44	17.9	–6.7
Actors, directors, producers	22	8.8	+19.9
On-air news personnel	19	7.6	+4.7
Photo/camera workers	14	5.8	+19.3
Writers and editors	6	2.4	+4.7
Sales workers	29	11.7	+4.7
Top managers/ executives	9	3.6	+1.6
Ad/market/ sales managers	5	2.1	+4.7
Technicians	23	9.2	–5.8
Administrative support	27	10.8	–5.7

Source: Bureau of Labor Statistics, 2001.

close to a quarter-million broadcast jobs existing nationwide around the end of the twentieth century. That's fewer jobs than in mortgage banking, fewer than in oil and gas extraction, and about one-tenth as many jobs as in U.S. department stores![15] A few thousand jobs are at major networks, but most are at local stations. A revealing statistic: More than 60 percent of all U.S. broadcast positions are in operations with 50 employees or more—toward the upper reaches of station size.[16] It's only in markets big enough to support numerous newscasts every day that a station needs a sizable work force (see Table 6.1).

Radio

Big or little, radio stations are inherently powerful instruments of communication, with important roles to serve in their communities. They may produce hours of daily "drive-time" music and talk shows and cover news across a vast metropolitan canvas. They can bring tailored programming to targeted audiences, such as talk shows for homemakers and rock music for teens. They can steer mass audiences by providing traffic alerts, air-pollution warnings, weather bulletins, and disaster reporting. They can wage editorial campaigns or provide air time to interest groups.

MANAGERIAL FUNCTIONS

Almost any radio station must have a leader, a *general manager* or *station manager* who supervises the operation. This person plans the broadcast day (often a 24-hour "day"), lays out an overall budget based on available or projected revenue, oversees all personnel, and finds ways to establish or enhance a public image for the station. Whether running a large-market organization of 50 workers or a tiny-market team of 5 (or even fewer), the top manager bears ultimate responsibility and sometimes fills several key roles.

The larger the station, the wider and deeper the array of management tasks and the greater the need to hire "middle" managers. Each must take on one or more key functions (see Figure 6.6):

- *Programming:* The construction of a schedule of programs is carefully fashioned to attract the largest and most desirable audiences. The programming manager not only designs the lineup but must oversee the production

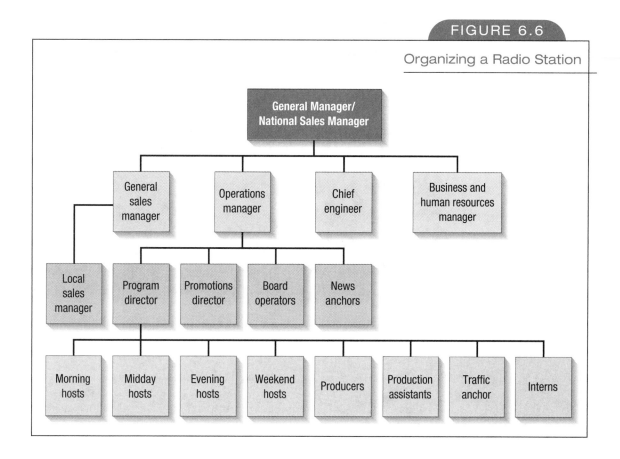

FIGURE 6.6

Organizing a Radio Station

of local shows and the acquisition of other shows from outside producers. Some general managers, keenly aware of their responsibility to make the business profitable, like to do their own programming.

- *Advertising Sales:* This function involves pursuing clients from among local or regional businesses that need (but don't always know they need) radio advertising to recruit customers. Once, the objective was to reach the largest audience; now, numbers remain important but demographic factors (age, gender, etc.) have grown more important as clients go after specific audience groups. Sales work is more complex as a result; even so, sales managers in smaller stations often have skeleton staffs and must do much of the time-selling themselves.
- *Business Affairs:* Monitoring and guiding where the money goes is the responsibility of the business manager. He or she controls or heavily influences the investment of precious revenue in station equipment and personnel—a fact that may put the manager at odds with department heads, but that also prepares him or her to move up to general management.

Radio Staffs. Economic pressures in the 1990s and early 2000s led radio stations to slash their workforce and increase their automation in efforts to cut losses.

- *Engineering:* The engineering manager maintains, upgrades, and operates all of a station's critical electronic systems. This is the heart of station operations. The engineering manager (or chief engineer) monitors all transmissions to be sure they meet the standards required by federal regulators, and thus safeguard's the station's license to operate. This manager knows the equipment and facilities intimately and always is brought into discussions of station design and expansion.

- *Human Resources:* This function involves recruiting and screening new employees as well as administering pay, benefits, company discipline, and the orderly departures of employees who leave. However, "HR" managers generally are excluded from hiring and firing key on-air "talent"; general managers and news directors handle that.

- *News:* The news director is responsible for the origination (or at least relay) of news reports and other important information for local listeners. News is the primary and sometimes only station department that generates content locally. Besides routine news reports, the news director arranges for critical traffic and weather alerts that can ease local emergencies. In many smaller stations, this manager is a news staff of one and takes on non-news duties as well.

- *Production:* This area usually involves the creation of local audio material that is not produced by the news department, which can include commercials, station promotion spots, and coverage of special (but non-news) events such as religious ceremonies or telethons. In addition, the production unit may be a valuable resource pool for general station use.

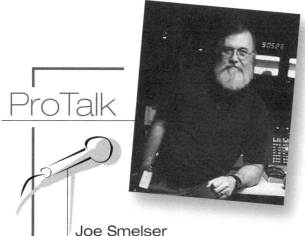

ProTalk

Joe Smelser
Broadcast Operations Manager, Chambers Communications

"It's been my life, and if I can take a fraction of the technology and the creativity I've learned and pass it on, I want to do that."

When Joe Smelser was a small boy, he played with building blocks. He believes now that they may have started him on a lifelong creative track that would include plenty of building. He has built television programs, production systems, and a 35-year career in broadcasting. He's now broadcast operations manager for Chambers Communications, a Eugene, Oregon, company that operates an ABC television affiliate and also does large productions of its own.

"I've seen television change in major ways three different times," Smelser recalls. "It changed from black and white to color, from film to video—with all that portability in the equipment—and now it's changing from analog to digital."

That's a pleasant experience arc for a man who recalls visiting a TV station for the first time when he was 5 or 6 years old and TV was still pretty new. He

was in Iowa, and it was at KWWL in Waterloo that Smelser later entered the business, in 1966. His job: projectionist—a specialty that vanished when TV stopped using film. He remembers the "film islands," where the bulky equipment stood, and the first video-tape he ever rolled. It was two inches wide.

The variety of his duties in the early years kept Smelser interested and soon broadened his skills. He handled zoomless Dumont studio cameras, ran commercials during basketball games, and worked the audio booth. The first real show he staffed was the local version of a classic children's program, *Romper Room*, with "Miss Bonnie." He went on to Peoria, Illinois, for 11 years as a TV production manager, after which he moved to Chambers in Eugene, where he's spent the past 23 years.

Smelser helped develop the Oregon Sports Network, which shoots and widely distributes University of Oregon games, and now is involved with DuckVision, which remotely switches among four stadium cameras over a fiber-optic cable system. He also has made or supervised "countless" commercials for the Chambers sales department. And he has kept a wary eye on developments in the industry.

"Because of the cost of programming," he notes, "our network 'comp' [compensation for running ABC shows] has been dwindling. It used to be that we'd be paid. Now the networks are pushing stations to pay for programming." That ping-pong relationship with networks is one of the reasons stations have sought other programming sources.

That's among the lessons Smelser carries into a studio at the University of Oregon where he teaches production classes. It's in the studio that he seems to flash back to the kid in Iowa, stumbling wide-eyed through a real TV station.

"It's been my life," says Smelser, "and if I can take a fraction of the technology and the creativity I've learned and pass it on, I want to do that."

THE RANK AND FILE

Personnel calculations were simpler when radio began: Working *alone*, an engineer in 1919 transmitted recorded music from his Pennsylvania garage. The subsequent rise of the medium nationally created demand for thousands of writers, performers, announcers, and technicians that lasted, largely undisturbed, well past mid-century. However, the 1980s brought industry reorganization and shrinkage of all sorts. Local broadcasters found ways to import much more content and automate many functions. This allowed them to reduce their staffs. Actions by the FCC virtually eliminated the need to do unprofitable public-service programs. U.S. local radio fairly rapidly became what it is today: a giant web of stations, most of which have absentee owners and drum-tight payrolls.

Television

The picture, so to speak, is somewhat different for television. Because its technologies are more numerous and complex and its projects are visual, TV almost always needs larger staffs than radio ever did. Still, its basic organization is roughly analogous to that of radio.

MANAGERIAL FUNCTIONS

Today, almost every TV station has a *general manager* to deal with owners, monitor the station's profitability, and make decisions about long-term projects, alliances, and business strategies. Many a station today, however, gets along without a traditional number-two person, the *station manager,* charged with shoring up community support of the license and providing day-to-day oversight of operations.

The station still needs its *business manager,* who, sometimes with a small staff, supervises the flow of spending and revenue. This person's targets often include major equipment purchases and upgrades, which may become bones of contention as technologies change and departments wrestle with tight budgets. There's a *sales manager* to keep advertising revenue flowing in. Sometimes, in fact, there are two managers: One for the sale of local or regional commercial time and the other for the sale of commercials to run in national programming, although that is often handled by a national account representative. In some cases, a *general sales manager* will oversee both areas. Sales, being the station's primary revenue source, usually gets the personnel it requires.

The management corps also might enlist a *community affairs director* to polish the station's local image. It almost invariably includes a *news director* to steer the coverage of daily local events. A *program director* usually is in place to locate and acquire programming from many sources, although some general managers do much of this work. The *production manager* guides technical operations with skilled assistance from the *chief engineer,* all the way to the final step in television work—transmission.

The promotion track for these managers varies widely. Sales managers, being the hunter-gatherers of station revenues and thus essential to the business, often seek to become general managers; many current "GMs" began their careers in sales. News directors generally have backgrounds as journalists but increasingly have had broader executive training, preparing them for general management. A chief engineer primarily must have talent and experience in designing, running, and trouble-shooting highly complex electronic systems. Without business or management training or experience, such technical experts find it difficult to ascend to the top station jobs.

THE RANK AND FILE

Most managers have not only important tasks but other people to help execute those tasks. In television, that means a wide assortment of professionals. It's mainly among their ranks that the action—and opportunities—can be found, and mainly in news. That's because, in most cities today, news is virtually the only locally generated programming; other forms proved too costly for the ratings they received.

From a business standpoint, as outlined earlier in this chapter, there are lots of reasons *not* to hire. One is pressure for profits. By the mid-1990s, fully three-fourths of the TV stations in the top 100 U.S. markets were owned by station groups.[17] Most general managers today know that corporate officers are, or might be, constantly looking over their shoulders. This tends to hold down all but truly necessary hiring.

Payrolls could shrink even further as advances in digital technology enable smaller teams to produce TV content. Already reporters at some stations edit tape at their desktops rather than handing it off to specialized editors. The industry can be counted on to keep developing ways of operating that will require fewer paychecks.

Access

Members of ethnic minorities and, to a lesser extent, women still face the greatest challenge getting full value from their broadcast careers. Studies consistently show that their hiring, pay, and promotion opportunities are significantly lower than those afforded to men. In a further setback to these disadvantaged workers, a federal appeals court ruled in 2000 that FCC actions to promote the hiring of women and minorities were unconstitutional.

The National Association for the Advancement of Colored People put heavy pressure on TV in 2001, using new survey figures to assert that the electronic media hire too few blacks (on screen and off) and give them too little authority in those positions. The NAACP threatened a boycott against at least one network, but did not immediately take such action.

Hopes of *ownership* of broadcast stations by minority members seem almost to have been swamped by broadcasting's trend toward bigger and bigger companies. One federal study in 2000 found that only 3.8 percent of commercial-station licenses were held by minority citizens, mostly in radio. Most of that tiny group were single-station owners. This means they face a disadvantage competing for financing and revenue against larger station groups and they have less than an equal crack at success.[18] Minority ownership figures have barely crept up from year to year.

Minority Workers. Electronic media employ relatively few members of ethnic minorities; some critics say that limits not only career opportunities but also the diversity of broadcast programming.

In December 2000, shortly before leaving office, FCC Chairman William Kennard urged the commission and Congress to put more effort and funding into lowering barriers to ownership for women and minorities. There was no immediate sign that major change of any kind for minorities was on the horizon, given recent court rulings against the FCC's policy. The new chairman, Michael Powell, introduced a new policy for hiring minorities (discussed in Chapter 14).

INTO THE FUTURE

Federal forecasters say employment in broadcasting probably will rise very little—less than 2 percent—by 2008,[19] although many jobs that managers consider expendable will be eliminated. If that holds true, blame will fall on the usual suspects: consolidation and new technologies that need less human participation and competition from other media that continue to place the bottom line first. Nonbroadcast media may become major job markets in their own right.

New Audience Paths

Forecasters at the media research company Veronis Suhler Stevenson predict that Americans will turn increasingly to electronic *diversions* that don't quite constitute "media." For example, the time people spend on video games—not a medium, as such, but perhaps a natural rival to TV—is expected to expand faster than time spent in any other media category. More significant is a forecast that time spent with direct *consumer*-supported media (cable and satellite TV, the Internet, recorded music, etc.) will rise by 29 percent in the 1999–2004 period, whereas time spent with *advertiser*-supported media (broadcast, newspapers, magazines) will remain flat.[20] That revolution in national habits evidently is under way now.

A big plus for broadcasters, Veronis Suhler Stevenson says, may be the arrival of digital opportunities to provide new services. One, just emerging, involves transmitting data to business clients over the additional channels granted to broadcasters in return for their conversion to HDTV.

Media Prospects

One way to begin gauging a future electronic-media industry is to consider what's already here or coming soon. Its variety, along with obvious possibilities for connecting and combining media forms, helps explain the merger and integration moves we see today and will see tomorrow:

■ The Internet has home-grown news and entertainment media as well as products from the broadcast networks (MSNBC, etc.), reaching new kinds of viewers/listeners/users.

- Broadcast stations still offer a constantly churning variety of programming (mostly sent to homes via cable systems) and have the strongest identities *locally*, where all consumers dwell.
- Digital TV's dazzling pictures and new screen shape (with a 16:9 width-to-height ratio, compared with today's 4:3) soon may alter the basic viewing experience.
- Interactive TV, now in limited use, is likely to spread as an adjunct to digital sets, providing not only video on demand but other services as demand grows.
- Cable television continues to show programming power, buying syndicated shows, offering all-news channels, and receiving premium movies via satellite; its potential as a media partner is huge.
- Satellite TV has become powerful by helping people watch local stations without cable, presenting alternative programming, and linking the U.S. media to valuable international material.

CAREER FOCUS

Electronic-media payrolls aren't growing as they did in earlier decades, but employers still search constantly for talented people—especially multiskilled types. Applicants who can perform conventional broadcast tasks and also are fluent at different technologies and varieties of programming are especially valued.

In smaller broadcast markets, one employee may be asked to do many different tasks in the course of a day. Even large stations and networks are being forced to do more with less. Still, some basic job descriptions remain, and can be targeted in high school training and in college, vocational schools, and internships. Here are a few of the opportunities available at the local level—and do bear in mind that a small radio station will have only a few of them.

Engineers(radio/TV) are licensed technical wizards who keep multimillion-dollar equipment focused, calibrated, aimed, and humming, as well as run live "remotes" for special events or news. (Without one or more broadcast engineers involved, radio and television don't happen.)

Control room personnel (mainly TV) include the director—a person miraculously capable of translating simultaneous streams of information and organizing them instantly—and his or her "crew," trained in audio, video, and graphics control and in how to carry out in

fractions of seconds every command the director issues. **Studio personnel (TV)** are the floor directors and camera operators who spruce up anchors and hosts, line up "shots" with seasoned precision, and maintain calm in the studio when chaos breaks out in the control room. **Advertising sales representatives(radio/TV)** seek out clients, persuade them to advertise, and help to place the resulting commercials in or around programs that attract potential customers.

Videographers (TV) are photographers and video editors who work on news, special programs, and commercials. **Producers (radio/TV)** are those who conceive, organize, and write newscasts and other local programming (if any), plus commercials.

Reporters (radio/TV) are the broadcast journalists who dig up news, write stories and edit them or supervise their editing, and present them on air. **Newsroom personnel (radio/TV)** include assignment editors, news planners, associate producers, writers, assistants, and, often, helpful interns from nearby colleges. **Administrative/clerical workers (radio/TV)** range from secretaries to accountants, from production assistants to traffic (ad-scheduling) clerks, from maintenance employees to news librarians, from security guards to drivers.

Convergence Joining or blending of older media forms with new, as when TV or radio pass through the Internet or a computer is used to edit animations digitally.

Beyond these obvious opportunities for electronic-media business lie satellite radio, a pay-to-hear medium offering uninterrupted music to cross-country motorists. Other digital forms of radio should lead to many more program sources and Internet channels, and extensions of the personal video recorders (PVR) now help viewers manipulate TV shows and eliminate commercials. Most near-future innovations, even in "conventional" broadcasting, probably will be digital at least in part; it's the key to multiplying applications—and profits—in an age underpinned by computers.

Summary

Like most U.S. industries, broadcasting for many decades had a stable structure within which predictable sets of employees did their work. Today, competitive pressures, new technologies, and financial strains are prompting massive industry change. Within it, broadcast employees do much of what they've always done, but often more rapidly and under heavier corporate pressure to perform efficiently and to adapt their products to new media. Shareholders gradually raise their profit demands, forcing networks and station groups to look for efficiencies such as common programming that can be purchased once and used by many stations in a system. Some of these shifts will help divert money and energy into quality broadcasting.

As federal deregulation proceeds, making it easier for companies to corner the market on entire categories of content, the trend toward concentration of ownership continues. Broadcasters still hire most of the same kinds of specialists they have always hired, but in smaller numbers and with a premium on versatility. The most successful job seekers will be those with college degrees or advanced training. The sophistication of today's radio or television station demands knowledge and flexibility—one reason that internships are a virtual necessity for some specialties. Another reason is that, amid media turbulence, no media worker—except perhaps the creator of content who can adapt to new forms—has a lock on lasting employment.

Industry growth for the next few years is projected to be slow, partly because ad revenues dropped sharply in 2000–2001 but also because consolidation is rampant and will swallow some current companies. However, the media can be counted on to expand their reach into American lives. Technological breakthroughs and "synergies" may generate frequent changes in media and in audience habits. Video streaming has already brought television to the Internet; it's displayed so far in less-than-perfect form, but much smoother systems for integrating old media into new are being developed.

This general process is called **convergence.** Still a buzzword today, the term probably represents much of the media's near future—the interweaving of broadcast, Internet-based, and even print media in ways that make more formats available to more people.

FOOD FOR THOUGHT

1. Is it reasonable to expect broadcasters to balance the profit motive against their public-service obligations? Evaluate arguments on both sides of the issue.
2. The FCC has worked to deregulate electronic media for the past two decades. Should it take a different approach? Explain your answer.
3. If you could buy a large share of stock in one electronic-media company, which one would you choose, and why?
4. Does it matter that most of us get our daily news from electronic-media units of big media corporations? Argue your case.

7

Programming and Distribution

Television is a gold goose that lays scrambled eggs; and it is futile and probably fatal to beat it for not laying caviar.

—Lee Loevinger, FCC Commissioner, 1963–1968

It's not true that I had nothing on. I had the radio on.

—Marilyn Monroe, Movie Star

Oprah. Wealthiest, most popular, most powerful—superlatives gravitated to Oprah Winfrey as she came to dominate talk-show TV and run many other ventures.

We can begin to study the aspect of electronic media most important to ordinary people—the **content**—through a true story. A veteran TV executive remembers one season years ago when a rather light-hearted experiment blew up in his face. His story involves movies, so let's "watch" it unreel:

The Time: The 1980s.

The Setting: A television station in New York—then, as now, the country's largest broadcast **market** (meaning ad-sales area, usually a city).

The Situation: "We had a 3 o'clock movie in those days, coming out of *The Guiding Light* (a long-running soap opera), and bridging right into the news, which started at 5:00 P.M. One summer we thought, 'There are a lot of kids home during the day right now, so maybe we should do some 3 o'clock movies for them.' "

The Wrinkle: "We happened to have some really bad black-and-white movies. They were like *Godzilla*, only not as good. They were sub-*Godzilla.* . . . So for a week, in that 3 P.M. movie slot, we held 'Mothra Week.' ["Mothra" was a low-budget Japanese mechanical monster.] We had those movies on every day."

The Climax: "Kids watched . . ."

The Twist: " . . . but we drove the 5 o'clock news right into the [ratings] tank."

It was just one week, but it had everyone howling: Youngsters in squirming delight at the appearance of Mothra, adults in dismay, and a station staff in pain over the sudden shrinkage of its postmovie news audience. At least it yielded a lesson.

The Lesson: "You have to work in the *flow* of what the **programming** is, of what the **demographics** are. . . . The key is adults 25 to 54. . . . You want to try to build a consistency."

Translation: Commercial broadcasters serve themselves and their advertisers best by building relationships with target audiences, and ill-conceived experiments can disrupt those cozy ties.

> Commercial broadcasters serve themselves and their advertisers best by building relationships with target audiences.

Content Catch-all term for all kinds of programming; often used to suggest need for a *quantity* of material, not specific qualities.

Market Community of potential customers for broadcast advertisers.

Programming The science and process of creating, acquiring, and/or arranging programs to serve the needs of a broadcast or cable outlet.

Demographics Key audience characteristics, such as age, gender, income level and ethnicity; knowing these factors helps programmers design daily schedules.

Horror stories like "Mothra Week" still occur occasionally at **networks** and at stations across the country, but not often. That's because, although the creation of programs themselves may amount to art, electronic-media programming—the selection and scheduling of content—usually is more like a developing *science* in support of a strategy. This chapter will examine programming and the ideas and forces behind it. It will also describe the distribution system, invisible to most of us, that keeps the content flowing from its sources to us— and that seems to give some programs eternal life.

WHAT PROGRAMS ARE

All electronic-media programming serves the purposes of media companies, and some of it goes beyond their immediate interests. In the course of a day—even a single hour—radio, television, and even the Internet can be undemanding roommates, amusing guests, sympathetic friends, and more. Studies have shown that families of air-crash victims find solace in watching TV coverage of the fatal events. The opposite can occur, as well. On September 11, 2001, almost before the terrible noise of the World Trade Center's collapse had died away, television executives were removing violent dramas from their program schedules to avoid upsetting viewers. Within a few weeks, most people seemed to be returning to their previous viewing habits. By December, movies with plots involving terrorism were starting to reappear. Recognition of television's potential effects on us had changed programming; awareness that we were ready to move toward our normal patterns changed it back.

Programming usually does not require such high levels of sensitivity. Nor is the production of a program always costly or complex. News dispatches yanked from a computer feed can become a short radio program with relatively little work or investment, much as they could in the mid-1900s. The spontaneous horseplay of teenagers caught by a roving camera can occupy half an hour on cable TV. Staging and scripting are not characteristic of all successful shows. Practically anything interesting could be program material. What will "work" with an audience at any time is the paramount question. Programmers try desperately to answer it correctly.

Networks ("Nets") Companies owning or affiliated with broadcast stations and supplying them with major programming.

> **Principle #2**
>
> Anything *interesting* could be program material.

Format Usually, a radio station's framework for broadcasting material geared to a target audience (e.g., the country format or Spanish-language format).

Radio

Most radio today presents a rather sparse menu of programs, measured against the rich diversity of its past. Between the 1920s and the 1950s, every sort of public spectacle, industrial announcement, musical performance, vaudeville act, moral/religious lecture, drama, suspense or adventure series, newscast, documentary, esoteric chat, and government information project seemed to make its way onto the airwaves. Properly timed and presented, almost any sort of radio program seemed to find an audience. As networks signed contracts with stage and movie stars, some of the biggest names in entertainment became huge names; other performers gained their first popularity from radio. News, sports, celebrity, and the intimacy of local voices brought the medium popularity with almost every age group.

Later, when television began sweeping the country a few years after World War II ended, commercial radio was financially threatened. It began to narrow its range of offerings to what its managers could do best and with the greatest commercial results. Today, great variety can still be found on the airwaves, but the majority of stations emphasize only a few program types.

MUSIC

Most radio today is built around recorded music, which means that musicians, producers, and audio engineers are its primary contributors. It's their creative products that draw most listeners, especially young ones, to radio and that begin to forge station-audience relationships. Although most never meet the people who make records, broadcasters depend heavily on their work. Similarly, record producers and distributors see broadcasting as one (often the most important) element in a comprehensive strategy for success. Without radio, the cheapest and most ubiquitous consumer medium, a large share of the music that hits the market annually would be virtually unknown and thus unheard.

Music accounts for most FM-radio programming and is found on AM stations, as well—all of it recorded except for the occasional radio-studio performance or live concert. Radio has divided music into dozens of well-defined types. It often turns one music type into a **format**—a programming framework that becomes a public signature for the station that adopts it, automatically drawing some listeners and providing a platform for promotion (see Table 7.1).

TABLE 7.1

Some Radio Music Formats

Adult Contemporary	Album-Oriented Rock
Beautiful Music	Classical
Classic Rock	Contemporary Hit Radio
Country	Dance
Easy Listening	Ethnic
Nostalgia	Oldies
Religious	Rock
Smooth Jazz	Standards
Urban Adult	Vintage

TALK

Apart from music, radio makes greatest use of people who talk on the air, attracting and engaging listeners who call in to comment. Launched widely in the 1960s but not a national phenomenon until the 1980s, talk radio dominates AM and ranks only behind music in drawing listeners to radio—partly because *their* comments get air time, too.

The hosts create radio content simply by doing some research, forming views, opening their microphones, and answering the phones. The more popular commentator-hosts are not only interesting but also controversial—Rush Limbaugh, G. Gordon Liddy, Dr. Laura Schlessinger, and raunchy humorist Howard Stern, for example. Still others are authorities in matters of personal or family concern to listeners: investing, health, spirituality, parenting, and so on. A few focus on fringe issues, such as debates about UFOs, a specialty of host Art Bell. Besides the national talkers, news/talk stations in major and middle-sized U.S. cities often air call-in programs of their own.

NEWS/INFORMATION

Complementing and fueling talk radio, news/information programs encompass all-news programming as well as newscasts within other formats. This category descended from the origins of U.S. radio and has been a vital link for listeners through the reporting of major historical events. Although stations wrap it into a package with talk in creating "news/talk" formats, news has a key distinction: It typically is free of overt opinion (other than what newsmakers say), restricted instead to delivering what journalists regard as a neutral presentation of current events. This may reduce its entertainment value but secures its status as public-service programming, something for which broadcasters are required to allocate air time. Thus, we can distinguish hourly newscasts from the discussions led by talkers such as Tom Leykis and Don Imus.

Local stations have sharply reduced their own news and locally produced information programs under financial pressure from radio's corporate owners. Some still make significant efforts: A number of big-city stations have all-news formats, and rural America boasts outlets such as WKAN-AM in Kankakee, Illinois, which airs nine newscasts a day and has a staff of news and agribusiness reporters. Overall, however, commercial radio seems to have yielded a measure of news supremacy to public radio. In that not-for-profit realm, we find in-depth reporting, documentaries, and offbeat information-essay programs such as "This American Life."

> **Principle #3**
>
> Broadcast news is free of overt opinion, and that secures its position as public-service programming.

SPORTS

Network and local radio carries all major professional and college sports, and "sports talk" has filled many hours in radio since the 1980s. Athletic competition remains a huge draw to male audiences. In today's commercialized sports environment, broadcasting brings in big ad revenues and—through contracts between stations or networks and the teams—returns some of it to amateur and professional franchises. Money that remains with broadcasters can be invested in future coverage, which often is promoted within the sports news/talk shows produced by ESPN and similar companies. This cooperative apparatus keeps this radio genre thriving and has spawned some all-sports stations, such as Detroit's Sports Radio 1130 AM (The Fan) and Los Angeles's Fox Sports 1150 AM.

Syndication Process, or marketplace, in which programs are "sold" (actually rented) to broadcast or cable companies for original use or reuse.

Television

At first, television didn't have to spread a smorgasbord of programs before its viewers. Some people were so excited just to have the new medium available that they would sit and watch the "test patterns" left on the screen between shows. Within a few years, though, TV programs ranged from civic conversations to soap operas to prime-time comedies to music to boxing matches to broadcasts of challenging plays. Today, purely in terms of programs available to watch, television is more diverse than in any previous time. New networks and hundreds of cable channels provide hundreds of shows a day, many of which never would be scheduled by over-the-air stations. At the same time, there's a constant countertrend: Competition has created a "copycat" environment. A TV network or station that sees a hit emerging on another channel is tempted to imitate the newcomer, and may drop one or more of its existing programs to make room. The effect of that, of course, is to *reduce* diversity.

> **Principle #4**
>
> **Program diversity works until one channel rushes to imitate another's hit show—thus reducing diversity.**

What once was simply the movie industry now is the leading maker of prime-time TV content. Its studios and production houses crank out thousands of hours a year of network shows and cable "originals." These producers also license programming—often former network hits—in an open market called **syndication** that helps fill many program slots every week across the United States.

The X-Files. With its blend of spooky events, paranoid chills, and star chemistry, this Fox series is headed for a long future on cable and overseas channels.

DRAMATIC SERIES

Some of the most popular programs in *prime time*, the viewer-heavy period from 8:00 to 11:00 P.M., are tautly scripted and elegantly produced stories. They depict ordinary people, families, public-safety officers or care-giving professionals facing life's challenges. Television revenues often get into this enterprise early. By the time a production is clearly conceived and at least partially planned, producers are meeting with electronic-media companies, setting up deals. Those involving a new high-budget show usually call for a "pilot," a test episode to help broadcasters gauge a new program's potential appeal. Even if enough appeal is established, the show still can do fabulously well, adequately, or poorly.

Behind the original network and cable series are inventive writer-producers. Many have their own companies and work under contract to the networks. All have developed ways of striking chords in television

David E. Kelley. A highly successful writer-producer of TV series, Kelley specializes in legal themes, often dramatizing situations where the law doesn't seem to work.

Sitcom Situation comedy (i.e., a comedy series with continuing characters, settings, and/or themes).

Licensing Sale of broadcast rights to a program, usually for a fixed period or number of showings.

viewers. Chris Carter, creator of the *The X-Files*, *Millennium*, and other spooky-realistic series, taps into apocalyptic lore from The Holy Bible. "There's lots of good stuff in there," Carter told an interviewer.[1] David E. Kelley (*Ally McBeal*, *The Practice*), said he portrays the legal system by noting what is absent, not what is present: "We take the law and we say, 'OK, as a general rule it works, but how about those individual equations where it doesn't?' "[2] By playing off real life, creators of prime-time television programs hold us in thrall.

SITUATION COMEDIES

Situation comedies get their name from the reassuring continuity of the situations in which their characters live, coping comically with problems and one another. Almost any situation can be harvested for laughs. Dating back to the 1940s–1950s series such as *The Goldbergs*, *Life with Luigi*, and *The Life of Riley*, "**sitcoms**" have been a staple of television's popularity and growth. Almost all are at a compact half-hour length and thus useful in many schedule slots. Some plots and styles become dated, yet many hold up well over time—perhaps due to their reliance on family roles (traditional and nontraditional) as well as their nostalgic power over viewers—an important factor in today's broadcast marketplace. Scores of sitcoms circulate through rerun seasons on cable channels and local stations for years after their network runs. They have far greater staying power than do dramas.

MOVIES

Hollywood creates feature-length productions specifically for TV, and also earns billions from the sale (or **licensing,** a sort of rental) of its theatrical movies to television. Movies still emerge from studios that have survived since film's golden age, as well as from newer production companies. They have found popularity across the moving-picture media, from TV to home video to continued theater runs. All of these forms seem to feed Americans' continuing love for long-form, fully resolved stories on the screen—especially the ones that end happily. Better movies not only fill two hours of key programming time but also attract big-spending advertisers consistently. Christmas 2001 brought huge audience response to warm family movies, three months after the September attacks on New York and Washington, DC.

However, after years of fat returns from airing films, networks after 2000 were scaling back their movie schedules. Lifetime and other cable channels had been using original movies (not ex-theatricals) to establish their identities and further divide TV audiences. Networks were making more room in their schedule for other attractions, including "reality" shows.

"REALITY" SHOWS

These programs feature nonactors in scenarios that generate drama or suspense, such as the placement of attractive young married couples on a desert island seeded with marauding (and attractive) singles. Producers claim that these programs, despite some unreal twists, are *not scripted*. That gives them a special scent of mystery—and also makes the programs relatively cheap to produce, a big factor when times are lean. Reality shows have had enough drawing power to keep networks reinventing them (even after denouncing them when Fox started the trend). CBS made **ratings** (audience-size) gains with *Survivor*. The 2001 terrorist attacks caused viewers to snub some of the more trivial shows and they were cancelled, but by January 2002, all major networks had new reality shows planned. NBC at first disdained the trend but then launched *Fear Factor*; its delights included an actress with her head in a box of worms and scorpions, and people eating buffalo parts. The show drew so many viewers that NBC decided to run a special episode—featuring "Playmates" from the *Playboy* titillation lineup—during halftime of Fox's 2002 Super Bowl game. It worked and it didn't work: *Fear Factor* proved to be the most successful adult counterprogramming to the game in years, but a huge majority of viewers stuck with halftime at the game, featuring a spectacular show by the Irish rock group U2.

NEWS

Journalism provides an inexhaustible source of TV programming, as demonstrated by the cable channels now covering stories 24 hours a day. News also emerges in conventional newscasts, morning and night on most stations and networks. Americans have access to a greater volume of television news than ever before. A fair amount of diversity of style and content is available on cable and satellite channels that bring us international and special-topic news. At the same time, networks in recent years have done much to tailor their flagship newscasts to popular tastes, covering emerging angles of familiar stories. That's because, in the current dynamic of broadcasting, news must compete with entertainment programs in terms of ratings and advertising revenues.

Most local stations generate most of their profits from news. Still, it must hold its own: Some stations around the country have dropped news altogether rather than invest heavily to make their newscasts competitive.

NEWSMAGAZINES

The newsmagazines genre is an answer to the competition problem that news faces across the major viewing hours. Slickly made newsmagazine TV programs now occupy plum spots in the prime-time schedule. They emphasize emotional storytelling, celebrity profiles, and consumer investigations. These shows do not always meet standard definitions of news, but with cheaply available human-interest material and high production values, they draw sizable audiences to nonfiction programming and help a network's financial "bottom line."

DAYTIME DRAMAS

Television started trying out generally slow-moving daytime dramas (often called *soup operas*) in the 1940s, and by the early 1950s they arrived to stay. Rich in vivid characters, unrequited love, and treachery unending, they continue to rule midday programming. One daytime drama, *The Guiding Light*, was half a century old

Ratings Usually, the gross number of viewers or listeners—often measured in "households"—tuned in to a program.

Sports Viewers. Audiences for TV's sports coverage aren't always huge, but tend to consist of fiercely dedicated viewers—who respond well to targeted advertising.

in 2002. Another, *As the World Turns,* is nearly as old. The 1980s and 1990s brought stronger sexuality and violence to some "soaps" as they sought to reach younger audiences.

TALK

Many daytime and early-evening hours on TV are filled with conversations between personable hosts and show-biz stars or newsmakers. Other popular shows expose the sad or tawdry stories of "ordinary" people, generating arguments and even physical combat. The talker-hosts can be as controversial as their programs are. One talker-host, Jerry Springer, caused an anchor walkout when he arrived at a Chicago station with a new job as political commentator (it didn't last). Another, Geraldo Rivera, resumed his role as a swashbuckling TV journalist for Fox News, but found his credibility challenged. A third host, Jenny Jones, landed in court as a witness after a murder resulting from a confrontation between two of her guests. The most successful talker—and one of the richest, most influential women in the United States—is Oprah Winfrey, whose sassy but sympathetic approach to solving women's problems has brought her years of huge audiences.

SPORTS

Networks continue to broadcast all major (including Olympics-related) sports, and full-time sports channels have subdivided to cover many specialties. There seems no end to the variety available on ESPN and dozens of other sports outlets. The 24-hour channels now reach so many viewers that some local TV newscasts have redesigned their sports segments to compete. They report far fewer game scores and cover more background features than they once did.

A RATINGS MOMENT

If every program delighted audiences and never lost its appeal, radio and television would be sleepy, unchanging media. That's far from reality, however; failure is at least as deeply embedded in the creation and presentation of programs as success is. We can see that in the fortunes of the TV talk shows. "Of 55 talk shows launched over the past 10 years, only three have survived," says Stephanie Drachkovitch, senior vice president of Telepictures (part of Warner Bros.) and a veteran program developer. "There's a high failure rate in daytime—more channels, more choices—and it's hard to get a program noticed, and to break existing habits."[3]

In commercial broadcasting, nearly every program's fate rests largely on a measurement system that generates ratings. The system is such an important force in the industry that this book devotes much of a chapter to it. However, since their most powerful impact is on programming, let's look briefly now at ratings and how they're used.

Objectives

Networks, *stations*, and *cable channels* all want and need to learn how many people tuned in to each of their programs. Among other things, knowing this helps them decide whether to stay with a program or give up on it and take it off the air. Reminder: The U.S. broadcasting system depends almost totally on the willingness of advertisers to pay money for commercial time to broadcasters, who use that money to make or acquire shows to attract *audiences*, who then will see or hear the commercials. That's why broadcasters strive to track the popularity of their programs as precisely as possible.

Measurement

The leading audience-measurement firm in radio is Arbitron; the primary ratings company in television is Nielsen Media Research. Each calculates the size of audiences by using a mix of two methods: diaries and meters. Listeners or viewers fill out *diaries* by noting which programs they were listening to or watching at specific times in the broadcast day. Critics of this method say it puts too much responsibility in the hands of media users, who may not remember their program choices or mail in their dairies promptly. Such critics usually prefer *meters*, electronic devices that record listening or viewing as it occurs; they can transmit data to the researchers' home offices, reducing chances of human error.

Broadcasters through the years pushed for technology that would tell them not just which programs drew an audience but who was in it. One answer was the Nielsen's Peoplemeter, which could be assigned individually to each member of a household. However, the meter depended on each user to identify himself or herself by entering a code. In 2001, Arbitron tested a portable Peoplemeter that electronically sensed any program airing *near* the user. The new device thus captured far more media consumption than previous systems had, causing excitement among broadcasters. All could anticipate higher ratings and ad revenues.

Results

When a measurement firm has meter or diary information in hand, it can calculate the ratings of a network or station program or **daypart** (segment of a broadcast day). In television, which mostly is metered, the first value to be established is called **HUT (homes using television)**—or just "the HUT level." It's the total number of households in the measurement area that had their sets turned on during a specific period. Once that's known, a program's **share** can be calculated—that is, the percentage of HUT that were tuned in to that specific show. The third value of importance is the rating itself. That's the percentage of the area's total number of homes that were tuned in to the program. So, programmers who learn that a

Daypart A distinct segment of the broadcast day; "early morning," "daytime," "prime time," "late night" and other dayparts feature programming tailored to their special constituencies.

HUT Homes using television, a quantitative factor in calculating TV ratings.

Share A station's portion (stated in percentage) of total viewers in the market at any given time.

Principle #5

The power of ratings lies in how programmers interpret them and act on them.

show received "an 8 rating and a 19 share" know that it was seen in 8 percent of all the homes in the area, which was 19 percent of all the homes using television.

Most critical, of course, is how programmers *interpret* and *act on* those numbers. Projected ratings come into play even before a show is born, and a record of ratings follows it until its last cancellation. In between, it can pull many millions of ad dollars into a network's coffers. It also can suffer the life of a vagrant, drifting from time slot to time slot, from cable channel to backwater station, at the whim of programmers carefully tracking the ratings.

HOW PROGRAMS MOVE

Broadcast programs move from their origins through a complex distribution system. A bit of history—what Hollywood writers might call a *backstory*—underlies how this works. Americans who now are middle-aged or older grew up with three broadcast networks, the big-city stations they owned, and many network-affiliated and independent stations. It was a simpler world in which most programming seemed to flow from the networks. Then, in 1970, the federal government barred networks from holding financial stakes in the production of programs and their later resale. This quickly reduced the networks' revenue and stripped away much of their power to shape and control programming.

These so-called fin-syn (financial interest and syndication) rules lasted more than two decades. During that period, program producers, networks, and other buyers set up new relationships and supply lines that in a sense replaced the old distribution system. Today, networks again are investing in programs from their inception, and still routinely supply many shows to the stations they own and to hundreds of affiliates. Yet, these once-cozy relationships have been strained and often weakened by battles over cost sharing and, especially, by the invasion of more and more powerful players in the trading game. There are so many stations and cable channels, so many new owners in radio and TV, and so many programs available from so many distributors that the industry seemingly has become a sprawling web of distribution channels among vendors and customers.

Who Delivers, Who Receives

Let's clarify: Much of what happens as programs leave their creators' hands and move through the marketplace is not really *buying* and *selling*; it's a variety of less permanent (and sometimes less secure) transactions. Whatever content somebody produces in a form fit for TV broadcast—fiction, sports, news, or special events—can be "sold" or syndicated. As in most industries, everything's negotiable. Figure 7.1 shows some of the ways in which distribution works.

The Radio Marketplace

Although it takes a back seat in volume and dollar value to TV syndication, the radio marketplace in some respects is more free-wheeling and vibrant. Most of the country's radio stations now acquire at least some programs from outside sources.

The industry magazine *Radio & Records* lists more than 200 suppliers of programming.[4] The old networks are there, from ABC to CBS and NBC (both syndicated by Westwood One), as are some sizable-to-large broadcasting companies, including Cox, Hubbard, and Jefferson-Pilot.

Some of the biggest radio names are in syndication. One is Paul Harvey, a pioneering commentator who at this writing is heard on more than 1,100 stations. Also sold to stations and regional networks are high-profile events, such as the 2002 Winter Olympics, once a major network has aired them.

Even one person with some audio equipment and a place to transmit can put a show into syndication. Companies have arisen to manage the work of performers and producers, promote their ad-revenue potential to stations, and broker the resulting deals. Cox Radio Syndication's offerings to stations include talker Clark Howard, billed as a positive, can-do source of solutions to everyone's daily troubles. Another syndication company, Murray-Walsh Radio Programming, distributes *Science Update*, a 90-second daily report that can be plugged into many different formats.

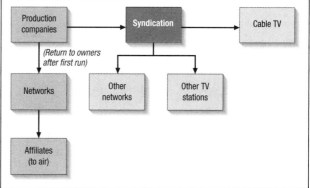

FIGURE 7.1

Paths to Profit

Production companies often create programs for TV networks (or sell movies to them), which pass the shows to their affiliated local stations to air. When air rights expire, the programs return to their owners—often the producers—who then can make more money by syndicating them to cable TV, other stations, or other networks.

A syndication contract between a supplier and a station (or station group) specifies very narrowly just what is being "sold." A station typically acquires the rights to broadcast a program for a certain length of time or through a certain number of repeated uses. It's possible to acquire not just individual features such as the Howard Stern or Don Imus shows but programming that fills *entire dayparts*. There are program suppliers that stand ready to provide everything stations need to fill their broadcast day—all on a *turnkey* (self-contained or "canned") basis. Such programming can be designed, of course, to fit seamlessly into a local format that previously was produced at a station with local hosts. Fed by satellite, the programming makes possible the near-total automation of everything listeners hear—even if most stations wisely insist on keeping local personalities at the microphone.

Major companies moving toward higher return per dollar tend to reduce their on-air lineups to the most marketable personalities and music programs, many of which are nationally syndicated, such as Premiere Radio's *American Top 40 with Casey Kasem*. If variety seems to disappear, syndication returns the medium overall to its feast-of-plenty status. Stations around the country offer everything from comedy shows to Spanish-language programming, trips through history, pet-talk forums, religious hours, jazz sessions, computing seminars, fishing shows, and much more. Live shows such as ball games, news specials, and music-awards ceremonies might seem to be "one-trick ponies," but even they can be sold for replay as "historical" events or as time-fillers on Sunday mornings.

Still, most of us lack the time, money, and will to travel endlessly in quest of radio's full range of programming.

The TV Marketplace

Television programs have especially large drawing power, production costs, ad-revenue value, and economic and social impact. They move through an especially high-powered, high-stress distribution system. Everyone bargains and competes for an edge. Some of the most experienced negotiators are at the fountainhead of dramas, comedies, and movies: Hollywood.

PRODUCTION COMPANIES

In one sense, Hollywood and other program makers provide their products to broadcasters in exchange for money. Often, however, something closer to a joint venture is involved. For example, as mentioned earlier, a network often enters production in the early stages and helps to pay for a pilot. Soon enough, the Hollywood studio or production firm asks the network to commit to buying a certain minimum of episodes. The license fee that goes with that commitment is in real money and pays for more production. Producers still may go into the hole—working on a deficit basis with borrowed money—until the new show goes on the air. That's a major reason that many programs are aired, then sold, then resold again and again: to pay off old debts.

A studio that retains ownership of a show will regain control of it after a network or station group's license to the show expires. Producers typically will make a show for a non-network customer only when stations or cable systems in 70 percent of the nation's local markets will clear air time for it. That helps guarantee its exposure to a broad enough audience to pay all the bills. In both network and non-network cases, it often takes a few years of licensing to foreign markets to bring in enough money to pay off all production costs.

Once production debt is erased and a network owns a program free and clear, it can go into "off-network" syndication and bring the owner big money. A single episode of a hit TV series often fetches more than a million dollars on the broadcast-and-cable market. Besides programs created expressly for television, Hollywood studios have huge libraries of movies to license for television use. In 2000, MGM licensed 13 of its always-popular James Bond movies to ABC for a period of two years, during which the network could use the films to attract millions of dollars in ad revenues. Studios also license batches of their lower-profile or older films to pay-TV and cable channels, where some seem likely to survive until television's last day on earth.

The rapid consolidation of media companies in the 1990s brought many syndication deals "in-house" and may have reduced competition. A case in point is the popular *Cops* series, in which cameras follow real police officers through their tense work days (and nights). The show's creator, John Langley, sued Fox, claiming it wrongly cut him out of his fair share of millions of dollars in profits by syndicating *Cops* between Fox's production arm and its own TV stations. That put the Fox company "on both sides of the bargaining table" in syndication, the lawsuit claimed. Fox reportedly had settled other suits involving *M*A*S*H* and *The X-Files*, while Disney—which produced *Home Improvement* and then aired it on its own ABC network—dealt with a similar legal assault.[5]

It's easy to infer from all this squabbling that the distribution of programs is a massive money-making enterprise, and that major producers have worked to maximize their gains from it. That's "good" business in pure economic terms. Whether it also is *fair* or even *legal* is for competitors and the courts to decide.

NETWORKS AND AFFILIATES

The world's greatest television program is worthless unless it gets on the air, and local stations continue to perform that function for producers. However, anyone who believes that networks supply their high-cost programs to stations for *free*, just to get them (along with commercials) on the air, is wrong. Here's how the system really works.

A network sets up contractual agreements with its affiliates, promising to make the same programs available at the same time, day after day, week after week, to all of them. Along with each program comes the network's cachet—its glittery brand-name power—as an aid to each station's local audience building. In return, the station promises to hold open ("clear") regular times in its schedule for the network show. Viewers in every market thus learn to schedule a regular weekly time to get to a TV set and see the show, or to set their video or digital recorders to capture and keep it for them to watch later. Thus, the network creates national viewing habits, making much of its money from exposure in many cities at once of its highly lucrative national commercials for cars, cereals, home-cleaning products, and, increasingly, prescription drugs.

These slick national commercials have the earmarks of the big-money network shows, but stations get selling opportunities, too. That's because the network leaves an agreed-upon amount of blank time within a program to allow a station to insert its own commercials for car dealerships or regional store chains. This is called **barter** time, since it's a noncash consideration. The amount of local barter time granted in a contract often is a point of disagreement between networks and affiliates and a lingering sore spot even after a deal is signed. A local station is not without any leverage, though. It often insists on the right to shift a network program from one time slot to another to make way for a sports event or other popular show purchased in syndication. A station also usually retains the right to reject an episode that it finds potentially offensive to audiences. Such issues are fluid and a constant source of disharmony. Besides the practical and financial impact, this tug-of-war between networks and stations amounts to little more than a power struggle.

Something usually called a "**comp**," compensation money that networks pay to stations to carry network shows, has become especially divisive in recent years. Cost and revenue pressures have led networks to cut, or threaten to cut, these payments. For example, the nine Scripps TV stations in 2001 were earning a total of about $10 million annually from network comp, down substantially from $13 million in the late 1990s.[6] No amount of compensation would pacify local broadcasters who accused the networks of pressuring them to carry all

Barter Commercial time in a program, "bartered" back to its distributor by a station programmer as partial payment for rights to broadcast the show; this practice gives both parties access to advertising revenues.

Comp Compensation that commercial networks traditionally have paid to stations to carry network shows.

network programs without fail. During the 2000 national election campaign, some leading stations refused to do this, spurning network sports coverage to carry presidential debates.

These and related trends helped force an alliance among more than 600 affiliates who petitioned the Federal Communications Commission in 2001 for help in curbing such network pressures. After that, NBC agreed to pay comp to affiliates in Detroit and Houston—with much of the money deferred over a 10-year period—some broadcasters entertained slim hopes that the network iceberg was finally melting.

Decade after decade, as the industry changes, so does the power balance in the distribution of programming. Networks no longer depend on their affiliates alone to carry network shows. They now are licensing programs for use by cable channels immediately after airing them for the first time, and sometimes *during* their debut runs, a practice called *repurposing*. Some of the licensing deals with cable and broadcast companies are commitments for many years to come.

SYNDICATION: TV'S AFTERLIFE

Syndication brings an endless stream of content to broadcasters. Stations have done away with so much of their own production capacity that many couldn't begin to fill their schedules without importing shows. One technology analyst, noting syndication in print media as well, asserts that "without syndication, the American mass media as we know it would not exist." One station general manager in the northwest explained some of the variables facing program buyers:

> You can see programs in this market running anywhere from no cost—"Hey, would you just run my show?"—up to $1½ million a year for an *Oprah*, or even more for something in **access,** maybe $4 to $4½ million for a *Friends* or a *Home Improvement*. . . . You're charged based on, first, market size—households, basically—then from there on, it's just a competitive marketplace and what it will **bid.**[7]

Home Improvement. The "everyman" comic Tim Allen used do-it-yourself situations to make this series a 1990s hit with a healthy afterlife in syndication.

Increasingly, program owners insist on being paid not only in cash license fees but also in barter time that the stations otherwise could sell to their own advertisers.

In a hot syndication market that could tie him up in 25 "pitch" meetings a week, that station chief shopped among programs priced at up to $3 million a year (e.g., *Oprah* for a daytime slot). Some command as much as $4 or even $5 million (e.g., *Friends, Home Improvement* for pre–prime-time hours).[8] Can a station afford such a show? Is it the right show for the job? To answer, the station must project the *cost per point*—in effect, how much money it would be paying for each audience-ratings percentage point the show brought in. Ratings over the two or three years of the "buy" would be predicted as accurately as possible, yielding an estimate of expected ad revenue.

"You take all of that gross revenue," says that northwest station executive, "and you deduct things like sales commissions and promotion spots that you're gonna put against that program to make it successful. And then you say, 'Well, what do we want our [profit] margin to be on this program?' Some stations are willing to accept a 5 percent margin if they really want the program, because it's going to help put them on the map. Others will accept only a 50 percent margin." *Only* a 50 percent profit? "Right. And then that dictates what license fee you're willing to bid for the program."[9]

The rise of station groups, with their superior buying power, has raised the bidding on many programs. Off-network comedies, in particular, seem to earn huge revenues in syndication. *Variety,* the entertainment publication, reported in 2000 that the famed situation comedy *Seinfeld* had earned $1.5 billion (yes, that's a *b*) in U.S. syndication alone. No drama had earned much more than $300 million—half a century after Milton Berle and *I Love Lucy*—a sign that laughter still rules nighttime television, even in reruns.[10]

For decades, the convention of the National Association of Television Program Executives (NATPE) provided an annual window into the state of syndication. At NATPE, programmers tour hundreds of exhibits by syndicators touting the merits of well-worn off-network programs as well as new shows. However, the turn of the twenty-first century brought sharp drops in attendance. With so many programs and shoppers on the market, many syndication deals were being made at other times of the year, leaving less need for a gigantic swap meet.

PROGRAMMING RADIO

What matters most to those of us watching television or listening to radio is what our local outlets *do* with the programs they've produced or acquired. We want to see and hear electronic-media presentations that meet our needs, at convenient times, and in predictable rhythms. Arranging that for us is the task of *programmers,* the managers who specialize in placing certain shows into certain time slots around the clock.

British television viewers in the mid-1960s enjoyed—but, judging from the shortness of its run, did not enjoy *greatly*—a satirical BBC series called *Not So Much a Programme, More a Way of Life.* That title, whether with satiric intent or not, captured the mission of programming in a market economy: to forge a way of life that will attract audiences. Once they're tuned in, a programmer's next objective is to keep people from reaching for their remote controls.

Basics

Radio is our oldest electronic medium, and its programming has helped to solidify and accelerate national change. In the 1930s, Irna Phillips and other writer-producers developed the daytime radio soap opera into a virtual addiction

Sponsor A person or company that pays for all ad slots in an entire broadcast.

for housewives—one that greatly spurred U.S. consumerism. This arose in a time when advertisers were gaining greater control over broadcasting, partly by agreeing to **sponsor** entire programs. Researcher Marilyn Lavin has written that Phillips "adjusted story lines to meet the selling needs of her sponsors; she used soap opera characters as effective product spokespersons; and she designed program promotions to stimulate product sales."[11]

Today, with advertiser influence as ubiquitous as radio itself, the manipulation of shows and their scheduling to attract and retain listeners as *consumers* is universal practice. Once consumer attention is assured, even the old practice of full sponsorship, rather than purchase of slots of time for ads, becomes feasible. For example, WCLV-FM, "Cleveland's only locally owned commercial FM station," has broadcast classical music for four decades and has originated Cleveland Orchestra concerts since 1965, building loyal listenership. The station in 1998 began broadcasting *complete* classical works every Monday. Who would sponsor a weekly classical marathon? Many an advertiser, as it turned out, since the charge for gaining five hours of access to a devoted audience would be just $2,750, the program's production cost.[12] Programming, like advertising, is a matter of dollars and sense.

One calculation—which programming fits best on *AM* (amplitude modulated) radio and which on *FM* (frequency modulated)—is over. Because of its superior sound quality, FM long ago became the radio band of choice for music lovers. There are some talk shows on FM, largely through public (noncommercial) radio, but AM commands most of the news/talk programming and sports on the air today.

Research

Early in 2002, the Arbitron audience-measurement firm released survey findings that formed a partial profile of U.S. radio listenership. It showed that, although virtually every home has radio, people with college degrees and household incomes of over $50,000 a year listen to more radio than do less affluent or less educated people. It also confirmed that adults do most of their radio listening in their cars, and mostly in morning or evening "drive time." That's good national information, but only a starting point for the local programmer.

A radio station's first step toward building an audience is to select a format, a particular category of programs that will become the station's signature "sound" and provide a strong platform for promotion and ad sales.

FORMATS IN USE

Formats in use refers to what the competition already has established in the market. If one station has done well with, say, an adult contemporary format, choosing the same format could touch off a wasteful struggle for listeners that a newcomer is likely to lose. A major Hispanic broadcaster reflected this when he told *Billboard* magazine that, in selecting a format for its new station in a fast-growing California market, his company would follow its standard blueprint: "We'll go in with no assumptions and find what's missing."[13] Still, a large city of-

Radio Dayparts

Radio dayparts are weekday periods of several hours each in which established lifestyles put certain groups of consumers near their radios. This is how they line up (in Eastern and Pacific time zones; one hour earlier in Mountain and Central):

- *Morning Drive:* Running from 6:00 to 10:00 A.M., this period is when most people are on their way to work; their car radios make this the first daypart that draws large audiences, often to news or to music-variety programs with joke-cracking hosts.
- *Midday:* Running from 10:00 A.M. to 3:00 P.M., this is a time when people in offices may listen to light rock or light classical music, while homemakers and retirees are taking in radio talk shows.
- *Afternoon Drive:* The period from 3:00 to 7:00 P.M. is when people head home from work, tired and leaning toward sprightly pop music, talk, and news.
- *Evening:* Spanning the hours between 7:00 P.M. and midnight is when stations schedule jock/talker/hosts to play music in a variety of formats.
- *Overnight:* These are the hours when night workers, insomniacs, and many college students search their radios for, among other things, edgy talkers and offbeat music formats. Like evening, overnight daypart brings far fewer people to radio than do morning and afternoon drive dayparts.

ten has a number of stations using the same program format and jostling constantly for listeners. No initial format is set in stone; managers occasionally see some weakness in a rival station's programming and abruptly adopt the same format, believing they can move in and lure away part of the audience. In general, however, a station that finds, attracts, and maintains a sizable and loyal audience segment for its advertisers becomes a successful business.

Most stations (or their group owners) continuously or repeatedly use audience or marketing **consultants**, surveys, focus groups, and other aids to acquire knowledge of the market. At many radio stations, recent downsizing has eliminated the program director and put the general manager directly in charge of programming. This links programming even more closely to overall business concerns and keeps the general manager's nose in trade publications that bring word of successful formats and strategies.

Television hits have helped to show that certain programming plays are almost certain to grab radio listeners, too. One such type is the "confessional" or highly personal show in which the stars or their quests expose to public view some of their most private moments or thoughts. Katie Couric of NBC's *Today*, whose husband had died of colon cancer, had her own 1999 colon exam televised on the show in an effort to spread health awareness; she also won ratings and a prestigious Peabody Award. In Los Angeles, KBIG-FM put the birth of disc jockey Leigh Ann Adams's baby on the air live and posted photos of the delivery on its website. Although the main purpose may have been promotional, the program director told of hearing from a listener who "had to pull her car off the road, so she could wipe away the tears" (women are the station's core audience).[14]

Consultants Professional advisers to broadcast stations; sometimes controversial for perceived negative influence on program quality.

Special Tools

Once its format is in place, a radio station must set up a program schedule that will reach listeners and hold them for as long as they're listening in the car or at home. Whether a station has a music, news/talk, or other format, its minute-by-minute and hour-by-hour programming strategy is important. Not everyone is able to listen closely at all hours of day or night; music or even news or talk often acts as background to work or study activities, reducing the power of commercials. Sometimes, listeners' involvement in having dinner or managing children prompts them to tune out radio altogether. For these reasons, a programmer must understand and work with *time*, a fact that places something called the *hot clock* chief among the arsenal of weapons to win the war for ratings.

A "HOT CLOCK"

Figure 7.2 displays the programming within any important segment of broadcast time, arranged around what looks like the face of a clock. There are many different ways to set up such a timepiece, and it can serve several purposes. One is to make visible the rotation of various types of programming around an entire 24-hour broadcast day. Another is to help a programmer see how his or her ideas might work to support the station's format within a given hour or period. Still another purpose of the hot clock is to show how well the station competes with its rivals in delivering certain features—blocks of music, news breaks, weather reports—and in showcasing commercials. Simply put, the hot clock shows how a station is doing its job, airing programs to suit appropriate consumers at times when they naturally gravitate to radio. Versions of the hot clock are useful in music and nonmusic formats.

PLAYLISTS

The *playlist* is a rundown of all the pieces of music featured in a music station's schedule (see Figure 7.3). These lists are useful to programmers evaluating their formats and comparing their "sound" with that of other stations. Playlists also help record companies discover how much air time their products are getting, and, increasingly, help corporate overseers fine-tune each station to reach its audience surgically.

Issues

Reducing playlists obviously reduces variety, as well; it already has taken much of the surprise out of tuning in stations at random. Now, some pro-

FIGURE 7.2

A Hot Clock

A "hot clock" is used to give a quick look at a radio station's programming plans. The clock can be designed to show an hour (shown here), day, or other time period.

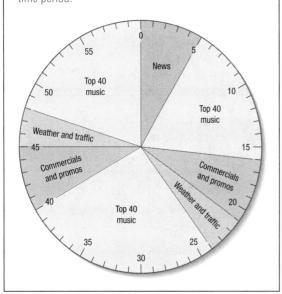

FIGURE 7.3

Country Hits Playlist

Radio stations sometimes publish their current playlists as a part of their promotional websites.

COUNTRY HITS PLAYLIST—Last Updated 2/5/02

Artist	Title	Artist	Title
Blake Shelton	All Over Me	Travis Tritt	Love of a Woman
Tim McGraw	Angry All the Time	Tim Rushlow	Love Will
Martina McBride	Blessed	Mindy McCready	Maybe, Maybe Not
Jo Dee Messina	Bring on the Rain	Travis Tritt	Modern Day Bonnie and Clyde
Sawyer Brown	Circles	Toby Keith	My List
Montgomery Gentry	Cold One Comin On	Brooks & Dunn	Only In America
Steve Holy	Good Morning Beautiful	Ashley Jay	Only When
Ty Herndon	Heather's Wall	Jeff Carson	Real Life
Chris Cagle	I Breathe In, I Breathe Out	David Ball	Riding With Private Malone
Tammy Cochran	I Cry	George Strait	Run
Steve Azar	I Don't Have to Be Me Til Monday	Sara Evans	Saints and Angels
Carolyn Dawn Johnson	I Don't Want You to Go	Kevin Denney	That's Just Jesse
Emerson Drive	I Should Be Sleeping	Phil Vassar	That's When I Love You
Trisha Yearwood	I Would've Loved You Anyway	Tim McGraw	The Cowboy In Me
Reba McEntire	I'm a Survivor	Brooks & Dunn	The Long Goodbye
Toby Keith	I'm Just Talkin About Tonight	Andy Griggs	Tonight I Wanna Be Your Man
Rascal Flatts	I'm Movin On	Cyndi Thomson	What I Really Meant to Say
Mark Willis/Jamie O'Neal	I'm Not Gonna Do Anything Without You	Tommy Shane Steiner	What If She's an Angel
Trace Adkins	I'm Trying	Kellie Coffey	When You're Next to Me
Joe Diffie	In Another World	Alan Jackson	Where Were You
Chely Wright	Jezebel	Brad Paisley	Wrapped Around
Tracy Byrd	Just Let Me Be In Love	Garth Brooks	Wrapped Up In You
Trick Pony	Just What I Do	Kenney Chesney	Young
Jessica Andrews	Karma		

moters of "satellite radio," which offers almost endless music variety, are using the popularity of conventional-radio playlists as a sales point in their own favor. They provide hours of uninterrupted music from almost any genre.

Clear Channel Communications owns some 1,200 outlets nationwide and, as of recently, a concert promotion company that helps the stations organize music events, plus an outdoor-advertising firm to give them wide exposure. Critics claim that Clear Channel's **vertical integration** of music-related businesses is sure to discourage dealings with outsiders, thus suppressing competition, and reducing listener choices. Already the company pays a relative few disc jockeys to record programs for many of its outlets, homogenizing content across those markets. That's a sensible financial move but no help to radio's content diversity or to the "localism" of which the industry often boasts.

Vertical integration Ownership by one company of all steps from production to distribution.

When a young radio show is cancelled, it's usually a clear sign that a programming decision went sour or a hotter prospect showed up. In Spokane, Washington, radio station KXLY-AM dropped the syndicated *Rick Emerson Show* barely six months after putting it on the air. According to a local journalist, "Few people listened, according to the station, and those who did only called to complain."[15] However, another factor also came into play: A more popular nationally syndicated show had become available as a quick replacement in Spokane. For radio personality Emerson, the incident held some irony. His show had been the replacement a few months earlier when another talk-based program was yanked from the air in Albuquerque, New Mexico, and other cities because of offensive language.[16] So it goes; such are the hazards of radio programming in a time of noisy, "edgy" competition.

PROGRAMMING TELEVISION

Unlike most radio stations, which must find content wherever they can, most television stations today are linked to networks. ABC, CBS, and NBC send programs to their affiliates that can fill all or most of a long broadcast day. Four newer networks—Fox, UPN, WB, and PAX—provide less than a full schedule of shows to their stations. Regardless of the amount, whatever the networks supply to local broadcasters is almost sure to have greater audience appeal than they could manage on their own. That's why a network's programming philosophy and practices are of vital concern to all.

Basics

One evolutionary note may be revealing: Under the eyes of their cost-conscious owners—and because the business has changed—many TV stations that once had full-fledged program directors and staffs have retrenched. Many a general manager does all the programming personally. It's relatively simple these days: Most larger TV stations produce lots of news and a sprinkling of other local programs, then plug a few syndicated shows into key schedule slots. For the rest of the long broadcast day, they run the networks' main programs just as the networks scheduled them to run. That's how the "nets" want it; if their nationally promoted programs come into viewers' homes in every city with rigid regularity, huge audiences congregate simultaneously. With that, the confidence of major advertisers is maintained and the ad revenues keep flowing in. Stations benefit from this as well, since they sell advertising within network shows.

A NETWORK'S BURDEN

This dynamic puts great responsibility on the shoulders of a network's programmer(s), who usually reports to a vice president or even a division president. He or she controls many millions of dollars in program expenditures—and must choose well from among program ideas. Networks don't just buy finished shows; they pay to have important shows developed by outside producers. Any big mis-

ProTalk

Helen Little
*President, U.S. Operations, RuffNation
Records*

"If it's a music-based format, the more narrow your focus, the more broad your results."

Helen Little embodies the close relations among different segments of the modern music industry. She went to college hoping to do research on sleep and dreams—an offbeat ambition for a person who someday would be charged with keeping people awake, not snoozing. Perhaps fortunately, she dropped her psychology major, switched to broadcasting, and today looks back on a 20-year record of radio programming that lifted her to the top of her field.

She also has a newer job: president of U.S. operations for RuffNation Records, a joint venture with the

Warner Music Group, part of the massive AOL/Time Warner empire. Now, instead of merely designing programming around available music, she plays a large role in *producing* that music, especially "urban" music, often working directly with R&B and rap groups. Her company's chief executive described her as having "an all-encompassing, across-the-board knowledge of the ever-changing urban landscape. She's a real music person."[17]

Proof of that came early. As the daughter of a theology professor, Little and her melodic family made a joyful noise; she played clarinet, piano, and guitar. While at the University of North Carolina at Chapel Hill, she landed a weekend job at a local station, and soon was off to her unexpected career in radio programming. Urban is a diverse and vibrant genre that includes hip-hop, and other rap music popular among young music fans. Little knew how to play it to maximum gain by applying a variation of the long-lived "top-40" format.

"If it's a music-based format, the more narrow your focus, the more broad your results," she says. "There are not but a few songs that people want to hear."

Following that simple principle, Little went on to help run Dallas, New York, and Philadelphia stations. As brand manager for Clear Channel Communications, the country's largest radio owner, she worked with programmers in San Francisco, Chicago, and Detroit. She won many awards; in 2000, she was ranked among the 15 "best program directors in America," large-market category, by *Radio Ink* magazine. In records and radio, Little has become a big name.

take can waste production money and cause a dip in ratings that might take months or longer to correct. Two or three flops in a season can taint a whole schedule, depress the rates a network can charge for commercial minutes, and damage its potential to attract future advertisers.

Thus, TV networks take few real programming risks unless someone else has taken them first. Nothing better illustrates this caution than the late 1990s arrival of network "reality" shows, those relatively low-cost, unscripted productions using nonactors.[18] The Big Three networks kept a lofty distance from the genre until it broke into CBS through *Survivor*. By then, even once-maligned Fox had loudly criticized reality shows, but almost no one was backing away from them. The size and loyalty of reality audiences were too powerful to resist.

NBC reportedly paid $13 million per episode for its long-running hospital hit *ER*.[19] That kind of spending required programmers to make sure that an already good show *stayed* good at bringing audiences to advertisers. Bullet-quick feedback on gross ratings and—more important—on viewer demographics tell a programming executive whether to order more episodes of a show as it is, have it retooled to increase its appeal, or put the program out of its expensively unwatched misery.

TARGETING VIEWERS

Programming obviously plays the lead role in establishing and maintaining a network or station's image among its desired viewers. This can be a tricky undertaking. Sometimes, when trends already have turned negative, it involves "damage control." CBS, for example, has a somewhat older audience than the other major networks—not a happy fact to advertisers who want to reach young adults and their families. How to remedy this?

The most obvious approach is to schedule shows filled with youthful actors in comic settings or dramatic predicaments. However, that could alienate the stable, loyal older audience on which many of the network's advertisers depend. Indeed, CBS aimed a 1995 show called *Central Park West* at younger viewers, but it failed to reach them and practically everyone else. In 2000, the network's fortunes began to change with the launch of *Survivor*, a reality show. Younger viewers flocked to it. The average age of CBS viewers dropped, while that of *other* networks' audiences rose. What once was regarded as the top-flight "Tiffany Network" came out of the shadows to beat its rivals in several ratings periods. Older viewers mostly stuck around. CBS suddenly had become the one to watch.

On another level, networks that reigned alone over broadcasting for many decades have yielded ground to spunky new rivals. A company that starts with a modest slate of shows and works systematically to appeal to a key audience can find success. In the late 1990s, the WB (Warner Brothers) network trained its sights on women ages 18 to 34. It launched youth-slanted *Dawson's Creek* and *Buffy the Vampire Slayer;* then, when each show had secured a solid following of young women, added *Felicity*, a series about a college student's troubles and triumphs. Soon, a 30-second commercial during *Felicity* was costing the advertiser more than $100,000 (based on what's called CPM—the cost per thousand viewers to whom an ad is exposed). This was vital revenue for the WB, since each episode of *Felicity* cost about $1.3 million to produce—only one-tenth as much as an *ER* installment, but a great deal of money to a fledgling network.[20]

Felicity. In a youth-oriented drama, actress Keri Russell coped with life as a New York college student and drew vital advertising revenue to the WB network.

Special Tools

Television programmers have developed an arsenal of tactics that's a good deal larger than radio's bag of tricks. Some of them involve the best placement of a single show in a schedule in order to reach certain viewers. Others focus on arranging several hours of programming to boost audiences for multiple shows, which in popular parlance, will "lift all boats." Still others are aimed simply and directly at knocking the competition off a single half-hour perch.

Television Dayparts

Like radio, television organizes its broadcast day into dayparts. However, TV's clock is more complex than that of radio. Here's how programmers usually divide a 24-hour day (times stated in Eastern and Pacific zones):

- *Early morning* runs from 7:00 to 10:00 A.M. and encompasses network morning news-interview shows led by NBC's *Today*.
- *Daytime* is a long stretch of hours, from 10:00 A.M. to 5:00 P.M. Its programming includes network (and syndicated) talk shows and soap operas aimed primarily at homemakers, as well as some children's programs in late afternoon.
- *Early fringe* lasts two hours, from 5:00 to 7:00 P.M., during which networks and stations typically air their early-evening newscasts while cable channels offer alternatives.
- *Prime access* runs from 7:00 to 8:00 P.M. and is usually filled with syndicated light entertainment or local programming. The term *access* is a legacy of the FCC's 1971–1996 prime-time access rule (PTAR), which pulled networks out of the 7:00 to 8:00 P.M. hour and granted stations the right to program it.
- *Prime time* is TV's crucial evening block from 8:00 to 11:00 P.M. This is when the networks trot out their strongest comedies and dramas (family-oriented first, then more adult), as well as newsmagazines.
- *Late fringe* is half an hour, from 11:00 to 11:30 P.M., and is almost always occupied by local newscasts except on non-network stations and cable.
- *Late night* is for viewers still up between 11:30 P.M. and 12:30 A.M. It offers mostly talk shows, comedy and fiction.
- *Overnight* on TV stations and cable channels of all sorts is an electronic Lazy Susan in which the viewer who's awake between 12:30 and 7:00 A.M. can find almost anything. Networks have attempted, with mixed results, to succeed with night-owl newscasts during this period.

HEAD-TO-HEAD PROGRAMMING

If a rival is getting high ratings from a particular program, a station may be tempted to schedule a similar show directly against it, at the same time in the schedule. This is not subtle; it's often called *blunting*. For example, CNN personality Greta Van Susteren jumped to Fox in 2002 to begin anchoring a program opposite CNN's main anchor, literally a face-off. Stations routinely schedule head-to-head local newscasts, which often leaves them scheduling their networks' newscasts head-to-head, as well.

COUNTERPROGRAMMING

When a network or station sees that its competitor will be airing a blockbuster show—such as the Super Bowl—the only answer may be to go after a different audience. Other networks for years have run female-oriented shows against ABC's *Monday Night Football*. That's called *counterprogramming*. Old episodes of a strong drama series might draw people who care little about sports. If a programmer's male and female friends all are planning to watch that "other" network, competing for adults might be hopeless, but that still leaves open the choice of children's shows to entertain other family members.

Friends. The show was a huge hit and its six stars each had $24 million salaries heading into their ninth and (reportedly) final season on NBC.

Hammocking The placement of a weak program between two strong ones.

Tentpoling The placement of a strong program between two weak ones.

HAMMOCKING

Sometimes a show that has yet to find its audience can draw strength from the programs that surround it. Putting a weak program between two stronger ones, hoping they'll pull it up in the ratings, is called **hammocking.** NBC tried helping a new show called *Jesse* by scheduling it between the hits *Friends* and *Frasier.* Early ratings indicated that most *Friends* viewers were hanging around for the new show, but later they drifted away and the hammock collapsed in the middle; *Jesse* was cancelled. Some observers are skeptical of hammocking, believing that impatient viewers with remote-control zappers simply won't linger through a so-so program.

TENTPOLING

To place one strong show between two weak ones, in hopes of helping them out, is the reverse of hammocking and is known as **tentpoling.** Sometimes one program is such a powerful audience draw that it lifts the ratings of shows that come before and after it; the long-running NBC sitcom *Seinfeld* achieved such a pinnacle. Fox's *Ally McBeal* and *The X-Files* are among recent TV tentpoles. Networks rarely can arrange for even a single evening's programming to be consistently first rate, although NBC's Thursday prime-time schedule arguably approached that summit. So the search for shows that can hold up the programming tent is perennial.

BRIDGING

When a program routinely ends a minute or more past the half-hour or hour mark on the clock, chances are the programmer behind it is engaging in *bridging.* This technique aims to hold viewers in place long enough to make them miss the start of a program on a competing channel. Local news departments sometimes schedule a strong feature story or personality to run from, say, 6:28 to 6:32 P.M. That can freeze some of the remote-control zappers that otherwise might have jumped to another channel at 6:30. A zap postponed is often a zap forgotten.

BLOCK PROGRAMMING

When a broadcaster strings together similar programs that can hold particularly interested viewers in place for hours. Prime examples of *block programming* show up on autumn weekends, when football fans may watch pregame shows, games, postgame shows, and then newscasts featuring game video. Soap operas march through daytime in similar fashion and for the same reason: to mesmerize loyal fans so that advertisers can reach them easily over an extended period.

STUNTING

Networks and stations *stunt* by breaking the mold. This can mean showing unusual attractions, or routine attractions at unusual times, to draw viewers away from competitors' favored programming. Any heavily promoted twist can have that effect. When the script of a drama series suddenly makes room for a quick visit from a hot movie actor, that's stunting. When a popular show suddenly moves one hour later to challenge a rival during a ratings "sweeps" period, that probably is short-lived, and it's stunting. NBC in 2001 briefly considered putting a celebrity-studded reality show against the sweeps-month premiere of a heavily promoted Fox series—a stunting idea. It died when NBC realized it had too little time to do its own promotion.

STRIPPING

Most often used with syndicated shows, *stripping* entails scheduling an episode of the same series—comedy, drama, game show, other—at the same time five days a week. Stations typically strip daytime talk shows and adventure programs such as *Xena: Warrior Princess.* Network programmers may decide to strip especially popular programs, such as *Who Wants to Be a Millionaire* before it faded (partly from overexposure). Cable channels endlessly strip old "off-network" shows; some specialists like the Sci-Fi Channel had little choice at first if they were to fill their schedules.

Remote Control. Remote-Control technology makes channel changing easy and forces programmers to use a variety of tactics to retain the attention of viewers.

The Role of Consultants

Programmers look for help wherever they can find it, and sometimes that means outside experts. A company called Frank N. Magid Associates, founded by a social psychologist in 1957, launched a subindustry of *TV consulting* that has advised stations and networks about their programming ever since. The central objective almost always is to increase the size and/or demographic desirability of audiences. Consultants have injected viewer-based thinking, derived from surveys and focus groups, into decision making about TV programs as historic as NBC's morning show, *Today.* National operations continue to use consulting; for example, Fox News in 2001 signed a contract with a veteran audience researcher to bring his expertise to the Fox News Channel and other programs. However, since networks are inclined to employ their own research directors,[21] most of the consulting firms' work is focused on local stations—especially their news programming.

After a New York news director named Al Primo launched his *Eyewitness News* concept in the late 1960s—putting street reporters on camera speaking directly to audiences—consultants helped to propagate Primo's seminal approach. They also spread the use of light "happy talk" between anchors and other attempts to keep news entertaining. In recent decades, TV consultants' proposals have raised ratings—but also eyebrows and, sometimes, hackles—in hundreds of towns and cities across the United States. Under names like Audience Research and Development (AR&D) and Broadcast Image Group (BIG), researcher-consultants have made norms and routines out of what once were experiments in audience appeal. This keeps the focus on satisfying viewers, a plus to them even if it often is a minus to broadcast journalists who find consultants likely to thin and even distort news content.

Issues

Television sometimes draws heavy criticism from advocates for children, families, ethnic groups, and other constituencies. This reflects the natural ability of all kinds of programs to flow into absolutely everyone's living room unless somebody gets in their way. Television often carries pictures, words, and themes that please some viewers while offending others. Top industry leaders deal with this challenge in public forums and congressional hearings. However, network and station programmers cannot hide from ongoing cries for a cleanup of television's sex and violence. The industry's latest response is a voluntary content-ratings system.

ProTalk

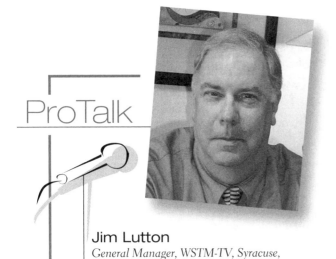

Jim Lutton
General Manager, WSTM-TV, Syracuse, New York

"People recommend a show . . . and if you haven't watched it, at the water cooler the next morning you feel deprived."

Jim Lutton knows programming. He's been doing it for 30 years at TV stations in large and middle-sized cities. He's even called the tunes for large station groups. One thing he knows is that many people don't like to see much change in television. They have habits, they like them, and broadcasters should be grateful for it. "That's why the most successful syndicated shows in history have been *Wheel of Fortune* and *Jeopardy*," Lutton says. "They're straightforward. They don't need a lot of promotion."

Promotion—including those loud and flashy little blurbs between commercials and programs—often goes unacknowledged, but for some shows, it's a necessary and powerful factor. As examples, Lutton cites two highly popular syndicated programs dealing with entertainment. "If we run *ET* [Entertainment Tonight] or *Access Hollywood*, we have to promote it topically," he says. "That's because every day brings a new audience. If Brad Pitt is taking his shirt off at the Cannes Film Festival, we have to get the word out.

"Prime time, on the other hand, changes a great deal. New shows come in, and soon people are watching in a very active way. . . . They figure out what the good programs are on the networks; they find what they like. People recommend a show—maybe *Survivor* or one of the other cult shows—and if you haven't watched it, at the water cooler the next morning you feel deprived."

When it comes to television news, adds Lutton, many viewers like to stay put: "People don't 'sample' news shows too much. They've usually been in the market too long. They follow an anchor, or they've just decided that somebody in town has the better news. News audiences move a lot less than some others audiences." So do older people in general: "Court shows were a big staple a few years ago—*Judge Judy* still is—and they got fairly big audience numbers in large markets. But the demos [demographics] were almost all [age] 50-plus individuals.

"In this PC environment, we don't talk about that much, but advertisers want viewers [age] 18 to 49."

Some of the most serious challenges to broadcasting's status quo come from advocates for more ethnic diversity in programming. Most prominently, the National Association for the Advancement of Colored People (NAACP) has pushed for more opportunity for African Americans and other minorities to own and develop programs, changing the face of television from the inside. In January 2002, a year after joining agreements for change with the four biggest networks, NAACP president Kweisi Mfume complained of slow progress and threatened economic sanctions against television.

Programming is the public surface of radio and TV, and as such draws the sharpest barbs. One of the earliest and most penetrating came back in 1961 from an FCC chair, Newton Minow, when he called nightly television a "vast wasteland." Although TV occasionally has reached great heights since then—the landmark 1977 mini-series called *Roots* and the early coverage of the 2001 terrorist attacks—much of its programming still seems expendable, and millions have stopped watching. With more and more new competitors for Americans' leisure time, the giants of commercial electronic media may have to become more responsive to critics. Whether these companies will respond fully to anyone other than audiences is the big question.

Tools for Parents

Since 1997, pushed by Congress, broadcast and cable TV have been labeling every program (except news) according to the potency of its sexual and violent content. This rating shows up in the upper left corner of the screen during a show's opening moments, giving parents a chance to change channels or divert their children from the set if they disapprove of the content.

Besides giving a visual cue, the rating signal on the screen interacts with the V-chip device that the FCC ordered included in virtually all new TV sets starting in 2000. The V-chip allows parents to set a rating level, and then all programs that have received that rating will be blocked out of their home. Here's how the rating scale looks:

RATING	APPROPRIATE AUDIENCE
TV-Y	All children (content is for the very young)
TV-Y7	Older children (content may be mildly violent or frightening)
TV-G	Anyone (nothing objectionable)
TV-PG	Parental guidance suggested (some foul words, mild sexuality)
TV-14	Parents strongly cautioned (too bloody or racy for many kids)
TV-M	Mature audiences only (too much of everything for those under age 17)

In addition to this scale, the TV-screen rating box displays one or more letters of the alphabet to tell viewers and parents a little more precisely what types of risky material may be present in a show. **D** is for dialogue that may have sexy undertones; **S** is for sex; **L** is for language that is probably offensive; **V** is for violence, and **FV** is for fantasy or cartoon violence. These symbols, too, can be programmed into the V-chip.

The Kaiser Family Foundation reported in 2001 that more than half of all parents were consulting the content ratings to decide on shows their children could watch. However, only 17 percent of parents with V-chips were using them to block offensive programs.

INTO THE (DIGITAL) FUTURE

Almost everything in this chapter has centered on traditional broadcasting, but there's a far larger story to tell, and it's still being written. Digital technology seems certain to revolutionize what broadcasters can do with their programming hours. It's likely also to turn a whole new program-delivery system, the personal computer, into a blessing for "electronic" audiences. So far, only the integration of digital tools and processes into conventional radio and television production has begun to show its potential.

TV Applications

Visual images in digital form resist interference, distortion, and deterioration as they pass from point to point. Satellite-TV companies already exploit this advantage in bringing new channels, often with new kinds of programming, into millions of U.S. homes. Nor will digital recordings of TV programs almost literally fall apart as they grow ancient, one of videotape's great weaknesses. Thus, television in the digital age could become a more effective expander and preserver of culture, worthy of fine program material and perhaps attracting more of it.

High-definition television (HDTV), although spreading slowly, is bringing the clearest video in history to the limited number of expensive sets now in use. It also brings the promise of a sea of change in how we view television programs. Much of the difference lies in the shape of the screen; rather than a traditional 4:3 "aspect ratio," in which every four inches of screen width brings three inches of height, the new digital sets will offer a 16:9 picture. With a frame that is much wider than its height, the television screen will cry out for new content and techniques. Producers then will have to develop new ways of handling fantasy and reality that will give greater spatial dimension and perspective to what we see.

All of this should expand the range of programming content as well as its value to viewers. It also may disrupt the cozy arrangements on which the broadcasting business depends. Digital video disk recorders now are in many homes, playing movies recorded on disks (DVDs). Also, new digital video recorders (DVRs) now make it possible for viewers to watch television programs while easily skipping commercials, hardly a happy development for the retailers who keep broadcasting afloat. Sometimes called personal video recorders (PVRs), these solid-state sets manufactured by SONICblue (Replay TV) and Tivo make it much easier for users to "time-shift" programs, viewing them in any order desired. This further disrupts the carefully crafted sequences of shows on which programmers make reputations and sales departments sell advertising time. That is one reason why a federal court case was filed regarding the legality of DVRs and their commercial-avoidance mechanism. The legal action was filed in Los Angeles U.S. District Court by ABC, NBC, and CBS in late 2001.

Some television companies have encouraged and even financed progress in user power through digital means, hoping it will lead to business opportunities in *interactive* television. Set-top boxes already make video-on-demand and other services available in some areas. Whether development will pay off in full-fledged, widely distributed interactive TV, rich in programming, depends on many unknowns. Among them is the degree of financial strength that broadcast and cable companies will be able to maintain as this complex media age evolves.

Radio Applications

Digital technology also is influencing radio programming. Stations play compact disks (CDs), which are recorded digitally and provide cleaner sound than older forms, even though they usually must travel through nondigital paths to reach the radio listener. Satellites relay some programs from their distributors to stations, digitally. There's software that makes the programming of a radio day quicker and easier than ever before.

Meanwhile, alternatives are developing that would work around the existing radio system to bring digital audio directly into the home. Already, two companies, XM and Sirius, are transmitting audio into their listeners' cars via "satellite radio," providing uninterrupted music and other programming even on coast-to-coast drives. All of this serves to expand and redefine the listening experience. In some ways, that already is happening: Many radio programs can be heard every day through that most intriguing of media, the Internet.

Programming the Internet

Some people made wild predictions about the potential of radio and television as those media were born. Much later, other people made extravagant claims about how the Internet might turn the desktop computer into a cornucopia of programming delights. That still might happen. The process has begun, yet there are solid reasons for its glacial progress.

For years, it's been possible to transmit video digitally over the Internet. At this writing, however, that video usually arrives on the home screen in jerky or flickering form. The main reason is that the "pipelines" and modems through which digital signals travel from source to recipient are, in effect, too narrow. Even without sitting before a computer, we can get that special digital-video feeling; TV-news correspondents increasingly are sending reports from remote places in digital form via the "videophone." It's basically a digital camera, a computer, and a satellite link. Even the rich old networks haven't cracked the bandwidth problem.

So-called *broadband* technology is starting to solve it, however. Cable modems, with greater capacity, also are helping. New compression techniques may try to squeeze the complex flow of digital video into bit rates small enough to get through current pipelines. Until the images are perfected, or match TV quality, the full range of television programming will not find a comfortable home on the Internet.

Lots of people work with the Internet and are impatient enough to push the medium's limits. Many are sending *streaming* video—digital video that plays when it's prompted to play—over the Internet, providing users with at least the raw materials of programming. The Public Broadcasting Service (PBS) has put video of venerable TV chef Julia Child onto the Web—not a show, but a chance to watch her and other chefs at work. Some TV game shows and other productions are on the Web. Again, the pictures aren't perfect, but their improvement has been rapid in recent years, so more programming appears on the horizon for Web users.

Summary

Programming is the face and voice of broadcasting, and over time will play the same role on the Internet as digital technologies advance. Programmers' essential principle is that their work must both attract audiences and hold them in place for as long as possible. That's largely because advertisers want their commercials to reach appropriate groups of listeners and viewers who are paying close attention. Success for the programmer depends on careful research into human traits and habits as well as the design and placement of program content to reach targeted audiences.

Ratings numbers, along with demographic analysis, are crucially important as the only generally accepted yardsticks of a program's effectiveness. Although some shows succeed, many more are cancelled after audiences sample and then

CAREER FOCUS

Jobs in programming provide fascinating opportunities to influence what we see and hear through our electronic media. However, *careers* in programming don't happen every day—partly because it takes years of experience to acquire the skills and insights to do the work consistently well. Most professional programmers have worked in other broadcasting jobs on their way up, learning how TV and radio affect audiences and what it takes to attract them.

A number of universities include programming courses in their broadcasting programs. Students and graduates are well advised to learn a variety of tasks as they move into the industry. It can be argued that nothing is more important than visible and audible *content,* but the greatest off-air financial rewards in commercial broadcasting go to general executives and to sales and marketing managers.

When a medium-market radio station advertised for a program director who also could go on the air, here's how the job ad described the array of skills needed:

Knowledge of Selector music scheduling software; building and maintaining working music systems; hiring and coaching air talent and morning shows; budgeting

and strategic planning; digital audio production and on-air studios; FCC regulations; on and off-air radio promotions. Ability to manage others, function as part of a strategic team and perform a daily air shift.

A large-market TV station advertising for a programming director stated these requirements, among others:

Must have three years' experience as a line producer or Executive Producer and current experience in executing local sports, entertainment, news documentaries, and current affairs programming. Works in conjunction with Sales, Creative Services and Community Affairs on station projects. . . . Responsibilities include all areas of local production—writing, producing, directing, editing, photography and creative thinking. . . . *Supervisory Responsibilities:* On a daily basis, directly supervises station Directors, both full and part-time. On a project basis, supervises Editors, Writers, Producers and Photographers.

Programming executives of large television companies can make hundreds of thousands of dollars a year, plus generous benefits packages. Some go on to fill top leadership posts in the industry.

reject them. This leads to a common charge that commercial broadcasting too often kills its young and that only the least challenging programs are sure to survive. The resulting sameness, along with television's failure to diversify its work force and program sources, add to ongoing critical pressures. Digital technologies are changing some key characteristics of conventional radio and TV. These changes, combined with expanded Internet power, could lead to entirely new experiences for media consumers.

FOOD FOR THOUGHT

1. How many *radio formats* have you heard that are *not* mentioned in this chapter? Does radio need to try new formats? Which ones? Why?
2. In this age of fast transportation and communication, does it really matter whether TV and radio produce any purely *local* programs? Explain.
3. Overall, does *syndication* benefit television and radio consumers? What's bad about syndication? Does the good outweigh the bad?
4. Are television programs compelling because they *surprise* their audiences — or because they *don't?* Explain.
5. Would broadcast programming be a good career for you? Why? Why not? Which parts of the work seem most challenging?

8

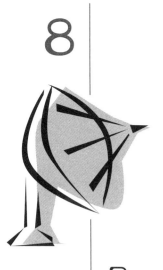

Broadcast
News

There is a weird power in a spoken word.

—Joseph Conrad, *Lord Jim*

What each man does is based not on direct and certain knowledge, but on pictures made by himself or given to him.

—Walter Lippmann, *Public Opinion*

Times Square/Election. Was it George W. Bush or Al Gore who had won the razor-close 2000 presidential election? Early and mistaken TV-network projections went back and forth on the night of November 7.

Broadcast news is a profession that seems to invite special moments of crisis. Consider, for example, NBC anchor Tom Brokaw, for whom the night of November 7, 2000, became an especially galling public trial. He is a rugged veteran of almost 40 years in journalism. He had won praise for his book, *The Greatest Generation*, honoring the courage of U.S. forces in World War II. Now, though, Brokaw himself could have been excused for taking cover.

For days, oddsmakers had pronounced the race in Florida "too close to call"; however, when the usual sources fed the TV **networks** the usual sort of data, they called the race anyway. NBC was first to project that Vice President Al Gore had won Florida and the presidency. Suddenly, the arrival of new exit-poll data prompted all networks to retract that projection. That move alone would have made for a rocky night, but there was worse to come. Looking at fresh data, NBC then gave the nod to President Bush, yet as more results flowed in, the network— embarrassed but trapped—had to withdraw that projection, too.

> Amid that gruesome night of uncertainty and error, NBC's Brokaw in effect confessed on the air for all the broadcast media.

Amid that gruesome night of uncertainty and error, NBC's embattled field general, Brokaw, in effect confessed on the air for all the

197

broadcast media. "We don't just have egg on our face," he said, "we have an omelet all over our suits." It was a sad admission from a man holding a job considered among the news media's most powerful. Indeed, if every episode were as hair-raising as Election Night 2000, perhaps few would answer the call to broadcast journalism. Yet every year, thousands do.

HOW NEWS MATTERS

Americans first snapped awake to broadcast news when one of radio's inventors, Lee De Forest, transmitted 1916 election results from his primitive New York station to perhaps several thousand listeners. By postwar 1920, Pittsburgh station KDKA was cutting a deal with the *Pittsburgh Post* to broadcast its news of election returns. These developments themselves were news. They showed that technology could transmit far and rapidly the kinds of information we had passed around slowly, from person to person, for thousands of years.

At Its Roots

Broadcasting basically is a process by which other humans give us the news *by word of mouth*; speech still seems essential to most communication. The modern electronic media thus have roots running back to ancient **oral cultures**; we can look to the "town criers" who shouted the news through England and colonial America. Some early news broadcasts were not much more sophisticated—just readings by radio actors using quite formal-sounding English. Soon enough, however, journalists with more of a man-in-the-street style were found or developed. Also, broadcasters learned to "write for the ear," meaning to break complex news stories into short, simple sentences that seemed almost *conversational*. Radio reports could therefore help the listener's brain create vivid images of events. All of this made news accessible and appealing to a wide range of listeners, turning radio into an all-American medium.

The correspondents assembled by CBS before and during World War II won particular notice for the clarity and directness of their reporting. Edward R. Murrow, broadcasting from the bombing blitz of London, set the standard. In waves of staccato phrases that sounded almost poetic, Murrow painted word pictures of war and suffering that carried the power of the European catastrophe through the listeners' ears and into their hearts.

Principle #1
The appeal of broadcast news rests on humans' ancient need to *tell* one another of the day's events.

The subsequent growth and branching of broadcast journalism turned it into a vibrant subindustry of the electronic media. It has been subordinated to broadcasting's main product—entertainment—and has swollen or contracted depending on ad revenue. However, as a practice and institution, it spans the nation, and today, U.S. radio and TV news operations provide livelihoods for about 20,000 on-air employees and thousands more behind the scenes.[1]

In Maturity

Not all news employees today have to take the sort of scary public risk that anchors such as Tom Brokaw face when they project election outcomes. They do, however, share in journalism's public *responsibility* to ask questions and report answers. Many news broadcasters theorize that viewers or listeners tune in to answer, first, the most urgent of questions: Is my world safe tonight? The fortunes of broadcast news ride heavily on the trust that people place in anchors and reporters who are paid to answer that question and others.

AUDIENCE SUPPORT

The relative intimacy of broadcast media compared with print media tends to create visceral relationships with audiences. They respond not only to news content but to the people who present it. Today's consumers seem less trusting of broadcasters than were generations past, with

Edward R. Murrow. The CBS correspondent's dramatic wartime radio reports and trailblazing TV documentaries turned his face and name into icons of modern journalism.

many people especially concerned about the *reliability* of journalists. After heavy coverage in 1998 of President Clinton's affair with a White House intern, two-thirds of respondents to one study said reporters were failing to check facts carefully before reporting them.[2] In that same study, three-quarters said they still supported network journalism. These two factors have shown up together often, and support the idea that radio and television reporters, whatever their flaws or mistakes, can generate *loyalty* in audiences.

This is critical today because of the business dynamic of commercial broadcasting, in which **ratings**—estimates of the number of households tuned in to a show—have remained so important. Operating revenues and profits come from advertisers who pay stations and networks to showcase products and services. To plan their sales campaigns, advertisers must believe that their commercials will reach large or especially desirable audiences. If programs aren't attractive enough—as demonstrated by ratings—audiences drift away. Some people are unlikely to return, given all the choices they now have in news and other programming.[3]

> **Principle #2**
> News consumers first want to know: Is my world safe?

> **Principle #3**
> To survive commercially, news must keep audiences involved the same way that entertainment does.

TECHNOLOGY'S ROLE

Broadcast journalists have employed techniques that would send an old-fashioned town crier into a swoon on the cobblestones. During the 1990–1991 Persian Gulf War, correspondents in hotel rooms and on rooftops in Saudi Arabia could go on camera and report *live* to U.S. audiences as missiles flew overhead. A national boom in use of cellular phones enabled radio journalists to outrace television, report instantly from news scenes and even reach traveling newsmakers.

Ratings Measurements of audience size.

News Satellite Trucks.
Bouncing TV images off of satellites, modern TV technology makes long-distance news coverage not only possible but common, even among local stations.

Satellite Space vehicle containing communication relay devices; broadcasting most often uses satellites in "geostationary" orbits—that is, in fixed positions relative to earth.

Principle #4

News technology has value beyond news.

Portable earth station Bundle of electronic equipment that fits in a truck and can "bounce" signals off satellite in space and back to a distant receiving station on earth.

Satellites in space, which have been around since the Soviet Union's *Sputnik* startled the world in 1957, have been relaying broadcast signals since Telstar's launch in 1962. Using **portable earth stations** that can be packed in their cars, TV crews bounce news reports off satellites more than 22,300 miles from earth and back to their stations or networks. Add field-to-base **microwave** technology—made familiar to us by those high-masted vans parked at news scenes—and there is little that television cannot show quickly. Stir in **digital** tools such as advanced cameras and editing systems, and both radio and TV reach the cutting edge of realism, precision, and speed.

As the United States went to war with terrorists in Afghanistan in 2001, network *videophones* went along, sending back live reports from remote places that a few years ago would be seen on maps and slides. By the mid-1990s, some TV stations were acquiring night video of police operations by using helicopters equipped with darkness-piercing **infrared** cameras. Live aerial coverage of developing crime or traffic dramas is now routine. Reporters with cameras as small as campaign buttons have probed commercial and government practices, sometimes exposing matters of real importance. Broadcasters tend to acquire new technical devices partly for journalistic reasons and partly to give their news programs a cutting-edge look, sound, and image.

TRADITIONAL PATHS

Radio

The twenty-first-century citizen can avoid television but so far has had great difficulty sidestepping radio; it reaches into almost all U.S. households, often through multiple sets (the average home has more than five radios). Radio thus permeates our environment and keeps most of us from falling utterly out of touch with important events. However, its news role has diminished and it rarely is heard above the other electronic voices in today's crowded universe of choices; this is ironic, in that radio started the whole process.

AT ITS ROOTS

One of the most memorable early demonstrations of radio's ability to present news dramatically wasn't live, but sounded like it and turned out to be very big news. In 1937, announcer Herbert Morrison broke into sobs as he watched and described the dirigible *Hindenburg* bursting into flames, killing 36 people. What was intended to be just an off-the-air event recorded as an experiment with disc technology for Chicago's WLS became a prolonged and heart-rending news report. Its subsequent broadcast on network radio is said to have been the first use of recorded sound in radio history. Recording technology good enough for routine field use didn't arrive until the 1940s.[4]

With radio spreading and World War II approaching, the networks organized strong teams of journalists and support staff. Their broadcasts emanated from New York stations, passing through telephone lines to the networks' affiliated stations—called **affiliates**—across the United States. This mimicked a pattern set earlier by **wire services** that fed stories to member or client newspapers (and to radio newsrooms). The networks even hired journalists who had honed their skills on "the wires." These fast, broadly informed writers could meet radio's demand for crisp news that, heard only once, could be clearly grasped. Their reports became familiar to Americans as Europe suffered through a German firestorm.

Hindenburg **Disaster.** The spectacular and lethal incineration of a German dirigible was narrated by a sobbing announcer; his recorded account made radio history.

After the war, networks extended their news capacity through more U.S. and foreign bureaus and a mushrooming web of local stations. By the 1950s, however, radio's primacy as a medium was overtaken by the raging growth of television, for which radio had paved the way by assembling audiences in the living room.

IN MATURITY

Today, ABC, CBS, and NBC continue to be brand names in radio news. However, where those brands fit in the industry picture has changed, because that picture has changed. Commercial broadcasting today is a marketplace not just for the sale and delivery of news and entertainment but for a brisk trade in radio *ownership*. A company called Westwood One now owns, partly owns, or distributes all radio newscasts under the CBS, NBC, Fox, and CNN brand names. Westwood One controls much of the "network" radio news we hear, and has many foreign clients as well. Its main rival is ABC Radio, which still distributes news, talk, sports, and entertainment programs to stations from within the ABC network.

Consolidation has affected local radio profoundly, as well. Station groups' acquisition of hundreds of stations has stilled many hometown news voices in favor of syndicated news. Radio-news air time and staffing have been reduced while opinion-rich talk shows proliferate. Disc jockeys frequently stand in for journalists. Some newscasts have shrunk to little more than copy from the wire

Microwave Electromagnetic wave of extremely high frequency; can be generated by a portable device to carry audio or video signals from one location to another.

Digital Technology that records and transmits sound and images through the use of numerical values or "digits."

Infrared Electronic technology that uses part of the light spectrum to create visible images from the heat given off by humans, cars, trees, animals, and so on.

Affiliate (noun) Local radio or TV station affiliated with—but not owned by—a network.

Wire service Journalistic company or collective that contracts with broadcast stations and other media to provide news material, sometimes including video.

services. New corporate owners have found ways to cut their newsgathering costs more severely. A group owner can tap into technology that permits one staffer to feed newscasts into several stations without ever going near their towns. Clear Channel Communications, the nation's largest owner of local radio with more than 1,200 stations, practices this new form of networking. In Ohio, for example, Clear Channel stations in Toledo and Lima feed stories to a hub station in Columbus, which feeds them back as part of a regional newscast.[5]

This approach has reduced efforts and costs by giving less and less attention to truly local reporting; it has also narrowed the diversity of news, in general. Former NBC News chief Lawrence Grossman, worried about the stability of broadcast news, found in 1998 that almost none of the radio stations in and around Washington, DC, was producing its own newscasts. Instead, companies named Metro Networks and (appropriately) Shadow Broadcast Services—subsidiaries of Westwood One—piped in identical national newscasts to all of the stations.[6]

On the other hand, some big-city stations maintain robust news operations. An example is Seattle, where KIRO-AM, owned by the Entercom station group, has struck a balance between local news and network newscasts. KIRO-AM has the largest radio news staff in the Pacific Northwest, with 13 reporters—an army by today's industry standards. By telephone and on foot, using digital audiotape recorders and other modern tools, these journalists dig the raw material of stories out of their bustling region, then write, narrate, edit, and present them.

Today's radio journalist usually is an all-around worker; she or he has to be. Not all of this is due to recent business changes; most radio stations never have been heavily staffed. The majority have no more than three news employees; many have only two; most probably employ only one, perhaps aided by a part-timer. A reporter typically covers at least two or three stories a day—often many more in a small market—and uses basic audio production skills in the field and the studio. The biggest rewards probably are psychological, not financial; salaries in radio are substantially lower than those in TV. Some radio journalists' greatest source of satisfaction is in "reach," which means that their newscasts are exposed to thousands of rush-hour commuters (in towns large enough to have rush hours).

Network Television

A network really is just a relationship among stations and a central production core that feeds them programming. In return for this bounty of content, stations agree to clear air time for *prime-time* (evening) shows and the commercials that accompany them—the networks' primary revenue source. Recent economic pressures have squeezed TV-network news, permitting rival news sources to compete. Still, the Big Three networks (ABC, CBS, and NBC) continue to dominate national news viewing through their local affiliates and cable TV, and have moved onto the Internet, as well.

NEWS STRUCTURE

Let's step back again, but only to the 1970s. By then, radio was drawing less than one-fourth of the broadcast-news audience nationally. CBS's Walter Cronkite

ProTalk

Heather Bosch
KIRO-AM Reporter, Seattle

"When there's something like an earthquake, you're running on adrenaline for three days. This is what a lot of reporters live for."

Seattle radio reporter Heather Bosch describes her often rigorous work day:

"I hit the ground running . . . I come in at 4:30 A.M. unless I'm called in earlier. . . . I usually have a couple of ideas I think will be good stories. The producer in charge also will have good ideas, and the producer will usually win. . . . I go on live at 5:00 A.M.—that is, the network news is at the top of the hour, then the local. Today, I covered the trial of an alleged terrorist, then followed up the death of a Des Moines [Washington] police officer. I was on live at 20 [minutes after the hour] and at 50.

"When the cop was shot, I was live at 4:00 A.M. My goal in radio is to get as much information as possible quickly and update continuously. By 4:00 that day I had information on the officer. I talked to people who were caught in roadblocks. I went to a coffee shop and interviewed local folks. I was on, live, 16 times that morning. You've gotta get different audio, angles, updates. Otherwise, it's the same old stuff, and why does anyone want to listen to that?

"Also, it's more interesting to me as a reporter to get more information. I was able to watch a huge public presence build up as they tried to find the cop killer. There are days like that, when I'm going from the get-go. There are other days when I'm just working the basics. Today, I did a phone interview with a terrorism expert early on. All of the early stuff goes on the air during 'morning drive,' 5:00 to 9:00 A.M. . . .

"When there's something like an earthquake, you're running on adrenaline for three days. This is what a lot of reporters live for. You get out there and get the pain of it, the visual picture, and you let people know what's going on. It must be similar to being an athlete in the playoff games. . . . Radio is so wonderful. Getting things on the air immediately, that's part of it. . . . News radio is baptism by fire; there's nobody to fall back on.

"The pieces I do for afternoon, I write and prepare. I do series pieces about once a month, maybe a five-day series, with each piece a minute and a half or so. That allows for more in-depth interviews. It's a wonderful privilege, as a journalist, that right to ask all kinds of questions, to sit down with all sorts of people."

and other big-name anchors pulled millions of people to their TV sets nightly. Network managers instituted news structures, routines, and specialties that, for the most part, persist today.

Each of the Big Three networks places news in a division with its own leadership, work culture, and budget. Until the 1970s, a news division had been an acceptable *loss leader* for networks; it could lose money but contribute prestige, and that was all right as long so entertainment programs were paying off. However, attitudes toward "loss" were already changing when CBS's *60 Minutes* turned that model on its head by gaining high ratings, those all-important viewer headcounts. Soon, the show was raking in a million dollars a week in advertising revenue versus only $150,000 in expenses, according to its founder-producer Don Hewitt.[7]

The network news divisions gradually came under pressure to follow in Hewitt's footsteps toward profit. Producing more television **newsmagazines** was one

Newsmagazine Radio or television program format that combines news and features in style analogous to print newsmagazines.

Soft news Human interest or secondary news stories.

Hard news Serious news of importance to a broad audience—on such topics as politics or foreign affairs—as distinguished from routine news items or features.

Public service Basic responsibility of U.S. broadcasters to create socially important programming without regard to ratings, in exchange for free use of publicly "owned" airwaves.

approach. ABC's *20-20* made a (disastrous) debut in 1977 and, after major retooling, became a staple. Other efforts did not fare as well; NBC News lost millions of dollars annually—perhaps more than $100 million, by some accounts[8]—until General Electric took over the network in the mid-1980s and cracked down on the budget. This was part of an unprecedented series of corporate acquisitions that triggered a sea of change in network economics. Takeovers of ABC (by Capital Cities Communications) and CBS (by Loews Corporation) pressed their news divisions to toe a new bottom line. They would have to cut costs as well as find more money-making ways to practice journalism.

The resulting drive for ratings generated newsmagazines rich in emotional stories and dramatic structure—similar to their fictional siblings in network entertainment—and very light on complex political and government-policy stories. The new programs fit nicely into prime time, their chosen stories rich in the same qualities as TV dramas. Meanwhile, the networks' morning shows moved increasingly into **soft news** and talk, emphasizing stories of *personal* interest to female viewers—not relatively abstract political or international stories. By the 1990s, NBC's one-time morning flagship, *Today*, was moving away from **hard news** and into chats with Hollywood stars, consumer-oriented discussions, crime and tragedy features, and more live music.

News remains important to the Big Three networks. One reason is that it's the most obvious response to television's **public-service** obligations—the non-commercial programs it's expected to provide as support to its communities. Moreover, startling or sweeping news events (topped so far by the September 2001 terrorist attacks) and long-running human-interest stories can attract massive viewership, raising a network's profile and its advertising revenues.

NEWS PROCESS

All across broadcasting, news systems and practices have evolved similarly. Managers and workers moving from company to company continuously reinforce this homogenization. Following are a few key functions that are common among networks and, in roughly this form, across most of television news.

Management.   Top executives are paid to keep a news division journalistically competitive, strengthen the "brand" of its programs, and watch the bottom line. A division chief (often with the title of news president) has subordinates who oversee areas such as daily news, political coverage, morning programs, and special events. Besides steering the ship, executives sometimes have to jump into topical issues affecting the image and integrity of the network. After Election Night 2000, news divisions assigned vice presidents to investigate the vote-projection errors.

News Selection.   The process of choice among many possible news stories begins many hours before a network newscast. Some stories have been hatching for days or longer. Assignment editors arrange for key bits of video, do research by phone and Internet, and set up interviews. In a morning story conference, editors who focus on different types of news (general, political, foreign, health, consumer) pool and debate their ideas. The lead anchor at networks and some stations may act as a managing editor, advocating some stories and discounting others. Then, hour by hour, early decisions are refined, revised, or discarded. To the degree that a single newscast provides all the news many people absorb in a day, its final shape is crucial, summarizing the most compelling or important situations and events.

Reporting and Production.   New technology, mostly of a digital nature, keeps reducing the number of people required to make a network newscast happen. Fewer employees perform more and more tasks. However, some general activities remain distinct: "Line" producers rank stories in importance, interrogate reporters, arrange supporting visuals, and turn the results into a newscast. **Photojournalists** shoot the pictures. Correspondents and field producers get the facts, write the scripts, catch the planes, and meet the deadlines. Many of these jobs may be blended together and probably will be over time.

Presentation.   Graphic artists create computer-generated charts and visual effects to enhance the storytelling on the TV screen. A director and his or her control-room crew plan the timing of special sound elements and the route of each rolling studio camera (a function sometimes handed to *robot* cameras these days). They also must consider the aesthetic values of the program; again, TV's entertainment shows keep the production-quality standard high, and news cannot escape it. The anchor—the only team member most viewers know—is the *last* link in the presentation chain. He or she must tell the day's stories while projecting conviction that all the stories are useful or important to the viewers.

Local TV Stations

The largest sector of American broadcast journalism is local television news. Newscasts flow from more than 800 TV stations. Some are in small towns and remain small themselves; others are in large cities and have grown with them. Most TV stations have large profit margins and are lucrative assets to their owners. One indication is that, in 1999, a station group bought San Francisco's KRON-TV and its local cable assets for an unprecedented $823.6 million.

STRUCTURE AND PROCESS

The local-news director must design, staff, and support a special kind of team. Its members maintain the flow of news programming. The size of the team varies from the smallest towns to the largest, but in general certain key players are in place everywhere, reporting to the news director. Briefly, an executive producer oversees all elements of newscast organization and assembly; line producers are in charge of one or two newscasts each; one or more writers merge visual and verbal skills to produce **voice-over** scripts for anchors to read live, among other material; an assignment editor deals with quick story checking and arrangements for interviews and other "shoots"; reporters and photojournalists stalk the landscape for story elements, and sometimes specialized videotape editors apply another sensibility to the storytelling.

Even many stations in small markets broadcast several hours of news every day. To the journalist, this means deadlines can arrive repeatedly from before

Photojournalist Professional news photographer who, in television, also edits material for on-air use; often called *videographer.*

Voice-over Video edited for use in newscast with anchor narrating the story live.

ProTalk

David Marash
Nightline Correspondent

"If, at the end of the week, you've told people something about the real world—that's the sine qua non.*"*

David Marash is that rare American journalist who sounds absolutely unpretentious finishing a sentence in Latin. Having once taught college (at Rutgers in New Jersey), Marash sees journalism as, in large part, education. He has worked for more than 12 years as a correspondent for ABC *Nightline* and is a tireless, convincing promoter of the show.

"*Nightline* is unique—alas—in American television and probably in the world," Marash says. "It's not just that we have an unlimited editorial ambition but that we have a *network budget*—which, even in the days when network budgets are shrinking, is still better than any other alternative."

The money pouring into the show's accounts comes from advertisers who appreciate reaching its four to seven million viewers every night. Marash claims a large blue-collar audience but also notes the nightly ads for expensive cars, "a tip-off that we have

educated consumers. . . . If you want to address the policy-making elite in America, there's no single more efficient vehicle than *Nightline*."

Marash travels widely and often, often bringing back eye-opening stories from Kosovo, Zimbabwe, and other points foreign and domestic. He takes pride in revealing ugly truths that governments often deny: "When I did a story on war crimes and concentration camps in Bosnia, we were able to detail two massacres and a death camp. For one of the massacres, which occurred with troops firing randomly into one of four warehouses, we have eyewitnesses in all four of them . . . we literally have the event encircled. The show offers us the opportunity and therefore the obligation to do this job to the fullest."

As a cum laude graduate of Williams College doing literature studies, Marash was not at first a likely broadcast journalist. However, he did small-town radio while at Rutgers and then held some New York radio jobs, a stint with ABC's *20-20* and other slots as a TV reporter and anchor. In 1989, he joined *Nightline*, where he does original reporting constantly and investigative projects 10 to 15 percent of the time.

"I am free to range from sports to profiles of people . . . to, now, nine years of continuing coverage of wars and their aftermath in the Balkans," Marash says. "I know that I will never have less than five minutes (of air time) and may have as much as 17½ minutes to tell my story."

In early 2002, Marash's lavish air time—indeed, *Nightline* itself—faced a challenge from ABC's own leaders. Coveting comic David Letterman's ratings, they tried to lure Letterman away from CBS by offering him *Nightline*'s time slot. Letterman turned down the offer, and the crisis soon passed, but for Dave Marash and the *Nightline* style of journalism, the corporate earth seemed to have shifted.

dawn until late evening or beyond. At most stations, the news day falls into roughly the same functions or phases as the network news process explained earlier. However, there are variations, including these:

- The morning meeting to consider potential stories embraces all ideas, national or local, that might interest large groups of viewers. This includes national stories with transcendent appeal or local "angles." It also includes situations that staffers discover in their neighborhoods or in the morning newspaper.

- Local anchors tend to work in pairs. By contrast, networks have had little luck pairing anchors since the glory days of NBC's Chet Huntley and David Brinkley decades ago.
- When a newscast ends, phones ring; viewers are calling. Many skip over substantive issues to complain that an on-screen name was misspelled or that the anchor's hairstyle was unflattering. However random or trivial, though, viewer calls are a window on community opinion and a link to grass-roots viewpoints that network journalists rarely hear.

> **Principle #5**
> The assumptions and processes of news are roughly similar across all local markets and in both local and network systems.

REWARDS—AND SHORTFALLS

Many TV journalists find the stresses they face daily to be a small price for all that they're allowed to do, and the chance they have to make a difference. A news job can provide some of the most intense and rewarding experiences available anywhere, which is why some choose to make it a career. Among the dividends, though not necessarily paramount, is money. Pay is highest at the networks, where anchors make millions annually while correspondents and top producers earn in the hundreds of thousands. Most budding journalists, however, begin in local news, where pay is good— eventually. On average, it starts at little more than $20,000 annually, the lowest in all of journalism, but salary growth outstrips cost-of-living increases and improves sharply as the TV reporter climbs to larger markets.[9]

At the top of local news, pay can be called lavish: A survey in 2000 by the American Federation of Television and Radio Artists (AFTRA) showed TV reporters in Los Angeles averaging $100,000 to $200,000 a year. Anchors fared even better, averaging more than $300,000 annually.[10] A few in big cities have multi-year, multimillion-dollar contracts. Besides Los Angeles, other top-10 markets

Local TV Reporter. Entry-level pay usually is low, but today's local-station TV reporter enjoys richly varied work and, in a large city, can earn a six-figure salary.

ProTalk

Shannon Dorsett
WAGA-TV Executive Producer

"I'd be lying if I didn't say my first instinct was to run screaming from the newsroom."

Shannon Dorsett didn't run. She had once thought she wanted to become a newspaper reporter, but tried television news through an internship while a student at the University of Oregon. She saw around her then what she soon learned was "organized chaos," and somehow adjusted to it.

In fact, Dorsett went into producing and became weekend executive producer for WAGA-TV in Atlanta—the Fox-owned station in a top-10 market. It's no job for a scaredy-cat, or for an anchor wanna-be, either.

"People joke that producers couldn't make it on camera," she notes, "but a lot of people I know are producers by design. It's tough work, and not everyone can do it—but there's a lot of creativity in producing, putting together an entire show instead of one story."

Stations place heavy pressure on executive producers such as Dorsett. Her fast-growing city, Atlanta, has a high crime rate and serious urban issues; it's a busy news town with highly competitive TV stations. As the only news manager at WAGA on weekends, she depends on others to command the field crews while she focuses on major matters, such as the shifting priorities of each newscast, often involving legal and ethical questions.

"I guess I really like having a lot of responsibility," she says. "Sometimes the calls are kinda tough to make, but I like making those tough calls. I like the daily 'gut check.' That's what journalism students don't know: You don't know how addictive it will become the longer you're in the business."

Dorsett adds that she wishes viewers understood how seriously broadcast journalists take their work: "[Viewers] imagine the news media or some evil secret society meeting daily to think up ways to twist the truth. What they don't realize is that journalists are real people telling real stories. We don't make them up to suit ourselves. We're in this because people have a right to *know*."

News set Table or arrangement of furniture where anchors sit or stand during newscasts; sometimes called a *news desk.*

such as New York and Chicago pay their "talent" highly. Even a few news workers in radio, which creates fewer celebrities, crack the $100,000 line annually.

Detracting from this on-air salary harvest is the fact that *women* do not share in it equally with men. The Los Angeles survey showed women earning, on average, 28 percent less than the men with whom they typically shared the **news sets** where anchors sit (or stand). Nor, in radio, did a woman *solo*-anchor any newscast; lone men anchored most of them. As for the racial balance among TV anchors and reporters, the landscape in many cities is even worse. A 1999 Gallup Poll showed that although 60 percent of whites believed the number of black anchors on TV was "about right," 57 percent of blacks said there were "too few." Progress has been slow; in many communities, the on-air racial mix does not reflect the local population, leading to some concerns about bias in news coverage, as well.

Fairly or unfairly, legally or illegally—and some cases do get to court—stations juggle race and gender among their on-air personnel. Producers, however, are less vulnerable to such manipulation and are in greater demand. TV economics in recent years heightened this: With competition intense and budgets tight, many stations now emphasize news *packaging* while holding the line on expensive newsgathering. To do this, they need producers with broad knowledge—especially of current events—and keen verbal and visual skills. They need them badly enough to pay some of them $50,000 a year and more in large markets.

CNN Effect Viewer compassion and charity after human suffering is shown on TV.

NEWER CHANNELS

Cable News Network

Cable News Network (CNN) was launched in 1980 and seemed to trigger an invasion of competition that would loosen the old networks' grip on the news market. At first, this 24-hour news channel seemed little more than a gamble by a rich, flamboyant Atlanta entrepreneur named Ted Turner. As CNN emerged in scores of cities through cable-TV systems, the insomniacs who wanted news at 4:00 A.M. could get it with *pictures*—as could the midday viewer otherwise trapped among the soap operas. CNN kept journalists—some of them citizens of newsy countries, not "parachuting" U.S. correspondents—working around the world even as ABC, CBS, and NBC cut back their foreign bureaus. From a starting strength of eight U.S. bureaus in 1980, CNN grew to nearly 40 bureaus worldwide over the next 20 years. Hiring local reporters and old-line-network journalists whose contracts had not been renewed, CNN defied the skepticism of veteran broadcasters.

Turner's brash network made a spectacular thrust during the Persian Gulf War by airing live reports from correspondent Peter Arnett behind enemy lines in Iraq. Some Americans complained that Arnett was an unwitting tool of Iraqi dictator Saddam Hussein, but they failed to prove it, and his network should at age 10 that it was ready to cover the world. Other big stories gave rise to what would be called the **CNN effect,** in which audiences moved quickly to help disaster victims worldwide, once their plight became visible on network TV news.

CNN has helped to bring extended live coverage of news developments to millions. It has reported continuously while television news in general stuck to the "appointment viewing" premise—a once-secure assumption that Americans could be enticed to sit down simultaneously for a single informative half hour each night. CNN also reached viewers in many other countries, broadening its business and scope by giving global exposure to U.S. culture and politics.

For several reasons, including cable's natural disadvantages in the ratings and the low star-power of CNN anchors, the network's audience numbers tend to be low except in high-voltage breaking-news situations. In 1996, Turner merged CNN and his other broadcast properties with Time Warner, later to become AOL Time Warner, as the age of media blending and merging raged on.

CNN News Abroad. Once mocked as the "Chicken Noodle Network," CNN grew to span the world with nearly 40 bureaus by 2000 and opened the U.S. marketplace to 24-hour news.

Peter Arnett
Baghdad, Iraq

In 2001, CNN, reorganizing, announced it was laying off 400 workers, and warned its remaining journalists to reach across craft lines and learn as many skills as possible.

Other TV Routes

Fox News Channel (FNC) was brought to cable TV by conservative Australian press magnate Rupert Murdoch, owner of the Fox entertainment empire. He said he intended it as a counterbalance to "liberal" network news. Its ratings went up sharply during and following the 2000 election, when Florida's unresolved ballot count triggered weeks of news, commentary, and debate. Surprising industry observers, FNC managed to keep its ratings high after the election dust settled: February 2001 ratings showed the news outpacing all of its rivals. Its *Special Report* was the top-rated weekday political show on TV.[11] FNC further heightened its profile (as did most channels) from the immense viewership generated by Osama Bin Laden's attacks on New York and Washington, DC. Its news-with-an-attitude approach also struck a chord with many viewers.

MSNBC—the Microsoft/NBC channel, a TV-Internet partnership—is an offshoot of NBC, using the network's anchors, repackaging stories from the network's newscasts, and also doing some reporting of its own. Like other cable-news channels, MSNBC made audience gains in the post-2000 election period, as did its Internet site; the political confusion moved millions of Americans to try new information sources. Also like other channels, MSNBC put a running title—a strategic "brand"—on its coverage of the aftermath of the 2000 terrorist hijack-bombings. Three months after the attacks, its title was "America at War."

CNBC (Consumer News Business Channel) was formed by NBC and Dow-Jones, owner of the *Wall Street Journal*. It hasn't gained high ratings—but, as an-

Combination News. TV/Internet enterprises such as MSNBC benefit from growing use of computers to find news, especially in complex situations like the 2000 election aftermath.

Bloomberg Newsroom. Feeding its products through cable television and the Internet, the news operation founded by Michael Bloomberg reaches business clients and broader audiences.

alysts have noted, *household* ratings don't capture viewing by people watching cable news at the office, club, or gym. One study reportedly found about 700,000 *Wall Street Journal* subscribers watching CNBC from such outposts.[12]

Bloomberg TV, part of a large media/financial enterprise owned by Michael Bloomberg, who was elected New York mayor in 2001, sells data services directly to businesses but also reaches broader audiences through cable TV. News about personal investing and business draws high-income viewers, readers, and computer users. Knowing this, Bloomberg, NBC, and others have worked to turn financial news into a powerful specialty.

Health, hobbies, sports, and other interests also have given rise to cable-TV channels catering to those enthusiasts. ABC-owned ESPN (Entertainment and Sports Programming Network), a 24-hour service, has spawned successful imitators, including Fox Sports,which runs a number of regional networks. ESPN rushes scores and video to sports fans so quickly that it has prompted some local-TV sports anchors to favor features and follow-ups over quick-action reporting.

On some cable systems, *regional* news channels, covering multicounty and even multistate areas, are gradually finding their audiences. In 2001, the National Cable Television Association listed 18 regional news channels—a third of them in the New York area. AOL Time Warner announced it would launch several more nationally. Some are 24-hour channels, aspiring to be regional versions of CNN.

One unique offshoot of interest in television and government is a nonprofit enterprise called *C-SPAN (Cable-Satellite Public Affairs Network).* Funded by license fees paid by cable systems that put it on the air, C-SPAN serves up unfiltered politics and policy by televising public appearances, live, unedited, and with little or no journalistic intervention. This appeals to Americans who've grown suspicious of the mainstream press—increasingly accused of drawing conclusions so quickly that it makes careless mistakes or even of reporting while under the influence of political bias. C-SPAN's audiences tend to be small but devoted, fond of watching uncut presentations on serious subjects. Interest in its coverage spreads wider, however, whenever developments drive people to seek more firsthand information than standard network newscasts provide.

Internet News

Since the 1970s, broadcasting in its original sense—the spread of messages over airwaves to a mass audience—has had to adjust to new competition. Resulting declines in network viewing have coincided with the growth of a whole bazaar of electronic news sources. The newest of these are *Internet news sites*. Unsure how large a market these sites may presage, broadcasters have been moving defensively to set up sites of their own, widely varying in the quality and scope of their coverage.

DEMAND

One ratings service found that 60 percent of the U.S. population (more than 169 million people) had access to the World Wide Web by January 2001. That was an 8 percent jump in three months' time, probably due partly to high interest in the 2000 election. News sites were among users' top destinations.[13] Enterprising business people made the Internet an accessible, broadly useful source of news. It's a source, however, that also requires the *user* to be enterprising; simply sitting on a couch and staring at a computer will, unlike watching TV, produce no information gain. This critical distinction has helped bring caution to the expansion of the Internet news business, as some experiments have failed.

> ### Principle #6
> Internet news invites the audience to become more active than it is when consuming broadcast news.

No one is sure how many Americans will become active seekers of news in the years ahead. However, one survey indicated that people who were consuming more Internet news were using passive news sources, including broadcasting, less frequently than before.[14] Even with their doubts, many broadcasters were afraid *not* to launch websites and appeared to be reminiscent of the "Doonesbury" cartoon character who, when asked why he was starting an Internet business, offered these reasons: "Fear. Greed. Take your pick." The Big Three TV networks now have comprehensive news sites, each with links to many other information sources. This is true also for smaller networks and hundreds of local stations. Some design and run their own sites; others "farm out" the work. One company, Internet Broadcasting Systems of Minneapolis, markets what amounts to a network of local news websites for its client stations.

A survey by the Pew Research Center for the People and the Press found that one-third of Americans in 2000 were clicking on the Internet to obtain news at least once a week. In fact, all key indicators of on-line appeal are rising. The central problem so far with TV-station sites is that few of them do what broadcasters are most focused on doing: make money. Certainly, there are exceptions: WMAQ-TV in Chicago claims to be both turning a profit and enhancing its station image with its website.[15] In Las Vegas, KLAS-TV's website begins with news, ranges through services from tourist aid to tax assistance, carries lots of advertising, and has long claimed profitability. However, not many other stations see revenue streams flowing from their Internet ventures.

STRUCTURE AND WORK

The front of an Internet news site often resembles a newspaper's front page; in fact, many sites are the Internet arms of major newspapers, supplying not only headlines and news briefs but also **hypertext** links to full stories. The viewer/reader who activates such a link is tapping the World Wide Web's capacity to open long, deep corridors of information. By combining broadcasting's brevity and visual allure with its ability to provide detailed background on a news topic, an Internet site can appeal to a large cross-section of news consumers. At least, that's the idea.

Many sites depend on advertising rather than charging subscribers directly; unfortunately, many potential advertisers have not yet developed confidence in the Internet. Even a brief economic downturn can cost a news dot-com lots of money, especially when it relies on advertising for its revenue and when advertisers suddenly cut back on spending. Such reversals have led big-name news sites—run by media giants such as the *New York Times* and Knight-Ridder—to lay off workers. Surprisingly, some promising sites went out of business early. Others began charging subscriber fees but later withdrew them; a few subscription sites survive, and more are promised.

CNN claimed in 2001 that its website, CNN.com, had reached that "wonderful and vital" stage and it began charging monthly fees to access its news video from the site. The company said it led the pack according to the number of *page impressions* and *gross usage minutes (GUM)*, both indicators (something like TV's **Nielsen** ratings) of just how and how much a site is used.[16]

Internet news publishers have recruited workers of all sorts. They include young, "computer-hip" journalists never initiated into traditional news media; mature ex-print journalists; a sprinkling of former broadcasters, and even some computer whizzes who aren't particular about content. Anyone with quick reflexes and information skills might find a place in this *avant-garde* realm. News sites employ reporters, editors, writers, graphic designers, and other print or broadcast specialists who can adapt quickly to packaging news for cyberspace. (Irresistible language from a help-wanted ad for a World Wide Website "anchor": "Ideal candidate is a female anchor in her twenties whose style is a mix of MTV and Fox News.")[17] Because some sites offer video clips of news stories, they also hire producers. Some come from fast-paced broadcast newsrooms, and yet they learn quickly how to organize and refresh multimedia sites.

Fortune can be fickle for the Web worker in this unstable marketplace. At Disney stockholders' annual meeting in 2000, chairman and CEO Michael Eisner said the company's Internet "portal" Go.com—which, among other things, led visitors to Disney-owned ABC news sites—had made the company "the sleeping giant of the Internet."[18] One year later, in February 2001, the sleep had turned to a coma: Disney announced more than 500 Go.com layoffs, about 25 percent of its Internet workforce. A general downturn in the fortunes of dot-coms also struck other news sites hard.

Still, the overall, long-term signs are better. On one day of that same February when Go.com was staggering, a single journalism-jobs website carried 81 ads for Internet news workers. They ranged from a web producer for WMFE-TV/FM in Orlando, Florida, to an on-line news editor for the *Santa Rosa (California) Press-Democrat*; from a reporter for a Chicago company that syndicates

Hypertext Collection of World Wide Web documents (or "nodes") containing cross-references or "links" that allow the reader to move easily among documents.

Nielsen A. C. Nielsen Co., a pioneering audience-measurement company.

Demographic Any audience segment as defined by its members' age, ethnicity, income, or other characteristics that may be targeted by advertisers.

auto-racing articles to 15 positions at National Public Radio Online.[19] If the future of Internet news had not yet been secured, at least many people were refusing to give up on it.

NEWS AND SOCIETY

There are some special influences on electronic journalism and its relationship with society, and there are some controversial issues involving news management and practice. Let's consider a few of these factors.

Ratings and Research

Because prices for commercial air time are pegged directly to ratings and to **demographic** targeting of listeners or viewers, these statistics have been a powerful force for decades. They apply to news just as to other kinds of programming. Much emphasis still is placed on sheer numbers of households watching a newscast or one of its segments. Ratings firms can estimate viewership in time periods of five minutes or less; this can be used to gauge viewer responses to an *individual story* in a newscast. One of the authors once heard a manager order an Emmy-winning investigative reporter to avoid a certain topic because her brief report on it the previous evening had drawn mediocre ratings. Question: If viewers knew of this, would they object to the notion that audience measurement can sway the judgment of news organizations?

Beyond just counting, the use of social-science analyses of audiences has accelerated the trend toward "news you can use" (or at least "want"). It's now possible to learn, for instance, how much an audience likes "live shots," which then can be added to or subtracted from the news menu accordingly. This can be harmless in regard to the live shot, which often is just a dramatic device that can be dropped without altering the substance of news. However, if viewers or listeners indicate little interest in foreign news or political stories, should they be dropped from the agenda, too? Journalists often claim an obligation under the First Amendment to tell even unpopular stories. It's a point they sometimes discuss with their own managers, who usually note that good journalism is useless if people aren't watching or listening and that a station has to maintain ratings and revenue. This issue is far more passionately debated within the broadcast community than among the general public—another ominous sign to journalists who fear that audiences' commitment to news is diminishing.

Technology

Technology has been a boon but it can also be double-edged. It has brought great speed to the transmission of news, but that speed has encouraged some journalists to skirt their profession's best practices, such as careful corroboration of tips from anonymous sources.[20] TV's resort to high-tech devices has helped attract audiences and inform citizens but has also put journalists under ethical scrutiny. They are criticized for invading privacy when hidden cameras or microphones expose unsuspecting characters. They are reviled for endangering hostages and police by looking over the shoulders of SWAT teams and showing their maneuvers on live television, which a hostage-taker could be watching.

With budget "bean counters" more empowered than ever before, managers who purchase expensive tools feel daily pressure to *use* them, whether news justifies it or not. The tension seems especially high when a helicopter is available.In Baltimore one evening in 2001, viewers of WBAL-TV were treated to live aerial views of a car fleeing police; the drivers were suspected only of car theft—one of thousands a year in that city, thus hardly a big news story. However, said the news director, "It was compelling to watch.[21] That thirst for spectacular drama, rather than importance or context, drives many news decisions today.

Behind the scenes, economic pressures are affecting news content. Merged media conglomerates are trimming payrolls in the newsroom, and are adopting new technology for greater efficiency. A Florida company, ParkerVision, has sold to some TV stations a computerized system that reportedly enables *a single employee* to perform most of the functions that make a newscast happen.

Trust and the Consumer

No challenge holds more long-term potential for disaster than the pressures to build ratings and reduce expenses, which go to the heart of electronic news media's purpose. The long-term usefulness of news to society hinges on its quality—that is, how well and truly it informs citizens—which depends, in turn, on its accuracy, its independence, and its credibility. In the end, the whole journalist-audience relationship hangs on a measure of trust.

CREDIBILITY

All values matter deeply, but credibility comes first in news and has suffered some serious blows. When forming general views of electronic media, Americans look not only to the steady performance they witness daily but to more negative and highly publicized events: the hiring of a sleazy-talk-show host to do news commentaries on a Chicago TV station; CNN's retraction of a report that U.S. troops used nerve gas during the Vietnam War; high-profile network anchors having to eat their words about who was winning on Election Night 2000; Fox TV dispatching the discredited journalist Geraldo Rivera to cover war in Afghanistan, where he promptly was accused of new distortions. A national survey in 2000 found CNN to be the "most believable" TV news source, but with only a 39 percent credibility rating. The Big Three networks scored lower, about 33 percent (like local TV news)—and much lower for their TV newscasts than for their Internet news sites.[22]

Clearly, not enough listeners and viewers believe or trust broadcast journalism. Beyond factual errors, ethical blunders, and blown projections, there are other contributors to the credibility problem. Both TV and radio make many on-air mistakes—but offer few on-air corrections, leaving the truth permanently in doubt. Worse, there are deep suspicions that broadcasters are finding new ways in their reporting to favor the people who pay their bills.

COMMERCIALISM

A study by the Radio-Television News Directors Association found 40 to 50 percent of consumers believing that radio news often is improperly influenced by "marketplace factors such as ratings, profits and advertisers."[23] That perception would be damaging even if there were no evidence to back it up—like the survey of TV news directors by the Project for Excellence in Journalism. It found one-third of them complaining of being pressured "to kill negative stories, or do positive ones, about advertisers."[24]

These issues inevitably contribute to overall perceptions of the *quality* of electronic journalism. Radio and television stations and networks do important work every day; this is what puts them ahead of newspapers in winning the largest audience. It also is the core reason for considering a career in broadcast or Internet news: Thousands of people strive to make it excellent. However, they meet with heavy resistance from commercial forces, from some of broadcasting's bosses, and from the high "dazzle" standard set by the entertainment that surrounds news.

COMPLEXITY

The older electronic media's limitations in handling abstract information have been a special, intractable problem. Most news of importance—that is, almost anything that can't be seen or heard and thus quickly understood, in all or most of its nuances—may be too complex to help broadcasters hold audiences. This rules out layered, long-form reports on or discussions of political, governmental, economic, and sociological topics, at least on most commercial channels. Television news, in particular, copes with the shrinking attention spans of consumers and the wispy, transient nature of broadcast messages. These factors seem to persuade some managers that only the most urgent, powerful, and possibly bizarre news will resonate in viewers' memories and make them loyal.

Consultants are developing strategies for making even complex stories attractive to listeners and viewers on the go. Meanwhile, however, CBS anchor Dan Rather has warned against false hope. Rather conceded in 2001 that television couldn't explain stem-cell research; he advised viewers instead to "read, in detail, one of the better newspapers tomorrow."[25] An unprecedented heresy by a broadcast icon? Hardly. Rather's predecessor, Walter Cronkite, had been saying much the same for at least 20 years. Cronkite refers to TV news as "a headline service."

Giving up on broadcasting's ability to convey more detailed and challenging fare does not mean giving up on the *newer* media, particularly those on the Internet. They may have the best opportunity to weave complicated narratives and help audiences—that is, individual computer users, scattered far and wide—follow the stories to their ends. This realization may be part of what has propelled broadcasters at least into the shallows of the Internet pool. Rather than settling for less and less substantive content, the next generation of Americans may insist on more, but from a different medium.

INTO THE FUTURE

There is no guarantee of eternal success for broadcast news. A major question of the Internet age is how audiences will respond as newer media blossom, compete for attention, and redefine the electronic-media world. As communication, in general, increasingly "goes digital," pressures to shift resources are likely to continue—but will not move far ahead of consumers.

Broadcast news remains not only a vital business but also a stimulating, satisfying career. Its current economic strains have forced radical notions to the surface—ideas for new ways of operating. In March 2001, *60 Minutes* originator Don Hewitt urged the three traditional networks to merge their three flagship evening newscasts into just one "blockbuster." The three big-name anchors at ABC, CBS, and NBC could take turns on the newscast, Hewitt said, and the money saved by eliminating needless competition could be plowed into other important news programs such as ABC's *Nightline*, NBC's *Meet the Press* and—yes—CBS's *60 Minutes*.[26] Hewitt's idea might not win many hearts, but it spoke to the choices at hand.

Another sign of the times was the ABC *Nightline* debacle. ABC executives decided to float a story in the press that *Nightline* had become "irrelevant," and that audiences might be better served by talk-show host and comedian, David Letterman. An embarrassing series of news articles ensued, and Ted Koppel, the show's anchor, was obviously incensed. Apologies were soon made and *Nightline* stayed put, but the indelible impression left by ABC's moves was that nothing mattered more than the bottom line.

Broadcast journalism may never reclaim the influence it held over our common information—and, to some degree, our imaginations—until late in the twentieth century. Today, it tends to be defined far more as a commodity, a product to be sold, than as a public service. In the rawest terms, it's whatever most viewers want to hear or watch at any moment. This trend produced an especially odd-looking network newscast in January 1997. One Tuesday evening, *NBC Nightly News* switched back and forth live for several minutes between the Washington site of President Clinton's State of the Union speech and the Los Angeles locale of ex-athlete O. J. Simpson's defeat in a civil trial resulting from his wife's murder. Electronic technology had enabled television that night to project the indecisiveness of its producers. One event, at the highest levels of government, held great potential meaning for the nation; the other clearly generated intense interest among many viewers. NBC declined to choose, trying to "serve two masters" with a split screen.

Wonderful opportunities await today's graduates—journalism never has been dull—but no one can yet see their precise nature or scope. Journalists of tomorrow might work in radio, TV, print, and the seemingly limitless Internet in the course of a single day. They might even throw off all traces of conventional broadcasting—but that seems unlikely, given the unique power of radio and television to tell some stories exceedingly well.

Videographer Professional news photographer who, in television, also edits material for on-air use; often called *photojournalist.*

Summary

Broadcast news is a demanding, sometimes scary line of work but a vital public service. Network television anchors such as Tom Brokaw suffer in the public eye when their "facts" turn sour. This signifies the importance of radio and television journalism careers as well as the pressures they bring. News has been a major component of broadcasting in the United States since early in the twentieth century. The value of radio information was compounded by its oral delivery, which drew on society's roots in the spoken word.

Modern broadcast news—still "writing for the ear" but also employing new electronic tools—can transmit human experience through both sound and pictures, sometimes enhanced by special graphic elements. Audiences bond to broadcast journalists as people telling them important things; and they deliver harsh judgments when they believe those people have failed to check facts and purge biases. Although local stations provide most people with most of their broadcast information, it is major networks that remain the most nationally prominent and often most controversial of news sources. In times of national crisis or simply elevated national interest—the Persian Gulf War, the illicit affair between a president and an intern—networks use their resources to showcase the news.

News no longer is permitted merely to break even or lose money; its profits must compete with those of the networks' entertainment programming. This has given birth to "newsmagazines" in prime time, a narrowing of news agendas, and cuts in newsgathering budgets. Critics say such moves have weakened broadcasting's commitment to providing public service, as it is required to do in exchange for free use of public airwaves. To reach audiences, the networks still depend on local stations as their outlets, and to create news programming, both network and local managers depend on a core of key workers. They include producers, assignment editors, reporters, photojournalists, and support staff.

Radio and TV networks and stations increasingly aim their news at specific, desirable audience groups, tailoring newscasts to "what people want" instead of traditional judgments of "what people need." Local TV news continues to be highly lucrative, and radio news often does well, but both sectors send their revenues up the "food chain" to a steadily decreasing nucleus of owners. One result has tended to be a sameness of news content, much of it shared among sister stations within station groups. Another result is relentless economizing that has cut many staffs to the bone. Still, newsrooms follow the same daily routines that broadcasting long has required: story conferences, deployment of reporters and **videographers,** writing and other in-house production tasks, and the convergence of those streams of effort in the execution of newscasts.

A major question is how much and how rapidly the growth of Internet news will affect broadcast news. Networks and many stations have established World Wide Web sites and use them to offer news and to promote programming. The developing audiences for news sites such as MSNBC.com and CNN.com reflect broadcasters' convictions that the Internet may become a more important news medium, and that they need to get into it early. This has meant new job opportunities for journalists—and pressure for them to learn new skills.

CAREER FOCUS

Local stations are the main entry points to a broadcast-news career. Radio journalists so often are "one-man bands" that they need prior or on-the-job news and production training. The makeup of a local TV-news team varies from small towns to large, but certain key players are found almost everywhere, reporting to the news director:

- An **executive producer** oversees the organization of newscasts.
- **Line producers** are assigned to construct each newscast.
- One or more **writers** (if available) write stories and lead-ins to reporter **packages.**
- An **assignment editor** pursues news leads and angles throughout the news cycle.
- **Reporters** follow up leads, generate new stories, interview sources, and write the self-contained narratives called packages.
- **Photojournalists** and, in larger stations, specialized **videotape editors** (or the two jobs combined in **videographers**) shoot and/or edit news footage, working alone or with reporters or producers.

Reporters and sometimes photojournalists may be assigned to **beats**—special areas of news interest, such as police, health, or city hall—or to general subjects in which they have expertise. Even if they do have beats, however—given the viewer appeal of live breaking news—reporters often are kept on a general assignment (GA) footing so that they can reach crime and accident scenes quickly. Similarly, in most stations, photojournalists move from story to story without regard to content (but must *know* content to do a good job).

The jobs mentioned here can be realistic targets for almost anyone who can complete college broadcasting courses. Most news directors want to see at least one *internship* on a job applicant's record; internships often are a deciding factor in hiring because of their value in orienting people quickly to the demands of broadcast news.

Anyone aspiring to an electronic-news career is well advised to read trade publications *(Broadcasting and Cable, Electronic Media, Columbia Journalism Review, American Journalism Review)*. These keep the reader abreast of ethical issues, economic realities, and hiring trends.

FOOD FOR THOUGHT

1. If broadcasting is an extension of our ancient oral culture—and reading among youth is in decline—then can it be that we still live in an oral culture? Argue your points.
2. Some critics and journalists argue that broadcast news would hold audiences and grow if it stuck to news, avoiding "infotainment." Would that work? Explain.
3. Do you believe that consolidation in radio has made most music stations sound alike? If so, how has that affected your own listening? Should consolidation be stopped? Why or why not?
4. What can our government leaders (or anyone) do to influence the news that broadcasters cover and how they cover it? Is that a good public-policy goal? Explain.
5. Is there real potential for Internet news sites to take the place of either broadcast news or newspapers? What role can these sites best play? Explain your analysis.

Package Self-contained report consisting of recorded images, sounds, and narration by reporter.

Beat Special-interest topic, geographic area, or agency to which a reporter is assigned.

9

Advertising and Promotions

> I do not regard advertising as entertainment or
> an art form, but as a medium of information.
>
> —David Ogilvy, Advertising Executive

Britney Spears's 2002 Super Bowl Spot for Pepsi. Celebrities promote advertising products in highly competitive venues such as the Super Bowl commercials, where audience interest is measured by both program ratings and public opinion.

Super Bowl ads are an American tradition not even a recession or war can entirely diminish. Since the National Football League championship game typically reaches one of the largest (if not *the* largest) TV audiences of the year, the price per commercial hovers around $2 million per half-minute. Approaching the 2002 contest, however, with a U.S. recession tightening advertising budgets, companies realized they could (1) pay Fox TV an average of $1.9 million or less per 30-second "spot," exposing their products to about 130 million viewers, or (2) advertise during the 2002 Winter Olympics starting later the same week, with NBC charging only $600,000 per 30 seconds and reaching smaller audiences in prime time over 17 days.

Ratings and audience characteristics influence advertisers differently, depending on their needs.

What followed was a demonstration of how ratings and audience characteristics influence advertisers differently, depending on their needs. First, many large companies stuck with the football game. It offered towering ratings and a chance to make a high-profile splash—especially helpful when launching a new product—with commercials that the audience was conditioned to enjoy. "You've got 130 million people watching who are actually looking forward to the ads," an executive of an Internet jobs site, HotJobs.com, told the *Atlanta Journal and Constitution*.[1]

Some other big advertisers, on the other hand, found the Olympics more attractive. One reason was *psychographics*. "We coined the term," said a Volkswagen spokesman. "It means lifestyle and attitude." His company decided to skip football and advertise during the snowboard and downhill-skiing portions of the Salt Lake City competition, sure to attract viewers with the "attitude" the car maker was targeting.[2]

The Super Bowl is also where the titans of Madison Avenue showcase the state of their art in commercial production. Whether it's friendly dolphins visiting with tourists at island resorts, or celebrities sipping their favorite sodas, these promotions are as competitive as the athletes on the field in their quest to establish ad dominance.

In 2002, Britney Spears took the spotlight for Pepsi in a 90-second retrospective depicting earlier commercial eras for the soft drink. The Internet converged with TV as Britney fans were invited to vote on their favorite era at pepsi.yahoo.com/britney. TiVo's Monitoring Technology also found the Britney spot was the favorite among 10,000 of its 280,000 subscribers who used their digital recorders to play it back again in slow motion.

The somber mood of post-September 11th America was also reflected in the Super Bowl spots. The White House Office of Drug Control Policy invested nearly $3 million in one message to discourage young viewers from taking drugs by linking their narcotics trade to global terrorism. In sum, the Super Bowl ranks among the top venues for TV commercials, reflecting state of the art in both business and technology.

A BRIEF HISTORY OF BROADCAST ADVERTISING

Any radio or TV station executive will gladly tell you that broadcasting is first and foremost a *business*—the object of which is to *make money* by reaching fickle audiences with commercial messages. The problem is they already see more advertisements each day than they can possibly remember. This explosion of advertising is a fairly new phenomenon.

The seed of commercial radio was not one everyone wished to see planted in the first place. Even trade publications such as *Printers' Ink* appeared wary at first. Radio was a privileged medium for the sanctity of the family circle, and "advertising has no business intruding there unless it is invited."[3] Once radio's ability to inspire the imagination and create devotion among listeners was recognized, advertising was invited and it grew to become the lifeblood of the business.

It actually began in 1922, as noted in Chapter 2, when a radio station in New York City helped to lease apartments on Long Island. Since then, broadcasters have found their way into American homes and cars, persuading us to open up our hearts and wallets. American television aired its first ad (for Bulova watches) in 1941 during a baseball game in New York City. Now, television ranks second only to newspapers in advertising volume, and it helps to look back to see how history shaped its strategies for success.

Radio's First Ads

So, who recognized the power of broadcasting to sell in the first place? You might recall it was the phone company. American Telephone & Telegraph's radio station in New York sold "toll time" to a Long Island realtor, the Queensboro Corporation. WEAF broadcast five "talks" to promote apartments for lease. Ten-minute spots aired—the first "infomercial," perhaps, but it worked. Big-name sponsors followed Queensboro to WEAF's microphones, including Colgate, Macy's, Metropolitan Life, and many more.

The demand for radio decorum inspired self-imposed limits on advertising at first. Until 1927, most radio shows were *sustaining*, which meant they aired without commercials. The shows that did advertise limited the pitch to one—that's right, only *one*—mention of the company name or product. No mention of prices was aired until 1932.

Advertising agencies such as J. Walter Thompson were undeterred. They dreamed up schemes for working sponsor names into talent acts. When vaudeville and radio merged, sponsors such as Eveready Battery, Gold Dust washing powder, and A&P groceries named performers after their brands. Each time an announcer thanked the Gold Dust Twins or A&P Gypsies, he inadvertently plugged the product. More creative sidesteps were contrived. Jack Benny greeted his radio audience, "Jello again." It was just a matter of time before major ad agencies on Madison Avenue overcame broadcasting's barriers against their enterprise and created radio slogans with catchy jingles: "LSMFT—Lucky Strike Means Fine Tobacco," and "you'll wonder where the yellow went when you brush your teeth with Pepsodent."

When the Depression darkened America's mood, radio spots resonated with appeals to "fear, shame and blame [that] conveyed a common message: 'If you don't buy this product, you will be sorry.' "[4] Profits sank during the 1930s, and marquee ad agencies found it hard to maintain their billings, their monetary measure of advertising accounts sold. When sales dropped, salaries were cut and personnel were laid off.

Audience distrust of commercials grew in response to the malaise—and to the growing repository of dishonest ads.

The Jack Benny Show. In 1934, General Foods signed on to *The Jack Benny Show* as its sponsor. Benny began greeting audiences with "Jell-O again" for every Sunday evening over a 10-year run. Radio audiences also became familiar with the J-E-L-L-O jingle.

Ma Perkins. Radio programming and products merged during the 1930s when Oxydol detergent sponsored the serial, *Ma Perkins.* The genre "soap opera" took its name from this family melodrama, which featured actress Virginia Payne in more than 7,000 broadcasts.

Principle #1

The business of commercial broadcasting is building audiences for exposure to advertising.

Puffery Advertising exaggerations not intended be taken seriously, but to make the messages more interesting and entertaining.

This dismal valley was charted by *Ballyhoo*, a 1930s magazine devoted to uncovering **puffery** (advertising claims too wonderful to be true).[5] Yet, radio sales people knew there was gold to be mined in broadcast time and they continued prospecting for it. At first, no one thought radio could sell commercials during daytime hours. That was until a Chicago ad agent came up with a plan to attract housewives in 1932. Frank Hummert drafted scripts for family melodramas while his assistant, Anne Ashenhurst, produced shows such as *Betty and Bob* and *Just Plain Bill*. It was *Oxydol's Own Ma Perkins* that gave the genre its name, *soap operas*.[6]

Saturday morning serials caught on with kids who tuned in for their favorite heroes. *Tom Mix and the Ralston Straight Shooters* kept cereal bowls full of Ralston's, while other youngsters gulped down Wheaties, "Breakfast of Champions," during episodes of *Jack Armstrong, the All-American Boy*. For the girls, Ovaltine went well with *Little Orphan Annie*, and there were more comedy, musical variety, and quiz shows for the rest of the family—all with commercials. Magazines saw their lead in total volume for advertising revenue overtaken by radio in 1938.

Rise and Fall of Single Sponsorship

The magic that worked for sponsors in radio fared even better on television. The strategy of producers in the 1950s was to match product ads with customer tastes in programs. The humor of the *Ernie Kovacs Show*, for example, appealed to the man who would light up a Dutch Masters cigar. American housewives would leave the kitchens to watch celebrities on *Betty Crocker's Star Matinee*. *Texaco's Star Theater* was one of many shows to carry the single-sponsor concept to television. Milton Berle's singing quartet of Texaco attendants entertained millions each week with "You can trust your car to the man who wears the star." Soon, the harmony turned to discord when a certain type of television program fell victim to corruption.

In 1958, news broke that *Dotto*, a CBS game show, was rigged. After other TV game show producers from *21* and *The $64,000 Question* were summoned before congressional committees, the networks decided to remove most of the single-sponsored shows from their schedule. They took over production and began selling shows to multiple advertisers who *participated* in shows instead of sponsoring them. Media planning became the name of the game where ratings proved to be the key to success.

COMMERCIAL ENTERPRISE

The object of the advertising game of media planning is defined both by the ratings and by the rules. They are familiar to people who have made it their career, but mystifying to others. The rules cover everything from how the spots are sold to where they're placed in the program schedules. The players may work out of a radio or television station office, an advertising agency, a network, or one of the many media groups that employ staffs to buy and sell time across the media marketplace.

> **Principle #2**
> Advertising begins with marketing—knowing the product, its benefits, and the target audience.

Advertising Forces

National businesses rely on different media to get their point across to potential customers. Mammoth firms such as IBM, General Motors, and Procter & Gamble often recruit advertising agencies to draw up their battle plans to win their market share and keep on growing. This is done by a strategy called the *media mix*, which identifies all of the channels used to attract new customers and build loyalty among old ones. Some firms employ in-house agencies to design commercials and campaigns. Regardless of where the ad team is located—in house or in Manhattan—it must be well equipped to reach the right audience, which means having the right players in the right positions.

Account executives
(AEs) Salespeople who serve as liaisons between agencies and clients, coordinating the specialists working on the account. Also, people in a broadcast or cable operation assigned to handle specific accounts and to act as marketing consultants.

ADVERTISING AGENCIES

Advertising agencies occupy the pinnacle of a much larger industry that crisscrosses among radio and TV production studios, web-design boutiques, and print shops. The full-service agency threads a number of duties—account management, creative tasks, media planning, and marketing research—into most of its projects. These employees report to a senior administrator, usually a vice president or president.

ACCOUNT MANAGEMENT

Account sales personnel act as both consultants and facilitators. They learn fully the client's promotional needs so they can intelligently advise him or her on the decisions to make with ad dollars. **Account executives (AEs)** are paired with client accounts, business people trying to build their industry through effective marketing. The AEs meet and consult with these clients about their firm's goals and how advertising can achieve them. Once message objectives are drafted and target audiences are identified, an advertising plan can be roughed out for execution. The account executives then go to their creative writers, artists, and media producers to embed the commercial message in words and images, while consulting with media buyers about the proper mix for broadcast and print distribution.

CREATIVE IDEAS

The creative department is where imagination holds sway. It is there that ideas are created and sold. *Creative writers, art directors,* and *producers* are the artisans responsible for choosing words and pictures to create compelling images for the client. *Radio* and *television producers* are responsible for making the spots, which demands creative and administrative talents. A great many details must be addressed in any commercial's production—everything from selecting the

Area of dominant influence (ADI) Arbitron's term to define the region and communities where an audience receives the same radio and television signals.

Designated market area (DMA) A. C. Nielsen's term for one group of communities where the audience receives the same radio and television signals.

Cold call Unannounced visit or phone call by an AE to an advertising prospect.

Inventory Total budget of available ads for a radio, television station, or cable system.

talent and location to budgeting, scheduling, recording, editing, and obtaining final approval of the finished spot.

MEDIA PLANNERS

Media planners and *buyers* are responsible for the planning and placement of advertising time. They draw up and present the media mix in a plan to fulfill the client's promotional goals. The agency's *media buyer* takes the finished campaign and places it in markets where it will do the most good, which may require buying time in local, regional, and even national media.

ADVERTISING MARKETS

The country is divided not just into cities but into markets that encompass more than one city. There are two terms used to describe markets: **area of dominant influence (ADI)** and **designated market area (DMA),** depending on the audience ratings employed. Nielsen prefers the term *DMA*, whereas Arbitron uses *ADI*. They basically mean the same thing—an area served by one group of radio and television stations, cable systems, and newspapers.

Meanwhile, researchers inspect circulation figures and rating levels to find the best stations for target audiences. Other forms of research, such as *focus groups*, gauge a commercial's readiness for air before it's ever broadcast. Afterward, telephone surveys check to see what type of impression the spots made. This research process is covered in greater detail in Chapter 10.

Broadcasting Forces

Inside the offices of local radio and TV stations, advertising and sales people work the telephones or get in their cars and visit clients. The general sales manager leads the station's sales force and is responsible for both local and national sales of commercial time. That team leader motivates the sales staff of the station by drawing up a plan of advertising goals and the best ways to achieve them. Like a coach, the general sales manager tries to build a winning team and project a positive image for the station.

Local sales managers focus on local clients and local advertising agencies. Their aim is selling the station's commercial **inventory** within the market area. They show AEs how to package and present the station's commercial time in order to maximize sales. They also prepare ratings presentations and research data on the competition, particularly cable systems that have managed to slice away at the TV advertising pie by offering lower rates per spot.

ACCOUNT EXECUTIVES

The principal envoys and consultants in radio and TV stations, as in the advertising agency, are the AEs. Account executives in local markets begin their day interviewing potential clients. They make planned or **cold calls,** either seeking out prospects from a core list or finding new ones on their own. They discover who each sponsor is and, more important, what the sponsor's needs are in terms

Cable versus Broadcasting

How serious is the battle between cable and broadcast television for advertising clients? Check out the websites of the Television Advertising Bureau and the Cablevision Advertising Bureau. In "TVB: Broadcast vs. Cable," television's national advertising bureau charges that "with highly selective use of Nielsen data and creative spin, the cable industry continues to mislead the advertising community about broadcasting vs. cable comparisons."

The site then offers 13 boxes to challenge cable's pitch for advertising accounts. Try a few choice quotes: "The latest Nielsen ratings show that of the top 100 television programs, 97 were on broadcast networks while only 3 were on cable,"[7] "Viewership of Top Cable Networks Down in '00–'01," and "Cable's Dirty Secret: No One's Watching." One quote borrowed from a writer for

Variety says "Spinmeisters for cable nets may boast of ratings gains and Big Four (ABC, CBS, NBC, and Fox) erosion, but faux wrestling and musty reruns aren't much to crow over."

Before you start to feel pity for the rough treatment cable gets from broadcasters, check out the stats on the Cablevision Advertising Bureau's website comparing all cable channels to four television networks. "Cable's U.S. household ratings far outdistanced the rating of any broadcast network in the 1999/2000 season," says the claim. What's left unspecified is how many cable channels combined to defeat the broadcast networks with a 24.0 rating. What has become clear to both cable and broadcasters is that advertising revenue has declined for network television while continuing to rise for less-expensive cable time.[8]

of promoting its business. When successful, AEs bring back signed contracts and place spots in the inventory of their program log.

NATIONAL REPS

National advertising sales usually are delegated to a firm outside the station. It simply is not practical for every radio and TV station to hire a sales person to represent the business in New York City or Los Angeles. That's the job of the national representatives who first made their appearance on the advertising scene more than 50 years ago. A revival of advertising swept through the nation after World War II, and it gave birth to a new type of broadcasting sales person. Two radio station salesmen, Ed Petry and John Blair, decided if they could represent several stations instead of just one, they could multiply their accounts and commissions. Blair and Petry found that their inspiration was on target. They were so successful, in fact, that the commercial networks took notice and opened their own national sales offices. The FCC took a sideways glance and saw a monopoly in the making. It ordered networks to represent only their owned-and-operated stations.

About a dozen firms followed Blair and Petry into the business of selling time for local stations to national sponsors—Petry Media, Katz, and Telerep, among others. National sales representatives (reps) contract with local stations for two or more years, and ask for commissions in exchange for their national spot sales. Rep profits are calculated according to the charge per spot.[9] It just makes good business sense for commercial sponsors to turn the chore over to one firm instead of having to negotiate with hundreds of stations around the country.

Avails Available time slots in a broadcast or cable schedule to be sold to advertisers.

Flight Commercial schedule from beginning to end when the advertiser places commercials with a station or cable system.

Reach Estimate of the percentage of the total audience exposed to a message, spot, or program at least once during its run.

Frequency Measure of advertising reinforcement—usually an estimate of how many times the audience has been exposed to a spot.

Best Time Available
(BTA) Flight of commercials where the TV station or cable system promises to run the spots in the highest-rated time period available.

For example, two of America's largest advertisers, General Motors and Procter & Gamble, divide their multibillion-dollar budget for advertising several ways, and television gets about 40 percent of it. The remainder is invested in advertising on radio and in newspapers, magazines, and outdoor advertising. In terms of TV time, these huge advertisers spend about one-fourth of their money placing commercials in network shows such as the evening news or situation comedies. They spend another 5 or 6 percent buying spots in syndicated vehicles—for instance, *Oprah* and *Wheel of Fortune*. Then they spend between 5 and 10 percent for cable channel placement. Even though a network television schedule reaches about 200 affiliates, sponsors aim for audiences outside the reach of those network stations, and that's where national reps come in. They make the investments for spot buys, commercials purchased on a regional or national basis in markets around the country. One wag called it the "spray and pray" approach.

ART OF THE DEAL

When account executives (AEs) seek to offer station time to a sponsor, they usually proceed in a logical fashion.[10] First, they secure the prospect's trust and respect. In the *approach*, AEs listen and learn of the client's business and marketing needs. Following that phase comes the *discussion*, in which the account executive will determine if, practically speaking, the station, cable system or website can effectively meet those needs. If that conversation is productive, the AE and client embark on the *negotiation* phase, in which advertising goals are discussed. If client and salesperson reach an agreement, there is a *closing*, where contracts are signed and commercials go into production.

Negotiating the Sale

In the negotiation phase, the AE and sponsor agree on the total *run* of commercials for the campaign. What that means is the number of spots to be aired over how long a period in what *dayparts* (separate periods of the day). They look for time in the station's inventory of slots available for advertising. These **avails** are unsold commercial minutes where AEs can place ads for clients, including hourly breaks and within programs. The AE then presents his or her plan in the form of a schedule or flight. A commercial *schedule* reflects dates and times when spots are scheduled for broadcast, whereas a **flight** suggests the entire period of time for a campaign. In some cases, AEs even have prospective spots produced; these "specs" are designed to encourage potential advertisers to buy.

Advertising sales are made on the basis of time sold and audience reached—to put it in the terms of the trade, *frequency* and *reach*. **Reach** equals the share of the target audience that actually was exposed to a advertising message based on the ratings, whereas **frequency** estimates the number of times the target audience was exposed to the spots.

The sales people and sponsor decide if the spots are to run within or next to network programs. They also may choose to place spots in local programs at the **best time available (BTA).** If the spots are scattered throughout the day at the

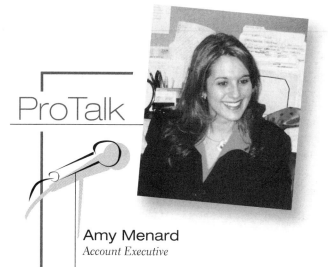

ProTalk

Amy Menard
Account Executive

"There are plenty of businesses that need the help of television advertising."

Advertising sales is a "people-person" job, says Amy Menard. She made the switch to television advertising sales after working in the news and promotion departments of the ABC affiliate in Lafayette, Louisiana. Menard's typical day involves working with many people—business managers, retail merchants, and potential clients interested in generating new business through advertising. She begins at 8:00 A.M. with a sales meeting in the station, at which the general sales manager outlines goals for the day, the week, the month, and even the quarter and year.

After the meeting is over, Menard begins making calls to advertising clients, including follow-up calls and cold calls for new prospects. Once she hits the streets, Menard has one idea in mind: "Sell, sell, sell!" At the end of the day, the station's general sales manager asks for her report. In that debriefing, she discusses the orders taken and the steps required to execute those orders. That includes getting the commercials produced and giving instructions to the traffic department about scheduling.

Menard's primary job is working her account list to build relationships with her station's customers and clients. She says advertising sales people are really the eyes and ears of the station—the first to learn what people think of the programming and the talent. In return, she informs her clients of special events, special programs, anything that might be of interest to them for promoting their businesses at her TV station. There is nothing like getting new businesses on the air, but there are times when the prospects seem lean and mean. She says, "Hearing NO never feels good. . . . Let's just say you have to know how to move on!" Menard adds, "There are plenty of businesses that need the help of television advertising, [so] there is no point in wasting time with those who don't."

---

station's discretion, they're getting the **run-of-schedule (ROS)** treatment. Most advertisers accept package plans offering discounts based on either the size of the package or the flexibility built into its schedule. That factor is called *preemptibility.* Lower prices are charged for spots that can be moved with advance notice as opposed to those holding **fixed positions.** There is even a difference in price according to how much notice the station must give before preempting a spot—a day, a week, or a moment's notice—all of this affecting the price per spot.

Naturally, rates vary by the time of day: The bigger the audience, the higher the cost for a *daypart.* The term *prime time*, for example, describes the evening daypart when more people are watching their television sets. If a sponsor wants to reach peak-audience numbers, the station charges its highest rate, perhaps described as a *triple-A (AAA)* rate or by a similar term. On the other hand, if the sponsor is willing to accept a *fringe daypart*, when fewer audience members are tuned in, the cost for advertising may be reduced to a *B* or *C* rate.

Advertisers need to know of station discounts before purchasing packages of spots. Sales people benefit from the extra commissions by selling longer

Run of schedule (ROS) Preemptible package of spots that can be moved wherever a station or system desires and is sold at lower rates.

Fixed position Guarantee to televise a commercial at the precise time requested by the advertiser.

Cost per thousand (CPM) Advertising charge for making an impression on 1,000 members of the audience.

Cost per point (CPP) Advertising charge for reaching an audience equivalent to 1 percent of the population.

Cume Cumulative, unduplicated total number of people who attend to a radio or TV station for at least five minutes over a period of time, usually a week.

Gross impressions (GIs) Total number of people reached by all commercials over a specified period of time.

Gross rating points (GRPs) Total of all ratings points received for all spots in a specified period of time.

Target rating points (TRPs) Percentage of viewers who saw the message or program within the target audience.

schedules, and discounts are also given to long-term clients for special occasions such as holidays. *Rate cards* are used to show advertisers the base rate, which is often the highest price charged per spot, and lower figures with discounts included for package plans. Some TV stations do not release their rate cards, but use them as tools for negotiations. Another factor figuring in the cost is commercial length. Obviously, 30-second spots are more common and more expensive than 10- or 15-second commercials.

Data for Dollars

The price tag of the audience for radio and TV advertisers is calculated in several ways. The most common method is **cost per thousand (CPM)** viewers or listeners; the *M* is based on the Latin term, *mille*, which is the Roman numeral for 1,000. The CPM, however, is not the only factor used to gauge cost. There is the **cost per point (CPP)**, which is computed by dividing the total number of rating points by the cost of the spots. Then there is the **cume** (short for cumulative unduplicated audience), which is the estimate of how many people were exposed to the spot just once during a portion of its run, usually a week.

Other calculations weigh the size of the audience for the sponsor in terms of the impressions they've made. The **gross impressions (GIs)** indicate the total number of people reached by the entire run. The **gross rating points (GRPs)**, or *grips*, show the gross or total ratings points for the flight. A. C. Nielsen Company also counts the total households within a particular demographic group that the sponsor wants to reach. This figure is called **target rating points (TRPs)**.

Audience Profiling

Conventional wisdom held that advertising was about collecting as many eyes and ears as possible to bring to each spot. It didn't matter to whom the eyes and ears belonged—just so long as they were counted in the audience. That, of course, creates "wasted circulation," advertising to people who are not interested in the product. What businesses really want is a way to reach their target audiences—people who would be more predisposed to hear a message in the first place. In order to solve the puzzle of finding the right viewer or listener to pair with the right ad, advertisers use the tools of demographics and psychographics.

Closing the Deal

When it comes to closing the deal, there are a number of ways advertisers can pay for their spots. Cash plans, trade-out deals, and bartering are available, for example. There are also co-op deals that allow a manufacturer and its retailers to share the cost of commercials. There are even packages of spots based on viewer response called *PI* for *per inquiry*. The emergence of cross-platform deals also has created a lot of interest. Major advertisers such as Kellogg's and Procter & Gamble are taking advantage of the growing concentration of media.

ProTalk

Sean Walleck
KTXA Sales Manager

"Learn how to read a ratings book."

Broadcast advertising can be a roving career and a rewarding one. Sean Walleck is the local sales manager for a television station in Dallas-Fort Worth. That's a position he has worked up to after stints at TV stations in Kansas City, Phoenix, and Chicago. Walleck, a philosophy graduate of Lake Forest College, got his foot in the door not with his diploma, but with his internship experience at a Chicago station.

Walleck has some advice for college graduates interested in broadcast advertising and sales: "Learn how to read a ratings book." What he means are those quarterly books measuring a TV station's audience from the A. C. Nielsen firm that serve as the basis for pricing spots. The rows of numbers are extremely important, whether you're working in radio, television, a full-service advertising agency, or a time-buying firm. "It's about knowing how to read the Nielsens," he says, "and what each point means for both your sponsor and your station."

At the macrolevel, Walleck sees both advantages and disadvantages in the trend toward industry consolidation. Mergers have made sales more efficient—his station's parent company is one example—but "people lose jobs" when those mergers are made. Economies of scale through consolidation make it easier to do business with a single media organization in a cross-platform buy (explained next). Procter & Gamble, for example, chooses to cover north Texas through a $300 million buy with Viacom Plus, which holds the keys to two TV stations, six radio stations under its Infinity umbrella, two broadcast networks and cable channels.

The value of nontraditional revenues (NTRs) as they apply to web promotions is another by-product. Walleck's advertisers have the option to buy spots and border ads that are displayed along the margins of his TV station's Internet site. "We sell spots and dots now," he says.

Walleck has a final piece of advice for aspiring professionals in broadcast advertising: "Learn how to sell." In television, that means learning how to become a careful consultant for your clients. This is a long-term relationship between the sponsors and the stations, and no one wins by just making a fast buck.

CROSS-PLATFORM DEALS

Cross-platform deals are the wave of the future, but just how big a wave no one knows for sure. What cross-platform deals have done is eliminate national reps and media planners by putting the sponsors in negotiation with media corporations, placing all their ads for national cable, broadcast, and print outlets under a single umbrella. Sometimes called *integrated marketing,* this technique feeds on two parallel but opposing forces: media consolidation and audience fragmentation. Proponents say it is more economical and convenient for the national advertiser to deal with one media department controlling multiple radio and TV stations.

The $300 million buy placed by Procter & Gamble with Viacom Plus is viewed as a harbinger of the future. The deal crossed more than 12 Viacom media platforms, including broadcast networks CBS and UPN; cable channels MTV, CMT, VH1, Comedy Central, and Nickelodeon; and syndicated shows from Paramount and King World.

Barter (or Trade-out) Deal for sponsors' products or services in exchange for advertising time.

Barter syndication Contract with local stations buying a syndicated program in exchange for an agreement to run spots it contains. Stations pay for the show in part or in whole by giving the syndicator an agreed-upon amount of commercial time to sell within the program.

Cooperative (co-op) advertising Agreement between local retailers and manufacturers to share advertising expenses.

Per inquiry (PI) Ads paid for by the number of units sold by audience response to the ad. These spots use a phone number or post office box number for a direct response.

Viacom Plus is not alone in its push for cross-platform advertising. Fox's parent News Corporation opened an integrated marketing bureau. ABC Unlimited is selling ads across Disney's media outlets, and NBC Connect sells spot packages for advertisers on its cable and broadcast networks in addition to NBC stations and websites.

Some advertising professionals, however, are concerned about this new paradigm. Allen Banks, executive vice president of Saatchi and Saatchi, one of the world's leading advertising firms with offices in 82 countries, says the fact that a cross-platform deal is efficient does not mean it's the best package. After all, stations outside Viacom's reach may better suit the sponsor's needs. Then who will find those stations? Banks says, "That's our role."[11]

BARTERING FOR TIME

When airtime is exchanged for sponsors' products or services, the deal is called a **barter,** or, in the case of radio sales, a *trade-out deal.* Barter or trade-out deals work best when a broadcaster needs a sponsor's products, such as vehicles or office furniture. The principal danger is that such deals can jeopardize the station's cash flow and thus undermine its payroll and schedule of debt payments.

In television, nationally syndicated shows such as *Friends* and *Entertainment Tonight* may be bartered to local TV stations. **Barter syndication** means the broadcaster "pays" for the right to air the syndicated program by giving the show's owner the commercial time slots to sell to advertisers. *Barter-plus-cash* seals the deal by requiring an additional cash payment from the broadcaster for the license to air the show. The show's producers have already placed commercials in the program directed at a national audience, but there are slots available for the local stations to sell, as well.

CO-OP DEALS

Cooperative advertising describes a method for paying for TV commercials where both the local retailer and a national manufacturer share the cost. Co-op spots are more common to radio than to television. They usually feature a 50-50 split of the cost between a national vendor, such as Coca-Cola or Ford Motor Company, and a local retail outlet.

PER INQUIRY

Sponsors buying **per inquiry (PI)** spots gauge the advertising rate by the number of phone calls in response to the ads. Per inquiries invite a direct response to order anything from rock music on compact discs to salad shooters. The spots usually close with, "Call now! Operators are standing by," or words to that effect. Sometimes spots don't reach as many people as promised, and that calls for a different solution.

MAKE-GOODS

When big stories break, such as the destruction of the World Trade Center or a major hurricane or other natural disaster, broadcasters clear their commercial

Advertising's Good Samaritans

Did you ever wonder where those spots for Smokey the Bear, Mc-Gruff the Crime Dog, or the Crash Test Dummies came from? Turn back to 1942, when the United States was at war on two fronts. One was in the battlefields against the Axis powers of Germany and Japan and the other front was here at home. At the White House's behest, the War Advertising Council was formed to fan patriotic flames through public service advertising.

Posters reminded citizens that "Loose Lips Sink Ships." When more help was needed in the factories, "Rosie the Riveter" recruited women to work at industrial jobs. In order to save the food supply for soldiers, public service advertising encouraged Americans to plant "victory gardens." Perhaps the War Ad Council's biggest victory came in raising $35 billion by promoting war bonds. After the war, President Truman asked the council to continue its peacetime mission, and the Advertising Council was formed.

In public service, the nation's top advertising agencies do the creative work *pro bono*—free of charge—while networks and local broadcasters join in by donating millions of dollars in free time. The National Association of Broadcasters is pleased to mention this fact whenever Congress takes up public-interest legislation threatening to impose new legal burdens on broadcasters.

The Ad Council receives hundreds of requests for campaigns each year but winnows out all of the ones that are political, religious, or commercial in nature. What's left are issues relevant to most Americans, from education to the environment, and the Ad Council creates about 40 campaigns each year to address those concerns.

---

schedules for "wall-to-wall" news coverage. Those spots missing their appointed times must be rescheduled as **make-goods.** The lost spots are broadcast at new times in agreement with the sponsor. These make-goods also are called for when broadcasters run the spot but something happens to the technical quality. Make-goods also are slated to make up for lost rating points when a show fails to net as large an audience as the sponsor was promised.

Make-goods Spots added or rescheduled when a television station or network fails to air them properly or to deliver a CPM guaranteed to the sponsor.

SUSTAINING TIME

If a program is *sustaining*, it means there are no commercials and the broadcaster is paying for the time. So, the broadcaster may choose to fill it with public service announcements or promotions (PSAs). The FCC encourages PSAs as a way of serving the public interest. They promote causes such as the American Cancer Society and the United Way.

ADVERTISING STRATEGIES

The goal of advertising sales is a fairly simple one: Persuade the client to buy time and build up the company's image in order to generate more business. Some commercials are directed at simply enhancing the sponsor's image; this is called *institutional advertising.* Other spots aim to increase customer use of a product or a service. There is an obvious reward for successful marketers, but to

Branding (or Brand imaging) Strategy to differentiate a product's name and logo from other competing brands in the market.

motivate the creative side of the industry, companies compete in contests each year and show off their best spots.

Building Brand Image

Whether selling a product or building a corporate image, **branding** is the name of the game—differentiating the sponsor and product from its rivals, giving it a personality and a name, and, most especially, showing what's in it for the buyers. Branding is mainly about images and perceptions. The reason Kellogg's Corn Flakes became such a popular item had more to do with Tony the Tiger's claim that they were "Grrrrreat!" than their actual taste. Is there any real difference in the way Kellogg's Corn Flakes taste from other brands? Advertisers claim what customers taste most is the brand's image.

> ### Principle #5
>
> Consumers buy a product when they perceive its brand image to be superior to the image of its competitors.

Unique selling proposition (USP) Facet of a product distinguishing it from rival brands and of benefit to its customers.

Clutter Excessive number of spots in a break, or general malaise of ads obscuring any single message.

Pods Several spots in a row—clusters of commercials broadcast on radio or television.

Unique Selling Propositions

Advertising success is tied to a second principle—**unique selling propositions (USPs).** This idea became the mantra of the 1960s after advertising executive Rosser Reeves convinced his colleagues that it was the best—if not the only way—to cut through ad **clutter,** the growing congestion of all media drawing on advertising for support. In his book, *Reality in Advertising,* Reeves argues, "The consumer tends to remember just one thing from an advertisement—one strong claim, or one strong concept."[12] Radio and TV producers interpreted Reeves to mean one strong benefit in a catchy slogan or jingle, as in:

"How do you spell relief? 'R-O-L-A-I-D-S.'"
"M&M's melt in your mouth, not in your hands!"
"Certs breath mints with a magic drop of retsyn."[13]

Branding and USPs ideally would place the product in a superior position to its competitors. Such theories are all well and good, but in the real world, advertisers need to know who the customer is, who the rivals are, and how to make the audience think the product is superior.

ADVERTISING CONVERGENCE

The vision of someone avoiding TV spots by either pushing the mute button on the remote control or surfing other channels during commercial breaks is beginning to bother some industry gurus. They also are concerned about a new type of digital video recorder (DVR) sold by Replay TV that allows viewers to completely skip the **pod,** the collection of commercials aired back to back. Advertisers prefer a future scenario where viewers simply click on an "enabled" (or interactive) 30-second spot to find out more about the product, especially how to buy it and use it.[14] Experiments with click-on TV spots suggest the audience will happily spend more time with advertising. These interactive spots are called *walled gardens,* because viewers can continue enjoying their programming of choice while dividing up the TV screen to learn more about the advertiser, products, and services available. Older forms of interactive television—home-shopping networks and infomercials—also have been successful.

Infomercials

Two forms of TV programming can fairly be called advertising: home-shopping networks and **program-length commercials (PLCs).** Other names—*paid programming, long-form advertising,* even *documercials*—have been used to describe the format. There are three ways to know you have stumbled onto an infomercial. First, it is trying to sell something by demonstration, display, testimonial, or a combination of all three. Second, it is at least a half-hour long. And third, it invites a direct response of some monetary investment.

Infomercials used to fill hard-to-sell time deep in the caverns of late-night TV, where only the graveyard shift, insomniacs, and bed-ridden patients reside. Now they occupy daytime hours on cable and most of the day on some stations. Not surprisingly, their popularity parallels the proliferation of cable and satellite TV channels.

Program-Length Commercials. Once considered an unacceptable form of advertising, infomercials have become a mainstay on cable and broadcast channels. These fitness fanatics are promoting the "Power Rider" for exercise at home.

Program-length commercials (PLCs) Thirty- to sixty-minute programs, usually called *infomercials,* that promote a single sponsor or product.

INFOMERCIALS INVESTIGATED

The FCC first turned its attention to program-length commercials in 1973 when it determined that the entire half-hour should be counted as advertising, and that the public interest was ill served by so large a chunk of commercial time. The government reversed itself in 1984, finding nothing illegal about infomercials, suggesting that viewers need only be aware that host celebrities and "experts" endorsing products are paid by the sponsor to do so. After the FCC lifted its ban on infomercials, a wide assortment of sponsors from star-gazing astrologers to home appliance dealers began producing their PLCs (program-length commercials).

Home-Shopping Networks

In 2002, the Home Shopping Network (HSN) celebrated its 25th birthday as the most widely distributed TV shopping network. Its annual sales exceed $1.8 billion, with "fulfillment centers" in Germany, Japan, China, Italy, and France, from which 1,300 HSN employees ship about 100,000 packages a day. Celebrities such as Suzanne Somers, Wolfgang Puck, and Susan Lucci present and endorse the merchandise on air.

The Home Shopping Network began as an improvised solution to an unpaid bill for radio advertising. In Clearwater, Florida, the AM station manager decided to help a sponsor pay his radio bill by auctioning off his product, 112 electric can openers, on the air. The station sold every can opener, and decided to start a regular call-in-and-buy show called *Suncoast Bargaineers.* The local cable access channel picked up the idea in 1981, and before long, the Home

Home Shopping TV. Operators take orders for products advertised on home television sets. Cable networks and independent stations produce a schedule for marketing items for viewers at home, and receive a percentage of the sales profits.

Banners Horizontal advertising blocks on the Web placed above content (like billboards).

Shopping Network had a cable channel of its own. Barry Diller, former chairman of the board of Paramount Pictures and Fox Inc., bought the shopping network in 1993. Four years later, it converged with HSN.com, combining e-commerce with television shopping.[15]

The nearest rival of the Home Shopping Network is QVC, a relative newcomer. It began promoting Sears products in 1986 from studios in West Chester, Pennsylvania. Like HSN, it integrated its TV and Internet commerce, and that helped QVC reach $1 billion in sales for the last quarter of 2000.

ADVERTISING IN THE INTERNET AGE

The Web began burgeoning into a billion-dollar industry in the late 1990s, and according to Wall Street, Internet advertising produced a record $8 billion in sales for 2000 before the downturn in 2001. It's become the central focus of both convergence and creativity. Websites have devised a new means for gauging the effectiveness of advertising based on the level of interactivity customers demonstrate while browsing online.

Creating Web Advertising

The original format for web advertising was called **banners**—static boxes across the top of the page, now considered somewhat passé. Jim Sterne, in *What Makes People Click*, says the boxes began as advertising billboards but were crowded out by banners everywhere and "traffic began going places where things were happening."[16] Next to come in vogue were *skyscraper* or *tower* ads down the side of the web page or *wallpaper* in the background. Then came the *pop-outs*—ads springing out from the borders of the computer screen. Recently, interstitial ads that appear while content is loading on the computer began fading in and out on web pages.

In the creative department, web designers recommend banners or towers be kept to seven words or less, featuring small but colorful art. Ads are most effective when they use animation and are interactive. They broadcast the equivalent of a call to action on the web when viewers are told to "click here" or "click now."

Debate has focused more recently on *pop-under exit panels* triggered by a viewer's attempt to leave a website or back out of it. These pop-ups have caused so much frustration for web users that even some advertisers want to see them scrapped. "When viewers make the decision to go off-line," says Mark Amado, an account director for a division of Initiative Media, "their mindset has already moved on to something else, and we should honor that decision by not hitting them with one more potentially out-of-context message."[17]

Tracking Web Viewers

Measuring web traffic has become a profitable industry for on-line audience analysis firms such as NetCount and Internet Profiles. Their software can keep tabs on every move a person makes on the Internet.[18] This technology consequently has raised privacy concerns among Internet observers.

LAYERS OF WEB BROWSING

Web advertising fostered new economic models based on the layered nature of web browsing from one click to the next. There are four levels of audience interactivity measured on the Internet. Ad placement may be counted by the traditional CPM basis, or it may be measured by the *cost per click* (CPC), the *cost per lead* (CPL), or *cost per sale* (CPS).

The first level, CPM, is based on impressions and charges for website billboards on a cost-per-thousand-viewers basis. More profitable are on-line ads that not only catch customers' eyes but their hands as well. Web sponsors pay more if viewers actually click on the link of the banner advertising to the website. This charge, the second level, is called the **click-through rate** or the cost per click (CPC).

The third level of advertising on the Internet is gauged by the number of times someone sees the banner logo and clicks through to a link on the website, and then begins to fill out a form. That is what is called a *lead*; no money has changed hands, no products have been purchased, but a potential customer has given his or her personal data on-line. Advertisers thus calculate the cost per lead, CPL.

The fourth level is measured by actual e-commerce sales. An example of interactive e-commerce would include the Broadway production *The Scarlet Pimpernel*. Its producers advertised on *Playbill*'s site (www.playbill.com), knowing that it would not only promote their play but sell tickets, as well. American Express also invested in *The Scarlet Pimpernel* site and reached audiences through that medium,[19] generating the cost per sale (CPS).

> **Principle #6**
> Internet advertising draws revenue based on the viewer's level of interactivity with the commercial message.

WEB ENTANGLEMENTS

There are good reasons why the blue skies of web advertising clouded over in 2001. There were hundreds of thousands of websites, but the average viewer visited only a few each week. As viewers became more familiar with those web pages, they developed "banner blindness," an inattentive attitude toward the ads. And as more web users headed for popular sites, loading times increased and crashes occurred. Finally, the Web saw a greater reluctance of users to give credit-card numbers for security reasons, although e-commerce proponents say the likelihood of fraud is no greater on-line than in conventional transactions.

The reach of the Internet is limited to those who have computers and an Internet service provider (ISP). Although most Americans now have personal computers in their home, many choose not to access the Internet at home. Americans access it at work, but employers are wary of personnel using computers for shopping during business hours.

Click-through rate Frequency at which viewers move from the Web advertisement to the sponsor's site to place an order.

ProTalk

ZZ Mylar
Internet Sales Coordinator,
MySanAntonio.com

"It's an amazing product that has people very excited—very revolutionary."

There is nothing new about proclaiming digital convergence for the future. What *is* new is finding ways to make money at it. That's where ZZ Mylar has joined a growing number of advertising pioneers charting new territory on the Internet. After working in sales and promotions for TV stations in Dallas, Houston, and San Antonio, she has made the transition to web advertising. "No one, including ad agencies, have much background or insight into how it all works," she says. "When an ad agency gives you the green light to contact their client directly, you know the information you have must be new." One thing is for certain: The move from television to the web has been an educational one for Mylar, and a lot of it has been self-taught.

Her website, MySanAntonio.com, merges media under the Belo umbrella, so she looks for effective ways to bring an on-line presence to what her former employer, KENS-TV, is selling, or she creates new promotions combining the website with the telecast. Just as before, Mylar spends a good part of the day making sales calls and writing new contracts—that is, when she is not checking on current campaigns and making sure they have the impact intended.

Mylar was able to break new ground in selling "News on Demand," a new way for MySanAntonio.com viewers to catch up with KENS-TV news at their leisure. It enables them to choose only the stories they want to see. "It's an amazing product that has people very excited—very revolutionary," says Mylar.

There's a lot to like about on-line sales, according to Mylar: "There is much more opportunity with the new inventory." Advertising selections can be made, different products can be sold, and her presentations are no longer confined to a single set of spots available during the 24-hour broadcast day. In other ways, however, it is quite similar to representing a television station. She still relishes the satisfaction of making big sales and reaching new customers with a product or service her clients have to offer.

Still, selling a product that is not "proven" has its risks. If a campaign fails, Mylar says, the client may jump to the conclusion that it's the web advertising that does not work rather than considering if the creative approach was effective. The bottom line for Mylar is that regardless of whether it's television or on-line media, advertising consultants have to be effective listeners. It's about discovering what a client's needs are and determining how to build that client's business. "It cannot be just about making the sale and getting a commission," she says; it has to be about giving honest advice to build their business. An attitude of service and the motivation of a self-starter who stays organized and up to date are prerequisites for a successful career in advertising across electronic media.

FUTURE GROWTH

The plusses for web advertising are that it does tend to reach 18- to 34-year-olds who are more affluent and well educated. It also reaches them at the point of purchase in the realm of e-commerce. In addition, web advertising allows sponsors to easily change their advertising. Some observers predict the Internet will become a more reliable source of advertising once broadband technology converges with interactive radio and television. "When full video streaming becomes a reality via broadband, it is going to change the entire economic model of free television, which is free only because it's a life-support system for commercials," says Dick Wolf, executive producer of NBC's *Law and Order.*

PROMOTION

It should come as no surprise that the merchants of media advertising would want to spend part of their broadcast budgets promoting themselves. Radio, television, and web promotion is used to sell a station or channel's personalities, programs, or brand image to the audience. It can be as small as an icon on a web page or as large as a hot-air balloon. There are promotion activities designed for every advertiser and every audience. Although there are advantages for stations who toot their own horns, it also helps to use other media so that promotion strategies involve both internal and external media, particularly when trying to attract new viewers to the audience.

Purposes of Promotion

Promotional spots can boost ratings if they are directed at the audience or if a sales promotion can encourage advertisers to buy more time. Promotional campaigns also unify sponsors and audiences through shared community projects or a particular theme. The terrorist attacks of 2001 and the war in Afghanistan prompted U.S. radio and TV stations to seize upon a national mood of patriotism in their theme promotions.

Image promotion or branding is like advertising used to give a media outlet a personality. It can be as humorous as the radio disc jockey who bills himself as an "idiot," or as sincere as an investigative news team that is reporting "on your side." Sometimes, the personality pitch may fall flat, as CNN discovered when it decided to use sex appeal to promote a news anchor hired from Fox. Paula Zahn was called "sexy" in the spot and a zipper was heard in the background. Red-faced CNN executives yanked the promotion shortly after its debut.

Themes, such as NBC's "must-see TV," reinforce both the network and the program's importance. *ABC News* was "uniquely qualified to bring you the world," and its global icon underscored that theme. Local stations promote daily newscasts by using unsold commercial time to tease stories with voice-over clips from the upcoming newscast.

Cable, Satellite, and Internet Promotions

Cable and satellite promos solicit subscribers for pay services by using a type of comparative advertising. DirecTV positioned itself as better than cable by virtue of its crystal-clear digital channels. Cable systems fought back by promoting the fact that satellite subscribers do not receive all local channels unless they switch to a regular antenna. Other promotions spotlight sports and movie packages or feature discounts for viewers. It's not surprising to see endorsements, logos, and themes used for media promotions, especially when expensive sports franchises are involved.

A multimillion-dollar sports pavilion in Dallas, for example, was looking for a way to get TV monitors installed throughout the arena without adding to its $420 million price tag. After all, patrons of the American Airlines Center would be more likely to sample the hot dogs, pretzels, and sodas if there were some way they could follow the action as they stood in line. The founders of the project sought and found a flagship sponsor, DirecTV, which promised to install hundreds of TV screens formatted in high definition in addition to many standard TV monitors. In exchange, the satellite TV firm secured the right to use the Dallas Mavericks and Dallas Stars in its promotional campaigns.

It is difficult to overstate the promotional uses of the Internet, as virtually all radio and television stations have established some presence accessible to web viewers. Websites also offer chances for promotional campaigns for causes. Sponsors generally like to be associated with a good cause, so stations take the opportunity to participate in campaigns such as the "Partnership for a Drug Free America" or the "Susan G. Komen Race for the Cure" for breast cancer, where they can note their sponsorship on the Internet.

ISSUES IN ADVERTISING

Critics of media advertising don't have to look far to find places where the loftier aims of informing the public and building business have missed the mark. Debates rage over issues touching on the honesty and quality of advertising. Critics also are concerned with subliminal advertising and the potential for deception and fraud.

Subliminal Advertising

Subliminal advertising, using barely perceptible words and images to move viewers, has been around since the 1960s. Yet, reliable evidence to confirm its effects is elusive. Jim Vicary brought it to the public's attention in 1957 when he conducted an experiment by splicing the quick messages "Eat popcorn" and "Drink Coca-Cola" into a movie reel. He reported upsurges in concession sales, but later replications failed to verify his findings. Vicary admitted his initial study was a hoax. Nonetheless, the idea generated interest and even one ardent supporter, Dr. Wilson Bryan Key.

In Key's first book on the subject, *Subliminal Seduction*, he observed sexual imagery rampant in subliminal advertising, noting that even Kent cigarettes were designed to appeal to women by their "strong masculine name, suggesting a solid distinguished WASP heritage." The cigarettes were actually named after Herbert Kent, president of the company that introduced the cigarettes.

Key's analysis could be described as more artful than empirical, given the lack of confirming evidence for subliminal ads. Nonetheless, the FCC imposed a rule prohibiting stations from using the technique. Some broadcasters keep experimenting with the idea, however. In fact, one department store in Seattle, Bon Marché, aired a four-frame ad for chocolates and paid $3,780 for less than a second of TV time.

Oh Rats! It's Subliminal Advertising

No contemporary campaign would be complete without a tempest over a TV spot. Presidential candidate George W. Bush's supporters were taken to task in 2000 for a commercial that seemed to be experimenting with subliminal advertising. The 30-second spot charged Bush's opponent Al Gore with placing American lives in bureaucratic hands by withholding prescription drug benefits from the elderly.

There on the screen Gore stood, and superimposed were the words: *BUREAUCRATS DECIDE*. That phrase bounced around the screen for a second or two but before it faded, the last four letters of *bureaucrats, RATS,* appeared in large white type over the Democrat's head. The commercial's producer, Alex Castellanos, insisted that the spot was innocent—that the word *RATS* appeared only by accident. The so-called RATS ad was withdrawn while pundits argued whether it was actually intended to implant a subliminal view of the vice president in the minds of the voters.

Commercial Clutter

How many TV spots are enough? For the first dozen years of commercial television, there were fewer than five minutes of advertising per hour, and almost all spots were 60 seconds in length. Then, in the 1960s, networks began boosting rates, and ad agencies answered the challenge by **piggybacking** spots, combining two product messages, each 30 seconds in length. The half-minute spot became the standard unit of sale by the 1970s, but TV stations and networks sold them at one-minute rates.

The American Association of Advertising Agencies (AAAA) found that for every 60 minutes of prime-time TV watched by viewers in 2000, they spent 16 minutes and 43 seconds viewing (or escaping) spots. While the number of commercials increased, their length diminished. Ten- and 15-second spots became common in the 1990s. Time limits imposed on commercials have been matters of debate within professional associations. At one time, the National Association of Broadcasters asked radio stations to sell no more than 18 minutes of ads per hour, and recommended that television limit ads to 9½ minutes an hour or less during prime time, and at other times, 16 minutes. Nowadays, network TV typically carries a 24-spot load per hour, but the load is even greater on cable, which often has 28 advertising messages or more per hour. When the Justice Department charged in 1984 that the NAB code's limits reduced competition, the NAB abandoned the code and its office for fielding complaints.

A former television program director has remarked that all the clutter "is killing the goose that laid the golden broadcast egg."[20] Ed Fulginiti, writing in one of the leading trade publications, *Electronic Media*, says if something doesn't change, "the advertiser will eventually dominate the list of things most annoying to Americans, bested only by guests of *The Jenny Jones Show* and telemarketers who call at dinnertime." He attributes clutter to the erosion of

Piggybacking TV commercial practice in the 1960s, when a single sponsor often presented two products in a 60-second ad.

Corrective advertising Correction of misleading spots by a new set of commercials that contain truthful information.

broadcast ratings, and ends by pleading to the broadcasters, "C'mon folks, the clutter has got to stop."

ADVERTISING AND THE LAW

In terms of First Amendment freedoms, commercial speech gets only mid-level protection—more than obscene or indecent words but less than political and private speech.[21] Consequently, there are three principles of law that advertisers must follow: The content of ads must (1) be truthful and not misleading, (2) show evidence to back up its claims, and (3) be fair. Case law has given rise to several remedies when the principles are not met, including corrective advertising and countercommercials.

> **Principle #7**
>
> Freedom of speech for advertisers is limited by their ability to substantiate the claims that their commercials make.

The FTC

The Federal Trade Commission predates the Federal Communications Commission. Congress established the FTC in 1914 to ensure the fairness of competition. Advertising was added to its purview in 1938 with the passage of the Wheeler-Lea Act, designed to eliminate "unfair and deceptive acts" of commerce.[22] The FTC's Bureau of Consumer Protection is the office directly responsible for protecting citizens from false or misleading ads.

DECEPTIVE ADVERTISING

Broadcast "advertisers must have reasonable support for all express and implied objective claims."[23] That is why TV spots no longer show Wonder Bread building bodies 12 ways, or Listerine not only making your breath smell sweet but preventing colds and sore throats.[24] The laws against "misleading" commercials have been interpreted to mean both what is included in a message and what is left out, and in the bread and mouthwash cases, the claims were judged to be misleading. If the "consumer's decision to buy or use the product" was based on false information or reasonable inference, if an ad "contains a statement or omits information that is likely to mislead consumers," then the advertisement is against the law. It's that simple.

COMPARATIVE ADVERTISING

For a time, TV networks rejected comparative commercials, but that was found to be unconstitutional. Now, the FTC encourages honest comparative advertising with some limits. A competing brand cannot be called "brand X," for instance, and all claims of comparison must be documented. Whenever advertisers have failed to meet their burden of proof, the government can apply a number of remedies, including cease-and-desist orders and a requirement corrective advertising.

CORRECTIVE ADVERTISING

Historically, **corrective advertising,** used to redress false impressions, has cost millions of dollars. One remedy imposed by the FTC, for example, had Ocean

Spray tell its customers that extra "food energy" promised in its cranberry juice was actually calories and not protein or vitamins. Profile diet bread had to correct the false impression that it had fewer calories per slice than regular brands of bread contained.

SAFETY

Do broadcasters have to make sure the spots their stations are running are safe? According to the FTC, if a spot "causes or is likely to cause substantial consumer injury that could not be reasonably avoided," then it may be judged unfair. If, for example, a food label failed to show its contents properly and caused a customer's allergic reaction, or if a child was somehow harmed while playing with a toy thought to be safe, then the advertising could be judged unfair.

The government's trade agency is not the only office that responds to complaints about advertising. The Federal Communications Commission has also reviewed allegations of unfairness and has even gone so far as banning some products from commercial broadcasts.

The FCC

The Communications Act requires that a line be drawn between advertising and programming. Stations must identify the sponsors of the advertising, as well. This identification rule is rarely violated except during campaign seasons, when political advocates may try to conceal their identity. For a time, the FCC tried to enforce a responsible measure of balance when the commercials that advocates aired concerned controversies.

COUNTERCOMMERCIALS

During the days of the Fairness Doctrine, broadcasters who sold time to special-interest groups for their "advertorials," pointed messages on controversial issues, were also required to broadcast countercommercials if asked. In one instance, smoking became the controverial issue, and the FCC deemed antismoking PSAs as an appropriate measure by broadcasters to counter TV commercials for cigarettes.[25] These countercommercials to smoking were effective for a while—broadcasters and tobacco companies noticed a drop in sales of more than 2 percent—so they turned to a different solution. Rather than continue to sustain a loss in business from counterads, some tobacco executives actually lobbied for the Federal Cigarette and Labeling Advertising Act banning broadcasts of cigarette ads on radio and television. The result was a shift in cigarette advertising from broadcasting to outdoor media and print—especially magazines.

DOUBLE BILLING

Co-op advertising has been subject to a fraudulent practice called **double-billing.** This usually occurs in radio when the station sales person and the local retailer conspire to inflate the reported cost of the spots in order to bill the

Double-billing Illegal advertising practice in which a station fraudulently bills a retailer at twice (or more) the normal rate. The retailer then sends the bill back to a vendor who pays twice as much as his share to relieve the local retailer of the excessive cost of the commercials.

national manufacturer a higher price than what the spots actually cost. The conspirators then split the gains. This was once an offense to be investigated by the FCC, but during the deregulation days of the 1980s, it was removed from the agency's purview except as a possible issue for license renewal. That left it up to national vendors to seek redress through civil claims if a local station bilked them on the cost of spots.

CLIPPING TIME

Sometimes, stations get into a jam by failing to run local spots at the right time, and may try to work their way out illegally. One form of chicanery, *clipping*, robs network or syndicated programs of program time. This occurs when someone at the local station decides to clip the closing credits of a network or syndicated program in order to put on a local ad. It also can involve replacing a network or syndicated spot with a local commercial played over it. This becomes fraud when the station signs a contract to air both network and syndicated programs in full.

Summary

Radio resisted commercialism at first, but the profit motive and the need to pay the bills won in the end. Television was more receptive, but held to certain limits in commercial minutes and formats. From their earliest days, broadcast advertisers were looking for a way to get ahead—ahead of other media and ahead of other sponsors. The strategy of targeting audiences evolved when single-show sponsors integrated ads into entertainment fare.

Meeting the client's marketing needs is fundamental to the success of the relationship between account executives and advertising clients. In exchange for those dollars in advertising investments, sponsors expect to see a picture of potential customers identified by both demographic and psychographic data.

In their quest for advertising sales, broadcasters price their most valuable commodity—time according to the number of spots sold, the time of day, adjacency to certain shows, and the time span. Before investing in electronic-media advertising, sponsors and agencies receive data based on the size of the audience. Just as people can be measured by several factors, including height and weight, the audience's size is gauged by several measures with the price of commercials in mind. There is the cost per thousand viewers (CPM), the cost per ratings point (CPP), gross ratings points (GRPS), and the cumulative number of viewers (cume). Broadcast time is priced by these measures of the size of the audience.

Commercials aim to secure customer loyalty by projecting a brand image that makes the sponsor seem superior to its rivals. Researchers know just how powerful imagery based on slogans and icons can be. Broadcast audiences will respond to advertising demonstrating unique personal benefits to them. It is a specialized enterprise at the national level, with major agencies and rep firms dividing accounts with networks, cable systems, and broadcast stations. Advertising is a team undertaking with different players in sales, marketing, creativity, and research.

CAREER FOCUS

Job opportunities in advertising are found in the offices of cable systems, radio and TV stations, as well as advertising agencies. Advertising agencies are just one part of a much larger industry composed of audio and video production studios, web design companies, and print shops, which act as suppliers to the industry.

The full-service ad agency typically defines its duties as servicing client accounts, creative tasks, media planning, and marketing research. These offices report to a senior administrator, a **vice president** or **president.** There also are **supervisors** or **directors of account management,** as well as **creative** and **media directors.**

Account managers monitor agency performance and handle long-term planning, personnel assignments, and revenue projections. They oversee **account executives,** who meet with agency clients in order to draw up advertising goals and strategies. **Account executives** are responsible for advising the agency on the client's product, the market, and relevant consumers. Their duties include client relations, project planning, and budgets.

Creative writers, art directors, and **producers** are responsible for composing the advertising message and choosing the right words and pictures to get across the target audience. **Radio and television producers** are responsible for recording and editing the spots, which demands creative and administrative skills. That includes everything from the selection of talent and location through budgeting, scheduling, recording, editing, and granting final approval of the commercial.

Media planners draw up and present the media mix, which is a plan proposing the specific channels to fulfill the client's promotional goals. They use ratings data and audience research to reach the target. They should have knowledge of the cost and effectiveness of print, electronic, and outdoor media available. Analytical skills based on reasoning from the ratings are necessary, since media planners must draft and defend the media mix to both the client and the agency. Some agencies also employ **marketing researchers** who analyze ratings data and conduct audience research.

After the client signs off on the media plan, **media buyers** make the purchases of the advertising space and time. For certain media, they use advertising rate cards. Newspapers, magazines, and some broadcasting outlets work this way. More often in broadcast advertising, particularly television, some back-and-forth bargaining over scheduling and pricing takes place.

Advertising or marketing researchers find, interpret, and evaluate the data about advertising and its audiences. These positions are in demand, drawing people from marketing research firms, government agencies, and media consultants.

Broadcast Sales Offices

General sales managers in radio and television motivate and lead the sales team, establish sales goals, and lead the station's effort toward increasing its share of the advertising revenue in the market. **Local sales managers** develop and direct the local advertising effort by working with account executives and keeping in touch with local clients and ad agencies.

Account executives serve as consultants for clients and sales people for the station. They make presentations and negotiate deals for advertising time. **Sales assistants** provide support from inside the station by taking orders for commercial time by phone either from account executives in the field or directly from clients over the phone.

Meeting the sponsor's marketing needs is fundamental to the success of the sales people and stations they represent. National advertisers, for example, like the idea of blanketing corporate logos and pitches across the country. This allows greater control over the content and time selection, and it's easy to seal the deal at once.

Public service announcement (PSA) Spot aired for free by a station or system promoting a nonprofit organization. PSAs are usually used to fill unsold avails, but some stations reserve slots specifically for PSA use.

Internet advertising potentially reaches a global audience, and is admired for its ability to gain attention and motivate action, but is criticized for being intrusive. Layers of interactivity go beyond ad recognition, producing new models for tabulating advertising effects and sales compensation. The question now is how to gauge advertising awareness when the Web and other media converge.

Several issues confront advertisers, including the problems involved with political attack ads, violent programs, and advertising clutter. The law is clear on issues of deception and fraud, but other areas of concern call for ethical choices. Advertisers reach toward the greater good when they program **public service announcements** designed to stimulate public awareness of issues such as drug abuse and domestic violence.

The future lies in cross-platform media packages that bring together national media groups and corporations to make international deals. The integrated marketing researchers give the sponsor a fairly clear snapshot of the audience, and there is a measure of prestige in having several national TV networks carry a company's banner. In order to chase the viewer of tomorrow across media platforms, national advertisers will go directly to parent corporations and make a buy. That's at the supply side of the curve. At the demand end, viewers will find their media experience enhanced by new venues of interactivity.

FOOD FOR THOUGHT

1. In the early days of radio, broadcast advertising met with resistance from people who thought it would lower the quality of the medium. Can you defend commercial radio from that charge? What arguments would you use?
2. Some countries use different economic models to support broadcasting, including purchase fees, taxes, and other public monies besides advertising. Do you think a different economic model for broadcasting in the United States could have worked? Why or why not?
3. Careers in advertising focus on sales, creative production, media buying, and research. If you were to pursue a career in advertising, what area would you choose and why?
4. Some stations allocate time for public service advertising, but most just use it as filler for unsold time. In your opinion, should broadcasters plan the slots devoted to public service time both in terms of quantity and their quality of position in the schedule? Support your answer.
5. The charge has been made that the majority of entertaining advertising is rarely the most effective. Can you think of any spots that made you want to buy the product? Were they award winners, in your opinion? Why or why not?
6. For a short time, the FCC banned infomercials (PLCs), suggesting that broadcasters would be spending too much time in marketing products and that was not in the public interest. Do you think such content controls are an infringement on the broadcaster's First Amendment freedoms? Explain.
7. Advertising on-line has led to what some researchers have called "banner blindness" and commercial clutter on the screen. What types of Internet advertising do you consider to be most effective and why?

8. In an effort to boost ratings, CNN used a sex-appeal approach for one of its anchors but pulled the promotion after only one day. Why do you think that appeal failed to win approval?

9. NBC-TV's decision to advertise liquor has met with controversy. Do you agree with the decision or not? Why?

10. Do you agree with the remedy of corrective advertising prescribed the government as a cure for deceptive or false advertising—or should it simply be a matter of "buyer beware"? Explain.

11. Do you think the law should be changed to allow cigarette advertising on radio and television? Why or why not?

10

The Audience

When the million applaud you, seriously ask what harm you have done; when they censure you, what good!

—Caleb C. Colton English clergyman

Who Wants to Be . . . *a Millionaire?* Fantasies of wealth turned into high ratings after programming experts polished a promising idea and launched the game show on ABC.

Even critics of *Who Wants to Be a Millionaire?* had to admit that the TV game show was a tidal-wave hit with audiences upon its premiere in August 1999. The program's title evidently spoke to hordes of wishful viewers. Stephanie Drachkovitch, who helps create hits, was there when the show was only a gleam in a programmer's eye.

"The idea was brought to me by an ABC executive who had found it," says Drachkovitch. At the time, she was a program developer for Disney, which owned ABC; it turned out that the *Millionaire* format already had been a hit in Britain. "He wanted to see if we'd go in on the development of the show." The answer was yes, and a pilot episode was produced to test the program on viewers. "I did my part on the studio side," Drachkovitch adds. Soon, *Millionaire* roared onto the national airwaves, knocking over ABC rivals in its time slot and spawning imitators.

Fast-forward to January 2002, when the *Hollywood Reporter* newspaper referred to leadership troubles at ABC: "An executive shuffle recently [occurred] after steep ratings declines for *Who Wants to Be a Millionaire?* and other veteran shows"[1] A veteran show after less than two and a half years? Other programs had their lives cut even shorter by "steep ratings declines." Why?

Knowing why **ratings**—a measure of how many **households** are tuned to a particular station or channel—rise and plunge, carrying with them the fortunes of most broadcast programs, is a core analytical skill in broadcasting. In programming, failure to earn adequate ratings leads to cancellation. That's the fate that ABC dealt *Millionaire* after it lost two-thirds of its total U.S. audience in the 2001–2002 season, including 70 percent of its younger viewers. It still probably would have a profitable future in syndication as local stations, cable channels, and others bought it to shore up their own audiences. All ABC knew was that, on the network, a show that sizzled in 1999 had guttered out like an untended campfire.

> Knowing why ratings rise and plunge, carrying with them the fortunes of most broadcast programs, is a core analytical skill in broadcasting.

Ratings Tally of households watching or listening to a particular station or channel.

Household Basic unit of measurement used in determining ratings.

THE MYSTERIOUS CROWD

By estimating the number of households tuned in, ratings indicate roughly how many potential buyers of advertised products are being exposed to commercials on a particular channel at a particular time. A specific program is being aired at that time, so the ratings are markers of the program's success at pulling in viewers or listeners. This determines how much a network or station can charge its advertisers to insert their commercials into that program. Will the show bring in the ad revenue needed to pay its own costs? The answer directly affects year-end profits.

A Necessary Evil?

Almost no one defends ratings as wholly reliable headcounts of the audience. A major buyer of commercial time said of the famous Nielsen ratings service, "It's riddled with faults, but it's the only game in town."[2] After three-quarters of a century, the art and science of counting and analyzing a broadcast audience represent works in progress. Even measurement professionals sometimes acknowledge that their techniques are imperfect, and worse. Yet, crucial decisions are based on them. Ratings have thus become a marker of the brutal economic universe in which our electronic media operate. They have made a lot of enemies, especially among people within the industry who place a higher value on public service than on profits.

"Why do you have ratings?" asks a news director, disgust in his voice. "To establish ad rates. There's no other reason for them. That's the bottom line. We have no better system."[3] He believes ratings have distorted news coverage. So do many others. When CNN anchor Bernard Shaw announced his retirement, he huffed to the *Hollywood Reporter*, "Don't talk to me about ratings. I'm a journalist."[4] To critics such as Shaw, ratings might as well be platoons of hostile space aliens taking over the planet.

Ratings Lingo

The term *ratings* is thrown around so loosely—sometimes as a curse against the ills of commercial TV—that it can cloud the terminology of audience measurement and research. Here are simple explanations of a few common terms:

- *Rating:* Measurement of an audience, usually as households. A single rating *point* equals 1 percent of all the households owning TV sets in the sample area.
- *Share:* The percentage of all households *currently using* TV sets that is tuned in to a particular channel.
- *Rating/Share:* A way of expressing a program's drawing power. "The show did a *9/16* yesterday"—means that the program was viewed in 9 percent of households owning TV sets and in 16 percent of households using TV sets at the time.
- *Sweeps:* A period several times each year when measurement firms calculate ratings. TV managers receive "**Nielsen** books" of ratings, so the May **sweeps** is often called the May *book*. Sweeps periods are February, May, and November.
- *Diary:* A viewing log kept by a member of a selected household as part of the audience-measurement process.
- *Meter:* An electronic device that records the channel choices of viewers (and sometimes more).

Calculations

Ratings play a powerful role in the lives (and deaths) of the most expensive entertainment series on television. They become a factor when a show is but a concept, still being "pitched" to networks or stations by a writer or producer or some other agent of new programs. Before production can go forward, broadcasters must assess how large and desirable an audience it can attract and hold. This projection must be presented to advertisers as they shop for what's called *upfront* commercial time in advance of a new season. It's a ritual that gives broadcasters the jitters because so much money is at stake. Before the 2001–2002 season, for example, the major networks managed to sell $6.8 billion in advertising time—a good total in a bad economic year that required them to lower their rates.

As noted earlier in this book, broadcasting's very name came from agriculture, where it referred to the widespread scattering of seeds. In electronic broadcasting, as in farming, no returns are guaranteed; one can only plan, cultivate, and hope. Early managers could be satisfied by reports that good numbers of people were tuning in; there was relatively little pressure to prove or generate higher head counts. Today, advertisers place great emphasis not only on raw numbers but also—and usually more important—on who the audience members are, what they like to buy, and how much they'll spend on it. It's in combination with such information that ratings have become immensely powerful in a highly competitive marketplace.

Two related specialties—audience *measurement* and audience *analysis*—contribute to research about what people watch and listen to, and why. Measurement of audiences, which generates numerical ratings, calculates how many people are

Nielsen Dominant TV-ratings firm.

Sweeps Period of intensive audience measurement three times a year.

> **Principle #1**
>
> Projecting future ratings is an early step in the development of programming.

ProTalk

Stephanie Drachkovitch
Senior Vice President, Telepictures

"The demo your're looking for is upscale. it's the $75,000-plus houshold with an educated female."

Seasoned TV-program developer Stephanie Drachkovitch finds *daytime* broadcasting—the long stretch between 9 A.M. and 4 P.M. weekdays—to be a challenging zone. Audience concerns make it so. Her company, Telepictures Productions, creates programs for networks and stations, often as "strip" shows to run at the same time every weekday. Their fate, says Drachkovitch, hangs on *ratings* (measurements of

audience size) and *demographics* (measurements of audience composition):

"Whenever you're in the 'daily' business, you have to be careful about how you respond to ratings.'What did we do yesterday? How do we do it again?' You have to take in all the factors: What was your lead-in yesterday? What competition were you up against? Were your HUT [homes using television] levels higher?

"There are certain topics and approaches that show a 'spike' [jump in ratings]. Think about it: Why are there so many episodes of the talk shows that deal with DNA testing for paternity, or troubled teens— 'My teen dresses like a slut,' or 'My teen's combative' or 'My teen's in trouble'? Because those themes do rate well consistently over *time*. . . .

"In daytime, we've lost a big share of audience to cable. Now it's hard to get above a 2 rating in daytime. A couple of years ago, if you got a 2, you were off the air. Now, if you're delivering a 'pure' demo [the targeted audience] in that rating, you're fine. . . .

"The demo you're looking for is upscale. It's the $75,000-plus household with an educated female. They make buying decisions and lifestyle decisions in families. They're the ones buying the new car, buying the PlayStation [an electronic game], buying the car, buying the Cokes. That's an attractive consumer, that woman who makes buying decisions for families."

---

tuned in. Analysis attempts to discover their characteristics in ways that can help to sell them advertisers' products, which first means selling them on programs. These tasks involve use of scientific methods, but the results never fully satisfy broadcast managers. One reason is that it has been impossible for them to look directly in on listeners and viewers to confirm which of them are watching each program and which may be ignoring it. Soon enough, even that may be possible.

The Early Listener

In radio's earliest days, audiences sometimes gathered in public halls to hear a broadcast over a single radio receiver. Anyone who wanted a "rating" could use his or her index finger to count heads. That sort of intimate communal approach to radio listening faded quickly as radio sets became affordable to most families. Within a decade after the end of World War I, radio people were needing and itching to know just who was "out there" listening and in what numbers. To find that out would be the mission of the field of audience measurement.

The United States was substantially different in those days from what it is now. The population was relatively small—about 123 million in 1930, less than half of today's total. Radio use had grown rapidly in the previous decade, but just how many people might be hearing any given show was beyond the knowledge of broadcasters. In fact, with one of every three Americans living on farms, some of the potential audience itself was beyond reach.

WAYS OF COUNTING

One of the first ratings services, **Cooperative Analysis of Broadcasting (CAB)**—created by and for radio advertisers—began trying in 1930 to measure the national audience. No special tools for this task had been invented yet. Most of those that would be invented later would only build on and refine the solid, basic approaches with which CAB started.

Science of the Sample

Archibald Crossley, CAB's lead researcher, directed squads of *telephone interviewers* who worked to identify radio listeners around the country and their favorite programs. A call to a home in a certain city, asking what people had listened to the night before, left the audience in the driver's seat: An interviewer had no choice but to trust the memory and candor of whoever was on the line. Still, the information was better than nothing. Armed with the phone-call findings, Crossley used a method called **quota sampling** to extrapolate national numbers from what local viewers had revealed.

Scientists understood that this was not the most statistically sound method. For one thing, it required the researcher to organize groups of listeners according to the proportion of their individual characteristics in the U.S. population as a whole. This might or might not yield results that accurately represented the whole radio audience. So quota sampling in radio soon gave way to **random sampling**, where everyone was supposed to have a chance at selection, which was intended to produce reliable cross-sections of the population. It reduced the likelihood that some of the results of this expensive research might be simply a matter of chance.

Whatever the sampling formula, the primary survey method in those days was the same: telephone calling. Even this basic information-gathering task could be approached in different ways, however. Within a few years, another media research firm, Clark-Hooper (later simply **Hooper**)—was commissioned by broadcasters to do **coincidental** calling of radio owners. That involved calling a home while a certain program was on the air to see who, if anyone, was listening. This method obviously helped people report their program choices more accurately, without depending on what sometimes were faulty memories. Hooper used it as well to help determine the *available* audience for any program by eliminating from the total of radio owners all those who weren't at home when the program was on the air.

The company gradually implemented other techniques to increase the credibility of radio ratings. As scholar Karen Buzzard has pointed out, Hooper's

Cooperative Analysis of Broadcasting Early audience-measurement cooperative among radio advertisers.

Quota sampling Study of a specified number of subjects of one type—say, 10 teenage girls or 20 male retirees; because subjects are not *randomly* recruited, results are open to challenge as not valid across a large population.

Principle #2
As an inexact science, audience measurement is open to challenge by its stakeholders.

Random sampling Study of subjects drawn from a larger group, with each individual chosen by chance; this gives all members of a population a chance of being chosen, making results potentially valid all across that population. In *simple* random sampling, all members of a population have an *equal* chance of being chosen.

Hooper Early ratings firm that pioneered use of coincidental telephone calling to determine radio listening patterns.

Coincidental Technique by which researchers call households *during* a program to see if they're watching or listening to it.

Telephone Interviewer. Using an earlier communication device, broadcast researchers since 1930 have probed audiences to learn what makes them listen or watch.

Diary Booklet in which a listener/viewer's channel choices are recorded for analysis by a measurement firm.

Arbitron Audience measurement firm, working primarily in radio.

A. C. Nielsen. Well before his name became synonymous with broadcast audience measurement, this researcher was tracking purchases of food and drugs to help marketers plot strategy.

ratings—typically much smaller totals than Crossley's, but more precise—tended to displease the broadcasters who were selling commercial time while pleasing the advertisers who were buying it.[5] In other words, Hooper provided better data per dollar on the real audience for a show, counterbalancing some of the broadcasters' grand claims.

Virtually from the start, a key to determining ratings was that it was neither possible nor necessary to count *every* listener. Instead, ratings consultants came to use *households* as the basic unit of numerical measurement—and didn't even count all of those, instead using samples.

What Nielsen Changed

In 1923, a company arrived that would come to be more closely associated with broadcast ratings than any other. Engineer Arthur C. Nielsen at first tracked retail food and drug purchases, but in the 1930s, he entered broadcast audience research. Two professors sold Nielsen rights to a mechanical "black box" that would become known as the *audimeter*. Placed inside someone's radio, it would record what station (frequency) was being tuned in and for how long. After several years of development, Nielsen put his audimeter into 800 homes in 1942—and the use of meters as a ratings method was born.[6]

Broadcasters who paid for the newly available data would know how many homes (at least homes with audimeters) had tuned into which radio programs. Such numbers could convince advertisers that their investments in commercial time would be sound. Soon, Hooper went further, using listener **diaries** to supplement its telephone interviews. The company was acquired in 1950 by Nielsen, which then stepped into a new medium through its Nielsen Television Index and its local Nielsen Station Index. The company had come to dominate audience measurement of a mushrooming sector of American cultural life.

Most of the emphasis in the rush for ratings had been on national broadcasting—that is, programming and advertising at the network level—but that soon would change. The Federal Communications Commission (FCC) in 1948 had imposed a four-year freeze on the expansion of TV, as a means of sorting out conflicting frequencies and letting the industry improve its technology. When the freeze ended in 1952, television began a growth spurt that carried with it new pressure to measure both national and local audiences.

The result was a mad scramble among ratings companies to establish beachheads across the landscape. A new company called *ARB*, for *Audience Research Bureau* (today's **Arbitron**), used viewer diaries and also pioneered the famous *sweeps*—regular samplings within TV markets in certain four-week periods of every year. Nielsen, meanwhile, worked to refine and extend the reach of its meters. The logistical demands of the interview technique tended to confine it to major cities. Meters had an edge in reaching far-flung audience sectors. Nielsen's electronic monitoring approach had gained a foothold that helped it lead the pack in measuring network TV.

The Numbers Now

Broadcasting's boom through the second half of the twentieth-century produced increasing demands on ratings services. They responded by developing more and better ways to measure audiences. Today, radio and television managers can browse among dozens of categories of ratings data in deciding which programs to produce, acquire, maintain, revise, or cancel.

A number of measurement firms are at work in both radio and television measurement—and, increasingly, in counting Internet-media customers—but the field is dominated by two large operations: Arbitron in radio and Nielsen Media Research in television. Each uses a mix of methods in tallying audiences, relying primarily on diaries and meters.

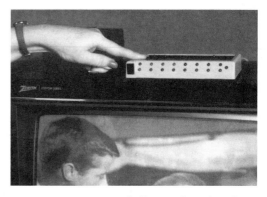

Audimeter. As early radio listeners enjoyed programs, Nielsen's monitor lurked inside their sets, recording channel choices and paving the way for audience meters in wide use today.

DIARIES

Far from being what most of us mean by "diary"—a private record of personal experiences—the ratings diary is a formally structured log to be filled out and returned to a measurement company for careful examination. The viewer or listener is supposed to record his or her program choices throughout each day and evening, usually a week at a time. Four weeks in a row make up each sweeps period, of which there are four per year.

The diary generally indicates when the TV or radio is turned on or off, which is helpful to the programmer or advertiser trying to pin down audience routines. Ratings firms compile that set-use information into totals called **HUT (households using television)**, **PUT (persons using television)**, or **PUR (persons using radio)**.

When the statisticians have added up how many of the people or homes in the sample were tuned to each show, they project that snapshot across the total potential audience to come up with a total viewing estimate. Stations receive that information as two numbers: the *rating*, the percentage of all homes *owning* radio/TV who tuned into the show; and the **share,** the percentage of all homes or users currently *using* TV/radio who tuned into the show. Either figure, or both, can prove critically important as broadcasters track the payoff for their investments in programs.

Nielsen Media Research reports that it contacts about one million homes in all 210 TV markets each year, asking viewers to keep diaries during the sweeps periods. Arbitron uses a similar process, then sends each willing household up to nine individual diaries, for each listener to use—paying a cash premium for every completed diary.

Diaries depend on audience response, which has fluctuated but never has been particularly high; in the late 1990s, Nielsen's diary response rate reportedly dipped below 20 percent in some markets, and it took cash payments to bring the figure above 30 percent.[7] Even that level of cooperation was inadequate, however. CBS's veteran research chief David Poltrack was quoted to the effect that a participation rate under 50 percent probably was "statistically invalid."[8]

> **Principle #3**
>
> Commercial broadcasters invariably press for closer surveillance of TV viewers' behavior.

HUT Figure indicating number of homes using television at a particular time.

PUT Persons using television.

PUR Persons using radio.

Share Percentage of homes using television (HUT) that are tuned in to a particular station or channel.

As measurement technology has advanced, the relative credibility of ratings drawn from diaries has slipped, due to their reliance on audience recall and reports. Yet, diaries continue to play an important role in audience measurement, in part because they cost less than other methods. They clearly remain valuable in obtaining age, gender, and some other demographic information from viewers and listeners. Arbitron (which abandoned its TV work in 1993) still claims that diaries are the most reliable source of ratings for radio.

For television, Nielsen still uses diaries in all 210 TV markets to generate crucial information for local broadcasters several times a year. However, for network ratings, Nielsen maintains meters in 5,000 homes nationally and draws data separately from 49 metered markets. Millions of dollars are being invested in this technology to improve its reliability and adapt it to the changing world that broadcasters—and, now, the Internet—face.

METERS

In the six decades since A. C. Nielsen installed his first audimeters in radio sets, electronic monitoring that records program choices automatically—not depending on viewers to report them accurately—has grown tremendously. This hasn't happened because the ratings companies specialized entirely in broadcast measurement—far from it: ACNielsen Corporation, now owned by a Dutch-based conglomerate, has grown to become the world's largest *market* research firm. Among its other lines of business, it draws floods of information from electronic scanners in stores to help the food industry work more efficiently.

Nielsen Media Research, the company's TV ratings unit, says its numbers are at the heart of $45 billion in commercial-TV-time sales every year in the United States and Canada. Its primary numbers come from meters installed in television sets. Arbitron, the eighth-largest market research firm in the world, now is noted primarily for radio ratings—for which it has been pushing a new kind of meter.[9]

Meters are intended to be not only accurate but convenient for TV households. Yet, when the audimeter arrived in radio in the 1940s, it required almost as much of viewers as diaries do. Because the device picked up signals and recorded them—rather than transmitting them electronically to Nielsen headquarters— each household had to mail the tapes in. This introduced human factors that left the metering totals incomplete, imprecise, and thus of limited usefulness to broadcasters and advertisers.

Nielsen threw millions of dollars into developing technology over the next few decades, making each new generation of meters more practical than the last, while its ratings dominated television decision making. In 1987, the company switched to *people meters*, automatic devices that allowed viewers to punch in personal codes whenever they began and stopped watching. This gave broadcasters a better reading on exactly who in a household that was tuned to a program actually was *watching* it, including the person's demographic details. However, it left open the possibility of human error or neglect, especially when children were the viewers entering the information.

Nielsen has beefed up its staff that persuades randomly selected families to cooperate with the people meter's needs. The company continues to aspire to

A Rush for Ratings: *Survivor*

Starting in 2000, CBS demonstrated how a single hit TV show can galvanize a broad, unified push for both high ratings and desirable demographics.

Survivor was a "reality" show in which real people lived out supposedly unscripted dramas in exotic places—and, week by week, were given opportunities to vote one another off the show. A large cash prize awaited the last player standing.

This premise might have seemed unthinkably lowbrow a few years earlier, but when *Survivor* suddenly went through the ratings roof in its time period, CBS saw grander possibilities, and pounced. Suddenly, it seemed that every division and tentacle of the one-time haughty "Tiffany Network" began cross-promoting *Survivor*.

In 2001, as rival networks aired knockoffs of the show, its format came roaring back on CBS. *Survivor: The Australian Outback* placed ever-more-colorful people in a seemingly hostile environment. How well did it do in the ratings?

- More than 29 million viewers caught the show one Thursday evening in February.
- In its last quarter-hour, as the Outback party's "tribal council" met about whom to eject, viewership shot up to 31.9 million. That was 12 million higher than NBC's audience in those minutes.

This happened even though NBC was broadcasting its perennially popular *Friends* series, plus part of the veteran *Saturday Night Live,* in a deliberate effort to keep *Survivor* from surviving.

On that Thursday evening, a long-running battle of the network titans ended without a knockout. *Survivor* and another show gave CBS a strong night, but NBC's lineup—including hospital-drama powerhouse *ER*—topped CBS in total Thursday prime-time numbers. NBC's share of the youth audience also grew a little.

So each network could claim competitive victories on a big night in February, a sweeps month. By appealing primarily to young viewers, both networks would attract higher ad revenue. More significant for the long run was that *Survivor* had created a groundswell. People were talking not only about the show but about its success, which brought it curious viewers and more success.

Critics still denounced the show as pandering to humanity's lower drives, and social scientists wondered aloud what *Survivor* said about *all* of our drives. This only helped to keep everyone talking.

CBS milked the popularity of this odd new programming genre. The network created a website to entertain fans with photos and profiles—while promoting future episodes and pushing show-branded merchandise. At that moment in TV time, *Survivor* and some of its clones seemed capable of surviving for years.

the dream of an entirely "passive" technology—requiring no viewer action at all. Since the late 1990s, Nielsen has been developing and testing an *active/passive meter.* This gauges newer home digital systems that combine different media, and it looks not at channels but at programs, each coming into the home carrying a distinctive electronic code. Nielsen also has joined Arbitron in testing the *portable people meter* (PPM). It's a hand-held device, designed to go wherever a radio listener goes, picking up the sounds of programs—even Internet-delivered programs—and identifying them. As television becomes accessible to viewers through more and more systems, some of them mobile, the PPM may come into play measuring TV audiences, as well.

ANALYZING THE AUDIENCE

In a hypercompetitive age, profiles of audience members have become far more important than mere head counts. Assuming that we know or believe that Viewer X is watching a particular show, many questions remain:

- What do we know about X's age, gender, race, income, and education?
- How about his (or her) preferences in personal-care products, cars, appliances, credit cards, and clothing?
- How much income would he or she be likely to spend on such a product or service?
- Is Viewer X retired? Disabled? A teenager? A retiree? Sedentary? Athletic?

Broadcasters know the mass audiences who built broadcasting have been shattered into fragments by cultural changes and new choices of entertainment and information. They work to cultivate those fragments as successfully as they once farmed the mass. Particular slices of the old mass audience are especially lucrative. A top NBC programming executive in 2001 could have been speaking for most networks when he said, "We need shows that draw a large audience that's desirable to advertisers—the eighteen-to-forty-nine demographic with high income and Internet usage."[10]

> ### Principle #4
>
> The characteristics of an audience usually are more important than its size.

With an extra minute's thought, the executive could have listed many more qualifications for his target audience, further narrowing it. That would make every dollar his network spent still more efficient in reaching the people likeliest to heed the commercials. That, in turn, would improve his own odds of succeeding, show by show, day after nervous day.

Demographics

Many years ago, it was widely believed that television and radio would be forces for unity on the U.S. landscape. Theorist Marshall McLuhan even spoke of a "national hearth" around which television would gather us all. For a while—through the 1950s, at least—this notion seemed valid. A small number of stations and networks designed the small number of programs that attracted most of the population.

Today, an army of networks, hundreds of cable-TV channels, thousands of broadcasters, and a growing but uncounted fleet of Internet sites are *dividing* the population. Statisticians chop it into into smaller and smaller units based on personal characteristics. Whether or not that's beneficial in civic and political terms, it has helped networks design programs that attract selected viewers or listeners, which helps advertisers find ready buyers for their goods. A few key markers sought by audience researchers are especially important:

AGE

In today's culture, fairly or not, age often determines how people are viewed by others; that's why a commercial in which a teenaged "slacker" tries to chat with his elderly aunt hits our laugh buttons.

Targeting age groups can perpetuate stereotypes. Still, people with similar (or just similarly short or long) track records in life do tend to band together and share discoveries about products and services. Some especially tight-knit groups may place high value on a single commercial item.[11] Age turns out to be a good indicator of a person's disposable income, interests, and other realities. It's hardly surprising, then, that advertisers and broadcasters do try to gather age-defined audiences and sell shows to them.

Like the NBC executive mentioned earlier, most broadcasters are out to find viewers in one particular bracket: ages 18 to 49. People in that group tend to have autonomy, consume media avidly, and spend money on their own. From a chronological standpoint, they're prime targets. Unfortunately for broadcasters and advertisers, heavy media competition has made that "demographic" harder and harder to attract consistently. As a result, the TV networks are pressing advertisers to broaden their prime target area to encompass people over age 50—baby boomers.

GENDER

Women buy more products of more types than men do. Men do shop passionately for certain items that reinforce the male image (as *Home Improvement* often noted), but, to many TV advertisers, women remain the most desirable demographic in most age groups. That's why female-oriented programming is manifest through much of the television day. Success has come to advertisers who pitch their goods to women during morning programs rich in domestic-issue stories, daytime soap operas, afternoon talk shows (where *Oprah* has reigned supreme) and prime-time newsmagazines that emphasize human interest. More women work outside the home these days than just a decade ago. That means they're not at home as much to watch television, and it means that audience researchers must keep unearthing information to help programmers and advertisers appeal to this moving target.

RACE AND NATIONAL ORIGIN

The unsteady march of racial integration in the United States has put more disposable income in the hands of many African Americans. What's more, the growing number and prospective success of immigrants from many lands will create stronger markets for goods and services. Now, for broadcasters—remember, the term suggests a *broad* arena—race, ethnicity, and national origin are not always crystal-clear indicators of who will respond well to advertising. Buying patterns within families fall into changing cultural patterns as the nation grows more multicultural.

The 2000 U.S. census brought in a few relevant facts: More black households than white households contain children; the traditional two-adult family grouping is more common among Asian Americans than among whites, and the number of black and Hispanic families with both parents present is relatively low but rising.[12] These sort of data are sure to influence programming strategies if it shows up as part of audience research. It also will cause advertisers to shift their aim—and their spending.

Psychographic Term for behavior profile of electronic-media users; psychographic research builds on ratings and demographics.

Cost per thousand (viewers or listeners) (CPM) Refers to cost of a commercial based on its expected audience reach.

INCOME, EDUCATION, AND MORE

Several key factors or variables round out the profile of a household and help to predict the behavior of viewers or listeners within it. Researchers find that income and education track rather closely together; the size of a home, its geographic location, the number of occupants, the number of TV sets, and so on, add to the picture. If interviews and questionnaires determine that generally small, well-educated families live on good incomes in comfortable homes in a middle-class neighborhood, certain advertisers will conclude that their messages will find a friendly reception there. When such attributes appear across larger populations, then research firms may create strategic maps for the same advertisers to follow.

Psychographics

Once broadcasters determine what viewers and listeners look like demographically, they can move toward discerning what viewers *feel*, *think*, and *do*. This information will bring advertising and programming much more precisely in tune with the audience.

So-called **psychographics** has been around since roughly the 1970s. Surveys and other methods already had made strides in linking the behavior of individuals to their demographic groups. Now, researchers began bunching broadcast consumers into clusters—who shared values and lifestyles and thus could be targeted by advertisers. It was advertisers who paid for much of this deep description, as a way of ensuring their future investments in commercial time. The prices for time, set by broadcasters, ultimately translate into **CPM**, or **cost per thousand**—what it costs an advertiser to reach each 1,000 viewers, as was noted in Chapter 9.

Pressure to make every dollar count has increased rapidly with the increased competition for select viewers and listeners. It makes good business sense to narrow the audience reach for some shows to people who are favorably inclined toward related products. This focus on how all of us consumers view the world has launched an almost surgically precise differentiation of some programs from others. For example, it was clear early that college graduates generally are less mesmerized by TV than are less-educated people. Still, both groups watch TV along rather similar patterns after work, so the same commercials theoretically would reach both. What if an advertiser, trying to spend money wisely, doesn't want to pay to reach both types, but wants only the more culturally upscale audience? To be able to sift through viewers' passions and prejudices and display them "psychographically" and in other dimensions, comparing one show's audience and time slot with that of another, can help achieve that goal.

Finding the Facts

No station, network, or advertiser can obtain all the audience data needed. Nor have ratings giants Nielsen and Arbitron provided a complete scan of each potential broadcast audience. Other companies with a complex array of experience have stepped into the field. Just like academics whenever they must furnish tables or charts, audience researchers tend to choose one or more proven methods before going about their work. That's because at some point, they must account for their methods' *validity* and *reliability*—two trusted yardsticks of how accurate and meaningful the data really are.

A central question to ask of any research report is: How did the observers extract data from their **sample**—all the people who cooperated in the study— through the specific questions they asked? One company, Mediamark Research Inc. (MRI), tries to allay concerns among broadcasters by stressing its systematic objectivity and "lack of interview bias," saying it reaches populations "difficult to survey through traditional means." Systematic and reliable methods applied to the same problem will yield the same results repeatedly—like a true set of scales or a good thermometer.

SRI CONSULTING BUSINESS INTELLIGENCE

SRI Consulting Business Intelligence is a broad-based research company that homes in on media audiences through a system called VALS ™ (VALS comes from an accepted abbreviation for *values, attitudes, and lifestyles.*) It claims to uncover the "underlying psychological makeup" of consumers—especially those traits that motivate buying—which strikes to the heart of what broadcasters and advertisers want to know. The VALS system approaches this by posing statements that encourage each person to think hard about his or her deeper impulses. Agreement or disagreement with such statements clearly can provide clues to what people might or might not buy, as well as to their tastes in programming. The VALS approach not only characterizes viewers and listeners through psychographics but identifies where they live and seeks out related patterns. This can be called **geodemographics,** and is practiced by other research firms, as well.

SYMMETRICAL RESOURCES

Symmetrical Resources is the parent company of Simmons Market Research Bureau, long noted for reports on how different demographic groups see broadcasting and the advertising it carries. In 2001, Symmetrical introduced a new way of "segmenting" television viewers according to their strongest preferences in programming—categories of shows with helpful labels such as Evening Soap Drama, Real Crime TV, Ethnic Sitcom, and Late Night Junkie. Through advanced statistical work, the system produces 23 types of viewer clusters that advertisers can locate within the great mass of viewers, using Nielsen ratings. Then the advertisers

Sample Group of subjects chosen for study in audience research.

Geodemographic Correlation of a household's location with demographics of its members; helps in determining broad patterns.

Digging in Our Brains

A VALS questionnaire asks: Do you agree or disagree with these statements?

- I am often interested in theories.
- I follow the latest trends and fashions.
- Just as the Bible says, the world literally was created in six days.

- I consider myself an intellectual.
- I am very interested in how mechanical things, such as engines, work.
- I am always looking for a thrill.
- I like my life to be pretty much the same from week to week.[13]

Viewers for Quality Television Citizens' group launched in 1984 to pressure networks to improve television; disbanded in 2000 when founder Dorothy Swanson became ill and retired.

are able to target these groups in their commercials and choose shows in which to run the commercials—obviously a matter of critical interest to broadcasters.

TVQ

For many years, TVQ has helped local stations decide whom to hire and fire, by canvassing audience members to see which performers—usually news anchors—are most "appealing." Critics often grouse that good anchors are fired because of imperfect "Q ratings" or because managers can use Q ratings as a cover for the real reasons. In addition, TVQ tests the popular appeal of specific products and brands. Each May and November, the company interviews 1,800 adults to learn what different brands mean to them and how loyal they are to certain products.

ISSUES AND CONCERNS

As noted at the opening of this chapter, nobody seems to be neutral toward ratings; for decades, ratings have seemed to hold almost absolute power over the content of the most popular mass medium in the world. Often forgotten is that ratings are simply numbers, buttressed by cold demographic facts—and by personal information that some of us give directly to media researchers. These bits of knowledge alone have no power, but they acquire great power, indeed, quite suddenly, when someone puts them to use.

That someone usually is a radio or TV executive weighing options for the near future, a situation often riddled with uncertainty and peril. Options include the launching of expensive programs that nobody may care about and the cancellation of ongoing shows that millions love dearly. Thus, while hoping conscientiously to serve his or her stockholders, superiors, advertisers, and possibly even the audience, the broadcast manager clenching a ratings sheet can probably smell its metaphorical fuse burning. If so, one of two important constituencies—the executive's own fellow broadcasters or the audiences they serve—may have lit it.

Consumer Interests

Consumers of radio and TV programming—and, at one time or another, that's *all* of us—have a stake in the system that gives such influence to ratings. However, we have little clear control over it. All commercial systems set up ways of measuring product effectiveness, and that's what ratings are. Consumers always can try to outshout the ratings—force a hearing of their arguments—by focusing public attention on them. In a few noteworthy cases, they have effectively done just that.

"QUALITY" OVER RATINGS?

More than three decades ago, the now-classic *Star Trek* was cancelled, then was kept on the air a couple of seasons longer after a reported 100,000 letters flooded NBC. In 1984, CBS put the buddy-cop show *Cagney and Lacey* on "hiatus," an often permanent status, but a group called **Viewers for Quality Television (VQT)** quickly rallied letter writers. Thousands wrote to the network, and the show was spared for another four seasons.

Another popular but ratings-challenged program, *Designing Women*, also won a reprieve; it lasted another six years. If those were gentler times, when the industry seemed kinder—reading and sometimes heeding viewer mail—they soon ended. With competitive and budget pressures mounting, only ratings held a firm enough tether for the prices the networks charged for commercial time. By the 1990s, television might as well have said to viewers, "Okay, from now on, it's no more Mr. Nice Network!" Shows would be cancelled and then stay cancelled. That happened in 1993–1994 when NBC removed a highly praised but lightly watched family drama, *Against the Grain*. Through the news media, the show's co-creator appealed directly to Nielsen households to rescue it from pending oblivion. He told a reporter, "No offense to all other Americans, but right now the only people we really care about who watch our show are Nielsen families, because that's the only thing that can keep us on."[14] It didn't happen: NBC stuck to its guns, replacing *Against the Grain* with the action show *Viper* (one newspaper dubbing that the year's "worst programming move").

Cagney & Lacey. This buddy-cop TV team benefited from audience activism when Viewers for Quality Television campaigned to keep the show on the air—and won.

Viewers for Quality Television, often in concert with independent viewers, mounted more letter-writing campaigns, but to little avail. Their founder, Dorothy Swanson, saw that viewers were most effective in strengthening shows early, not trying to save them later. Still, grass-roots action did keep a popular young-pal series called *Party of Five* on the air *somewhere* for awhile; launched on Fox in 1994 and cancelled six seasons later, it moved to the Lifetime cable channel but then faded from the lineup.

When Swanson became ill and disbanded VQT, it was succeeded by another national audience group, Wisconsin-based Viewers Voice, which had been pressuring broadcasters on its own. It, too, faced long odds.

> **Principle #5**
>
> **Broadcasters do not give all audience members equal weight in programming decisions.**

DIVERSITY CAMPAIGNS

Besides campaigns to promote "quality" broadcasting, there are crusades to bring more prominence to various minorities in the program content and management of television in particular. In 2001, the National Association for the Advancement of Colored People (NAACP) demanded that the networks give nonwhites more authority over programming. The move came nearly two years after the NAACP held heavily publicized meetings with top TV executives, and even though overall casting of nonwhite actors improved, some movement leaders held out for more lead roles and greater influence behind the Hollywood scenes. Pressure also has come from advocates for Hispanic Americans, an especially fast-growing population group. Cable and satellite channels—looking for niches and seeing diversity as less of a ratings risk than the networks do—have created some notable minority-based shows and offer extensive Spanish-language programming.

Concerned viewers and career activists can work more surgically toward their goals, as demonstrated in 2000 by the Gay and Lesbian Alliance Against

Defamation (GLAAD). With support from other homosexual groups, GLAAD campaigned against Dr. Laura Schlessinger, who had been controversial on radio and was now launching a TV advice show. The campaign worked: Complaints that Schlessinger was antigay cost her advertisers, then low ratings helped push her off the screen before she had completed a season. Conversely, gay and lesbian organizations have been fervent backers of shows such as ABC's mid-1990s *Ellen*, featuring a gay comedian-lead-character, and the Showtime cable hit *Queer as Folk*, adapted from a popular British program.

IN PUBLIC BROADCASTING

It may seem incongruous to think of ratings in connection with public broadcasting—that special web of stations and program suppliers that depends on individual donors, foundations, and government for most of its financial support. The official ethos of public broadcasting holds that it can take on topics and treatments that commercial broadcasters wouldn't dare touch. However, audience research has influenced decisions in public radio and television for years. That's a source of simmering controversy as public stations creep toward a commercial model under which they would run true commercials—not just brief "underwriting" spots—to bring in revenue.

Since the mid-1990s, the Corporation for Public Broadcasting has used Arbitron ratings as a basis for granting funding to community and public radio stations. Critics of this practice say it tends to knock the corners off programming, pressuring stations to take fewer risks in their choice of issues to tackle and the content they air. The role of ratings was a factor in recent turmoil at the nation's first community radio station, KPFA, in Berkeley, California. The social activists who made the station a fixture in community life wanted less emphasis on audience size, as dictated by Arbitron, than KPFA's leadership preferred.

The Radio Research Consortium publishes ratings and listener demographics for many major public-radio programs, to help stations find and nurture shows to hold local audiences—prospective donors—in place. Consultants now advise public TV programmers to keep viewers engaged in the weeks before on-air "pledge drives," through which most membership donations flow in. In general, audience size and loyalty have not kept pace with programming costs, leaving a yawning and persistent financial gap. Nor has Congress been consistently supportive. In this environment of need, the use of ratings and audience analysis seems likely to grow in public TV and radio.

Broadcaster Interests

At this writing, a combination of ratings and audience-analysis data governs the daily content of TV and radio programming across the United States. That's hardly news; what may seem more surprising is that pressure to follow ratings has intensified in recent years. At the same time, resistance to the old ways of tallying audiences has grown within the industry. Broadcasters accept the need to "count the house," but they want Nielsen, Arbitron, and other researchers to do their jobs better. Behind that drive lies a need to deal with issues that range from annoying to threatening.

ProTalk

Pat Cashman
Disc Jockey, KOMO-FM, Seattle, Washington

"I was called into the general manager's office. After that meeting, doing the final show was a little tough."

Audience power can rise up against broadcasters at the drop of a pink slip. Angry calls and e-mails poured in after Seattle radio station KIRO-FM cut a comic "personality" named Pat Cashman from its lineup in favor of syndicated programming in 1999. One listener told a newspaper that when he heard of the change, "I felt as though a member of my family had died." Two major advertisers cancelled their commercials.

The station's program director was left to explain that he took Cashman off the air because he clearly appealed to two audience segments: female listeners and families. Why was this a bad thing? Because it detracted from the sex-talk of the station's raunchy afternoon performer, whose show commanded a huge young, male audience. KIRO didn't want to blur its macho image.[15]

Now, Cashman recalls, with a kind of sardonic wonder, the day he lost his job: "It was April of 1999, my day of reckoning. I was called into the general manager's office. They had the human-services guy there, and the PD (program director), and the GM. I said, 'Gee, I don't believe I've seen you all in the same room together before.' After that meeting, doing the final show was a little tough. . . .

"But the most unusual thing about the firing was what happened next. . . . There was a group that formed as a result of my dismissal. They were big fans of the show, and formed the 'Pat Pack.' These people found a collective gathering place on a website. They'd use it to hold rallies. Even the PD who fired me said he had never seen anything like this. People just deluged that station with cards, and even picketed outside the building."

Before long, Cashman—highly popular on Seattle radio for years—found himself behind a microphone at another major station, KOMO-FM. Now, from that comfortable perspective, he looks at the radio industry and finds fault with the relationship between its decision making and its analysis of audiences. Consolidation bears much of the blame, says Cashman:

"I guess one of my biggest lamentations is about the size of these radio companies. It means the disappearance of local ownership for the most part. This station is still locally owned, by Fisher Broadcasting, and the difference is that you can touch and feel something out there, and you're part of the community." Local stations at their best are part of the fabric of a town, says Cashman, "so there can be quirky types that populate your shows. You're part of the local scene, the local uniqueness. But when the people making the decisions are back in Dubuque, they don't have an appreciation of that. All they look at is what the rating book says."

DRIFTING ATTENTION

The added pressure to generate high ratings was produced largely by two related trends: the upsurge in competition from other media and the rapid reorganization of the broadcast industry. First, the proliferation of broadcast, cable, and Internet competition has split the attention of millions of media users across the United States. Although a relative few channels dominate most viewing, the scores of TV options today obviously make it difficult for any one network or station to rule the field. Moreover, for viewers armed with today's rapid-fire remote-control devices, "surfing" can turn a widened spectrum of choices into a colorful

System for Measuring and Reporting Television (SMART) Unsuccessful 1990s effort by TV networks to design alternative ratings system to Nielsen's.

blur; it's the despised enemy of something broadcasters love: viewer loyalty. When forces like that drive ratings down, they're hard to win back.

The migration to cyberspace for entertainment and information poses an even greater challenge for broadcasters. For example, the viewer who buys her or his first Internet-empowered computer may well become infatuated with the new world of bits and bytes and watch less TV.[16] As their enthusiasm spreads through the population, it has diverted one viewer after another from his or her usual viewing diet—certainly not all viewers, but many. Some may return to the old shows, but ratings still slip in the meantime. This, of course, keeps many executives struggling to give advertisers a large enough and eager enough audience to justify their spending on ads. The result can be either a me-too imitation of successful programs or a risky innovation in search of demographic appeal.

AN ECONOMIC JAM

The reorganization of the industry largely involves wealthy media (and nonmedia) corporations that buy up weaker companies. These include networks, station groups, and local stations. This power shift upward tends to harness small-market broadcasters to Wall Street players who own the parent corporations' stock. The effect is to place greater pressure on stations to hit ratings home runs at every opportunity.

> **Principle #6**
>
> Industry consolidation increases pressure for high ratings.

If a station can't raise ratings, and thus ad revenue, high enough to meet profit demands, it must cut costs—which can involve laying off workers. It also can drive stations toward look-and-sound-alike syndicated programs, though a few stand out from the crowd. One of these, Rush Limbaugh's mostly political talk show, has been a particularly productive choice for radio managers eager to gain ratings. Since 1989, Limbaugh's success reportedly quadrupled the number of AM talk-radio stations, and was capable of single-handedly turning a ratings-losing station into a winner.[17] One former station-group chief is quoted as calling the impact of ratings on local radio "fabulous for shareholders, but terrible for listeners and employees."[18] Many industry voices have been raised against this web of financial causes and consequences, but almost always behind a mask of anonymity and to little lasting effect.

DOUBTS ABOUT NUMBERS

Broadcasters often blame the ratings methods for costly shortcomings that keep "the numbers" too low. An example appeared in March 2001, when the head of CBS Sports complained publicly that Nielsen was "undercounting" TV audiences for sports events. He said this was because many fans watched not just from homes—including "Nielsen homes"—but from other venues, ranging from bars to college dorms. Technology may remedy some ills, but unfortunately, over time, ratings advances have failed to stave off broadcasters' concerns.

Discontent with the quality of Nielsen's numbers boiled over in 1996. A Wisconsin broadcaster confided starkly to the *Washington Post*: "It's about time we called the baby ugly."[19] The Fox network threatened legal action against Nielsen; ABC, CBS, and NBC put money into an effort to develop a ratings alternative called **SMART (System for Measuring and Reporting Television)**.

The networks' main complaint was that Nielsen's sampling process underreported the young viewers. If true, this was bad for all broadcasters. Another beef was that Nielsen *over*counted cable-TV homes, giving cable higher ratings than it deserved and putting over-the-air TV at a disadvantage.

In 1999, assured by Nielsen that its in-house tinkering would improve ratings, the networks withdrew their money from the SMART project, and it folded. This did not discourage two other companies—the cable-system operator Comcast and the home-shopping network QVC—from pushing another alternative. Called **TargetTV,** this would use set-top boxes to record program choices. It would not answer demands for a mobile device like Nielsen's Portable People Meter, and had other limitations; but it would record channel use *every five seconds* to keep up with channel surfing. By spring 2001, TargetTV was in 60,000 homes and its developers were planning to install it in many more.

Rush Limbaugh. He's the ratings hero of commercial radio. That's why Rush Limbaugh's voice can be heard across America, squeezing less magnetic hosts and their views off the AM dial.

TargetTV Effort by Comcast Cable and QVC (shopping channel) to develop alternative to Nielsen techniques, using set-top boxes to track TV-channel choices.

Diaries still are a widely used tool for obtaining demographic data. Stations have complained—evidently with some validity—that very low response rates from diary households were distorting results. In some cities, those responses reportedly dropped below 20 percent. Nielsen answered this in 2001 by giving viewers $5 apiece for sending in their diaries during the May sweeps, and it worked: The response rate began to rise. Still, fewer than one in three viewers provided Nielsen with data, which seemed to support charges that the all-powerful ratings system was badly flawed.

Early tests of the Portable People Meter—designed to track viewing wherever highly mobile Americans engage in it—reportedly went well. Arbitron announced that more than 80 percent of test subjects in a Wilmington, Delaware, test were using the device properly. This meant taking it out of a special carriage container in the morning, wearing it all day, and returning it at night to its holder, from which PPM data could be uploaded automatically to Arbitron.

The audience-counters strive to improve, but in the superheated cauldron of broadcasting today, measuring audiences may be a no-win proposition. When the National Association of Broadcasters asked TV stations nationwide to indicate their overall level of satisfaction with Nielsen, 23 percent said "low," 40 percent said "neutral," and about 30 percent said "fair."[20] This reinforced impressions that broadcasters feel deflated by the system. Worse, many emphasize—they're paying for it.

A COLLISION OF VALUES

The deepest concern about ratings-driven broadcasting is aimed not at measurement firms but at the industry's own managers. It is they who convert ratings into decisions that sometimes confound the values of their own programming. It also is the top managers who, critics say, have ceded all control over broadcasting to its advertisers—as in the early days when sponsors dictated content.

Nowhere is the impact of audience numbers more onerous than in the newsroom. Journalists who complain that the ratings obsession is diluting news

Book Another word for *sweeps*, a period of intensive audience measurement three times a year.

run the risk of being branded mavericks; still they complain. News executives often privately criticize (or curse) the influence of ratings over their upper management. Too often, some say, a single low **book** (sweeps period) leads the boss to order staff cuts; since the news department usually is the station's largest, it's the most inviting target for layoffs.

Carping about the power of ratings is a familiar refrain in the news business, and has been so at least since Edward R. Murrow and his producer, Fred Friendly, made CBS a temple of journalism at mid-century. Murrow the journalist chafed at business pressures on landmark news programs such as *See It Now*—then gave way to Murrow the entertainer, the chain-smoking host of a celebrity show, *Person to Person*. Friendly, on the other hand, became president of CBS News, only to quit in 1966 when the network dumped live coverage of Senate hearings on Vietnam, cutting to the ever-popular *I Love Lucy*—in reruns. Ratings realities could overpower even the icons of journalism.

In the 1970s, as ABC News sought stability and respect, stars Ted Koppel and Sam Donaldson beamed their pride in the network's news coverage and paid little heed to its huge audience deficit, according to one account.[21] As the seventies ended, veteran news executive Richard Wald could still say, "The question always is, will you put something on that may not get ratings, but may be important? So far, television news, like other news organizations, has always said yes."[22] Today, Wald could not honestly say "always." Unable to escape the ratings trap, news managers do their best in its grip. Prime-time newsmagazines cater to curiosity about family violence and Hollywood, dispensing gossip amid the "news-you-can-use" format. Not just individual stories, not just entire newscasts, but news *departments* may be thrown out if the ratings go sharply against them. In 2001, years of low numbers led Indiana's WEVV-TV to cancel all of its newscasts, as some other stations had done.

The Grim Sweeper

Like salmon in the Pacific Northwest, local TV news directors are a perenially threatened lot. Their departments produce what in most stations is the only locally generated programming. Sometimes news directors lose their jobs after developing "creative differences" with their superiors. More often than not, it's ratings that usher them to the exit. Their average job tenure is not much over two years; nobody is immune. John Mussoni is a case in point. Summer 2001 was his season of reckoning. He had spent almost 15 years running the news operation at the Fox station in Philadelphia. But the general manager fired Mussoni, and told a reporter why: "It's ratings, pure and simple."[23]

Such dismissals usually occur in either December or June, soon after the end of one of the two most important sweeps periods of the year. Arbitron invented sweeps and Nielsen continues the practice, counting viewers in all 210 TV markets during those anxious target months. This is when stations' ratings are recorded for the purpose of setting rates for advertising time, so fortunes are at stake.

During sweeps, local managers quickly obtain minute-to-minute feedback on any newscast's ratings; this enables them to tweak a show in time to get better results the following day. Because tweaking is possible, it has become routine.

(One of the authors listened as a major-market news director informed an award-winning consumer reporter that ratings had dipped during her five-minute segment the previous night. "Don't go back to that subject again tonight," the news director strongly advised.)

Sweeps periods are noted for the loud hyperpromotion of news and for the prevalence of sensational, even salacious, material. There are promotion firms that specialize in fashioning sweeps promos, and TV consultants who track stations' ratings and pick up their highest-scoring sweeps ideas to peddle to other clients. Many viewers do respond to sweeps hype, which now includes contests and cash inducements to viewers, a kind of reverse pay-per view. When these intense periods are over, ratings typically tail off, making it as hard as ever for stations—and their advertisers, who have big money at stake—to determine a newscast's true drawing power.

Some executives say they yearn for a better, calmer, longer-lasting way to raise their ratings and revenues. They disdain the necessity to do garish, low-common-denominator programming four times a year, "but we have to put on our party clothes, because that's when they take the pictures," said one general manager.[24]

ProTalk

Matthew Zelkind
News Director, WKRN-TV, Nashville, Tennessee

"Make no mistake, . . . if we weren't pushing ratings here, you'd be talking to a different guy."

He has a good track record, a respected staff of journalists, and a growing audience. In several ways, however—all related to ratings—Matthew Zelkind is trapped. "We are at the mercy of a flawed system," he says, "a monopoly on how the numbers are determined. Our viewer base is diminishing, and that creates almost a situation of desperation to attract viewers."

Zelkind lives under the tyranny of audience ratings. Nielsen Media Research has reported an overall decline in local-news viewing in the Nashville market. It probably is tied to cable and satellite-TV competition. Whatever the cause, it's damaging to Zelkind's enterprise, and he believes that ratings companies make such trends worse by only *sampling* newscasts, exaggerating the importance of short time periods.

"It unfortunately has turned into a situation where sound journalism is secondary to attracting reviewers in a metered market for 300 seconds at a time," Zelkind says. "You need five minutes [of channel-choice tracking] per quarter-hour to get credit for a quarter hour in the ratings . . . for that meter to register that people have watched you."

Zelkind saves his heaviest barrage for rival stations that "stunt" during ratings sweeps, not only airing sensational material but also running contests to draw viewers. "They literally bribe viewers to watch their newscasts four times a year," he says. "They give away cash, trips, houses—$500 every half hour."

Zelkind can't control his competitors' actions. Nor can he alone revamp the entrenched ratings system to make it, in his view, fairer. He is required to take it as it is, if he wants to keep his job, and he is keenly aware of that. "Make no mistake," he says, "local TV news is big business. If we weren't pushing ratings here, you'd be talking to a different guy."

THE DIGITAL FUTURE—NOW

At the outset of this chapter, we posed several questions: Should the rating system be changed? How? Should people change the way they *use* ratings?

> **Principle #7**
>
> No modern media—even "new" media—can escape the imperative to count and evaluate audiences.

Beyond any conclusions the reader may have reached thus far, other possible answers are stirring in the minds, offices and laboratories of ratings specialists. Some broadcasters believe new approaches to measuring and evaluating their audiences must be found as media competition increases. Otherwise, they warn, radio and television will not be sufficiently self-aware and nimble to anticipate consumer desires and hold their own against future alternatives.

The wild card in these projections is that new players with new game plans are contributing to rapid technological change across all electronic media. This already has begun to restructure broadcasting, and it could necessitate entirely new approaches to every aspect of all media—including the assessment of their audiences.

The Internet as Medium

The success of the Internet in reaching Americans focuses more audience research on the Internet every year. Several veteran ratings companies, as well as some new players, are mapping the growing audience for on-line news, information, and entertainment. At this writing, the most popular news sources on the Internet are established newspapers and magazines. When the World Trade Center was attacked in September 2001, researchers measured the audience's news quest to see if websites belonging to traditional news organizations such as CNN and BBC were preferred (they were), and if network TV news coverage exceeded the Web's popularity (it did).

As expansion comes—and it's coming rapidly—audience measurement and analysis will grow with it. Already, among others, ACNielsen Company, its now-separate offshoot Nielsen Media Research, and an Internet specialist called Nielsen NetRatings are collaborating to survey the fan base across this widening landscape. Nielsen/NetRatings says it's charting "actual click-by-click Internet user behavior measured through a comprehensive, real-time meter installed on the computers of over 225,000 individuals in 26 countries worldwide both at home and at work."[25]

Besides the established audience-measurement companies, there are new-media research firms that already take the pulse of a variety of on-line communication channels, for a variety of purposes. For example, Jupiter Media Metrix analyzes the impact of the Internet and e-marketing on consumers.[26] Jupiter's "top 50 Web and Digital Media Properties" ranks the websites of companies such as Microsoft, Yahoo! and AOL Time Warner by number of visitors and minutes of usage.

Lines of Convergence

Unlike broadcasting's viewers and listeners, computer users operate interactively through individual links to the Internet. This makes them easier to count and identify. The difficulty of obtaining demographic profiles of them could depend on the users' willingness to answer questions—an update of the decades-old diary-response issue—and on researchers' ability to analyze these consumers through surveillance methods if interviews and surveys fail.

Interactive television is becoming available to consumers, offering them more control than ever before over the media they use. Many of these media will draw support from paid subscriptions, from per-use charges such as movies-on-demand, and from the purchase of time and screen space by advertisers pushing their wares. For the advertisers, companies such as Nielsen/NetRatings can be expected to supply audience measurement and related guidance. These companies will track users electronically, probably far expanding the power of the People Meter, since the personal computer inherently is tied to individuals, not a crowd.

Summary

Ratings show managers of electronic media how many households are tuned in to their channels. Audience research extends that knowledge to encompass many of the personal characteristics of viewers, listeners, and Internet users. Armed with this information, managers reach some of their biggest decisions about what we see and hear over radio, television, and now the Internet.

It's an imperfect system of estimates and extrapolations, since no one (so far) has discovered how to sample *every* user of an electronic medium at once with reliability. Measurement and research firms have experimented for decades with methods to improve their audience snapshots. Systems have come far—from simple telephone calls to 1930s radio listeners to see if they remembered their recent listening patterns, to today's sophisticated monitoring of TV viewers' behavior through electronic sensors. In demographic and psychographic research, greater texture and detail define media users. Meanwhile, the digital age has given birth to new media and is spawning new kinds of data-gathering techniques to identify their audience and its desires.

FOOD FOR THOUGHT

1. ABC dropped *Who Wants to Be a Millionaire?* after several successful seasons. Why did the show lose its ratings (or demographics) power? Are audiences really so prone to impatience or boredom, or do they just give way to *new* audiences?
2. Broadcasters who change their programming in response to ratings or research usually say they're simply giving audiences what they want. Is this good, bad, or both? Why?
3. What are the practical limits of meter-based audience measurement? Experimental meters can see or sense who's in the room and who's watching or not watching TV. Is that invasive or not? How and why?
4. When radio or television presents programs targeted to narrow slices of society instead of the mass audience, is it threatening our social fabric? Why? Does broadcasting have enough power to do harm to social cohesiveness? Explain.

11

Theory and Research

> The truth of a theory is in your mind, not in your eyes.
>
> —Albert Einstein

> It is a capital mistake to theorize before one has data.
>
> —Sir Arthur Conan Doyle

Marshall McLuhan. McLuhan was a Canadian scholar who founded technological determinism based on the concept that our personal interactions with media alter our sense ratios, depending on means of statement—radio, television, films.

It is the sort of book that would make a conservative talk-show host like Rush Limbaugh smile—an insider's indictment of the TV networks' liberal bias, full of barbed comments and juicy anecdotes from a former CBS News correspondent. The book quickly found its audience and rocketed up the *New York Times* best-seller list, even making its way into President George W. Bush's hands. Bernard Goldberg's *Bias* took deadly aim at what he saw as the reason for the shrinking network news audience—networks' liberal slant on the news. He cited as evidence network television's propensity for ignoring the repugnant qualities of AIDS victims, drug addicts, and the mentally ill. Portrayals of such people on the nightly news with Dan Rather, Peter Jennings, and Tom Brokaw were calculated to inspire compassion, said Goldberg, rather than justly regarding their suffering as "personal problems."

Goldberg is a study in contrasts. He confesses that he joined his network cohorts in routinely "prettifying" the news, showing attractive people as homeless and suffering. However, he says that he has seen the error of his ways, while his former colleagues continue blithely veering toward the left each night. For the angry white male, Goldberg's book was a godsend. At last, someone was criticizing network news for its egregious acts of unrepentant bias: women network hosts lustily describing male private parts, morning news anchors joking about castration as an intended bride's just revenge for being jilted at the altar, and angry divorced moms robbing ex-spouses of their children and life savings in court with little sympathetic coverage. Goldberg saw it all as part of network news overkill directed against the privileged white male on behalf of the underclass. He did note one noble exception, the networks' reporting on the tragedy of September 11, 2001. For once, he said, they got it right.

Bias represents a type of research classified as *participant observation*, a form of qualitative study—that is, it would be if the author had taken the rigorous steps necessary to put a check on his *own* bias. That would mean, first, strictly defining the problem and its terms, then conducting a thorough review of the literature and clearly explaining the problem and procedures so others could follow and replicate them. Finally, the researcher would have to consider alternative explanations before announcing conclusions. Good research rises above personal bias by answering questions systematically, with passion held in check and reason in control.

> Good research rises above personal bias by answering questions systematically, with passion held in check and reason in control.

Research Process of systematically observing and collecting evidence in order to answer specific questions in a scientific manner through controlled and repeated measures.

PURPOSES OF RESEARCH

Very little can be taken for granted in the information age, but one thing is for sure: Major decisions are not made—whether about merging corporations or making new laws—without research. Media problems are solved not by guesswork and hunches but by data analysis. Before making major investments of time or talent in broadcast or broadband media, managers see *what the research shows*. It's about reducing uncertainty and having a firm foundation for predicting the future. So important is this business of research—collecting data, analyzing them, and interpreting them—that the best jobs in terms of salary and security in electronic media often go to researchers. Without knowing the basics of research, reaching the top of the media pyramid is difficult for power brokers and policymakers.

The systematic structure of mass communication **research** grew out of academic laboratories as well as consulting and research within the media business; both sides apply the scientific method to develop theories and principles. Research is about answering questions and solving problems. It also involves testing theories about the way things work and predicting likely outcomes. So, it's all just based on common sense—correct? Not exactly, Einstein observed: "Conclusions obtained by purely rational processes are, so far as reality is concerned, entirely empty."[1] Building a good theory is about discerning what happens *beyond* your perceptions.

So, how can you tell a good theory from a bad one? First, you must ask several questions: Does it build on what is already known to be true? Can it be proved false? Is it simple and practical enough to be tested? What researchers must avoid is testing any theory that *reinvents the wheel* and fails to push back the frontiers of knowledge.

A previous chapter on ratings offered a brief overview of applied audience research. This chapter focuses on academic studies and gives some attention to what is often called *administrative research*. Private consultants strive to yield immediate profits for the companies they serve. Scholars test theories that yield more in understanding than in profits. In so doing, they seek to reveal media processes and **effects,** and to answer important questions.

What are the influences of propaganda, and how does this process of persuasion work? What are *gatekeepers* thinking when they allow certain messages into the channels of media while holding others back? How does TV violence affect children's minds and shape their worlds? Can the media function to gratify the audience? These are just a few of the fields of inquiry scholars have tried to resolve in theory and research, and in the information age new questions are needing answers.

COMMUNICATION MODEL

It was not social scientists but an engineer and a mathematician who gave the early study of **communication** its first structural model. Claude Shannon at Bell Labs and Warren Weaver at the Sloan-Kettering Institute for Cancer Research collaborated on technical questions concerning the communication phenomenon. Could there be a logical way to trace its distinct parts and evaluate its processes? Shannon and Weaver drew up a mathematical model resembling an engineer's schematics, which became "widely accepted as one of the main seeds out of which communication studies has grown."[2]

This powerful model begins with an information source selecting a message, encoding it, and then sending it through a **channel** to be received as a signal and decoded back into a message. This has proved relevant in the digital era of convergence. Shannon and Weaver's model has addressed technical questions concerning how many bits per second are needed to transmit audio and video messages to computer screens.

The model (Figure 11.1) looks simple enough, but *noise* enters the process and threatens the message. Noise is basically anything that can interfere with the **source/sender** or the *receiver*, or simply can interrupt at points in between. Noise may be generated by people, machines, and sometimes both.

Later researchers felt the model was missing one element in the communication process: feedback. A scientist from Massachusetts Institute of Technology, Norbert Weiner, added the feedback loop while developing weapons systems for the U.S. Defense Department. He saw it as necessary to either correct or confirm that the sender's signal was

Effects Approach to mass communication theory and research that measures the impact media have on members of the audience, either collectively or individually.

Communication Gathering, ordering, encoding, and transferring information from one source to a receiver.

Channel Means used to carry a message from a source to a receiver, including electromagnetic waves, light, sound, or other media.

Source/Sender Message originator who encodes information and prepares it for transmission.

Principle #1

The structural process of communication must be understood before the meaning of content is considered.

FIGURE 11.1

Communication Model

Shannon and Weaver's model of communication is the basis for a wealth of research. It was the first attempt to quantify the communication process and has been revised and expanded over the years.

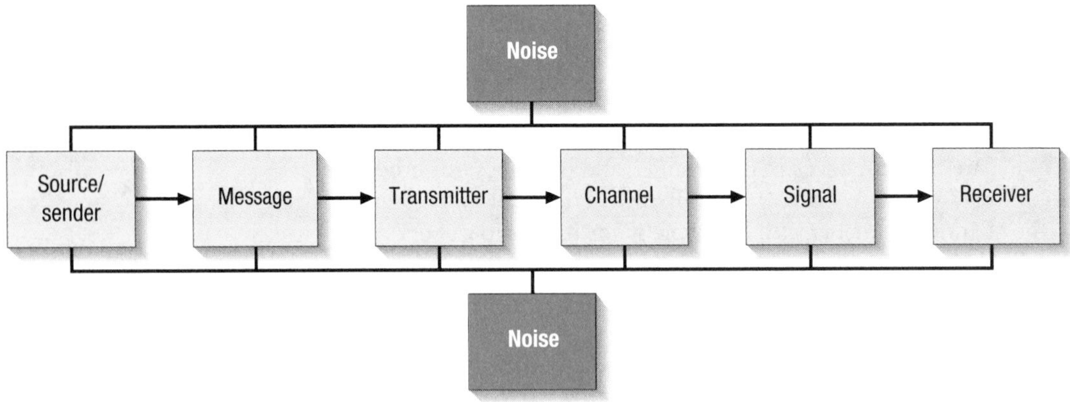

Magic bullet (Hypodermic needle) Metaphor to describe how persuasive messages will strike target audiences with such dramatic impact to penetrate conflicting attitudes like a bullet or hypodermic needle.

properly received. So how is feedback different from a new cycle of communication? It is focused on the initial message; only when a new subject is introduced does a new cycle begin. Notice that this model does not attempt to define *meaning*. Meaning has been of interest to theorists who have investigated how people initiate and respond to certain ideas and discard others. This research has been especially important during times of war, when messages may motivate people to fight for a cause, or perhaps even to surrender.

Propaganda Studies

When U.S. military planes prepared for deployment over Afghanistan in late 2001, their payloads consisted of more than explosives and missiles. Stacks of leaflets were placed on board the planes, to be air-dropped to the citizens of Afghanistan. The leaflets stressed that the invasion was aimed not at harming citizens, but at ridding their country of "Arab-Afghans" who were guilty of exporting global terrorism. It was not the first time mass distribution of propaganda had been used as a means of persuasion. The early impetus for investigating communication activities came from the national interest during wartime, when Americans needed to know how to win both on the battlefield and in the hearts and minds of people.

A student at the University of Chicago became curious about how propaganda was used to help win World War I. Harold Lasswell studied the leaflets dropped from planes flying behind German lines to see how they encouraged enemy soldiers to surrender. He undoubtedly considered this form of persuasion to be effective, but later scholars attributed to him the **"magic-bullet"** or "hypodermic-needle" theory. This suggests that a stimulus message is followed by a direct response. Just as a bullet pierces barriers or a needle injects something under the skin, a message works powerfully in convincing an audience to accept its "truth." The trouble was that it failed to account for the fact that most people simply do not accept messages without challenging them first.

So did Lasswell truly believe in the bullet theory for which he was credited? Communication scholar Wilbur Schramm doubted whether Lasswell or any other professor ever had put much stock in it: "I have never known a serious scholar to endorse or make research use of the so-called bullet theory of communication effects." It may have been part of the popular wisdom of the era, but Schramm added dryly, "If any scholar did make serious use of this concept, it signaled the childish side of the act of passage."[3]

Lasswell's propaganda work was published as a book in 1927,[4] drawing details from interviews with European leaders in World War I and using a form of content analysis. In it, the researcher defined four goals for propaganda: galvanizing hatred against the enemy, strengthening ties to allies, recruiting the co-operation of neutral parties, and demoralizing the enemy. He did believe **propaganda** was effective as "management of collective attitudes by the manipulation of significant symbols." Lasswell viewed it, though, in neutral terms—simply as a strategy to shape people's personal convictions through mass messages and socially derived information. Not everyone agreed with his position.

Public relations pioneer Edward L. Bernays referred to propaganda as a means for manipulating and maintaining control of the masses. After the Nazis repeatedly broadcast the "Big Lie" (that the Jews were to blame for Germany losing World War I, and that pure Germans were a master race) through the late 1930s and early 1940s, propaganda took on even darker connotations. One book reviewer, Foster R. Dulles, labeled Lasswell's book a "Machiavellian textbook which should promptly be destroyed!"[5] Regardless of how it was perceived, however, propaganda and its wartime deployment inspired much early study in mass communication.

Lasswell posed another key question for mass communication theorists. It contained just five elements: "*Who* says *what* to *whom* through what *channel* with what *effects*?"[6]

Persuasion Studies

Just as Lasswell opened the door to the study of World War I propaganda through his use of content analysis, Carl Hovland, a Yale social psychologist, charted the impact of World War II propaganda through his experiments. The emphasis shifted from social processes of propaganda to the psychological processes of persuasion. Hovland and his fellow psychologists manipulated messages to see how they might reinforce or change an *attitude, belief,* or *behavior* that had affective (emotional) and cognitive (thought) components. He believed each could be altered through learning.

Propaganda Spreading viewpoints or doctrines by government authority through the use of media.

Nazi Propaganda. Wartime propaganda has produced landmark studies in media research. Communication scholars and social psychologists have used experiments and content analyses to measure the effects of propaganda on the audience.

Selective exposure/attention/perception/retention Tendency to organize and interpret messages to establish a coherent perspective consistent with preexisting beliefs and values.

Cognitive dissonance Research theory predicting human reaction to information that is contrary to felt attitudes and convictions.

Credibility Measure of trust an audience invests in a source, based on perceptions of character quality, including honesty, expertise, and sincerity.

SELECTIVE BARRIERS

Persuasion theorists have explored the nature of *cognition*, which is how personal knowledge can influence communication effects. They have tried to determine how the behaviors leading to knowledge—**selective exposure/attention/perception/retention**—influence the impact of messages. Selective exposure is the tendency for people to expose themselves to messages in agreement with their personal beliefs and to avoid disagreeable ones that cause dissonance. Selective attention/perception suggests a personal attraction to messages that reinforce strong convictions and, conversely, a repulsion from contrary messages. Selective retention refers to how the memory functions in this process—calling to mind supporting facts while avoiding unpleasant ones from experience and learning.

Scholars have organized these mental defenses into four barricades. Selective exposure serves as the outer barrier. Selective attention is next, then perception, and finally selective retention is the most intimate barrier. They all work to maintain cognitive consistency by filtering out messages that create what social scientists have called **cognitive dissonance.** That's when people try to maintain cognitive balance by avoiding or reordering real-world information that contradicts their beliefs or behavior.

WHY WE FIGHT RESEARCH

The U.S. War Department, needing advice about how best to train soldiers for the mental rigors of combat, hired Carl Hovland as its chief psychologist and director of experimental studies in 1942. Hovland studied the influence of Army training films on U.S. soldiers who were preparing to go to war. He experimented with the *Why We Fight* series created by Hollywood director Frank Capra. The Army wanted to know if these films increased soldiers' awareness of events leading up to the war. How long would this learning last, and would the films motivate soldiers to fight?

Hovland discovered that the 50-minute documentaries did heighten soldiers' awareness of events leading up to the war. However, the films failed to motivate men to fight or even to hate the enemy. Mere exposure to a documentary on the evils of Nazi Germany produced only the first step in a persuasion process. Starting at awareness, the soldiers went on a cognitive journey that ended with a shift in attitude and behavior. This became known as the *hierarchy of effects*. Because persuasion is a process that occurs in phases, each step must be completed separately and successfully before the next one can occur. In the initial phase of knowledge acquisition, a viewer's *attention, comprehension, acceptance,* and *retention* must be obtained, each in its turn. To complete his theory of persuasion, Hovland added other key components, including the *sender's characteristics* (credibility), the *qualities of the message* (persuasive appeals), and the receiver's *cognition.*

Credibility Research

The ancient Greek rhetorician Aristotle spoke of **credibility** as the speaker's *ethos.* He noted that rhetorical appeals to emotion (*pathos*) and to reason (*logos*) contributed to a speaker's success. Audiences believe credible speakers, but tend to discount those who lack knowledge, goodwill, or status. Such judgments are based on perceptions of the source, which, to be credible, must be viewed as believable, knowledgeable, and sincere.

Early research in persuasion theory revealed a **sleeper effect,** in which arguments actually produce a stronger impact after the source is forgotten and credibility is no longer relevant. The audience begins to trust Hovland's information a few weeks later—after forgetting where it came from.

Research in credibility on the Internet found a division between audience members and media workers with regard to on-line news. The Online News Association discovered from its survey that journalists were wary of the practices and standards of reporting on the Web, whereas the readers logging on considered it just as credible as news from other sources.[7]

> **Sleeper effect** Delayed impact persuasive messages have on attitude formation, based on time needed for arguments to be "awakened" in the subconscious after source is forgotten.

> **Principle #2**
> The basis of credibility is formed by audience perceptions of expertise, honesty, and sincerity.

> **Recall tests** Means of gathering data by asking members to remember information disseminated by a media source, usually within a brief period afterward.

> **Random sample** Group of people or items selected for study in which every member of this portion of the larger group has an equal and independent chance of selection.

MESSAGE APPEALS

Hovland experimented with other persuasive appeals, such as varying levels of fear. His aim was to find out which would be most effective—*low, moderate,* or *high* doses. The quiet scholar from Yale conducted experiments that yielded surprising results. He measured human response to dental hygiene messages, and discovered that *high*-fear appeals were actually less effective than *minimal*-fear messages. Subjects told to brush daily after seeing graphic examples of badly rotted teeth were less likely to comply than were subjects urged to brush after viewing x-rays and drawings of cavities.[8]

Later research in this area by Hovland and his associates favored a *moderate* rather than *minimal* approach to fear appeals. Subsequent studies formed the basis of what is called *protection motivation theory.* It suggests audience attitudes shift in response to the magnitude of the threat, its likelihood of occurring, and the appropriateness of the prescribed defense. This research has proved useful to politicians mounting media campaigns and to health professionals warning the public of outbreaks of disease.

RECALL TESTS

Researchers believe that memory holds the key to attitude change, and have used a variety of methods to test memory's impact on media consumption. Surveys have identified which types of messages are easier to recall. **Recall tests** ask audience members which commercial appeals come to mind. **Random samples** are drawn to give potential respondents an equal chance of selection.

Archibald M. Crossley and his Cooperative Analysis of Broadcasting (CAB) conducted the first radio surveys. As noted in the previous chapter, Crossley's interviewers typically asked a family whether its radio was tuned to a sponsored show on NBC or CBS. That was because the Association of National Advertisers was paying for the research. The advertisers needed information to figure where to buy commercial time. Consequently, the questions veered away from noncommercial (sustaining) programs.

Two-step flow Model of opinion flow devised by Lazarsfeld, based on presidential election studies of 1940 and 1948 supposing that media information flows from opinion leaders to individuals.

Empiricism Foundation of science based on seventeenth-century philosophy that our knowledge of the world could be accurately measured by our sensory experience.

Two-Step Flow

Research is about probabilities. One unlikely probability is that an Austrian socialist and mathematician would become the founder of applied research at CBS. Paul Lazarsfeld of the University of Vienna fled the Nazis prior to World War II, and established research centers in the United States at Princeton and Columbia Universities. CBS hired him to conduct radio audience research with an Ohio State University professor, Dr. Frank Stanton, but he also conducted social science research.

One of Lazarsfeld's contributions to mass media research grew out of a series of voter studies in the 1940s. He wanted to find out how much impact news coverage of presidential campaigns had in making up the minds of voters. Were radio and newspapers as influential as people seemed to think?

A panel study of the 1940 presidential race in Erie County, Ohio, between Franklin D. Roosevelt and Wendell Willkie, provided the data for Lazarsfeld's conclusions in *The People's Choice*. The book showed how powerful people were in filtering the media's impact on voting decisions. Lazarsfeld and his team noticed a tendency for some citizens to base their ballot choices not on what they learned directly from radio and newspapers but on secondhand interpretations by friends and family. The Lazarsfeld team called this a **two-step flow** from the media to "opinion leaders" and then to primary social groups.

As with any discovery challenging the existing order, this provoked a fair amount of criticism. Critics charged that Lazarsfeld failed to properly measure the direct flow of news and that he overemphasized the role of so-called opinion leaders in the process. Lazarsfeld bolstered his argument for a *limited-effects* perspective in mass communication research based on data collected in Decatur, Illinois, during the 1948 race between Harry S Truman and Thomas E. Dewey. *Voting: A Study of Opinion Formation in a Presidential Campaign* also concluded that opinion leaders were interpreting news for primary social groups—friends and family.

Principle #3

The two-step flow theory says that opinion leaders interpret news for others, thereby limiting the media's direct impact.

CRITICAL STUDIES

Early critical theorists shaped contemporary studies about the prevalence of racial and gender stereotyping in the media and about the western media's influence over other societies and cultures. Critical perspectives have led the way in European scholarship of media and have grown more popular in recent times. Postmodern criticism has created a new approach for this research.

Frankfurt School

Lazarsfeld's faith in **empiricism**—gathering data from people in order to test theories and predictions—stood in stark contrast to the critical ideas that his European colleagues preferred. Marxist scholars Max Horkheimer, Theodor Adorno, and Herbert Marcuse were trained in philosophy and political economy in Austria and Germany. They formed the Institute for Social Research at the University of Frankfurt. Like Lazarsfeld, their religious and intellectual heritages forced them into exile when the Third Reich began to tighten its grip. They fled to New York City but continued to publish articles that challenged capitalist-based systems.

Lazarsfeld tried to persuade one of his comrades, Theodor Adorno, to join him in conducting statistics-based research, but failed. Instead, the Marxist scholar went to work on a popular-music project at CBS, and announced to anyone who cared to listen that he detested "jazz" and believed that reporting radio listeners' likes and dislikes was basically a waste of time. American audiences should be taught to appreciate serious music, Adorno said; treating art as a commodity was absurd.

Critical scholars from the Frankfurt tradition saw empirical research as a servant to the status quo. They challenged the empiricists' lack of concern over who owns the media, the nature of their goals, which ideas they promote and which ones they suppress—all evidence of submission to the capitalistic elite. What difference does it make what radio programs people choose to listen to if there is no choice about who produces them? Lazarsfeld responded to the attacks written by Horkheimer in *Traditions of Critical Theory* with his own case in favor of "administrative communication research." He believed that both traditions, administrative and critical, should be nurtured in U.S. colleges and universities.

Postmodern Critique

Postmodernism is part of the critical movement that crosses disciplines of philosophy, education, communication, art, and architecture. In its broadest strokes, postmodernism conceives of western civilization in three phases.

■ First, there is the premodern era, which generally begins with early civilization and follows through to the Renaissance. That age brings an emphasis on authoritarian leaders, such as the church and royalty, who give meaning to civilization and its expressions in art and architecture. The premodern era generally lasts from antiquity through the Dark Ages until the dawning of the Renaissance and the Reformation in the fifteenth and sixteenth centuries.

■ The modern era begins when the thinkers of the Enlightenment begin to reject ecclesiastical and royal authority, preferring the individual's power of reason and creativity. This modern period lasts until the late nineteenth or twentieth century, depending on the scholar and discipline consulted. Mass communication scholar James Carey, for example, contends that the postmodern age begins with the fragmentation of the media audience through such developments as pay television over satellite, cable, and the Internet: "The integration of cable, satellite and computer not only permitted but also imagined new conceptions of time and space, beyond those rooted in the national system: a world of microseconds and global villages."[9]

■ The postmodern age moves beyond individualism to what some scholars describe as "neocollectivism," focusing on electronic means of interpersonal communication eventually creating a collage of virtual communities, which are fragmented, asymmetrical, and defined more by personal role than by place.

South Park. Postmodern conventions were played out on cable television through cartoon characters like Kenny, Stan, Kyle, and Cartman, with Elton John (behind). They appear in this 1998 episode of *South Park*.

The influence of this digital age on content in postmodern media has been wide ranging, influencing both style and substance. In the modern age, a story line was drawn to punish villains in the last part of a linear plot that progressed from beginning to middle to end. Postmodern stories escape this traditional form and narrative by blurring the lines between good and evil in a nonlinear fashion.

Cable cartoon show *South Park* stood as one example of postmodernism, with animated characters—jerking and jumping like cardboard cutouts—that were actually products of sophisticated computer animation. The cartoon attacked the modernist **paradigm** lampooning notions of childhood innocence, sexual mores, family and religion. *South Park* ridiculed Mr. Garrison, a pedantic teacher in the modernist mode, who manipulated puppets as part of his regime. Even religious notions of Jesus were parodied; he was portrayed as a talk-show host on public access cable. If there is a goal in postmodernism, it is to rebel against the cultural moorings of the modernist paradigm.

Critics of this style of "commodification of transgression" in media say it pushes the bounds of decency beyond tolerance. It requires an increase in the level of outrage with each episode in order to be effective. Postmodern transgressions lose their impact once they become predictable. *Beavis and Butthead*, for example, another cartoon contrivance on TV, grew tiresome after its "gross-out" humor became predictable. The success of such programming requires the audience to be clued in to the conventions that give the cultural violations their significance. Postmodern content does not always "travel well," since foreign audiences play by different cultural rules than the ones that are mocked by western media.

Cultural Imperialism

JAG. Some American television programs are more successful overseas than others. JAG, for example, found a niche with international audiences who responded favorably to the military setting and the use of courtroom drama.

The globalization of media has fostered a new critical perspective that tends to divide the world into exporting and importing countries. **Cultural imperialism** suggests that western values have dominated the world's cultures through exported radio and TV programs. Underdeveloped countries have trouble competing with the sophistication of western media, so the issue boils down to which country has the newest technology and the highest-quality production. This argument is countered, however, by evidence that even third-world countries prefer programs produced by their citizens in native languages. The United States, for example, successfully exports programs such as *JAG* and *ER*, but they are less popular than indigenous shows.

A professor of sociology, Stuart Hall, has written extensively about intercultural media with an emphasis on the "haves and have-nots." Hall finds that audiences don't simply accept a TV or radio program at face value without evaluating some or all of its subtext. That is, they choose to embrace or dismiss a writer's message based on filters from their cultural heritage, including family values and personal beliefs.

TECHNOLOGICAL DETERMINISM

In terms of theory building, the digital age has drawn inspiration from *media determinism*. This is a theory developed by a Canadian scholar of English, Marshall McLuhan, whose ideas about the medium being the message shook up the communication research world of the 1960s. Through McLuhan's eyes, the message is relevant only as "the juicy piece of meat carried by the burglar to distract the watchdog of the mind."[10] It is the communication activity itself that forms a lasting impression on our attitudes and behaviors. So how does the Internet factor into this vision of a world transformed by television into a *global village?* Would McLuhan speak now of the "global village" as a product of the Internet, or should we envision many global villages—virtual communities, to be sure—where old distinctions based on common interests, culture, and citizenship are preserved? The short answer is yes to both questions.

Television Determinism

In order to accept McLuhan's point about the "juicy meat" of content drawing us away from the media activity itself, we need to understand how his "sense ratios" or "patterns of perception" influence our media habits. In this perspective, the age of movable type enhanced the singular sense of vision beyond hearing, taste, touch, and smell. As a result, our thinking conformed to this sensual reemphasis on sight and the relative deprivation of other senses. Literacy moved society in logical and linear directions. In political terms, it gave rise to nations over tribes, according to McLuhan.

Television turned Gutenberg on his head by engaging aural and tactile senses and reordering our *sense ratios.* This is the term McLuhan used to describe the varying degree of reliance people have on their five senses (sight, hearing, taste, touch, and smell) due to their communication experience. McLuhan saw the shared TV experience of electronic imagery as the opposite of the typographic experience. It had a retribalizing influence on humanity, constructing a *global village* as society began to conform to the nonlinear world of TV viewing.

The reason digital convergence has been so important may be related to the quest for *control, convenience,* and *speed* in our daily communication. Interactive media give us more power over environment, enabling us to browse websites or change channels in an instant. We can quickly exchange roles as senders and receivers of information by voting in a web poll prompted by a sports question on television. Digital media are flexible and convenient, allowing access at what McLuhan called "electric speed."

Internet Determinism

The Internet is more than a new language for the third millenium, inviting millions of global tongues into chatrooms and e-mail discourse each year. It poses a challenge to scholars because it merges forms of both interpersonal and mass media. The Internet is used for one-to-one or one-to-many communications.

Paradigm Way of conceiving reality based on expectations fostered by cultural norms, social institutions, and personal beliefs.

Cultural imperialism Term applied mainly to U.S. domination of global media production, resulting in (real or threatened) spread of consumerism and other American values and practices to vulnerable societies elsewhere.

Gatekeeper Individual who has the power to control message flow from source(s) to receiver(s) through the media.

Web writers project their ideas by merging words with pictures through audio and video channels. How should we approach this new medium, given both its traditional qualities of print and its additional facets of interactivity with layers of visual and audio messages?

Interactivity defines the Internet to the degree that users easily change roles and control the conversation from their computers. Clicking on hyperlinks invites viewers to pursue their curiosity boundlessly by selecting highlighted terms and phrases and by visiting virtual pages of new information. This style of web reading embraces intuition over logic. However, whether the web viewer reads or scans content is based as much on the individual's personality as it is on the nature of the medium. There is one concept that has tried to broadly define the web experience.

Mediamorphosis is a term coined by Roger Fidler, who, like McLuhan, emphasized media activity over message analysis. The Internet, said Fidler, evolved from older forms of media, replicating some of their dominant features while introducing new ones.[11] Research on the Internet has shown how it appeals to playfulness, reciprocal communication, and mastery over the environment—in other words, speed, convenience, and control. The Internet represents just the latest challenge, testing a number of earlier theories concerning how and why we communicate through electronic media.

JOURNALISM THEORIES

For years, media scholars have tracked reporters and editors to see how they shape politics and society. What professional norms and practices do they follow, and why? They have tried to find out why certain stories seem so important while others are barely mentioned. They have wondered what impact news media have on politics and the outcome of elections.

A research perspective summoning the ancient idea of a walled city where a **gatekeeper** stands watch, choosing which visitors should gain entry, has produced numerous studies of media. Acting as gatekeepers, news editors, producers, and writers allow certain stories to flow through gates, creating the agenda of entertainment and information. Is this agenda shaped, then, by *personal choice, professional training,* or *organizational routines?* Additional questions probed how journalists *frame* their reports. Framing deals with editorial decisions about how a problem or issue is to be defined by its news coverage.

Gatekeeping Research

The idea of gatekeeping in journalism first appeared in the work of Lewin's research assistant, David Manning White, at the University of Iowa. In 1950, White interviewed a wire editor for a small-town daily newspaper to uncover the thinking behind story selection. White called his editor "Mr. Gates," borrowing the *gatekeeping* metaphor of his mentor, as he took note of the journalist's compliance with accepted news routines, jotting down his comments about each story's merits.

Kurt Lewin and Group Influences

Archives of the History of American Psychology— The University of Akron

One beloved scholar who established key concepts for mass communication research was a stereotypical European professor, from his thick accent to his coffeehouse seminars. Kurt Lewin was born in 1890 to Jewish farmers in Mogilno, East Prussia, in what is today Poland. The deepening chill of anti-Semitism did not discourage him from earning a Ph.D. in psychology at the University of Berlin in 1914.

In the tradition of German professors, Lewin met informally with his students to discuss their ideas. At one Sunday-morning session in a Berlin cafe,[12] he noticed that the waiter had an uncanny ability for recalling everyone's order and collecting the check without writing down any of the information. Lewin saw this as an opportunity to test his "field theory," based on the idea that personal intention to carry out a task creates a psychological field that is unbalanced until the task is completed. After the waiter collected everyone's bill for the coffee and pastry, the professor asked him to recall what each student had ordered, but the indignant waiter could not do it. The field of mutually dependent facts had evaporated. Lewin maintained it was because the waiter's task had been completed and the equilibrium of his field restored.

Prior to World War II, Lewin was so eager to leave Germany that he accepted a two-year appointment in home economics at Cornell University in New York. That meant an unmistakable drop in status for a rising star among European scholars. Lewin later moved to the University of Iowa to conduct psychological experiments with the Child Welfare Research Station. There, he coined two key terms, *gatekeeper* and *channel,* to describe the selection and preparation of food menus for the family. His students adapted the concepts to the study of mass communication. Lewin is best remembered, though, for his observation, "There is nothing so practical as a good theory."

After White's landmark study, gatekeeping evolved as a vital area of research. Scholars have shown how the mix of news items carried on national wires tends to be replicated in daily newspapers. If the Associated Press devoted about half the day's news to politics, the local newspaper's portion would be about the same. In television, gatekeeping studies have considered the visual, dramatic, and other news by which producers choose stories for their lineups. So, where do their criteria come from?

Scholars have identified a hierarchy of gatekeeping influences starting at the microlevel and working up to the macrolevel: *Individual, social, organizational, institutional,* and *ideological* forces all play a part. The news routines of the organization tend to influence story decisions more than do the personal traits of the gatekeeper, including personal ideology. So how does this *gatekeeping* activity influence the audience?

Powerful effects Perspective of media effects suggesting media have strong influence over individuals.

Agenda-Setting Studies

The idea of agenda setting arrived at a time when scholars were questioning the **powerful effects** notion of media. The notion came from one of Paul Lazarsfeld's colleagues, Joseph Klapper, who suggested that personal differences and intervening circumstances moderate media influences.[13] Klapper believed that

American Columnist and Author Walter Lippmann.

reading newspapers or listening to the radio does not produce any singular effects, but acts in concert with other "mediating factors and influences."[14]

Agenda-setting studies emerged as new evidence that the media are powerful; issues are either brought to prominence by news attention, relegated to lesser importance, or discounted as irrelevant. Two quotes appear as trademarks in this early line of research.[15] Walter Lippmann's title to the first chapter in his book *Public Opinion*, "The World Outside and the Pictures in Our Heads," resonated with scholars. Lippmann believed that those "pictures in our heads" are created by journalists who assemble facts to entertain as much as to inform.

The second quote comes from a University of Wisconsin political scientist who felt that the press "may not be successful much of the time in telling people what to think, but it is stunningly successful in telling its readers what to think about." Bernard C. Cohen's qualifying remark is frequently overlooked: "And it follows from this that the world looks different to different people, depending not only on their personal interests, but also on the map that is drawn for them by the writers, editors, and publishers of the papers they read."[16]

LIMITED VERSUS POWERFUL EFFECTS

Cohen's reference to individual differences and mitigating circumstances seems to support Klapper's conclusion about limited effects. The primary challenge to Klapper's thesis came from Professors Maxwell McCombs and Donald Shaw, who held that the priorities behind the news media's agenda are detected and adopted by the audience. McCombs and Shaw drew a yardstick on issue salience by comparing media and audience priorities in the news. Their survey in Chapel Hill, North Carolina, produced path-breaking results.

> **Principle #4**
>
> Agenda setting is how news media influence the public's attention to particular issues.

The two researchers counted 15 issues ranking high in news coverage of the 1968 presidential race between Vice President Richard M. Nixon and Senator Hubert Humphrey. They ranked the items on a scale of important to not-so-important. The rank order was calculated according to each story's share of time or space and its prominence in placement—whether it was in the front or back of the newspaper or newscast. Researchers then interviewed undecided voters to determine their opinions about what was important. The result was a good match between news media and audience priorities, lending support to the agenda-setting hypothesis and the case for powerful-media effects.

AGENDA-SETTING EVOLUTION

The agenda-setting model helped reveal much about *salience* and its relationship to audience priorities. However, it also raised another issue: Do some important stories languish in obscurity until dramatic events make them "marketable" and significant to the news agenda? It took a dramatic event of catastrophic proportions to move a Washington scandal off the front pages and out of the lead position in TV news in 2001. Only after September 11 did terrorism replace a congressional intern's disappearance at the top of the news media's agenda. The second level of agenda-setting research analyzes such issues to determine how they contribute to the stories' ranking.

INFORMATION NEED

Agenda-setting research has taken another direction in assessing how an individual's need for orientation within society influences his or her reliance on news in the first place. A person's motivation for seeking information—based on personal relevance and need for knowledge—may intensify the agenda-setting effect. One reason presidential elections generate so much scholarship is that researchers know that many voters lack personal knowledge of the candidates and have a need for orientation about them. The agenda-setting phenomenon then becomes more visible.

Framing Analysis

A good deal of study has been devoted to the question of bias in the news, such as the liberal-versus-conservative slanting of stories. The research evidence suggests that bias is actually in the eyes of the beholder more than in the views of the news media. Whether the viewer is watching Fox News or CBS, bias is actually a reflection of personal agreement or disagreement. Scholars have proceeded in a different direction by probing how issues may be changed in the audience's mind by their **framing**.

Todd Gitlin, a Berkeley political scientist, said framing shows "persistent patterns of cognition, interpretation, and presentation, of selection, emphasis and exclusion, by which symbol-handlers routinely organize discourse."[17] Sociologist Erving Goffman defined *frames* as a **schema** of interpretation for the audience to "locate, perceive, identify and label" issues they have heard, read, or watched.[18] Gitlin focused on the "symbol-handlers," whereas Goffman stressed the *audience's* frames for interpreting news.

The greatest power of framing is not in defining problems but in suggesting who or what is to blame for them. That inevitably leads to questions about what must be done to remedy a situation and who must be held accountable. It is possible that framing can even influence public policy. For example, a U.S. Surgeon General's report framed the debate over lung cancer by linking it to cigarette smoking. Congress acted in 1971 to ban cigarette commercials from television.

FUNCTIONS AND DYSFUNCTIONS

So far, this chapter has explored what the media try to do and what happens after they do it, but what about the audience's intentions? In **uses and gratifications** research, scholars emphasize the idea of an *active* audience. The underlying premise is that the media do *not* have ultimate control in the flow of information and entertainment. Harold Lasswell is the intellectual founder of this perspective, since it's anchored in his functionalist paradigm.

What are the principal functions of media use? To inform the audience is defined as *surveillance of the environment*, to formulate opinion is described as *correlation of events*, and *transmission of the social heritage* is how media trans-

Framing Organizing structure of news defining parameters of an issue, including causes and effects of a problem and the people responsible.

Schema Attitudinal basis for explaining how an individual approaches a communication experience.

Uses and gratifications Perspective based on an active audience seeking to satisfy personal needs through media rewards; involves the idea of functions and dysfunctions of media use.

late cultural values. Charles Wright, a sociologist and follower of Lasswell's, added the function of *entertainment*, and also indicated that there were *dysfunctions* arising from media use.

Uses and Gratifications

Research into uses of the media was actually an outgrowth of the debate over limited versus powerful effects. Professor Bernard Berelson, a member of Paul Lazarsfeld's Bureau of Applied Social Research, wrote in 1959 that the well of thought in media research had gone dry. Elihu Katz, another Lazarsfeld colleague, disagreed and countered that only persuasion theory was spent; the functionalist paradigm was flowing with new ideas. To support his point, Katz pointed to one of Berelson's own studies. This research had revealed how readers cope with a newspaper strike and respond to missing their daily newspaper.[19] Katz reinforced his argument by referencing other active-audience findings, such as the importance of adventure heroes to children at play.

> **Principle #5**
>
> Personal needs motivate media exposure and limit media effects.

Would the emergence of *uses and gratifications* then be classified as a new theory of communication? Katz did not think so. He called it a *perspective* for discovering the social and psychological *needs* that generate *media exposure* and result in *gratifications* or other *consequences*.

GRATIFICATIONS OBTAINED

Studies in *uses and gratifications* have produced some interesting results. One study asked how a person's mood might affect his or her choice of TV programs. It found that "stressed subjects watched nearly six times as much relaxing television as did bored subjects [while] bored subjects watched nearly twice as much exciting fare as did stressed subjects."[20] British scholars wondered why voters tuned in to political broadcasts on the eve of a general election. Most of the viewers simply wanted to know more about the candidates and their platforms, but one-third wished to identify with a political party.[21]

Uses researchers typically rely on self-reports prompted by asking audiences to reveal personal motives and rewards for choosing what they watch, read, and browse. The difficulty that communication scholars have encountered is not only getting audience members to identify personal motives but also determining how successful they are in obtaining gratifications.

UNINTENDED CONSEQUENCES

One theme of *uses* research is that people choose to scratch a real or imagined "media *itch*" in ways that can produce unintended consequences. One dysfunction is called *media dependency*, which is a study of how much people get hooked on favorite media fare: talk shows, soap operas, violence, and even pornography. A higher level of exposure, preoccupation, and disregard for harmful effects are the traits of media dependency.

One feature of this theory is called *parasocial interaction*. This phenomenon was introduced in a 1956 edition of the journal *Psychiatry*. That study found audience members developing imagined relationships with real and fictional characters on television. TV viewers fancied strong ties with glamorous personas. They imagined understanding the characters and their motives better than the viewers' own real-life relationships.[22] A motion picture, *Nurse Betty*, played on an extreme case of parasocial interaction involving a soap-opera devotee. A lovestruck waitress fantasized about becoming a nurse for a handsome doctor in a soap opera, and drove to Hollywood to fulfill her fantasy. Media dependency shares some theoretical territory with ideas about the *cultivating* effects of heavy television viewing. (This term describes how media can "cultivate" a view of reality that the audience will accept as accurate if that is its dominant source of information.)

Media Violence

Violence is familiar to both fiction and nonfiction forms of entertainment. Scholars have defined *television violence* as scenes of "intentional physical harm, compelling force against one's will, or the infliction of pain." In metropolitan areas across the nation, anchors on television narrate video of murders and mayhem. Reality crime shows such as *Cops* and *America's Most Wanted* play back videotaped scenes of aggressive acts, punctuated by pleas from law enforcement officers to help bring fugitives to justice. It is easy to understand how violence has become an attractive scenario for screenwriters spinning spectacular narratives. TV producers claim that the pervasiveness of violence on the screen is due to its popularity. "We-just-give-'em-what-they-want" rationalizations defending the use of violence to meet audience expectations do not always square with ratings success. The economic argument is easier to accept, since violence in television costs less to produce.

Researchers have pursued questions about media violence since the 1920s, when the Payne Study and Experimental Fund sponsored a study on the impact violent movies had on children. Media violence has come to be associated with a number of contradictory theories predicting that it can relieve tension, stimulate acts of aggression, desensitize viewers, or engender an exaggerated fear of reality.

Renee Zellweger as "Nurse Betty." Parasocial interaction studies describe how people invest personal emotions in imagined relationships with media characters. Nurse Betty dramatized this concept, showing a waitress who no longer distinguished her media-inspired fantasy from reality.

Cultivation Theory suggesting heavy television viewing tends to distort people's perceptions of reality.

CULTIVATION OR CATHARSIS

The effects of media violence are *emotional*, *behavioral*, and *cognitive*, theorists have concluded. The most familiar cognitive theory dealing with media violence is the *mean-and-scary-world hypothesis* advanced by **cultivation** research. It suggests that heavy exposure to television violence cultivates an exaggerated perception of danger in the real world.

The primary emotional theory is based on the *catharsis* perspective, which holds that therapeutic effects may be derived from watching actors engage in violent and hostile activities on screen—that it somehow purges the audience of hostility toward others. This theory has little support in experiments. Similarly, the *excitation transfer theory* proposes that media excitement may be imparted by neural transmission. The responses need not be hostile or violent but can be warm and friendly, depending on the motivation of the viewer.

IMITATIVE EFFECTS

In the 1960s, social psychologists conducted experiments by watching children after they had viewed violence on television. They saw children beat up a large bobo doll that rocks back and forth after being punched. *Imitative* effects or modeling theory was used to explain the children's aggression. *Modeling theory* is based on four prerequisites: First, the viewer remembers the violence (*retention*). Then, if given an *opportunity*, and with sufficient cause, the viewer becomes *motivated*. Finally, he or she will *act out* based on his or her imitation of TV violence.

DISINHIBITION OR DESENSITIZATION

Another theory is defined as *disinhibition*, which predicts that people will feel freer to express aggression after viewing harmful acts on television. It suggests that audiences relax their control by rationalizing their tendencies toward aggression using media portrayals as justification.

Desensitization supposes that a lack of empathy or concern results from viewing violence. The viewer can become so callous to acts of brutality on TV that she or he shrugs and turns away when confronted with a brutal act in reality.

SOCIAL PSYCHOLOGICAL APPROACHES

Communication has been described as the fundamental social process. Because interpersonal processes affect media processes (as the two-step flow established), social psychologists interested in media look at how people behave in particular groups. Theorists have studied how some types of people suffer in silence on certain subjects if they have been convinced that their opinions will isolate them. These theorists have traced the spread or diffusion of new technologies to different social groups. Varying levels of knowledge have been analyzed according to age, education, income level, gender, and ethnicity.

Spiral of Silence

Viewers may experience *feelings* of aggression or fear through repeated exposure to violence, but there is a theory suggesting that television, radio, and newspapers also may inhibit verbal expressions. This theory is also based on fear—the fear of social isolation. Public opinion is reflected in the media's lens, but can these snapshots stifle *unpopular* views? Elisabeth Noelle-Neumann, a German professor from the University of Mainz, believed that was more than likely. She defined *public opinion* as a constraining force that allows people to express only acceptable feelings if they wish to avoid isolating themselves.

BASIC TENETS

Noelle-Neumann's *spiral of silence* had its origin in the conformist cults of pre–World War II Germany. She began as a publicist writing for *Das Reich*, a German magazine supporting Hitler's reign. The basic tenets of her theory are fairly easy to follow: Even though people harbor private opinions, they generally want to share them in public—that is, until their "quasi-statistical organ or sense" zips their lips by telling them they're about to let loose an unpopular idea. The desire to be accepted by the dominant group as well as the fear of being shunned are incentives to this self-censorship.

James Carville and Mary Matalin. The "spiral of silence" theory proposes that people refrain from speaking their minds to avoid social isolation when they perceive their views are unpopular. Couples like Carville and Matalin, however, publicly disagree apparently without alienating each other.

Ubiquity Key element in spiral of silence theory suggests media are available to everyone almost all of the time.

Consonance Presentation of a consistent image or message, usually concerning public issues or current events.

The media play an important role in self-regulation, according to Noelle-Neumann. Their omnipresence, or **ubiquity,** and their narrow range of opinion, or **consonance,** actually discourage free expression. Media consumers gather essentially the same type of information and opinions on the same subjects regardless of where they turn—newspapers, magazines, television, or the Web—or so the theory holds. The *cumulative effect* of this consonant exposure is to exercise self-censorship, according to the theory.

Noelle-Neumann agrees that some people are exceptions to the rule—able to withstand social pressure and go against the grain—people she describes as "hard cores." There is, in addition, the possibility that unpopular opinions may reemerge as acceptable, depending on revised treatment in the media. Cues given by characters, actors, and story lines about cultural values—including moral codes, social roles, and other customs—encourage viewers to adopt similar attitudes.

RESEARCH EVIDENCE

Testing the *spiral of silence* has not been easy, given the need to first identify ideas quashed by the media and then relate them to people's reports of being stifled. Historical evidence offers some clues, though. For example, during the 1930s, it was acceptable to defend U.S. proposals for socialism as a remedy to the ills of the Depression. During the 1950s, however, this defense became tantamount to treason. Did media play a role in stifling socialists from speaking out? Critics doubt it, and accuse this theory of exaggerating media's power over dissent. They also question the power of social sanctions over unpopular expressions. The upshot of this theory is that only expressed opinions can be translated into public policy. Otherwise, they are invisible, and, as far as the public agenda is concerned, nonexistent.

Diffusion of Innovations

For years, historians and anthropologists have charted the spread of new ideas through literary and cultural exchanges wrought by war and commerce. At the dawn of the twentieth century, French lawyer and sociologist Gabriel Tarde observed how his society was ordered by paths of personal influence linked to education and rank in society.

In the study of communication, diffusion theory follows the flow of ideas through media and social institutions. Its special emphasis is on the adoption of new ideas and technologies. In Iowa, agricultural scientists tested diffusion theory to find out how farmers chose to adopt hybrid seed corn.[23] The choice was attributed to both media and personal ties. Diffusion's initial premise is that audiences find news of innovation stimulating and, given their heightened need for orientation, will find out more before deciding whether to adopt something new.

As in persuasion theory, diffusion follows several steps: *awareness, attitude formation*, and *decision making*. Researchers gauge the length of time it takes for audience members to move through each one of those phases in the process, and investigate the rationale that they use. The decision to adopt is based on five factors: the innovation's relative *advantage*, its *compatibility* with existing conditions, its *simplicity*, its *accessibility* to experimentation, and the *benefits* it reveals to others.

ADOPTER CATEGORIES

Diffusion theorists divide people according to their rates of adoption. First, there are the *innovators*, adventurous and savvy people, who look for new ideas to try them out. They take seriously the invitation to be "the first ones on their block." Coming in a close second are the *early adopters*. They are adventurous but more cautious. The curve then thickens to form two groups: *early majority* and *late majority*. They will try an innovation only after it becomes clear that it has been tested and accepted. Finally come the *laggards*, who adopt an innovation only after tried-and-true methods become obsolete.

The diffusion of innovations in electronic media has seen transitions from film to videotape, typewriters to computers, pay phones to cell phones, broadcast to cable—and the list goes on. Interest in the theory grew from Everett Rogers's *Diffusion of Innovations*, published in 1962. Columbia University's Bureau of Applied Social Research gave its seal of approval to diffusion theory in 1966. That's when Pfizer Pharmaceuticals needed a study to find out how its advertising campaign for tetracycline, an antibiotic for skin disorders, was faring with physicians. The Columbia researchers agreed to do the study by applying diffusion theory. They established a link between doctors who adopted tetracycline and their level of social activism. Physicians who were involved in professional networking adopted the medicine sooner than socially isolated ones did.[24]

Diffusion theory suggests that the media's influence will be strongest during the awareness phase, after which social contacts become more relevant. An individual decides *not* to innovate if he or she concludes that the innovation's costs exceed its benefits, or that it poses unfavorable consequences.

MEDIA DIFFUSION

Diffusion research in media has shown the point at which a crucial level of saturation is achieved among audience members. Studies of e-mail and fax diffusion focused on the take-off point when a critical mass of knowledge was formed and created momentum for those two innovations to become self-sustaining.[25] In 1960, researchers began charting the diffusion of news stories. News of public affairs did not always reach a critical mass, but filtered through quickly to citizens in leadership positions and could bypass other strata of society. This made researchers wonder if education and income combined to create a "knowledge gap" between those in the know and those left outside the loop.

Knowledge-Gap Hypothesis

Communication is essential to acquiring the basic needs of shelter, clothing, food, and most human essentials. Social scientists find that information empowers people by giving them the means of satisfying those needs. Those with personal influence enjoy a safer and easier existence than those without. British Prime Minister Benjamin Disreali once observed, "As a general rule the most successful man in life is the man who has the best information."

Social divisions based on socioeconomic status (SES) have distinguished the line between the information-rich and information-poor. This is a way of describing people who have access to the facts they need for making good decisions versus those who do not. Studies have found that people are denied the blessings of prosperity simply because they do not know where to turn for help.[26] These blessings include day care, welfare assistance, medical aid, and other services. Why would anyone accept information poverty? A team of University of Minnesota researchers related such acceptance to levels of literacy and access to channels of communication. In 1970, the researchers published their study of the socioeconomic status of population groups, linking status deficits to knowledge deficits. The knowledge gap is especially evident in news of general interest, such as public affairs. The gap is less noticeable in areas of personal interest, such as hobbies or sports.

STATUS AND PARTICIPATION

The **knowledge-gap hypothesis** predicts that people of higher socioeconomic status will have more opportunity for education and greater access to sources of quality information. They also tend to associate with people of similar backgrounds who offer useful tips for solving problems. To further widen the knowledge gap, media tend to target upscale audiences for advertising based on buying power. Targeting neglects impoverished viewers, since they are regarded as "wasted circulation."

A representative democracy depends on an informed electorate to choose candidates and participate in civic affairs. Swedish scholars found there is not only a knowledge gap for lower SES citizens but an "influence gap" as well. In Sweden, well-educated citizens gain access to policymakers through social channels denied to those of lower social status.

DIGITAL DIVIDE

Knowledge-gap theory has been applied to the use of the Internet and has found that some of the same disparities have worked their way into the information age.

Knowledge-gap hypothesis Prediction that people with more education and higher incomes tend to acquire better and more information on public issues and other necessities than those of lower socioeconomic status.

Qualitative research Methods including interviews, study of documents, and observation; developed in social sciences to study social-cultural phenomena.

Quantitative research Methods including surveys, experiments, and numerical methods; developed in natural sciences to study natural phenomena.

Validity Quality-control check researchers use to determine their methods and means are correctly measuring the phenomenon intended for observation.

Reliability Quality criterion of research observation indicating the method used will consistently give over time at various intervals the same information.

Survey research Sampling opinions from part of a population by questionnaires, telephone calls, interviews, or electronic means.

Sample Portion of total population based on their representative or special qualities chosen to generalize about the larger group.

The differences are most apparent across income levels and ethnic lines, where nearly half of the white households have computers but less than a third of African Americans do. The exception is in households above the $40,000 income level, where African Americans were more likely to own a computer than whites at the same income level. Knowledge-gap research has been criticized for appealing to notions about racial and class divisions, and for failing to regard variables such as personal and professional interests.

RESEARCH METHODS

The scientific method of scholarship can unlock the mysteries of attitudes and behaviors by collecting evidence and processing it in a systematic manner. A variety of data-gathering techniques have gained acceptance and are broadly classified as **quantitative** and **qualitative research.** The obvious difference between them is that quantitative research draws on statistical tools, whereas qualitative scholarship collects facts and opinions from relevant sources before extrapolating to a greater principle. Both approaches are founded on problem-solving techniques and logical reasoning.

It's tempting to distinguish quantitative research as *inductive* rather than *deductive*, because it first gathers data in an open-ended quest to solve a problem or answer a question. Deductive reasoning, on the other hand, is often linked with qualitative research, since it can begin with a stated premise and then seek evidence to support it. Such distinctions are not entirely accurate; both types of reasoning play roles in quantitative and qualitative research. Qualitative research is often applied in historical or case studies.

Three principal methods are involved in quantitative research of electronic media: surveys, experiments, and content analysis. Whenever tables or charts are furnished and statistical analysis is made, the methodology must be explained and defended. Specifically, an accounting must be given for the research method's **validity** and **reliability.** In other words, did the research method—like a good set of scales—give the correct weight (validity), and will it be able to do so again and again over time (reliability)? Just how did the observers extract the specific data desired from their sample, and will other researchers come to the same conclusion if they use those methods?

Survey Research

In the quantitative approach, one of the most familiar methods is **survey research,** which draws data from a **sample** of respondents. A day rarely goes by when the news media do not present a poll claiming to show how the American people feel about a particular issue or event. For example, *Newsweek* highlighted coverage of President George W. Bush's State of the Union Address with polling data. The figures showed that 64 percent of the American people felt the president's speech was a warning that the United States was watching Iraq, Iran, and North Korea closely, whereas 10 percent said it was just tough talk.[27] Below this survey snapshot of American opinion, the magazine cited the source of its

ProTalk

Joan M. Barrett
*Vice President and Executive Director,
Broadcast Image Group*

*"It doesn't do anyone a service to pay for a research
project and then lock it away in the drawer."*

Joan Barrett knows from personal experience how important it is to be able to interpret the data that tell the story of the TV news audience. She has seen enough research as a news director in Phoenix and in other television newsrooms to know what's needed to diagnose the strengths and weaknesses of a station's news programming.

Barrett consults with news directors and station managers in her role as vice president and executive director of the Broadcast Image Group. She knows audience studies are not all created equal. The viewers who reach for their remote controls to change channels when TV news is on may have opinions to offer, but none carrying the same weight as those of regular viewers. An initial step in Barrett's research method is to identify regular news viewers and then further define that group by their viewing habits and preferences.

Students preparing for broadcasting careers are well advised to understand the differences among research methods using either qualitative or quantitative data or both. *Quantitative research* is the numerical breakdown of percentages reflecting audience opinions, media content, or ratings. *Qualitative data* are the words and descriptions used to paint the picture of the phenomenon of interest. Sometimes a random (quantitatively chosen) sample of viewers interviewed by a researcher (a qualitative process) can solve problems hidden beneath the ratings and demographics.

The research consultant's role involves quality control. For example, Barrett makes certain that Nielsen services are properly sampling the viewers for the stations with whom she consults. "You must check audience meters to be sure they are connected and running," she says, to gain a valid and representative picture of the audience.

Barrett believes in the importance of briefing all departments of a TV station on research findings so that all those involved can help ensure the station's success. "It doesn't do anyone a service to pay for a research project and then lock it away in the drawer," she says. The station's staff needs to know how decisions are made. It will have a much better chance of successfully implementing a strategy if it understands the research behind the strategy.

polling data, the firm, its methodology, sample size, and margin of error. Princeton Survey Research Associates interviewed 1,008 adults by telephone between January 31 and February 1, 2002. The degree to which the statistics varied from the population at large was plus or minus 3 percent.

Surveys permit comparisons based on the demographic elements discussed in Chapters 9 and 10, such as age, education, and income level. Surveys can be administered by telephone, mail, in person, or over the Internet, but researchers need to follow scientific safeguards before generalizing from the data. Obviously, interactive polls conducted via televised questions, such as those on the screen during the Super Bowl, do not draw a representative sample of an audience.

In selecting a sample to be surveyed, researchers work to assure that it reflects the makeup of the whole population of interest. They ask either open-ended or closed questions, allowing respondents to originate personal answers or give multiple-choice responses. In either case, percentages are compared to determine which answers are most favored, whether the question involves a candidate, an issue, or a course of action.

The main advantage of sample surveys is that it's possible to generalize to a larger group by interviewing representative members. This is helpful but poses a problem, given the tendency for certain types of people to be near their phones and available to answer questions while others are more elusive (occupied with children and careers). The remedy often is to give additional weight to data collected from hard-to-interview types. What surveys do not reveal are cause-and-effect relationships. Social scientists have designed another method to deal with the problem of causality—that is, causes and effects.

ProTalk

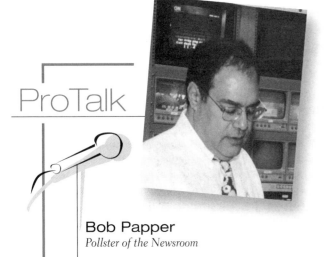

Bob Papper
Pollster of the Newsroom

"Researchers who fudge their findings hurt the credibility of survey research."

There is something about human nature that likes to see itself in the mirror—even at the professional level. Broadcasters need to know how they fare among their peers in terms of the issues confronting their business. When broadcast journalists want a bird's-eye view of the newsroom, they typically turn to surveys conducted for the Radio-Television News Directors Association (RTNDA) by Bob Papper of Ball State University.

Papper leads a research team that draws up annual questionnaires on such varied subjects as newsroom salaries, diversity profiles in the work force, and Web use. One statistical chart that is popular among news professionals is the annual salary scale for broadcast journalists. It often appears on a newsroom's bulletin board, posted either by management to show how well everyone is doing or by employees to show how far they're lagging behind their peers elsewhere.

Papper's review of gender and ethnicity in the newsroom has charted progress (and lack of it) around the country. Years ago, women were less likely to be hired as news directors of major-market TV stations than as bosses in smaller markets. Papper's survey showed that, more recently, women had an equal opportunity to supervise a newsroom regardless of its market size. That trend may be changing, though: Another university study showed women losing ground at the national networks, with female news correspondents slipping from 33 to 29 percent of the correspondent corps between 2000 and 2001.[28]

The RTNDA research on the Internet shows broadcast news directors struggling to turn a profit from station websites. Successful sites mostly have gained an edge by breaking the news first, before the stations' TV anchors have a chance to report it. Local news and weather rank high on the list of what Web users want, according to the research.

Like any researcher, Papper must be careful about what data he uses to make his projections, and says he will discard information if it is flawed. Data that are questionable in terms of validity or reliability will not get into his reports, he says. Researchers who "fudge" their findings, Papper adds, hurt the credibility of survey research.

Experimental Designs

Experimental design research originated in agriculture as a means for determining what factors—such as seeds, sun, rain, and fertilizer—would make crops grow. It became a valuable tool in social science for determining how media exposure may influence different people in a variety of ways.

In such experiments, **key variables** are defined as *independent* or *dependent*, which means they contribute either to the cause (independent) or to the effect (dependent). For example, studies in television violence expose audiences to the *independent variable* of knifings and shootings on the TV screen, to see how that exposure might produce a reaction in the *dependent variable* of attitudes or acts of aggression.

Experiments involve two or more groups, one of which serves as a *control* for reasons of comparison. The control group is *not* exposed to the independent variable, so that researchers may compare the group with those subjects who received the stimulus. The groups that are exposed to the independent variable are called *treatment groups*, and there are often multiple levels of the treatment condition.

Experiments can be conducted either in the field or the laboratory. The laboratory gives the researcher more control so that he or she can shield subjects from what are considered *confounding* or **intervening variables** that can interfere with the outcome. The field experiment, however, eliminates the artificiality of placing subjects in front of a TV monitor in a classroom with strangers. Instead, it allows the researcher to measure media effects in a natural environment.

Content Analysis

Just as a survey researcher or experimenter draws conclusions from a set of data that represents a larger group, content analysts infer findings from media materials—video- and audiotapes, scripts of commercials and so on—by organizing them into meaningful blocks of data. Each piece of tape or paragraph of copy is coded according to definitions described by the category choices. For example, a researcher might be interested in the way women are portrayed in commercials as wives, mothers, professionals, or combinations of those roles. The coder will classify by operational definition each portrayal per spot and count it. Rather than sending out questionnaires or exposing subjects to stimuli, the researcher draws inferences from samples of those ads or other programming.

Content analysis is a systematic technique for examining elements of a message to draw some inferences either about the message's nature or its source. Before counts are taken and comparisons are made through

Experimental design Controlled means for varying a condition or treatment on experimental subjects in order to determine the effects such exposure has on their status.

TV Violence. One of the most extensively researched questions in electronic media concerns how depictions of violence have affected both children and adults. Social psychologists believe intense viewing of media violence produces aggressive and imitative behavior among children, and cultivates distorted ideas about the threat of violence among adults.

Key variables Measurable influences responsible for stimulating or causing particular effects or consequences in a phenomenon.

Intervening variables Influences that serve to mitigate and interfere with what is believed to be a cause-effect relationship between variables.

Content analysis Research method for objectively and systematically studying elements of a message in order to draw inferences about the nature of the content and/or the source.

statistical analysis, researchers check the *reliability* of the coding method. For example, if one coder found a televised portrayal of a woman in a commercial to be as a professional, would a second coder share that opinion? The level to which they agree is called *intercoder reliability*, and it is the standard required for scientific content analysis.

Content analysis has become popular as a means for studying television and other electronic media content—whether the question concerns the prevalence of gender and ethnic stereotypes in TV shows or the political opinions of talk radio. So popular has content analysis become as a tool for researching media messages that an entire edition of the *Journal of Broadcasting and Electronic Media* in 1997 was devoted to articles using this research method. Scholars measured the extent to which ethnic diversity had become a part of network TV programming from 1966 though 1992. The findings: In terms of race, 88 percent of the characters were white; only 10 percent were black, and only 2 percent were Asian or Hispanic.[29] The journal also featured articles on TV news and the degree of emphasis given sensational content.

Historical and Qualitative Methods

Whenever a researcher employs qualitative techniques, the methodology is justified in much the same way as in quantitative research. That means the scholar must make a good-faith showing that the evidence addresses a larger question, and that the study's generalities are valid because they include a complete and representative set of data. It also means that the qualitative technique for reasoning from the evidence can be proved valid and reliable.

Qualitative studies include historical analysis, a kind of cultural research called *ethnography*, and case studies. Historical research is often a mix of words and numbers, but its primary mission is to extrapolate ideas by collecting enough incidents from the historical record to distinguish an emerging pattern. The historical scholar must consider alternative explanations, especially when trying to show cause-and-effect relationships. Historical research is most carefully judged by its overall literature review, and whether the scholar used comprehensive references in assembling primary and secondary sources to answer the research questions. The literature review is critical because it establishes the depth of information that has already been gathered relevant to the question at hand.

CASE STUDIES

Qualitative research may involve participant observations or case studies. Daniel Berkowitz at the University of Iowa, for example, decided to undertake a case study of gatekeeping by spending more than 200 hours in a local TV newsroom. He spent the time observing work and conducting interviews to discover how TV news producers decided which story ideas to pursue and which ones to discard. He discovered that the criteria of importance and visual impact, as well as the producer's personal instincts, were brought to bear on the story selection process. Berkowitz concluded that the driving purpose of TV news gatekeepers was to achieve a balanced mix of stories, similar to a healthful meal.[30]

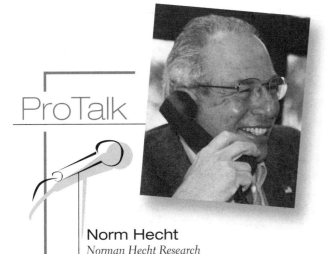

ProTalk

Norm Hecht
Norman Hecht Research

"Qualitative data can provide very actionable insight into promotion and programming strategies."

Television news is usually the primary budget item for local TV stations, so ratings success is critical to their profits and financial stability. That means that the news competition within each market is a key concern of station managers, and it's the reason they turn to consultants to find out how to beat their rivals for ratings.

Norman Hecht says his research team evaluates its methods to assess their effectiveness for client stations and to keep pace with the dynamic media landscape. When Hecht entered the field of news measurement about 10 years ago, TV stations and research firms used focus groups as one of their leading measures for gathering feedback. He has since shown clients newer methods that provide better data to guide their winning strategies.

The challenges facing focus-group research include drawing a representative picture of the audience. This is complicated by any failure to achieve random selection and by a group's vulnerability to dominant members. Hecht believes other methods produce more valid and useful results. He cites, for example, the "recruit-to-view" method, in which samples of about 10 to 15 viewers are recruited each night over a given period of time—usually one or two weeks. The subjects are screened for their viewing behavior, and then are asked to watch one of the client's newscasts on a specific evening. Fans of both competitive stations and the client station are recruited. That way, a variety of newscasts are included in the sample, and the findings are more representative of the larger scheme of things. Viewers participate in the privacy of their own homes—the environment in which they would normally watch TV. This kind of "qualitative data can provide very actionable insight into promotion and programming strategies," enabling the station to serve its audience and attract new viewers, says Hecht.

Most leading stations in the top 50 television markets hire research analysts to work in their sales departments. These researchers analyze and compile ratings data as well as developing sales materials based on Nielsen and other data sources. There are hundreds, if not thousands, of attractive jobs involving all sorts of media research, according to Hecht.

Summary

Communication research relies on sound theoretical explanations of media activities, including social effects and how media teach values, influence views, and shape personal behavior. The drive to build practical theories to explain the nature of communication involves academic, administrative, and critical scholars. They have helped to decode and focus the information age.

Whether conducted by independent firms or academic institutions, media research is fundamental to decision making by programmers, advertisers, producers, and writers. It may be used "after the fact" to justify personal decisions or, more appropriately, as a building tool for strategies in media planning. In any event, it is vital in shaping global channels for the future.

CAREER FOCUS

Job-seekers can find research positions in both the private and public sectors. There is work to be done—or for—advertising agencies, cable systems, cable networks and services, radio stations and networks, television stations and networks, station sales representative firms, and the syndicated data companies themselves, such as Arbitron and Nielsen. The positions involve both primary and secondary media research. Primary researchers harvest their own data from which to draw conclusions, whereas secondary analysis draws on statistics compiled by others, such as rating companies.

The top 50 markets usually have positions for **research directors** at local TV stations. These lucrative positions go to people who know how to compile statistics, write presentations (sometimes with the help of staff) and present their findings. In some cases, research directors "bid out" data collection to other companies, which conduct the field interviews.

Research directors need a thorough understanding of Nielsen data, as well as the statistics other firms supply. For example, they may have to interpret reports and surveys from such services as TVScan or Scarborough, which offer stations specialized data on their performance in sales, advertising, programming, web traffic, and the audience. Researchers usually have at least a master's degree in communication or a marketing degree with relevant professional experience. Research directors demonstrate their broader skills in management and budgeting by supervising staffs assigned to help them.

Researchers track a station's ratings success, make audience estimates for future program schedules, and prepare station position papers involving rating patterns for advertisers and for show producers, including newswriters and reporters. They provide data to help stations promote their news and community work. Researchers advise sales managers and account executives on ways to increase revenue. In addition, researchers adopt a teaching role by training station employees (and their own assistants) in research methods.

Researchers must be able to explain in print and personal presentations what a station or network audience is watching, and why. They must write effectively and present their findings in meaningful ways. They are also asked to monitor the competition and its sponsors; advise their employers on copyright and contract issues; formulate market strategies; and analyze the growth potential of the station, cable system, or network. Researchers for media polling firms are hired for survey design, methodology, and report writing.

In public broadcasting, consultants often enhance fund raising and membership drives as well as public relations and internal communications.

Writers/Researchers work on network or documentary projects, on topics as diverse as global business and nature/science series. Production studios and network news organizations use researchers on creative projects and programming scripts.

Academic Positions

Colleges hire researchers as instructors and professors at the assistant, associate, and full-professor ranks. Virtually all such faculty jobs require research, publication, and service to the college and community. Professors teach theory and research in the classroom and work in collaboration with other scholars. A school that advertises for a professor to teach media theory and research gives special attention to a candidate's record of publications and scholarship.

Assistant professors in broadcasting and electronic media usually have experience in various aspects of radio and television. They establish research track records by investigating the theories discussed in this chapter and by applying new theories to their fields of expertise. Professors at all ranks serve as reviewers and editors on publication boards where their knowledge of theory and research is essential to the task of screening journal articles. In addition to writing for journals and books in their fields, professors review scholarly papers for academic conferences.

From the early days of the bullet theory to recent research in framing, the nature of media study has been to address key questions. Theories of persuasion have asked what types of emotional and logical appeals motivate audiences. Theories of cognition have asked how people learn and apply information. Social theorists have asked how group norms and values influence media content and create two-step flows of information. Critical theories and approaches veer from the empirical tradition of data analysis, but they still address key questions: How is media power consolidated in wealthy conglomerates? How do media depict members of the minority community? What happens when western culture collides with foreign television?

The process and effects of research have produced theories on how media cultivate aggressive behavior and harmful perceptions of the world. Research has shown how news agendas and frames are established, and who controls the gates through which news and programming pass. Digital convergence has brought with it a need for new theories and methods to explain the principles of electronic media. In the future, scholars will have an opportunity to see how smaller segments of society engage in digital media. While more channels and choices vie for scattered and shrinking audiences, the traditional debate of limited-versus-powerful effects has given way to a moderate-effects perspective. It defines audiences in all types of communities, "de-massified" but still connected.

FOOD FOR THOUGHT

1. Propaganda studies focus on persuading people during times of war. If you were to conduct a study of U.S. propaganda in the Middle East, what research questions would you ask?

2. The two-step flow theory suggests that people get their news from other people's accounts of what they heard or saw in the news media. When was the last time you heard news from a friend or family member before checking it out for yourself? How did your friend or relative influence your attitude toward the news?

3. News reporters are sometimes charged with exaggerating, or "hyping," the facts of their stories. If that's the case, do you think it harms the credibility of the reporter, the news story, the station or network, or all of the above? Explain your answers.

4. Media researchers deal with problems involving stereotyping in the media. Do you consider the stereotyping of women and minorities to be a problem, and if so, what should be done about it?

5. Gatekeeping, agenda setting, and framing research have examined news media's decisions about what stories to cover, how much importance to attach to them, and how the stories define the issues. Can you think of a case where the news media gave too much attention to a story or framed the issue in such a way that did not seem fair to you? Explain.

6. The diffusion-of-innovation model suggests that social networks play a greater role in making an innovation viable than media do. Are there times when media would be more powerful than friends or family in persuading you to adopt an innovation? Explain.

7. The knowledge gap predicts that people with more education and higher socioeconomic status will learn more about political affairs than people at the lower end of the spectrum. Do you agree with that assumption? Why or why not?

12

Public Broadcasting

The noblest motive is the public good.

—Sir Richard Steele, English essayist, 1744

Broadcasting really is too important to be left to the broadcasters.

—Tony Benn, English politician, 1971

Sesame Street. No program compares with *Sesame Street* in long-term exposure to children and influence on many of them. This TV icon also generates "tie-in" merchandising revenues for public broadcasting.

Jenny Newtson looks around the cramped offices of KLCC-FM, a public radio station in Eugene, Oregon, and usually sees no one in a suit and tie. When asked what distinguishes her field from commercial radio, however, men's apparel figures in her metaphor.

"There are people behind the suits," says Newtson, a paid staffer since 1988. "People actually count for something in public radio. In commercial radio, you're just numbers. Those stations are bought and sold . . . with little concern for whose lives are being affected. Public radio has a commitment to the community and to the people we serve. We've been a *family.*"

It may read like a pat pitch, but it sounds like a message from the heart. To hear it from someone who has worked the 5:00 A.M. shift for a decade is impressive. Among other duties, Newtson, owner of a strong, reassuring voice, does local-news "cut-ins" to National Public Radio's (NPR) *Morning Edition* for four hours a day. She is not highly paid. Single and 36 years old, Newtson supplements her income by making and selling jewelry.

Volunteers bear much of the load at this community college–based station. Their satisfactions seem to lie in freedom to

> Public radio has a commitment to the community and to the people we serve. We've been a *family.*

meet Eugene's listeners' eclectic tastes without commercialism. On weekdays, after Newtson and *Morning Edition* go off the air, two local programs of wildly varied music selections, under the rubric *Fresh Tracks*, fill the next six hours. Then comes a run of public-affairs shows—NPR's *Fresh Air* interview program, followed by the local *Northwest Passage* newscast and NPR's evening flagship, *All Things Considered*. Weekends are more of a smorgasbord.

KLCC doesn't have to meet advertising and profit goals that require a mass audience. On the other hand, the lack of profit pressure can lead to supernarrow programming for audiences too small to add up to much of a donor base. Public broadcasting depends on donors, as well as on tax-based government support and corporate underwriting. Its noncommercial economic basis is under constant stress as programming costs rise faster than revenue streams. Overall, the most potent attraction of this institution is that its purpose, programs, and culture differ substantially from those of commercial radio and TV. To provide an *alternative* like none other is the mission that keeps KLCC humming.

Jenny Newtson, *Morning Edition* Local Host, KLCC-FM, Eugene, OR.

Corporation for Public Broadcasting Body established by Congress in 1967 to launch and develop public-broadcasting stations and programming.

PUBLIC BROADCASTING ROLES

Public television stays busy airing historical and investigative documentaries, long-form displays of the arts, offbeat comedies and dramas, and public-affairs shows from the local to the national level. Public radio keeps up a hectic pace of its own, offering quiz-and-comedy programs, interview shows, extended daily newscasts, quirky exercises in social criticism, and a rainbow of music to satisfy the eclectic tastes of listeners and the whims of hosts.

This content may explain why some avid fans of commercial television and radio find public television and radio to be pompous, dull, or simply irrelevant to their lives. It also may explain the opposite—why a 2001 poll by the **Corporation for Public Broadcasting** found about 60 percent of audience members surveyed rank public broadcasting among their best tax-dollar values. They placed it behind defense and medical research, but—remarkably—ahead of law enforcement, a hint of the power of programs that take on important issues more often and more deeply than do commercial broadcasters.[1]

The enterprise of public broadcasting has been shaped by motives and impulses that often seem quite contrary to those of stations in the profit-making

Beyond Making Money

It's easy to underestimate the importance of public broadcasting amid the clatter and dazzle of commercial radio and TV. However, there's more to this alternative field of electronic media than many people may realize. First, even though there are *fewer* public stations than private ones, FCC figures (for September 2001) show that both categories are substantial:

Radio	Television
AM Stations 4,727	Commercial 1,319
FM Commercial 6,051	Public 377
FM Noncommercial Educational 2,234	

Note that radio stations are categorized differently from TV stations. In radio, some AM and all FM educational stations are noncommercial. However, religious and some other formats are not part of *public* broadcasting. As of 2001, about 2,200 radio stations and 377 TV stations, as listed here, were doing what is known as *public broadcasting.*

Public broadcasting is in most U.S. cities and in many sizable towns, especially those with college-run stations. Newcomers may have to search the spectrum to discover public broadcasting, but it's usually there to be found.

Public broadcasting deserves close examination for at least two reasons: It draws on tax dollars and donations, demanding enough from its audience to warrant scrutiny; and it pursues programming well beyond the chosen range of most commercial stations. It thus challenges the capitalist dynamic underlying our society. There are signs that money-pinched public broadcasting is mimicking some commercial practices, but so far, it remains a national experiment in *differentness.*

mainstream. To interpret all of this, apart from its larger context and purposes in the tangled thicket of American cultural life is risky at best—but we will try.

Public Service

To the dismay of many broadcasters, media consumers tend to recall only the biggest national names: People often say "NBC," for example, when referring not to the national network but to the local NBC-affiliated station. The same holds true with public broadcasting. When fans refer to its institutions, they usually mention one of two acronyms: *PBS* or *NPR*. These terms stand for television's Public Broadcasting Service and for National Public Radio. If these institutional names don't raise strong mental images, the titles of particular programs often do: *Morning Edition, Austin City Limits, Frontline, The World of National Geographic, Masterpiece Theater, Car Talk,* and *NOVA.*

Not all of these programs are unique; variations of them can be found occasionally on commercial stations and cable TV. Commercial broadcasters, too, are committed formally to serving public needs; that's the price exacted for their otherwise free use of publicly owned airwaves. In reality, however—because they are businesses—they are neither consistently inclined nor consistently expected to serve cultural or educational needs first. Public broadcasters claim to do that

> **Principle #1**
>
> The first objective of public broadcasting is to survive—but the second is public service.

routinely. Under pressure to attract funding, even they don't stick exclusively to programming that's edifying. What they aim for is a high batting average.

Education

Education was the very first concern of public broadcasting, dating to 1917, and has been a vibrant component of the field ever since. It arose from desires to make conventional schooling more effective and to extend it to Americans who could not make their way to classrooms. Those goals still are in place in many parts of the United States today.

Most early programming was *educational* broadcasting because it was produced by schools and colleges and often took the form of instruction—classes delivered over radio waves. However, as entrepreneurs worked to turn radio into a business, the term *educational* became broader. It came to suggest broadcasting done primarily in the public interest and not for private gain. In practice, as the landscape of topics and programs expanded, this has meant noncommercial as opposed to commercial broadcasting. Furthermore, because of its dependency on direct public support, what used to be called only educational broadcasting is generally called simply *public* broadcasting today.

Shows now vary widely, from the radio comedy-quiz *Whad 'Ya Know?* to TV wildlife specials to gavel-to-gavel congressional hearings coverage to *Exxon/Mobil Masterpiece Theatre*, a series of dramatic performances. At its core, much public-broadcasting fare still seems intended to educate in a broad sense—to feed, stretch, and stimulate the mind. However, hot controversies over federal funding can erupt when broadcasts "go too far," offending audiences' (or at least politicians') values and tastes.

Today, some programming flows through closed systems run by schools or colleges that serve their students or wider communities with daily lessons and not much more. Other public-broadcasting fare arrives in homes via standard broadcast channels and is nationally celebrated. For example, researchers have found the long-running series *Sesame Street* to be a good preparation for prekindergarten children. Other studies, however, indicate that television can inhibit early learning and benefits affluent children more than poor ones. Still *Sesame Street* is one of public broadcasting's greatest success stories.[2]

Inclusion

Commercial networks primarily have pursued mainstream-white-middle-class-family audiences, only gradually making room on their airwaves (and staffs) for diverse ethnic groups and perspectives. Public broadcasting, on the other hand, has long offered time and resources to the expression of minority views, some arising from the "counterculture" that grew out of the turbulent 1960s. This does not mean, though, that it has lived up to its early promise. The **Carnegie Commission** on the Future of Public Broadcasting—one of a series of blue-ribbon study groups on public broadcasting—said in 1979, "Public broadcasting is a major cultural institution that can play a decisive role in bringing together the pluralistic voices and interests of the American community." On the other hand, the commission also noted that many interest groups found public broadcasting to be "closed, unwilling to change, and afraid of criticism and controversy."[3] Years later, in 1992, James T. Yee of the National Asian American Telecommunications Association said public broadcasters had adopted "multiculturalism," but with little acknowledgment of the past: "Such things as racism, discrimination, and oppression are assumed not to exist or to have never existed."[4]

> **Principle #2**
> Public broadcasters have to struggle as hard to achieve diversity as commercial broadcasters do.

Public broadcasters' increasing need for large audiences with money to donate may work against multicultural programming in a nation often split by race and economics. In addition, shortfalls of diversity in programming seem to be matched in areas of labor and management. Some of the ways in which public broadcasting works seem to discourage racial diversity within its ranks. The controlling boards of stations, as well as of the foundations that provide so much of their funding, tend to be mostly white, and that mirrors employment figures.

The Corporation for Public Broadcasting reported in 1998 that, although the ethnic-minority share of public television management nationwide had doubled over the previous two decades, the leadership still was only 12.5 percent minority—87.5 percent white. The total public-broadcasting force was more than 80 percent white.[5] (That was higher than the white share of the U.S. population in 2000, just 75 percent and declining.[6])

Public Affairs

The largest public-broadcasting entities, PBS and NPR, have encouraged thorough newsgathering and provocative programming that reveals social needs and examines cultural boundaries. This has ranged from critical documentaries and investigative reports under prominent labels, including *Frontline* and *P.O.V.* Some are daring: A 1991 *P.O.V.* presentation of "Tongues Untied," a film about black gay life in America, drew critical praise, but in some cities, public-television stations refused to show it.

Public broadcasting's news programs, often cited among the critics as favorites, are less flamboyant than that of network TV, with its high-drama reporting and anchor-stars. With less concern about alienating audiences and advertisers, public broadcasters tend to produce more substantive journalism. This earns them respect but—along with their programs' relatively measured pace and often complex subject matter—denies them mass popularity.

THE DOLLAR DILEMMA

Public broadcasting faces an abiding dilemma: If it sells ads or accepts too much corporate money, it will lose its special freedoms; but if it stays mostly independent of commercial forces, it will be doomed to struggle for money. In some countries, economic survival is a less daunting struggle for public broadcasters. Some systems that are at least partly tax funded have almost universal popular support and thus manage to establish long-term stability. This is not the case in the United States, where philosophies and rivalries contend vigorously in the

Tentpole Metaphor used to describe lift in ratings that a strong program can give to weaker programs surrounding it on the schedule.

political arena. American public broadcasters cling to their noncommercial status with a stubborn if sometimes tenuous grip.

Competition

One aggravating factor in the public-broadcasting struggle is the wide spectrum of program choices available to most audiences today. The digitally tuned car radio and the ever-more-versatile TV "zapper" have made precise selection of programming so easy that many people, like migratory birds, tend to visit certain nesting spots. Thus, they become *niche* audiences, flocking repeatedly to the same channels.

That's fine with public broadcasters if those digital tuners are locked onto public stations. Things aren't always that simple, though. Commercial radio, dominated by popular music and political talk, may appear to program mainly for demographic groups that tolerate advertising and wouldn't choose public radio on a bet. Still, in some respects, public and commercial radio compete head to head.

KLCC program director Don Hein certainly would like larger audiences. He can speak in the same jargon commercial programmers prefer, and did so when reporting happily in spring 2001: "In the last two 'books' [ratings "sweeps" periods], we've raised the **'tentpole'** [ratings level] between the morning news and the late afternoon programs."[7] In other words, the station's mid-day audiences had grown. For commercial radio, larger audiences mean more support for a station's advertisers; in public radio, they mean a greater field of listeners from whom to seek donations and whose presence may attract corporate underwriters.

Today's radio dial is jammed with commercial choices, some of which outshout the more genteel tones of public stations. In the public-radio universe—more than 2,000 stations across all the 50 states—a spare dollar is as rare as a country-club membership. Meanwhile, public television has suffered even more serious blows from the explosion of cable and satellite TV since the 1980s. Public stations used to be almost alone in airing tough, edgy documentaries and offbeat cultural fare. Now, with about 230 national cable networks operating and the number growing, viewers find many of the same features on specialized cable channels, virtually around the clock.

Politics

Largely due to political controversy over programming, government support for public broadcasting has fluctuated. Donors and underwriters could take its place, but most people who listen to public radio never contribute a dime to it. To pay their bills, public radio stations might like to sell advertising, but are not allowed to do so.[8] These distinctions, among others, sharply separate public radio and TV stations from the business model of broadcasting described elsewhere in this book. That is why, overall, this unique electronic enterprise survives with fewer resources than commerical broadcasting.

With this relative poverty, though, comes one common advantage tied into public broadcasting's goals: Most public stations are locally owned and don't have to send money flowing up a corporate food chain to distant investors on

Wall Street. In soliciting help from audiences and lawmakers, stations can (and often do) claim a moral high ground that places public good above business goals. The downside—a serious concern to some broadcasters—is that public broadcasting has little hope of ever getting off the fund-raising treadmill or out from under politicians' thumbs.

Public interest, convenience, and necessity Phrase in Radio Act of 1927 setting out purposes of broadcasting; used at the time mainly in a *commercial*-broadcasting context.

BIRTH AND GROWTH

Broadcasting has two histories—one of them primary and prominent, and the other a far less flashy narrative. Although public (educational) broadcasting evolved at about the same time and out of the same technologies that built commercial stations, it always has played the secondary role of a smart but outcast cousin. Its programming is precious to its fans, but they are relatively few. It's a mass-media sector that sometimes rejects the mass. Showing us things of substance, its programming is labeled *elitist*; taking on tough political and social issues, it's branded as *liberal.* The history of public broadcasting is mostly an epic of high hopes and low ratings.

Foundations

Public broadcasting was born in a classroom. Its history is that of an educational project that "morphed" into a broader cultural phenomenon. Millions of families still know the network mainly because of *Sesame Street,* a show that attempts to embed basic learning skills through entertainment for children.

> **Principle #4**
>
> Public broadcasting's roots in education provide a natural mission that separates it from commercial media.

GOING TO COLLEGE

The first educational radio station, known as 9XM, was established experimentally at the University of Wisconsin in 1917. That was the year the United States entered World War I—the year after broadcast pioneer Lee De Forest broke ground by transmitting national election results from his primitive New York station. In the infancy of broadcasting as a popular medium, public radio's precursors were just as determined as their commercial counterparts.

Soon, college lectures turned into radio programs. Educators—starting in 1921 with Latter Day Saints University in Salt Lake City, Utah—received many of the first radio licenses from the government. In 1922, University of Wisconsin station 9XM became WHA. Soon, business interests and entrepreneurs eager to control the new mass medium posed formidable opposition to nonprofit visions of broadcasting.

A DOUBLE-EDGED LAW

The Radio Act of 1927, setting up a commission to regulate radio, borrowed a phrase from a piece of railroad legislation that still is quoted today when the purposes of broadcasting are discussed: Stations were to be licensed to use the airwaves according to the **"public interest, convenience, and necessity."** This

University of Wisconsin 9XM/WHA The *X* in its original name marked it as an experiment in 1917, but the University of Wisconsin station (later named WHA) inaugurated educational radio.

Public service Ill-defined concept cited as primary goal and value of public broadcasting; generally suggests not-for-profit enterprises or efforts to serve civic goals.

Frequencies Specific "spots" on the electromagnetic spectrum (airwaves) on which stations transmit their programs, as assigned by the FCC.

AM (Amplitude modulation) Method of impressing a signal on a radio carrier wave by varying its amplitude.

FM (Frequency modulation) Method of impressing a signal on a radio carrier wave by varying its frequency.

seemed to position **public service** as a commanding goal. However, the other edge of the Radio Act disappointed educational broadcasters. To win political support, the Federal Radio Commission offered the choicest **frequencies** to commercial broadcasters—who had, as it happens, virtually designed key elements of the act.

The frequency problem would hamper educational stations. Many were trying to reach listeners not just with high-level instruction in useful subjects but with unique cultural and entertainment shows. Others sought to fulfill important missions—for instance, transmitting agricultural information, as no other medium was.[9] By 1930, the State University of Iowa's station WOI would be broadcasting agricultural market data across a state in which half the farmers had radio sets.[10] Government regulators and politicians did encourage commercial stations to air more educational programming. Because they were already hampered by the cost of broadcast facilities and operations, educators were being marginalized. Without strong positions on the radio dial, many soon gave up their licenses, disappointed that they had neither attracted crowds of open-minded listeners nor generated much publicity for their colleges.[11]

In the early 1930s, the growth of unions and other interest groups prompted Congress to focus on a fundamental question: Who should be permitted to use the airwaves "owned" by—that is, controlled by the government of—the people of the United States? It was clear that to avoid technical chaos, access would have to be limited, but to *whom?* In the end, the Communications Act of 1934 largely protected the interests of commercial broadcasters. An amendment that would have reserved good frequencies for public broadcasting was defeated. But in 1938, after a series of hearings over what to do with unassigned radio frequencies, the Federal Communications Commission (FCC) created a new class of "noncommercial educational" stations. It set aside **AM (amplitude modulation)** airspace for them in 1940 and promised that **FM (frequency modulation)** channels—with better sound quality—also might be available soon.

FM PROMISE

The new FM bands did emerge as cheaper and thus favored routes for education. Major public school districts and universities in the 1940s began building FM stations, newly eager to provide learning to children and adults. Development—tied mainly to money supplied by schools and colleges, rarely a rich set of backers—proceeded slowly, however. Technically, FM was a weak stepchild; it was still inaccessible to most potential listeners because few homes had FM sets. Commercial broadcasters boosted AM radio into a dominant position in American radio that lasted into the 1970s.

In this environment, most people didn't mind hearing radio ads, which, after all, kept introducing new wonders into everyday life. So it's unsurprising that a spasm of well-intended efforts to promote public service over private gain in the nation's media drew little attention from the American people. Some of these efforts came from a government-appointed group called the Hutchins Commission. This blue-ribbon panel studied the media, including radio specifically, and in 1947 urged them to follow a "social responsibility" standard in all things. Meanwhile, the FCC's own staff produced a report (known as the "Blue Book" for the color of its cover) that could have led to a blueprint for regulation that would encourage programming in the public interest. These outcomes were largely ignored, however. "Despite mounting evidence to the contrary," one scholar has noted, the notion that commercial broadcasters would answer important public needs was by now deep-seated.[12] After all, broadcasters would be regulated. Meanwhile, they were delivering exciting radio shows, some of them straight from Hollywood.

The FCC set aside frequencies for educational radio, but it languished as a colorless, sparsely available, mostly low-power medium through the 1940s and into the 1950s. Its stations, when they could be found on the local dial at all, offered a short menu of programs. Meanwhile, attention was shifting toward a newer, more glamorous medium—television. It seemed likely to create tremendous opportunities for public broadcasting in an open society.

Acceleration

By the early 1950s, the FCC was holding hearings on **spectrum** space for television stations nationally. One commissioner, Frieda Hennock, earned an honored place in public-broadcasting history by insisting that a fourth of the channels be reserved for noncommercial stations. In the end, the stations won fewer than 10 percent of the available channels, but that was enough to launch educational TV. A Houston, Texas, university station received the first license in 1953.

THE LURE OF TELEVISION

The **Ford Foundation**—a legacy of the great Ford auto-making fortune—now had started supplying educational TV with its first regular outside funding. The foundation, which would become public broadcasting's most faithful and generous friend, wanted to put useful cultural and intellectual material before audiences that they wouldn't find elsewhere.

At this point, public broadcasting should have been gaining a splashy new position in modern society. After all, **test patterns** (on-screen graphics used to tune transmissions) and still-primitive programming looked pretty much the same, whether they appeared on commercial or public TV channels. To most families of that day, TV was an almost unbelievably attractive novelty. In their journeys around the dial, they should have discovered and watched many interesting public broadcasting shows.

Spectrum The electromagnetic spectrum, which is used to carry radio signals.

Ford Foundation Major financial backer of public television from its earliest years onward.

Test pattern Graphic pattern of fine and dark lines, usually printed on card or sheet, with which technicians focus and calibrate television cameras.

Frieda Hennock. Businesses wanted television to themselves, but FCC commissioner Hennock made history by holding out for educational channels.

VHF (Very High Frequency)
Refers to any frequency between 30 and 300 megahertz; denotes TV channels 2–13.

Markets Term for communities or metropolitan areas served by broadcast stations.

UHF (Ultrahigh Frequency)
Refers to any frequency between 300 and 3,000 megahertz; denotes TV channels 14–69.

National Educational Television Consortium of broadcasters that became major program producer for public TV; assets acquired in 1970 by owner of New York station, renamed WNET.

Vast wasteland Term coined by FCC Chairman Newton N. Minow to describe commercial television programming in 1961 speech to broadcasters.

There was one big problem: Public TV was nowhere to be found on most TV sets. In the largest U.S. cities, every spot on the standard **VHF (very high frequency)** band, from channels 2 through 13, had been granted to commercial broadcasters. To see public TV, viewers in New York, Los Angeles, and other huge **markets** would have to buy **UHF (ultrahigh frequency)** equipped TV tuners, since it wasn't accessible through existing models.[13] Many educational station projects simply stalled as a result.

Such obstacles typified the early years of public television—but so did its advocates' stubborn commitment to public goals. Aided by Ford Foundation construction grants, people did build stations, aggressively on the VHF band, though less so on UHF. There was enough political support for reserving future space for educational channels to set off a vehement debate in the U.S. Senate in the mid-1950s. Before long, the government was starting to provide funding for public-TV programming. The FCC worked with broadcasters and manufacturers to design TV-set technology that would bring in all channels. In 1962, President Kennedy signed a law stating that this requirement must be met in all new television sets. By this time, major educational stations were on the air several hours a day—ambitious at that time, if unimaginably limited today. They had begun early to pool their resources; a *consortium*—or alliance—that would become **National Educational Television (NET)** accepted programs from stations, made copies, and distributed them to other stations.

NUDGING THE CULTURE

President John F. Kennedy took office in 1961 and urged citizens to throw off Eisenhower-era complacency and pursue higher arts and ambitions. Even with respect to popular culture, the young president wanted action and activism on a national scale. He found inclinations toward both in a still younger man, a lawyer named Newton N. Minow. As the new Democratic chairman of the FCC (and a strong backer of educational TV), Minow made it clear that prime-time TV did not square with his view of public service. He complained memorably to commercial broadcasters at their national convention: "Sit down in front of your television when your station goes on the air . . . and keep your eyes glued to that set until the station signs off. I can assure you that you will observe a **vast wasteland.**"

Newton Minow. President Kennedy's FCC chairman became famous by labeling TV programming "a vast wasteland" and pressing the commercial broadcasters for higher public-service standards.

Minow threatened not to renew licenses of broadcasters who failed to meet public-service needs. *Vast wasteland* soon would become a popular epithet for television, despite (or, perhaps, because of) the support it was winning from millions of viewers. With an FCC chair denouncing commercial TV, educational broadcasting suddenly looked even better. Moreover, there clearly was growing demand for the more varied public-television programming beyond mere classroom instruction.

The national public-TV distribution group became National Educational Television in 1963, and soon switched its emphasis from the classroom to the living room. The Ford Foundation provided money, much of it funneled to a two-year experimental program called **Public Broadcasting Laboratory (PBL)**, in which NET generated cutting-edge content. Some of it was high-culture entertainment, including dramas as socially challenging in the sixties as the TV stage plays aired "live" by commercial networks had been in the fifties. There also were programs that boldly showcased the nation's ethnic diversity; some went so far as to examine the lives of black Americans during a period of violent civil-rights confrontations in the South. Other programs delved into volatile national issues, including key government actions in Vietnam. Public broadcasting was displaying its power to tackle important and controversial issues of American life and culture.

CARNEGIE'S GIFT

Under Kennedy and his successor—Lyndon B. Johnson, a Texas commercial broadcaster—the government was encouraging the growth of this alternative medium. A 1964 meeting between broadcasters and the U.S. Office of Education created the Carnegie Commission on Educational Television, charged with charting its future path. The Carnegie recommendations, announced in 1967, would come to be viewed as historically significant.

The commission declared noncommercial broadcasting to be a vitally important communication asset of the American people. It held that public stations "should be individually responsive to the needs of the local communities and collectively strong enough to meet the needs of a national audience. Each must be a product of local initiative and local support." Moving from the general to the specific, the commission members called for greatly increased federal support for public broadcasting—specifically for funding to be drawn from a new 2 to 5 percent excise tax on the sale of television sets. The commission asked for the creation of a semipublic corporation to administer the funds.

President Johnson was listening: He introduced a bill to that effect in Congress. Hearings and debate soon brought radio into the process as well, and on November 7, 1967, the **Public Broadcasting Act** became law. It retired the term *educational* from popular use. Besides committing federal financial aid, the act established the Corporation for Public Broadcasting (CPB), a 15-member board drawn from civic and cultural organizations. It would use tax dollars to help create high-quality radio and TV programs, set up interconnections, develop stations, and generally promote the growth of noncommercial broadcasting.

The corporation could not govern stations; the FCC licensed them individually, so power in public broadcasting remained formally at the local level. (Even NET, a vital program supplier to stations, never had managed to organize stations together.) So there was less to CPB's formal authority than its title might suggest. It was not to be the hub of a national network. Still, some local stations and regional public-TV networks objected to the idea of a central power interconnecting them all; they insisted on autonomy.

Moreover, there was the specter of political influence from Washington—not at all welcome in many communities. An earlier plan under which the U.S. Department of Health, Education and Welfare would issue directly all public-broadcasting grants—keeping the purse strings out of CPB's hands—had given way to full grant-making power for the corporation's board. One of its central tasks was to shield stations from direct government pressure—but would they need to be shielded from CPB itself?

Public Broadcasting Laboratory Two-year experimental program (in 1960s) to generate innovative programming for public television.

Public Broadcasting Act Law enacted in 1967 committing federal money for public broadcasting and establishing Corporation for Public Broadcasting to develop system.

Principle #5

If centralized funding = centralized power, then federal funding = the threat of federal interference.

National Association of Educational Broadcasters Main organization and program supplier of public broadcasting until demise in 1981.

THE CPB FACTOR

Money from the new corporation seemed certain to make stations attentive to the leanings of its board members. They would, of course, have leanings: The board was to be appointed by the president—initially, at least, in a brutal political climate. The Vietnam War polarized national politics; battered Kennedy's successor, President Johnson, into announcing that he would not run for re-election, and brought Republican Richard Nixon back to the forefront. Once elected, in 1968, Nixon quickly appointed a long-time political supporter and Johnson critic, Albert L. Cole, to the CPB board. In this political environment, many local station managers became nervous about possible "top-down" pressure on them to accept certain types of programming.

Pressure certainly would come in the years ahead, especially from members of Congress, goaded by constituents and special-interest groups, and from the White House. In the turbulent late sixties, with the Public Broadcasting Act taking effect, the main questions about public broadcasting had to do with how independently and how rapidly the newly elevated field would grow to serve public needs. Speed was important partly because of how television in particular was permeating American life. Fewer than 1 in 10 homes had TV sets in 1950, but one decade later, in 1960, 87 percent of homes had acquired "the tube."[14] A few years after that, the Carnegie Commission recognized that only with large quantities of federal and other noncommercial dollars could public broadcasting be seen and heard through a growing mass of commercial programming.

The Corporation for Public Broadcasting (CPB) began dispersing funds to pay American Telephone & Telegraph (AT&T)—at that time still the country's dominant "Bell" telephone system—to interconnect the public TV stations. It wasn't as if they hadn't been exchanging programs for many years, however; their primary collective, the **National Association of Educational Broadcasters (NAEB)**, had organized interstation shipping by mail back in 1950. (The process was known as *bicycling tapes*.) But universal movement of programs *through phone lines* (and, very soon, satellites) would standardize operations and help move public TV into the big leagues.

After a six-month test to prove the distribution web would work, the next job was to set up a guiding organization to push programs through it. With support from the older entities NET and NAEB (soon to begin receding from their leadership roles), CPB in 1969 created the Public Broadcasting Service. The Corporation for Public Broadcasting would become a central force in both public television and public radio, facilitating their growth. It would also help them evolve into a sort of counterindustry to commercial broadcasting, and would become a bull's-eye for critics.

Triumphs and Troubles

Public Broadcasting Service (PBS) arrived on the scene at a historical moment that in some ways would symbolize its future. In 1969, the country was torn by dissent. The Nixon White House seemed suspicious of all mass media. Young people marched in the streets; older people argued at work about the war and politics, and many found it difficult to get through the day without ideological headaches. Most got home from work and chose one among their few channels of *commercial* television. So the creation of a potentially mind-expanding broadcast service that would feed on tax dollars, replacing "educational" TV with "public" TV, invited close attention as an alternative.

LOCALISM'S PULL

In late 1970, PBS launched its live-feed web among local stations. The Nixon White House—whose Office of Telecommunications Policy kept a wary eye on perceived "liberal" bias—resisted the prospect of a fourth network that might use federal money to infiltrate America's communities with antigovernment attitudes. President Nixon vetoed a CPB funding request in 1972. Meanwhile, public broadcasting had developed internal conflicts. More than its commercial counterpart, it had been rooted in **localism.** That principle held that local stations should retain power over programming, even when shows came in from a national source. Now the rising influence of CPB and PBS alarmed some local broadcasters, especially in conservative regions that were wary of Washington's ways and New York's producers. They resented even the possibility that PBS would force unified scheduling on them, requiring them to show programs that didn't fit their communities in schedule slots when other shows would do better.

The Public Broadcasting Service was revamped in 1973 to foster creation of programming, not just distribute it—but under control of a PBS board packed with local-station executives. Thus, perhaps paradoxically, a national network was being assigned to maintain localism. Stations would be able to influence, if not rule on, program topics and treatments. Moreover, each station would continue to be free to design its own schedule and to reject any network-distributed program.

Along the way, radio joined the network trend. Unlike TV, educational radio generally had received little federal funding and had remained generally poor, weak, campus based, and heard by few. However, more than 400 stations were on the air, a substantial base for a national system. In 1971, with CPB backing, National Public Radio was established and gave those stations—at least the 90 that signed on as charter members—a program service that would be their version of a network.

THE TRUST-FUND OPTION

The single most nagging problem of public broadcasting was—and is—its lack of assured long-term financing. Broadcasting is an expensive medium to run. Without the sort of revenue streams enjoyed by commercial broadcasters, public outlets might have to live every day on the verge of literally begging for sustenance. From the beginning, educational stations had to get by on meager college stipends and whatever donations or bake-sale proceeds they could gather. With national interest in education increasing, federal and foundation grants came intermittently through the mid-century years. Even after CPB began funneling tax money to them, public broadcasters knew that every dollar could turn out to be their last from Uncle Sam.

Soon, broadcasters were giving on-air mention to commercial enterprises that made donations. Stations gave this kind of financial support a dignified

Localism Regulatory principle declaring that the broadcast system is based on local stations meeting local needs.

Underwriting Usually, financial support of public broadcasting by a company or institution.

Trust fund Money set aside and held "in trust" for a specific purpose.

Lobby Lawyers or other advocates for a particular cause or industry before Congress or regulatory agencies (e.g., the "broadcast lobby").

name: **underwriting.** The funding problem was a key factor in prompting the formation of still another commission, the Carnegie Commission on the Future of Public Broadcasting. Its report in 1979 pressed the government to pay about half of the estimated $1.2 billion needed annually to run public broadcasting by 1985. The balance would come from state governments, businesses, audience members, and other sources. Rather than set up special taxes to supply the federal share, the commission said, the government should charge commercial broadcasters for their use of the public airwaves and put the proceeds into a **trust fund** that would protect the money for use in public broadcasting.

That didn't happen. Among other reasons, the commercial broadcast industry had a strong, sophisticated **lobby** in Washington, the National Association of Broadcasters. The NAB once had supported public broadcasting, but came to perceive it as a threat. The broadcast lobby had encouraged President Nixon to veto a CPB budget proposal in 1972, and now—feeling some real competition from public TV—lobbied away any hope that Congress would approve a commercially supported trust fund. Nor did other revisions proposed by "Carnegie II" bear fruit.

THE REAGAN EFFECT

Instead, in 1981, Ronald Reagan became president. During his administration, taxes were cut and federal spending increased, though generally along politically conservative lines. The CPB's budget consequently was cut by tens of millions of dollars.[15] Throughout the 1980s, public broadcasting struggled. After a near-disastrous deficit in 1983, National Public Radio reordered its financial arrangements with NPR stations and with CPB, and then continued to expand its programming.

Public radio and TV experimented with the definition of *noncommercial*, stretching the limits of the short, restrained sponsor messages they were allowed by law to air. Ten TV stations, with special dispensation from Washington, DC, even broadcast commercials. The FCC eventually authorized something called *enhanced* underwriting, in which companies donating to public broadcasting could receive up to 30-second plugs in return. Meanwhile, the most popular programs on public TV spun off some aggressive "tie-in" merchandising. Dolls and other replicas of characters from *Sesame Street* and other programs were up for sale across the country—often in stores bearing public-broadcasting logos. None of this looked very "noncommercial," but it did help the stations and networks to remain solvent. It also laid the groundwork for a future of truly modest federal funding—a future that seemed almost certain.

In 1990, as competitive pressures from cable TV mounted, PBS made a radical change in its strategy that would prove controversial within the broadcast community. The network's national programming chief was given sole control of decisions over which new programs to fund for station use. Previously, stations—especially large ones producing many PBS programs—had had a voice in that process, as had independent producers and minority representatives. It cost the stations much of their autonomy in program choice, but PBS promised that more and better shows would reach more stations under the new system.

WASHINGTON WOES

The 1990s saw conservatives mounting new attacks on the content and financing of public broadcasting. After a Republican landslide in the 1994 congressional elections, House Speaker Newt Gingrich and other top Republicans led an attack. They wanted cuts in funding to the "liberal" CPB—in fact, Gingrich said he wanted to "zero it out"—and public broadcasting wound up with a two-year funding freeze. Controversy erupted again in 1999, centering on the security of each donor's name once he or she had sent money to a public station. There were reports that some stations were turning over donor

Pledge Drive. Public-broadcasting loyalists are used to "pledge breaks," which interrupt programming several times a year and bring in tens of millions of dollars annually. © Maryland Public Television.

Pledge break Interruption of programming to ask viewers or listeners to donate money.

lists to political organizations. Public broadcasters long had obtained lists *from* political groups in order to tap their members for contributions. To provide unwitting donors' names *to* the political parties, however, seemed well beyond public broadcasting's mission.

The Corporation for Public Broadcasting—which had its own inspector general—investigated and reported that 53 stations had in fact exchanged the names of their contributors for other names from political fund-raisers. One, Minnesota Public Radio, a source of many popular programs aired by stations nationwide, handed over 10,000 donor names during the 1990s and got more than 46,000 names in return (a profitable ratio, at least). When CPB reported that most donor lists had gone to Democratic organizations, the old accusations of liberal bias echoed again.[16] Congress threatened to withhold funding unless the practice ended, and CPB cracked down on those involved.

Little had occurred to calm the stormy seas of public broadcasting by the dawn of the twenty-first century. Federal support remained touch-and-go, subject to political shifts, and the "dollar dilemma" was unresolved. Nonetheless, large foundations kept giving, businesses kept underwriting, and public broadcasters were covering more than 80 percent of their expenses with money from private sources. These included the viewers and listeners. Because of them, the **pledge break**—an interruption in programming during which staffers or volunteers repeatedly invite the audience to donate money—entered the language. Giving by individual supporters (members) has been impressive: In 1997, they contributed an estimated $140 million to public stations, about twice as much as the checks drafted by private underwriters.[17]

PROGRAMMING

Very little about public broadcasting today is as simply stated and as easy to define as it is in the commercial sector. After much deregulation and drift from lofty public-service goals, commercial stations have been asked to do little more

Principle #6

In a consumer economy, public broadcasting cannot escape the mandates of marketing if it is to compete for funds.

than entertain the people. By contrast, the mission of public stations and their programs arouse debate over their value to the public and the increasing need to keep the whole enterprise running fairly independently. Today's managers watch Nielsen and Arbitron ratings closely, paying special attention to demographics—not how many are watching, but who. Some stations have begun to create large mosaics of little "niche" audiences, ready with their checkbooks, who in turn will lure richer underwriters.

Television

When *TV Guide* magazine announced its "20 top shows" of the 1980s, the fifth-ranked program was PBS's *Brideshead Revisited.* As the writer noted, "Who'd have guessed this British drama about two young Oxford men who might be lovers—one of whom carries a teddy bear—would become a cult classic, one of the most popular public television shows ever made?"

COURTING THE KIDS

Who knew, indeed. Certainly some things are expected of public broadcasting's programs: They are expected to be high-quality exercises; to have a tone that is gentle but tough, sensitive but probing; to be rich in learning and lore; to be serious; to be droll. A very few are expected to be just a little racey (in a British sort of way). Almost no program, though, is expected to be wildly popular—except with children. Kids were the first core audience, and not just in the classrooms served by early educational broadcasting.

Years before PBS was founded, *Sesame Street* was a gleam in the eye of Joan Ganz Cooney, a young public-TV producer. She got some foundation money, she brought a puppet-making genius named Jim Henson into the fold, and she tried out her new idea on youngsters in Philadelphia. The show didn't work. Cooney took its failure with the trial group as a spur to success, retooling it. *Sesame Street* hit the air nationally in November 1969. This time it worked, and well. In fact, it quickly had children reciting their letters and numbers while parents chuckled in the background at witty remarks from Henson's "Muppets."

Today, the program is a fountain of stunning statistics: It has encompassed more than 4,000 episodes; it's the longest-running children's show on television; and it's seen in 150 other countries. In short, it's an American national fixture. Moreover, its educational role has spawned years of debate and miles of research papers. *Sesame Street* also has lent hope and inspiration to the creators who followed Cooney. The Public Broadcasting System now airs a slowly churning mix of programs for youngsters, from *Clifford the Big Red Dog* to *Reading Rainbow* to *Zoom* to *Tots TV* to *Barney and Friends* to *Teletubbies.*

ANGLING FOR ADULTS

For adults who enjoy the arts, public television offers a richly varied schedule. One showcase, *Great Performances*, ranges from opera to comedy to "performance biographies" of figures such as composers Rodgers and Hart. Another stalwart success, *Austin City Limits*, presents Texas-style concerts, often by big-name country and pop performers with baby-boomer appeal.

Public TV loved history and Americana even before producer Ken Burns became the equivalent of an auteur through his poetic, entrancing documentaries *(The Civil War, Baseball, Jazz)*. *The American Experience* also has reexamined major periods, issues, and characters, from female pilots *(Fly Girls)* to the Great Depression *(Riding the Rails)* to an antislavery fanatic *(John Brown's Holy War)*. Another kind of history—natural history—occupies many prime-time hours. *The Living Edens* takes great cinematographers and, through them, the viewers into enchanting places. NOVA, the network's most-watched ongoing documentary series, explores the sciences vividly. Although the highly popular series *Cosmos* died along with astronomer Carl Sagan, another genius deconstructs the heavens for viewers in *Stephen Hawking's Universe*.

The Hawking show emanates from New York's public television station WNET, another reminder that although PBS gets most of the publicity and attention, stations around the country own, control, and supply it. The programming enterprise is a collective. Indeed, without a few large stations—WNET (New York), WGBH (Boston), WETA (Washington), and KQED (San Francisco)—producing most of the major shows, PBS might have little programming to offer.

A timely assignment for public television early in the twenty-first century is to serve an audience that's getting older, as well as younger adults who need tips for living better. *The Perennial Gardener* is among regular visitors to homeowners, as is the entertaining home-renovation show *This Old House*. Advice-and-information programs in the long PBS lineup include *In the Prime* (on aging well), *The Whole Child* (parenting), *HealthWeek* and *Body &Soul* (health), and *Religion & Ethics Newsweekly*. These, too, are produced by local stations or independent companies.

The NewsHour with Jim Lehrer, a program that helps public television fulfill its imperative for news and public-affairs content, airs each weeknight. It presents an opening news summary and then typically examines no more than four or five issues. It does so at a pace that contrasts sharply with the dizzying rush of an ABC, CBS, or NBC newscast. The show's tempo may be short on excitement but is long on information, which gives it the added authority and credibility needed to book important guests, who know they usually will be allowed to finish their sentences. *NewsHour* is produced in Washington, where it's seen by lawmakers who control federal funding and who often sit at its microphones.

There's much more in the public-affairs bag: Documentaries of *Frontline* highlight important yet often ignored problems (uncontrolled trade in imported guns, marketing of popular culture to teenagers, the HMOs' toll on conscientious doctors). *P.O.V.*, sometimes working with minority or activist filmmakers, focuses on

Jim Lehrer. His *NewsHour* moves deliberately through a few issues every weeknight, giving public television a prestigious presence in Washington, DC, where many funding decisions are made.

Some PBS-Distributed Programs

American Experience (documentaries on events that shaped the country)

Antiques Roadshow (traveling "show-and-tell" about antiques)

Austin City Limits (concerts of American music in every genre)

EGG the Arts Show (people making art in America)

ExxonMobil Masterpiece Theatre (dramatized novels and teleplays)

Frontline (long-form investigative journalism)

Great Performances (music, opera, dance, movies)

In Julia's Kitchen with Master Chefs (cooking with culinary legend Julia Child)

The Living Edens (natural history from "isolated, undisturbed corners of the globe")

Mystery! (British mystery teleplays)

Nature (animals and more in wild places)

The NewsHour with Jim Lehrer (news briefs, in-depth reports, discussions, essays)

Newton's Apple (science experiments for the family)

NOVA (documentaries that decode science for the layperson)

P.O.V. (showcase for independent nonfiction films)

Reading Rainbow (wide-ranging show encouraging children to read)

Religion & Ethics Newsweekly (news and perspectives on moral-spiritual matters)

This Old House (home improvement series tracking long-term projects)

Washington Week (journalists in discussion of major news events)

Source: Program listings at www.pbs.org.

rugged individualists, including a 12-year-old boy who challenged the Boy Scouts' antigay policies, and on interesting back roads of society.

LOCAL INITIATIVES

Although audiences enjoy nationally distributed programs, they also favor local shows with local hosts who appeal to community tastes. "Localism" remains an official service priority for public broadcasting. Stations approach it in a variety of ways. For starters, there are some utterly local public-TV programs. Among them are those noteworthy news inquiries and discussions, mainly in large cities where commercial stations might scan complex issues quickly—if at all—but where public stations can develop topics and issues through long-form programs.

At the other extreme are vigorous small operations delivering news and public service programming. In Alaska, *Anchorage Edition* tackles public-affairs issues and is broadcast simultaneously (simulcast) on public TV and radio. At Northern Michigan University, WNMU brings in medical specialists 17 times a year for *Ask the Doctors*, a live call-in show. Television production is expensive, however, and ambitious shows sometimes require more specialists or equipment than a small station can afford. That's why producers are often asked to bring in a private-funding proposal, complete with named potential donors, before a station will commit airtime to a specific show. Programs about regional history and culture, always popular among public-TV fans, are often produced by a station

ProTalk

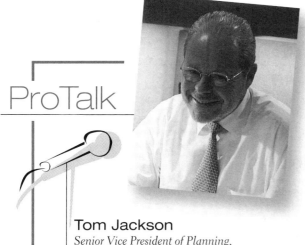

Tom Jackson
Senior Vice President of Planning,
KETC-TV, St. Louis

"We need . . . to build more long-term relationships with people who are totally aware of the highest aspirations of the organization."

Tom Jackson knows business. He has been a leader in advertising. His job now is in marketing. And he doesn't mind pointing to what he sees as a historic mistake. "Public TV's biggest failing in the deep distant past was when someone found out that you could turn on a camera, ask for money, and people would send it," Jackson says, implying that a passive approach to fund-raising has persisted ever since.

Jackson has been with KETC-TV, St. Louis's public station, since 1986. He had held major jobs with large commercial broadcasters. In his current role as senior vice president for marketing and planning, he's in charge of fostering ever-closer relations between the station and its donors. He also scouts constantly for "new business" and "development" opportunities—ways of earning, or raising, more money from an expanding field of sources to keep the station going. Does that lead KETC toward meek policies and bland programming that won't rock its benefactors' boats? Jackson says no.

"Financial stability lies in working with people who don't necessarily agree with you but can tolerate other views," he says. "We have to take on tough issues

in a fair way, and not be purely escapist or reduce our programming to the lowest common mental denominator."

Controversies over programming often prove helpful to a station that's trying to make ends meet. When KETC in 1999 decided—alone among Missouri public-TV stations—*not* to broadcast a debate between U.S. Senate candidates, the *St. Louis Post-Dispatch* moaned editorially that such events were "precisely the kind of programming that public television is created for."[18] The station said then that the debates would not be useful to voters. Jackson says now, "I think we definitely made a mistake."

Overall, marketing and development cannot hang on one decision or one program at a time—and Jackson asserts that for public broadcasters, long-term cultivation of donors and "underwriters" (quasi-advertisers) is essential. He compares a public station to a university: "A university really grooms its alumni over many, many years to stay active in the life of the organization. They become more and more involved. Those alumni who can, support the organization. Public TV, on the other hand, too often said, 'We'll send you a tape . . . there, don't you like this program?' 'We need to move into a model more closely akin to the university, to build more long-term relationships with people who are totally aware of the highest aspirations of the organization."

Jackson credits the Public Broadcasting Service (PBS) with creating special opportunities for local fund-raising. One example is *Egg, the Arts Show*, into which stations may insert their own underwriting messages, as they do in the PBS children's program *Zoom*.

While bringing in money, KETC is striving to save money, as well. Jackson says that field cameras used to cost $55,000 to $60,000 each, but now cameras costing $5,000–$6,000 generate acceptable video. A digital editing suite used to cost up to half a million dollars; now, he says, adequate equipment can be purchased for $20,000. All of which, says Jackson, brings closer to reality something that all of public broadcasting badly needs: "There must be a new economic model," he says.

and then circulated widely to diffuse the cost. Oregon Public Broadcasting airs minidocumentaries on the state's past, from immigration surges to train robberies; University of Oregon students research and produce the pieces to gain experience. Other statewide shows view the present: A Fargo station provides

North Dakotans with kids' education programs while its website alerts residents to flooding on the Red River.

Public-television's viewers aren't always obsessed with the *serious*. Leisure pursuits make for good TV, and any state that's interesting or attractive enough to generate an outdoors or tourism show can peddle it to stations around the region or even the country. One good example is *Outdoor Idaho*, produced by Idaho Public Television and marketed widely. There are also a few big-name shows with strong local roots. The highly popular PBS series *This Old House*, produced at WGBH in Boston, is viewed nationwide but reveals a cultural trait rarely heard on commercial networks: Some of the craftspeople have rich New England accents.

For all the productivity of some public-TV stations, many smaller operations produce little beyond fund-raising shows and occasional community discussions.

Radio

Radio has a unique ability to create worlds in our heads, even as it frees us from the grip of the visual and encourages abstract thought. That's a fancy way of explaining why public radio is alive and fairly well across the country. Its use of the airwaves to broadcast effective programming has made it important to millions (about 1.8 million people a day hear *All Things Considered*). Like public-TV viewers, they endure pledge breaks—but they listen.

THE RISE OF NPR

Through the Public Broadcasting Act of 1967, the federal government set the stage for the creation of National Public Radio. Unlike PBS, the new radio network was intended from its inception to be a program service to local stations, and CPB helped give birth to NPR. Its debut, in April 1971, was live coverage of U.S. Senate hearings on the Vietnam War—important in terms of public broadcasting's civic mission, since stations all over the country picked up the feed. Less than a month later, the news program *All Things Considered* went on the air, its reporters covering antiwar demonstrations. The show's then-director and now-host Linda Wertheimer would remember that day as "scented with spring flowers and tear gas."[19]

All Things Considered. As National Public Radio's evening flagship program, this news/discussion program is a major factor in local stations' fundraising success.

For KLCC in Eugene, Oregon, it was NPR's second important show, not its first, that made a dramatic difference. "The biggest impact NPR had on us was *Morning Edition*," recalls program director Don Hein of the arrival of a new public-affairs show in late 1979. "We were running classical music in the mornings up till then. We just dumped the classics . . . and inserted the new show." Hein was lucky: After the arrival of *Morning Edition*, his audience grew. "Inside the station, we thought everybody wanted classics," he says, "but *outside* the station, people wanted morning news."

Today, *Morning Edition* is public radio's top audience draw nationally, making it one of many programming "brands" that distinguish NPR. Its programs can be heard on hundreds of local stations, and other suppliers also contribute to the rich public-radio mix. One syndicator of programs, Public Radio International (PRI; formerly American Public Radio), provides stations with shows including *A Prairie Home Companion*, the well-rounded business report *Marketplace*, a getaway guide called *The Savvy Traveler*, and a popular Canadian public-affairs show, *As It Happens*. Public Radio International also distributes *From the Top*, hosted by pianist Christopher O'Riley, featuring classical musicians from ages 9 to 19 who hold the promise of virtuoso careers. In that respect, PRI is a direct rival to NPR—which in 1997 briefly sought to merge with it.

Most stations mix such material with local programs that reflect local tastes. An example is in Louisville, Kentucky, where WFPL-FM was launched in 1950. As the first station anywhere to be owned by a public library, the station focused on culture and learning, in contrast with the formats of nearby commercial outlets. Besides its classical music, WPFL aired lectures, language lessons, and other educational material. Later, it became "your jazz and information station." Today, the station works in partnership with two others and with the University of Louisville, and its schedule looks typical of most: NPR programs all morning, local issues and music in the afternoon, and a partly local but largely national-programming menu on weekday evenings.[20]

A FOCUS ON PEOPLE

Much public-radio programming is aimed at well-educated audiences—but not all of it. A show called *A Prairie Home Companion* hit the air in 1974, concentrated on programming for the common people, and set a standard few programs could match: It became the most popular show in public-radio history. Host Garrison Keillor quit in exhaustion in 1987, ran the show from New York under a different title, then returned it to its birthplace of St. Paul, Minnesota, under its old name in 1993. The *Prairie* format ranges from music to comedy to Keillor's quirky, folksy tales of the imaginary town of Lake Wobegon. Other people-centered programs, such as the jokey auto advice show *Car Talk*, the quiz show *Wait Wait . . . Don't Tell Me!* and comic Michael Feldman's *Whad'ya Know?*, sprang up to engage wider audiences than music or public-affairs programs might have reached.

Garrison Keillor. Minnesota-based, he became a *Prairie Home Companion* to hordes of public-radio listeners, putting Lake Wobegon on the nation's mythic map.

An especially bright critical and popular success has been *This American Life*, a Chicago-based show born in 1995 and blossoming ever since. Its host, Ira Glass, addresses urban angst and other modern issues, using vivid language and sound, and its storytellers often combine the funny with the bittersweet. The show is one of many that have originated at local public-radio stations, often with the help of government or foundation grants. Some of these funds come from the Corporation for Public Broadcasting. More than many hosts heard nationwide, Glass has given voice to people who feel disadvantaged if not disenfranchised—like the people who depend on yet a different wing of noncommercial radio.

COMMUNITY RADIO

Public broadcasting primarily is practiced in towns and cities, not in Washington, DC; still, it's in the nation's capital that most of the big financial and political battles must be fought. That helps explain the orientation of the best-known NPR programming toward matters of interest to listeners in business, government, and the professions. Predictably, this fails to appeal to some members of racial minorities, to the poor, to certain political factions, to aggrieved immigrant groups, and to others who feel trapped on the fringes of a capitalist society.

Noncommercial radio long has given air time to such people's views, but in its earliest years only from small college-campus stations. A breakthrough came in 1949, when the Pacifica Foundation established KPFA in Berkeley, California, and opened the medium to new kinds of content. KPFA would become a megaphone for liberal-to-radical-left causes, giving airtime to communists, gays, and marijuana smokers in the fifties. In the sixties, as protest welled up around the Vietnam War, KPFA broadcast rallies and rhetoric, some of it coming close to inciting rebellion. The station styled itself (and still does) as a "community" station that never would lose touch with the common people. It rejected both advertising and government funding. Pacifica later added stations in Los Angeles, Houston, Washington, DC, and New York.

However, Pacifica has been torn by the money pressures that all noncommercial broadcasters face—exacerbated by Pacifica's left-leaning political history. Starting in the late 1990s, internal battles raged between anticorporate political

Some NPR-Distributed Programs

All Songs Considered (on-line only; music, text, pictures)

All Things Considered (afternoon news program)

Car Talk (car advice and humor)

The Connection ("street-smart conversations about events and ideas")

The Diane Rehm Show (public affairs and call-in program with news analysis)

Fresh Air with Terry Gross (interview/magazine of arts and issues)

Jazz from Lincoln Center (exclusive live concerts)

Latino USA (issues and events affecting Latino communities)

Living On Earth (in-depth news, features, and interviews on environmental issues)

Morning Edition (NPR's morning news program)

NPR Playhouse ("classic" and current radio dramas)

NPR World of Opera (performances by top opera companies)

Only A Game (weekly sports magazine show)

Performance Today (classical music with background notes and talk)

Public Interests (call-in show on politics, science, popular culture, and social issues)

Talk of the Nation (discussions of day's "most compelling" issues)

2000x (futuristic radio plays centered on third millennium)

Wait Wait . . . Don't Tell Me! ("fast-paced and irreverent" review of past week's news)

World Radio Network (English-language reports overnight from around the globe)

Source: Program listings at www.npr.org.

"progressives" and more pragmatic managers who disagreed sharply over issues, including how to raise money. A newspaper columnist in 2000 called the feud "a tedious, slow self-immolation that has involved firings, resignations, court intrigue, lost listenership and a protest of more than 10,000 people in Berkeley."[21] By 2002, the dissidents had taken charge of Pacifica and were charting a new future.

Other community stations found prominence in the sixties, propagating and thus, in a way, creating the music and speech of what antiwar youth called "the revolution." As that movement became more broadly antigovernment, it became more popular with its constituents. Pacifica stations pioneered "listener-sponsored" radio by calling for donations. Much later, noted singer-songwriter-activist John McCutcheon reminisced at his website about that yeasty period and its programming:

Ira Glass. Like many top shows on public radio, Glass's Chicago-centered *This American Life* started local, but its reputation for insight and vivid storytelling elicited national popularity.

> Then, sometime in the late 1960's, like commandos of the airwaves, young people started taking over the lowest regions of the FM dial. Public radio was born. It was Mozart and Muddy Waters, Newgrass and New Wave, Cajun and Coltrane. It was a radio revolution giving us what they called "alternative" music, news, information, and commentary. But, to me, it seemed like the whole picture.[22]

Today, the **National Federation of Community Broadcasters (NFCB)**, an umbrella group for community stations, advocates change in a radio landscape over which it claims great reach, with *rural* stations comprising 40 percent of its membership. Among other goals, many of these stations want relief from CPB funding rules. They charge that those rules force them to meet minimums of paid staffing, audience ratings, and other factors that make the stations behave too much like commercial operations.

> **Principle #7**
>
> As an activist, volunteer-oriented fringe of public broadcasting, community radio is a true alternative to commercial media.

A NEW PATH: LOW-POWER FM

Even community radio stations fall short of serving every constituency that would like—and believes it has a right—to participate in broadcasting. A thriving subculture of unlicensed (thus illegal) stations long ago emerged from coast to coast. They're called *microbroadcasters*, or, more commonly, *pirate* stations. These often are one-person enterprises using inexpensive, compact equipment and broadcasting furtively; exposure can bring arrest on federal charges. Their signals reach listeners within a radius of a few blocks or a mile or more, spanning neighborhood and small towns.

By no means do all of these pint-sized stations run on radical political principles. A *Village Voice* writer described microbroadcasters this way: "They range from Latin evangelicals and right-wing fanatics preaching conspiracies about the World Bank, to black liberationists, hippy treehuggers, techno ravers, and punk-rock anarchists—and even middle-American, mom-and-pop types broadcasting updates about the high school basketball team from town hall."[23] Most had not

National Federation of Community Broadcasters Umbrella advocacy group for community radio stations.

Low-power FM FM broadcasts of 50 to 100 watts and reaching from one to three miles.

Interference Disruption or dissonance caused when two radio signals overlap; FCC prohibits interference and penalizes violators.

even tried to get FCC licenses. The stations usually were poorly funded, in part because CPB could hardly be expected to channel federal funds to unlicensed operators.

For those who supported the tiny radio mavericks, however, the story has a happy ending. Microbroadcasters would become a new, legal FCC class called **low-power FM (LPFM)**—operating at 100 watts of power or less, compared with a minimum of 6,000 watts for commercial FM. In 2000, under then-chairman William Kennard, the FCC authorized licensing for low-power FM stations but would not grant licenses to anyone who had been operating as an illegal microbroadcaser. However, a U.S. Court of Appeals ruled that the ban violated the First Amendment. Commercial broadcasters also fought hard to defeat the plan and later persuaded Congress to scale it back, on grounds that the tiny stations would interfere electronically with existing stations. Even National Public Radio opposed low-power FM, saying its own broadcasts might also be endangered by electronic **interference,** the intrusion of signals from another frequency—although FCC engineers claimed such interference was unlikely.

National Public Radio also may have been concerned that microbroadcasters pushing legitimate civic causes, or programming inventively, would lure away many of its own local donors across the country. It was—and is—a legitimate concern for fans of the well-entrenched public-radio system that in fact has brought the nation much high-quality programming. However, the door had been opened: By May 2002, more than 3,000 applications for low-power FM licenses had arrived at the FCC, and about 10 stations were on the air.

INTO THE (DIGITAL) FUTURE

Public broadcasting has become one of the most closely investigated and extensively analyzed sectors of the modern mass media. Its mission, structure, and history have brought that about. Now in its ninth decade, public broadcasting as an altruistic enterprise sometimes soars but often displays the faltering movements of a newborn. Like the nation, it's an experiment, and its near and long-term future will be subject to some strong crosswinds.

Internet Approaches

Public broadcasting has been a technological pioneer—in satellite distribution of radio, for instance—and public TV and radio stations have pushed "webcasting" forward. A major reason is to stimulate interest in their programs among computer-addicted teenagers and young adults; they are among the least likely to check into conventional public broadcasting at all. New PBS president Pat Mitchell began making inroads into youthful indifference when she bought the reality-documentary series *American High* after it crashed on the Fox network. Rather than merely promoting and airing the program, Mitchell saw to it that youth-oriented websites began creating "buzz" about the show. It drew zealous youth audiences—as much as 150 percent larger than normal—after it went on the air in spring 2001. The normally calm PBS website reportedly topped

100,000 visits a week. Certainly, the nature and quality of *American High* accounted for much of the enthusiasm, but it was clear that synergy between on-air content and the on-line habits of teenagers did its work, as well.

In another experiment with cyberspace, public TV in early 2002 began airing *American Family*, a drama about a Latino clan in East Los Angeles. One of the characters, young Cisco Gonzales, kept an Internet journal on the Web, and—in a migration from fantasy to reality—the show's viewers could enter the site and read the diary for themselves. This convergence, which once might have seemed bizarre, captured a mood of media transition that was rippling throughout the popular culture of the nation. Even though one critic called it "a sentimentalized, idealized, sanitized soap opera," *American Family* had a fair chance of bringing new viewers to a branch of television with a white, middle-aged image.

The Public Broadcasting Service also was aggressively seeking reasons to use the Internet not only to support but also to complement broadcasting. The network claimed to be putting 135,000 pages of *program content*, not just promotional "cross-plugs," at its website, and to have set up companion sites for more than 450 TV shows. Public radio also was engaging Web users: National Public Radio acquired *Justice Talking*, a show that examined important court cases in front of a live audience, and made it the first public-radio program ever to have its premiere on the Internet. At the same time, many local public-radio stations already were operating websites as alternative receivers for radio listeners. With few people buying their way onto "broadband" paths that could carry clean, smooth video, the relative ease of Internet audio transmission put radio well ahead in that new medium.

Some of the greatest technical boons to public broadcasting probably still are in the future—possibly the near future. If the government lets all public broadcasters use extra digital channels indefinitely to run ads or for other purposes, the size, shape, and definition of programming could change along with the amount of incoming revenue. More revenue combined with new technology and (most important) ideas could open many doors. Of course, it also could change the *values and practices* of this noncommercial answer to the values and practices of for-profit broadcasters. In the meantime, there are many concerns to address.

General Concerns

There's no neat way to sort, divide, and categorize the potential problems that public broadcasting faces; they are too tightly interwoven and too dependent on the unknown. However, it's fair to predict that the toughest challenges ahead will be recognizable extensions of the past. As William Faulkner noted, the past isn't over; it isn't even past. Sure enough, several fundamental concerns loom ahead—just as they always have.

IDEALS

Some public broadcasters may be forced by economic and political pressures to admit—like alcoholics entering AA—that their lives have become unmanage-

Bob Edwards. The deep, steady voice of this anchor/interviewer has helped to make *Morning Edition* a clock-radio destination for public-broadcasting fans.

able. Certainly their mission is extraordinarily demanding. Over time, it may require a special breed of civic heroes.

There are signs that such people exist, people who would commit themselves to public broadcasting—perhaps as a challenge or, worse, a gamble—no matter what the odds. Even if Congress in 1967 had not ordered public broadcasters to hew selflessly to the public interest, some say they would have done so. It's not often that a person speaks openly and without apparent guile about having such noble impulses. It happens, though: With evident sincerity, *Morning Edition* host Bob Edwards told how he felt after visiting CBS News to discuss a possible job one day in 1975, just as the Vietnam War was ending in a Communist victory:

> I felt ashamed of myself. I should have been back in my own newsroom putting together a story on the fall of Saigon . . . with lots of time to review the history, lots of time for analysis, lots of time to capture the full impact of such an important story. . . .
>
> I returned to NPR a changed man. For the first I time realized what we had there. What we were doing was a lot more important journalistically than anything Walter Cronkite or anyone else was putting out.[24]

It did not seem to bother Edwards that his moral certainty could be interpreted as condescending toward commercial broadcasters; his focus was on a mission of public service. Some public broadcasters fear that focus is getting fuzzier. True, audiences still inhabit the cozy clubbiness of high ground, as when someone insists; "I watch only PBS." In more substantive terms, however, it can be hard to winnow out the public service qualities of some noted programs. *Car Talk*, for example, often is less an advice show than an extended comedy routine by its hosts. On the other hand, no one ever said public broadcasting must avoid entertaining its listeners.

PUBLIC NEEDS

Scholars and philosophers have argued for ages over just what a *public* is. Small wonder, then, that for public broadcasting, the notions of *public interest* and *public service* often have proved too soft-edged to define and visualize, much less bring to life or defend.

Clearly, public service is in play when broadcasters extend their gifts to poorer, weaker, or more ethnically diverse communities than typically are served by—or seen in, or heard in—commercial broadcasting. Some improvement has occurred: One study indicates that at least 12 to 15 percent of mainstream public-radio listeners regard themselves as "other than 'White/Caucasian.' "[25] As noted earlier, the most dramatic results occur when members of underserved communities practice public broadcasting themselves. This has happened—for example, in Anchorage, Alaska, where a comprehensive daily radio report called *National Native News* originates and is fed daily to 130 noncommercial U.S. stations. It also has happened for *Latino USA*, out of Austin, Texas, heard on more than 200 stations.

One interpretation of *public interest* would lean toward honoring that other core value we've noted, localism. That is not just a future concern but a present one. Some public-TV station managers complain that, although they are the ostensible masters of public broadcasting, their community priorities are muffled by top-down pressures on them to behave like commercial affiliates.

MONEY

Hope for success in fulfilling their mission hinges partly on how well public broadcasters resolve their money-and-power issues in the years ahead. They may not be *of* the world of commerce but they are undeniably *in* it—paying for buildings, electronic equipment, phone service, programs, and expertise at prices set by an aggressive commercial marketplace. That marketplace also is making it difficult for public television to guard its special realm: Cable-TV channels now run programs so much like the prize offerings of PBS and its stations that they are struggling to hold onto their audiences.

Car Talk. What can you say about a couple of Massachusetts mechanics and brothers who've made a call-in show about pings and pistons into a public-radio phenomenon? It's about family and fun.

Meanwhile, the availability of money to public broadcasters rises and falls, much as it does for commercial broadcasters. In the 2000 election period, Arbitron ratings for public radio rose just as ratings rose for commercial radio; that meant underwriters reached more listeners in the same way advertisers did. After the election, when the national advertising market softened, both donations to public broadcasting and the purchase of advertising time from commercial media went down. There seemed to be no way to beat that curve.

Beyond underwriting, an inability to make large, long-term audience gains makes it all the more important for public broadcasters to tap the viewers and listeners they already have. Research tells public radio that "programming causes audience," that "public service causes giving," and that news-public affairs listeners give the most money of all. NPR's *Morning Edition* and *All Things Considered* account for almost one-third of money donated by listeners.[26] So, local programs are shuffled and eliminated as stations try to mirror audience desires. Whether this will work before some stations are forced to thin their budgets and staffs further is in question.

The researchers also say that once plenty of listeners are in place, appeals to them must be efficient and effective. For some audiences, star power helps: When WEDU in Tampa broadcast a concert by Donny Osmond, the singer himself went on the air from the studio to seek pledges of support.[27] Viewers who pledged $250 apiece to Los Angeles station KCET heard their requests played by pianist Roger Williams.[28] For its part, PBS is pulling out all the quasi-commercial stops. It now employs an under-40 woman, Lesli Rotenberg, as

ProTalk

Margaret Drain
Executive Producer, American Experience
(PBS)

"These 'pledge period' things, they upset me. They're more linked with product placement than ever before—with merchandising."

Margaret Drain is a true believer, with a lot to believe in. As executive producer of *American Experience,* one of public television's most admired programs, she has reached a pinnacle of quality—a pinnacle she helped to build from the ground up.

"I went to *American Experience* [produced at Boston's WGBH-TV] in 1987," she says. "I helped put the show on the air. . . . There are very few opportunities to start a series from scratch. . . . There was a concept for the show, and we had to sell it to stations around the country. . . . It was conceived as an 'anthology' series that could cross time and geographic location and ethnic communities and gender. . . . We had some story ideas."

The central theme, though, was to be—drum roll—American history, a thin and scary thread to

some producers. "The reaction of my old colleagues at CBS was, 'History? On TV?,'" Drain recalls. "We started a little before the History Channel was hatching." At first, *American Experience* had few producers who knew how to do history, Drain says, and no one had thought of the presidential biographies that would become a staple in later years.

The program's inaugural year featured shows on the 1906 San Francisco earthquake, on Geronimo and the Apache "resistance," on rhythm 'n' blues music, and more. "I was surprised at how well we did in that first year," says Drain. "We got some terrific reviews." Ratings weren't as important; this was *noncommercial* broadcasting. Good stories from the past seemed to do well enough—unless they were overly controversial like, say, the history of abortion. "It's risky to get funding for shows like that," she notes.

Funding is fundamental. Fifteen years after its debut, in a new century, *American Experience* is going strong. More and more people enjoy watching history on television. Still, "the biggest problem we face is that we don't have enough money," says Drain. She helps to solicit money from foundations and to do coproductions with filmmakers and producers in other countries, a separate revenue source. Drain also knows she must popularize history to draw viewers and funding, but resists the naked marketing for which public TV has been criticized.

"These 'pledge period' things, they upset me. They're more linked with product placement ["tie-in" products] than ever before—with *merchandising.*" Such a comment doesn't suggest dissatisfaction, Drain adds: "I'm a total supporter of public broadcasting. It's getting more and more important to have a commercial-free environment."

If only it were just a little easier to pay the bills.

"senior vice president—brand management and promotion"; she is in charge of such ventures as plugging *American High* on websites favored by the young.[29]

GOVERNMENT

Although the federal government has long paid less than a quarter of public broadcasting's bills and recently has cut the percentage lower, it still clings to its right to oversee the service and sometimes to intervene. That's what it did during the Nixon years and threatened to do again when Ronald Reagan and then

George Bush held the presidency. Intervention from *state* government can afflict local and regional public broadcasters, as well. When Idaho Public Television aired a PBS-supplied documentary on children with gay and lesbian parents, outrage exploded among Republicans in the state legislature. Lawmakers required the public-TV network to air daily warnings that some acts depicted in its programs violated Idaho laws (including a ban on homosexuality—"sodomy").

Local and regional cultural issues can lead to such assaults, or threats of them, at any time; public broadcasting is especially vulnerable because of its dependence on government support. This situation shows no sign of abating. It's one reason that, again and again, friendly critics have urged that public broadcasting's finances be built and protected within a permanent trust fund of some sort. The second Carnegie Commission suggested a *trust fund* well insulated, if possible, from politics, as did a task force of the Twentieth Century Fund (now the Century Foundation) in 1992; activist Jerold Starr and his **Citizens for Independent Public Broadcasting,** an advocacy group trying to get corporate-donor influence out of the public media; the Gore Commission in 1998; and, in a 2001 book, ex-PBS-chief Lawrence Grossman and his coauthor, Newton N. Minow. (Yes, the same man who looked at commercial television more than 40 years ago and coined the term *vast wasteland.*) All advocate some form of financial security for public broadcasting.

Then, there are the listeners and viewers, who in occasionally waspish tones support the mission of public stations more fervently than anyone else does. When St. Louis's PBS station, KETC, decided against airing a political debate, a letter-writer to the *St. Louis Post-Dispatch* noted that the station did manage to find airtime for less important material. Acidly, he cited "the repeated broadcast of a year in the life of a badger or the broadcasts, re-broadcasts and re-re-broadcasts of lectures by New Age gurus." The *Post-Dispatch* itself took the issue

Citizens for Independent Public Broadcasting Activist group focused mainly on freeing public broadcasting from corporate money and influence.

CAREER FOCUS

Careers in public broadcasting probably appeal to some job-seekers at least as much as commercial broadcasting does. Fortunately, since the disciplines and technologies of broadcasting are fairly similar everywhere, public radio and TV require little special training. Only a few positions—largely at upper levels and involving fund-raising or external relations—are likely to differ much from commercial jobs. Unfortunately, however—because they run on contributions, not on a business model, and inhabit a smaller wing of the mass media—public-broadcasting stations tend to offer fewer and lower-paying jobs than do commercial media. Despite this, thousands of applicants each year try to enter public radio or television, hoping for careers or at least rewarding experiences. Some have studied in college broadcast-production programs and are ready for work upon graduation. They may already have entered public stations, as volunteers, interns, or part-time employees—a definite plus, but not a requirement.

Because public broadcasting's mission still includes its first purpose, education, it's a good fit with schools and universities that work it into their own curricula. For example, KECG-FM, owned by a school district in El Cerrito, California, broadcasts music and news while training high school students to enter the field. Its emphasis on multicultural programming not only fills a need in the San Francisco Bay Area radio market but,

importantly, encourages minority students to aspire to public-broadcasting jobs. At Northern Michigan University, broadcast students may work for WNMU-FM and WNMU-TV, both public-broadcasting stations.

Perhaps the most critical question for prospective public broadcasters is whether they are a good fit for this demanding arm of the electronic media. Many university-based stations offer good public-employee benefits. Mostly, though, the field features low pay, relatively scant public attention, decent job security (there is no ongoing flood of glamour-crazed applicants), and a chance to spread culture and sometimes give voice to neglected sectors of society. Bottom line: If that combination suits you, try it—but study it carefully first.

Jobs

Account executive	Production
Announcer/Producer	coordinator
Assistant manager	Program director
Development director	Promotions director
Maintenance	Reporter
technician	Sales manager
Managing producer	Secretarial assistant
News anchor	Station manager
News writer	Systems engineer
Producer	Weekend on-air

further, declaring editorially, "Political debates, whether highbrow, lowlife or sleep-inducing, are precisely the kind of programming that public television is created for."[30] The debates were heard on public radio, at least.

Summary

Public broadcasting has grown out of early experiments in education via radio, and has brought with it for eight decades that public-service mission. Nationally, local public stations "own" and—on paper—control the medium. Yet, recent economic stresses and political pressures have increased the chances that top-down, commercial-style management and distribution of programming will take over as public broadcasting defends its privileged territory.

The medium lives, meanwhile, with a growing mandate to welcome many voices to its work and programs as the United States becomes a more ethnically diverse country. That need and others will bring changes, which in turn will draw attention from federal overseers who complicate broadcasting even in a free society. Experts agree that continued noncommercial operation is the best if not only plan for the success of public broadcasting's mission. However, this has not ruled out experiments in marketing, promotion, and ratings-oriented programming in a heavily commercialized age.

FOOD FOR THOUGHT

1. Look up the word *public* in a dictionary and ask yourself (and some friends) if the definition you find rings true. How well does the term fit public broadcasting?
2. What are the qualities that seem to distinguish an hour of public television from an hour of commercial TV? How important are those differences, and why?
3. Why should government help to support broadcasting as it exists today? Can you organize a persuasive argument?
4. Does public broadcasting meet the objectives of the Carnegie Commission on Educational Television's 1967 report (http://www.current.org/pbpb/index.html)? In what ways does it succeed or fail in meeting them?
5. In your view, what would be a "perfect" program on public radio or public TV? (Remember that it must represent an *alternative* to commercial programming.)

13

The World

> Societies have always been shaped more by the nature of the media by which men communicate than by the content of the communication.
>
> —Marshall McLuhan, media scholar

Slobodan Milosevic. The Serbian strongman tried to silence a rebellious radio colony by taking over its station, repeatedly—but the station outlasted him.

Radio B92 might have turned out far differently. It was, after all, founded by young Yugoslav fans of rock music. However, they also were political dissidents. It was 1989, the year Slobodan Milosevic took power and began brutally imposing Serbian rule over the country's minorities. This was no time to sit back and broadcast dance tunes or wander idly into hip-hop. Radio B92 would pump out music, all right, but it also had more serious work on its playlist.

"The main goal was to criticize the regime," recalls founder Veran Matic."But we did it in a totally new manner, above all by . . . making fun of that dogmatic and conservative spirit which was spreading hate-speech and intolerance toward everything that was different from the imposed politics."

[Milosevic's] troops soon came, and came repeatedly, to arrest staffers and shut down B92.

The station sniped at Milosevic on the air and organized public events with a clear dissident touch. His troops soon came, and came repeatedly, to arrest staffers and shut down B92. In its place, the regime even briefly launched its own government-line station, trying to "sound like" B92—but without the dissent. Nothing worked. The independent station kept bouncing back, unrest grew, the world pressed in, and the "butcher of Bosnia" was hunted down and put on trial in an international court for hate crimes.

B92 is still on the air; it has more time for music now. It will stand in history as having helped to spawn an uprising that eventually pushed aside an internationally dangerous dictator—one of the more dramatic examples of broadcasting as politics.

A WORLD CONNECTED

Although they may seem vividly "American" to many of us, electronic media are international in origin and impact. As scholar James Carey has pointed out, the French were the first to use a preelectric telegraph—in the eighteenth century, just as the United States was coming into existence.[1] As noted earlier in this text, an Italian, Guglielmo Marconi, would pioneer "wireless" communication— radio. In Canada, the Marconi Company's XWA (later CFCF Montreal), hit the air after World War I. Russian Vladimir Zworykin and Briton John Logie Baird (with American Philo Farnsworth) made breakthroughs to television. More recently, it was Tim Berners-Lee, a British-born inventor working in Switzerland, who gave birth to the World Wide Web.

The role of any medium is interwoven with the customs, values, and economic-political history of the people using and operating it. What's more, there are sharp differences between rich and poor countries in their ability simply to *afford* electronic media. Expressed in millions of U.S. dollars, for example, the money required to set up and run just one television station for a substantial audience puts it virtually beyond reach for many nations. Nor are skilled broadcast or computer personnel available everywhere. Today, however, electronic messages of all sorts criss-cross continents and oceans. In so doing, they express and may even be blending human communities that only recently seemed literally worlds apart.

> **Principle #1**
>
> Electronic media can transmit across borders and thus are inherently international.

Radio

An American living atop a mountain or driving through a desert can use a short-wave radio to pick up the programming of stations overseas. It's even easier for people with Internet access to hear overseas broadcasts through their stations' websites. International demand never seems to slack off; people think of radio as basic and, in some places, essential. Nearly every country in the world has many radio stations, with good reason: There are at least 2.5 billion radio sets in use around the planet—about one-third of them in the United States (and still more in Asia).[2] This gives radio the greatest "penetration" into households and communities of any mass medium.

A SPECTRUM OF PURPOSES

Advanced industrialized nations—including the United States—transmit programming to huge sections of the globe, often through special international services. A growing array of radio programs travels by satellite from cities everywhere to listeners everywhere else. For example, just one source, Radio France Inter-

ProTalk

Veran Matic
Radio B92, Belgrade

"Often the people stated that our radio was the only reason for them to stay in the country."

As chief editor of Belgrade's most celebrated radio station, Veran Matic has seen much excitement—sometimes a bit *too* much, perhaps. Here, he recalls some of the tactics that the free-speech movement, represented by Radio B92, and the repressive regime of Slobodan Milosevic used against each other:

"The most popular method that the regime was using against us was electronic jamming of our programs. When that failed, they would simply turn off our transmitters. In December 1996, during mass anti-regime protests [by] the citizens, they turned off our transmitter . . . On that occasion, even Cathy Morton, the president of CPJ [Committee to Protect Journal-

ists] back then . . . came all the way from New York to Belgrade to express her protest personally to Milosevic.

"Milosevic gave an extensive explanation, using numerous technical terms, about 'the water leakage within our cable system' which caused the disruption of our radio transmitter. Many jokes and funny stories were made about that [on the air] afterwards, and technical description of program disruption was used upon every action that the regime took against the independent media. Of course, lots of journalists and editors were receiving threatening warnings; some of them were even physically attacked. We were faced with the classic methodology of police work in totalitarian regimes.

"We put on the air many 'silly' clips. Our listeners expected something like that from us . . . In addition, we made so-called serious shows as well, which can be considered mere travesty. For instance, in 1992, we changed the whole program agenda during a single evening, along with the style and manner of speaking, so that it seemed as though the ruling party took over the radio station. We intended to continue with this for the whole 24 hours, but we were forced to stop as the listeners started smashing their radios in anxiety. . . .

"Radio was extremely important primarily for persevering . . . for the common sense of the most of the people. Often, the people stated that our radio was the only reason for them to stay in the country. People . . . easily identified with our radio, and we have often been under [the] impression that we became part of the family. That fact imposes a higher level of responsibility for every single word that we put on the air."

nationale (RFI), beams programs in many languages to Africa, India, and the Middle East and also reaches the United States via cable radio.

Some countries where broadcasters were under severe restrictions until a decade ago are reaching out. In former territories and "client" states of the communist Soviet Union, pent-up urges to broadcast have been exploding onto the airwaves. The Republic of Belarus, formerly part of the Soviet Union itself—and hardly a Western household name—now sends its programs to much of Europe and to North America. Just as in the United States, some radio stations abroad are commercial, working to win listeners who will buy advertisers' products. Young people often are the primary targets. In Norway, Radio 1 has drawn youthful audiences with what U.S. programmers call the "hot adult contemporary" music genre. In Bangladesh, Radio Metrowave attracts younger people by sponsoring rock concerts.

Radio Martí. For two decades, this U.S.-government-funded radio operation has beamed anti-Castro messages into Cuba, an overt use of an electronic medium for political ends.

Even though U.S.-style mainstream radio is broadly popular, many stations choose to pursue unique "niche" approaches, some based on geography and ethnicity. In the Hungarian capital city of Budapest, for instance, Radio C had to struggle to find start-up money. It has a social mission: To be the world's first radio outlet aimed at the Roma people—often called Gypsies, an ancient ethnic group—who comprise Hungary's largest minority. Meanwhile, Radio Terunajaya is the sole broadcaster in a poor, hilly district on the south coast of Java in Indonesia. The privately owned station broadcasts folktales and modern music originating in that region and also allows listeners to send urgent messages to neighboring villages; there's little doubt that someone they're targeting is tuned in.[3]

POLITICAL GOALS

Radio in many countries is still sponsored and, sometimes, constrained by national leaders. Some governments run their own stations and networks and reach out to other countries for public-relations or diplomatic reasons. Elsewhere, hybrid public-private corporations operate quite freely with only general instructions from government. Radio Canada International broadcasts continuously in seven languages, supplementing radio with a daily "cyberjournal" for Internet users worldwide. From Britain, the famed British Broadcasting Corporation (BBC, informally "the Beeb") sends its World Service broadcasts to 60 countries via satellite, providing news and cultural information in 35 languages.

The U.S. government supports and directs several kinds of international radio programming. Most notable are three services whose overall goals are distinctly political:

> ### Principle #2
> Electronic media internationally attract both government support and government controls.

Radio Free Europe/Radio Liberty (RFE/RL) A semiprivate, government-funded broadcast news service that carries U.S.-oriented news and information into other countries.

Radio Martí Organization created by Congress to transmit radio news into Cuba despite its limits on freedom of information.

1. **RFE/RL (Radio Free Europe/Radio Liberty)** is a news service founded privately in the early 1950s to broadcast news into Soviet-controlled countries where media had been silenced. RFE/RL now is government-financed and is a broadly useful U.S. policy tool. Its president, launching an Afghan radio service in 2002, promised "accurate, objective and comprehensive news and analysis about local developments" in Afghans' majority languages, Dari and Pashto.[4] Its funding, however, came from the U.S. "war on terrorism" following the September 2001 attacks on New York and the Pentagon, so its commitment to objectivity might prove tenuous.

2. **Radio Martí** was created by Congress in 1983 to beam radio news into Cuba in defiance of Fidel Castro's controls on Cuban media. In its two decades as an American tool to promote anti-Castro sentiment among Cubans, this service has provoked criticism that it's mismanaged and circulates biased news; consequently, its listenership has plunged. President George W. Bush has backed Radio Martí, which costs about $25 million an-

nually to run. The Cuban government answers with its own international radio broadcasts in nine languages, plus a website in four.

3. **Voice of America** is a radio-TV-Internet service transmitting what it calls "a balanced and comprehensive projection of significant American thought and institutions"[5] to an audience of 91 million worldwide in 53 languages. Voice of America is government funded and also filters U.S. policy through news and entertainment programs. Established on radio during World War II, the service has spent decades building a close-to-neutral journalistic reputation; it has a staff of 1,200 and a $147 million budget. However, it has been prone to political interference. In late 2001, Congress moved to keep the service from broadcasting interviews with officials of terrorism-linked nations. Voice of America's director said it would keep doing appropriate interviews to maintain balance in the news.

Pure government entities such as VOA are not the only model under which political ideas are broadcast internationally. Hybrid public-private systems have developed around the world, especially in nations accustomed to strong central control. In Estonia, for example, Radio Tallinn must depend on government support and has been seeking more funding to expand its Internet programming; its health as a broadcaster has become a national issue.

Conversely, there is a place in history for *anti*government broadcasting. During World War II, broadcasting systems in Europe became virtual captives of Hitler's occupying forces, which used radio to assert domination. The "resistance" in that war used radio to send demoralizing messages into each other's military camps. Most important to citizens of the occupied lands, clandestine radio stations kept them apprised of the war's true progress and alerted them to threatening troop movements. Meanwhile, anti-German broadcasts from abroad easily passed into the nation's airwaves, building grass-roots resistance to Hitler.

Television

At least 1.4 billion TV sets were in use worldwide by 2001[6]—almost one set for every four people. That may seem amazing, considering the size, diversity, and uneven access to resources of all the world's cultures. An appetite for on-screen entertainment in the home now seems common to them. However, one's access to television has a lot to do with where one lives.

GAINING ACCESS

Although by 1995 homes in ultramodern Japan had more TV sets than flush toilets,[7] there also are places where a quiet evening before the "tube" is an unattainable luxury. As of 2001, Pakistan had about 135 million people—equal to nearly half the U.S. population—but fewer than 3 million TV sets, or less than 1 for every 45 people. In Africa in the late 1990s, the figure was about 60 sets per 1,000 people. (By the end of the century, perhaps 99 percent of all U.S. homes had at least one TV set.) Poverty, distance, and cost all are factors. Perhaps surprisingly to many Americans, large regions of the world, including much of South Asia, do not yet have home electricity, which often precedes electronic media access.

Voice of America Radio-TV-Internet network under U.S. government control that attempts to send objective news reports to other countries but sometimes suffers political interference.

Overseas TV Viewers.
While 99 percent of U.S. homes have television, access to it abroad varies wildly, and it's still a rare luxury in much of the developing world.

NHK Japan's quasigovernmental broadcast company, run by governors approved by the nation's parliament; like Britain's BBC, NHK is funded primarily by license fees paid by TV viewers.

EuroNews International satellite-TV news channel broadcasting in numerous languages.

By contrast, some countries have been generating television as long as, or longer than, the United States has. The United States initiated programming in 1939—three years after the British. Postwar France adopted it in 1948, and half a dozen Latin American and European nations had TV by 1951—about the time American television was establishing its first national icons on the air. Early programming in most lands conformed to their own societies' tastes (and their governments' wishes), just as the brisk Westerns, hard-bitten "teleplays," and mild white-collar comedies of the 1950s conformed to our tastes. However, most of Asia had no access to television at all until the 1960s.

One huge Asian country, India, showed how politics could delay even history's most widely sought-after leisure technology. After the English pulled out at mid-twentieth-century, the country's post-colonial leaders frowned on TV as a time-waster for a newly independent nation, so the medium stayed black and white until the early 1980s.[8] Since then, however, with the help of a vigorous domestic film industry, Indian TV has become rich and colorful. About 140 other nations also have their own television systems.

WHAT TV CAN DO

Programming internationally ranges far beyond the forgettable entertainment that Americans experience nightly—not that there isn't plenty of frivolous programming on every continent. Countries originate TV newscasts and nonfiction programming that suit their own purposes, including the need to promote tourism and prepare their citizens for greater global interchange. Turkish viewers can see not only their indigenous programming but also Turkish newscasts in several languages. In Japan, the ubiquitous **NHK** network has aired programs in English since 1925 and currently in seven other tongues, as well.

Like other mass media, television occasionally forces a wedge into a tight political situation. This happened in 2001, when **EuroNews**—a European satellite-news service—gained permission to send programming into Russia. It was the first time a Western media outlet had won the right to serve Russians through their own network. At last they would have the chance to hear outside perspectives on their country's affairs. In return, President Vladimir Putin agreed to supply Russian programming to the all-news channel.

Some television operations abroad, especially in Britain and Australia, produce first-rank entertainment of general appeal that is exported, as is, to the United States. Similarly, European networks turn out fine programs that need only translation into major languages to attract large audiences abroad. It's U.S. programming, however, that packs the greatest marketing punch worldwide. European channels sign deals to bring American sports to eager new audiences. Some countries acquire U.S. network newscasts because of their exotic appeal, wide-ranging content, and relative savings compared to originating newscasts. Hollywood movies, of course, are the hottest TV import in many lands.

There also is a healthy traffic in "borrowed" ideas. European formats (*The Weakest Link* and *Who Wants to Be a Millionaire?*) have been popular among copycat U.S. producers who adapt them for American audiences. The British put *Robot Wars* on the air in the late 1990s and made it a hit in Sweden, Italy, and Germany. Then the National Network (TNN) brought the humans-and-fighting-terror-machines spectacle to U.S. viewers, calling it *Robot Wars: Extreme Warriors.* The National Network tapes the show with American performers and the same independent producer who created it for the British. Meanwhile, the United States has been rather quietly supplying a familiar channel to consumers around the planet: Its Home Shopping Network (HSN) proclaims itself "the world's most distributed television retailer, with services in eight languages reaching 155 million homes globally."[9]

NHK (Japan) Program. Government-run and viewer-financed, giant NHK covers Japan with news and entertainment, broadcasting in English and seven other languages.

Internet

Of all international electronic media, perhaps the hardest to encircle with a clear definition—or with limits of any kind—is the Internet. It knows no borders and, being digital, can move its cargo in a variety of ways from user to user via satellite, telephone wires, fiber-optic cable, new wireless technologies, and more. In its purest sense, it's utterly anarchic; nobody's in charge. It's the product and fiefdom of its individual contributors, moment to moment.

At its simplest level, the Internet is a messaging service; an estimated 610 billion e-mail messages are sent every year.[10] However, even e-mail can carry informative or entertaining content from one person to many. At higher levels of complexity, the Internet already carries radio and TV programming from Iran, Lebanon, China, and other countries to still other countries through sites on the World Wide Web. Europe is constructing a fiber-optic system that will carry the Internet and many other types of electronic media across many borders. It's part of the world's projected—and to some extent already realized—information superhighway.

With complex interactivity—connections permitting interaction with electronic systems—users from around the world can sign onto computer games and play them simultaneously with others. The success of games already has helped make *gambling* an Internet sport; a tiny British island community has raked in money by selling licenses for a "virtual casino" to entrepreneurs from Europe to Australia to Las Vegas.[11] On another front, a man named Jay Cohen in 1996 launched an operation on the Caribbean island of Antigua—where gambling is legal—that encouraged Americans to bet on sports over the Internet. The U.S. government charged him with a crime under an old telephone-based law.

Digital divide Gap between people who have computer and Internet access and those who do not; used to describe both domestic and international rich-poor divisions.

AOL Time Warner Giant corporation formed by merger of America Online (AOL), largely an Internet company, and Time Warner, a diversified media company with movie, TV, and publishing interests.

Cultural imperialism Term applied mainly to U.S. domination of global media production, resulting in (real or threatened) spread of consumerism and other American values and practices to vulnerable societies elsewhere.

Cohen was convicted; he appealed—and lost in 2001.[12] Clearly, the Internet has been making international waves.

For ordinary users, the simple act of "surfing" the Internet for surprises, or pursuing flimsy leads toward some fascinating and elusive bit of information, is entertainment enough—so far. Unfortunately, most of the world's citizens can't indulge even in these simple pleasures, because of a vexing problem: They currently have little or no access to computers. The gap between larger masses of cyber-challenged people and the relatively few who do have on-line access has been termed the **digital divide.** This ephemeral boundary runs along the immense plains, deserts, and mountain ranges that separate one city and its electronic technologies from the next. It also distinguishes the world's urban upper classes from the urban poor, and poor countries from rich ones.

At least half of U.S. households are connected to the Internet, but many countries lag well behind that. For example, by one account, 80 percent of the information about Africa is generated *outside* Africa; but by 1995, only about one of every four countries on the continent had the Internet access they needed to reach much of that information.[13] Lack of money was the dominant reason. Meanwhile, communications giant **AOL Time Warner** asserts that unfettered commercial media can close the digital divide by themselves: The company says it's working toward "privatization and liberalization of national telecommunications and communications marketplaces, so the Internet is affordable for the greatest number of people."[14]

In the face of what some fear is **cultural imperialism** perpetrated by rich countries through their media products—that is, an imposition of Western tastes and ideas on other cultures—this sort of lack of access to broad information sources poses a serious threat of global disparity. In sum, then, the Internet is a potential smash as an international mass medium, already pleasing a rapidly growing user community; yet millions remain out in the cold.

> **Principle #3**
>
> Cultural imperialism and the "digital divide" are built-in issues for international electronic media.

AUTHORITY OVER MEDIA

Nowhere on earth, not even in the freedom-loving United States of America, are electronic media permitted to operate entirely and exactly as they wish. Usually, government gets in the way. In colonial America—long before the arrival of electronic media—mobs angered by news or agitated by politicians sometimes wanted to shut down printing presses. On more than one occasion, Benjamin Franklin's grandson, Benjamin Franklin Bache, felt the politicians' fury over something he had printed about the day's events. This is how it has been in the rest of the world, too; governments in particular have complicated life for media producers even in the age of international broadcasting and the Internet.

Forms of Governance

Besides holding a stick, political authorities often hold the carrot necessary to the success of electronic media. It is public agencies that can launch and support sta-

ProTalk

María Paz Epelman
Communications Manager, VTR GlobalCom, Chile

"You open the newspapers every day and you don't know what you'll see there . . . we try cable TV, telephony, Internet—through the same connection."

It seems inadequate to apply the word *challenge* to a task that Maria Paz Epelman has faced: to get the Playboy Channel onto the daily viewing menu in a staunchly Catholic country in Latin America. "You don't have the media on your side, you don't have the Church on your side," says Epelman. "The Church and the government are not going to take risks. But the population is more neutral—not so conservative."

The people—the prospective customers—were Epelman's compatriots as well as her business targets. She's communications manager for VTR Global-Com, S.A.—the Chilean arm of United Global Com,

a telecommunications company operating in 26 countries.

However eager some of her compatriots were to view American sex kittens via satellite, important members of the Chilean establishment had their doubts. So Epelman, a journalist turned corporate spokesperson, made speeches and used her knowledge of the news industry to try to separate "skin" from "sin." "The way we did it in the press helped us to introduce [the Playboy Channel] very smoothly," she says. "After that, when anybody was against it, there was an explosion in the press, pictures of Playmates in the paper. It was very funny. Our sales went crazy."

Chilean individualism worked in her company's favor: "Lots of people bought that programming not really for viewing it. They did it as something symbolic, in the same way that people who choose VTR [for general TV service] choose it because they don't want to be censored."

Cultural tensions have not kept Chile from attracting a large and competitive set of foreign-based media companies over the past decade. This long, slender nation on South America's Pacific Coast had a closed economy under former military ruler Augusto Pinochet. But since a civilian government replaced him in 1990, the country has welcomed more outsiders.

United Global Com, based in Denver, Colorado, acquired VTR and with it Chile's largest cable-TV system, providing digital and telephone services, as well. It claims 60 percent of the cable-TV market nationwide and 40 percent of subscribers in the largest city, Santiago. Its customers can choose from 45 to 50 "basic" channels and 5 "premium" channels—Playboy among them.

tions and networks. Governments always like to keep their hands near the media power levers; even when they don't repress, they regulate. One scholar has identified three rationales for regulation: *technical*, under which government controls use of frequencies to prevent chaos on the airwaves; *monopoly*, which assumes that dominant media left unregulated would provide poor programming at high prices; and *political*, which holds media accountable to certain standards that range from venal to virtuous, depending on the government in charge.[15]

Coup d'etat Sudden political action, usually resulting in change of government by force.

AUTHORITARIAN RULE

The power to broadcast is often seen by *authoritarian* leaders—who place the power of the state above individual freedoms—as central to their control of citizens. Usually, in a ***coup d'etat*** attempt (an effort to overthrow authorities), both

Paternalistic Fatherlike—in both the good and the stern sense—in dealing with people, groups, or nations; some governments tend to behave paternalistically toward business.

rebels and government rush to occupy the broadcast stations, pushing journalists aside to reach the microphones. Fierce skirmishes often result, as in Romania and Lithuania when the Soviet Union was collapsing.

In a "pure" authoritarian regime, media have no independent power to begin with; the government owns and tightly manages the broadcast stations (while keeping newspapers on a short leash, too). Again, such controls flow organically from the political situation of the times, and certain times seem to last far longer than others. The communist revolutionary Fidel Castro took over Cuba in 1959 and now, in his 70s, remains in charge. After more than 40 years of Soviet-style rule, some Cubans' frustration with news controls has led to an Internet "underground." Although computer access is limited to a favored few, 100 independent journalists or more manage to file antigovernment "news" with overseas websites. The government knows of this illegal journalism and harasses the independent journalists, but tolerates them.[16]

> **Principle #4**
>
> Authoritarian governments always gravitate toward control of electronic media.

Apartheid Racially based political system in which white rulers of South Africa discriminated against black citizens in most aspects of life; this included forcing them into all-black "homelands."

This sort of tension between government domination and breakaway broadcast media—usually led by one station—is often part of the unofficial political calculus in authoritarian countries. In some, such as sub-Saharan Africa's fragile nations, governments hold only tenuous power. Perhaps in compensation, they tend to crack down when broadcasters get out of line (rarely, as a rule) in order to restrict citizens' access to "destabilizing" ideas. One of the more severe examples is North Korea. With just a handful of domestic channels operating, the politically isolated country's 21 million people are forbidden by their government to watch foreign TV. Next door in South Korea, by contrast, nearly all homes have television sets and people use electronic media avidly. Westward across Asia, the Taliban sect of ultraconservative Muslims that once ruled Afghanistan was burning television sets in the streets in 2001—until U.S.-aided Afghan rebels drove the clerics from power.

Only the least fortunate societies live under such iron-fisted rule, of course; government pressure on free speech and media in democracies is usually subtle. Since the disintegration of Soviet communism, which had created authoritarian regimes on several continents, many nations have edged toward "western" models. For them, broadcasting and the Internet is used not merely to wage political warfare but also to develop well-rounded entertainment and information programs and content.

MODERATE RULE

Many nonauthoritarian countries tend to have **paternalistic** policies—applying stern controls to the media while supporting their growth. Radio and television can spend less time battling repression and more time providing news and entertainment. An example of such progress is South Africa, a predominantly black nation once run by a white minority. In 2001, one popular TV entertainment show was *Madam and Eve*, in which Madam was a wealthy white woman and Eve her black maid. Their struggle to shed old prejudices and inhibitions in order to get along together seemed to help South African viewers work through their own post-**apartheid** (white-run discrimination) anxieties. The program

"An Arrow in the Dark"

After the September 2001 terrorist attacks, Americans learned much about the harsh world of the Taliban. The Muslim sect that then ruled Afghanistan routinely beat women in the streets and denied them the right to go to school, and forbade everyone from listening to music. It was almost enough to make an outsider forget that some governments try only to keep dissenting political ideas away from their people. Soon enough, a reminder came from another nation: Iran.

Six weeks after the World Trade Center toppled—with countless TV cameras trained on it—the *Iran News* reported a government raid on citizens' satellite dishes. Iranian police confiscated about 1,000 dishes in 48 hours, with most people giving them up quietly. The radical Islamic regime explained the move as a way of heading off "bankrupt elements abroad" that were plotting to use TV to mount a political challenge in Iran.

This wasn't new; the country once run by Persian royalty had outlawed the use of satellite dishes in the 1990s. However, they generally were tolerated after the election of reform-minded President Seyed Mohammad Khatami in 1997. Now, however, the international journalism group *Reporters Sans Frontieres (RSF)* protested that some 7,000 dishes had been confiscated since March 2001, and that "satellite dishes are, along with radios, one of the rare means for Iranians to have access to foreign information." That, of course, seemed to be the point. The RSF said that most Iranians routinely hide their dishes under tarps or in air conditioning units.

One government official spoke out against the confiscations. "It does not make sense in this day and age (2001) to block information, because ultimately citizens, using various means and methods, will gain access to the information they seek," said Mohammad Reza Saidee, a parliament deputy from Tehran. "Trying to negate information is like shooting an arrow in the dark." Predictably, Iran's government hadn't switched off the power to its own satellite broadcasters, who stuck to their global schedule. It included shows with such promising titles as *Khomeini Epic, Good Morning Compatriot,* and *Love's Dregs.*

Sources: "Iran Crackdown," *Global News Wire,* 1 February 2002; "Iran: Hardliners Target Internet, Satellite Dishes," *Inter Press Service,* 27 December 2001; Islamic Republic of Iran Broadcasting (www.irib.com).

would have been suppressed less than a decade earlier, when the country's old political system still was in place.[17]

Apartheid had other effects on broadcasting, at least one of them memorably bizarre. The government-controlled South African Broadcasting Corporation aired newscasts in English, Afrikaans (the unique tongue of the country's white Dutch settlers), and the indigenous (native) languages Xhosa and Zulu. However, the few black anchors who were permitted to deliver news in English and Afrikaans reportedly had to do so utterly free of "black" accents, to avoid offending white viewers. Even in this subtle way, the media were forced to acknowledge publicly who was in charge of the country.[18]

LAISSEZ-FAIRE RULE

A number of economically advanced countries have *laissez-faire* governance, which entails neither sponsoring media nor getting in their way at every turn. The media in these countries usually are run as private concerns and have a large mea-

Laissez-faire Noninterference in the affairs of others; in governance, tolerance of autonomous action by citizens or organizations.

sure of freedom in what they transmit. This approach prevails in the United States, where business goals generally hold sway. Political appointees to the Federal Communications Commission (FCC) have power to thwart broadcasters' moves—to buy up competitors, for example—but in recent years have tended to facilitate and even encourage them. While Congress could pass restrictive laws, it must work within the bounds of the media-shielding First Amendment to the Constitution; anyway, lawmakers depend on broadcasting to transmit their campaign messages.

Still, even progressive countries find they must impose some rules: U.S. law prohibits the broadcast of material that is judged to be obscene, for example. Yet, in every country with multiple stations there's a traffic-directing function for the government, since broadcast signals occupy the publicly "owned" airwaves and can interfere with one another. This has led to regulation, including licenses that specify the conditions under which radio and TV stations may operate. Licenses usually do not set very specific limits or requirements on programming content, instead obligating broadcasters to honor general principles such as "the public interest." Indeed, truly daring adventures rarely happen in commercial radio and television, because broadcasters want most to keep operating without interference; it's a basic urge that mainly reflects economic interests.

> **Principle #5**
>
> Even *laissez-faire* systems need some controls to keep electronic media working smoothly.

Economic Factors

Broadcasting, especially television broadcasting, is expensive everywhere. Even the basic technical tools are beyond the financial reach of most people. That's a double burden on those who would own and operate electronic media: They must acquire money constantly, and they often must do so by complying with—or at least not openly defying—the wishes of their country's political leaders.

Government Funding

In the United States, most broadcasters meet expenses and make profits by charging advertisers money for using the airwaves to push their products. However, lightly regulated commercial broadcasting is but one economic model. Another, generally known as *public service* broadcasting, draws substantial funding (and, with it, close scrutiny) from the government.

When governments demand total control of their country's media—which have the built-in power to reach and possibly arouse the "masses"—the most direct approach is to run them. A government that wants to *be* a broadcaster can use a routine tax or whatever other revenues it has to underwrite the costs. Iraq, a former monarchy that gave way to a dictatorship, is an example of this. Half a century before military ruler Saddam Hussein challenged the western powers, Iraq's king launched a national radio station. The revolution that overthrew the royalty in the 1950s expanded radio and launched television—supported by funds from the Soviet Union. The government used broadcasting mainly to transmit messages and to reinforce cultural, religious, and political norms that would strengthen the regime's hold on power. Later, Saddam Hussein poured oil money into the purchase of powerful transmitters to give Iraq a louder radio voice in the Middle East. Most of its programming remained political in nature and thus of little appeal beyond the Iraqi people. Still, today, Saddam retains control of both radio and television as government-run propaganda tools.[19]

MIXED MONEY SOURCES

Broadcast economics around the world is a patchwork quilt, varying from one country to the next. Government often seeks both to influence and to support the growth of broadcasting by **subsidizing**—contributing money to—private companies. Then, often, the companies may sell advertising to gain other revenues. With government blessings, they also may charge citizens license fees on their home receivers. Japan's vast NHK network subsists on such fees; it's a public-service network like the BBC, barred from amassing profits.

Different forces are at work in every country, however. Consider, for example, Argentina. When TV arrived in the 1950s, three private channels tried to do business in a country which, in one researcher's words, has had "a jagged history of military intervention and populist dictatorship."[20] Dictator Juan Perón **nationalized** broadcast outlets in the 1970s (turned them into government property) and then they were **privatized** again in the 1980s (returned to private hands). Since then, aided greatly by U.S. and other foreign investors, Argentine

Saddam Hussein.

Different—And Yet . . .

Britain's approach to financing broadcasting is a function of its political and economic history. The famous BBC (British Broadcasting Corporation) was set up in 1922 as a cooperative within the radio industry, which already was growing through commercial means. It was the *government,* however, that pressured private companies to accept the BBC in their midst; it was the government that permitted it to thrive on license fees paid by radio-set owners. The BBC (affectionately called "the Beeb") thus became a sort of public monopoly with a clear, officially sanctioned edge over its commercial rivals.[21] This approach spread across Western Europe, tying the fortunes of broadcasters to license fees.

More recently, the BBC has strayed from its roots as a noncommercial public-service entity that draws sustenance directly from the people. Like U.S. public broadcasters, it has suffered mushrooming costs, increasing competition, and limits on its chief revenue source (license fees). The result is that the Beeb is selling more and more of its programs and many "tie-in" products on the international market in an effort to create a wide and reliable income stream. This is controversial among many BBC fans and employees who have resisted commercial infiltration, but the British government has acquiesced and leading politicians support the Beeb's new strategy. It includes alliances with foreign broadcasters and draws on commercial tools; in the United States, for example, the cable/satellite service known as BBC America carries advertising.[22] In January 2002—to the chagrin of traditionalists—the BBC announced the creation of its second commercial-TV division.

Subsidizing Financially assisting persons or organizations; for example, governments sometimes subsidize needy farmers to help them keep producing food, or subsidize broadcasters to help them stay on the air.

Nationalize To convert private property (often companies or industries) to government or public property.

Privatize To convert public property to private property, as when a state or school system turns over some of its responsibilities to private business.

Unification The uniting of different forces or groups; a number of European countries have moved toward unification by agreeing to use a common currency.

TV and radio have expanded and grown affluent on advertising dollars—but remain politically cautious.

In France, as in other European countries, advertising does not bear the full financing burden. The information ministry subsidizes broadcasters, providing part of their income while at the same time practicing paternalism by controlling their programming and limiting their competition from foreign broadcasters.[23] Many other nations grant economic protection to their broadcasters. This helps domestic operators monopolize the advertising marketplace. European **unification** moves—lowering economic barriers among generally friendly countries—plus international media mergers since the fall of communism have helped to expand consumer markets and boost expenditures on advertising. Robust demand for products and services can feed enough money into a radio or TV system to reduce its reliance on government funds.

The world broadcasting map shows both progress and stagnation. Most of Western Europe has pushed privatization in recent years as Europe's unification advanced. The trend extended to postcommunist countries: Hungary began privatizing broadcasting in 1995 and now has nine commercial TV stations that run advertising. However, Estonia, another of the old Soviet-bloc nations, has taken steps recently to *halt* its movement toward a commercial broadcast norm. Estonian radio and TV systems will have to wait until after 2005 to carry advertising, except when they win the rights to air international programming that *obligates* them to carry ads.

Croatia, part of the former Yugoslavia, is still tense over its region's future, and has yet to set broadcasting free. State-owned broadcasting does accept advertising and does acquire satellite-fed programs from other countries. The operating key is that Croatia's three TV channels have a 95 percent market share in their country—that is, they command 95 percent of the viewership and the ad market.[24] A country that so effectively discourages foreign competition can avoid taking the controversial step of banning it.

GLOBAL REACH

When astronaut Neil Armstrong walked on the moon in July 1969, 600 million others watched on earth via live television. They could do so because a huge satellite dish had been placed in a small Australian town named Parkes. Pictures and sound sent by *Apollo 11* were bounced from that dish to other, smaller dishes that pulled the signals into TV networks everywhere. The moon walk was new then, but this technology wasn't. The United States had launched its first communications satellite nine years earlier. Live TV pictures from the United States were reaching England via satellite by 1962. So, by the sixties, television had become extensively international, spanning oceans with live signals sent into space and relayed back to the home planet.

Decades later, humans work in space stations, and thousands of satellites have been launched, many for communications use. Media companies increasingly are leaping across continents, racing one another to connect the right services to the right populations and maximize their profits.

Global Dollars

Beyond selling programs, the new global companies are investing in many nations' media and sometimes are acquiring them. This helps less developed countries, giving them quicker access to the modern media cornucopia than they might have enjoyed otherwise. Of course, it also guarantees that many of the proceeds from broadcasting in such countries will profit capitalists *elsewhere*.

CORPORATE POWERS

While hundreds of thousands of people work in global media corporations, the progress of the privately owned media is most clearly understood by tracking the moves of a few leaders. These are men who spotted immense business opportunities and were in position to act on them.

As large as it is, Rupert Murdoch's News Corporation isn't the biggest media enterprise in the world. That title belongs now to AOL Time Warner, with more than $100 billion in annual revenues. Because America Online was an Internet-focused company before merging with Time Warner, the merged company depends less on uncertain advertising income—and more on paid subscriptions—than some media giants do. Thus, it may have financial room to keep extending its global reach, which before the merger accounted for only about 20 percent of its annual revenue.

Among AOL-TW's holdings were Turner Broadcasting (including CNN); Home Box Office (HBO), with movie-channel joint ventures in Asia, Latin America, and Europe; and the Warner Bros. and New Line Cinema movie companies, whose products are part of the world's favorite U.S. entertainment export: movies. The two minds that merged to create this immense enterprise were those of Stephen Case, founder of AOL, and Gerald Levin, who had run Time Warner. Case and Levin shared a business vision that contrasted with Rupert Murdoch's: to expand their international reach through an on-the-ground, company-to-customer mode of **localism**. The strategy spoke to their success in on-line commerce and local cable systems, but no one was sure how they would carry out the new plan—especially after financial trouble struck AOL-TW in mid-2002. Levin had abruptly retired, the company's Internet revenues had plunged, its stock prices were down, and federal investigators were looking into the company's accounting practices.

THE SPREADING WEB

Profit-oriented people on every continent have been jumping into the global game. They see revenues in it at many levels, from advertising (products known and purchased globally) to subscription fees to side deals with foreign companies. To reach millions of new customers with broadcast programming and high-tech communication services—one often leads to the other—has proved difficult for even long-established businesses trying to act alone. Instead, companies moving wisely and quickly to execute mergers or acquisitions have found it easier to bring together the resources needed to ring the planet.

Localism Broadcasting term for commitment to serve the interests of local citizens first.

> **Principle #6**
>
> Successful global media ventures tend to be created by mergers and acquisitions.

Spanning the World

Rupert Murdoch. His name became synonymous with global reach as the Australian-born media baron gained programming footholds in more and more countries.

The most aggressive media globalizer, Rupert Murdoch, began life in Australia but has succeeded beyond any borders. He reigns over a $14 billion media empire and is one of the world's very richest men. He also, at this writing, is over 70 years old, with two sons and a daughter already in major roles in the family firm, **News Corporation.** Adding to the air of corporate royalty, Murdoch became a father again in November 2001, when his third wife gave birth to a girl—fifth in line to his throne.

Murdoch built his empire with passport in hand. Starting with a newspaper chain in Australia, he moved on to England and assembled a tabloid empire, getting into broadcasting with a "superstation" sending programs around Europe. Murdoch migrated to New York in the 1970s and by 1985 was becoming a U.S. citizen in order to buy the six Metromedia TV stations for $1.55 billion. He then created Twentieth-Century Fox Film Corporation, acquiring what would become the Fox TV stations.

By mid-2002, Murdoch's News Corporation owned 23 U.S. television stations and was buying 10 more. The corporation also owned British Sky Broadcasting, a leading European satellite-TV carrier. It had stakes in pay-TV services covering Germany and Italy. News Corporation supplied programming to Asia—a reported 300 million viewers in 53 countries—through STAR TV, with Murdoch's son James at the helm.[25] Its joint venture in China had bundled U.S. cable channels like Fox Sports and Fox News and claimed to have become China's most-watched foreign source.[26] News Corporation had moved into programming vacuums from Mexico to Europe to its Australian homeland.

Adding the company's interests in cable networks, the National Geographic Channel, and other enterprises, it seemed possible that an aging Australian could snap his fingers and darken screens across several continents. Murdoch had one more angle: a growing corporate arm called NDS, which was exploiting new technologies. It sold electronic gateways that denied viewers access to pay-TV channels unless they'd paid, and also had launched a business allowing Brazilians to do interactive banking and helping users in the Chinese province of Sichuan trade stocks via satellite.

News Corporation Large international media conglomerate founded by Rupert Murdoch.

This, of course, results in companies owning or controlling other companies, and the layers can stack up high. Consider the 2001 bidding war for a satellite company called DirecTV. DirecTV beamed hundreds of channels of TV programming directly to small receiving dishes at subscribers' homes; the company claimed 9 million U.S. subscribers. In addition, DirecTV supplied TV to another 1.4 million homes in 27 Latin American countries as part of a multinational business. DirecTV was owned by Hughes Electronics Corporation, which in turn was a division of General Motors. News Corporation was hoping to buy Hughes in order to enter the U.S. satellite-TV market. Rupert Murdoch wanted to merge DirecTV satellite operations with his own.

However, another company, EchoStar, also wanted DirecTV and made offers to buy its parent, Hughes. EchoStar sweetened the offers with cash in an effort to beat back Murdoch. The trouble with that idea was that EchoStar already owned DirecTV's main U.S. competitor, the Dish Network. Federal regulators might not approve putting the two big satellite providers under one corporate roof. Indeed, in February 2002, the FCC still was posing tough questions about the possibly anticompetitive nature of an EchoStar-DirecTV deal—estimated as being worth $25 billion. By then, out of the bidding, the scorned Murdoch was issuing documents claiming that an EchoStar-DirecTV merger was a bad idea and asking the FCC to reject it.

Ripples run through many corporations—and, by extension, the markets they serve—every time large deals are cut or even proposed. When the mammoth News Corporation is involved, almost any transaction creates international aftershocks because it draws money from, or adds money to, one or more of the corporation's divisions. On the other hand, due to consolidation—companies growing larger and larger by consuming other companies—the international media map has become easier to follow.

This integration certainly can result in what Murdoch called **synergy** for subscribers—multiplying the services they receive. Modern media owners like to combine product lines so that they boost one another and make a corporation generally more efficient and profitable. If the Disney Company's ABC-TV network promotes the Disney World theme park, or if Disney movie studios provide films based on Disney rides such as "Pirates of the Caribbean" that are eventually shown on the Disney Channel and sold to its advertisers, that's synergy—it brings in profit that stays in the corporation.

GLOBAL AT HOME

One of the more striking aspects of international life in the twenty-first century has been the acceleration of immigration, legal and otherwise, into the United States. This is forcing the nation's electronic media to serve rapidly changing audiences and, in doing so, to join cultural and political dialogues with global implications. Indeed, census figures tell us that the United States increasingly is a meeting ground for people in need of news about their homelands, about America, and about the rest of the world—often in their native languages. This situation, in its way, requires an *international* approach to the operation of electronic media within our borders.

Politics provides a sharp spur to media action. If a democracy requires an informed electorate, then future American leadership—in foreign affairs and other matters—will depend on information reaching a different electorate from what we have known in the past. Researcher Robert Leiken predicts that election campaigns are likely to focus increasingly on new Hispanic voters "who are concentrated in the electorally rich states of California, Texas, Illinois, New York, and Florida."[27]

Like Latin American immigrants, Asians, Africans, and Europeans slowly if ever let their home cultures slip away or lose interest in international issues. A channel called ZEE-TV has brought Indian-language TV programs to more than 110,000 U.S. households. A young Liberian journalist has started a pan-African cable TV show—in Minneapolis.

Synergy Cooperative action, greater than the sum of its parts, as when two divisions of a media corporation supply goods or services to one another, aiding their common enterprise.

Cultivating Change

For years, broadcast networks based in Latin America—and some that have sprung up in the United States—have aired news and other programming in Spanish. When one such company, Telemundo, joined in broadcasting a live U.S. telethon for survivors of the 2001 terrorist attack on the World Trade Center, it reflected the presence of new immigrants as well as millions of Hispanic natives of the United States. The network translated the event into Spanish for 7.7 million Hispanic households.

Telemundo, founded in 1986 (and later reborn after a bout with bankruptcy), is the nation's second-largest Spanish-language broadcaster, claiming to reach 85 percent of all Hispanic Americans. The good news for advertisers is that total buying power for Hispanics increased by 84 percent to $383 billion during the 1990s. The Latino boom in broadcasting has raised an issue common to both Telemundo and its larger rival, Univision. In general, the question concerns assimilation; in particular, a soap-opera genre called *telenovelas* that has thrived, in Spanish, on both networks. It reminds viewers of their foreign heritage. In the view of Hispanic critics, however, including some in the media, such programming may be delaying immigrants' full transition into American life while excluding many of those who have completed it. The end result is a cultural divide, even within the Latin community. TV advertising reaches all, however, which helps explain why, in fall 2001, NBC paid $2.6 billion to acquire Telemundo.

News That Travels

The power of electronic media can be detected almost everywhere humans live today, and at no time more dramatically than when news breaks. CNN war reporter Christiane Amanpour told a national audience of news directors that she feels it as she travels: "I am so identified over the world—because CNN is seen all over the world . . . that wherever I go, people say jokingly, or maybe not so jokingly, that they shudder when they see me: 'Oh my god. Amanpour is coming. Is something bad going to happen to us?' "[28]

FILLING THE SKIES

CNN is based in the United States, but has TV outlets in more than 100 countries and claims to reach a *billion* viewers. This path-breaking enterprise sprang from the fertile mind of a media visionary, Ted Turner, whose story by now is well-known. He launched the cable network in 1980, used foreign journalists to supply news from abroad, added his own staffers, and dominated coverage of the 1990–1991 Persian Gulf War. In the process, Turner forced national leaders around the world to watch Atlanta-based CNN (recently absorbed by AOL Time Warner). This was because the network often acquired important information before their governments did and fed it via satellite to their own constituents. Satellites have been used to cover the biggest international TV stories—and radio stories, too, generating pictures in our heads that reach beyond mere "news."

Picture one memorable moment: A young Chinese man standing bravely in front of an oncoming tank in Beijing's Tienanmen Square. CNN transmitted that image via satellite in August 1989 as a pro-democracy revolution bubbled over.

It turned out that the strength—or brutality—suggested by a large piece of military equipment in proximity to a human would shake China's world image, spurring outrage. Once again, too, as Lewis A. Friedland has noted, the subsequent live coverage made CNN temporarily "the primary source of information for much of the U.S. government" in an international moment of tension.[29]

One of the more important effects of those events in China was to demonstrate the danger of taking television lightly in an increasingly connected world. At least during crises, global leaders no longer could afford to wait for their aides to prepare a neat summary of the day's stories (as President Ronald Reagan preferred in the 1980s). More than a dozen years later, news that's happening now can be captured and transmitted from almost anywhere.

Now other sources of TV news—many of them based outside the United States—populate the global marketplace. A sample of the smorgasbord: Via satellite, DirecTV carries news from the U.S. networks ABC, CBS, and NBC; the United Kingdom's BBC; CNN International; Canadian-run News World International (offering foreign newscasts in their own languages or English); Galavision, broadcasting from Mexico; Univision, from Mexico and Venezuela; the nonprofit Worldlink TV, and other programming sources that at least occasionally provide international news. A world as closely linked by news as this needs coverage that is shared quite openly and fluidly. On the contrary, U.S. journalists working abroad constantly rediscover that their country's free-press model is the exception to the international rule.

Christiane Amanpour. CNN's most conspicuous globe-trotter is recognizable—and, she says, a little unnerving to the locals—wherever she shows up around the world.

Industrialized countries routinely send reporters, cameras, and microphones into the world's news "hot spots." Any globetrotting journalist who walks into one of these hot zones is potentially in danger. Journalists—whether foreign or domestic—sometimes meet their death or capture while reporting in developing countries torn by political turmoil or civil war. A nonprofit support organization called the Committee To Protect Journalists (CPJ) compiles the annual death toll. In 2001, it added up to 37 journalists killed worldwide. Among them were nine journalists killed in Afghanistan by Taliban forces or hired gunmen as the Western "war on terrorism" moved into gear.[30] The dead also included four radio journalists—in Costa Rica, Thailand and the Philippines—who had criticized powerful forces or commented on political scandals and were killed by unknown assailants. In 2002, Islamic militants in Pakistan captured Wall Street Journal reporter Daniel Pearl; officials announced a month later that he had died in his captors' hands. His murderers later released a video to document their atrocity.

TECHNICAL WIZARDRY

Overall, newsgathering technology has played a huge role in international journalism. In fact, without the development of increasingly sophisticated gear for sending pictures and words over land and through the sky, reporters would have

Man, Tank, Tienanmen Square. TV cameras fed the drama to the world when a Chinese man stood up to a tank during protests in 1989—an image that moved millions.

Videophone Field transmission kit that allows TV correspondents to send video and voice via satellite from remote news locales to their home countries.

Computer-assisted reporting (CAR) All forms of on-line research that help journalists investigate and report news.

transmitted far less news to us over the past 150 years. The telegraph, telephone, and wireless communication helped supply us with foreign dispatches from the mid-nineteenth century through the mid-twentieth century. During the Persian Gulf War of 1990–1991, small network news teams with truckloads of technology and portable satellite dishes transmitted live pictures to the United States from embattled Kuwait before Allied liberation troops arrived. As the legendary broadcast journalist Daniel Schorr noted, such techniques could confound government censors on both sides by literally flying over them.[31] Veteran CNN correspondent Jim Bittermann put it this way: "Where earthquakes, coups and crises happen, the satellite dish is there, for better or worse."[32]

Critical to coverage of the Kosovo conflict in the late 1990s was the satellite phone. It predated the videophone and handled only voice communication, but it was a ramp into space, where no official was standing ready and eager to intercept and censor digital signals.[33]

Foreign correspondents expect discomfort, and modern advances have made that likelier than ever. Bittermann said that the portability of today's satellite gear means that, rather than hustling back to safe hotels after a day's action, reporters "are very often eating and sleeping in the disaster they are covering."[34] When he made that comment, he hadn't even worked with the **videophone.** It was not until April 2001 that this device—actually a data-handling package the size of a small suitcase—gave CNN a big international news "exclusive." It came when an enterprising TV crew furtively photographed a U.S. plane being held on a Chinese island, using a digital camera and the videophone to feed live pictures and sound to the world via satellite.

Much cheaper and smaller than previous video-feed systems, the videophone promised to be useful at especially sensitive news scenes. Rival networks quickly placed orders with the British manufacturer. The videophone came into use again all too soon—when TV journalists sent pictures from deep within the maelstrom of dust and blood at the World Trade Center in New York after terrorists destroyed it on September 11, 2001. Conventional ways of getting video out of the "ground zero" area had been destroyed as well.

Today, besides the videophone, a whole array of electronic tools comes into play, especially in television. From the world's more remote corners—remote only because they're seldom covered, and not "corners" at all—correspondents can make wireless connections to the Internet. They then can dig up background facts through what's generally called **computer-assisted reporting (CAR)** and transmit their stories as audio or video files, to be converted to voice narration for radio or television. Secure paths through the Internet are also playing a larger role in relaying news from reporters to newsrooms. Many news services, and some radio and TV stations, use the same technology to forward reporters' work to consumers. Advances in wireless technology and in **bandwidth**—a controlling factor in sending video over the Internet—will improve such processes rapidly.

INTO THE FUTURE

Everything the electronic media do, and are, has consequences, and some of them are global. For a quick example, we needn't look beyond the September 2001 terrorist attacks on the World Trade Center and the Pentagon. Broadcast images of the horrific physical and emotional impact of the attacks gave Americans a new and disturbing sense of vulnerability that would linger long. And because of the nation's role as a world power and New York's image as a world city, that vulnerability was palpable to viewers all over a satellite-connected globe. The result was sure to shape international perceptions and behavior for years to come. It might push or pull the media themselves into new ways of scanning and probing human affairs.

Some of the most intense concerns for the future of international electronic media are directed at the growth of the corporations that increasingly shape what people view and hear around the world. Another issue addresses the quality of journalism and the influence of news technology.

Control, Cultures, Economies

The world map of media control is changing slowly, but clearly most of the power over programming is in American, European, and Australian hands. This leaves several continents relatively weak in influence over media content and thus—some argue—exposed to whatever cultural messages the richest nations wish to force on them.

This argument includes the cultural-imperialism claim that global media will tend (or attempt) to convert every listener, viewer, and Internet consumer to western values, including a desire for consumer products. The effect, it is asserted, could be to undermine strong indigenous cultures and to stimulate desires that would be shallow and, worse, unrealistic in less-developed countries. After all, as media scholar Robert McChesney points out, "infomercials" and TV shopping channels are among the hottest-selling programming on the world market.

McChesney also declares that some traditional criticisms of global media are beginning to lose their relevance. For instance, it's undeniable that Hollywood films and U.S.-made sitcoms and dramas remain wildly popular worldwide. They're better produced, with more recognizable performers, than are many other countries' programs; and U.S. exporters of entertainment, like most others, sell to foreign markets at discounted prices. Regardless, some analysts perceive these productions as rushing into nonproducer countries and filling their channels with western culture. What's more, say such critics, this drains away revenue that indigenous media should be earning for themselves.

Changes are afoot, some of which could redistribute the wealth derived from global media sales. As competition grows, western media are cutting deals that bring local distributors and producers into the revenue stream. This change begins to deposit money in other countries, not just send it back to the producers'

Bandwidth Refers to size of electronic "band" allocated to a communication system; progress in improving quality of TV transmission via the Internet has been limited by available bandwidth.

Internet User (World). Still incalculable are the effects of spreading Internet use on nations and cultures that have lacked U.S.-style access to the fruits of electronic media.

own bank accounts and shareholders. Among other results, if this trend grows, it could encourage the "localism" that some believe is the key to global media that will satisfy all. In the meantime, western-generated entertainment and information continue to have negative effects on much of the world, says McChesney; one effect is that, because they see consumerism as equal to democracy, young people in postauthoritarian countries such as Chile are buying more and voting less.[35]

Another analyst, Dietrich Berwanger, argues that cultural imperialism through media has done little to impose the will or values of rich nations on the world's less affluent societies—at least "compared with the effects of Western religion, economy, and weaponry" throughout history.[36] Recently, important media producers have begun to emerge in some of the global media's client countries: India's Kishore Lulla has sold his subscription TV channel featuring Bombay-made movies and music to 170,000 South Asian-immigrant subscribers on six continents—a sort of reverse cultural imperialism.[37]

Journalism

News, if narrowly defined as "breaking" events, can burst out anywhere, anytime. But seen more broadly, news is occurring continuously; it's the running analysis of issues, the "first rough draft of history," as the late *Washington Post* publisher Philip Graham once described it. Will future journalism explain the world to itself consistently and conscientiously? If not, how will new international relationships and entanglements—economic, cultural, political, even military—be understood and evaluated by world citizens?

Some answers may be found close to home—anyone's home. A country's own journalists often are best able to tell its stories fairly, accurately, and thoroughly. Indeed, when they've been silenced by their own governments, reporters who know "where the bodies are buried" sometimes serve as tipsters to arriving foreign correspondents. After all, if local journalists can't report what they know by conventional means, why not give it to the world any way they can?

Unfortunately, many serious developments go unreported by either domestic broadcasters or the sparse and busy corps of globe-trotting journalists. True, globalization may begin to lift some government pressures off the shoulders of indigenous journalists. Until such progress appears, however, our common knowledge of many regions and nations is bound to remain sketchy and spotty—unless global media corporations begin to invest in a larger and more experienced international news corps.

That's improbable, given the U.S. experience: Guided by constricting budgets and audience research—some of it from what CNN's Christiane Amanpour has called "hocus-pocus focus groups"[38]—TV networks since the 1980s have shifted toward human-interest and consumer news. The networks have cut back on government coverage (except during crises or scandals), slashed overseas staffs, and reduced the amount of foreign news on TV by more than half.[39]

Still, as the Murdochs and other media magnates extend their global grasps, building larger and deeper conglomerates across the map, new hopes arise. Perhaps more journalists will be assigned, or will go on their own, to the most neglected or misunderstood regions of the world. These should include the Middle East and Africa, where relatively few western broadcast correspondents are stationed permanently and where governments are reluctant to let news escape—or, for that matter, to let it circulate within their own borders.

Summary

Our electronic media are the products of more than a century of international invention—and themselves are inherently international, thanks to their ability to vault over borders and oceans. Radio is as pervasive on other continents as it is in the United States. It has connected citizens at the village level and across cultural boundaries, and has served governments and social movements. Private money, public funds, and sometimes a blend of the two have helped broadcasting thrive

Television, although less readily accessible than radio, is now beamed into almost every corner of the earth. Propagated via satellite, animated by Hollywood movies and tailored to regional cultures, TV is at the heart of a global commercial enterprise. Corporations have grown fabulously wealthy transmitting U.S. media products around the world. Although some of their work draws criticism on intercultural grounds, the infrastructure and technologies created and used by global electronic media help to move news from almost anywhere to almost anywhere else. Internet initiatives have given millions of world citizens a new tool with which to acquire information and exchange culture, in more self-tailored ways than the traditional media provide.

FOOD FOR THOUGHT

1. Is *cultural imperialism* by media-producing countries a serious threat to less-developed nations and communities? How? Give examples.
2. How important is *news* in most of the world's societies? How does it compare with entertainment as a driving force in the spread of global media?
3. Why do Americans, in general, show little interest in TV and radio programs from other lands—when those countries show great interest in U.S. media?
4. Is the global transmission of government propaganda—including deliberately deceptive reports from the Pentagon and State Department in their "war on terrorism"—a legitimate use of electronic media? Explain.
5. If you had the opportunity to begin a dialogue with an African, Asian, or European person via radio or the Internet, would you do so? Why or why not?

14

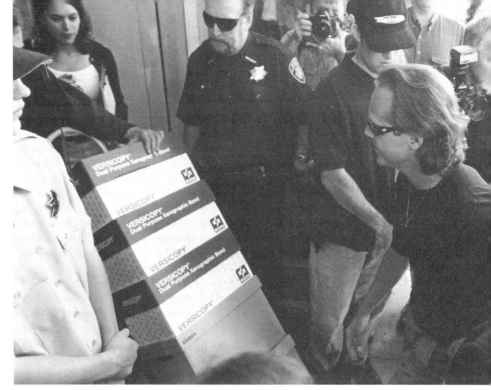

Law

The life of the law has not been logic; it has been experience . . . to know what it is, we must know what it has been and what it tends to become.

—Justice Oliver Wendell Holmes, 1881

Napster Case. Rock drummer Lars Ulrich from the band Metallica wheels boxes of documents containing the names of Napster users as evidence in a copyright infringement case. Shawn Fanning's online music service (named after his "nappy" hair) lost in federal court in February 2001.

ederal agents fanned out through Miami for several days in July of 1998. They were not looking for drug traffickers or nabbing illegal aliens. They were overturning *pirate* radio stations. In the largest siege of unlicensed stations, agents of the Federal Communications Commission netted 15 pirate broadcasters and confiscated 2,000-watt transmitters as well as assorted microphones, consoles, and recording decks—all flouting federal law.[1]

Miami had become a hotbed of radio pirates, but had plenty of company in this enterprise. A quick web search found pirate flags flying boldly, the skull and crossbones protesting the FCC and the "corporate radio structure" that had overtaken America. One pirate broadcaster claimed to be just exercising First Amendment rights. In Texas, Radio Free Austin ignored federal licensing of radio stations, asserting that the FCC was "an entrenched authority," dealing dishonestly with the public and confiscating what rightfully belonged to citizens—the airwaves.[2]

Broadcasting without a license carries a fine of up to $100,000, a year in jail, or both, for first-time offenders. Pirate radio waves collide with licensed transmissions of aviation channels, public safety transmitters, and legitimate broadcasters. So pirates may identify themselves as anarchists, Robin Hoods, or just rebels, but their brand of "microbroadcasting" underscores two principles of media law: First, broadcasters do not *own* the airwaves; the public does—you and I. Second, broadcasters must be granted licenses promising they will not ignore the greater good of their local communities. At that point, they become *public trustees* in the eyes of Congress, the courts, and the Federal Communications Commission.

> Broadcasters do not *own* the airwaves; the public does—you and I.

BEGINNING WITH THE BASICS

The rule of law is a commonly heard phrase when an actor, celebrity, or politician finds his or her fate shifting in the scales of justice. What it means for the rights of the governed is that their will counts as much as the will of those who govern. American **jurisprudence** in electronic media upholds this principle through three branches of government: executive, legislative, and judiciary. Each one checks the others to see that they honor this line between tyranny and democracy. What does it mean for electronic media? Because broadcast waves are a natural resource—one both scarce and limited—their use is guarded in laws drafted by Congress and enforced through the FCC.

Less room is available for broadcast channels than for people who wish to secure them, so the FCC faces a formidable task in assigning frequencies. The agency received more than 26,000 inquiries for broadcast licenses in 2000 alone. In the past, broadcasters' resources and their promises to serve the community interest helped the FCC decide between competing applicants. Now, money matters most, despite the fact that the public's rights are paramount. The Communications Act of 1934 stresses the national interest *"in communication by wire and radio so as to make available, so far as possible, to all the people of the United States a rapid, efficient, Nation-wide, and world-wide wire and radio communication service with adequate facilities at reasonable charges."* So the ideas of public airwaves, spectrum scarcity, and local service are in flux, subject to interpretation by the Congress, the courts, and the FCC against the dynamic landscape of electronic media. To prepare for the future, let's see how we arrived at this point in time.

> Principle #1
>
> **The government licenses broadcasters to serve the public interest.**

Wireless Rules

Beginning the ledger of radio law is the Wireless Ship Act of 1910. The U.S. Navy requested a rule for the "apparatus and operators for radio communications on certain ocean steamers" carrying "50 or more persons."[3] The tragic oversight of this law was that it failed to prescribe how many hours a day wireless operators had to stay at their posts. On April 14, 1912, that omission came to light when, with no radioman on duty, a jagged iceberg sent the "unsinkable" *Titanic*

The *Titanic*. The maiden voyage of the famous luxury liner in April 1912 had an impact on American radio law. If wireless operators had been required to stay on duty all night, more of the ship's 1,517 passengers might have been saved.

into maritime history. Congress was roused to spell out a law requiring staffing of every ship's radio room both day and night.

Radio stations were silenced during World War I. Soldiers trained in wireless technology returned home and managed to wreak havoc with homemade transmitters and crystal sets. Their huge clash of signals was inevitable, because only one frequency was available. Early stations were assigned one spot on the radio dial at 360 meters, the length of the wave, but that channel—833 kHz—grew so crowded that early pirates seized another one that bad been reserved for government weather and crop reports.

The radio spectrum was in disarray, so Herbert Hoover, U.S. Secretary of Commerce and Labor, summoned leaders to a national radio conference to straighten out this mess. The 1922 session produced a new channel for broadcasting at 750 kHz. Still, two frequencies were not enough and some stations were forced to share their time on the air just to be heard.[4]

The spread of wireless sets inspired eager operators ready to broadcast across the national map. By 1923, the number of radio stations exceeded 560, and they had exhausted the government's file of three-letter combinations for call signs. Secretary Hoover needed new advice on how to nurture radio's continued growth. After three more meetings with hundreds of engineers and station owners from companies such as AT&T and Westinghouse, the government cleared more channels—from 550 to 1500 kHz. Telltale noise from radio interference had been alleviated, but enforcing the law became next to impossible.

INTERCITY AND ZENITH CASES

Secretary Hoover found his authority lacking when two court cases went against his department. The first ruling reversed an earlier decision to deny Intercity

Radio Company a license. Its broadcasts would infringe on government channels, so the secretary saw no option but to refuse the application. However, a federal court held that Hoover had no power to refuse a license.[5]

In the second case, a Chicago station trespassed on a wavelength reserved for Canadian radio. Zenith Radio's station, WJAZ, was denied its license, but company president Eugene F. McDonald was not taking no for an answer. He ignored the federal refusal and resumed programming at 910 kHz.[6] In both cases, *Hoover* v. *Intercity Radio* and *Hoover* v. *Zenith-WJAZ*, judges reached fundamentally the same conclusion: The department's power to deny licenses was written nowhere in law. Congress had failed to empower Hoover to orchestrate radio frequencies, power, and hours of operation.[7]

FEDERAL RADIO COMMISSION

After hearing from radio engineers and industry leaders in 1926, Secretary Hoover was ready to see something written in law that would give him authority over this chaos. The Radio Control Bill of 1927 granted his wish. Representative Wallace H. White (R-ME) and Senator Clarence C. Dill (D-MT) pushed through a bill legislating a new, *temporary* agency to remedy radio's problems. The Federal Radio Commission (FRC) would, "consistent with the public interest, convenience, and necessity, make reasonable regulations governing the interference potential of devices . . . emitting radio frequency energy."

CASUALTIES IN THE PUBLIC INTEREST

There were new problems to be resolved beyond the noise of interference and unruly station owners. When word reached Washington of medical charlatans and evangelists hawking their wares by radio, the FRC stepped in to establish legal precedents. One huckster, John R. Brinkley, had signed on a remarkable station, KFKB (Kansas First Kansas Best) in 1923. The license for the station in Milford, Kansas, was granted to a hospital association. "Doc" Brinkley specialized in a cure for lost male virility—he surgically implanted goat glands in his male patients. Over his 5,000-watt station, Brinkley counseled midwesterners through the *Medical Question Box* show. He read their letters, diagnosed their symptoms, and prescribed cures—all sight unseen. Once the FRC got a whiff of his methods, it moved in with a second opinion—close down the station.

Another medical marvel was broadcasting farther north, in Muscatine, Iowa. The voice of Norman "TNT" Baker rang forth from Know-The-Naked-Truth (KTNT) radio. "Doc" Baker sold his "penetrating oil" over the air for those suffering from appendicitis whenever he was not shilling for an instrument with the "newest musical tone in 40 years," the *calliaphone*. His more orthodox colleagues took a public position against his radio carnival, incurring his wrath. After the American Medical Association (AMA) denounced TNT's sideshow, Baker charged that the AMA's members were the "Amateur Meatcutters of America," and said M.D. only meant "More Dough!"

The FRC, honoring free speech and its mandate not to censor broadcasting, was reluctant to turn off Baker's or Brinkley's radio transmitters. It did have the power to deny their petitions to renew their radio licenses, and did deny them in 1931. Undaunted, the mesmerizing doctors packed up their antennas and moved to warmer climes. Baker and Brinkley were heard broadcasting cures from Mexico, using the airwaves to reach desperate and unwary patients.[8]

Perhaps more than medicine, religion persuaded radio listeners, but early evangelists found the government could draw the line on their sermons. The FRC took action in 1931 against Rev. Robert Shuler, a California evangelist famous for his attacks on the Roman Catholic Church. After hearing an appeal to recover his license for KGEF in Los Angeles, the Court of Appeals found "Bullet Bob" Shuler's incendiary broadcasts were not subject to First Amendment protection due to their defamatory nature. He lost the privilege of using the public airwaves.[9]

Another spiritual star of California radio was Aimee Semple McPherson. She preached from the Four Square Gospel church in Los Angeles, where her radio broadcasts wandered up and down the dial like a sojourner lost in the wilderness. She was warned in 1925 that KSFG had better find its rightful frequency and stop interfering with other stations; this only angered the charismatic minister. McPherson's telegram to Secretary Hoover stated: "Please order your minions of Satan to leave my station alone. You cannot expect the Almighty to abide by your wavelength nonsense."[10]

EMERGENCE OF THE FCC

Remember: Congress never intended for the FRC to spring to full life for the future regulation of radio. There was just a one-year plan designed to allow the agency to "function only occasionally," then hand back its chores to the Commerce Department. That hand-back never took place, though. Instead, the FRC evolved to become the Federal Communications Commission. Congress extended the commission's reach over rule making in 1934 to encompass telephones, telegraphs, and all electronic media. The FRC was given a broad canvas, with the media landscape barely sketched.

> **Principle #2**
>
> Public ownership of the spectrum requires government oversight over the use of its frequencies.

ADVERSARIES AND ASCERTAINMENT

Because a democracy draws its breath from the consent of the governed, early attempts at dictating regulatory issues to broadcasters were ill-fated. One notable flop was an FCC policy statement attacking broadcasters for giving away too much air time to networks for their programs and advertising. The statement was titled *Public Service Responsibility of Broadcast Licensees*, but became known by its colorful nickname, the Blue Book, inspired by its binding and cover. Charles A. Siepmann, a British consultant to the FCC, composed the prescriptive commentary on U.S. radio, taking aim at the lack of public-affairs shows and "sustaining" programs free of commercial interruption. American broadcasters were livid. They found the tone and tenor of the Blue Book demeaning and its threat of government oversight intimidating. Leading the resistance was *Broadcasting Magazine*, which called Siepmann's work as "masterfully evasive as it is vicious."[11] The Blue Book was never actually enforced.

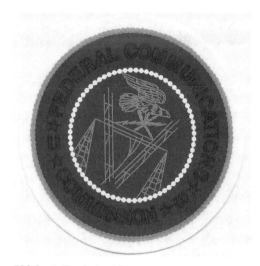

FCC Seal. The Federal Communications Commission stands as the authority over licensing and regulation of electronic media in the United States. Although prohibited from censorship, the agency's authority does ensure that broadcast licensees serve the "public interest, convenience and necessity."

In 1960, the FCC took a new tack. It published a program policy statement endorsing programming that it considered to be in the public interest. Fourteen favored items included community news of political affairs and programs on religion. There were to be educational and children's shows, farm reports and business news, and editorials and minority access. This statement placed entertainment programming at the bottom, though.

The document also called for an *ascertainment* of community problems to be dealt with by each broadcaster through programming. By interviewing civic leaders and conducting surveys, broadcasters would discover issues of importance. Most important, this 1960 policy was enforced as part of broadcasters' renewal process for their licenses. That was true until the 1980s, when President Reagan's appointee to lead the FCC, Mark Fowler, called for an overhaul of such rules. In terms of the public's interest, he likened radio and television to a household appliance—"a toaster with pictures."

DEREGULATION

Under Fowler, the FCC found its ascertainment policy—and others like it—offensive to the First Amendment. He dropped the policy into the "circular file" of discarded rules, to be replaced by the marketplace's wisdom. First, commercial radio was deregulated in 1981, followed by commercial television in 1985. Congress joined in the retrenchment by reducing the size of the FCC from seven to five members. Things changed during the 1990s, when deregulation was no longer supported as a one-size-fits-all formula for FCC action. In 1996, Congress passed the Telecommunications Act, which lifted the limits on station ownership, but provided parental control of program content through the V-chip.

FCC Structure

The FCC is first responsible for administering and enforcing the laws passed on Capitol Hill. It does so by delegating its regulatory powers to its bureaus and offices. Each one functions under the agency's procedures for rule making and policy enforcement. The agency examines license applications and leads aspiring broadcasters through the maze of the federal bureaucracy. To understand this branch of administrative law requires knowing how it is organized.

THE COMMISSION

The FCC consists of five men and women appointed by the president and confirmed by the Senate. They exercise the will of Congress, which has given them quasi-judicial and legislative powers to draft and enforce rules governing elec-

Chairman Michael K. Powell

When it came time for President George W. Bush to tap a commissioner to lead the FCC, his choice was between a friend in Texas and a sitting commissioner, Michael K. Powell. Bush chose the 38-year-old Powell to succeed William Kennard as the new chair. The two men were the first African Americans to hold that position of leadership, though it was not in Powell's original trajectory. As the son of General Colin Powell, U.S. Secretary of State, he had seen military stars in his future. Michael Powell's path took an abrupt turn when his Army jeep rolled off the German autobahn and crushed his pelvis. This ended his military career, but signaled the start of a new one in law. Upon graduation from Georgetown University School of Law in 1990, he accepted a job with the Washington, DC, offices of a California firm. Powell then made his way into the antitrust division of the Department of Justice. President Clinton summoned him to the FCC as a Republican commissioner in 1997. His experience and conservative philosophy led President Bush to appoint him chair in 2001.

Powell's actions veer occasionally from traditional GOP policy. For example, he favored low-power FM radio—advocated by Kennard—to give churches and schools a chance to broadcast. Yet, when asked by reporters about the so-called digital divide, the gap between the *haves* and *have-nots* in computer technology, he sounded a more cynical note: "I think there's a Mercedes divide. I'd like one, but I can't afford it."[12]

Powell's distaste for dictating content to broadcasters simmered below the surface during one indecency controversy. The FCC in 2001 issued a notice of apparent liability and forfeiture (in other words, a fine of $7,000) against a Pueblo, Colorado, radio station for playing an edited version of one of Eminem's rap songs, *The Real Slim Shady.* That move echoed an earlier era when New York shock jock Howard Stern managed to tally up $1.7 million in fines for his brand of radio sleaze. In 2002, however, the FCC's Media Bureau reversed the indecency decision against KKMG-FM in Pueblo, in a move troubling to one commissioner. In a matter of such importance, Michael J. Copps said, "the Commissioners themselves, rather than the Bureau, should be making the decision about whether to reverse the initial finding. Issues of indecency on the people's airwaves are important to millions of Americans; they are important to me. I believe they merit, indeed compel, Commissioner-level action."[13] Another FM station, KBOO in Portland, Oregon, was fined $7,000 for playing *Your Revolution* by rap artist Sarah Jones. That FCC decision against a community radio station for playing a song attacking sexual arrogance and materialism has *not* been overturned.

Powell's biggest battles may be over ownership limits. His rule of thumb is to act only after finding a compelling reason for federal intrusion in telecommunications; otherwise, leave it to the marketplace. One example is his support for lifting ceilings on broadcasting and cable ownership. A Democratic predecessor, Reed Hundt, found Powell's deference to media mergers difficult to accept. Said Hundt: He "is promoting the most radical view of media consolidation that any democracy has ever supported. It's an experiment with the underpinnings of democracy. There isn't any consumer demand for this consolidation. Not a single person in America would say it's a good idea. It's exclusively driven by ideology and business interests."[14]

tronic media. All commissioners are sworn to serve five-year terms, though few actually stay on that long. The president appoints them, selecting three of them from his own party, and choosing one of the three to preside as FCC chair and to set the agenda.

Notice of Inquiry (NOI) Public statement by the FCC, designed to create awareness of a legal problem or issue and to invite informed comments on how it should be resolved. The Federal Register is responsible for publishing the NOI.

Notice of Proposed Rule Making (NPRM) The FCC takes this second step in the regulatory process to show it is planning to make or amend its rules, and inviting further comments.

Report and Order (R&O) FCC statement explaining new rules or changes in old ones. The R&O is published in the Federal Register.

BUREAUS AND OFFICES

The old slogan at the ballpark was "You can't tell the players without a program," and at the FCC you need an organizational chart to tell what's going on. Its bureaus are shuffled and reshuffled to match the priorities and policy views of each new chair. Chair Kennard, for example, believed that each compliance and information bureau should be split into two bureaus. Before him, Chair Hundt saw the need for an international affairs bureau and another for wireless telecommunications.[15] More recently, Powell took audio and video services from the old Mass Media Bureau, and moved them in with Cable Services to form the Media Bureau. He created the Wireless Competition Bureau to replace the Common Carrier Bureau, as Figure 14.1 shows.

THE FCC'S WATCH

Congress delegates the powers of the Commission to ensure the technical quality of broadcast signals while preserving the U.S. stake in their use. To reach as many communities as possible, the FCC assigns call letters, monitors frequencies, inspects stations, and even sees that TV towers are properly lighted and painted.

RULE-MAKING PROCESS

Electronic media change faster than new rules can be drafted or old ones revised, but the agency honors its procedures for changing rules or adding new ones. It begins by calling attention to a perceived problem. That issue is framed in a document called the **Notice of Inquiry (NOI)**. The NOI alerts broadcasters by telling them that the FCC has deemed a question to be of special importance, and invites their comments on its answer. The next step signals that there's a good chance that a change of rules is on its way. The **Notice of Proposed Rule Making (NPRM)** will give broadcasters a second chance to speak their minds. When the agency arrives at the third stage, it publishes a **Report and Order (R&O)**, announcing a decision. The R&O defines in detail how and why any new rule was adopted and whether amendments were tacked on, or may simply explain why the status quo was preferred. All R&Os are in the *Federal Register*, published by the U.S. Government Printing Office in Washington, DC.[16]

Licensing Process

The most basic power delegated to the FCC is the licensing of broadcast stations. If you sought to own a radio or TV station, the steepest hill you would need to climb is finding an available frequency. If you doubt that frequencies are in short supply, check out the FCC website: "The FCC is not accepting applications for (AM, FM commercial, FM educational, TV) broadcast stations at the present time."[17] The Media Bureau does tantalize potential broadcasters with the promise of a "filing window period at intervals during which new station applications and major change applications may be filed," though it's anyone's guess when that will be. During the past decade, the FCC did expand the AM radio band by

Principle #3

The scarcity of spectrum space limits broadcast frequencies and station licenses.

FIGURE 14.1

Organization Chart, Federal Communications Commission, 2002

As part of its reform plan to become more effective, efficient, and responsive, the Federal Communications Commission approved the reorganization of several of the agency's bureaus. In making these changes, the FCC was guided by the following principles: Develop a standardized organizational structure across the bureaus; reflect changes in regulation and workload; recognize that dynamic industry change will continue; and use the reorganization to improve the technical and economic analysis in decision making.

Source: FCC News, Federal Communications Commission.

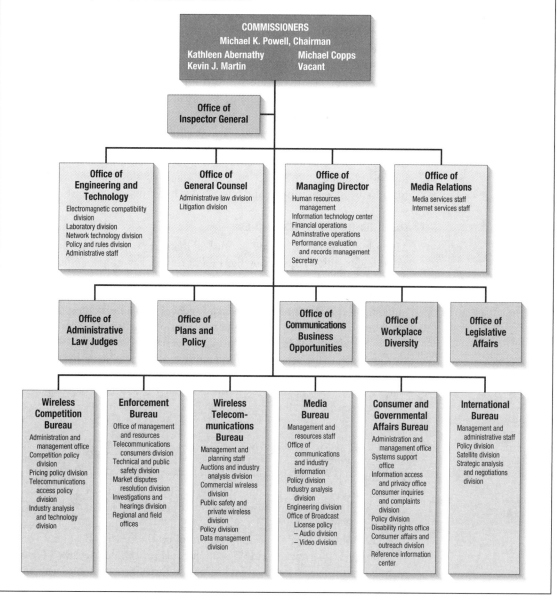

Construction permit (CP) Authorization by the FCC to build a broadcast facility or to make substantial changes in an existing one.

Renewal expectancy FCC's stated commitment to favor existing broadcast licenses over competitive applications at the time of renewal, unless given cause to do otherwise under the Telecommunications Act of 1996.

10 channels (it now stretches to 1705 AM) and granted licenses for 700 new FM channels.

To improve your chances of winning a license, an engineer *and* a communication lawyer will help by watching for public notices indicating that stations or frequencies are up for grabs. If they find one, you'll fill out forms from the Media Bureau. A new station begins with a **construction permit (CP).** That document confirms your citizenship (only U.S. citizens may apply), the quality of your character (no convicted felons), and the depth of your pockets (sufficient resources). The latter ensures that you have enough cash to keep your new station running for 90 days without commercial sponsors.

LICENSE RENEWAL

Once you have a license in hand, how long do you think that will last? License terms have been expanding, from two years in the earliest days to three-, five-, seven-, and now eight-year terms.[18] Revisions to the Telecommunications Act in 1996, included a value-added bonus for broadcasters: **renewal expectancy.** That meant that licenses were safe and secure until someone could show that the broadcaster was treading on the public's interest. To express its good faith, the FCC introduced in 1985 a postcard form for license renewal, containing just five questions, only one of them needing more than a yes-or-no answer. That form was beefed up in the 1990s, but the stacks of files once required for keeping a transmitter humming and tower lights blinking are now history.

PUBLIC INSPECTION FILE

Mounds of paperwork may have vanished thanks to deregulation, but one document folder still is required by the FCC's rulebooks: the *public inspection file.* These records are available for all to see, and include a station's license applications and reports to the agency, contour maps of the station's coverage area, letters and e-mails from the audience, and a list of local issues and of programs designed to address them. Failure to make the public inspection file available during business hours for anyone to thumb through—even rival broadcasters—can draw an FCC fine, or, as the agency calls it, a *forfeiture.* What's not included in the public inspection file are the station's financial documents, including profit and earnings statements, payroll records, tax forms, and other business records. The government respects the fact that broadcast stations compete as private enterprises.

PENALTIES

The agency may fine a station or revoke its license for putting *obscene or indecent language* on the air, *soliciting money under false pretenses, advertising illegal lotteries,* or other violations of the public trust. The FCC almost never revokes a station license; it renews licenses about 98 percent of the time. The few exceptions show the dark taint of lying to the government (lack of candor), often compounded by a miserable record of public service. Beyond revocation or forfeitures, the agency employs other tools to uphold the law. License renewals can be okayed for the short term, until the station has found ways to solve its problems. Letters of reprimand also may be placed in the station's public file.

Fees, Auctions, and Lotteries

It sounds like a lot of money—$250 million dollars a year—but to budget one agency overseeing U.S. telecommunications in the information age, it's not much. President Bush asked Congress to approve an FCC spending plan of $248,545,000 in 2002. More money than before was needed to replace the commission's old computers and upgrade the agency's technology systems. Forty percent of the budget was earmarked for pay raises and benefits for about 2,000 employees. Now—before presuming that tax dollars fund the agency—understand that the FCC rakes in a lot more than its budget each year. Some of the surplus comes from a variety of fees. Satellite television, for example, chips in at least $130,000 per satellite; cable systems pay half a dollar per subscriber; and radio and TV stations add hundreds of thousands in their annual fees.

The FCC has grown to become one of Uncle Sam's favorite nephews through spectrum auctions that have been used to raise money from a natural resource: electromagnetic frequencies. For example, cellular and wireless personal communication systems (PCSs) have bid competitively for government licenses since 1994. Overall, more than $23 billion was raised for the U.S. Treasury by spectrum auctions in less than eight years.

Media conglomerates know their chances of gaining licenses are no longer based on public-service proposals or random luck but on cold, hard cash. In times past, administrative law judges held comparative hearings and chose between competing broadcasters by applying public-service criteria. However, a federal court in 1992 found that system's rationale wanting, and the agency never drafted a new plan. Instead, it moved on to lotteries for licensees. Next, spectrum auctions threw open the door to virtually anyone who could submit an advance payment. In 1997, Congress expanded this money-making program by essentially doing away with the lottery as an alternative means.

> **Principle #4**
>
> Competitive bidding—not the promise of performance—determines who gains access to the telecommunications channels.

OWNERSHIP: CONCENTRATION AND DIVERSITY

You may have noticed how multibillion-dollar enterprises owning dozens of radio and TV stations have been growing larger in size but fewer in number. When Ben Bagdikian wrote *The Media Monopoly* in 1983, half of the broadcasting, newspaper, magazine, music, film, video, and publishing groups were in the hands of 50 companies. In less than two decades, that number has shrunk to fewer than 10 media conglomerates. More liberal caps on broadcast ownership took effect with the passage of the Telecommunications Act of 1996, which accelerated the trend toward media mergers. Consider this statistic: From March 1996 to March 2001, the number of U.S. radio stations grew by 7 percent while the number of owners fell 25 percent. Six years after the Telecommunications Act, a federal appeals court granted the largest media corporations power to extend their ownership beyond anything seen before. In 2002, the FCC created a task force to study all rules pertinent to ownership and to issue a proposal by the end of the year. The panel was to consider regulations regarding how many radio stations, TV stations, cable systems, and newspapers one company may own.

Ownership Regulation

Early in 2002, a three-judge federal panel told the FCC that it needed to rethink how many TV stations one owner could buy. The District of Columbia Circuit Court of Appeals also was ready to lift the bar preventing groups from owning both cable systems and TV stations in the same town. Unless overturned on appeal, that decision would allow a multiple-system operator (MSO) such as AT&T Broadband to supply viewers with the channel of its newly acquired TV station as well as those of its competitors. The ruling was a setback for smaller owners of broadcast stations and for consumer groups concerned with the growing power of the networks and their corporate owners.

The big corporation owners applauded the end of limits on station ownership and cross-ownership of cable, saying they were no longer needed to preserve competition and diversity, and were outdated in the first place. AOL Time Warner's general counsel called the restrictions "an anachronism." NBC chose to use the term *antiquated*, while Fox's parent News Corporation preferred *outdated*.[19] Just how far will network owners reach in collecting radio and TV stations and other media, including newspapers, magazines, and cable channels? CBS/Viacom and Fox Broadcasting now hold title to enough TV licenses to reach more than 40 percent of the households in the United States. If media ownership rules are abandoned completely, their reach could go even further. One thing is certain: The next 50 years of broadcast ownership will look quite different from the past 50 years.

FIRST LIMITS

The FCC placed its first cap on ownership of radio and TV stations in 1952 with the "rule of sevens." This simply meant that the maximum number of broadcast outlets for any one person or corporation to own was seven AM, seven FM, and seven TV stations. The rationale was that more broadcast owners meant more differences of opinion and more diversity in the marketplace of ideas.

The nation's news media policy was founded on what the Supreme Court identified as an underlying assumption of the First Amendment: that "the widest possible dissemination of information from diverse and antagonistic sources is essential to the welfare of the public."[20] That thinking was challenged, however, during the deregulation era, when the government created a friendly environment for media mergers. The rule of sevens became the rule of eights, and then twelves, and then twenties, until it was expanded by Congress in 1996.

The Telecommunications Act of 1996 put in place an "all-you-can-own" rule for radio stations on a national basis, but it left in place some limits at the local market level. Radio was placed on a sliding scale so that no more than *eight* stations would come under one tent in the largest markets (45 stations and up). The limit would be only seven stations in cities with 30 to 44 radio stations, six in smaller markets with 15 to 29 stations, and five in towns with 14 or fewer stations.

DUOPOLY RULE

In television under the old rules, no single group owner could broadcast to more than 35 percent of the U.S. audience. A group also could not own two TV stations in one city. The **duopoly** rule, however, was relaxed in 1999 to allow common ownership of two TV stations, but only under certain circumstances. Lawyers for AT&T, AOL Time Warner, Fox, Viacom/CBS, and Sinclair Broadcasting petitioned in 2001 for abolition of the duopoly rule in order to acquire more stations.

Duopoly Refers to the FCC restriction on ownership of two electronic media of the same type in the same community.

Cross-Ownership

The cross-ownership rule, forbidding partnerships between newspapers and broadcasters in the same city, was written into law in 1975. Over the years, new cable and satellite channels as well as Internet sites have been added. Network owners maintain that marketplace reality has done more to protect diversity and competition than outdated law ever did. Citizen groups agree that more channels are available, but assert that they are often owned by the same huge corporations, and that the ones that are not so well supported discover it difficult to compete.

Newspaper companies such as Tribune, Belo, and Post-Newsweek owned both dailies and broadcast stations in the same cities before the 1975 cross-ownership rule was adopted. In most cases, the rule allowed them to hold on to those properties. Now, major media groups would like to buy new TV stations in other markets where they own newspapers or cable systems, and one court appears to be on their side. In *Fox Television Stations* v. *Federal Communications Commission* (No. 00–1222), the District of Columbia Court of Appeals threw out the rule that barred one media enterprise from owning both cable systems and television stations in the same market. It also asked the FCC to rethink its rule that kept one business from buying TV stations that could reach more than 35 percent of American households.

Local Station Reaction

Networks and their affiliated stations differ on this quest for more media mergers. The National Association of Broadcasters board of affiliates voted in favor of the 35 percent audience limit before the federal court ruled that it should be lifted. The affiliated stations fear the commercial networks could grow so powerful that they no longer would be obliged to pay stations to air network commercials. This has become such a controversial topic that some observers decline to take sides publicly. Former FCC Chair Richard Wiley of Wiley, Rein and Fielding mused, "I have clients on both sides of that issue, and let me just say that I am always with my client."

> **Principle #5**
>
> Media consolidation leads to monopoly if left unregulated.

Diversity in Ownership

Before 1978, the government granted one-half of 1 percent of all broadcast licenses to minorities—only 40 stations out of more than 8,500. After 1978, the

FCC deployed a tax certificate program designed to encourage the sale of cable systems and radio and television stations to minorities. The program did this by deferring or eliminating the capital gains tax that station sellers would have to pay on their profits from a sale. If you owned a broadcast or cable property and were willing to sell it to a female or minority, you would get a tax break. During the next 17 years, more than 350 broadcast and cable systems lined up to take advantage of that offer.

There was another push toward the goal of diversity in ownership established during President Jimmy Carter's administration. The FCC encouraged distress sales of broadcast and cable properties to minority and women licensees by allowing the sellers to recover some of the market value of "intangible assets," a recovery of their investment not normally allowed under other circumstances.

In 1995, Congress and the courts did away with both programs. In *Adarand* v. *Pena*, the U.S. Supreme Court ruled against federal programs' applying racial criteria except to remedy specific cases of discrimination—not to solve the general social ills of prejudice.[21] Congress acted that same year to repeal the tax certificate program.[22]

The result was a slip in the number of TV stations owned by minorities. Figures for 2000 showed fewer than 2 percent of the nation's full-service TV licenses were controlled by minorities. Minority ownership of radio stations fared better, with about 4 percent of AMs and FMs, but U.S. Commerce Secretary Norman Mineta said, "Clearly there is reason for concern."[23] A report prepared for the Office of General Counsel of the FCC called it a serious situation.[24]

Minority Employment

In the three decades the FCC's equal employment opportunities (EEO) rules were on the books, minority employment in electronic media jumped from 9.1 to 20.2 percent. Women fared best, holding more than 40 percent of available jobs, but only 15 percent of the women were counted as general managers.

The EEO rules required broadcasters to consider minorities and women for job vacancies: "No person shall be discriminated against in employment by such stations because of race, color, religion, national origin, or sex." The rules did not set quotas or specify types of people to be hired. However, the rules did allow the FCC to pass judgment on hiring decisions after the fact. For example, the agency in 1991 fined two Georgia radio stations $10,000 each and granted only short-term renewals of their licenses due to inadequate minority recruitment.[25]

A severe blow was dealt to the FCC's guidelines when the government lost two court cases. *Lutheran Church-Missouri Synod* v. *Federal Communications Commission*,[26] involved FCC notices to two radio stations at Concordia Seminary in Clayton, Missouri, that their hiring of minorities failed to comply with EEO guidelines. An appeals court overturned those notices. A second case turned on whether an outreach program for hiring minorities crossed the line from expanding opportunities to disadvantaging nonminorities. The courts agreed with the latter conclusion in January 2001.[27]

So it was back to the drawing board for the EEO guidelines, and a new plan was presented to the FCC in December 2001. That one would require broadcasters and cable systems to send job-vacancy notices to groups representing minorities and women. The proposed guidelines also called for reporting of statistics on the race and gender of job applicants. This policy provided no sanctions for poor performance, and once data on the percentages of women and minorities hired in electronic media were reported to the government, the process would be over.

REGULATION BY DELIVERY SYSTEM

It's no surprise to TV station managers that few viewers receive their signals via rabbit ears or rooftop antennas anymore. Most U.S. households (70 percent) subscribe to cable and about 15 percent use satellite dishes. The broadband road to the digital future looks uncertain for over-the-air broadcasters. They're under pressure to convert to digital formats but wonder when competing media and manufacturers will join in the transition. Broadcasters say they want a level playing field to face intense future competition from telephone companies, satellite, cable, and the Internet.

Digital Television (DTV)

A major magazine for broadcast journalists posed an intriguing question: "How and When Will HDTV (High-Definition Television) Affect TV News?"[28] The article was published 15 years ago, and the answer could've been "not anytime soon." Digital television (DTV) was finally approved for U.S. homes in 1997, but high-definition TV, an advanced format, was left up in the air. Congress set a deadline of 2006 for stations' conversion to DTV, but did not force the issue of high definition. TV station owners blinked at the cost of building new facilities and worried about getting digital equipment in time. They had further doubts about winning enough DTV viewers to justify their expenses.

The FCC tore a page from its color TV manual by declaring that DTV signals must be compatible with analog (conventional) sets. As the law stands now, TV stations can broadcast in analog channels until 85 percent of U.S. viewers have digital sets in their homes.[29] The agency assigned 6 MHz of spectrum for stations to establish new digital channels.

Leaders in Congress began growing restless about the digital transition in 2001. One committee chairman sent a terse message to the television industry: "Get moving on DTV because if you do not, we [Congress] will force the issue." The barriers to DTV conversion were several: no digital set-top boxes were compatible with broadcast DTV signals, TV manufacturers had not installed digital TV tuners in most models, and practical copyright protection for digital program content was nowhere in sight. Congressional leaders, once peeved about TV station owners' "cold feet," began taking note of how cable and consumer-electronics firms had delayed installing digital receivers and making cable-compatible TVs.[30] Congress pushed cable and electronics industry leaders to find a standard that would work and to make the digital-TV transition by 2006. In 2002, the FCC adopted a plan to require DTV tuners on nearly all TV sets by 2007.

ProTalk

Richard E. Wiley
Dean of the FCC

"It [DTV] needs some overall guidance, and I am hopeful that the Commission will provide that."

Commissioners of the FCC may come and go every five years or less, but one FCC chair has played a pivotal role in policy for more than three decades—that's three decades after the end of his tenure!

In an era of digital convergence, Richard E. Wiley moved the nation closer to high-definition television, but he now confesses that it has all been a bit frustrating: "I think the transition has been very slow and uncertain, and I am concerned about it. I am not sure it is coming together. It needs some overall guidance, and I am hopeful that the Commission will provide that."[31]

Part of the problem, as Wiley sees it, is a lack of compelling high-definition programming from the major networks. "There is CBS and AOL Time Warner and cable, but you know the other networks really haven't done anything . . . so I just don't know what would cause people to go out and buy a digital television set." The other factors troubling the former FCC chair are digital's lack of compatibility with cable and the need for copyright protection for Hollywood movies. While TV station managers strive to make the DTV conversion, Wiley admits that it will be difficult and says he presumes the FCC will grant waivers in certain cases.

Cable Regulations

Congress appeared to be whipsawed by rival groups when it drew up its cable regulation acts. First, there was the 1984 law the cable industry wanted to see enacted to keep franchising authorities from imposing outlandish service requirements and levying exorbitant franchise fees. Then, Congress heard the protest of consumers in 1992, and served notice on the cable industry to begin offering rate relief. The Cable Television Consumer Protection and Competition Act sought to control the charges for both basic and expanded basic tiers of cable channels. One thing seems certain: There will be more legislative attempts to satisfy both parties.

FRANCHISING THE SYSTEM

To get a better view of how cable systems differ from broadcasting, look at one basic difference: federal licensing does not apply to cable because it operates under agreements that bring it under local governing bodies—city or county. The franchise contract is adopted as an ordinance, a local law specifying length of the deal (10 to 15 years is standard); terms of service fees charged; number of channels offered; scheduled time for public access, educational and government channels; and other technical issues.

The city or governing agency is entitled to ask for up to 5 percent of the cable system's gross revenues in fees, so there's a built-in incentive to select the operator most qualified to generate more revenue. In most instances, the process for selecting a cable system starts with a Request for Proposal (RFP). Then, hearings are held with representatives from competing companies before the local agency reaches a franchise agreement with one of them. Some civic leaders forced rival cable systems into unreasonable terms for service contracts in exchange for awarding them franchises, which is why Washington stepped in.

1984 CABLE LAW

Congress passed the Cable Communication Policy Act in 1984 to set the ceiling for municipal franchise fees at 5 percent. The act also prevented cities from specifying just how much money a cable system could or could not charge its customers. It also added a new title to the Communications Act. Title VI coded into law most of the earlier FCC rules for cable, and gave the FCC power to issue guidelines for franchise agreements, including renewals and fees. It freed cable systems from aggressive franchisees hoping to increase their revenues through the franchise fees.

On the other hand, some cable operators saw the 1984 act as a green light to begin raising their rates for basic and premium tiers. The General Accounting Office (GAO) measured a 43 percent hike in the average cable bill from 1986 to 1989. So Congress stepped in again, this time drafting a plan with the consumer in mind.

1992 CABLE LAW

The 1992 Cable Act put a cap on local cable rates, and ordered every system with 36 channels or more to set aside at least 3 channels for lease to outside parties. This **leased access channel** provision gave power to the franchising authority to set maximum rates for special lease customers. The Cable Act (1992) allowed competition among cable systems, and even allowed "overbuilds," in which two cable lines pass the same neighborhood, which is still more the exception than the rule.

Congress asked the FCC to cap the number of cable systems one owner could control. The FCC adopted a rule barring any company from acquiring more than 30 percent of all cable subscribers in the United States. A federal appeals court rejected that action, holding that the 30 percent limit was at crosspurposes with the First Amendment.

MUST-CARRY RULE

The 1992 Cable Act also took a new turn with regard to the "must-carry" provisions for local broadcast channels. You may recall from Chapter 3 that the **must-carry** rule requires cable operators to carry every TV station within a certain radius of their systems. The act had barely become law when Turner Broadcasting, joined by several cable groups, appeared in court to challenge the law's provisions. In two rulings, *Turner I* and *Turner II*, the U.S. Supreme Court held that the must-carry rule was acceptable because it protected noncable homes from losing broadcast TV stations that might be forced out of business if taken off cable's basic tier of channels.[32]

Leased access channels Legal requirement that cable systems reserve some channels for leased commercial use for parties not affiliated with the TV system.

Must-carry Rule requiring that broadcast stations be carried on cable, satellite, or other subscription video service.

A broadcaster could choose to negotiate a "retransmission consent agreement," which charged the cable operator a fee for carriage. Except for a few major cities, most cable systems were unmoved by this option. Television stations needed the exposure on cable anyway and, in most cases, accepted must-carry without imposing fees. This meant the stations' signal would be carried for free, as usual.

Now, if all local TV stations banded together and chose to take their channels off a cable system until the operator agreed to pay a retransmission consent fee, what do you suppose would happen? The U.S. Justice Department stepped in and essentially said, "Cut it out," when KRIS-TV, KIII-TV, and KZTV attempted that ploy in Corpus Christi, Texas. The government warned stations not to "band together and collude in their dealing with cable companies."[33]

Satellite Regulations

If radio and TV stations are licensed and cable systems are franchised, then does satellite television operate without controls? No. Satellite systems are licensed, and have been since the Satellite Home Viewers Act required licenses in 1988. The next time Congress acted, in 1999, the Satellite Home Viewers Improvement Act granted satellite television equitable access to all cable channels available. The new law gave DISH and DirecTV the right to carry local channels, as well. Satellite television also came under the purview of the 1992 Cable Act. Political rules requiring DISH and DirecTV to offer equal opportunities for the campaign spots of federal candidates were applied, in addition to public-service obligations for programming.

Telco Laws

After Bell Telephone was broken into seven regional Bell operating companies (RBOCs), or "baby Bells," in 1982, a new playing field for telecommunications emerged. First, the FCC's video dial tone (VDT) decision of 1992 opened the door for phone companies to deliver TV shows through their wires. Second, the 1996 Telecommunications Act lifted the cross-ownership ban on telephone and cable services. That act allowed the baby Bells to begin offering video programs, while the cable company began selling telephone service to its subscribers.

The FCC now oversees what are called open video systems (OVS) for phone companies. These systems replaced the VDT option, which failed to be profitable through copper-wire distribution. Where fiber-optic lines have been installed, telephone companies deliver data and video through broadband networks. These networks require certification by the FCC, however, and may be subject to a fee charged by local governing bodies.

SMATV and Wireless Systems

Private apartment complexes and some residential communities draw from satellite master antenna television (SMATV). Because SMATV systems usually do not cross public right-of-ways or use broadcast spectrum, they are subject neither to licensing nor to franchise agreements. They are required, however, to follow the same must-carry rules that apply to cable systems. There are other competitors to cable and satellite television as well.

MMDS

Television broadcast by multipoint multichannel delivery systems (MMDS) uses the public airwaves and requires a license from the FCC. Dubbed "wireless cable," MMDS uses microwave channels between 5 and 10 GHz. First sold as an alternative to cable programming, MMDS began to promote its broadband Internet services in the late 1990s. In 1999, Sprint took over one major MMDS company, American Telecasting Inc. (ATI) of Colorado Springs. ATI held MMDS licenses for systems in Denver, Las Vegas, and Portland (Oregon), covering an estimated 10 million households.

CONTENT STANDARDS

As practiced in the United States, media law may be divided into two areas: structural and content regulation. Discussion of mergers and acquisitions focuses on the industry's structure, in terms of legal administration and media ownership. Take a look now at matters of content, beginning with two rules sometimes erroneously tied to the term *equal time*. Both rules were meant to ensure balance and fairness in terms of the broadcaster's obligations to citizens, politicians, and issues of public importance. Neither rule, however, guaranteed *equal time*. The third area of content law covers children's programming.

Fairness Doctrine

The **Fairness Doctrine** grew out of the FCC's longstanding commitment to "the free and fair competition of opposing views."[34] The struggle to define *fairness* goes back to a report issued by the agency's predecessor, the Federal Radio Commission (FRC). In the *Great Lakes* case of 1929, the FRC emphasized the fairness principle, applying it to addresses by political candidates and to all issues of importance to the public.[35] Twenty years later, the FCC adopted the Fairness Doctrine in a special policy statement titled *In the Matter of Editorializing by Broadcast Licensees*.[36] It repealed the FCC's pre–World War II ban on editorials, replacing it with an affirmative obligation to cover "public issues in the community." As the doctrine evolved, it spoke forcefully to debates about the dangers of nuclear energy, pollution of the environment, and even cigarette smoking. However, after decades of contentious hearings, contradictory decisions, and uneven enforcement, the FCC abandoned it. The commission's Fairness Report in 1985 deemed the Fairness Doctrine a failure. Congress disagreed and tried to codify the doctrine into law. President Reagan's likely veto and radio talk-show host Rush Limbaugh were all that stood in the way—but they were enough. The conservative Limbaugh called the fairness legislation the "Hush-Rush" bill, and persuaded his audience to lobby Washington. The listeners protested to lawmakers that the Fairness Doctrine

Fairness Doctrine A doctrine that evolved as a rule requiring broadcasters to report and discuss controversial issues of public importance and to present opposing viewpoints on those issues. The FCC rescinded parts of it in 1987 and 2000.

Equal opportunities Federal requirement that candidates have the same degree of access to local radio and television stations, including advertising rates and time available prior to an election.

deserved to die. President Clinton invited a new Fairness Doctrine bill, but Congress lost both the initiative and the votes needed to enact one. Finally, prompted by two lower court rulings—one involving a nuclear plant in Syracuse, New York, and the other a labor dispute in Arkansas—the FCC stopped enforcing "fairness."[37]

Some loose ends of the doctrine had to be addressed in court. A federal panel ordered the FCC to rescind the doctrine's personal attack and editorializing rules because they "entangle the government in day-to-day operations of the media."[38] Although the doctrine is destined to become an historical footnote, "equal time" has a healthy future as long as politicians demand airtime for their candidacies.

Section 315: Equal Opportunities

The second rule, **equal opportunities,** affects the election campaigns of members in Congress. It holds that if a broadcaster permits any person "who is a legally qualified candidate for any public office to use a broadcasting station, he shall afford equal opportunities to all other such candidates."[39]

At the dawn of radio regulation, the bill that created the Federal Radio Commission advised broadcasters that they must afford equal opportunities to all candidates to air their campaign spots. The law added that stations "shall have no power of censorship over the material broadcast." Congress moved the rule to Section 315 of the Communications Act when the FRC became the FCC, and the 1934 law put some teeth in its enforcement. Radio licenses could be revoked if stations were caught willfully and repeatedly failing "to allow reasonable access to . . . a legally qualified candidate for Federal elective office."[40]

Through the years, Section 315 has produced a number of frequently asked questions (FAQs). For example, broadcasters asked how much to charge politicians for their campaign spots. The answer came in the FCC's "lowest unit charge" rule, which gives candidates the bargain-basement rates offered to a station's most favored advertisers. Stations routinely skirt that rule's little secret: If a candidate wants a particular time slot with a substantial audience—say, a slot next to the local newscast—the station can and often does raise the rates for that ad to guarantee that it won't be preempted. One study of 17 media markets found the price per political spot tripling in the three months prior to the election—the closer to the ballot box the costlier the spot.[41]

The next FAQ: Can a campaign spot for a candidate be edited? Section 315's no-censorship clause proved controversial in 1972. The case in point was the gubernatorial race in Georgia, where a white supremacist decided to spew poison against blacks in his radio spots. Broadcasters felt disgust airing J. B. Stoner's slurs and challenged his political ads, but to no avail. The political spots posed no "clear and present danger of imminent violence," the court held, and had to be broadcast without censorship.[42]

Hustler magazine publisher Larry Flynt threatened to push the limits of the no-censorship clause even further by promoting pornography in his campaign for U.S. president in 1984. The FCC answered that challenge by advising sta-

Campaign Reform

Here's a riddle for you: How does a successful candidate get elected without broadcast advertising? Answer: Only by running unopposed. From 1980 to 2000, the amount of money invested in political advertising in the United States quadrupled from $200 billion to $800 billion. One of the reasons corporate giant Enron became a darling of politicians was its generosity in making campaign contributions to help them buy TV time. Broadcasters are in no hurry to see such situations change.

After the U.S. Senate passed campaign reform legislation putting teeth in the lowest-unit-charge rule, broadcasters launched a lobbying blitz to see that the House of Representatives pulled those threatening teeth. The National Association of Broadcasters expressed its deep appreciation to the House for erasing that rule, which threatened stations' income during election years. Even though "soft money" (cash contributions falling outside federal election laws) may be one day eliminated from the campaign process through congressional reform, the need for money to buy commercial time is a hardy perennial. Some reformers argue that that won't change until the United States joins the rest of the world's democracies in offering *free* television time for candidates to discuss political issues.

tions that the law against obscenity and the federal rules on indecency should be honored even if it meant censoring Flynt's ads.

Obscenity is defined by a three-part test that asks if the questionable material appeals to the "prurient interest," if it depicts sexual conduct in a "patently offensive" way, and if it lacks "literacy, artistic, political, or scientific value." *Indecency* is defined somewhat differently by the FCC as "language or material that, in context, depicts or describes, in terms patently offensive as measured by contemporary community standards for the broadcast medium, sexual or excretory activities, or organs." The key difference is that obscenity is always illegal, but indecent material may be broadcast during the "safe harbor" of hours between 10:00 P.M. and 6:00 A.M. (18 U.S.C. 1464 and 47 CFR Section 73.3999).

When antiabortion activists asked to show dead fetuses as part of their campaigns, broadcasters faced another dilemma. Should the gruesome pictures be censored or broadcast without edits? WAGA-TV in Atlanta elected to channel the graphic spots to "safe-harbor" time slots after midnight, and a U.S. District Court backed up that decision.[43]

Then came the question of newscast coverage: Was equal time needed for every minute that radio and TV reporters covered political incumbents? That certainly would have prompted some news directors to ban most political reporting during campaign season. So the law was amended in 1959 to exempt newscasts, news interviews, news documentaries, and spot news coverage.[44]

What about political debates and press conferences? A special exemption was made for the famous Kennedy-Nixon debates in 1960, but otherwise debates were considered fair game for equal-time requests. Congress eventually understood that if stations were supposed to cover political news to the "fullest degree," debates and press conferences must be added to the exemptions, which they were in 1975.[45]

Warren Beatty. Actors who become candidates for public office find that their appearances on radio or television—even in non-political venues—may trigger legal obligations for broadcasters. Federal law provides equal opportunities for candidates to have access to air time.

One final question: When a candidate appears in a situation comedy or a televised motion picture, does it trigger equal opportunities for his or her political opponents? In 1980 and 1984, because of concern about this issue, Ronald Reagan's movies were routinely yanked from TV program schedules while he campaigned for the White House. The FCC reinterpreted the word *use* to mean broadcasts for political purposes in 1992, thus exempting movies and entertainment programs, but that could change again. Hollywood actors contemplating a race for high office may consult with the FCC to see if it interprets *use* to mean the campaign or the showing of earlier films and TV appearances.

Children's Television

Rules for children's television have long been of interest to parents and politicians. Action for Children's Television (ACT) was formed in the late 1960s in response to cartoons with host characters gulping down brand-name cereals, and with action heroes teaching youngsters violent solutions to social conflicts.

Action for Children's Television had entered the arena after it saw that television had veered from the vision articulated by FCC policy statements. In 1974, the FCC urged broadcasters to provide air time for youth-oriented educational shows and to be wary of how advertisers approached young viewers. Five years later, the commission checked in to see how its *Children's Television Report and Policy Statement* had fared with broadcasters.

The verdict was mixed. Broadcasters were curbing commercial time, but the educational content of children's programming left something to be desired. TV station managers described *Leave It to Beaver* as a learning experience. At that time, deregulation of broadcasting was reaching a zenith in Washington, so the FCC looked the other way. Alternative media, cable, and videocassettes would help mold young people's minds, reasoned broadcasters.[46] Not surprisingly, ACT refused to accept this rationalization and went to court to turn up the heat. The mothers' group lost its first battle over children's programming in 1983, but mounted a second charge that met with success.[47] The FCC reversed its position by drafting new controls for children's television. Meanwhile, Congress drew up the Children's Television Act and passed it in 1990.[48] Six years later, the FCC amended its rules to strengthen its enforcement of the act (see Report in Order in the Matter of Policies and Rules Concerning Children's Television Programming; MMDocket No. 93-48, FCC 96-355, released Aug. 8, 1996).

The new children's TV rules limit advertising time to 12 minutes per hour during the week and 10 ½ minutes an hour on weekends. Television stations must locate three hours in their weekly lineup for educational content. Licensees failing to comply are invited to explain why, or to pay thousands of dollars in forfeitures.

Principle #6

Advocacy groups influence policy and law for electronic media, including children's television.

A Boston Mom's Tea Party

Few people are confident enough to believe they can make a difference in the nature and enforcement of federal law. Those willing to work at it find that they can. Consider the group of Boston area mothers who formed Action for Children's Television (ACT) in 1968. The women first decided to close ranks in support of *Cap'n Kangaroo* after a local TV station announced it would be cutting his morning show in half. The ACT group initiated a letter-writing campaign. Some 2,500 letters later, Cap'n Kangaroo had his full hour back in Boston.

Action for Children's Television then trained its sights on the nation's capital. The FCC had no detailed policy for children's programming, so ACT leader Peggy Charren and her friends decided to help the agency complete its homework. For more than a year, they had prepared studies and talking points on what could be done to improve children's television. Charren led her group to Washington, DC, in order to meet with the FCC commissioners.

They were impressed with ACT's depth and understanding of the broadcast issues.

At first, ACT focused on excessive violence in children's programs, but knew that raising the flag of censorship might jeopardize their cause. They chose instead to focus on TV advertising, arguing that children should not be "dismissed by the medium simply as a market—a group of naive little consumers."[49] The membership of ACT grew slowly and steadily while its leadership developed a sense of what would and would not work in dealing with lawyers, network executives, and Congress. The group secured backing from the Ford and Carnegie foundations, allowing it to get better organized and hire a staff.

The pinnacle of ACT's record of accomplishments was the passage of the Children's Television Act of 1990. Soon after that event, ACT closed its offices, but Charren remains outspoken on children's issues. Her efforts include a campaign to direct indecent content to "safe harbors" (time periods when children are not expected to be watching television).

COPYRIGHT AND PROMOTIONS

A media lawyer recalls that when he began his career, it took about 15 minutes a week to deal with *copyright* litigation. Now, such litigation fills most of his working days. In the digital age, no avenue of law has seen as much new traffic as intellectual property rights. In light of the ease with which any computer can transmit words, pictures, and sounds across global borders, it's easy to understand why. Digital convergence of media has made it easy to copy and distribute material, and the owners of creative property have gone to court to protect their rights. Here's some background on the subject.

Copyright Origins

The eighth section of the first article of the U.S. Constitution delegates to Congress the power to "promote the progress of science and the useful arts." Congress has enacted laws to secure for authors and inventors exclusive rights (for limited periods) to their own writings and discoveries. The U.S. government

Damages Monetary compensation a person receives for injury to his or her property or rights because of the willful act or negligence of another.

Fair use Limited legal permission to use copyrighted materials without the owner's consent, particularly when news, criticism, or scholarship is involved.

recognizes three areas of ownership—slogans, logos, and brand names—as suitable for trademark protection. Inventions are eligible for *patents*, and copyrights are reserved for a "fixed tangible medium of expression." This could mean a play, news story, record, or script, all of which can be copied in some fashion. The fixed expression of ideas may be protected, but the ideas themselves are not.

In 1976, a patchwork of cases and acts converged in a single law to protect ownership rights for creative artists in seven areas: (1) literature; (2) musical compositions; (3) drama; (4) choreography and pantomime; (5) pictures, graphics, and sculpture; (6) films and audiovisual works; and (7) sound recordings.

In order to ensure that a work is protected by copyright, the creator must follow a few rules: Label the work with the author's name, provide the date of publication, and use the symbol for copyright or just add the word *copyright* to the work. Original works need not be registered to receive legal protection. However, making the extra effort to register secures an advantage in court when an artist seeks to recover costs or **damages** for infringement.

Principle #7

There is no absolute protection for one's ownership of original and creative content.

The law defines one pertinent exception to protection: A "work made for hire" falls outside the bounds of personal ownership. "For hire" describes any creative work within the scope of an artist's paid employment. Ownership then belongs to the employer.

Fair Use

Sometimes it's legal to use other people's "fixed expressions." **Fair use** is the term for a privilege to use copyrighted material in a reasonable manner without the owner's consent. Before the copyright expires and the creative expression enters the public domain, scholars, journalists, and other artists may make *limited use* of the material as long as doing so has some *useful literary purpose*.

The Copyright Act of 1976 gave the courts four criteria by which to tell the difference between fair use and infringement: (1) Did the original work fall under copyright protection? (2) How much of the substantive content was exploited? (3) Was that secondary use intended to make a profit? and (4) Will that use affect future profits for the copyright holder(s)? The courts have been reluctant to permit fair use for certain types of commercial spin-offs, such as when a singer imitates Bette Midler on behalf of Ford Motors or when Samsung Electronics uses a Vanna White robot to sell its products.[50]

In Texas, a political parody on the Internet raised a copyright question. A Democrat loyalist set up a website called www.EnronOwnsTheGOP.com using imagery resembling the Texas Republican Party's trademark symbol. The twist was that the corporate logo of bankrupt Enron, Inc., was plastered over the GOP symbol. The Texas Republican Party's at-

Bette Midler. Celebrities have a right of protection to their personal talents and images. When Ford Motor Company used a sound-alike of Bette Midler in a TV commercial, the court ruled in her favor in order to protect her copyright ownership.

torney wanted the website shut down, but its owner refused, pointing to legal precedents protecting satire and parody.[51] The parody site is still up, and so it seems the "cease and desist" letter was to no avail.

Royalties Monetary compensation given to the author, composer, or inventor of a product or work, calculated according to a percentage of its sales receipts.

Royalties and Music

Radio and TV stations don't get their music for free. They negotiate a license fee with the rights-owners, based on the station's audience size, how many times it plays a song, and the music selected. The license requires that **royalties** be sent to either the American Society of Composers, Authors, and Publishers (AS-CAP); Broadcast Music Incorporated (BMI); or the Society of European Stage Actors and Composers (SESAC). What happens when those royalties are not paid?

DIGITAL PIRATES

Copyright pirates have kept especially busy stealing digitally transmitted music over the Internet. That practice led to legal action by the recording industry to stop the pirates, and Congress responded in the 1990s by passing two major laws. The Digital Performance Right in Sound Recordings Act (DPRA) became law in 1995, giving copyright holders royalties from the digital performance of their records over satellite and pay-cable services.

Three years later, the Digital Millennium Copyright Act (DMCA) extended music copyright protection to Internet sites. The DMCA also spread the ban on illegal distribution to include motion pictures, software, and even magazine photos. The law also lengthened copyright periods through the Sonny Bono Copyright Term Extension—named for the California congressman and musician. (Bono was a rock artist who teamed up with Cher during the 1960s to create a number of popular hits. After he died in a 1998 skiing accident while still in office, his widow, Mary, served out his term and brought the bill to passage.) The Bono provision extended ownership protection from the author's life plus 50 years to life plus 70 years. The Bono Act was advocated by the Disney Corporation, which was seeking to maintain ownership of

International Hit List

Artists and copyright holders were glad to see President George W. Bush's administration crack down on countries harboring alleged copyright criminals. Topping the list of renegade nations in 2001 was Ukraine, which developed into a major trafficker of pirate CDs, according to the U.S. government. Other countries on the "priority watch list" were Russia, Taiwan, Indonesia, and the Philippines. One country received a good notice: The United States commended Egypt for taking steps to put a stop to pirate CD and DVD markets. What is the punishment for countries that ignore this law? Trade sanctions are one penalty; denial of membership in the World Trade Organization is another.[52]

Achieving Musical Parody

Fair use has been taken to mean that a parody of original content does not infringe copyright if permission is obtained in advance. The musical comedian Weird Al Yankovic parodies pop artists, but not before getting their permission to do so. Appropriating an artist's music and using it for profit without permission can lead to disaster in copyright court—but doesn't always.

When members of the rap group 2 Live Crew wanted to record a parody of Roy Orbison's rock classic, *Oh, Pretty Woman,* they tried but failed to get permission from Acuff-Rose Music, Inc. So the rappers decided to record their parody without permission and put it on the album *As Clean as They Wanna Be.* The piece featured lyrics such as "Baldheaded woman you got a teeny weenie Afro." Acuff-Rose Music sued for infringement. The U.S. Court of Appeals ruled in 2 Live Crew's favor, concluding that its musical parody was "like less ostensibly humorous forms of criticism, is [of] social benefit, by shedding light on an earlier work, and in the process, creating a new one."[53]

A different outcome developed when comedian Joe Piscopo performed a parody of a rap group known as "The Fat Boys" for a beer commercial. The district court held that Piscopo's act did not qualify for fair-use protection, since it satirized no original work and violated the Fat Boys' right of publicity.[54]

***Oh, Pretty Woman* Case.** 2 Live Crew parodied Roy Orbison's *Oh, Pretty Woman* without permission, and was sued for copyright infringement. The rap group prevailed in court because of the satirical nature of its song.

Mickey Mouse. The American Library Association challenged the law on the basis that it kept "an extraordinary range of creative invention" from entering the public domain just when the Internet was enabling more and more people to draw on this work. The case is currently set for hearing by the U.S. Supreme Court.[55]

The new law gave webcasters a choice between two types of licenses. Web-streaming stations could either negotiate a license with SoundExchange, an organization representing more than 2,000 record labels, or obtain a statutory license from the U.S. Copyright Office. The statutory license carried restrictions that the SoundExchange contract did not. The DMCA also freed Internet service providers (ISPs) from corporate liability stemming from copyright abuses by subscribers illegally downloading and sending music over the Web. The DMCA, however, required ISPs to take action once they became aware of this type of music piracy.

NAPSTER AND FRIENDS

Napster, a website created and incorporated in Boston by a former Northeastern University student, Shawn Fanning, attracted multiple legal claims of copyright infringement. Fanning had composed an index of titles allowing users of the Web to browse and then download records from other members' computers. New artists appreciated this chance to distribute their songs without record companies intervening in the process. Established musicians and record companies, however, considered the downloads to be illegally depriving them of their royalties.

In a San Francisco courtroom, Chief District Judge Marilyn Patel dealt with the Napster litigants. She placed the burden on the music industry by ordering the **plaintiffs**—the petitioners in a legal action—to identify all songs to be removed from the record-swapping service. Napster had just three days to comply with the order.[56]

Napster proponents had hoped the Audio Home Recording Act (AHRA) of 1992 allowed the web-swapping service to do business. After all, the U.S. Supreme Court had ruled in the *1984 Betamax* case that VCRs were a technology capable of noninfringing uses.[57] However, the AHRA prohibited serial copying—making multiple duplicates—but did not cover computers at all. When a three-judge panel from the Ninth Circuit Court of Appeals ruled early in 2001 against Napster, the writing was clearly on the wall. Napster effectively shut down its service on July 2, 2001, and subsequently filed for bankruptcy.

Major music labels rushed in to fill the Napster void with subscription-based on-line music services. Sony Music Entertainment and Universal Music Group formed a service called "Pressplay," and AOL Time Warner, EMI Group PLC, and Bertelsmann AG unveiled a music download service titled "Music-Net." Pressplay's Gold Plan offered 75 songs downloaded to a hard drive and 750 streamed (to be heard once) for $19.95. Pressplay and MusicNet licensed their music, but instead of paying artists a licensing fee, they offered a royalty fee per song, amounting to less than one-fourth of a penny per download.

The lesson to be learned from the Napster case is how dangerous it is to ignore copyright legislation such as the DMCA, even though some musicians and libertarian groups suggest ignoring these laws. Other digital services, including Scour, RecordTV, and iCraveTV, were shut down for taking other people's property and transferring it for free on the Internet. There was even an arrest of a computer programmer for designing software to decode electronic books.[58]

Payola or Promotions?

During the "Happy Days" era of the 1950s, when rock 'n' roll radio was booming, a sleazy business in darkened control rooms came to light. News broke of

Plaintiff One who claims injury to his or her person or property and brings forth a lawsuit.

ProTalk

Heidi Constantine
Media Lawyer

"I don't think the First Amendment gives us the right to exploit the ideas of others without compensating them."

Heidi Constantine enjoys being on the cutting edge, and in her law office in Manhattan that's where she's is, working cases in new media, intellectual property, and "Ibusiness." Her communication studies at the University of Louisiana sparked a special interest in media law, but it was while interning in a Hollywood film and television studio that she found her niche in intellectual property rights. "It was then I realized that this was an area that would never get boring for me due to the constant evolution within the field," says Constantine.

Professionals in electronic media work at the intersection of technology and creativity, and can easily lose the fruits of their labor due to ignorance of property law. "Knowing how to protect your ideas is key to success in today's economy," Constantine says, and that's why she works to keep her clients from losing the benefits of their ideas.

Constantine predicts that the law will continue to evolve toward favoring "big business" through the protection of copyrights, trademarks, and patents. She sees the Sonny Bono provision as a good example. Its extensions of copyright time periods will keep U.S. copyright laws on par with those of the European Union. Constantine supports this, seeing no reason why creative people (or their heirs) should not benefit from their work. "I don't think the First Amendment gives us the right to exploit the ideas of others without compensating them," she says.

Intellectual property law will continue to progress in terms of use of the Internet as test cases such as Napster unfold. "These cases are important because they will set our boundaries for use of the Internet," Constantine says.

Media law provides graduates with the opportunity to combine their interest in communication with a study of our legal system and perhaps effect change in society. Constantine enjoys the perks of working in a fairly stable profession in which she can learn from bright people. That makes the long days filled with writing briefs, letters, and settlement agreements seem worthwhile.

---

record labels trying to manufacture hits for their artists by slipping cash under the turntable to disc jockeys. The deal was that a radio station would play an artist's record so listeners would want to go out and buy it. After this practice, known as *payola*, was revealed in 1959, Congress moved to amend the Communications Act with a section (#508) prohibiting it. The story does not end there, though.

In 2002, the recording industry called on the U.S. government to crack down on a new method for pushing records onto the airwaves. An independent music promoter, or "indie," pays a radio station for the right to represent it exclusively. The promoter's fee paid to the broadcaster can range between $100,000 and $400,000. That would be a big sum for one person to pay, but the indie easily recovers that amount by billing record companies for each song added to the station's playlist. Placing one record on the air can cost a label from a few hundred to 5,000 dollars based on the size of the market and the popularity of the station. The recording industry estimates that major record companies pay promoters millions of dollars each year in such "promotion fees." Lawmakers in Congress drafted legislation to end the practice, but a partisan split stalled that move as conservatives fought for the status quo.

When the largest radio group in the United States, Clear Channel Communications (owner of 1,244 stations), announced in 2002 that is was going to deal exclusively with "indies" and not others, things began to happen. The Recording Industry Association of America (RIAA) and nine artist groups and unions called on the FCC to investigate the practice surrounding indie promotions, record companies, and radio stations. Now that this chasm divides the record and radio business, tougher laws and stricter enforcement may be forthcoming.

FREE SPEECH AND FREE PRESS

Something was missing in the new U.S. Constitution, and Thomas Jefferson knew it. He advised his friend James Madison in 1787 that the document drawn up in Philadelphia that year had a gaping hole where a statement of individual rights belonged. The Bill of Rights, the Constitution's first 10 amendments, was adopted four years later. The First Amendment sets forth the legal principle for communications law by stating in part that "Congress shall make no law . . . abridging the freedom of speech or of the press." The First Amendment protects free speech, but lawmakers in Congress have wrestled with where to draw the line on areas such as defamation and privacy. Meanwhile, electronic journalists hope the amendment will help them to gain access to courtrooms to report on trials, using the tools of their trade — cameras and microphones.

Defamation

Not all free speech deserves protection, since it must be balanced with other rights, including the right to personal reputation. *Defamation* in modern times branches out to form two types of **torts** (**civil suits**). **Slander** refers to oral utterances, and in some states, defaming a person over the air by radio or television is treated as slander. **Libel** refers to printed publications, and suggests that something written caused the injury. Whether a statement amounts to a "publication" depends principally on the message's permanence and whether it may be passed on to others. Most states have adopted the judicial definition of *libel* for broadcasting. It states that speech modulated by electronic media is a type of publication, and any such libel carries heavier penalties than slander does.[59] Either category of offense falls mainly under civil law. Criminal libel statutes are on the books in some states, but rarely are enforced.

A plaintiff seeking to restore his or her good name through a libel action must show the court that the publication did falsely malign the plaintiff through ridicule, contempt, or scorn in a way in which his or her identity was discernible. Even if a name is not mentioned, if the subject's identity can be detected, then the statement may be libelous.

Tort A wrong that breaks the implied social contract of behavior toward others. Torts include libel, slander, and invasion of privacy. Relief is usually sought in the form of money damages.

Civil suit Action involved in petition for monetary damages as the result of a personal wrong or injury. It differs from criminal prosecution that seeks justice for crimes against society.

Slander False expression in speech, gestures, or signs that harms the reputation of an individual.

Libel Published information that is false and injures a person's reputation. If it is an obvious libel, it is called *libel per se*, but if it injures only by implication, it is *libel per quod*.

Defendant Person who is the object of either a criminal or civil action. The defendant must answer the charges in criminal court or the plaintiff's complaint in civil court.

Fair comment A traditional defense in libel or slander suits, dating back to the common law.

Actual malice Defamatory statements made with knowledge of their falseness or with reckless disregard for their truth or falsity.

LIBEL DEFENSES

When media lawyers are asked to defend a broadcast journalist or performer against a claim for defamation that seeks thousands or perhaps millions of dollars, they begin by asking the **defendant** several key questions. First, they need to determine whether the offending statements that were broadcast could be considered true. Truth is an absolute defense, but it is often difficult to prove in a court of law. The second question, then, concerns the defendant's sources for the information. Did it originate from reliable sources, or was it nothing more than secondhand gossip and rumor? Third, lawyers need to discover whether the broadcast information was *privileged*, which means it was spoken or written in a public forum where reporting such material is permissible. Statements are privileged if they are part of a public record, such as debates in the halls of Congress or on the floor of a courtroom. Finally, did the announcer or reporter simply state his or her opinion or was the person asserting a fact? If opinion, the offending words may be protected as **fair comment** and criticism. Fair comment permits some types of satire or humorous exaggeration if the audience would not reasonably infer it to be a fact.

One example of humorous exaggeration is the Carl Sagan case. The famous television astronomer refused to grant Apple's request to name one of its personal computers after him. So as a joke, Apple announced that it would call its new machine the "butt-head astronomer." Sagan sued, but the ruling went against him, since the slur implied opinion, not an objective fact.[60] Therein lies the key to whether humor crosses the line between fair comment and defamation. If it does imply a fact, it crosses the line and can be actionable. In the famous *Hustler Magazine* v. *Falwell case*,[61] an advertisement parody indicated the Virginia evangelist had a drunken rendezvous with his mother in an outhouse. The court held that the advertisement could not be taken seriously.

After the defense has addressed the key questions, it is time for the plaintiff to state his or her case. The plaintiff's lawyers must first ask if their client is a public figure or a private citizen. If the plaintiff is a private citizen, the bar of evidence is lower for the attorneys seeking damages. All they have to show is that the media defendant was negligent in his or her investigation of the alleged facts. On the other hand, if the plaintiff is found to be a public figure, the bar of evidence is higher. The plaintiff's attorney must show **actual malice** was involved in order to secure an award of damages. Be careful, though; *actual malice* is not defined as hostility or a vengeful attitude. It describes circumstances where the journalist or announcer knew beforehand that the defaming information was false, or at least showed a reckless disregard in determining its truth.

The landmark case in this area, *New York Times* v. *Sullivan* (1964), involved a political advertisement. It appeared in the *Times* on behalf of Rev. Martin Luther King Jr.'s legal defense fund.[62] The U.S. Supreme Court agreed that Police Commissioner L. B. Sullivan (though not identified by name) did represent the Montgomery police. The ad falsely accused him, in that official capacity, of trying to "starve students into submission" at Alabama State College. In his opinion, Justice William Brennan declared that a public official should not recover damages for a libel directed at his official conduct unless the statement was made with actual malice—that is, with knowledge that it was false or with reckless disregard for whether it was true. The ruling thus placed libel against public officials on a different level from libel against ordinary citizens.

PUBLIC FIGURES

Some people may lack formal titles or standing in public office, but are viewed as *public figures* in the eyes of the law. Las Vegas entertainer Wayne Newton, for example, brought suit against the NBC television network for a report implying that his purchase of the Aladdin Casino involved Mafia money. At first, a Nevada court found that Newton, a public figure, was owed $5.2 million in damages because the network television story had clearly harmed his persona. NBC appealed the verdict to a higher court, which reversed the decision. The Nevada jury's verdict in favor of its "hometown hero" was overturned because actual malice had not been proved.[63]

> **Principle #8**
> Public officials and figures receive less protection for their reputations than private citizens do.

Privacy

When celebrity gossip passes for news, journalists risk intruding on personal privacy. Two Boston attorneys writing in a law journal expressed that sentiment more than a century ago. Samuel D. Warren and Louis Brandeis claimed that stories of personal gossip had crowded out news items that mattered, and consequently were destroying readers' "robustness of thought and delicacy of feeling."[64] Warren's wealthy family, in particular, had been subjected to some unwanted coverage in Boston's dailies. In an 1890 edition of the *Harvard Law Review*, the two men proposed a law to protect citizens from embarrassing intrusions into their private lives. In 1916, President Woodrow Wilson appointed Brandeis to the U.S. Supreme Court, where he sought to lay the legal foundation for privacy protection. He ultimately succeeded through the "restatement of torts," where the harm of privacy invasion was formally outlined.

Justice Louis D. Brandeis. This Supreme Court Justice, considered one of the founders of privacy law, coauthored a journal article describing the necessity for personal protection from intrusion by the news media.

OFFENSES AND DEFENSES

Courts consider four circumstances to be legitimate invasions of privacy. First, celebrities who find their personal images or likenesses used to sell a product without permission may sue for *misappropriation*. Second, paparazzi who fire a barrage of camera-shutter clicks toward public figures on their private property are *trespassing on personal solitude*. Third, disclosure of *embarrassing private facts* is an unjust invasion of privacy. Finally, if the media place someone in a *false light*, a jury can award damages based on privacy invasion.

The two defenses against privacy are proof of newsworthiness and consent. In other words, the media have to justify their intrusive behavior by showing how important the person is to the public, or must get his or her permission. Celebrities such as Clint Eastwood, Christie Brinkley, Cher, and Jackie Collins have won suits when the media have failed to show either newsworthiness or consent.

CYBERPRIVACY

On the Internet, privacy has moved to center stage in cases involving e-mail searches without warrants and the use of pseudonyms. When the Georgia legislature in 1997 tried to prevent people from using nicknames in their e-mail addresses, the American Civil Liberties Union moved to protect such anonymous communication. A federal district court overturned the Georgia statute for being vague and overly broad.[65]

Congress stepped in to stop unreasonable searches and seizures of e-mail messages found on a personal computer's hard drive. The Electronic Communication Privacy Act (ECPA, 1986) held that such computer evidence requires either a search warrant or a court order before police may seize it. The ECPA also keeps law enforcement agents from intercepting e-mails without a magistrate's signature. A petty officer in the United States Navy, Timothy McVeigh (not the Oklahoma City bomber), sued and won under the ECPA when the government, without a magistrate's approval, investigated his sex life through an America Online e-mail account.[66]

Cameras in the Courtroom

Given the unpredictable nature of the presidential election of 2000, no one knew what the U.S. Supreme Court would say when the Radio and Television News Directors Association (RTNDA) asked for permission for broadcast journalists to cover *Bush* v. *Palm Beach County Canvassing Board*. Justice David Souter announced, "The day you see a camera come into our courtroom, it's going to roll over my dead body."[67] It was a historic occasion when network anchors announced they had audio of that unprecedented hearing, supplied by the U.S. Supreme Court from its chambers. (Audiotape cassettes usually are released, but only after the year's term has ended.)

Barbara Cochran, RTNDA president, called the audio release a victory for her organization and urged members to continue their fight for wider access to courts: "Now is the time for RTNDA and its members to push for access to courts as never before. We will continue to lobby actively for the federal Sunshine in the Courts Act."[68]

TRIALS UNDER THE BIG TOP

Some judges are happy to grant access to photographers and broadcast journalists, whereas others are not so inclined. Those opposed cite trials in which judicial decorum was destroyed by media frenzy. Throughout the twentieth century, the Sixth Amendment's guarantee to a fair trial came into conflict with freedom of the press, and overturned convictions often were the result.

Dr. Sam Sheppard's famous murder trial in Ohio inspired the dramatic TV serial and motion picture, *The Fugitive*. The case now stands as an argument against cameras in the courtroom. In a noisy chamber crowded with radio and television reporters, Sheppard was convicted in 1954 of murdering his wife. The U.S. Supreme Court faulted the trial judge for failing to maintain dignity and order, and overturned Sheppard's conviction. He was later retried and convicted for the crime. The judiciary has viewed cameras as a threat to a defendant's right to a fair trial, not only during the prosecution of a case, but beforehand as well.

Harrison Ford in the Movie Version of *The Fugitive*. The conviction of a Cleveland physician for the murder of his wife inspired both television and motion-picture portrayals of the "Fugitive." To journalists, however, the 1954 trial of Dr. Sam Sheppard was notorious for the circus atmosphere created by reporters covering it.

CAMERAS BANNED

A family tragedy involving the great aviator Charles Lindbergh has a direct bearing on the broadcast coverage of trials. In 1937, the American Bar Association (ABA), reacting to the sensational trial of Bruno Hauptmann for the kidnapping and murder of the Lindbergh baby, moved to prevent courtroom access to photographers and broadcasters. That ban on access came into being as Canon 35 of the ABA Code of Conduct. The canon came under scrutiny after *Chandler v. Florida* was appealed in 1981.[69]

In that case, two Miami police officers had been charged with burglarizing a restaurant. The city's news media followed the case from arrest to prosecution. TV cameras covered the trial, and though only a few minutes of video actually appeared on the screen, the defense claimed the coverage had interfered with justice. The U.S. Supreme Court reached a different conclusion and ruled that the presence of cameras was not enough to deny defendants their right to a fair trial. Afterward, the ABA dropped its ban on cameras from its code. Today, 38 states allow televised trials and 48 states permit judges to decide when access by electronic and photographic media is warranted.

> **Principle #9**
>
> In granting electronic media access to the courts, jurists balance the right to a fair trial against the freedom of the press.

Obscenity and Indecency

Precedent Decision that serves as the authority for subsequent cases in an area of law.

This is a difficult area of law. Should words and pictures be prohibited that incite lust ("prurient interest"), offend the senses ("patently offensive"), and show little in the way of substance ("lacking in serious literary, artistic, political, or scientific value")? These criteria for obscenity emerged in the **precedent**-setting case of *Miller v. California*.[70] There are three sections of federal law under which electronic media may be found in violation for obscene or indecent content.[71] The difference between obscenity and indecency is that indecency has some redeeming social value, but according to the law, obscenity has none.[72]

George Carlin. The king of iconoclastic comedy has come a long way since 1973 when the case arising from his "Seven Dirty Words" monologue established indecency standards for broadcasters. The former disc jockey was cited for lifetime achievement at the American Comedy Awards in 2001.

Principle #10

Obscenity always is illegal, but "indecent" communication is permitted when children are not in the audience.

THE CARLIN CASE

On an October afternoon in 1973, a father was driving with his young son around New York City. He had tuned the car radio to Pacifica Foundation's WBAI-FM. A routine by comedian George Carlin featured a litany of profane and sexual terms that supposedly had been banned by the FCC. Carlin presented them in a rendition of comic free verse titled "Seven Dirty Words."

The father was a member of Morality in Media (MIM), and he wrote a letter complaining of that experience to the FCC. The agency agreed that Carlin's monologue, broadcast at that time of day, was a faux pas of legal magnitude. Rather than slap a fine on WBAI-FM, however, the agency issued what amounted to a warning—a "declaratory order." Pacifica Foundation appealed that sanction, and the FCC welcomed this court challenge in hopes of gaining some judicial guidance.

What came down from the U.S. Supreme Court affirmed the FCC's opinion that radio references to "excretory or sexual activities or organs" were patently offensive during daytime hours. The court ruled that such expressions were a nuisance rather than a high crime, and declared them best channeled to a "safe harbor" in the broadcast schedule—a period when children normally would not be found in the audience.[73]

INDECENCY AND CABLE

The Cable Act of 1984 gave franchising cities the power to ban shows criticized as either obscene or indecent. A cable subscriber in Miami, however, successfully had that law overturned. His complaint was based on the fact that cable subscribers are inviting particular channels into their homes, and therefore should be entitled to watch what they want.[74]

Similarly, the courts nullified two of three provisions in the Cable Television Consumer Protection and Competition Act of 1992 on First Amendment grounds. The Supreme Court prohibited cable operators from either censoring public access channels or segregating indecent programming to certain channels and blocking access to them. The high court did, however, allow cable systems to prohibit indecent programs reserved for lease to third parties. (Part of that 1992 cable act required system operators to lease their channels to home security services, computer data exchanges, or other businesses not to be viewed by cable subscribers.) The Internet and indecency is a different story.

INTERNET INDECENCY

When Congress passed the Telecommunications Act of 1996, the Communication Decency Act (CDA) was attached to keep any form of interactive computer or cable services from transmitting "obscene, lewd, lascivious, filthy, or indecent" material. Even before the digital record had been made of President Clinton's computerized pen signing the measure, the American Civil Liberties Union (ACLU)—joined by a host of publishers, citizen groups, and librarians—challenged the CDA's constitutionality.

The Court of Appeals in *ACLU* v. *Janet Reno* (then the U.S. attorney general) ruled that the CDA was a content-based restriction on speech and this was impermissible. The court said that whether "indecent" or "patently offensive," speech was entitled to constitutional protection. Justice John Paul Stevens delivered the majority opinion in a 7–2 ruling that held that the CDA placed "an unacceptably heavy burden on protected speech." The ruling also said the act was not worthy of rewriting to save an otherwise "patently invalid unconstitutional provision."[75]

Congress responded by passing another bill aimed at the Internet, this time designed to protect children. The Child Online Protection Act (COPA) banned content harmful to minors based on the obscenity definition rendered in *Miller* v. *California*. However, COPA fell to the same fate as the CDA after the ACLU and digital activist groups filed suits against it. The Third Circuit Court of Appeals held that COPA's reliance on community standards in cyberspace was impractical, and pinned its ruling to the belief that computer technology blocking access to minors would be a better solution than government intervention in free speech.[76]

Summary

Electronic-media law has roots in two contrasting traditions: One encompasses the freedoms afforded by the First Amendment, while the other is an obligation to use the airwaves in the public's interest. In the 75 years since the first public-interest standard was incorporated into law, the broadcast media have seen an influx of competition from cable, satellite, and Internet companies. This new playing field has shifted the debate from enforcement of the public-interest standard to the role of law in a broadband future in which delivery systems will overlap and require different solutions in terms of legal protections. Broadcasters are hoping for rules that will let them compete with rivals who are less hemmed in by regulation in the marketplace.

The debate over ownership restrictions has focused on whether cross-ownership and duopoly rules will still afford a diversity of voices and on whether those rules are necessary in the age of digital convergence. Requirements regarding political communication, indecency, and even children's television show how important it is for broadcasters to recognize the special obligations of their public trusteeship. As long as the number of radio and television station applicants exceeds the number of channels available, and free radio and television prevails, a public-interest standard will be applied to licensees. The FCC no longer looks mainly at content in deciding on license renewals, but has not entirely sacrificed the key principles undergirding the Telecommunications Act.

CAREER FOCUS

The transforming influence of telecommunications has created a high demand for attorneys specializing in information and communications law. Career opportunities are expanding in the Federal Communications Commission, the Federal Trade Commission, and a host of other offices in the federal government. New career paths also are available in state agencies involving utilities that deal with telecommunications, as well as in firms specializing in information and communications law.

Law schools intent on meeting the needs of the information economy are adding study "concentrations" in communication, entertainment, media, and information law. Indiana University, for example, offers a degree in information and communications law.

Fortunately, people who pursue law as a profession are generally interested in communication. Many obtain undergraduate degrees in that field before going to law school. They thus have taken courses relevant to a legal career, including public speaking, media law, debate and rhetoric, persuasion, and ethics. Later, as

lawyers, they must extend and refresh their education, partly through continuing legal education (CLE) courses. Because the laws regarding computers, digital networks, and all electronic media are so dynamic, increasing education is particularly important in media law.

The law school graduate specializing in some aspect of communications law can find work in major law firms, the U.S. Patent and Trademark Office, the FTC, the FCC, or other communication-related state and federal agencies. Legal jobs are identified by a variety of titles, including **attorney in communications and media law,** for example, which could focus on public utilities, telecommunications, and administrative law. Another title in this field is **telecommunications associate,** which also would cover regulatory communications and special knowledge of the technology and technicalities of the industry. Careers in law and communication also include **legal researcher, paralegal, legal secretary, legal reporter,** and **legal educator.**

In the digital future, new dilemmas will require new solutions. Concentration of ownership raises the specter of monopoly, but some observers see it as the wisdom of the marketplace winnowing the field. Copyright protection demands solutions that will keep digital pirates from making money off of others' creative works. New technology will call for new laws to protect the old principles of freedom and democracy.

FOOD FOR THOUGHT

1. The FCC has moved toward selling spectrum in auctions rather than giving it away. Do you think that this system unfairly advantages the rich and powerful in electronic media? Why or why not?
2. The FCC has proposed new guidelines to increase diversity in employment by having stations keep records and reporting the ratio of minorities and women to Congress. Do you think that it will be effective in increasing equal employment opportunities? Why or why not?
3. Technical and copyright issues have hampered the transition to digital television. How would you solve the problem in terms of new rules and policies?
4. Do you think that cable companies should be required to pay broadcasters for carrying their channels to cable subscribers? Why or why not?

5. Do you think the V-chip has been effective in curbing children's viewing of violent or sexually oriented programming? What alternative solutions would you propose?

6. Napster's music swapping service is now a matter of history, but would you be willing to subscribe to a pay-service for computer-downloads of music? Support your position.

7. If you owned a record company, would you allow new artists to post their music for free on the Internet? Why or why not?

8. Do you think cameras in the courtroom hamper a defendant's ability to get a fair trial? How would you balance the competing interests in this matter?

15

Professional Ethics

> We are what we repeatedly do. Excellence then is not an art, but a habit.
>
> —Aristotle

Al-Jazeera Television. The agreement between American cable network, CNN, and Al-Jazeera television raised ethical questions regarding the use of videotape of alleged terrorist, Osama bin Laden.

Network TV news coverage of the 2001 air strikes in Afghanistan was titled and promoted like the movie of the week: "America Strikes Back," "America's New War," and other branded newscasts. Images poured forth of live, breaking news covering the U.S. campaign to "root out terrorists." Unlike made-for-TV movies, though, the narrative did not always follow the script.

Two news organizations from opposite ends of the earth joined in a pact to share video. CNN of Atlanta, Georgia, and Al-Jazeera in the tiny kingdom of Qatar forged a deal for exclusive footage of Osama bin Laden, the alleged mastermind of September 11, 2001. Al-Qaeda's chief merchant of terror produced a videotape of himself surrounded by his lieutenants outside a cave in Afghanistan. Bin Laden's monologue was beamed up to Al-Jazeera's satellite after the U.S. air strikes in Afghanistan began.

CNN held exclusive rights to those pictures for at least six hours, but when rival networks such as CBS saw the images, they felt compelled to download and rebroadcast the footage. CNN's exclusivity was effectively nullified, but CBS News spokeswoman Sandy Genelius said her network was simply serving the public's interest "by putting its right to be informed above petty competitive issues."[1]

There is more to this story than just network rivalry. More than a decade earlier, when Saddam Hussein of Iraq was the adversary, U.S. news coverage in the Middle East was virtually dominated by CNN. Anchor Bernard Shaw and correspondent Peter Arnett televised the bombing of Iraq live from Baghdad, courtesy of Iraqi censors. But that was then, and this was 2001. The field of 24-hour news competitors had blossomed in the 1990s. Fox and MSNBC, on cable, plus a host of websites, in addition to the traditional networks, were vying for the same viewers as CNN. Naturally, they all wanted the best footage, and so they simply took the shots of bin Laden. What were the consequences of their actions? CNN chief Walter Isaacson threw up his hands and said, okay, his competitors could use the pictures. A "compelling national interest" was involved. This courtesy in the battle for ratings was unusual, but CNN's next move in covering the war on terrorism drew a firestorm of attention.

Her network was simply serving the public's interest "by putting its right to be informed above petty competitive issues."

The all-news network joined in a plan with Al-Jazeera to interview bin Laden by supplying a list of questions in advance. Radio talk-show hosts and conservative websites went ballistic. "CNN wanted *face time* with the enemy? Boycott CNN and its sponsors!" was heard from coast to coast. Angry Pakistanis burned CNN's logo in effigy, while the network got "flamed" at home—all because it recognized a respected journalism principle: Get both sides of the story. When an interview was finally staged with bin Laden, Al-Jazeera refused to telecast it. Its journalism ethics prevented it because the questions had been orchestrated by bin Laden. CNN, on the other hand, telecast the interview over its Arab partner's objections.

Who was right—CNN, Al-Jazeera, or the viewers who found the whole episode disgusting to the extreme? The point is that there is no avoiding tough calls on deadline. What's more, each media decision is in full view for the audience to applaud or hiss, until questions are resolved or until it just blows over. So it can help to have a solid grasp on principles from professionals when those storms of second-guessing begin.

WHY STUDY ETHICS?

There is a school of thought that believes principles and ethics to be an indelible product of childhood rearing, social influence, and cultural mores—so why bother teaching them if they are instilled in the first place? Another school holds that principles and ethics are irrelevant to professional conduct—easily forgotten because, in essence, don't we all do what we must do to survive? If that means sacrificing some moral high ground—then, so be it.

Both viewpoints dismiss the part that ethical reasoning and professional standards play in determining conduct. We are committed to the idea that people who reach pinnacles in their professions by unscrupulous means are exceptions that prove the rule, and true success is not contradictory to either character or conscience. This chapter will examine the evidence of this and will explain our ethical heritage. After all, what contemporary professionals have to say about tough calls and the standards they rely on to make them, indicates what is useful to know for a future career.

Ethics Defined

When you look up the word *ethics*, you find the Greek word, *ethos*, denoting custom or character. Your ethical choices become part of your custom by what you practice everyday. *Ethics* is actually what happens in your thoughts, whereas *morality* is what others see on display. One simple question sums it up: What is the best way to think and behave in a particular situation?

Generally, ethics fall below the level of law, but certain ethical choices do lead to litigation, particularly when personal wrongs are alleged in civil court. Both areas—ethics and law—deal with questions of right and wrong. The roots of our legal and ethical heritage spring from the same source: ancient and medieval philosophy, science and the Scriptures, and even the cultural and moral trends of the day. The journey usually begins in Athens, where Greek philosophers tried to define the good life in terms of duty and purpose.

Teleology

Two theories shape much of what we know and think about ethics. The first one looks at what is called *telos*, the Greek root word of **teleology,** and it suggests an *end* or *purpose*. In other words, what are we trying to accomplish here? Greek philosopher Aristotle (384–322 BC), an early teleologist, taught that we must understand what is our purpose. As the U.S. Army used to say in recruitment posters, "Be all that you can be."

To achieve your *telos*, you must make choices by reasoning from principles. One principle helps to narrow the options: Aristotle called it the *golden mean*—the middle point between extremes. The goal of moderation avoids extremism, advocating self-discipline over self-denial. Aristotle's lessons were instructions for virtuous living, which is why his way is called *virtue ethics*. Temptations to sloth, fraud, murder, or adultery would never enter the discussion since, by definition, they are *vices*.

Even more central to Aristotle's philosophy is the work of ethical analysis. As scholar Martha Nussbaum once put it, "you or I, coming

Teleology Ethical theory based on *telos* for end or purpose. Assumes the purpose of our lives is discernible and is ordained either by divine powers or by our own will.

Aristotle, Greek philosopher and ethicist.

Principle #1

The golden mean recommends a middle ground between extremes.

German idealist Immanuel Kant.

into a complex ethical situation, have to have our faculties open and responsive, ready to shape ourselves to the complex, perhaps unique and non-repeatable demands" for each decision.[2] We reason from principles in order to make good decisions. Rival Greek philosophers, known as the "Sophists," promoted more attractive solutions. Their philosophy, known as *sophistry*, describes seductive but *not* well-reasoned choices.

Deontology

A second foundation theory in ethics is rooted in the Greek word *deon* for duty, which is said to be the essential moral value ensuring happiness. **Deontology** elevates *duty* over *purpose*, and originates in the scriptures and commandments that recommend service to a higher principle. Deontology is how we often define our heroes. When personnel of the New York City police and fire departments rushed into the World Trade Center on September 11, 2001, to save lives at the loss of their own, it was a sense of duty summoning them onward.

Two millennia after the Greeks, German idealists put a new face on deontology. Their quest was for philosophical ideals that would show how each person could embrace the good life by acting on principle, which is why they were called German idealists. One of their leaders, Immanuel Kant (1724–1804), searched for universal maxims known as **categorical imperatives**. These include obligations such as being fair and truthful. Kant also believed correct motives produce happiness regardless of their success—like the old saw about winning or losing not being as important as how you play the game.

In terms of ethical theory, the problem with the deontological approach is that it forms no basis for resolving conflicts between loyalties. Journalists, for example, may find their professional duty at odds with their general duty as citizens. What happens then? One reporter was writing about a struggling immigrant in the United States carefully saving his earnings to send back to his family in Mexico. The reporter's story tipped off authorities that the man was an undocumented alien, and brought about his deportation. Should the journalist have concealed the man's illegal status and ignored federal law? If your answer is, "do your duty," the obvious question becomes, "which duty?" Ethicists suggest that a reasoned analysis of the situation based on principles and consequences will reveal the correct solution.

Consequentialism

An offshoot of teleology, (emphasis on purpose) devoted to the impact of ethical choices on the end result, called **consequentialism**. The writings of Jeremy Bentham and John Stuart Mill, nineteenth-century British philosophers, are cited as sources of this perspective. Mill's classic treatise, *On Liberty*, spelled out another simple notion—the greater the freedom, the greater the happiness. However, he argued that because personal liberty expands our choices, it gives

---

> **Principle #2**
>
> Categorical imperatives such as fairness and truth guide ethical decisions.

Deontology Ethical theory based on *deon* for duty, which is the essential moral value (rather than happiness or virtue).

Categorical imperative Ethical theory based on discoverable principles or laws that can guide *all* human behavior.

Consequentialism Ethical theory that holds that the correct moral choice is the one that produces the best results.

us more opportunity to act for the greater good. In Mill's **utilitarianism,** there is a healthy sense of moral duty. Twentieth-century ethicists Bertrand Russell and John Dewey agreed with Mill that considering outcomes is essential in making moral choices.

Consequence-based ethics have spawned other self-seeking theories, such as egoism, relativism, and situationism. **Egoism** asks first what might be in your own best interest, and beckons self-interest instead of sacrificing for some greater good. **Relativism** and **situationism** place emphasis on personal goals and circumstance—the specifics of the ethical delemma at hand. These perspectives minimize the role of duty, and can even lead to moral decay, warned one media scholar. If carried to its outer limits, "relativism can lead to moral anarchy in which individuals lay claim to no ethical standards at all."[3]

So, in choosing among ethical theories, is it necessary to select one perspective based on deontology or teleology or can we consider all of the above? Ethical dilemmas call for an assessment of goals and duties, as well as of moral responsibilities and consequences. The more careful the reasoning based on principles, the greater the chances that a wise decision will be reached.

Utilitarian John Mill.

PROFESSIONALISM

> **Principle #3**
>
> Ethical decisions are based on an assessment of duty, purpose, and consequence.

When it comes to working in the media, the question of whether it is a profession, craft, or trade is far from settled. The answer usually depends on whom you ask, and how that person defines the term *professional.* If you were to describe a profession as a career grounded in formal degrees with some system of certification, as in medicine or law, then a career in electronic media probably would not qualify. However, if a profession is defined by a set of standards or ethics, then a career in electronic media would fit that description.

Generally, volunteer members of professional associations draft or revise codes of ethics in committees, which hold little or no power to enforce them. The codes are simply statements of principle, designed to encourage ethical conduct. Lawyers may even try to discourage radio and television stations from defining their moral principles for fear of having to defend them in a court of law. However, dedicated professionals do not shy from stating their ethical beliefs simply because lawyers warn them that this may exact a price in civil damages. Ethical codes are one element of professionalism, and education is another.

Historical and Contemporary Perspectives

When famed newspaper publisher Joseph Pulitzer exchanged letters in 1904 with Harvard University's president about teaching ethics as a prerequisite for a professional career in journalism, it was clear that the two men did not quite see eye to eye. President Charles Elliot was enthusiastic about teaching students the journalist's duty to the public. He proposed classes at Harvard that would be designed to show how editors and publishers influence public policy. Pulitzer preferred

Utilitarianism Ethical theory that determines the correct moral choice based on choices and behaviors that produce the greatest good for the most people.

Egoism Ethical theory that holds that the primary beneficiary of an action should be he or she who takes the action, and that sacrifice is not necessary.

Relativism Ethical theory based on principles accepted according to circumstance rather than on universally applicable principles.

Situationism Ethical theory that approaches each situation as unique and holds that absolutes are simply too inflexible.

Normative ethics Branch of ethical theory that determines which human actions are right based on moral values, principles, and conduct.

Egalitarianism Ethical theory based on the notion that people are entitled to the same rights and privileges without respect to extraneous factors such as religion, gender, or race.

Prescriptive ethics is a normative approach and involves taking a stand about what standards and principles ought to govern behavior.

another approach: "Ideals, character, professional standards . . . a sense of honor should be the motif of the whole institution," he replied.[4] Pulitzer shifted the emphasis from the newspaper office (in Elliott's proposal) to the world at large.

Ethical Applications

Regardless of the source—the Bible, the Quran, family instruction, or cultural mores—**normative ethics** are the general principles governing moral behavior. They are based in the philosophies and translate virtues such as *charity*, *fidelity*, and *truth* into everyday choices. One such virtue, **egalitarianism**, holds to the idea that people are created equal with certain inalienable rights.

Political theorist John Rawls was interested in achieving justice for all through what he called "the veil of ignorance."[5] This metaphor suggested that questions of justice may be resolved without regard to race, creed, color, gender, or status and ensure the rights of liberty and equality of opportunity. For the media, this *veil* is similar to the blindfold of the goddess Justice, who weighs only the issues relevant to a dispute so that all people are treated as equals.

Normative or **prescriptive ethics** have been translated into codes developed by associations and professional groups. The National Association of Broadcasters (NAB), the Society of Professional Journalists (SPJ), and the American Advertising Federation (AAF), among others, present their members with these guides of professional behavior. They contain ideals that are both prohibitive and affirmative.

> **Principle #4**
>
> Prescriptive ethics draw on higher principles to point us toward actions.

Codes of Ethics

The first National Association of Broadcasters (NAB) code of ethics was adopted in 1929 and consisted of only eight rules, half of which were designed to alleviate concerns about the commercialization of radio. Broadcasters, for example, who subscribed to the code promised to air no promotion that was "fraudulent, deceptive or obscene." Over the years, the NAB code was expanded to address a variety of issues in news, politics, religion, and children's programming. Not all broadcasters subscribed to it, but for those who did, NAB staff members were assigned to investigate complaints made against them or their station.

In terms of advertising, the early code banned radio commercials between 7:00 P.M. and 11:00 P.M. to make room for "relaxing nighttime listening, often as a family."[6] That ethic lasted only until 1937, when nine minutes of commercial time were allowed per daytime hour, and six minutes at night.

Violations of the NAB code carried only one penalty: removal of the NAB seal from the wall of the broadcast station office. The code was revised in 1952 to include television, but 30 years later was eliminated altogether. The scene of its demise was a court battle over the so-called *piggybacking* ban, preventing a sponsor from squeezing two product messages into a one-minute spot.

Alberto-Culver, a cosmetic firm, complained that this restrictive rule kept it from getting the commercial schedule it needed for its advertising. The NAB asked the Department of Justice if the code violated antitrust laws, since the ban on piggyback spots appeared to be in restraint of trade. The government affirmed that position, and a federal court judge agreed. In November 1982, the 53-year-old NAB code was dropped.

For eight years, there was nothing on the books resembling a statement of good behavior at the NAB. In 1990, the NAB's executive committee, working in concert with its attorneys, came up with a voluntary statement of principles covering just four areas: *children's television, indecency* and *obscenity, violence,* and *drug abuse.* Gone were all of the rules and prescriptions of the old NAB code, replaced by a statement of the broadcasters' rights under the First Amendment, and "the desires and expectation of its audiences and the public interest."[7] This "general and advisory" statement asked broadcasters to "exercise responsible and careful judgment" when considering programming dealing with those issues. Washington lawmakers and one member of the FCC, Michael Copps, asked for a new NAB Code in 2002, but the response from the broadcast community was decidedly adverse.

Broadcast Journalism Ethics

Among careers in electronic media, it is broadcast journalists who most often confront ethical issues and dilemmas when making decisions. They have relied on their own codes of ethics for over half a century. In 2000, the RTNDA adopted six normative values for its code, including *"public trust, truth, fairness, integrity, independence,* and *accountability."*

When first meeting as the National Association of Radio News Directors (NARND) in 1946, broadcast journalists approved a guideline to "accurately and without bias . . . within the bounds of good taste" report the news. They further endorsed a reporter's duty to "journalistic principles and ideals," and duty as well to the general manager of the station.[8] In its postwar resolve, the NARND vowed to move radio reporting beyond its "rip 'n' read" phase, petitioning station managers to hire independent journalists to cover local news.

SENSATIONALISM

Just two years after that first code of ethics was drafted, broadcast journalists became concerned with what might be called *sensationalism.* Excessive play of the terms *bulletin* and *flash* on radio was the problem then. News directors called on their colleagues to avoid this practice in reporting, writing, and announcing the news. Today, the association's professional standards reject all reporting "that fails to significantly advance a story, place the event in context, or add to the public knowledge."

Sensationalism, however, is defined in different ways. The RTNDA advises anchors and reporters to avoid "techniques that skew facts, distort reality, or sensationalize events." The code of ethics for the Society of Professional Journalists (SPJ) asks reporters to "show good taste. Avoid pandering to lurid curiosity." The National Association of Broadcasters advises programmers "to avoid presentations purely for the purpose of sensationalism or to appeal to prurient interest or morbid curiosity." The Advertising Principles of American Business also calls for ads "free of statements, illustrations or implications, which are offensive to good taste or public decency." The term raises questions about exaggeration and distortions as well as decency and taste.

STEREOTYPING

Ethical codes have spoken to the rights of minorities by reminding journalists to gather a diversity of opinions from all informed members of the community and, in the name of fairness, to avoid stereotyping minorities. In 1950, broadcast journalists codified their concern with stereotyping in the United States for the first time. They stated, in what became the eighth standard in the revised code, that "the race, creed, color or previous status of an individual in the news should not be mentioned unless it is necessary to the understanding of the story."

Today the SPJ code is both broader and more specific in attacking prejudice in reporting. It asks the press to "avoid stereotyping by race, gender, age, religion, ethnicity, geography, sexual orientation, disability, physical appearance or social status." The SPJ ethic further advises its journalist members to "be a voice for the voiceless."[9]

JUDICIAL DECORUM

When the RTNDA revised its code in 1966, broadcast journalists were asked to "conduct themselves with dignity" in court, and to "keep broadcast equipment as unobtrusive and silent as possible." That action followed two sensational court trials—one of a doctor accused of murdering his wife in Ohio, and another involving the fraudulent sale of fertilizer in Texas. Reflecting on the carnival atmosphere created by such trials, RTNDA members vowed to place greater emphasis on each citizen's right to a fair trial.

PRIVACY

The RTNDA's rewrite of its code in 1966 also marked the beginning of its professional concern with the privacy of individuals in the news. Broadcast reporters were pledged to "display humane respect for the dignity, privacy and well-being of persons" with whom the news dealt. In addition, the amended code called for a special sensitivity to the privacy of children.

The SPJ code calls for "compassion to those who may be affected adversely by news coverage" and for recognition that gathering and reporting the news "is not a license for arrogance." Only an overriding public need, in SPJ's view, "can justify intrusion into anyone's privacy."

DIVIDING NEWS AND ADVERTISING

The first code of standards for radio news recommended a wall of separation within a station, between its newsroom and the sales office. The code said commercials must be kept separate from news content and required a someone other than the newscaster to deliver them. This separation was endorsed by the Society of Professional Journalists, which saw hybrids of advertising and news as violations of the *truth* principle and thus to be avoided. The SPJ ethic urges journalists to "distinguish news from advertising and shun hybrids that blur the line between the two." The Advertising Principles of American Business includes eight ethics, seven of which deal with truth and verification in commercials.[10]

PRESCRIPTION TRUTH

CBS newsman Edward R. Murrow put it this way: "To be persuasive, we must be believable. To be believable, we must be credible. To be credible, we must be truthful."[11] University of Illinois ethicist Clifford Christians says that all principles of ethics begin with a promise. In electronic media, the most fundamental promise is to tell the truth to the audience. *Truth* naturally summons to mind the need for accuracy and diligence in reporting, but it also suggests the danger of distortions, plagiarism, and false and misleading information. Over the years, hasty mistakes have cost more than one member of the electronic media professions a loss in credibility.

Scooping the Scandal

A study commissioned by the Committee of Concerned Journalists found lapses in reporting during the Monica Lewinsky scandal in 1998. That's when President Clinton found his administration under siege by "hypermedia" that gave around-the-clock coverage to speculative opinions, rumors, and conjectures about his relationship with a White House intern. During one six-day period, when the focus was on Ms. Lewinsky's dress, 30 percent of what was reported was effectively based on no attributed sources, and 41 percent of the reporting contained no facts but was grounded in "analysis, opinion, speculation, or judgment."[12]

Scandal Mongering. Media coverage of President Clinton's liaison with Monica Lewinsky raised questions of professional ethics concerning the use of rumor, speculation, and unverified sources in reporting.

What had been the standard for investigative journalists—interviewing two independent sources to verify all allegations—was often ignored. Former CBS correspondent Marvin Kalb found that news networks and websites were citing each other as sources, or simply leaving audiences in the dark about the identity and integrity of their sources. It seemed to be a contest to keep up with a new journalistic contender, Matt Drudge's Internet mill of fast-breaking gossip. Kalb perceived that standards of journalism were being undermined not just by Drudge but by media mergers, in which staffs are cut to help bottom-line investors—making fact-checking shortcuts inevitable. It seemed that verifying stories with two independent sources simply was becoming too costly in time and personnel.[13]

Promotions and Propaganda

The drive for audience ratings threatens the principle of truth if media reporters are willing to exchange hyperbole and fiction for reality. A syndicated TV news magazine, *Inside Edition*, promoted a show in 1999 entitled *Opening the Lost Tombs Live from Egypt*. The title seemed to suggest that live TV cameras would carry the audience to a dramatic moment of first discovery. What actually took place was the opening of several tombs prior to the telecast. An archaeologist responsible for the excavation explained that his preopening of tombs was necessary in order to avoid ruining the contents. *Reopening the Tombs* would have been a more accurate title for the program.

In November 2000, a Cincinnati radio station broadcast a story so amazing that the press was eager to report it. One of WEBN-FM's fans had become so devoted to its programming and personalities that he bequeathed $10,000 to the station, and WEBN-FM put his widow on the air to verify her husband's generosity. The station later admitted it was all just a hoax—a female staffer had impersonated the widow—much to the surprise of the *Cincinnati Enquirer* and other news media reporting the story. The fiction invented by WEBN-FM's program director broke no federal law, but it clearly betrayed the principle of truth.[14]

President Bush's administration in 2002 announced plans for two offices that would be dedicated to propaganda. The Office of Strategic Influence would operate in the Pentagon, and, reported the *New York Times*, would rely on both information and *disinformation* for its propaganda campaign.[15] A second office of global diplomacy was to be dedicated to "intense shaping of information and coordination of messages." The reaction by the press to this announced betrayal of the truth principle was decidedly unfavorable. Texas columnist Molly Ivins wrote that you do not have to go "very far out on a limb to predict this will be a disaster. It will wreck our credibility in no time. . . . As any journalist can tell you, when you put out misinformation, all it does is poison the well of public debate."[16]

Shortly after the news broke of the military's plans to plant fake stories overseas, the Hollywood press reported that Washington would be teaming up with a top action-movie producer to produce a 13-episode "reality" series on ABC, profiling U.S. troops abroad. An ABC Entertainment executive claimed that the Pentagon was eager to "produce what Americans want to see" because the military regarded it as

> **Principle #5**
>
> Without truth there is no trust, and without trust meaningful exchanges of information are lost.

an Army recruiting film. CBS anchor Dan Rather told the *New York Times* he was outraged over the "Hollywoodization" of the military.

Indecent Content

Lurid, indecent, and sensational content has provoked lawmakers and watchdog groups to recommend changes in television commercials and programming. FCC Commissioner Michael Copps and Senator Robert Byrd (D-WV) criticized broadcasters for violating standards of good taste by airing objectionable programming. Broadcasters countered by claiming that the FCC was trying to bully them, and announced their hopes that Senator Byrd's complaints would fall on deaf ears at the FCC.

Why all the fuss over television decency? The Parents Television Council (PTC) conducted a content analysis indicating that sexual activity was more prevalent and raunchier than ever before. The most popular "family hour" show in early evening was *Friends*, focusing on sex in each episode with characters making the rounds among multiple partners. A show with animated creatures for kids had one repeatedly saying, "Kiss my butt." Fox scheduled a prime-time special featuring "the largest metal object ever impaled in and removed from a human."

WWF *Smackdown*. Several advertisers withdrew their commercials from one of the World Wrestling Federation's popular programs after children begin harming each other by imitating the moves in the ring.

UPN airs *WWF Smackdown* which averages 18 incidents of crude or coarse language or sexual and violent content per hour, and is a huge success on cable television. The World Wrestling Federation even went to court and sued a group of concerned parents for millions of dollars in lost revenue after the parents persuaded sponsors to desert *Smackdown*.[17] The PTC announced on its website that four children were killed by imitating wrestling moves viewed on *WWF Smackdown*. The PTC blamed the violent deaths on kids' mimicking the "clothes line" and the "jackknife power bomb."

Are broadcasters just giving audiences what they want? "Look, we're not saying we love the fact that kids are exposed to a lot more adult concepts and language a lot earlier than they used to be," editorialized *Broadcasting & Cable*. "But whether it is the inevitable and healthy maturing of the culture or an unseemly coarsening of the fabric of society, it is a fact of life." Senator Joseph Lieberman's (D-CT) advice to parents: "Turn off the television if you find [shows] inappropriate for your children or offensive to their values."[18]

FAIRNESS FOR ALL

The study of professional standards is important because in a free country, self-governance determines action more than law does. Radio and television journalists are called on to protect people subject to the ravages of prejudice and stereotypes by fostering an atmosphere of tolerance and respect.

Prime Minister Tony Blair.
Britain's Prime Minister argued against lumping believers in Islam with those who practiced terrorism in order to achieve destructive goals.

Hispanics on TV. In terms of television, Hispanics are America's forgotten minority with far fewer appearances than their percentage of the population. Pop stars such as Ricky Martin and Christina Aguilera stand as exceptions.

September 11, 2001: A Wake-Up Call

In his plea to stave off the impact of misguided prejudice, British Prime Minister Tony Blair blamed the September 11 attacks not on "Muslim terrorists" or "Islamic terrorists" but on "terrorists" period. Journalists had begun to feel the need to portray the Islamic community in a positive or at least neutral light.

For decades, Americans of Arab origin were brought into the vortex of news coverage in times of war or terror, but virtually were ignored on a day-to-day basis. A Los Angeles reporter heeded the SPJ ethic, "Be a voice for the voiceless."[19] Jennifer Sinco-Kelleher heard local Muslim leaders charge U.S. media with adding fuel to the fires of hatred against their congregations. Sinco-Kelleher thought she should do something about it. Keenly aware of her lack of knowledge about one of the world's great religions, she headed for a mosque.

There, she found something surprising: Despite negative media images of Middle Easterners and skewed stories of Palestinians celebrating the attacks of September 11, Moslems were happy to welcome Sinco-Kelleher into their house of worship. Her prejudices soon melted in the glare of experience and reason.

Diversity Deferred

Egalitarian principles are supposed to prevail in the United States, but, by nature, people tend to think first in terms of their own social group, gender, and ethnic origins. So diversity becomes a challenge for media writers and producers.

Hispanic Americans, for example, represent 12 percent of the U.S. population, but appear in fewer than 3 percent of the shows on television. When they do appear, it is not often in a flattering light. ABC News correspondent Elizabeth Vargas believes it is especially important to counter negative stereotypes whenever people of color are depicted as criminal suspects hiding their faces. Vargas said one ethical remedy would be to interview role models from the minority community—for example, to seek out physicians of color for health news "to show that, indeed, blacks and Hispanics are well represented in the successful, affluent, educated part of our society."[20]

It would be reassuring to believe that major strides have been made toward perfecting a diverse picture of the United States. Fifty-five years ago, Robert L. Hutchins of the University of Chicago convened a commission of 13 scholars and professionals to investigate the ethical performance of media. The commission resolved that journalists need to draw a "representative picture of the constituent groups of society." Other media obligations, the commission said, included giving a truthful and fair account of the day's events, providing a forum for comment and criticism, reflecting the goals and values of society, and offering full access to the day's intelligence.

Researchers have been tracking coverage of minority groups in local television news to see how well stations perform in terms of this diversity ethic of social responsibility. Professor Don Heider of the University of Texas found evidence that news reporters fail to see beyond their personal ethnicity to collect "information from, or perspectives of, people of color." Journalists face an uphill fight in their efforts to achieve diversity of coverage, but Heider says they "must resolve whether they want to struggle with mostly Anglo, male managers over what will be covered and how it will be covered, and whether these fights may be worth jeopardizing their careers."[21]

> **Principle #6**
>
> Being fair means being blind to individual differences that are irrelevant to the issue.

INDEPENDENCE AND SELF-INTEREST

Journalists are often subject to pressures from both news sources and advertisers. Professional ethics require them to report stories in an impartial and disinterested manner. Notice that the term is not *uninterested* but *disinterested*. A vexing challenge arises when journalists are pressured to hold back on a story, either by advertisers or by their own bosses.

Advertising Pressures

Television members of the Investigative Reporters and Editors (IRE) organization have found that advertisers carry a big stick but do not always speak softly. One survey asked those journalists if TV sponsors had ever "tried to influence the content of news on local commercial stations?" Almost 75 percent of the sample said yes, and more than half said they had seen sponsors try to kill a story. Fifty-four percent in the IRE survey said they knew of businesses that had withdrawn their advertising because of the content of news reports.[22] Dollars are potent weapons that sponsors can use against electronic journalism.

JOB SECURITY?

Television reporters who tackle tough consumer topics—especially issues directed at automobile dealers—may even risk their job security. Consumer reporter David Horowitz was released from KCBS-TV in Los Angeles after raising the question of automobile safety one too many times.[23]

A husband-and-wife investigative team in Florida found its coverage of Monsanto's synthetic growth hormone for cows upsetting to lawyers for the station's

Corporate Ethics. As a member of the Disney family, ABC News has had to make difficult decisions on what stories to cover about Disneyland and other corporate properties.

parent company. The couple's reporting for WTVT-TV (Fox) in Tampa Bay raised the possibility of carcinogens in milk. The problem was that the report never aired, and the couple lost their jobs. Steve Wilson and Jane Akre alleged in their suit that upper management had intervened in their news judgment.[24]

COVERING THE MOUSE

The question of corporate influence over news policy came into play when ABC News blocked the broadcast of a 20/20 segment in 1998. In the story, investigative reporter Brian Ross described Disneyland's hiring practices, raising the question of whether pedophiles were effectively screened out by the Disney Company, which owns ABC. Network news managers defended their decision to kill the story, denying that corporate pressure was involved. ABC News had covered negative stories before about its parent company. Eileen Murphy, ABC News spokeswoman, says reporting on one's corporate bosses is never an easy task. "Whatever you come up with [regarding the parent company], positive or negative, will seem suspect."[25]

Hybrid Content and Commercials

Advertisers also may try to blend their products in with news coverage, leaving journalists to decide the ethics of covering stories saturated in commercial content. Tough decisions over what to do about video news releases, product placement, and the use of digital technology to rent part of the screen for marketing purposes are not uncommon.

VIDEO NEWS RELEASES

The use of video news releases (VNRs) is a familiar practice to politicians with an eye on reelection, or to advertisers interested in selling their products over television. A typical VNR release runs about a minute and a half in length and appears to be a typical reporter's story. Video news releases are produced for broadcast on local TV stations during their evening newscasts.

These informational pieces usually come prepackaged as reports on health tips, consumer affairs, and even political events. Fortune 500 companies sell products with them; political candidates use them, and they continue to grow in popularity as a public relations tool. If done well, these news/promotion pieces are hard to distinguish from a regular TV story—that is, unless the station chooses to identify the source.

So, where is the problem? Video news releases are neither created by journalists nor intended to cover the news from an independent and impartial viewpoint. If TV stations choose to use video provided by outsiders such as public relations or advertising firms, the truth standard requires that the stations disclose that use. Some TV stations simply shovel VNRs to the audience without checking either their facts or their sources. In so doing, they treat their responsibility to the public's trust lightly and risk damaging their credibility.

"NEWZMERCIALS"

Another type of broadcast news material that exudes a commercial scent could hardly be mistaken for news. A station's employees produce these "newzmercials," which seem designed to please clients or sponsors, with little or no news value. Miami University's Professor Sam Roberts noticed one example of this disturbing trend while viewing a story on wine tasting: The expert interviewee praised the quality and price of a particular wine. The station cut to a commercial, and lo and behold, it was for that very wine sold by a local wine merchant. "It was a blatant infomercial disguised as a news story," says Roberts.

In New York City, a reporter produced a humorous piece about a portable chair to use at outdoor events such as golf tournaments. It seemed a harmless feature story until the anchors tagged it by reporting a toll-free number that viewers could call to order the chair. "Again, a shameless infomercial disguised as a news story in the middle of a newscast," observed Roberts.[26]

DIGITIZING THE SCREEN

Baseball fans watching the World Series on TV in 2001 were rubbing their eyes—because the view from behind the pitcher's mound kept changing. Fox digitally overlaid part of its picture of the backstop with rotating promotions for its lineup of new programming. The commercial invasion does not stop there, though.

Network advertisers are buying corners of the screen for airing their transparent sponsored logos, known as "bugs," to be viewed during particular segments of a show. Would such a practice run afoul of the SPJ ethic that says "Distinguish news from advertising and shun hybrids that blur the line between the two"?

Bank of America was the first sponsor to place its logo on the screen during "Marketwatch" business reports whenever they were followed by Bank of America commercials. After its makeover in 2001, *CNN's Headline News* began broadcasting corporate logos on the lower half of the screen during business, sports, and weather updates. The president of sales at CNN, Larry Goodman, said the combination of the screen logo and spot sales gave *Headline News* a competitive edge that it needed. He dismissed the idea that dividing the screen between news and commercials interferes with journalistic integrity. "Viewers understand that television is ad supported," he says. "They [the logos] are solely sponsors and don't have anything to do with editorial content."[27]

PRODUCT PLACEMENT

Advertising sponsors also pay huge sums to have their products mentioned in story lines and shown in scenes of entertainment programs. Product placement has become but one means for circumventing digital video recorders such as Tivo that enable viewers to zap past conventional ads. Ford's line of sports utility vehicles, for example, was to be displayed prominently on the WB network's

2002 reality show, *No Boundaries*, in exchange for Ford's picking up the tab for the show's production costs.[28]

WEB-WEAVING ADS

The programming language of the Web enables particular words to be under-lined or highlighted so that viewers who click on them can be seamlessly trans-ferred to other websites. Such is the beauty of HTML, hypertext markup language, and sponsors have shown their appreciation by investing in links. By paying search engines, sponsors can convert key-word searches on the Web into detours to their advertisements. One group bought the rights to 55 keywords re-lated to its political perspective, just to be sure it showed up on the highlighted lists of search engines.[29]

Sponsors also have tried *bridge pages* in order to link viewers from a radio or TV station's website to the advertiser's homepage. How do the links work? Suppose a TV news viewer enjoys a regular travel feature, but becomes curious about additional information promised on the website. When the viewer goes on-line to get the information, he or she sees a travel agency's bridge page, a pro-motional advertisement that appears before the link to the news material.

Conflicts of Interest

Broadcasters are asked to govern their lives in such a way that charges of conflict of interest, real or apparent, cannot be justly made. Turner Broadcasting System hands its employees a manual of ethics aimed at preventing them from publicly promoting, advertising, or endorsing "any product, service or organization with-out the prior written consent of an executive vice president, or the president, of CNN."[30]

POLITICAL ACTIVISM

Local TV stations uphold similar policies, some times to the surprise of their own personnel. Kelly Harvey was the weekend anchor at WTKR-TV in Norfolk, Virginia, when she found out about her station's conflict-of-interest policy. She arrived at work one day to discover she had been relieved of her anchor duties, placed on two-week suspension, and reassigned to the early-morning shift that began at 4:00 A.M.

The reason? She had donated $1,000 of her own money to Democratic Senator Chuck Robb's reelection campaign. WTKR-TV's policy holds its em-ployees accountable for any "conflict of interest, or appearance of a conflict of interest that may cause any public question about the journalistic integrity" of the employee or the station. The news director said ignorance of the rule was no excuse, since this policy of professional conduct was fairly consistent among television stations.[31]

PATRIOTISM, PINS, AND RIBBONS

During times of national crises, patriotic passions run high and questions of prin-ciple take on new force. It seems uncanny that something as small as a lapel pin could move to the center of an ethical debate, but after the terrorist attacks of September 11, that became the case.

The TV news director for the NBC affiliate owned by the University of Missouri advised employees to keep their flags and lapel pins at home while reporting on the air. News Director Scott Woelfel said it was their business to cover events as impartial observers, and that meant eliminating badges from the TV picture, even those expressing national pride. Because the people of Missouri own the TV station, a state lawmaker was incensed by this ban on patriotism and threatened legislation against the university.

On the same issue but from a different perspective, a newspaper columnist saw no reason for hiding her patriotism as an American journalist. Michelle Malkin refused to bow to whom she called "media snobs" who were "wrinkling their noses at flag pins and patriotic ribbons."[32] "Hey newsies: Get off your high horses," she wrote. "Impartiality is no excuse to behave like four-star ingrates."

Roy Peter Clark, senior scholar at the Poynter Institute, called for the retirement of red, white, and blue ribbons and lapel pins. He compared the journalist's obligations to that of a public defender bound to represent accused criminals, even those known to be guilty. The flap over displays of patriotism by journalists reveals how professionals may have to balance particular ethics of their profession with general duties to their country. Some would argue that the highest form of patriotism is found not in wearing pins but in fully informing the public of all sides in a debate, even those positions adversarial to our nation.

> **Principle #7**
>
> A journalist who shows partisanship compromises his or her own credibility.

MODELS OF MORAL REASONING

Professional ethicists hand out lists of questions to ask before making tough calls. The Poynter Institute, for example, which serves as a school of higher learning for journalists, lists 11 questions for photojournalists to answer. They include "What are my ethical concerns?" and "What is my journalistic purpose?" These questions can be broken into basic areas dealing with purpose, ethics, and outcome. We offer here a general model for handling tough calls. We begin with a traditional model of moral reasoning called *Potter's Box.*

Potter's Box

Ralph M. Potter was a doctoral student at Harvard who based his dissertation on a step-by-step procedure for making moral decisions. He began by first defining the situation, assessing the particular *values* and *principles* involved, then reaching a *decision* based on an assessment of *loyalties* (see Figure 15.1). Potter's box may have limited application to media dilemmas because it tends to

FIGURE 15.1

Potter's Box

Quadrant #1 **Situation** (finding of facts)	Quadrant #2 **Values** (issues at stake)
Quadrant #3 **Principles** (ethics involved)	Quadrant #4 **Loyalties** (order of priorities)

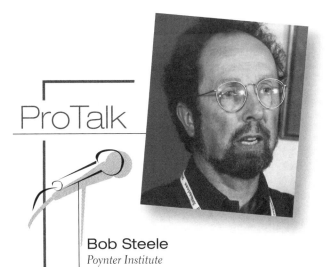

ProTalk

Bob Steele
Poynter Institute

"There are lots of ethical land mines in the digitally convergent environment."

When journalists look for answers to on-the-job dilemmas, they often come to the Poynter Institute for Media Studies, where they can get additional training from professionals such as Bob Steele. Steele became interested in how good ethical decisions were made as a reporter, producer, and news director for television stations in Maine and Iowa. He chose ethical decisions as the topic of his Ph.D. dissertation, and examined both the principles of ethics and the process news people follow in making their decisions. Steele takes the position that ethical decision-making is a learned craft, much like writing, reporting, editing, and other media skills.

Electronic media play a special role in our society, and obviously professionals in the field have duties reflecting that difference. The freedoms enjoyed under the First Amendment, Steele says, carry "both significant rights and great responsibility."

Digital convergence in media has increased both flow and speed of information across multiple platforms. Steele says that makes it even more important for journalists to distinguish their work with credibility and reliability. "It calls for quality craftsmanship and strong values," he says.

"There are lots of ethical land mines in the digitally convergent environment," says Steele. Some of these have to do with technology that allows on-line media to link to sources of questionable credibility. Other concerns have to do with the commercial side of the business—drawing a clear distinction between advertising and editorial content.

Some would argue that professional ethics are too costly in a competitive world where speed and impact are at a premium and quality control is not. Steele would disagree. He does not regard "cost" as part of taking the high road. "I believe it's our duty to honor important principles that guide our work as journalists in service to citizens and community," he says. The "reward" for high ethical behavior may be intangible, measured mainly in the pride of rendering excellent service to others. "Granted, this journalism can also be financially lucrative to those who run media organizations," Steele says, "but that shouldn't be our driving force."

avoid discussions of consequence. The emphasis is on loyalties rather than on weighing the potential outcome of alternatives, as a teleogist might propose.

PEACE Model

The authors propose an original approach, aimed directly at media decisions, that embraces both deontological and teleological perspectives. It forms the acronym *PEACE*, and is based on questions of *Purposes, Ethics, Alternatives, Consequences,* and *Execution* (see Figure 15.2). The following scenario will suggest one possible application of the Davie/Upshaw PEACE model.

What happens when media fail to heed their professional duty? Ethical accountability is usually a personal matter. Rather than censure violators, media organizations simply encourage observance of the professional codes. As one RTNDA leader, Jeff Marks, put it, "There are, indeed, many cases in which we would like to reprimand our colleagues publicly. However, in practice, a voluntary membership association cannot act as a prosecutor of its members."[33]

SUCCESS PRINCIPLES

Professionalism is more than just making the right choices, although that is certainly a part of the equation. It is also about developing habits of success in one's chosen field. We consider now the work ethics that leaders in professions claim to be important. Clichéd as it might sound, competition is often called "cut-throat" by media veterans in describing their rough-and-tumble careers. A former president of CBS News, Van Gordon Sauter, characterized network news rivalries as "trench warfare, only without the mustard gas." Leaders in the media say they owe their success to knowing how to capitalize on their talents, opportunities, passions, and principles of conduct. What it takes to stay on top of the game is covered here.

FIGURE 15.2

Davie-Upshaw PEACE Model

- Purpose
- Ethics to Consider
- Alternatives at Hand
- Consequences of Choice
- Execution and Explanation

Seizing the Moment

Carpe diem: It became almost a slogan for the 1980s after the release of a movie about a New England prep school, *The Dead Poets Society*. In the film, Robin Williams plays a poetry teacher who wants his students to realize the importance of seizing the day and teaches them the Latin phrase for it, *carpe diem*. This same lesson has served well the leaders of many industries, particularly the electronic media. It led to the creation of one of television journalism's more successful endeavors, *ABC News Nightline*.

CNN anchor Judy Woodruff was majoring in political science at Duke University when she asked the news director of the ABC affiliate in Atlanta for a job interview. That was in 1968, and after a brief discussion of her interest in political science and mass communication, she was ready to leave the news director's office. Woodruff had moved to the door when the news director remarked, "Well, I think we can work something out. Besides, how could I turn down somebody with legs like yours?" She just gulped and said, "Thank you. I'll look for your letter in the mail," and left. Woodruff was stunned.

CNN's Judy Woodruff.

Solving Ethical Problems

National Security Adviser Condoleeza Rice.

Scenario:
On October 10, 2001, the White House took an unusual step with regard to press coverage in the war on terrorists. In a conference call, National Security Adviser Condoleeza Rice made a plea to television networks to curb the terrorist group al-Qaeda's access to the U.S. people. Rice said Osama bin Laden and his cohorts might achieve two goals through videotaped propaganda: First, the terrorists could incite hatred against Americans by promoting bin Laden's cause. Second, the terrorists might encrypt messages to communicate secretly with members of their network living in the United States. In a later interview with al-Jazeera, bin Laden scoffed at the possibility he would need such a method to reach his confederates—pointing to all the other media available to him.

Purposes: To think this problem through from the media's perspective, let's analyze it using the five steps. With the first, *Purposes,* we review what the media are trying to accomplish in their role and what others may be trying to achieve in theirs. We begin by asking what is known about the situation, and what more needs to be known before taking action. It is essential to consider the purposes of the actors with regard to the audience.

The White House asked network executives not to air full, prerecorded statements by Osama bin Laden or his aides. The administration's dual purpose was to prevent unchecked propaganda from reaching citizens and to keep coded messages from reaching terrorist cells in the United States. Americans were obviously troubled by the terrorist attacks and also perplexed by them. Citizens wondered how such hatred could be taking root on American soil. The network's purposes included not only informing the public but doing so without alienating the audience. Therein lies the dilemma: How much, if any, of the terrorist generated pictures and messages should be conveyed to the viewers?

Ethics: With this step, the media should analyze the ethics involved in this scenario. What professional guidelines or company policies should be consulted? For journalists, Condoleeza Rice's appeal to TV network represented a case in which key principles were in conflict. Both the Society of Professional Journalists and the Radio-Television News Directors Association advocate diligently and thoroughly investigating all sides of a controversy. Here, professional duties had to be weighed against loyalties to country and citizenship.

Alternatives: In the present example, the choices ranged between full disclosure and complete secrecy. If the media air al-Qaeda's videotaped messages in full, would they jeopardize lives and assist people antagonistic to the United States? Would this in turn soften our national resolve to deal effectively with the menace of terrorism? What was to prevent the terrorists from putting their videotape on the Internet, with or without coded messages? The choices boiled down to decisions about gatekeeping of both pictures and words.

Consequences: This fourth assessment step is necessary to assess both long- and short-range outcomes. It calls for a reasoned prediction of the impact a decision might have on all parties involved, including actors in the event, the media,

Solving Ethical Problems *continued*

and the audience. In considering the administration's request to limit terrorists' air time, the networks had to weigh how much Americans needed information from and about their enemies in times of war. What would be the outcome of any choice available, from full disclosure to complete censorship of the al-Qaeda videotape?

Execution: Finally, in this step, a decision must be made and action taken, but not until a rationale is fully developed and explained. This last step serves to recheck all the previous ones in terms of the appropriateness of the choice and its presentation.

In the bin Laden tape scenario, the question involved how much of a message should be abridged; what parts to air and which ones to cut; how long to leave videotape on the screen, and when to run it. The TV networks agreed to edit the tapes, eliminate inflammatory language, mute the Arabic content to prevent encrypted messages, and avoid repeatedly showing clips.[34]

ProTalk

Deborah Potter
Executive Director of NewsLab

"Ethical journalism means excellent journalism."

Deborah Potter believes the practice of ethical journalism is not an oxymoron. "It's essential, in fact, for journalists to ensure the credibility of their work, without which journalism itself is pointless," she says.

As a journalist and educator who spent 16 years as a correspondent for CBS and CNN before taking charge of NewsLab, a nonprofit organization in Washington, DC, Potter now helps TV journalists learn to tell difficult stories and to make tough ethical calls.

"Ethical journalism means excellent journalism," Potter declares. "It's difficult for one to exist without the other, because no matter how extraordinary a story may be, unethical behavior by journalists in developing that story will call into question the end result." That's why she finds the truth principle to be basically nonnegotiable. "Journalists who lie or dissemble to gather information may get what they're after, but at what cost to their credibility?" Readers and viewers may legitimately wonder: If a journalist would lie to a source, why wouldn't he or she lie to the audience?

So Potter teaches journalists how to navigate the ethical minefields that await them in their careers. She helps them develop and follow their own guidelines for making sound ethical decisions, especially on deadline. "Guidelines work better than rulebooks," she believes, "because they allow journalists to consider individual circumstances" and to discuss a problem among themselves rather than blindly follow any rules.

Some professionals think they can trust their "gut" to know the right thing to do in all circumstances, but Potter doesn't trust that type of decision making. "It is better for journalists to reason their way through an ethical dilemma," she says, "and be prepared to justify their actions, not just to themselves and their bosses, but also to the public."

ABC's Sam Donaldson.

She accepted the job as a secretary, and for more than a year did everything from making coffee to cleaning film. This was not her dream. "I was chomping at the bit to get some reporting experience," she said, but the only on-air job available was a part-time slot doing Sunday-night weather. She had decided to pass on that opportunity when the news director pulled her aside and said, "If you're serious, you better get some experience. This is the way the real world works." Woodruff took the job.[35]

ABC's Sam Donaldson learned the same lesson, but credited his military school background to his belief in seizing the moment. Donaldson had to get over his dislike of military discipline, however, before he began to learn the important principles of that experience. He soon felt the competitive urge and found that "you want to excel, you want to win the best cadet award, you want to beat someone in swimming, you want to demonstrate your proficiency at the Queen Anne drill on the M-1 rifle."

Based on that experience and others, Donaldson's advice is, "Take every opportunity that comes along, even though it means more work, more responsibility—clearly you want that. Take the opportunity. Don't shrink from it, particularly in your early years," He says.[36] In other words, *carpe diem.*

Marlene Sanders was the first woman to anchor a network newscast (in 1964), eventually, she became a vice president at ABC. She says her success was due not to any concrete plans or goal-setting, but, like Donaldson and Woodruff, to seizing opportunities when they came. "You stumble into jobs or you find yourself in a happy confluence of events that give you an opportunity," says Sanders. "That's how it works. Lightning does not suddenly strike."[37]

Teamwork

This maxim may sound overly familiar, but hidden behind its well-worn exterior is an essential truth: Teamwork either makes an organization a success or creates a failure in its absence. ABC News Anchor Ted Koppel offers an anecdote about how teamwork contributed to the success of *Nightline*. At some point, a planned story for one evening's program showed little promise of development, and everyone seemed to know it. So all members of the *Nightline* staff were summoned together to see what could be done about it. They each took a piece of paper and jotted down a new idea for the evening's topic.

Each staff person deposited his or her slip in a hat and waited for the winning idea to be announced by the executive producer, Rick Kaplan. The winner was a suggestion to cover a play, accused of racism, that was based on Mark Twain's novel, *Huckleberry Finn.* The winning idea came from the show's researcher, who was excited to hear her idea chosen, though her mood changed somewhat when she realized that she was expected to help produce the show.[38]

Never Stop Learning

Some creative talents in television take the do-it-yourself approach by reading everything they can about their profession. Brannon Braga knew what she wanted to become at the age of 10, and so she decided to do something about it. She had no idea how to become a "Hollywood professional," but devoured every book she could find on the subject and began writing screenplays. She went to film school in California, and, most important, kept practicing her craft by working on scripts every day.

After being turned down for a scriptwriting internship with Paramount Pictures, she applied again the following year and found that her persistence paid off. Like so many others, she converted her internship into a successful career, moving from writer to story editor to executive producer for *Star Trek: Voyager.*[39]

Seizing a pivotal role in the planning of one of the country's most popular newsmagazines requires an attitude of learning. Brad Bessey became coordinating producer for *Entertainment Tonight* after learning from his mentors. "Everyone you meet along the road can and will be a mentor to you," says Bossey, "full of teachers and students who can be both in the same moment." He singles out *ET*'s executive producer, Linda Bell Blue, as a "mentor, friend, and inspiration."[40]

CBS correspondent Susan Spencer found useful learning experiences both in college and on the job. She graduated with a double major in German literature and television/radio production at Michigan State University before tackling a master's degree in journalism at Columbia University. With two degrees from respected institutions in her field, Spencer might have seemed able to could write her own ticket, but such was not the case. She went to work first at a film production house in Louisville, Kentucky, and wrote advertising copy. Then local public television station hired her to work on a public-affairs program. Spencer shot film, wrote and voiced copy, and covered hard news and features. It was enough to give her the training she needed, and she became coanchor at WCCO-TV in Minneapolis, Minnesota. Five years later, she was hired as a correspondent at CBS News.[41]

What does it take for a woman to achieve the pinnacle of leadership in network television? Ask Jane Cahill Pfeiffer how her education evolved. She became president of NBC by learning all she could from each move she made in college and career. Cahill Pfieffer credits excellent professors and her desire to participate everywhere she could on campus: "In the theater department, I worked diligently—directing, writing, and even acting." Upon graduation, she sought a life of religious devotion, but after a year in a convent, she abandoned her ambition to become a nun. Instead, she moved up the corporate ladder to hold directorships of of directors for oil, paper, insurance, and retail companies. After turning down an offer from President Carter to join his cabinet, Cahill Pfeiffer was invited to join NBC by President Fred Silverman in 1977.

There, she made important strides in NBC's news coverage, improving the quality of the programming and making the management system more efficient. Cahill Pfeiffer advanced to network chair at a time when women were still not accepted in the head office. She gives advice to others entering the field, saying, "Recognize you'll always be learning, because technology is driving so much change."[42]

Passion Wins

In the world of advertising, Ted Bell is no lightweight. As former vice chairman and creative director of Young & Rubicam worldwide, one of the largest ad agencies in the world, he developed the heart to win in a fiercely competitive business. He advises other newcomers, "Be the most passionate person in the room. Not the smartest, not the cleverest, but the most passionate. Care more than anybody and you'll be the one that wins."[43]

Those who know Bell say his passion translates into a love for his work. He has loads of self-confidence, and his enthusiastic vision for projects seems to infect his colleagues. Bell is quick to explain that you can't be stingy with your time or your concern for others and hope to make it. His colleagues felt Bell's desire to work with them and they naturally responded with positive support and enthusiasm. Creativity and talent help, of course, but passion is the key. Small wonder that Bell admires another passionate executive—Sumner Redstone—who rose to the top of one of the largest media conglomerates in the world.

In his seventies, Redstone stands among the wealthiest and commanding figures in American media. He engineered Viacom's takeover of Paramount, Blockbuster, and CBS. He controls interests in publishing giant Simon & Schuster and in New York's professional hockey and basketball franchises. A self-made man? Perhaps, but Redstone is careful to credit his education first. Trained at Harvard and the famous Boston Latin School, he is one of the finer intellects in global media's corporate offices. One other facet of his career stands out in an uncommon way: his determination brought him through a harrowing brush with death.

In 1979, Redstone was awakened by a fire in a Boston hotel and had to crawl out on a ledge to survive. He survived the midnight blaze only by clenching a window-sill with one hand while flames scorched the other hand and arm. After being lifted down by firefighters, he spent 60 hours on the surgery table to repair half of his body using skin grafts from the other half.[44] One might expect that such a fearsome encounter might change a person's perspective on life. "Nonsense," says Redstone. The same man Boston firefighters lifted off that hotel ledge continues to lead his enterprise each day as the head of CBS/Viacom. "I have always been driven, he says, I have a passion to win, and the will to win is the will to survive."

Summary

Success is one of those funny terms that almost defies definition. Some professionals define it by status, personal wealth, or respect from their peers. However, success more basically is this: what you think of yourself at the end of the day. Media success may be defined in corporate terms such as ratings and dollars, but after the accountants have gone home and the Nielsen numbers tallied, there is another inventory to take. This personal accounting evaluate whether you've done the right thing that day. Such moral "gut-checks" are really what success is all about.

The professionals who lead electronic media vary somewhat in their standards and practices, but their personal decisions are subject to the same principles of truth, fairness, and responsibility that guide other careers. Your personal blueprint as a professional will mark your success in the end. Textbooks and teachers, family and friends, corporate manuals and common sense—all will help to draft that blueprint. After that, the nature of your character will direct your decisions and define your future. This chapter has tried to show how important it is to consider your duty to principle, your sense of purpose, and your reasoning about consequences in those defining moments.

FOOD FOR THOUGHT

1. If you were to identify two students cheating in class, and were considering whether to tell the professor, what principle would you follow:

   Duty. Tell the teacher to preserve honor and integrity of the test.
   Purpose. Tell the teacher to avoid other student's getting unfair grade.
   Consequences. Don't tell, to avoid appearing as a snitch and to keep favor with other students.

2. Someone argues that codes of professional ethics are unnecessary because the only ethics that matter are personal ethics anyway. What is your opinion?
3. Do you think government is ever justified in distributing dishonest propaganda, and if so, under what circumstances?
4. Do you think that television does a poor, adequate, good, or excellent job in portraying minority members of U.S. society? Please explain the reason for your answer.
5. Some citizen groups advocate boycotts against commercial sponsors of programs that violate standards of taste and decency. Would you ever participate in such a protest, and under what circumstances?
6. If you were a broadcast journalist and were put under pressure by an advertiser to change or kill a story, how would you reason your response to the problem, using the PEACE model?
7. Discuss a time when you saw an opportunity to achieve a goal and seized the opportunity to your advantage, or perhaps had such a chance but failed to recognize it.
8. If you discovered that a radio station had perpetrated a hoax to stimulate publicity and attract listeners, how would you feel? Do you consider such behavior unethical? Why or why not?

NOTES

CHAPTER 1

1. "Perspectives," *Newsweek*, 1 October 2001, 17.
2. For a profound discussion of this process, see Walter Lippmann, *Public Opinion* (New York: Harcourt Brace, 1922).
3. " 'Year of Recognition': LPTV to Remain Secondary Service—Sikes," *Communications Daily*, 29 November 1990, 2.
4. *Market Conditions and Public Affairs Programming: Implications for Digital Television Policy* (Washington, DC: The Benton Foundation, 2000), 3.
5. *Random House Dictionary of the English Language*, 2nd ed. (New York: Random House, 1987), 1539.
6. John Omicinski, "New War Not Media-Friendly," Gannett News Service, *The Advertiser*, 2 October 2001, 5a.
7. An exception is the low-power FM radio stations that in 2001 were granted permission to seek FCC licenses; their coverage areas can be as small as a single neighborhood.
8. *Random House Dictionary*, 647.
9. Pamela J. Shoemaker, "Hardwired for News: Using Biological and Cultural Evolution to Explain the Surveillance Function," *Journal of Communication* 46/3 (Summer 1996): 32.
10. For more insights on news and fear, see David L. Altheide, "The News Media, the Problem Frame, and the Production of Fear," *Sociological Quarterly* 38/4 (Fall 1997): 647.
11. Nielsen Media Research, via Television Bureau of Advertising website, 30 October 2001, http://www.tvb.org/tvfacts/tvbasics/basics32.html.
12. The term *ads* here refers to many types of nonprogramming material, most of it persuasive in nature. The American Association of Advertising Agencies defines *clutter* as "network and local commercial time, public service announcements (PSAs), public service promotions (PSPs), promotions aired by broadcast and cable networks, program credits not run over continuing program action, and 'other' unidentified gaps within a commercial pod."

CHAPTER 2

1. Ronald Kline, "Reconstructing Tesla," Review: Wizard: The Life and Times of Nikola Tesla, *Scientific American* (April 1997). http://www.sciam.com/0497issue/0497review1.html.
2. Robert L. Hilliard and Michael C. Keith, *The Broadcast Century and Beyond*, 3rd ed. (Boston: Focal Press, 2001), p. 26.
3. Federal Communications Commission, *Report on Chain Broadcasting* (Washington, DC: U.S. Government Printing Office, 1941). See also Frank J. Kahn, *The Network Case*, 4th ed. (Englewood Cliffs, NJ: Prentice-Hall, 1984).
4. Interestingly, while the so-called NTSC standard cleared the way in 1941 for a U.S. broadcasting system, it made the system *inferior*. American television would transmit images at a resolution of only 525 horizontal lines, but most countries would have higher-resolution TV. This would cause problems as television's orbit grew. Videotapes of U.S. shows were incompatible with foreign playback systems—but not until the 1990s did serious work begin on high-definition television (HDTV) in the United States. By then, the arrival of digital technology had both brightened and complicated the process of moving to a new broadcast-image standard.
5. "WTVR-Channel 6 Turns 50; Its History Parallels Television's," *Richmond Times-Dispatch*, 18 April 1998 (Green Section), F4.
6. Reuven Frank, *Out of Thin Air: The Brief Wonderful Life of Network News* (New York: Simon & Schuster, 1991).
7. Jay Perkins, "Television Covers the 1952 Political Convention in Chicago; an Oral History Interview with Sig Mickelson," *Historical Journal of Film, Radio and Television* 18, no. 1 (March 1998): 95.
8. Melvin Patrick Ely, *The Adventures of Amos 'n' Andy—A Social History of an American Phenomenon* (New York: Free Press, 1991).
9. Ben Fong-Torres, "Like a Rolling Stone Richard Fatherly Knows Best," Special to the Repository of Reel Radio Presents a Special Report: Todd Storz and Radio's Revolution. http://www.reelradio.com/storz/index.html.
10. David T. MacFarland, "Up from Middle America: The Development of Top 40," in *American Broadcasting—A Source Book on the History of Radio and Television*, 2nd ed., ed. Lawrence W. Lichty and Malachi C. Topping (New York: Hastings House, 1976), 399–403.
11. Ben Fong-Torres, *The Hits Just Keep on Coming—The History of Top 40 Radio* (San Francisco: Miller Freeman Books, 1998).
12. "America's Long Vigil," *TV Guide*, 25 January 1964.
13. Norm Pattiz, telephone conversation, November 11, 2000.
14. Amanda Barnett, "Satellite Radio Lifting Off," CNN.com, 24 July 2001. http://www.cnn.com/20001/TECH/ptech/07/24/satellite.radio/.

15. Larry McShane (Associated Press), "DJ Pursues Liberated Radio on Internet," *Albany Times Union*, 8 July 2000, D8.

16. "Web Worries," *Communicator* (Radio-Television News Directors Association), August 2000.

CHAPTER 3

1. Spot-beam satellites will allow limited coverage of local markets. See "Sats Pitch 'Must Carry,' " *Broadcasting & Cable*, 31 July 2000, p. 38.

2. See "Pioneers," at Cable Center web page http://www.cablecenter.org.

3. Mary Alice Mayer Phillips, *CATV—A History of Community Antenna Television* (Evanston, IL: Northwestern University Press, 1972), 7–8.

4. Ibid., 9.

5. George Mair, *Inside HBO—The Billion Dollar War between HBO, Hollywood, and the Home Video Revolution* (New York: Dodd, Mead & Company, 1988).

6. Howard J. Barr, "Commission Releases Report on 2001 Cable Industry Prices," Womble Carlyle web page, 11 April 2002, http://www.wcsr.com/FSL5CS/telecommunicationmemos/telecommunicationmemos1252.asp.

7. Ibid., 30.

8. See David H. Waterman and Andrew A. Weiss, *Vertical Integration in Cable Television* (Washington, DC: American Enterprise Institute, 1993), 9.

9. *Cable Communications Policy Act of 1984, U.S. Code*, vol. 47, sec. 531 (1984).

10. William R. Davie and Jung-Sook Lee, "Handling Hate Speech on Public Access Television," *Feedback* 40, no. 3 (1999): 33–41. See also Mark D. Harmon, "Hate Groups and Cable Public Access," *Journal of Mass Media Ethics* 6, no. 3 (1991): 149, 153.

11. James Roman, *Love, Light, and a Dream* (Westport, CT: Praeger, 1996), 241, 248.

12. See Robert W. Crandall and Harold Furchtgott-Roth, *Cable TV: Regulation or Competition?* (Washington, DC: Brookings Institute, 1996).

13. 26 F.C.C. 403 (1959).

14. First Report and Order, 38 F.C.C. 683 (1965).

15. Second Report and Order, 2 F.C.C. 2d 725 (1966).

16. *United States v. Southwestern Cable Co.*, 392 U.S. 157 (1968).

17. *Quincy Cable TV, Inc. v. F.C.C.* (D.C. Cir. No. 83-1283, 1985).

18. "Alternative Delivery Systems," *Electronic Media*, 31 July 2000, 14.

19. FCC, CC Docket 87-266, July 16, 1992, Local Telephone Companies to be Allowed to Offer Video Dialtone Services; Repeal of Statutory Congress.

20. F. Leslie Smith, John W. Wright II, and David H. Ostroff, *Perspectives on Radio and Television*, 4th ed. (Mahwah, NJ: Lawrence Erlbaum, 1998), 139–140.

21. "Western Show Attendance Down," *Multichannel News International*, 30 November 2001. http://www.tvinsite.com/multiinternational/index.asp?layout+story&doc_id= 58879&display=breaking News.

22. See "Industry Statistics," National Cable & Telecommunications Association, http://www.ncta.co . . . _overview/ind-Stats.cfm?statID=7.

23. See "Career Opportunities with Cable Systems," National Cable & Telecommunications Association, http://www.ncta.com/careers/careers.cfm?careerID=2.

CHAPTER 4

1. Nicholas Negroponte, *Being Digital* (New York: Knopf, 1995).

2. "Why the Name 'Wink'?" What Is Wink: The Name Web Site. http://www.wink.com/contents/name.shtml

3. Irwin Lebow, *The Digital Connection* (New York: Computer Science Press, 1991), 167, 170–174. Also "Harry Nyquist," http://www.geocities.com/bioelectrochemistry/nyquist.htm.

4. Steven Lubar, " 'Do not fold, spindle or mutilate': A cultural history of the punch card," May 1991, http://ccat.sas.upenn.edu/slubar/fsm.

5. Internet Society, "A Brief History of the Internet," *All about the Internet*. http://www.isoc.org/internet-history/brief.html

6. Preston Gralla, *How the Internet Works*, 4th ed. (Indianapolis: Que–Macmillan, 1998).

7. William Gibson, *Neuromancer* (New York: Ace Publishing, 1984).

8. M. Mitchell Waldrop, "No, This Man Invented the Internet," Forbes.com, http://www.forbes.com/asap/2000/1127/105.html. Also "Part I: The History of ARPA Leading Up to the ARPANET," *History of the ARPANET*, http://www.dei.isep.ipp.pt/does/arpa—1.html

9. Tim Berners-Lee, with Mark Fischetti, *Weaving the Web: The Original Design and Ultimate Destiny of the World Wide Web by Its Inventor* (San Francisco: Harper, 1999).

10. Adam Cohen, "Coffee with Pierre—A Better World—That's the Dream of eBay Founder Pierre Omidyar," *Time.com: 1999 Persona of the Year*, 27 December 1999, http://www.time.com/time/poy/pierre.html. Also, Susan Moran. "The Pro," *Business 2.0 Magazine Indepth*, Auction Watch Daily—Viewpoint—The Insider, http://www.auctionwatch.com/awdaily/viewpoint/inside/3-082399.html.

11. Saul Hansell, "Demand Grows for Net Service at High Speed," *The New York Times*, 22 December 2001, C1, C4.

12. See "Advanced Television Enhancement Forum," http://www.atvef.com/press/releases/1999_09_09_02.thml.

13. Ku-band satellites differ from the lower C-band frequencies in that its waves are shorter, more vulnerable to attenuation, and require smaller receiving dishes. C-bandrepresents the lower frequencies in microwave communication between 1 and 10 gigaHertz. Unlike Ku-band, it is also used for terrestrial microwave signals.

14. Steve McCannel, "Bluetooth: It's All the Rage." *Webreview,* 2 February 2001, http://www.webreview.com/2001/02_02/developers/index01.

CHAPTER 5

1. Joel Brinkley, *Defining Vision—The Battle for the Future of Television* (San Diego: Harcourt Brace, 1997), pp. 146–148.
2. Ibid., p. 146.
3. Ralph Donald and Thomas Spann, *Fundamentals of Television Production* (Ames: Iowa State University Press, 2000), pp. 138–139.
4. In video, RGB colors are kept isolated and delivered from their source to the display device over separate wires, resulting in higher-quality pictures.
5. Originally, UHF was channels 14 to 83 after the freeze was lifted in 1952 on new station licenses. This UHF plan provided for more than 2,000 stations in about 1,300 communities, including 242 noncommercial and educational stations. Since the UHF band represented much higher frequencies than the original VHF channels, it presented a problem—most existing TV sets could not receive UHF channels. The FCC then mandated that all new TV sets must be able to receive both VHS and UHF channels.
6. Stephen Labaton, "255 Licenses Are Awarded for Low-Power FM Radio," *The New York Times,* 22 December 2000, C5.
7. "What Is iBiquity Digital?" http://www.ibiquity.com/01content.html.
8. Joan Van Tassel, "Digital Video Compressions," in *Communication Technology Update,* 3rd ed., ed. August E. Grant (Newton, MA: Butterworth Heinemann, 1994), p. 9.
9. NTSC also refers to the television system called *composite video,* wherein sync, luminance, and color are combined into a single analog signal.
10. Fred Lass, personal interview by phone, November 17, 2000.
11. Closed captioning text for the hearing impaired takes only one line of the VBI. Broadcasters use other lines of the VBI to communicate with local stations and cable systems, for purposes such as clock signals and commercial timing.

6. Ken Auletta, *Three Blind Mice: How the TV Networks Lost their Way* (New York: Random House, 1991), p. 4.
7. "NBC Sees Earnings Surge 10%; But Fourth-Quarter Revenue Falls as Net Feels Ad Slowdown," *The Hollywood Reporter,* 18 January 2001.
8. "Clearly, It's Clear Channel," *Broadcasting and Cable,* 18 September 2000, 50.
9. "Who Owns the Airwaves? Ownership Ranks Rapidly Thinned by Consolidation," *Electronic Media,* 18 May 1998, 1A.
10. Corporate history at Citadel website: http://www.citadel-communications.com/about/history.html.
11. "Sinclair Seeks to Refinance Loan to Avoid Default," *Electronic Media Online,* April 3, 2001, http://www.emonline.com/.
12. Transcript, hearing of Senate Commerce, Science and Transportation Committee, Federal News Service, July 17, 2001.
13. "Powell Sees Big Change in Broadcast Environment," *Television Digest,* 29 October 2001.
14. "Independent Production Companies," Museum of Broadcast Communications, http://www.mbcnet.org/ETV/I/htmlI/independentp/independentp.htm.
15. "The Employment Situation," Table B-1, news release from Bureau of Labor Statistics, U.S. Department of Labor, March 9, 2001, viewed at http://stats.bls.gov/news. release/empsit.t11.htm.
16. *Career Guide to Industries,* Bureau of Labor Statistics, U. S. Department of Labor, http://www.umsl.edu/services/govdocs/ooh20002001/512.htm#employment.
17. Herbert H Howard, "TV Station Group and Cross-Media Ownership: A 1995 Update." *Journalism & Mass Communication Quarterly,* 72, no.2 (Summer 1995): 390–401.
18. *Changes, Challenges, and Charting New Courses: Minority Commercial Broadcast Ownership in the United States,* National Telecommunications and Information Administration (Dept. of Commerce), December 2000.
19. *Career Guide to Industries,* Bureau of Labor Statistics, U.S. Department of Labor, http://www.umsl.edu/services/govdocs/ooh20002001/512.htm#occupations.
20. Industry spending projections, *Communications Industry Forecast,* Veronis Suhler Media Merchant Bank, 2001.

CHAPTER 6

1. "Vivendi Signs Second Big Deal to Create Vertical Integration," *Communications Daily,* 18 December 2001.
2. 'The Global 1000," *Business Week,* 9 July 2001, 46.
3. Willard Sterne Randall, *A Little Revenge: Benjamin Franklin at War with His Son* (New York: Quill/William Morrow, 1984), p. 42.
4. Disney news release on *Business Wire,* January 5, 2000.
5. http://disney.go.com/investors/.

CHAPTER 7

1. Chris Carter, closed-circuit television interview (satellite-fed to NATPE affiliates), National Association of Television Program Executives Educational Foundation, 1997.
2. David E. Kelley, closed-circuit television interview (satellite-fed to NATPE affiliates), National Association of Television Program Executives Educational Foundation, 1998.
3. Stephanie Drachkovitch, conversation with author, November 2001.

4. http://www.rronline.com/.
5. "Langley Collars Fox on 'Cops' Deals," *The Hollywood Reporter*, 11 July 2000.
6. "Network Affiliation and Programming," E. W. Scripps Co. annual report for 2000, http://www.scripps.com/2000annualreport/financials/08.html.
7. Peter Maroney, conversation with author, 29 June 2000.
8. Show syndicators typically base their prices on a station's audience size; thus, New York and Los Angeles stations would be charged much more for the same show than Portland stations would; small-city stations would pay much less.
9. Maroney, conversation with author.
10. "Laughter Is Best Syndie Medicine," *Variety*, 27 March–2 April 2000, 59.
11. Marilyn Lavin, "Creating Consumers in the 1930s: Irna Phillips and the Radio Soap Opera, " *Journal of Consumer Research*, June 1995, 75.
12. "WCLV to Play Full Pieces on Monday Marathons," *Cleveland Plain Dealer*, 2 August 1998, 31. Also WCLV website, www.wclv.com.
13. "Tuning in to Hispanic Music," *Billboard*, 8 December 2001, LM-1.
14. "Vying for Listeners: KBIG Tunes in to Likes, Needs, Habits of Women," *Los Angeles Times* (On the Air column), 30 May 2000, B4.
15. " 'The Basket' Shoots . . . Will It Score?" *Spokane Spokesman-Review*, 30 April 2000, F3.
16. "Citadel Yanks 'Don & Mike'; Replacement Show Sought," *Albuquerque Tribune*, 28 August 1999, D5.
17. "Little to Head RuffNation; Radio Vet Assumes President's Post Jan. 15," *Billboard*, 30 December 2000.
18. Young viewers may not have realized that TV "reality" arguably began half a century earlier, when a CBS program called *Candid Camera* started capturing ordinary people in mildly embarrassing situations. Passing through many adaptations before Fox launched *Cops* and similar shows in the 1980s, reality also brought us *When Animals Attack* and similar thrill-fests.
19. Dyan Machan, "Barry Diller's Next Course," *Forbes*, 9 March 1998, 122.
20. Michael Stroud, " 'Felicity' Voted Most Likely to Succeed," *Broadcasting & Cable*, 7 September 1998, 22.
21. This has been true in prosperous times; in the past few years, however, as consolidation and competition tightened TV budgets, networks have trimmed back some of their research staffing and investment.

CHAPTER 8

1. *Occupational Outlook Handbook*, Bureau of Labor Statistics, U.S. Department of Labor, http://stats.bls.gov/oco/ocos088.htm#employment.
2. "Popular Policies and Unpopular Press Lift Clinton Ratings," report by Pew Research Center on People and the Press, 6 February 1998, http://www.people-press.org/content.htm
3. For an overview of research into TV audiences' behavior and the industry's attempts to hold onto viewers, see Robert Abelman, David Atkin et al, "What Viewers Watch as They Watch TV: Affiliation Change as Case Study," *Journal of Broadcasting and Electronic Media*, Summer 1997, 360.
4. Peter Fornatale and Joshua E. Mills, *Radio in the Television Age* (Woodstock, NY: Overlook Press, 1980).
5. "Big Radio Airs: The Sound of Sameness," *Cincinnati Enquirer*, 28 March 2000, p. ARC.
6. Lawrence K. Grossman, "The Death of Radio News: Will TV Be Next?" *Columbia Journalism Review*, September–October 1998.
7. "Why the Overhaul of TV News Shows," *U.S. News and World Report*, 20 November 1978, 51.
8. Ken Auletta, *Three Blind Mice* (New York: Random House, 1991), 341.
9. Deborah Potter, "Getting What You Pay For," *American Journalism Review*, October 2000, 94.
10. "Female Anchors on Local TV Paid 28% Less," *Los Angeles Times*, 1 June 2000, A1.
11. "Fox Trots Ahead of the Rest," *Houston Chronicle*, 8 March 2001, 4.
12. "Diverse Auds Just Want to Be Shown the Money," *Variety*, 26 April–2 May 1999, 36.
13. "Wired U.S. Population Grows Steadily," press release from Nielsen/NetRatings, 28 February 2001.
14. *Internet Sapping Broadcast News Audience*; *Investors Now Go Online for Quotes, Advice*, report posted June 11, 2000 at Pew Research Center for People and the Press website, http://www.people-press.org.
15. Cherie Richardson, "TV Stations Follow Viewers to Web; Battle to Capture Eyeballs Goes Online," *Crain's Chicago Business*, 29 January 2001, SR20.
16. CNN news release, January 3, 2001.
17. Ad published in *ShopTalk* (Internet newsletter for TV-news industry), July 12, 2000.
18. Disney news release on *Business Wire*, February 22, 2001.
19. Notices posted February 28, 2001, at http://journalismjobs.com/.
20. Bill Kovach and Tom Rosenstiel, *Warp Speed: America in the Age of Mixed Media* (New York: The Century Foundation, 1999).
21. "Aired Live but Was It News?" *Baltimore Sun*, 7 March 2001, 1E.
22. "Internet Sapping Broadcast News Audience," report of Pew Research Center for the People & the Press, 11 June 2000.
23. *American Radio News Audience Survey*, Radio-Television News Directors Association, 2000.
24. *Local TV News Project—2001*, Project for Excellence in Journalism, 15 November 2001.
25. *CBS Evening News*, 9 August 2001.
26. "Merge Network Newscasts, Says Hewitt," *New York Post*, 15 March 2001, Business, read 3/19/01 at http://www.nypost.com/03152001/business/26506.htm.

CHAPTER 9

1. "Many Firms Pass Over Chance to Advertise During Super Bowl," *Atlanta Journal and Constitution*, 2 February 2002.
2. "Games Grabbing the Gold," *San Francisco Chronicle*, 13 December 2001, B1.
3. *Printers' Ink* (April 12, 1922) in Juliann Sivulka, *Soap, Sex, and Cigarettes* (Belmont, CA: Wadsworth, 1997), 183.
4. Sivulka, *Soap, Sex, and Cigarettes*, p. 201.
5. An early version of AdBusters, today's Media Foundation publication, is dedicated to counteradvertising.
6. Sivulka, *Soap, Sex, and Cigarettes*, p. 222.
7. "The Case against Cable," in *TVB: Broadcast vs. Cable*, http://www.tvb.org/selling/broadcast/cablecase.html.
8. See "Ad Spending by Media," *Electronic Media*, 31 December 2001, 6. It shows that advertising spending for the first quarter of 2001 declined from the previous quarter for Network Television (–8.0%), Spot Television (–17.9%), but rose for Cable TV (+2.1%).
9. Charles Warner and Joseph Buchman, *Broadcast and Cable Selling* (Belmont, CA: Wadsworth, 1993), 306.
10. Warner and Buchman, *Broadcast and Cable Selling*.
11. Steve McClellan, "Advertisers Buy into One-Stop Shopping." *Broadcasting & Cable*, 12 March 2001, 22–23.
12. Rosser Reeves, *Reality in Advertising* (New York: Knopf, 1960), 34.
13. Sivulka, *Soap, Sex, and Cigarettes*, p. 276.
14. Louis Chunovic, "Cable Getting Ready for Future of TV Ads," *Electronic Media*, 18 June 2001, 14, 35.
15. "Home Shopping Network," 6 July 2001, http://www.hsn.com/content/article.
16. Jim Sterne, *World Wide Web Marketing*, 2nd ed. (New York: Wiley Computer Publishing, 1999), p. 259.
17. "Pop-Under Ads Fuel Negative Perception for Internet," http://www.unicast.com.
18. "Cookies," http://www.illumintus.com/cookie/.
19. Sterne, *World Wide Web Marketing*, p. 259.
20. Ed Fulginiti, "Television Collapsing under Clutter's Weight," *Electronic Media*, 31 December 2001, 9.
21. Jean Folkerts, Stephen Lacy, and Lucinda Davenport, *The Media in Your Life: An Introduction to Mass Communication* (Boston: Allyn and Bacon, 1998), 362.
22. Sec. 52 Stat. 111 (1938) and 38 Stat. 717 (1914).
23. F.T.C. Policy Statement on Deception, Appended to Cliffdale Associates, Inc. 103 F.T.C. at 174.
24. *Warner-Lambert v. FTC*, 562 F.2nd 749, cert. denied, 435 U.S. 950 (1978).
25. Cigarette Advertising, 9 FCC 2d 921, 949 (1967), aff'd *Banzhaf v. FCC*, 405 F.2d 1082, 1091 (DC Cir. 1968), cert. denied, 396 U.S. 842 (1969). Congress enacted the Public Health Cigarette Smoking Act of 1969 banning tobacco ads from television and radio. Because of congressional ban on cigarette commercials, the FCC ruled in 1970 that counterads were no longer required. Mothers Against Drunk Driving appealed to the FCC in 1997 to have it apply to alcohol spots, as well. MADD argued before the FCC for counter-commercials to drinking based on the extraordinary impact on health and safety.

CHAPTER 10

1. "Freshman TV Class Grades High; Four of Seven Newcomers Honored; HBO Extends Domination," *Hollywood Reporter*, 22 January 2002.
2. Walter, Staab. "A New Way to Play the TV Polling Game," *New York Times*, 21 April 1996.
3. Matthew, Zelkind. Personal conversation, July 11, 2001.
4. "Newsman Shaw Signing Off CNN," *Hollywood Reporter*, 13 November 2000.
5. Karen S. Buzzard. *Chains of Gold: Marketing the Ratings and Rating the Markets* (Metuchen, NJ: Scarecrow Press, 1990), 15.
6. A. C. Nielsen Co.; also Museum of Broadcast Communications.
7. "Response-Rate Drop Stopped," *Mediaweek.com*, published 25 June 2001, http://www.mediaweek.com.
8. "Who Needs the Sweeps? TV's Periodic Race for Ratings Seems to Have Lost Its Purpose," *New York Times*, 24 April 2000, C1.
9. "Annual Report on the Global Research Industry," *Marketing News TM*, 4 June 2001, H4.
10. Scott Sassa, NBC, in "The Next Big Bet: Is a Family of Depressed Morticians HBO's Best Hope for Life after 'The Sopranos'?" *New Yorker*, 14 May 2001, 80.
11. For example, in 2002, the Nike shoe company introduced the *Air Jordan XVII*, a $200 pair of basketball shoes that came in a metal briefcase-style box with an interactive CD-ROM showing how the shoes were made. The target audience was teen-aged boys, who, said a retail analyst, "basically keep it under their bed and, when friends come over, show it to them." (From "Nike's New Air Jordans: $200 a Pair," *Register-Guard* (Eugene, Oregon), 2 February 2002, 5B.
12. "A Multicultural Family Affair: If Your Target Is the Traditional American Family, Make Sure Your Message Is in Many Languages." *American Demographics* Forecast, June 2001, 4.
13. Questionnaire posted on SRI Consulting Business Intelligence website, July 2001, http://future.sri.com/.
14. "'Grain' Pleads for Nielsen Families' Help," *Chicago Sun-Times*, 22 December 1993, 51.
15. "Advertisers Join Fans in Protesting Dumping of KIRO-FM's Cashman," Seattle *Post-Intelligencer*, 8 April 1999, Entertainment, 1.
16. Joseph M. Kayany, and Paul Yelsma, "Displacement Effects on Online Media in the Socio-Technical Contexts of Households." *Journal of Broadcasting and Electronic Media*, 44, no. 2 (Spring 2000): 215–229.
17. *Lou Dobbs Moneyline*, CNN, 17 July 2001.
18. "One Big Happy Channel?" *Salon.com*, 28 June 2001.
19. "A Dim View of the Ratings: Broadcasters Say the Nielsen Numbers Don't Add Up," *Washington Post*, 11 April 1996, D9.

20. National Association of Broadcasters, *Survey of Nielsen Ratings Service Quality Issues, Nov. 2000.* Stations queried: 1,069. Responding: 506 (47.3 percent). Sample was all full-power commercial TV stations with known fax numbers, not a random sample; NAB stresses that views of nonrespondents cannot be known.

21. Marc Gunther. *The House That Roone Built: The Inside Story of ABC News* (Boston: Little, Brown, 1994), 31.

22. Interview with Richard Wald, in *Inside the TV Business* (New York: Sterling Publishing, 1979), 215.

23. "Ch. 29 News Chief 'Had a Great Run,' Not So Great Ratings," *Philadelphia Inquirer*, 28 June 2001.

24. "Nielsens Schmielsens: TV Ratings System Is More Unpopular than Ever, But Executives and Advertisers Have Nowhere Else to Turn," *Minneapolis Star Tribune*, 20 April 1997, 1F.

25. Posted at Nielsen//NetRatings website, July 2001, www.nielsen-netratings.com/. The PTC also hands out a grade card for the TV networks by charting the "influx of adult-themed programming infiltrating the 'family hour.'" There were only two networks (CBS and WB) with passing scores in 2000. ABC, UPN, and NBC received unsatisfactory grades, and the Fox network flunked PTC's criteria for wholesome entertainment.

26. http://www.jnm.com, 8/16/01.

CHAPTER 11

1. Albert Einstein (1933), cited by Don W. Stacks and Michael B. Salwen in *An Integrated Approach to Communication Theory and Research* (Mahwah, NJ: Lawrence Erlbaum, 1996), p. 3.

2. John Fiske, *Introduction to Communication Studies* (London: Routledge, 1982), p. 6.

3. Wilbur Schramm, *The Beginnings of Communication Study in America—A Personal Memoir* (Thousand Oaks, CA: Sage, 1997), p. 111.

4. Harold D. Lasswell, *Propaganda Technique in the World War* (New York: Knopf, 1971). (Original work published 1927).

5. F. R. Dulles, Review of *Propaganda Technique in the World War. The Bookman*, 1968. cited by Wilbur Schramm, *The Beginnings of Communication Study in America—A Personal Memoir* (Thousand Oaks, CA: Sage, 1997), p. 35.

6. Harold D. Lasswell, "The Structure and Function of Communication in Society," in *The Communication of Ideas*, ed. L. Bryson (New York: Harper and Brothers, reprinted in Wilbur Schramm, ed. *Mass Communication* (Urbana: University of Illinois Press), pp. 117–130.

7. "Journalists, Public Disagree on Digital Credibility" *Newsbytes*, 31 January 2002. http://www.newsbytes.com/news/02/174132.html.

8. Carl Hovland, Irving L. Janis, and H. H. Kelley, *Communication and Persuasion* (New Haven, CT: Yale University Press, 1953).

9. Ev Stryker Muson and Catherine A. Warren, eds. *James Carey: A Critical Reader* (Minneapolis: University of Minnesota Press, 1997), pp. 323–324.

10. Marshall McLuhan, *Understanding Media: The Extensions of Man* (New York: McGraw-Hill, 1965), p. 12.

11. Roger Fidler, *Mediamorphosis: Understanding New Media* (Thousand Oaks, CA: Pine Forge, 1997).

12. Rogers, *A History of Communication Study*, p. 321.

13. Joseph Klapper, *The Effects of Mass Communication* (New York: Free Press, 1967).

14. Ibid., p. 8.

15. Professors Werner J. Severin and James W. Tankard have noted other scholars referencing this phenomenon. In 1958, Norton Long, for example, referred to the newspaper's role in "setting the territorial agenda," which influences "what most people will be talking about, what most people will think the facts are, and what most people will regard as the way problems are to be dealt with" (*American Journal of Sociology*, 64: 260). The husband and wife team of Kurt and Gladys Lang the following year discussed how "mass media force attention to certain issues" and "are constantly suggesting what individuals in the mass should think about, know about, have feelings about" (Kurt Lang and Gladys E. Lang, "The Mass Media and Voting," in *American Voting Behavior*, ed. E. Burdick and A. J. Brodbeck [Glencoe, IL: Free Press, 1959], p. 232, cited by Werner J. Severin and James W. Tankard, Jr., *Communicaton Theories—Origins, Methods, and Uses in the Mass Media*, 3rd ed. [New York: Longman, 2001], pp. 221–222).

16. Bernard C. Cohen, *The Press and Foreign Policy* (Princeton, NJ: Princeton University Press, 1963), p. 13. Walter Lippmann, *Public Opinion* (New York, Macmillan, 1922).

17. Todd Gitlin, *The Whole World Is Watching: Mass Media in the Making and Unmaking of the New Left* (Berkeley, CA: University of California Press, 1980), p. 7.

18. Erving Goffman, *Frame Analysis* (New York: Harper and Row, 1974), p. 21.

19. Bernard Berelson, "What 'Missing the Newspaper' Means." In *The Process and Effects of Mass Communication*, ed. Wilbur Schramm (Urbana: University of Illinois, 1965), pp. 36–47.

20. Jennings Bryant and Dolf Zillman, "Using Television to Alleviate Boredom and Stress: Selective Exposure as a Function of Induced Excitational States," *Journal of Broadcasting*, 28 (1984): 1–20.

21. Jay G. Blumler and Denis McQuail, *Television in Politics: Its Uses and Influence* (Chicago: University of Chicago Press, 1964).

22. D. Horton and R. R. Wohl, "Mass Communication and Parasocial Interaction: Observation on Intimacy at a Distance," *Psychiatry*, 19 (1956): 216.

23. Bryce Ryan and Neal C. Gross, "The Diffusion of Hybrid Seed Corn in Two Iowa Communities," *Rural Sociology*, 8 (1943), 15–24.

24. Everett M. Rogers and Arvind Singhal, "Diffusion of Innovations," in *An Integrated Approach to Communication The-*

ory and Research, ed. Michael B. Salwen and Don W. Stacks (Mahwah, NJ: Lawrence Erlbaum, 1996), p. 417.

25. Rogers and Arvind, "Diffusion of Innovation," p. 418.
26. T. Childers and J. Post, *The Information-Poor in America* (Metuchen, NJ: Scarecrow Press, 1975).
27. Michael Hirsh and Roy Gutman, "Powell's New War," *Newsweek*, 11 February 2002, p. 25.
28. "Women Journalists Appearing Less on Evening News," *New York Daily News*, 6 February 2002. www.nydailynews.com/20002-02-06/New_York_Now/Television/a-140420.
29. Bradley S. Greenberg and Larry Collette, "The Changing Faces on TV: A Demographic Analysis of Network Television's New Seasons, 1966–1992," *Journal of Broadcasting and Electronic Media*, 41, No. 1 (1997): 14–24.
30. Daniel A. Berkowitz, "Refining the Gatekeeping Metaphor for Local Television News," *Journal of Broadcasting & Electronic Media*, 34 (1990): 55–68.

CHAPTER 12

1. Press release and survey detail (PDF) accessible June 2001 on CPB website: http://www.cpb.org/about/media/releases/2001/0105_roper.html.
2. R. T. Murphy, *Educational Effectiveness of Sesame Steet: A Review of the First Twenty Years of Research, 1969–89.* (ERIC Document Reproduction Service No. ED 385 553) and Angela Teresa Clarke, and Beth Kurtz-Costes, "Television Viewing, Educational Quality of the Home Environment and School Readiness," *Journal of Educational Research*, 90, no. 5, (May/June 1997): 279–285.
3. *A Public Trust: The Landmark Report of the Carnegie Commission on the Future of Public Broadcasting* (New York: Bantam Books, 1979), pp. 281–282.
4. James T. Yee, "Background Statement on Minority Needs," in *Assessing the Public Broadcasting Needs of Minority and Diverse Audiences* (Queenstown, MD: The Aspen Institute, 1992), p. 39.
5. "Minority Job Share Doubles in Pubcasting, But Still Lags behind Progress of Women," *Current*, 18 September 2000.
6. "Overview of Race and Hispanic Origin," Census 2000 Brief, accessible at http://www.census.gov/prod/2001pubs/c2kbr01–1.pdf.
7. Personal interview with author.
8. Federal regulators always prohibited blatant commercials in public broadcasting but permitted "underwriting" messages of limited length acknowledging support from specific businesses and briefly mentioning their products or services. Expansion of underwriting messages into full-blown commercials was proposed frequently, debated hotly, and never approved—until a 2001 FCC ruling involving digital channels took some controls off public TV, as will be explained later in this chapter.
9. George H. Gibson, *Public Broadcasting: The Role of the Federal Government, 1912–76* (New York: Praeger, 1977), p. 10.
10. John Witherspoon and Roselle Kovitz, *A History of Public Broadcasting*. With an update by Robert K. Avery and Alan G. Stavitsky (Washington, DC: Current Newspaper, 2000), p. 58.
11. Witherspoon, *A History of Public Broadcasting*, p. 6.
12. Willard D. Rowland, Jr., "Public Service Broadcasting in the United States," in *Public Service Broadcasting in a Multichannel Environment: The History and Survival of an Ideal*, ed. Robert K. Avery (New York: Longman, 1993), p. 160.
13. Erik Barnouw, *Tube of Plenty: The Evolution of American Television* (London: Oxford University Press, 1975), p. 202.
14. Stanley Lebergott, *Pursuing Happiness: American Consumers in the Twentieth Century* (Princeton, NJ: Princeton University Press, 1993), p. 137.
15. That stands as the most severe one-year federal-budget setback for public broadcasting since 1969. Researchers Robert K. Avery and Alan G. Stavitsky note that, overall, federal funding rose from $5 million in 1969 to more than $300 million by 2000—but that, adjusted for inflation, CPB's 2000 funding amounted to 5 percent *less* than it received in fiscal 1990. See Witherspoon, *A History of Public Broadcasting*, pp. 82–83.
16. "CPB Inspector General Finds Minor Role in Political Mailings," *Communications Daily*, 10 September 1999.
17. Audience Research Analysis, *Audience 98*, accessible June 2001 at http://www.ara.com.
18. "Showdown at Grizzly River" (editorial), *St. Louis Post-Dispatch*, 11 October 2000, p. F8.
19. From 30th anniversary article at NPR website, June 2001, www.npr.org/atc/atc30.
20. WFPL website http://www.wfpl.org/.
21. "Tiny Pacifica's Big Troubles: Influential Network Continues Slow Self-Immolation," *Washington Post*, 8 February 2000, p. C2.
22. John McCutcheon, "Folk Music and Public Radio," *The International Musician*, January 1990. Reproduced and accessible June 2001 at http://www.folkmusic.com/archive/z_radio.htm.
23. "Rebel Radio," *Village Voice*, 19 May 1998.
24. Bob Edwards, *News and Views from National Public Radio: The M. L. Seidman Memorial Town Hall Lecture Series* (Memphis, TN: Rhodes College, 1987), p. 7.
25. Audience Research Analysis, *Audience 98*.
26. Audience Research Analysis, June 2001, http://aranet.com/.
27. Sarasota (Florida) *Herald-Tribune* (TV Diet), 19 March 2001, p. E1.
28. *Los Angeles Times* (Calendar), 4 December 1999, p. F2.
29. "PBS Promo Chief Does Homework," *Advertising Age*, 4 June 2001, p. S14.
30. *St. Louis Post-Dispatch* (Editorial), 11 October 2000, p. F8.

CHAPTER 13

1. James Carey, "Time, Space and the Telegraph," in *Communication in History: Technology, Culture and Society*, 3rd ed., ed. David Crowley and Paul Heyer (New York: Longman), p. 135.

2. *UNESCO Statistical Yearbook 1999*, Institute for Statistics, United Nations Organization for Education, Science and Culture.

3. Krishna Sen and David T. Hill, *Media, Culture and Politics in Indonesia* (Melbourne, Australia: Oxford University Press, 2000), p. 92.

4. RFE/RL news release, 30 January 2002.

5. Language from Voice of America charter, at VOA website, www.ibb.gov/pubaff/voacharter.html.

6. *UNESCO Statistical Yearbook.*

7. Maynard Parker, *Mixed Signals: The Prospects for Global Television News* (A Twentieth Century Fund Report) (New York: Twentieth Century Fund Press, 1995), p. 5.

8. "India's Television History," Indiantelevision.com, http://www.indiantelevision.com/indianbrodcast/history/historyoftele.htm.

9. Home Shopping Network press release, *Business Wire*, 25 July 2001.

10. "How Much Information?" (research report), School of Information Management and Systems, University of California at Berkeley, 2001. http://info.berkeley.edu/research/projects.

11. "Alderney Proves a Safe Bet for Gamblers," *M2 Presswire*, 24 August 2001.

12. *United States v. Cohen*, No. 00-1574 (2nd Cir., July 31, 2001), reported in "Net Gambling Business Owner Not So Lucky in Court," *E-Business Law Bulletin*, September 2001, p. 17.

13. Carla Brooks Johnston, *Global News Access: The Impact of New Communications Technologies* (Westport, CT: Praeger, 1998), p. 81.

14. From "Public Policy: Developing Media and Communications Policy in the Internet Century," AOL Time Warner website, http://aoltimewarner.com/about/policy.html#8.

15. Peter J. Humphreys, *Mass Media and Media Policy in Western Europe* (European Policy Research Unit Series) (Manchester, England: Manchester University Press, 1996), pp. 112–116.

16. "Faint Voices Rise from Cuba," *WIRED.COM*, 29 May 2001.

17. "New, Multiracial Beginning in Story of 'Madam and Eve,'" *Los Angeles Times*, 7 March 2001, p. F6.

18. Report from correspondent Phyllis Crockett on *All Things Considered*, National Public Radio, 27 November 1993.

19. For excellent overviews of broadcasting in Iraq and neighboring countries, see Douglas Boyd, *Broadcasting in the Arab World: A Survey of the Electronic Media in the Middle East*, 3rd ed. (Ames: Iowa State University Press, 1999).

20. John Sinclair, *Latin American Television: A Global View* (Oxford, England: Oxford University Press, 1999), p. 84.

21. Humphreys, *Mass Media and Media Policy*, p. 112.

22. Lucy Küng-Shankleman, *Inside the BBC and CNN: Managing Media Organisations* (London: Routledge, 2000).

23. Priscilla Parkhurst Ferguson (translator's note) in Pierre Bourdieu, *On Television and Journalism* (London: Pluto Press, 1998), p. 83.

24. "Croatia" Country Profile, *Quest Economics Database, Europe Review World of Information*, 23 August 2001.

25. STAR's main India channel dropped English to go all-Hindi in 2000, strengthening its foothold in what is the world's largest democracy and one of the largest media markets.

26. News Corporation 2000 Annual Report at website www.newscorp.com/report2000.

27. Robert S. Leiken, "With a Friend Like Fox," *Foreign Affairs*, September/October 2001, p. 91.

28. Speech to Radio-Television News Directors Association annual convention, Minneapolis, MN, 15 September 2000.

29. Lewis A. Friedland, *Covering the World: International Television News Services* (Perspectives on the News series). (New York: Twentieth Century Fund, 1992), p. 6.

30. Committee to Protect Journalists website, http://www.cpj.org.

31. Daniel Schorr, "On National Security, Five Ways to Respond to Restraints," *Nieman Reports*, 52, no. 1 (Spring 1998): 42.

32. Bittermann, Jim, in *Live from the Trenches: The Changing Role of the Television News Correspondent*, ed. Joe S. Foote (Carbondale: Southern Illinois University Press, 1998), p. 123.

33. Kevin McAuliffe, "Kosovo: A Special Report," *Columbia Journalism Review* (May/June 1999): p. 28.

34. Bitterman, p. 123.

35. Robert W. McChesney, *Rich Media Poor Democracy: Communication Politics in Dubious Times* (Urbana: University of Illinois Press, 1999), pp. 100–112.

36. Dietrich Berwanger, "The Third World," in *Television: An International History* (Oxford, England: Oxford University Press, 1998), p. 192.

37. "A Passage from India," *The Economist*, U.S. edition, 21 October 2000.

38. Speech to Radio-Television News Directors.

39. Garrick Utley, "The Shrinking of Foreign News," *Foreign Affairs*, (March/April 1997): 2.

CHAPTER 14

1. "Radio4all's Micro-Radio News: FCC Raids 15 Miami Stations," http://www. radio4all.org/news/bombs_over_miami. html, June 10, 2001.

2. "Free Radio Austin Rejects FCC License," www.infoshop.org/news5/radio2.html.

3. "Regulation," Lawrence, Lichty and Malachi Topping (Eds.), "Regulation," in *American Broadcasting—A Source Book on the History of Radio and Television*, 2nd ed. (New York: Hastings House, 1976), p. 527.

4. Andrew F. Inglis, *Behind the Tube—A History of Broadcasting Technology and Business* (Stoneham, MA: Butterworth, 1990), p. 84.

5. *Hoover v. Intercity Radio Co.*, 286 F. 1003 (1923).

6. Marvin R. Bensman, "Regulation of Broadcasting by the Department of Commerce, 1921–1927" in *American Broadcasting—A Source Book on the History of Radio and Television*, 2nd ed., Lawrence Lichty and Malachi Topping (New York: Hastings House, 1976), p. 554.

7. *Hoover v. Intercity Radio Co., Inc.*, 286 F. 1003 (D.C. Cir.), February 25, 1923, and *United States v. Zenith Radio Corporation et al.*, 12 F. 2d 614 (N.D. Ill.), April 16, 1926.

8. Maurice E. Shelby, Jr., "John R. Brinkley: His Contribution to Broadcasting," and Thomas W. Hoffer, "TNT Baker: Radio Quack," in *American Broadcasting: A Source Book on the History of Radio and Television*, 2nd ed., ed. Lawrence W. Lichty and Malachi Topping (New York: Hastings, 1976), pp. 560–577.

9. *Trinity Methodist Church, South v. Fed. Radio Comm.*, 62 F.2d. 850.

10. Telegram from Aimee Semple McPherson, KFSG Radio, 1925, cited by Erik Barnouw, *A Tower in Babel: A History of Broadcasting in the United States to 1933* (New York: Oxford University Press, 1966), p. 180.

11. As cited by Richard J. Meyer, "Reaction to the 'Blue Book'," in *American Broadcasting—A Source Book on the History of Radio and Television*, 2nd ed., ed. Lawrence Lichty and Malachi Topping (New York: Hastings House, 1976), p. 590.

12. Frank Ahrens (*Washington Post* Staff Writer), "Michael Powell: The Great Deregulator." *Washtech News*, 18 June 2001, www.washtech.com/news/regulation/10574-1.html.

13. FCC statements. 8 January 2002, http://www.fcc.gov/Speeches/Copps/Statements/2002/stmjc201.html.

14. David Lieberman, "Media's Big Fish Watch FCC Review Ownership Cap," *USA Today*, 4 December 2001, http://www.usatoday.com/money/covers/2001-07-09-bcovmon.htm.

15. PCS is the abbreviation for personal communications services, which is regarded as the next generation of two-way wireless after cellular phones functioning digitally at a different frequency (1900 MHz) with data as well as voice transmission.

16. *The Federal Register* is also found on the Web at http://fr.cos.com.

17. See "How to Apply for a Broadcast Station," Mass Media Bureau—Federal Communications Commission, http://www.fcc.gov/mmb/asd/.

18. Until the Federal Radio Commission was formed in 1927, the Commerce Department issued radio licenses for two-year terms, then extended it to three-year terms with the creation of the FRC. The extension to eight-year terms came with the 1996 Telecommunications Act. See W. Jefferson Davis, "The Radio Act of 1927," *American Broadcasting—A Source Book on the History of Radio and Television*, 2nd ed., ed. Lawrence Lichty and Malachi Topping (New York: Hastings House, 1976), p. 556.

19. Seth Scheisel, and Bill Carter, "Court Ruling May Change Landscape for Media," *The New York Times*, 20 February 2002, c1, c6.

20. *Associated Press v. United States*, 326 U.S. 1, 20 (1945) as cited by Philip M. Napoli, "Deconstructing the Diversity Principle," 49 J. Comm. 7 (1999).

21. *Adarand v. Pena*, 515 U.S. 200 (1995).

22. 109 Stat. 93 (1995), Pub. L. No. 1044-7 (1995).

23. Kalpana Srinivasan, (Associated Press), "Entertainment: Number of Minority-Owned TV stations drops." 16 January 2001, http://www.nandotimes.com.

24. Ivy Planning Group LLC, *Historical Study of Market Entry Barriers, Discrimination and Changes in Broadcast and Wireless Licensing 1950 to Present.* Document prepared for the Office of General Counsel, Federal Communications Commission, December 2000.

25. "EEO Forfeitures and Short Term License Renewals Continue," Haley, Bader, and Potts Memorandum 16 (February 14, 1991): 6, cited by Kenneth C. Creech, *Electronic Media Law and Regulation*, 3rd ed. (Woburn, MA: Butterworth-Heinemann, 2000), p. 104.

26. D.C. Cir. No. 97-1116, April 14, 1998.

27. *DC/MD/DE Broadcasters Association v. FCC*, 236 F.3d 13 (D.C. Cir. 2001).

28. Rob Puglisi, "How and When Will HDTV Affect Television News?" *RTNDA Communicator* (May 1988): 12, 14–15.

29. "Advanced Television Systems and Their Impact upon the Existing Television Broadcast Service," MM Docket No. 87–286, FCC 97–115 Orel. April 21, 1997 (Sixth Report and Order).

30. "Capitol Hill Appears to Be Warming to Broadcaster Pleas for Help with the Digital-TV Transition," *Broadcasting & Cable* online, 14 February 2002.

31. Telephone Interview, May 31, 2001.

32. *Turner Broadcasting Inc. v. FCC*, 819 F. Supp.32 (D.D.C. 1993); *Turner Broadcasting System, Inc. v. FCC*, 512 U.S. 622, 114 S. Ct. 2445 129 L. Ed. 2d 497 (1994).

33. Bill McConnell, "Band of Colluding Broadcasters?" *Broadcasting & Cable*, 5 November 2001, p. 30.

34. In Re-Application of Great Lakes Broadcasting Co., FRC Docket 4900, 3 F.R.C. Ann. Rep. 32 (1929).

35. Federal Radio Commission. Third Annual Report 33 (1929).

36. 13 FCC 1246 (1949).

37. See *Syracuse Peace Council v. FCC*, 867 F. 2d 654 (D.C. Cir. 1989) cert denied, 493 U.S. 1019 (1990); *Arkansas AFL-CIO v. FCC*, 11 F.3d 1430 (8th Cir. 1993).

38. *Radio-Television News Directors Association and National Association of Broadcasters v. FCC et al.*, United States Court of Appeals for the District of Columbia Circuit October 11, 2000 No. 98–1305, consolidated with No. 98–1334 On Motion to Recall the Mandate or for an Order Pursuant to 47 U.S.C. 402(h).

39. Title III, Part I, Sec. 315.

40. 47 U.S.C. Sec. 312 (a) (7).

41. David Broder, "A Word from Our TV Stations," *Washington Post* syndicate, *Fort Worth Star-Telegram*, 24 February 2002, 5E.

42. *Atlanta NAACP*, 36 FCC 2d 635 (1972).

43. *Gillett Communications of Atlanta Inc. (WAGA-TV5) v. Becker 21* (DC N.Ga), Med. L. Rptr. 702 (1992) cited by Kenneth Creech, *Electronic Media Law and Regulation*, 3rd ed. (Woburn, MA: Butterworth-Heinemann, 2000), pp. 60–61.

44. See 47 U.S.C.A. Sec. 315(a)(1)-(4).

45. *Aspen Institute Program on Communications and Society Petition*, 35 R.R. 2d 49 (1975).

46. See "Children's Television Programming and Advertising Practices," 75 FCC 2d 138 (1979).

47. See *Washington Association for Television and Children* v. *FCC*, 712 F. 2d 677 [D.C. Cir. 1983); *ACT* v. *FCC*, 821 F. 2d 741 (D.C. Cir. 1987).

48. 47 U.S.C. Sec. 303(b), *Consideration of Children's Television Service in Broadcast License Renewal.*

49. Barry Cole, and Mal Oettinger, *Reluctant Regulators: The FCC and the Broadcast Audience* (Reading, MA: Addison-Wesley, 1988), pp. 248–250.

50. See *Midler* v. *Ford Motor Company*, 849 F.2d 460 (9th Cir., 1988); *Vanna White* v. *Samsung Electronics America Inc.*, 971 F.2d 1395, 20 Med.L.Rptr.1457 (9th Cir. 1992), cert. denied, 508 U.S. 951, 113 S.Ct. 2443, 124 L.Ed.2d 660 (1993).

51. Neil Strauss, "Record Labels' Answer to Napster Still Has Artists Feeling Bypassed," *The New York Times*, 18 February 2002, A1-A11.

52. The U.S. Trade Representative Robert Zoellick under a "Special 301" section of federal trade law identified countries failing to afford protection to America's intellectual property rights.

53. *Luther R. Campbell a.k.a. Luke Skywalker* v. *Acuff-Rose Music, Inc.*, 510 U.S. 569, 114 S.Ct. 1164, 127 L.Ed.2d 500, 22 Med. L. Rptr. 1353 (1994).

54. *Tin Pan Apple* v. *Miller Brewing* (DC So. NY, 1990) 17 Med. L. Rptr. 2273.

55. Linda Greenhouse, "Justices to Review Copyright Extension," *The New York Times*, 20 February 2002, c1, c6. The case is *Eldred* v. *Ashcroft* (No. 01–618).

56. See *A&M Records* v. *Napster, Inc.*, 114 F. Supp. 2d 896, 900 (N.D. Cal. 2000).

57. *Sony Corporation of America* v. *Universal Studios*, 464 U.S. 417, 1984.

58. Laura Hodes, "The DMCA, The Death of Napster, and The Digital Age: A Review of Jessica Litman's Digital Copyright," *FindLaw's Book Reviews*, 20 July 2001, http://writ. news.findlaw.com/books/reviews/20010720_hodes.html.

59. Restatement (Second) of Torts Section 568A (1977), cited in Roy L. Moore, *Mass Communication Law and Ethics*, 2nd ed. (Mahwah, NJ: Lawrence Erlbaum, 1999), p. 322.

60. *Sagan* v. *Apple Inc.*, 22 Media Law Rptr. 2141, 874 F. Supp.1072 (D.C.C.Cal. 1994).

61. 485 U.S. 46, 1987.

62. 376 U.S. 279–80 (1964).

63. *Newton* v. *NBC.* (D.C. Nev., 1987) 114 Med. L. Reptr. 1914.

64. S. D. Warren and L. D. Brandeis, "The Right to Privacy," 4 *Harv. L. Rev.* (1890) 193.

65. *American Civil Liberties Union of Georgia* v. *Miller*, 977 F. Supp. 1228 (N.D.Ga.1997).

66. *McVeigh* v. *Cohen*, 983 F.Supp. 215 (D.C. Cir. 1998).

67. Kathleen Kirby, "Public Trials Mean Televised Trials," *Communicator* (February 2001): 32.

68. Barbara Cochran, "President's Column," *Communicator* (February 2001): 17.

69. *Chandler* v. *Florida*, 449 U.S. 560 (1981).

70. *Miller* v. *California*, 413 U.S. 15 (1973).

71. Federal law prohibits obscene content on broadcast television (18 USC 1464) cable (18 USC 1468; 47 USC 559) and satellite television (18 USC 1468). The provision of federal law prohibiting "indecent" material on broadcast TV is enforced only between the hours of 6:00 A.M. and 10:00 P.M. Congress passed a law in 1996 (47 USC 561) requiring cable operators to scramble the signals for channels dedicated to sexually oriented programming.

72. The FCC issued a new policy statement on indecency in April 2001—one that had been promised since 1994, when the FCC found itself at a stalemate with a Chicago radio station, WLUP-AM. The station's owner, Evergreen Media Corporation, responded to an indecency complaint from the FCC by challenging its process regarding indecency on constitutional grounds.

73. *FCC* v. *Pacifica Foundation*, 438 U.S. 726, 98 S. Ct. 3026, 57 L. Ed. 2d 1073, 3 Med. L. Reporter 2553 (1978).

74. *Cruz* v. *Ferre*, 571 F. Supp. 125 (S.D. Fla. 1983).

75. *Reno* v. *ACLU (CDA)*, 521 U.S. 844 (1997); *ACLU* v. *Reno (CDA)*, 929 F. Supp. 824 E.D.Pa. 1996).

76. *ACLU* v. *Reno (COPA)*, 217 F. 3d 162 (2000).

CHAPTER 15

1. Ed Bark, "Scrambling Networks Score in Laden Footage," *The Dallas Morning News*, 8 October 2001, 17A.

2. Bryan Magee, "Aristotle," in *The Great Philosophers* (New York: Oxford University Press, 1987), p. 52.

3. Louis A. Day, *Ethics in Media Communications: Cases and Controversies*, 2nd ed. (Belmont, CA: Wadsworth, 1997).

4. Joseph A. Mirando, "Lessons on Ethics in News Reporting Textbooks, 1867–1997," *Journal of Mass Media Ethics*, 13, no. 1 (1998): 26–39.

5. John Rawls, *A Theory of Justice* (Cambridge, MA: Harvard University Press, 1971).

6. Val Limburg, *Electronic Media Ethics* (Newton, MA: Butterworth-Heinemann, 1994), pp. 49–59.

7. NAB, July 9, 1990, as cited by Limburg.

8. Vernon Stone, *Evolution of the RTNDA Code of Ethics*, 7 October 2001.

9. Jennifer Sinco-Kelleher, "Story from Mosque Inspired Me to Be a Voice for the Voiceless." Newsroom Diversity Freedom Forum.org, 25 September 2001, http://www.freedomforum. org/templates/document. asp?document=149m.

10. See *Advertising Principles of American Business* at http://www.aaf.org/about/principles.html.

11. Alexander Kendrick, *Prime Time: The Life of Edward R. Murrow* (Boston: Little, Brown, 1969), p. 466.

12. Lawrence K. Grossman, "Monica Lewinsky, Clinton, The Dress," *CJR*, Nov/Dec. 1998.

13. Marvin L. Kalb, *One Scandalous Story: Clinton, Lewinsky, Thirteen Days That Tarnished American Journalism* (Boston: The Free Press, 2001).

14. "Slate Writer Fired Over Hoax Story," *NOLA.com*, http://www.nola.com/rose/tp/index.ssf?/livingstory/rose28.html.

15. Maureen Dowd, "Lights, Camera, Wartime TV Action," *The New York Times in the Fort Worth Star-Telegram*, 26 February 2002, 11B.

16. Molly Ivins, "A Bad Idea and Some Better Ones," *Fort Worth Star-Telegram*, 24 February 2002, 5E.

17. Louis Chunovic, "WWF, TV Council Go to Mat in Court," *Electronic Media* 7 July 2001, www.emonline.com/advertise/.

18. Joe Scholosser, "Family-Hour Feud," and "More Sound and Fury, *Broadcasting & Cable*, 6 August 2001, 8, 46.

19. Sinco-Kelleher, "Story from Mosque."

20. Natalie Cortes, "Latinos Woefully Underrepresented in U.S. Media, Panelists Say," Freedom Forum Online, 8 October 2001, http://www.freedom forum.org.

21. Don Heider, "Completeness and Exclusion in Journalism Ethics: An Ethnographic Case Study," *Journal of Mass Media Ethics*, 11, no. 1 (1996): 4–15.

22. Lawrence Soley, "The Power of the Press Has a Price," *Extra!* July/August 1997, http://www.fair.org/extra/9707/ad-survey.htm.

23. Bob Steele and Al Tompkins, *Newsroom Ethics: Decision-Making for Quality Coverage*, 2nd ed. (The Radio and Television News Directors Foundation, 2000), p. 42.

24. "We Paid $3 Billion for the Stations. We'll Decide What the News Is." *Extra!* June 1998, www.foxbghsuit.com and www.monitor.net/rachel/r593.html.

25. Lawrie Mifflin, "ABC News Reporter Discovers the Limits of Investigating Disney," *The New York Times*, 19 October 1998, http://www.corpwatch.org/trac/corner/worldnews/other/226.htm.

26. Sam Roberts, "Infomercials Disguised as News," 9 September 2001, rtvj.l@server2. umt.edu.

27. Allison Romano, "Grist from CNN More Subtle than Some," *Broadcasting & Cable Online*, 30 July 2001, http://broadcastingcable.com.

28. "Advertisers to Implant Products in Shows?" 29 August 2001, http://interactive. wsh.com/articles/SB999033866131846899.htm.

29. Wendy S. Williams, "The Online Threat to Independent Journalism—On the Web, Where Does News End and Ads Begin?" *Extra!* November/December 1996, http://www.fair.org/extra/9611/internet.html.

30. Jay Black, Bob Steele, and Ralph Barney, *Doing Ethics in Journalism—A Handbook with Case Studies* (Boston: Allyn and Bacon, 1999), pp. 145, 159.

31. "Anchor Fired for Giving Political Money," *Editor and Publisher Online*, 14 November 2000, http://www.media into.com/ephomo/news/newshtm/stories/20400 or 2.htm.

32. Roy Peter Clark, "The Invisible Uniform. The Journalist's Role in Democratic Life," Poynter Org, 10 October 2001, http://63.208.24.134/terrorism/roy.19.htm.

33. Stone, *Evolution of the RTNDA Code of Ethics*, p. 9.

34. Bill Carter, and Felicity Barringer, "Networks Agree to U.S. Request to Edit Future bin Laden Tapes." The New York Times, 11 October 2001, 1A.

35. Shirley Biagi, "Special Perspectives from . . . ," *News Talk II* (Belmont, CA: Wadsworth, 1987), p. 41.

36. Ibid., p. 88.

37. Ibid., p. 124.

38. Koppel, *Nightline*, p. 10.

39. Dan Weaver and Jason Siegel, *Breaking into Television* (Princeton, NJ: Peterson's, 1998), pp. 9–10.

40. Weaver and Siegel, *Breaking into Television*, p. 189.

41. Biagi, "Special Perspectives," (News Talk pp. 5–6.

42. Lucinda Watson, *How They Achieved* (New York: John Wiley and Sons, 2001), pp. 35–43.

53. Ibid., p. 54.

44. Sumner Redstone, (with Peter Knobler), *A Passion to Win* (New York: Simon & Schuster, 2001), p. 20.

INDEX

Photo Credits